NEW ENGLAND DISCOVERY

A Personal View

NEW ENGLAND
DISCOVERY
A Personal View

NANCY HALE

COWARD-MCCANN, INC.

NEW YORK

"The Landing at Plymouth," from *Plymouth Plantation* by William Bradford, edited
by Samuel Eliot Morison. Reprinted by permission of Alfred A. Knopf, Inc., publisher.

"Sermon Aboard the Arbella," by John Winthrop, reprinted from *The Winthrop Papers*
by permission of the Massachusetts Historical Society, Stephen T. Riley, Director.

"Everyday Life in Massachusetts Bay Colony," by George Francis Dow. Reprinted by
permission of the Society for The Preservation of New England Antiquities.

"Last Will and Testament of Andrew Hodges," from *Records and Files of Quarterly
Courts of Essex County, Massachusetts*, volume 3, pp. 314–315, 1913. Reprinted by
permission of the Essex Institute, Dean A. Fales, Jr., Director.

"Upon Wedlock, and Death of Children," by Edward Taylor. Reprinted by permission
of the Yale University Library.

Selection from the *Diary of Cotton Mather*, volume I; a letter from Cotton Mather to
John Cotton; a letter from Cotton Mather to John Richards from *The Mather Papers*,
volume VIII; "The Big Snow of 1717," a letter from Cotton Mather to Mr. Woodward.
All reprinted by permission of the Massachusetts Historical Society.

Selection from *The Autobiography of Benjamin Franklin*, from the Albert Henry
Smythe text published 1906. Reprinted by permission of The Macmillan Company.

"The Puritan State and Puritan Society," by Perry Miller from *Errand into the Wilderness*. Reprinted by permission of the publishers, Harvard University Press, Cambridge,
Massachusetts, copyright © 1956 by the President and Fellows of Harvard College.

"John Adams' Graduation from Harvard" and "The Other Adams," by Catherine
Drinker Bowen from *John Adams and The American Revolution*, copyright © 1949,
1950 by Catherine Drinker Bowen. Reprinted by permission of Little, Brown and
Company, Atlantic Monthly Press.

"Paul Revere's Own Account of His Ride," from a letter to Jeremy Belknap, *Proc.*,
1879, pp. 370–376, edited by Charles Deane. Reprinted by permission of the Massachusetts Historical Society.

"Diary of an American Soldier," selections from *The Journal of Simeon Lyman*, volume
8, copyright © 1899. Reprinted by permission of the Connecticut Historical Society
Collections, Thompson R. Harlow, Director.

"Bunker Hill," from *The Diary of Amos Farnsworth*, 1899, pp. 74–107, edited by Dr.
Samuel A. Greene. Reprinted by permission of the Massachusetts Historical Society.

"Boston Evacuated," from *The Diary of Timothy Newell*. Reprinted by permission of
the Massachusetts Historical Society.

[iv]

To My Father
Philip L. Hale
1865–1931
painter, art critic, teacher
who knew hundreds of tales of old New England
and told them to his daughter

Introduction

An anthology of any literature is, properly, a collection of valuable items selected from the wide reading of an authority in that field. The present anthology is something quite other. It is, in fact, an almost direct opposite, for instead of being culled from accrued knowledge, it has been, for its editor, a search and a discovery.

I was brought up near Boston in a family much given to telling stories of the past. My father had an uncanny memory for tales, both historical and family, and I grew up with a strong, definite myth of New England in my mind. It was a myth that included such archetypes as the Puritan, exemplified for me by my ancestor John Hale of Beverley, persecutor of witches until his own wife was cried out upon. The Revolution seemed to me almost a family affair; when I was six, we were asked one day at school to tell what our ancestors had done in the American Revolution and I reported with pride, "I had a great-uncle who was hanged." Calvinist theology was made real for me by the story of my great-great-grandfather, Lyman Beecher, of Litchfield, who arranged to exchange pulpits one Sunday with the minister of a neighboring Connecticut town. As the two divines passed each other on horseback on the road, the other said, "Dr. Beecher, is it not marvelous: since the beginning of time it was ordained that you and I should exchange pulpits today." "Is that so?" cried Beecher, wheeling his horse about. "Then I won't do it."

In Cambridge I was shown the old yellow wooden house where Edward Everett lived when he was president of Harvard and his nephew, Edward Everett Hale, was serving as his private secretary. As for the Civil War, a child could only feel a vested interest in a conflict of which Abraham Lincoln had said to one's great-aunt, "So you are the little woman who started this great war."

Such so to speak dinner-table education is the veriest myth, for, like the ancient myths, it is gained from word of mouth, from hearing the praises of famous men sung, and from the personal connection that exists between the listener and the heroes of the lays. A sort of false confidence informs the possessor of a myth. He thinks he knows; but he doesn't. He only feels. It can be tempting, if one was brought up in New England, to feel that one knows something about, say, Emerson, when really the source of one's feeling is no more than a familiar photograph of Emerson seated on a sofa with one's grandfather. It is easy to feel one knows about the Plymouth Plantations just because one was taken to see the Rock as a child and, at school, sang on so many mornings, "The break—ing waves—dashed high!" Brook Farm, not five miles down the road, seemed almost as familiar a place as home. But to be familiar with is not the same thing as knowing.

When I grew up and went away to live, first in New York and later in Virginia, it was gradually borne in upon me that my vast store of anecdotes and songs and jokes and legends about New England were not always, in every case, accurate. The Boston Massacre turned out to be not the bloody outrage that, viewing the Revere print of it in my father's study, I had always assumed; British regulars who fired on the Americans did so only after the most extreme provocation by determined agitators. Unitarianism was not, after all, the last sweet word in liberation of the mind; the Transcendentalists had felt they needed to liberate themselves from its dry rationalism.

But there is no more Yankee sentiment than that summed up in the vernacular rejoinder, "Well, I want to know!" Since I still loved New England as much as ever I had, it behooved me, in talking to people in the rest of the country, to find out what, actually, I was talking about. There was no sense singing New England's praises if, in doing so, I was making a fool of myself. I began to try to substantiate the myth I carried about with me. The greater part of my task proved to be just that: substantiation of what I already believed. But where the myth turned out to be untrue I found I could lop it off; where it was cloudy I could clarify it; where it was in part true I could fill in legend with history.

When I was asked to edit this anthology of writing about New England by New Englanders, it was, therefore, upon this dual background of myth and the revision of myth I had to draw. My life is spent in the company of scholars—real scholars—and I hesitated for a long time before accepting an assignment for which I seem classically so unprepared. Since in the end I took the job, it might not be inappropriate to give some of the reasons why I decided I might not be wasting my readers' time with the results of such an undertaking.

In the first place, there are plenty of first-rate conventional anthologies by authorities in the field; Perry Miller and Van Wyck Brooks are names that spring instantly to mind. No one need ever want for the final word from the scholarly horse's mouth where New England is concerned. In the second place, there can never be enough anthologies of New England writing. It sometimes seems as though every son of New England, and half her daughters too, had been born articulate and had a pen thrust into his fingers on his first birthday. Everybody wrote. The rest of the country, in comparison, was stone mute.

Until one comes to edit a New England anthology one can have no idea of the mountains of material three centuries and a bit over have produced—some of it, of course, not worth saving. But there is so much that is worth saving! There is the great writing, which has for the most part already been saved, and should be saved again. There is the awfully good writing, which will always be worth saving a little more of. And there is the interesting, the odd, the curious—worth saving if only for its antiquarian flavor.

In the present volume some of all three categories is included. The test for inclusion has been simple: The item must be connected in some way with that private myth of New England of which I have spoken. The item may be the verification of something I had always heard about as a child. It may be some poem or story often repeated to me, here discovered in black and white. It may be an account that corrects an early misapprehension of mine, or shatters some illusion. In the commentary, I have tried to suggest the associations each item evokes in my mind. It is, thus, a very personal anthology.

I felt considerable doubt about including in it selections from the writing of members of my family, for such is not considered correct procedure by professional compilers of anthologies. But I am not a professional anthologist. Although I have certainly not included any writing of my own, I have included family writing mostly because it is a part of the myth on which this book is founded.

I have tried to give the reader a taste of what an interest, what a pleasure it is to convert myth—phantasy—into reality. For everyone, I think, grows up carrying within him a myth of his own environment—a myth about his family, his community, his city, right up the line to his country and his world. Among the gifts of maturity none gives greater satisfaction than to find oneself able to distinguish between myth and fact and to engage in modifying the one by means of the other.

Modifying, not demolishing; for if fact is the reasonable part of the truth, myth is its imaginative side. Much truth is in the myth, always. It is fact that has made New England great. But it is her myth—that blend of staunchness, brains, courage, toil, loneliness, wild beauty, independence, and style—that makes her children want to kneel to kiss her earth. Not to do so, of course; such behavior would seem most unsuitable, to a New Englander.

Contents

1689–1730

1812–1824

CONTENTS

1862–1885

Illustrations Follow Pages 134 and 358.

NEW ENGLAND DISCOVERY

A Personal View

1620-1643

A TRUE RELATION OF THE MOST
PROSPEROUS VOYAGE

JAMES ROSIER

———◆◆———

*November 11, 1620, goes down in fame as the date of the founding of
New England when the* Mayflower *anchored in the harbor of Cape Cod.
The Pilgrims aboard her were Puritans who carried Puritanism to its ultimate extreme (unlike the main body of Puritans, who were to make their
landing at Salem in 1630). Puritanism was a Protestant reform movement
within the Church of England; some Puritans, the Pilgrims among them,
desired actually to split off from the national church—an act tantamount
to treason. Such "separatists" had to flee for their lives; the Pilgrims had
taken refuge in Holland for some years before they came to Plymouth.*

*But even before 1620 New England was a shore familiar to seafarers.
Captain John Smith gave the region its name in his map of 1616. Still
earlier trips had been sent out from England, among them one which explored the coast of Maine and was described by James Rosier (c.1575–
1635) in* A True Relation of the Most Prosperous Voyage Made This
Present Yeere 1605 *by Captain George Waymouth. The following is an
excerpt.*

*Note that the taking of a cod in Maine waters is here described. The
importance codfish was to have in New England's future economy, symbolized by the so-called Sacred Cod which hangs today in the State
House at Boston, is inestimable. I remember an old aunt of mine saying
with great severity to a little boy who came around to our Cape Ann back
door selling cod for ten cents, "Little boy, never, never sell codfish for
less than twenty-five cents."*

THURSDAY, the 13 of June, by two a clocke in the morning (because our
Captaine would take the helpe and advantage of the tide) in the light-

[1]

horseman with our Company well provided and furnished with armour and shot both to defend and offend; we went from our ship up to that part of the river which trended westward into the maine [the St. George's River], to search that: and we carried with us a Crosse, to erect at that point, which (because it was not daylight) we left on the shore untill our returne backe; when we set it up in maner as the former. For this (by the way) we diligently observed, that in no place, either about the Ilands, or up in the maine, or alongst the river, we could discerne any token or signe, that ever any Christian had beene before; of which either by cutting wood, digging for water, or setting up Crosses (a thing never omitted by any Christian travellers) we should have perceived some mention left.

But to returne to our river, further up into which we then rowed by estimation twenty miles, the beauty and goodnesse whereof I can not by relation sufficiently demonstrate. That which I can say in generall is this: What profit or pleasure soever is described and truly verified in the former part of the river, is wholly doubled in this; for the bredth and depth is such, that any ship drawing 17 or 18 foot water, might have passed as farre as we went with our light-horsman, and by all our mens judgement much further, because we left it in so good depth and bredth; which is so much the more to be esteemed of greater woorth, by how much it trendeth further up into the maine: for from the place of our ships riding in the Harbour at the entrance into the Sound, to the furthest part we were in this river, by our estimation was not much lesse than threescore miles.

From ech banke of this river are divers branching streames into the maine, whereby is affoorded an unspeakable profit by the conveniency of transportation from place to place, which in some countries is both chargeable; and not so fit, by cariages on waine, or horse backe.

Heere we saw great store of fish, some great, leaping above water, which we judged to be Salmons. All along is an excellent mould of ground. The wood in most places, especially on the East side, very thinne, chiefly oke and some small young birch, bordering low upon the river; all fit for medow and pasture ground: and in that space we went, we had on both sides the river many plaine plots of medow, some of three or foure acres, some of eight or nine: so as we judged in the whole to be betweene thirty and forty acres of good grasse, and where the armes run out into the Maine, there likewise went a space on both sides of cleere grasse, how far we know not, in many places we might see paths made to come downe to the watering.

The excellencie of this part of the River, for his good breadth, depth, and fertile bordering ground, did so ravish us all with variety of pleasantnesse, as we could not tell what to commend, but only admired; some compared it to the River Severne, (but in a higher degree) and we all concluded (as I verily thinke we might rightly) that we should never see the like River in every degree equall, untill it pleased God we beheld the same againe. For the farther we went, the more pleasing it was to every man, alluring us still with expectation of better, so as our men, although they had with great labour rowed long and eat nothing (for we carried with us no victuall, but a little cheese and bread) yet they were so refreshed with the pleasant beholding thereof, and so loath to forsake it, as some of them affirmed, they would have continued willingly with that onely fare and labour 2 daies; but the tide not suffering us to make any longer stay (because we were to come backe with the tide) and our Captaine better knowing what was fit then we, and better what they in labour were able to endure, being verie loath to make any desperate hazard, where so little necessitie required, thought it best to make returne, because whither we had discovered was sufficient to conceive that the River ran very far into the land. For we passed six or seven miles, altogether fresh water (whereof we all dranke) forced up by the flowing of the Salt: which after a great while eb, where we left it, by breadth of channell and depth of water was likely to run by estimation of our whole company an unknowen way farther: the search whereof our Captaine hath left till his returne, if it shall so please God to dispose of him and us. . . .

Tuesday, the 18 day, being not run above 30 leagues from land, and our Captaine for his certaine knowledge how to fall with the coast, having sounded every watch, and from 40 fathoms had come into good deeping, to 70, and so to an hundred: this day the weather being faire, after the foure a clocke watch, when we supposed not to have found ground so farre from land, and before sounded in about 100 fathoms, we had ground in 24 fathomes. Wherefore our sailes being downe, Thomas King, boatswaine, presently cast out a hooke, and before he judged it at ground, was fished and haled up an exceeding great and well fed Cod: then there were cast out 3 or 4 more, and the fish was so plentifull and so great, as when our Captaine would have set saile, we all desired him to suffer them to take fish a while, because we were so delighted to see them catch so great fish, so fast as the hooke came down: some with playing with the hooke they tooke by the backe, and one of the Mates with two hookes at a lead at five draughts together haled up tenne fishes; all were generally very great, some they measured to be five foot long, and three foot about.

This caused our Captaine not to marvell at the shoulding for he perceived it was a fish banke, which (for our farewell from the land) it pleased God in continuance of his blessings to give us knowledge of: the abundant profit whereof should be alone sufficient cause to draw men againe, if there were no other good both in present certaine, and in hope probable to be discovered. To amplifie this with words, were to adde light to the Sunne: for every one in the shippe could easily account this present commodity; much more those of judgement, which knew what belonged to fishing, would warrant (by the helpe of God) in a short voyage with few good fishers to make a more profitable returne from hence than from Newfoundland: the fish being so much greater, better fed, and abundant with traine; of which some they desired, and did bring into England to bestow among their friends, and to testifie the true report.

THE LANDING AT PLYMOUTH

WILLIAM BRADFORD

The first permanent New England colony was founded in 1620 by the Pilgrims at Plymouth. The following passage is excerpted from the Journal *of William Bradford (1590–1657) who led the 1620 expedition. A year later Bradford was elected governor of the Plymouth Colony and continued to serve for thirty years—without salary until 1639, and after that for 20 pounds a year.*

BUT to omit other things (that I may be brief), after long beating at sea they fell with that land which is called Cape Cod; the which being made and certainly known to be it, they were not a little joyful. After some deliberation had amongst themselves and with the master of the ship, they tacked about and resolved to stand for the southward (the wind and weather being fair) to find some place about Hudson's River for their habitation. But after they had sailed that course about half the day, they fell amongst dangerous shoals and roaring breakers, and they were so far entangled therewith as they conceived themselves in great danger; and the wind shrinking upon them withal, they resolved to bear up again for the Cape and thought themselves happy to get out of those dangers before night overtook them, as by God's good providence they did. And the next day they got into the cape harbor where they rode in safety. . . .

Being thus arrived in a good harbor, and brought safe to land, they fell upon their knees and blessed the God of heaven who had brought them over the vast and furious ocean, and delivered them from all the perils and miseries thereof, again to set their feet on the firm and stable earth, their proper element. . . .

But here I cannot but stay and make a pause, and stand half amazed at this poor people's present condition; and so I think will the reader, too,

died sometimes two or three of a day in the foresaid time, that of one
hundred and odd persons, scarce fifty remained. And of these, in the time
of most distress, there was but six or seven sound persons who to their
great commendations, be it spoken, spared no pains night nor day, but
with abundance of toil and hazard of their own health, fetched them
wood, made them fires, dressed them meat, made their beds, washed their
loathsome clothes, clothed and unclothed them. In a word, did all the
homely and necessary offices for them which dainty and queasy stomachs
cannot endure to hear named; and all this willingly and cheerfully, without any grudging in the least, showing herein their true love unto their
friends and brethren; a rare example and worthy to be remembered.
Two of these seven were Mr. William Brewster, their reverend elder, and
Myles Standish, their captain and military commander, unto whom myself
and many others were much beholden in our low and sick condition. And
yet the Lord so upheld these persons as in this general calamity they
were not at all infected either with sickness or lameness. And what I have
said of these I may say of many others who died in this general visitation,
and others yet living; that whilst they had health, yea, or any strength
continuing, they were not wanting to any that had need of them. And I
doubt not but their recompense is with the Lord.

MERRYMOUNT

JOHN LOTHROP MOTLEY

———◆◆———

*The Pilgrims were soon scandalized by goings-on at Merrymount, near
what is now Quincy. Thomas Morton, Gent. (1590?–1647), started there
a rum- and gun-running establishment, plus what William Bradford
termed "a schoole of atheisme" where were carried out "the beastly practices of the madd Bachanalians." The Piligrims sent Myles Standish to
take Morton into custody, and he was sent to England under arrest in
1628.*

*The following account by the Boston historian John Lothrop Motley
(1814–1877) is taken from his historical romance* Merrymount *and concerns the celebration of old-style May-Day rites. To an Elizabethan
mind, a Maypole had certain connotations that had little in common
with modern schoolgirl festivities. The nature of what went on at "the
New English Canaan," as Morton himself described the place, is probably the reason why so few New Englanders have ever heard of the place.*

CONTINUATION OF THE MAY-DAY REVELS

THE sun rose brightly from the sea upon May-day morning, and Maudsley, who had found but slight and unsatisfactory repose within his hut, stood upon the summit of the mount, and refreshed his weary soul with a contemplation of the majestic scenery around him. Although he was by nature of a wayward and impetuous disposition, and although his prejudices, from the earliest period of his life, had enlisted him strongly against the gloomy and austere principles of Puritanism, he could not but confess, as he looked upon that solemn and impressive wilderness scene, so full of fresh and uncontaminated beauty, that it were indeed a prostitution of nature, if the virgin purity, the cool and shady loveliness of this sylvan world were to be profaned forever by orgies such as he had already witnessed. . . . At a moment when he was struggling to shake off the thoughts which were again thronging to his brain, he was awakened at once to a vivid perception of the world about him, by a variety of shrill and uproarious sounds which issued from the forest. At first, so entirely had he forgotten the mummery of the preceding evening, and the promised sports of the present day, he was at a loss to account for the sounds, but as soon as he observed one or two of his late companions emerging from the woods, he recollected that the May morning had arrived, and he descended from the eminence towards the open glade.

In a few moments the whole wild crew, who had passed the night in the forest, had entered upon the open field, and after a short pause formed a procession and moved slowly towards the mount. They were bringing home the May-pole, which was a vast pine nearly a hundred feet in length. The tree had been stripped of its bark and branches, ornamented with garlands of wintergreen and forest-tree blossoms, and placed upon rudely constructed wheels. In place of oxen, some fifty savages were yoked together, each wearing May garlands upon their swarthy brows, and evidently taking a grave satisfaction in thus assisting at a solemn ceremony, which Bootefish had assured them was an initiatory step towards their conversion from paganism, and which was sure to require copious besprinklings of the strong water, which they worshipped as the white man's God.

Thus harnessed, the savages drew the mighty May-pole slowly along, with the Lord of Merry-Mount seated upon it in solemn state. The rest of the company thronged around him in his triumphal progress, marching in unison to the braying of trumpets and the thump of drums, whose rude music sounded strangely among those ancient woods. After a time, and with great efforts, the May-pole was at last brought to the top of the Merry-Mount, where, after a pair of elk antlers had been fastened to its top, and the red cross banner of England, with a variety of other pennons, added to its other decorations, it was triumphantly erected upon the summit. Many shouts of congratulation now rent the air, and then the company, a little wearied with their exertions, threw themselves upon the ground for a few moments' repose. Morton and several of his adherents now withdrew for a time from the mount, leaving the company under the charge of his lieutenant and grand master of the ceremonies; who, after serving out to them what he considered a sufficient quantity of liquor, soon after retired himself. A grand arbor was now constructed of green branches upon the hill, not far from the May-pole, and another of lesser dimensions near it. A considerable time had thus been spent, and sun was already approaching the zenith, when suddenly the music again was heard advancing from the neighborhood of the palace, and presently a fantastically attired company were seen advancing gravely toward the mount. The procession was led by the sovereign of Merry-Mount himself, who, as Lord of the May, was attired according to immemorial custom in the green forest garb of Robin Hood. He wore moreover upon his head a gilt and glittering crown, and held a gilded staff in his hand, as symbols of his supremacy. Hanging upon his arm, came a dark-eyed, dusky daughter of the forest, who, for lack of a fairer representative, was arrayed as Maid Marian, the May Lord's favorite dame. She too, as Queen of the May, wore a gilded crown upon her swarthy brows, with her glossy black tresses floating almost to her feet, and was arrayed in gaily colored robes of purple and crimson cloth. They were followed by Cakebread, who had recovered from the effects of the flagellation received at Mishawum, and who now figured as court jester. The respectable buffoon wore a fool's-cap and bells, a motley coat, with tight-fitting Venetian pantaloons, whereof one leg was of flame color and the other of purple. He held a bauble or fool's baton in his hand, and his dress was hung with little bells, which jingled merrily as he danced along, occasionally refreshing himself and the spectators with one of his favorite somersets. Next came the grave and dignified Bootefish as Friar Tuck, his short but portly person arrayed in a monkish robe bound about his ample waist with a cord from which hung a rosary and cross, and his rubicund physiognomy looking particularly effulgent, as it broke out like the rising sun from the dark and cloud-like cowl which covered his venerable head. Rednape followed as the lover of Maid Marian, wearing a tawdry cap, ornamented with a wreath of violets, fastened securely to the right side of his head, and a sky-blue jacket; while his long legs were daintily incased in scarlet breeches and hose, cross gartered, and with countless ribbons and true lover's knots streaming from every portion of his dress. Next came the Spanish gentleman and the Morisco, personated by less distinguished members of the company, and wearing immoderately loose breeches, curling shoes of a yard's dimension, and enormous, empty sleeves hanging from their gaily colored jerkins. The principal musical performer followed, with a drum hanging from his neck, a tamborine in his hand, and a lathe sword at his side. Next came a creature with a wolf's head and a fox's tail, with half a dozen green and golden snakes wreathed round his waist; after him, a kind of goblin wearing the grim head and portentous teeth of a shark, with a dragon's tail; then several palmers masqued and cloaked; then a jack-in-the-green, or living pyramid of blossoming branches, dancing grotesquely along to the wild music which accompanied the procession. Last of all came the merry Bernaby Doryfall, riding the hobby-horse, the animal's head and shoulders artistically contrived of pasteboard, while an ample housing, or rather petticoat of parti-colored cloth, descended to the ground, and effectually concealed the rider's legs. The amiable Centaur wore a pumpkin helmet of formidable appearance, and flourished a wooden dagger in his right hand, while with the other he reined in his restive steed as he gaily pranced and capered about, bringing up the rear of the pageant in a very effective style.

The procession ascended the mount in an orderly manner, and arranged themselves about the May-pole, while the rest of the revellers arose from their recumbent positions and stood, awaiting the orders of their sovereign. That potentate now took a roll of paper from his bosom, upon which he had inscribed a short poem, setting forth, in very high flown and classical doggerel, an allegorical description of the ceremony, combined with many enigmatical allusions to the present and prospective condition of the nascent empire of the Massachusetts. This, after he had read it in a sonorous and impressive voice, he gravely affixed to the May-pole, that it might serve for the edification of his guests, whenever they felt inclined for literary relaxation. Then, with an indescribable air of majesty, he again extended his hand to the dusky Queen of the Revels, and conducted her with stately step to the great arbor, where he seated her upon a rustic throne. Then advancing once more in front of the verdant tent, he exclaimed,—

"With gilded staff and crossed scarf, the May Lord, here I stand."

"Know ye, therefore, my faithful subjects, that your sports are to be conducted in an orderly and reputable guise, so as in no wise to cast discredit upon the court of your sovereign, or to invoke a blush upon the tender cheek of our loving queen,—

　　" 'Music, awake! ye lieges all advance,
　　　And circling join in merry Morrice dance.' "

NEW ENGLAND'S PLANTATION 1630

FRANCIS HIGGINSON

———◆•◆———

Francis Higginson (1586–1630) had been minister of the advance guard of 1630 landings of the Puritans at Massachusetts Bay. During the perilous voyage, whenever storms threatened the tiny craft, Mr. Higginson would appoint a fast, whereupon the tempest would abate and seasickness cease. In the following passage Higginson describes the terrain upon which the voyagers landed from two points of view, one extolling its advantages, the other deploring its lacks.

THE COMMODITIES OF NEW ENGLAND

Iт is a land of divers and sundry sorts all about Masathulets Bay, and at Charles river is as fat black earth as can be seen anywhere; and in other places you have a clay soil, in other gravel, in other sandy, as it is all about our Plantation at Salem, for so our town is now named.

The form of the earth here, in the superficies of it, is neither too flat in the plainness, nor too high in hills, but partakes of both in a mediocrity, and fit for pasture or for plough or meadow ground, as men please to employ it. Though all the country be, as it were, a thick wood for the general, yet in divers places there is much ground cleared by the Indians, and especially about the Plantation; and I am told that about three miles from us a man may stand on a little hilly place and see divers thousands of acres of ground as good as need to be, and not a tree in the same. . . .

The fertility of the soil is to be admired at, as appeareth in the abundance of grass that groweth every where, both very thick, very long, and very high in divers places. But it groweth very wildly, with a great stalk, and a broad and ranker blade, because it never had been eaten with cattle, nor mowed with a scythe, and seldom trampled on by foot. It is scarce to be believed how our kine and goats, horses and hogs do thrive and prosper here, and like well of this country.

In our Plantation we have already a quart of milk for a penny. But the abundant increase of corn proves this country to be a wonderment. Thirty, forty, fifty, sixty, are ordinary here. Yea, Joseph's increase in Egypt is outstripped here with us. Our planters hope to have more than a hundredfold this year. And all this while I am within compass; what will you say of two hundred-fold, and upwards? It is almost incredible what great gain some of our English planters have had by our Indian corn. Credible persons have assured me, and the party himself avouched the truth of it to me, that of the setting of thirteen gallons of corn he hath had increase of it fifty-two hogsheads, every hogshead holding seven bushels of London measure, and every bushel was by him sold and trusted to the Indians for so much beaver as was worth eighteen shillings; and so of this thirteen gallons of corn, which was worth six shillings eight pence, he made about £327 of it the year following, as by reckoning will appear; where you may see how God blesseth husbandry in this land. There is not such great and plentiful ears of corn I suppose anywhere else to be found but in this country, being also of variety of colors, as red, blue, and yellow, &c.; and of one corn there springeth four or five hundred. I have sent you many ears of divers colors, that you might see the truth of it.

Little children here, by setting of corn, may earn much more than their own maintenance. . . .

This country aboundeth naturally with store of roots of great variety and good to eat. Our turnips, parsnips and carrots are here both bigger and sweeter than is ordinarily to be found in England. Here are also store of pumpions, cowcumbers, and other things of that nature which I know not. Also, divers excellent pot-herbs grow abundantly among the grass, as strawberry leaves in all places of the country, and plenty of strawberries in their time, and penny-royal, winter-savory, sorrel, brook-lime, liverwort, carvel, and watercresses; also leeks and onions are ordinary, and divers physical herbs. Here are also abundance of other sweet herbs, delightful to the smell, whose names we know not, and plenty of single damask roses, very sweet; and two kinds of herbs that bear two kinds of flowers very sweet, which they say are as good to make cordage or cloth as any hemp or flax we have.

Excellent vines are here up and down in the woods. Our Governor hath already planted a vineyard, with great hope of increase.

Also, mulberries, plums, raspberries, currants, chestnuts, filberts, walnuts, small-nuts, hurtleberries, and haws of white-thorn, near as good as our cherries in England, they grow in plenty here.

For wood, there is no better in the world, I think. . . .

Also here be divers roots and berries, wherewith the Indians dye excellent holding colors, that no rain nor washing can alter. Also we have materials to make soap ashes and saltpetre in abundance.

For beasts there are some bears, and they say some lions also; for they have been seen at Cape Anne. Also here are several sorts of deer, some whereof bring three or four young ones at once, which is not ordinary in England; also wolves, foxes, beavers, otters, martens, great wild cats, and a great beast called a molke, as big as an ox. I have seen the skins of all these beasts since I came to this Plantation, excepting lions. Also here are great store of squirrels, some greater, and some smaller and lesser;

there are some of the lesser sort, they tell me, that by a certain skin will fly from tree to tree, though they stand far distant.

New-England hath water enough, both salt and fresh. The greatest sea in the world, the Atlantic Sea, runs all along the coast thereof. There are abundance of islands along the shore, some full of wood and mast to feed swine, and others clear of wood, and fruitful to bear corn. Also we have store of excellent harbours for ships. . . .

The abundance of sea-fish are almost beyond believing; and sure I should scarce have believed it except I had seen it with mine own eyes. I saw great store of whales, and grampuses, and such abundance of mackerels that it would astonish one to behold; likewise codfish, abundance on the coast, and in their season are plentifully taken. There is a fish called a bass, a most sweet and wholesome fish as ever I did eat; it is altogether as good as our fresh salmon; and the season of their coming was begun when we came first to New-England in June, and so continued about three months' space. Of this fish our fishers take many hundreds together, which I have seen lying on the shore, to my admiration. Yea, their nets ordinarily take more than they are able to haul to land, and for want of boats and men they are constrained to let a many go after they have taken them; and yet sometimes they fill two boats at a time with them. And besides bass, we take plenty of scate and thornback, and abundance of lobsters, and the least boy in the Plantation may both catch and eat what he will of them. For my own part, I was soon cloyed with them, they were so great, and fat, and luscious. I have seen some myself that have weighed sixteen pound; but others have had divers times so great lobsters as have weighed twenty-five pound, as they assured me. . . .

The temper of the air of New-England is one special thing that commends this place. Experience doth manifest that there is hardly a more healthful place to be found in the world that agreeth better with our English bodies. Many that have been weak and sickly in Old England, by coming hither have been thoroughly healed, and grown healthful and strong. For here is an extraordinary clear and dry air, that is of a most healing nature to all such as are of a cold, melancholy, phlegmatic, rheumatic temper of body. . . .

In the summer time, in the midst of July and August, it is a good deal hotter than in Old England, and in winter January and February are much colder, as they say; but the spring and autumn are of a middle temper.

Fowls of the air are plentiful here, and of all sorts as we have in England, as far as I can learn, and a great many of strange fowls which we know not. . . .

Though it be here somewhat cold in the winter, yet here we have plenty of fire to warm us, and that a great deal cheaper than they sell billets and fagots in London; nay, all Europe is not able to afford to make so great fires as New-England. A poor servant here, that is to possess but fifty acres of land, may afford to give more wood for timber and fire as good as the world yields, than many noblemen in England can afford to do. Here is good living for those that love good fires. And although New-England have no tallow to make candles of, yet by the abundance of the fish thereof it can afford oil for lamps. Yea, our pine trees, that are the most plentiful of all wood, doth allow us plenty of candles, which are very useful in a house; and they are such candles as the Indians commonly use, having no other; and they are nothing else but the wood of the pine tree cloven in two little slices something thin, which are so full of the moisture of turpentine and pitch that they burn as clear as a torch.

A SETTING-FORTH OF DISCOMMODITIES

Now I will tell you of some discommodities, that are here to be found.

First, in the summer season, for these three months, June, July, and August, we are troubled much with little flies called mosquitoes, being the same they are troubled with in Lincolnshire and the fens; and they are nothing but gnats, which, except they be smoked out of their houses, are troublesome in the night season.

Secondly, in the winter season, for two months' space, the earth is commonly covered with snow, which is accompanied with sharp biting frosts, something more sharp than is in Old England, and therefore are forced to make great fires.

Thirdly, this country being very full of woods and wildernesses, doth also much abound with snakes and serpents, of strange colors and huge greatness. Yea, there are some serpents, called rattlesnakes, that have rattles in their tails, that will not fly from a man as others will, but will fly upon him and sting him so mortally that he will die within a quarter of an hour after, except the party stinged have about him some of the root of an herb called snake-weed to bite on, and then he shall receive no harm. But yet seldom falls it out that any hurt is done by these. About three years since an Indian was stung to death by one of them; but we heard of none since that time.

Fourthly and lastly, here wants as yet the good company of honest Christians, to bring with them horses, kine and sheep, to make use of this fruitful land. Great pity it is to see so much good ground for corn and for grass as any is under the heavens, to lie altogether unoccupied, when so many honest men and their families in Old England, through the populousness thereof, do make very hard shift to live one by the other.

SERMON ABOARD THE ARBELLA

JOHN WINTHROP

In 1630, even before the Massachusetts Bay Colonists had reached shore, they were preached a lay sermon, on board the flagship Arbella, *which laid down the terms of the social contract under which they would undertake a new life. In words as serious as they are stirring, John Winthrop (1588–1649), the fleet's commander and later governor of the colony, told them that the settlement would be a model of Puritanism upon which the eyes of the world would be fixed, that this was to be no search for economic prosperity or social advancement, but an experiment in religious society. The following is an excerpt from Winthrop's discourse.*

WHEN God giues a speciall Commission he lookes to haue it strictkly obserued in every Article, when hee gaue Saule a Commission to destroy Amaleck hee indented with him vpon certaine Articles and because hee failed in one of the least, and that vpon a faire pretence, it lost him the kingdome, which should haue beene his reward, if hee had obserued his Commission: Thus stands the cause betweene God and vs, wee are entered into Covenant with him for this worke, wee haue taken out a Commission, the Lord hath giuen vs leaue to drawe our owne Articles wee haue professed to enterprise these Accions vpon these and these ends, wee haue herevpon besought him of favour and blessing: Now if the Lord shall please to heare vs, and bring vs in peace to the place wee desire, then hath hee ratified this Covenant and sealed our Commission, [and] will expect a strickt performance of the Articles contained in it, but if wee shall neglect the observacion of these Articles which are the ends wee haue propounded, and dissembling with our God, shall fall to embrace this present world and prosecute our carnall intencions, seekeing greate things for our selues and our posterity, the Lord will surely breake out in wrathe against vs be revenged of such a periured people and make vs knowe the price of the breache of such a Covenant.

Now the onely way to avoyde this shipwracke and to provide for our posterity is to followe the Counsell of Micah, to doe Justly, to loue mercy, to walke humbly with our God, for this end, wee must be knitt together in this worke as one man, wee must entertaine each other in brotherly Affeccion, wee must be willing to abridge our selues of our superfluities, for the supply of others necessities, wee must vphold a familiar Commerce together in all meekenes, gentlenes, patience and liberallity, wee must delight in eache other, make others Condicions our owne reioyce together, mourne together, labour, and suffer together, allwayes haueing before our eyes our Commission and Community in the worke, our Community as members of the same body, soe shall wee keepe the vnitie of the spirit in the bond of peace, the Lord will be our God and delight to dwell among vs, as his owne people and will commaund a blessing vpon vs in all our wayes, soe that wee shall see much more of his wisdome power goodnes and truthe then formerly wee haue beene acquainted with, wee shall finde that the God of Israell is among vs, when tenn of vs shall be able to resist a thousand of our enemies, when hee shall make vs a prayse and glory, that men shall say of succeeding plantacions: the lord make it like that of New England: for wee must Consider that wee shall be as a Citty vpon a Hill, the eies of all people are vppon vs; soe that if wee shall deale falsely with our god in this worke wee haue vndertaken and soe cause him to withdrawe his present help from vs, wee shall be made a story and a by-word through the world, wee shall open the mouthes of enemies to speake euill of the wayes of god and all professours for Gods sake; wee shall shame the faces of many of gods worthy seruants, and cause theire prayers to be turned into Cursses vpon vs till wee be consumed out of the good land whether wee are goeing: And to shutt vpp this discourse with that exhortacion of Moses that faithfull seruant of the Lord in his last farewell to Israell Deut. 30. Beloued there is now sett before vs life, and good, deathe and euill in that wee are Commaunded this day to loue the Lord our God, and to loue one another to walke in his wayes and to keepe his Commaundements and his Ordinance, and his lawes, and the Articles of our Covenant with him that wee may liue and be multiplyed, and that the Lord our God may blesse vs in the land whether wee goe to possesse it: But if our heartes shall turne away soe that wee will not obey, but shall be seduced and worshipp [serue *canceled*] other Gods our pleasures, and proffitts, and serue them; it is propounded vnto vs this day, wee shall surely perishe out of the good Land whether wee passe over this vast Sea to possesse it;

> Therefore lett vs choose life,
> that wee, and our Seede,
> may liue; by obeyeing his
> voyce, and cleaueing to him,
> for hee is our life, and
> our prosperity.

JOURNAL

RICHARD MATHER

———◆•◆———

When one is shown models of the tiny ships in which the colonists came to America, one is baffled by how so many people, in such cramped quarters, necessarily carrying so much food and water for so long a voyage, endured their trips at all. The following passage from the Journal *of Richard Mather (1596–1669) gives an intimation of the kind of spiritual support the colonists relied upon.*

To a modern New Englander there is something touching about Mather's mention of familiar seaside spots: Saugust is Saugus, Marvil head is Marblehead, and Nantascot is Nantasket, a beach where, for generations now, children have played on the yellow sand and dabbled in the little waves.

FRIDAY, wind still northerly, but very faint. It was a great foggy mist, and exceeding cold as it had been December. One would have wondered to have seen the innumerable numbers of fowl which we saw swimming on every side of the ship, and mighty fishes rolling and tumbling in the waters, twice as long and big as an ox. In the afternoon we saw mighty whales spewing up water in the air, like the smoke of a chimney, and making the sea about them white and hoary (as it is said, Job xli. 32),—of such incredible bigness that I will never wonder that the body of Jonas could be in the belly of a whale. . . . On Friday, in the evening, we had an hour or two of marvellous delightful recreation, which also was a feast unto us for many days after, while we fed upon the flesh of three huge porpoises, like to as many fat hogs, struck by our seamen and hauled with ropes into the ship; the flesh of them was good meat with salt, pepper and vinegar; the fat like fat bacon, the lean like bull-beef; and on Saturday evening they took another also. . . .

The Lord had not done with us, nor yet had let us see all his power and goodness which he would have us to take knowledge of. And therefore on Saturday morning about break of day, the Lord sent forth a most terrible storm of rain and easterly wind, whereby we were in as much danger as I think ever people were; for we lost in that morning three great anchors and cables, of which cables, one (having cost fifty pounds) never had been in any water before, two were broken by the violence of the waves, and the third cut by the seamen, in extremity and distress, to save the ship and their and our lives. . . . The Lord let us see that our sails could not save us neither, no more than our cables and anchors; for by the force of the wind and rain the sails were rent in sunder and split in pieces, as if they had been but rotten rags, so that of the foresail and spritsail there was scarce left as much as an hand-breadth, that was not rent in pieces, and blown away into the sea. So that at this time all hope that we should be saved in regard to any outward appearance was utterly taken away, and the rather because we seemed to drive with full force of wind and rain directly upon a mighty rock standing out in sight above the water, so that we did but continually wait, when we should hear and feel the doleful rushing and crushing of the ship upon the rock. In this extremity and appearance of death, as distress and distraction would suffer us, we cried unto the Lord, and He was pleased to have compassion and pity upon us; for by his overruling providence and his own immediate good hand, He guided the ship past the rock, assuaged the violence of the sea, and the wind and rain, and gave us a little respite to fit the ship with other sails. . . . In all this grievous storm, my fear was the less, when I considered the clearness of my calling from God this way, and in some measure (the Lord's holy name be blessed for it) He gave us hearts contented and willing that He should do with us and ours what He pleased, and what might be most for the glory of his name, and in that we rested ourselves. But when news was brought unto us into the gunroom that the danger was past, oh, how our hearts did then relent and melt within us! And how we burst out into tears of joy amongst ourselves, in love unto our gracious God, and admiration of his kindness in granting to his poor servants such an extraordinary and miraculous deliverance! His holy name be blessed forever!

This day we went on towards Cape Anne, as the wind would suffer, and our poor sails further, and came within sight thereof the other morning; which Sabbath, being the thirteenth we kept on shipboard, was a marvellous pleasant day, for a fresh gale of wind and clear sunshine weather. This day we went directly before the wind, and had delight all along the coast as we went, in viewing Cape Anne, the bay of Saugust, the bay of Salem, Marvil head, Pullin point, and other places; and came to anchor at low tide in the evening at Nantascot, in a most pleasant harbor, like to which I had never seen, amongst a great many of islands on every side. I was exercised on shipboard both ends of the day. After the evening's exercise, when it was flowing tide again, we set sail, and came that night to anchor again before Boston, and so rested that night with glad and thankful hearts that God had put an end to a long journey, being a thousand leagues, that is, three thousand miles English, over one of the greatest seas in the world.

ANNE HUTCHINSON'S EXILE

THOMAS WELDE

————◆◆————

*Most people assume that the Puritans were hypocritical to seek "freedom
to worship God" while denying a similar freedom to any other religious
persuasion. Actually, convinced that they were possessed of "the one and
only truth," the Puritans would have considered it hypocritical to grant
freedom to any other faith. According to their lights, such tolerance
would have been grave error.*

*Anne Hutchinson (1591–1643) seems a romantic figure, a martyr to Puri-
tan rigidity. What really happened to Mrs. Hutchinson? She arrived in the
colony in 1634, an admirer and follower of the theologian John Cotton
(1584–1652). In three years "after a career like that of Madame Récamier
in her salon in Paris," Mrs. Hutchinson was involved in a religious crisis
over denial of the "phases of conversion" in the soul's "preparation for
Christ," as the Rev. Thomas Hooker had laid them down to demonstrate
a point fundamental to Puritan theology that there is order in God's
plan. "I like not his spirit," Mrs. Hutchinson said of Hooker. She took the
position that revelation could be received directly from the Holy Ghost
without preparation, in accordance with Antimonian notions of salvation
by grace.*

*Her hearing before the General Court—which handled both religious
and civil cases, the two being not distinguishable in Puritan New England—was in effect a heresy trial. Throughout it, Perry Miller tells us,
"Cotton was clearly trying to save Mrs. Hutchinson," and, "Like the good
man he was, he tried to get her to distinguish between such a Christian
hope as anyone might entertain, and a false revelation . . . [but] he had
no choice but to bring her to her defiant assertion that it was supernatural
intervention she counted on."*

*The account of the trial John Winthrop left admits that at this he "ex-
ulted that the Jezebel delivered herself out of her own mouth, showing
that she . . . believed in bottomless revelations above reason and Scripture." She had also come close to delivering poor Mr. Cotton out of her
own mouth as well; but Winthrop himself rescued the divine by asserting
he was not obliged to answer any questions from the court, whose duty
was simply to judge Mrs. Hutchinson.*

I have chosen another voice to tell of the trial, that of Thomas Welde (1595–1661), a minister who took a leading part in the persecution of Mrs. Hutchinson. He, with John Eliot and Richard Mather, was one of the authors of the Bay Psalm Book.

HOW THE HERESIES CAME TO AN END

A GREAT while they did not believe that Mistress Hutchinson and some others did hold such things as they were taxed for, but when themselves heard her defending her twenty-nine cursed opinions in Boston church, and there falling into fearful lying, with an impudent forehead in the open assembly, then they believed what before they could not, and were ashamed before God and men that ever they were so led aside from the Lord and his truth, and the godly counsel of their faithful ministers, by such an impostor as she was.

Now no man could lay more upon them, than they would upon themselves in their acknowledgments.

Many after this came unto us, who before flew from us, with such desires as those in Acts ii.: "Men and brethren, what shall we do?" and did willingly take shame to themselves in the open assemblies by confessing (some of them with many tears) how they had given offence to the Lord and his people by departing from the truth and being led by a spirit of error, their alienation from their brethren in their affections, and their crooked and perverse walking in contempt of authority, slighting the churches and despising the counsel of their godly teachers.

Now they would freely discover the sleights the adversaries had used to undermine them by, and steal away their eyes from the truth and their brethren, which before (whiles their hearts were sealed) they could not see. And the fruit of this was, great praise to the Lord, who had thus wonderfully wrought matters about, gladness in all our hearts and faces, and expressions of our renewed affections by receiving them again into our bosoms, and from that time until now have walked, according to their renewed covenants, humbly and lovingly amongst us, holding forth truth and peace with power.

But for the rest, which (notwithstanding all these means of conviction from heaven and earth, and the example of their seduced brethren's return) yet stood obdurate, yea, more hardened (as we had cause to fear) than before; we convented those of them that were members before the churches, and yet labored once and again to convince them, not only of their errors, but also of sundry exorbitant practices which they had fallen into; as manifest pride, contempt of authority, neglecting to fear the church, and lying, etc., but after no means prevailed we were driven with sad hearts to give them up to Satan. Yet not simply for their opinions, for which I find we have been slanderously traduced, but the chiefest cause of their censure was their miscarriages, as has been said, persisted in with great obstinacy.

The persons cast out of the churches were about nine or ten, as far as I can remember; who for a space continued very hard and impenitent, but afterward some of them were received into fellowship again, upon their repentance.

These persons cast out, and the rest of the ring-leaders that had received sentence of banishment, with many others infected by them, that were neither censured in court nor in churches, went all together out of our jurisdiction and precinct into an island, called Rhode Island (surnamed by some, the Island of Errors), and there they live to this day, most of them; but in great strife and contention in the civil estate and otherwise; hatching and multiplying new opinions, and cannot agree, but are miserably divided into sundry sects and factions.

But Mistress Hutchinson, being weary of the Island, or rather, the Island weary of her, departed from thence with all her family, her daughter, and her children, to live under the Dutch, near a place called by seamen and in the map, Hell-gate. (And now I am come to the last act of her tragedy, a most heavy stroke upon herself and hers, as I received it very lately from a godly hand in New-England.) There the Indians set upon them and slew her and all her family, and her daughter's husband and all their children, save one that escaped (her own husband being dead before), a dreadful blow. Some write that the Indians did burn her to death with fire, her house and all the rest named that belonged to her; but I am not able to affirm by what kind of death they slew her, but slain it seems she is, according to all reports. I never heard that the Indians in those parts did ever before this commit the like outrage upon any one family, or families; and therefore God's hand is the more apparently seen herein, to pick out this woful woman, to make her and those belonging to her an unheard of heavy example of their cruelty above others.

Thus the Lord heard our groans to heaven and freed us from this great and sore affliction, which first was small, like Elias' cloud, but after spread the heavens; and hath (through great mercy) given the churches rest from this disturbance ever since; that we know none that lifts up his head to disturb our sweet peace, in any of the churches of Christ among us. Blessed forever be his Name.

I bow my knees to the God of truth and peace, to grant these churches as full a riddance from the same or like opinions, which do destroy his truth and disturb their peace.

EVERYDAY LIFE IN MASSACHUSETTS BAY COLONY

GEORGE DOW

The following is a modern account of forms of punishment that were administered to, and accepted by, grown-up people in the new colony as an appropriate atonement for error. It is taken from Everyday Life in Massachusetts Bay Colony, *by George Dow.*

It is interesting to discover that such punishments were no more severe than those meted out in Virginia at the time, and less so than those in England. During the first half of the seventeenth century, Virginia laws against Sabbath breaking and other religious contempts were almost as strict as in Massachusetts. Days of fasting and humiliation were appointed in one colony as in the other. Witchcraft was persecuted in Virginia, even though she hanged no witches.

EXPIATION OF CRIMES

To sentence a culprit to expiate his crime before the congregation in the meetinghouse was a common thing. The publicity, in theory, induced shame and thus served as a future deterrent. To sit in the stocks and then make public acknowledgment before the congregation was a favorite penalty. Sometimes the offender was ordered to stand at the church door with a paper on his hat inscribed with the crime he had committed. If for lying, a cleft stick might ornament his tongue. Whipping was the most frequent penalty, closely followed by the stocks, and after a time imprisonment became more common. The bilboes were used only in the earliest period. The use of the stocks and whipping post was discontinued in 1813 and not a single example seems to have survived in either museum or attic. The pillory was in use in State Street, Boston, as late as 1803, and two years before, John Hawkins stood one hour in the pillory in what is now Washington Street, Salem, and afterwards had one ear cropped—all for the crime of forgery. Branding the hand or cheek was also inflicted, and Hawthorne has made famous another form of branding, the wearing prominently upon the clothing, an initial letter of a contrary color, symbolizing the crime committed. This penalty was inflicted upon a man at Springfield, as late as October 7, 1754, and the law remained in force until February 17, 1785. As early as 1634 a Boston drunkard was sentenced to wear a red D about his neck for a year.*

Massachusetts did not purge her laws from these ignominous punishments until 1813 when whipping, branding, the stocks, the pillory, cutting off ears, slitting noses, boring tongues, etc., were done away with.

There lived in Salem, nearly three centuries ago, a woman whose story is told by Governor Winthrop and the records of the Quarterly Courts. She was, in a sense, a forerunner of Anne Hutchinson and we may fancy at heart a suffragette. Her story gives you an outline picture of the manners of the times in a few details. Her name was Mary Oliver and her criminal record begins in June, 1638. Governor Winthrop relates: "Amongst the rest, there was a woman in Salem, one Oliver, his wife, who had suffered somewhat in England by refusing to bow at the name of Jesus, though otherwise she was conformable to all their orders. She was (for ability of speech, and appearance of zeal and devotion) far before Mrs. Hutchinson, and so the fitter instrument to have done hurt, but that she was poor and had little acquaintance. She took offence at this, that she might not be admitted to the Lord's supper without giving public satisfaction to the church of her faith, etc., and covenanting or professing to walk with them according to the rule of the gospel; so as upon the sacrament day she openly called for it, stood to plead her right, though she were denied; and would not forbear, before the magistrate, Mr. Endecott, did threaten to send the constable to put her forth. This woman was brought to the Court for disturbing the peace in the church, etc., and there she gave such peremptory answers, as she was committed till she should find surities for her good behavior. After she had been in

* At the Court of Assize, at Springfield, the 2d Tuesday of September last, Daniel Bailey and Mary Rainer, of a Place adjoining to Sheffield in that county, were convicted of Adultery, and were sentenced to suffer the Penalty of the Law therefor, viz. to sit on the Gallows with a Rope about their Necks, for the Space of an Hour; to be whipt forty Stripes each, and to wear for ever after a Capital A, two Inches long, and proportionable in bigness, cut out in Cloth of a contrary Colour to their Cloaths, and sewed upon their upper Garments, either upon the outside of the arm, or on the back. —*Boston Evening-Post*, Oct. 9, 1752.

A case of incest in Deerfield: "the man was set upon the Gallows with a Rope about his Neck for the space of one Hour, to be whipped in his Way from thence to the Goal 30 stripes, and to wear a Capital I of two Inches long, and proportionable Bigness on his upper Garment for ever. Sentence against the Woman, for special Reasons, we hear, is respited for the present."—*Boston Evening-Post*, Oct. 7, 1754.

At the Superior Court held in Cambridge last week, one Hannah Dudley of Lincoln was convicted of repeatedly committing Adultery and Fornication with her own Mother's husband, an old Man of 76 years of age. She was sentenced to be set upon the Gallows for the space of one Hour, with a Rope about her Neck, and the other end cast over the Gallows, and in the way from thence to the Common Goal, that she be severely whipped 30 stripes, and that she for ever after wear a Capital I of two inches long and proportionable bigness cut out in Cloth of a different Colour to her Cloaths, and sewed upon her upper Garment on the outside of her arm, or on her Back, in Open View. [No further mention is made of the step-father.]—*Boston News-Letter*, Aug. 16, 1759.

prison three or four days, she made means to the Governor and submitted herself, and acknowledged her fault in disturbing the church; whereupon he took her husband's bond for her good behavior, and discharged her out of prison. But he found, after, that she still held her former opinions, which were very dangerous, as, (I) that the church is the head of the people, both magistrates and ministers, met together and that these have power to ordain ministers, etc. (II) That all that dwell in the same town, and will profess their faith in Christ Jesus, ought to be received to the sacraments there; and that she was persuaded that, if Paul were at Salem, he would call all the inhabitants there saints. (III) That excommunication is no other but when christians withdraw private communion from one that hath offended." September 24, 1639, this Mary Oliver was sentenced to prison in Boston indefinitely for her speeches at the arrival of newcomers. She was to be taken by the constables of Salem and Lynn to the prison in Boston. Her husband Thomas Oliver was bound in £20 for his wife's appearance at the next court in Boston.

Governor Winthrop continues: "About five years after, this woman was adjudged to be whipped for reproaching the magistrates. She stood without tying, and bore her punishment with a masculine spirit, glorying in her suffering. But after (when she came to consider the reproach, which would stick by her, etc.) she was much dejected about it. She had a cleft stick put on her tongue half an hour for reproaching the elders."

March 2, 1647–8, Mary Oliver was fined for working on the Sabbath day in time of public exercise; also for abusing Capt. Hathorne, uttering divers mutinous speeches, and denying the morality of the Sabbath. She was sentenced to sit in the stocks one hour next lecture day, if the weather be moderate; also for saying "You in New England are thieves and Robbers" and for saying to Mr. Gutch that she hoped to tear his flesh in pieces and all such as he was. For this she was bound to good behavior, and refusing to give bond was sent to Boston jail, and if she remained in the court's jurisdiction was to answer to further complaints at the next Salem Court.

It appears from depositions that she went to Robert Gutch's house in such gladness of spirit that he couldn't understand it, and she said to some there, not members, "Lift up your heads, your redemption draweth near," and when reminded what she already had been punished for, she said that she came out of that with a scarf and a ring.

November 15, 1648, Mary Oliver for living from her husband, was ordered to go to him before the next court, and in December she brought suit against John Robinson for false imprisonment, taking her in a violent manner and putting her in the stocks. She recovered a judgment of 10s. damages. The following February Mary Oliver was again presented at Court for living from her husband, and in July, having been ordered to go to her husband in England by the next ship, she was further enjoyed to go by the next opportunity on penalty of 20 li.

November 13, 1649, Mary Oliver was presented for stealing goats, and a month later she was presented for speaking against the Governor, saying that he was unjust, corrupt and a wretch, and that he made her pay for stealing two goats when there was no proof in the world of it. She was sentenced to be whipped next lecture day at Salem, if the weather be moderate, not exceeding twenty stripes. Capt. William Hathorne and Mr. Emanuel Downing were to see the sentence executed. At the same court George Ropes complained that Mary Oliver kept away a spade of his and she was fined 5s.

February 28, 1649–50, Mary Oliver thus far had escaped the second whipping, for at her request Mr. Batter asked that her sentence be respited, which the Court granted "if she doe go into the Bay with Joseph Hardy this day or when he goeth next into the Bay with his vessell" otherwise she was to be called forth by Mr. Downing and Capt. Hathorne and be punished. If she returned, the punishment was to hold good.

The next day Mary Oliver's fine was remitted to the end that she use it in transporting herself and children out of this jurisdiction within three weeks. And there ended her turbulent career in the town of Salem, so far as the Court records show.

REPENTANT SINNERS AND THEIR MINISTERS

REV. THOMAS HOOKER

There were powerful forces at work in men's hearts to make them accept such harsh atonements as a part of their way of life. The sermon about repentance excerpted here is by the Rev. Thomas Hooker (1586–1647). As a theologian, Hooker was the rival of John Cotton.

After being pastor at Cambridge, Massachusetts, Hooker led his flock into Connecticut to found Hartford (where Hookers have abounded).

His is a good sample of a Puritan sermon in the "plain style," as opposed to the ornate rhetoric of the Laudian preachers in England. It is constructed on a firm basis of logic, so that the congregation could follow its progression through "doctrine" to "reasons" to "uses."

*I have appended to the sermon an anecdote told of Hooker by Timothy
Dwight (1752–1817), a president of Yale, in his* Travels in New England
and New York.

REPENTANT SINNERS AND THEIR MINISTERS

DOCTRINE: They whose hearts are pierced by the ministry of the word,
they are carried with love and respect to the ministers of it.

Men and brethren, they be words of honor and love, and they spoke
them seriously and affectionately. They mocked them before, and they
now embrace them; they cared not what terms of reproach they cast upon
their persons, they know not now what titles of love and tenderness to put
upon them; they now fall at their feet as clients, who flouted them before as enemies. So it was with the jailor; (Acts 16. 30, 31, 34) how kindly
doth he Paul and Silas, whom, erewhile he handled so currishly,
beyond the bounds of reason and humanity, he entertains them in the
best room of his house, who before thought the worst place in the prison
too good for them. He bathes their wounded parts which he had whipped
and stocked before, fears and trembles before them as his counselors,
whom he handled most harshly before as prisoners; he feasts them as his
guests whom he had struck as malefactors; the wind was in another door,
the man is of another mind, yea, is another man than he was. God had no
sooner opened the heart of Lydia to attend the word but her affections
were exceedingly enlarged towards the dispensers thereof (Acts 16. 15),
so that the cords of her loving invitation led Paul and held him captive;
he professed, "She compelled them," *i.e.*, by her loving and affectionate
expressions, prevailed with them for a stay. And while Paul had the
Galatians under the pangs of the new birth and Christ was now forming in
them, they professed they "would have plucked out their eyes" and have
given them to the apostle (Gal. 4. 15).

Naaman hath no sooner his leprosy healed, and his heart humbled and
cut off from his corruption, but he professed himself and what he had is
at the devotion of the prophet, and that not out of compliment but in
truth: (II Kings 5. 15) "Take a blessing from thy servant."

Reasons are two:

They see and know more than formerly they did, when happily the
crooked counsels of others deceived them, and their own carnal reason
cozened and deluded their own souls that they misjudged the men and
their doctrine also. As that they did not speak the truth, or else had
some crooked and self-seeking ends in what they spoke: as either to
gratify other men's humors whom they would please or else to set up
their own persons and praise and esteem in the apprehensions of others as
singular men and more than of an ordinary frame; and therefore would
wind men up to such a high pitch of holiness, and force them to such a

singular care to fly the very appearance of all evil, when it's more than needs and more than God requires, and more than any man can do. But now they find by proof and are forced out of their own sense and feeling to acknowledge the truth of what they have spoken and what they have heard, and themselves also to be the faithful ambassadors of the Lord Jesus, and therefore worthy to be believed and attended in their dispensations and honored of all. So Paul: (II Cor. 4. 3) "We hope we are made manifest unto your consciences." Thus the woman of Samaria, when our savior came home to the quick and met with the secrets of her heart, she then fell from her taunting and slighting of our savior to admiring of him: "Come, faith, she beheld the man that told me all that ever I did: is not he the Christ" (John 4. 29)? Look as Nebuchadnezzar said: (Dan. 4.) "Now I know the God of Daniel is the true God, and now I praise the living God." So when they have been in the fire, and God hath had them upon the anvil: now I know what sin is, now I know what the danger is, now I know what necessity there is to part with sin. When the patient hath found the relation and direction of the physician hath proved real, it makes him prize and honor his skill and counsel forever, and forever to have his custom. As the pythonist was compelled from the power of Paul's administration to confess, "These are the servants of the living God which show unto us the way of salvation"; so here.

As they see more and can therefore judge better of the worth of persons and things, so their conscience now hath more scope, and the light of reason hath more liberty, and allowance to express that they know, and nothing now can withstand and hinder. For while men are held captive under the power of their lusts and corruptions of their hearts, in which they live and which for the while they are resolved to follow— though their reason happily do yield it, and their own hearts and consciences cannot but inwardly confess it, the persons are holy, the sins are vile which they condemn and dangers dreadful which they forewarn—yet to profess so much openly to others and to the world were to judge themselves while they would acquit others, and condemn their own courses while they should praise and honor the carriages and persons of others, and therefore darken the evidence of the word by carnal cavils and reproaches, stifle the witness of conscience, and stop its mouth that it cannot speak out. Thus (Rom. 1. 18): "They hold down the truth in unrighteousness." When the truth that is by their judgments assented unto and by their hearts yielded, and therefore should break out and give in testimony to the good ways of God, their corrupt and unrighteous and rebellious hearts hold it prisoner, will not suffer it either to appear unto others or prevail with themselves; as it fared with the scribes and Pharisees when the wonder was wrought by Peter, say they: (Acts 4. 16) "That indeed a notable miracle hath been done by them is manifest to all that dwell in Jerusalem, and we cannot deny it" (*q.d.* they would have

done it if they could) "but that it spread no further, let us charge them
straightly that they speak no more in this name." But here when the
conscience of a poor sinner is convinced and the heart wounded, and that
resistance and gainsaying distemper is taken off and crushed, now conscience is in commission and hath his scope, and the coast is now clear
that reason may be heard. Now the broken-hearted sinner will speak
plainly: these are the guides that God hath set up, their direction I will
attend, these are the dear and faithful servants of the Lord whom I must
honor, and with them I would betrust my soul; not with the blind guides
and false teachers, who daub with untempered mortar and are not
trusty to God nor their own souls, and therefore cannot be to me. Oh,
send for such, though in their lifetime they could not endure the sight,
abide the presence, nor allow them a good word, reviled their persons
and proceedings and professions (yea, that they will confess), but it was
directly against their own judgment and knowledge and conscience.
Mine own heart often gave my tongue the lie, when I did so speak and
so disparage their conversation; otherwise I must have condemned mine
own course and conscience also. But the Lord is with them, and the truth
is with them, and a blessing will undoubtedly follow them. Ask why these
poor pierced sinners did not go to the scribes, they would tell the truth.
Oh, it was they that deceived us, led and drew us to the commission of
this hellish wickedness; we cannot call them teachers but murderers; they
could never help themselves, therefore not help us.

Instruction: Sound contrition and brokenness of heart brings a strange
and a sudden alteration into the world, varies the price and value of
things and persons beyond imagination, turns the market upside down,
makes the things appear as they be, and the persons to be honored and
respected as they are in truth, that look what the truth determines, reason approves, and conscience witnesseth. That account is current in the
hearts and apprehensions of those whose hearts have been pierced with
godly sorrow for their sins. Because such judge not by outward appearance as it is the guise of men of corrupt minds, but upon experience,
that which they have found and felt in their own hearts, what they have
seen and judged in their own spirits, they cannot but see so and judge so
of others. Those who were mocked as "men full of new wine" are now the
precious servants of the Lord; flouted to their faces not long since, now
they attend them, honor and reverence them—yea, fall at their very feet.
It was before men and drunkards, now men and brethren; the world you
see is well amended, but strangely altered. It was said of John Baptist,
the forerunner of our savior, and the scope of whose doctrine was mainly
to prepare the way for the Lord—it's said of him that Elias is come and
hath reformed all, set a new face and frame in the profession of the
Gospel: (Matt. 17. 11) "Turned the disobedient to the wisdom of the
just men, the hearts of children to the fathers." That though they were so

degenerate that Abraham would not own them had he been alive, yet when the ministry of John had hammered and melted them for the work of our savior, they became to be wholly altered, their judgments altered and their carriage also. For in truth, the reason why men see not the loathsomeness of other men's sins, or else have not courage to pass a righteous sentence upon them, it is because they were never convinced to see the plague sore of their own corruptions, never had their hearts affected with the evil of them in their own experience, but their own conscience was misled out of authority, and stifled that it durst not outwardly condemn that which inwardly they could not but approve. They therefore who either do not see their own evil or dare not proceed in open judgment to condemn, they will either not see or not pass a righteous judgment upon others; so Paul intimates to Agrippa: (Acts 26. 8, 9) "Let it not seem strange, oh King, for I myself did think I should do many things against the name of Jesus, which I also did." *Q.d.:* whilst thou so continuest thou wilt see as I did and do as I did, but after God had entered into combat with him and spoken dreadfully to his soul, see! he is another man and of another mind. He destroyed the churches, now takes care of them; he that hated the name and Gospel of Jesus counts all things dung and dross for the excellent knowledge of Jesus; the world is well amended but it's marvelously altered, and therefore "We have found this man a pestilent fellow" (Acts 24. 5); he hath subdued the state of the world.

Terror: This shows the dreadful and miserable condition of all those who after all the light that hath been let into their minds, conviction into their consciences, horror into their hearts touching the evils that have been committed and come now to be discovered unto them, they loathe the light that hath laid open their evils, distaste those persons and preachers and Christians most, that have dealt most plainly to discover the loathsomeness of their distempers. It shows the irrecoverable corruption of the mind and heart that grows worst under the best means, and cleaves most to its sins under all the choicest means that would pluck their sins from their heart, and their heart from them. They are either fools or madmen that cannot endure the presence of the physician without whose help they could not be cured. This is made an evidence of the estrangement of God's heart from a people, and an immediate forerunner of their ruin: (Isa. 9. 13, 14, 17) "For this people turneth not unto him that smote them, neither do they seek the Lord, therefore the Lord will cut off from Israel head and tail, branch and rush, in one day; therefore the Lord shall have no pity on their young men, nor mercy on their fatherless, for every one is an hypocrite." It takes away all pity in God, all hopes in themselves of any good. After Pharaoh had many qualms and recoilings of spirit by Moses' dealing with him and the miracles which he had wrought for his repentance, and at last sides it with the hellish stiffness of his own stubborn heart, so that he cannot endure the speech or presence of Moses any more, (Exod. 10. 28) "Get thee from me, see my face no more, for the day thou seest my face thou shalt die," God sends Moses no more, but sends His plagues to destroy his first-born. He will not see the face of Moses, he shall feel the fierceness of the wrath of the Lord.

MINISTER HOOKER'S CHRISTIANITY

TIMOTHY DWIGHT

THE following anecdote, transmitted among his descendants, is in several particulars strongly expressive of his character. In the latter part of autumn Mr. Hooker, being suddenly awakened by an unusual noise, thought he heard a person in his cellar. He immediately arose, dressed himself, and went silently to the foot of the cellar stairs. There he saw a man with a candle in his hand, taking pork out of the barrel. When he had taken out the last piece, Mr. Hooker, accosting him pleasantly, said, "Neighbor, you act unfairly; you ought to leave a part for me." Thunderstruck at being detected, especially at being detected by so awful a witness, the culprit fell at his feet, condemned himself for his wickedness, and implored his pardon. Mr. Hooker cheerfully forgave him and concealed his crime, but forced him to carry half the pork to his own house.

THE BAY PSALM BOOK

RICHARD MATHER

◆◆◆

Psalm singing was an integral part of Puritan religious services. Back in England, in fact, the Cavaliers called the Puritans "blue-nosed psalm-singers." One of the several projects on which the newly arrived Massachusetts Bay Colony set to work was a new translation of the Psalms. Richard Mather headed the work on the Bay Psalm Book—the name generally given to The Whole Booke of Psalmes Faithfully Translated into English Metre. *Published at Cambridge, in 1640, this was the first full-sized book to be printed in the colony. The few copies which endure, of the first edition of 1,700 copies, today fetch phenomenal sums.*

Mather's preface, excerpted below, displays the scruples of the Puritan

*mind faced with frivolities like rhyme and meter in matters of religion.
It is followed by a sampling of the verse Psalms themselves, which in turn
are followed by a short excerpt from the treatise by John Cotton,* Singing
of Psalms a Gospel Ordinance, *which worries the question of whether
one or all should sing in meeting, whether in lively voice, etc.*

PREFACE

THE singing of psalms, though it breathe forth nothing but holy harmony and melody, yet such is the subtlety of the Enemy—and the enmity
of our nature against the Lord and His ways—that our hearts can find
matter of discord in this harmony, and crotchets of division in this holy
melody.

For, there have been three questions especially stirring concerning
singing: First, what psalms are to be sung in the churches—whether
David's and other scripture psalms or the psalms invented by the gifts of
godly men in every age of the church? Secondly, if scripture psalms,
whether in their own words or in such meter as English poetry is wont to
run in? Thirdly, by whom are they to be sung—whether by the whole
church together with their voices, or by one man singing alone and the
rest joining in silence and in the close saying amen?

Touching the first, certainly the singing of David's psalms was an acceptable worship of God, not only in his own but in succeeding times. . . .

As for the scruple that some take at the translation of the Book of
Psalms into meter, because David's psalms were sung in his own words
without meter, we answer: First, there are many verses together in several psalms of David which run in rhythms, . . . which shows at least the
lawfulness of singing psalms in English rhythms.

Secondly, the psalms are penned in such verses as are suitable to the
poetry of the Hebrew language and not in the common style of such
other books of the Old Testament as are not poetical. Now, no Protestant
doubteth but that all the books of the scripture should by God's ordinance be extant in the mother tongue of each nation, that they may be
understood of all: hence the psalms are to be translated into our English
tongue. And if in our English tongue we are to sing them, then, as all our
English songs according to the course of our English poetry do run in
meter, so ought David's psalms to be translated into meter, that so we
may sing the Lord's songs, as in our English tongue, so in such verses as
are familiar to an English ear—which are commonly metrical. And as it
can be no just offense to any good conscience to sing David's Hebrew
songs in English words, so neither to sing his poetical verses in English
poetical meter. Men might as well stumble at singing the Hebrew psalms
in our English tunes, and not in the Hebrew tunes, as at singing them in

English meter, which are our verses, and not in such verses as are generally used by David according to the poetry of the Hebrew language.
But the truth is, as the Lord hath hid from us the Hebrew tunes, lest we
should think ourselves bound to imitate them, so also the course and
frame, for the most part, of their Hebrew poetry—that we might not think
ourselves bound to imitate that; but that every nation without scruple
might follow, as the grave sort of tunes of their own country songs, so the
graver sort of verses of their own country poetry.

Neither let any think that for the meter's sake we have taken liberty or
poetical license to depart from the true and proper sense of David's words
in the Hebrew verses. No, but it hath been one part of our religious care
and faithful endeavor to keep close to the original text. . . .

If therefore the verses are not always so smooth and elegant as some
may desire or expect, let them consider that God's altar needs not our
polishing (Exod. 20). For we have respected rather a plain translation
than to smooth our verses with the sweetness of any paraphrase: and so
have attended conscience rather than elegance, fidelity rather than poetry,
in translating the Hebrew words into English language and David's
poetry into English meter; that so we may sing in Sion the Lord's songs
of praise according to His own will—until He take us from hence, and
wipe away all our tears, and bid us enter into our Master's joy to sing
eternal halleluiahs.

PSALME XLVI

God is our refuge, strength, & help
   in troubles very neere.
Therefore we will not be afrayd,
   though th' earth removed were.
Though mountaines move to midst of seas
   Though waters roaring make
and troubled be, at whose swellings
   although the mountaines shake. Selah.
There is a river streames whereof
   shall rejoyce Gods city:
the holy place the tent wherin
   abideth the most high.
God is within the midst of her,
   moved shee shall not bee:
God shall be unto her an help,
   in the morning early.
The nations made tumultuous noyse,
   the kingdomes moved were:
he did give forth his thundering voyce
   the earth did melt with feare.

The God of Armies is with us
 th' eternall Iehovah:
the God of Iacob is for us
 a refuge high. Selah.
O come yee forth behold the works
 which Iehovah hath wrought,
the fearfull desolations,
Unto the utmost ends of th' earth
 warres into peace hee turnes:
the speare he cuts, the bowe he breaks,
 in fire the chariots burnes.
Be still, & know that I am God,
 exalted be will I
among the heathen: through the earth
 I'le be exalted hye.
The God of armyes is with us,
 th' eternall Iehovah
the God of Iacob is for us
 a refuge high. Selah.

CONCERNING THE SINGERS: WHETHER WOMEN, PAGANS, AND PROFANE AND CARNAL PERSONS

JOHN COTTON

THE third question about singing of Psalms concerneth the Singers. For though vocal singing be approved and also the singing of David's Psalms, yet still it remaineth to some a question who must sing them. And here a threefold scruple ariseth. 1. Whether one be to sing for all the rest, the rest joining only in spirit and saying Amen; or the whole Congregation? 2. Whether women as well as men; or men alone? 3. Whether carnal men and Pagans may be permitted to sing with us or Christians alone and Church-Members? . . .

The second scruple about Singers is "Whether women may sing as well as men." For in this point there be some that deal with us as Pharaoh dealt with the Israelites, who though he was at first utterly unwilling that any of them should go to sacrifice to the Lord in the Wilderness yet being at length convinced that they must go, then he was content the Men should go but not the Women. So here, some that were altogether against singing of Psalms at all with a lively voice, yet being convinced that it is a moral worship of God warranted in Scripture, then if there must be a Singing one alone must sing, not all (or if all) the Men only and not the Women.

And their reason is. "1. Because it is not permitted to a woman to speak in the Church (I. Cor. xiii. 34.) How then shall they sing? 2. Much less it is permitted to them to prophesy in the Church (I. Tim. ii. 11, 12.) And singing of Psalms is a kind of prophesying."

One answer may at once remove both these scruples and withal clear the truth. It is apparent by the scope and context of both those Scriptures that a woman is not permitted to speak in the Church in two cases: 1. By way of teaching, whether in expounding or applying Scripture. For this the Apostle accounteth an act of authority which is unlawful for a woman to usurp over the man, II. Tim. ii. 13. And besides the woman is more subject to error than a man, *ver.* 14. and therefore might soon prove a seducer if she became a teacher.

2. It is not permitted to a woman to speak in the Church by way of propounding questions though under pretence of desire to learn for her own satisfaction; but rather it is required she should ask her husband at home.

For under pretence of questioning for learning sake, she might so propound her question as to teach her teachers; or if not so, yet to open a door to some of her own weak and erroneous apprehensions, or at least soon exceed the bounds of womanly modesty.

Nevertheless in two other cases, it is clear a woman is allowed to speak in the Church: 1. In way of subjection when she is to give account of her offence. . . .

2. In way of singing forth the praises of the Lord together with the rest of the Congregation. For it is evident the Apostle layeth no greater restraint upon the women for silence in the Church than the Law had put upon them before. For so himself speaketh in the place alleged: "It is not permitted to the women to speak, but to be under subjection, as also saith the Law." The Apostle then requireth the same subjection in the woman which the Law had put upon them—no more. Now it is certain the Law, yea, the Law-giver Moses, did permit Miriam and the women that went out after her to sing forth the praises of the Lord, as well as the men, and to answer the men in their song of thanksgiving: "Sing ye to the Lord for he hath triumphed gloriously: the horse and his rider hath he thrown into the Sea." Which may be a ground sufficient to justify the lawful practice of women in singing together with men the praises of the Lord.

DINNER AT THE WINTHROPS

CATHERINE MARIA SEDGWICK

————◆•◆————

Home life with the Puritans was not always as bleak as the stereotype would have it; it could be cozy, even elegant. The following excerpt is from a nineteenth-century novel called Hope Leslie, Or Early Times in the Massachusetts, *a fairly reliable depiction of Puritan social customs by Catherine Maria Sedgwick (1789–1867), bearer of a great New England name.*

THE governor's house stood in the main street (Washington-street), on the ground now occupied by "South Row." There was a little court in front of it; on one side a fine garden; on the other a beautiful lawn, or, as it was called, "green," extending to the corner on which the "Old South" (Church) now stands, and an ample yard and offices in the rear....

"In the principal houses was a great hall, ornamented with pictures; a great lantern; velvet cushions in the window-seat to look into the garden: on either side a great parlour, a little parlour or study, furnished with great looking-glasses, Turkey carpets, window-curtains and valance, picture and a map, a brass clock, red leather-back chairs, a great pair of brass andirons: the chambers well furnished with feather beds, warming-pans, and every other elegance and comfort: the pantry well filled with substantial fare and dainties, Madeira wine, prunes, marmalade, silver tankards and wine-cups not uncommon."

If any are incredulous as to the correctness of the above extract, we assure them that its truth is confirmed by the spaciousness of the Pilgrim habitations still standing in Boston, and occupied by their descendants. These Pilgrims were not needy adventurers nor ruined exiles. Mr. Winthrop himself had an estate in England worth seven hundred pounds per annum. Some of his associates came from lordly halls, and many of them brought wealth, as well as virtue, to the colony....

Our humble history has little to do with the public life of Governor Winthrop, which is so well known to have been illustrated by the rare virtue of disinterested patriotism, and by such even and paternal goodness, that a contemporary witty satirist could not find it in his heart to give him a harsher name than "Sir John Temperwell." His figure (if we may trust to the fidelity of his painter) was tall and spare; his eye dark blue, and mild in its expression: he had the upraised brow, which is said to be indicative of a religious disposition; his hair and his beard, which he wore long, were black. On the whole, we must confess, the external man presents the solemn and forbidding aspect of the times in which he flourished; though we know him to have been a model of private virtue, gracious and gentle in his manners, and exact in the observance of all gentlemanly courtesy.

His wife was admirably qualified for the station she occupied. She recognised, and continually taught to matron and maiden, the duty of unqualified obedience from the wife to the husband, her appointed lord and master; a duty that it was left to modern heresy to dispute, and which our pious fathers, or even mothers, were so far from questioning, that the only divine right to govern which they acknowledged was that vested in the husband over the wife. Madam Winthrop's matrimonial virtue never degenerated into the slavishness of fear or the obsequiousness of servility. If authorized and approved by principle, it was prompted by feeling; and, if we may be allowed a coarse comparison, like a horse easy on the bit, she was guided by the slightest intimation from him who held the rein; indeed, to pursue our humble illustration still farther, it sometimes appeared as if the reins were dropped, and the inferior animal were left to the guidance of her own sagacity.

Without ever overstepping the limits of feminine propriety, Madam Winthrop manifestly enjoyed the dignity of her official station, and felt that if the governor were the greater, she was the lesser light. There was a slight tinge of official importance in her manner of conferring her hospitalities and her counsel; but she seemed rather to intend to heighten the value of the gift than the merit of the giver. . . .

We return from our long digression to the party we left in Governor Winthrop's parlour.

The tables were arranged for dinner. Tables, we say, for a side-table was spread, but in a manner so inferior to the principal board, which was garnished with silver tankards, *wine-cups,* and rich china, as to indicate that it was destined for inferior guests. This indication was soon verified; for, on a servant being sent to announce dinner to Governor Winthrop, who was understood to be occupied with some of the natives on state business, that gentleman appeared, attended by four Indians: Miantunnomoh, the young and noble chief of the Narragansetts, two of his counsellors, and an interpreter. . . .

Governor Winthrop motioned to his Indian guests to take their seats at the side-table, and the rest of the company, including the elder Fletcher and Cradock, surrounded the dinner-table, and serving-men and all reverently folded their arms and bowed their heads while the grace or prefatory prayer was pronouncing.

After all the rest had taken their seats, the Indians remained standing; and although the governor politely signified to the interpreter that their delay wronged the smoking viands, they remained motionless, the chief drawn aside from the rest, his eye cast down, his brow lowering, and his whole aspect expressive of proud displeasure.

The governor rose, and demanded of the interpreter the meaning of their too evident dissatisfaction.

"My chief bids me say," replied the savage, "that he expects such treatment from the English sagamore as the English receive in the wigwam of the Narragansett chief. He says that when the English stranger visits him, he sits on his mat and eats from his dish."

"Tell your chief," replied the governor, who had urgent state reasons for conciliating Miantunnomoh, "that I pray him to overlook the wrong I have done him: he is right; he deserves the place of honour. I have heard of his hospitable deeds, and that he doth give more than even ground to his guests; for our friend, Roger Williams, informed us that he hath known him, with his family, to sleep abroad to make room in his wigwam for English visiters."

Governor Winthrop added the last circumstance partly as a full confession of his fault, and partly as an apology to his helpmate, who looked a good deal disconcerted by the disarrangement of her dinner. However, she proceeded to give the necessary orders; the table was remodelled, a sufficient addition made, and the haughty chief, his countenance relaxing to an expression of grave satisfaction, took his seat at the governor's right hand. His associates being properly accommodated at the table, the rest of the company resumed their stations.

NEW ENGLAND'S FIRST FRUITS

ANONYMOUS

———◆•◆———

Harvard seems as integral a part of the New England scene as its glacial boulders, and almost as old. In 1636 the General Court appropriated 400 pounds to found a college, and the first of its classes, composed of nine members, graduated in 1642. There wasn't another college founded in America until William and Mary, in 1693. That gap of years, noted on the program of any academic celebration today when representatives of American colleges march, in full regalia, in procession in order of the founding of their respective colleges, is enough to make a New England heart beat fast.

New England hearts were proud from the beginning. The tract New England's First Fruits, *describing the new college, was published in London in 1643 to prove to the Puritans at home that the colony had not fallen behind in intellectual achievement. An excerpt follows.*

AFTER God had carried us safe to New England, and we had builded our houses, provided necessaries for our livelihood, reared convenient places for God's worship, and settled the civil government, one of the next things we longed for and looked after was to advance learning and perpetuate it to posterity, dreading to leave an illiterate ministry to the churches when our present ministers shall lie in the dust. And as were thinking and consulting how to effect this great work, it pleased God to stir up the heart of one Mr. Harvard (a godly gentleman and a lover of learning, there living amongst us) to give the one half of his estate (it being in all about £1700) towards the erecting of a college, and all his library. After him, another gave £300, others after them cast in more, and the public hand of the state added the rest. The college was, by common consent, appointed to be at Cambridge (a place very pleasant and accommodate) and is called (according to the name of the first founder) Harvard College.

The edifice is very fair and comely within and without, having in it a spacious hall (where they daily meet at common lectures, exercises), and a large library with some books to it, the gifts of divers of our friends, their chambers and studies also fitted for and possessed by the students, and all other rooms of office necessary and convenient, with all needful offices thereto belonging. And by the side of the College, a fair grammar school, for the training up of young scholars and fitting of them for academical learning, that still as they are judged ripe they may be received into the College. Of this school, Master Corlet is the master, who hath very well approved himself for his abilities, dexterity and painfulness, in teaching and education of the youth under him.

Over the College is Master Dunster placed as president, a learned, conscionable and industrious man, who hath so trained up his pupils in the tongues and arts, and so seasoned them with the principles of divinity and Christianity, that we have to our great comfort (and in truth, beyond our hopes) beheld their progress in learning and godliness also. The former of these hath appeared in their public declamations in Latin and Greek, and disputations logical and philosophical, which they have wont (besides their ordinary exercises in the College hall), in the audience of the magistrates, ministers and other scholars, for the probation of their

growth in learning, upon set days, constantly once every month, to make
and uphold. The latter hath been manifested in sundry of them by the
savory breathings of their spirits in godly conversation, insomuch that we
are confident, if these early blossoms may be cherished and warmed with
the influence of the friends of learning and lovers of this pious work, they
will, by the help of God, come to happy maturity in a short time.

Over the College are twelve overseers chosen by the General Court: six
of them are of the magistrates, the other six of the ministers, who are to
promote the best good of it, and (having a power of influence into all persons in it) are to see that every one be diligent and proficient in his
proper place.

Rules and precepts that are observed in the College:

1. When any scholar is able to understand Tullius [Cicero] or such like
classical Latin author *extempore,* and make and speak true Latin in verse
and prose, *suo ut aiunt marte* ["to stand, as they say, on his own feet"],
and decline perfectly the paradigms of nouns and verbs in the Greek
tongue, let him then, and not before, be capable of admission into the
College.

2. Let every student be plainly instructed and earnestly pressed to
consider well: the main end of his life and studies is "to know God and
Jesus Christ, which is eternal life" (John 17. 3), and therefore to lay
Christ in the bottom, as the only foundation of all sound knowledge and
learning.

And seeing the Lord only giveth wisdom, let everyone seriously set
himself by prayer in secret to seek it of Him (Prov. 2. 3).

3. Everyone shall so exercise himself in reading the scriptures twice a
day that he shall be ready to give such an account of his proficiency
therein, both in theoretical observations of the language and logic, and
in practical and spiritual truths, as his tutor shall require, according to his
ability: seeing "the entrance of the word giveth light; it giveth understanding unto the simple" (Psal. 119. 130).

4. That they, eschewing all profanation of God's name, attributes,
word, ordinances and times of worship, do study with good conscience
carefully to retain God and the love of His truth in their minds. Else, let
them know that (notwithstanding their learning) God may give them up
"to strong delusions" (II Thess. 2. 11, 12), and in the end "to a reprobate
mind" (Rom. 1. 28).

5. That they studiously redeem the time, observe the general hours
appointed for all the students, and the special hours for their own classes;
and then diligently attend the lectures, without any disturbance by word
or gesture. And if in anything they doubt, they shall inquire as of their
fellows, so (in case of "non-satisfaction") modestly of their tutors.

6. None shall, under any pretense whatsoever, frequent the company and society of such men as lead an unfit and dissolute life.

Nor shall any, without his tutor's leave or (in his absence) the call of parents or guardians, go abroad to other towns.

7. Every scholar shall be present in his tutor's chamber at the seventh hour in the morning, immediately after the sound of the bell, at his opening the scripture and prayer; so also at the fifth hour at night, and then give account of his own private reading (as aforesaid in particular the third), and constantly attend lectures in the hall at the hours appointed. But if any (without necessary impediment) shall absent himself from prayer or lectures, he shall be liable to admonition, if he offend above once a week.

8. If any scholar shall be found to transgress any of the laws of God or the school, after twice admonition, he shall be liable, if not *adultus*, to correction; if *adultus*, his name shall be given up to the overseers of the College, that he may be admonished at the public monthly act.

The time and order of their studies (unless experience
shall show cause to alter):

The second and third day of the week, read lectures, as followeth:

To the first year, at eight of the clock in the morning, logic the first three quarters, physics the last quarter.

To the second year, at the ninth hour, ethics and politics, at convenient distances of time.

To the third year, at the tenth, arithmetic and geometry the three first quarters, astronomy the last.

Afternoon:

The first year disputes at the second hour.

The second year at the third hour.

The third year at the fourth, every one in his art.

The fourth day, read Greek:

To the first year, the etymology and syntax, at the eighth hour.

To the second, at the ninth hour, *prosodia* and *dialects*.

Afternoon:

The first year, at second hour, practice the precepts of grammar in such authors as have variety of words.

The second year, at third hour, practice in poesy. . . .

The third year perfect their theory before noon, and exercise style, composition, imitation, epitome, both in prose and verse, afternoon.

The fifth day, read Hebrew and the Eastern tongues: Grammar to the first year, hour the eighth.

To the second, Chaldee at the ninth hour.
To the third, Syriac at the tenth hour.
Afternoon:
The first year, practice in the Bible at the second hour.
The second, in Ezra and Daniel at the third hour.
The third, at the fourth hour in Trostius's New Testament.

The sixth day, read rhetoric to all at the eighth hour:
Declamations at the ninth. So ordered that every scholar may declaim once a month. The rest of the day, *vacat rhetoricis studiis* [is given over to the study of rhetoric].

The seventh day, read divinity catechetical at the eighth hour; commonplaces at the ninth hour.
Afternoon:
The first hour read history in the winter, the nature of plants in the summer.

The sum of every lecture shall be examined before the new lecture be read.

Every scholar that on proof is found able to read the originals of the Old and New Testament into the Latin tongue, and to resolve them logically, withal being of godly life and conversation, and at any public act hath the approbation of the overseers and master of the College, is fit to be dignified with his first degree.

Every scholar that giveth up in writing a system or synopsis, or summa, of logic, natural and moral philosophy, arithmetic, geometry and astronomy, and is ready to defend his theses or propositions, withal skilled in the originals as abovesaid, and of godly life and conversation, and so approved by the overseers and master of the College at any public act, is fit to be dignified with his second degree.

1646-1662

THE COVENANT OF GRACE

THOMAS SHEPARD

———◆◆———

The Puritans followed a Covenant theology. Covenant, I always won-
dered, with whom? With God. Covenant theology held that God prom-
ised Adam and his posterity eternal life in exchange for obedience to
moral law. When Adam broke this Covenant of Works, God made a new
covenant with Abraham, which required more labor and reason on man's
part, in return for less freedom. This was the Covenant of Grace. One
sometimes thinks of the God of the Puritans as harsh and arbitrary; but
the concept of the covenants makes Him seem rather a Being with whom
man could bargain. In the Covenant of Grace, God agreed to abide by
ideas that man could grasp. Perry Miller says, "the Covenant is the intelli-
gible medium between the ultimate and undecipherable mystery of God's
original purposes and His ultimate performance, between the beginning
and the end of time."

Thomas Shepard (1605–1649) was among the greatest of the preachers
to the first generation of Massachusetts Bay Puritans, and one of those
most active in suppressing the Antinomians. I append two paragraphs
from his preface to The Covenant of Grace, *to give the flavor of the*
language.

PREFACE

THE blessed God hath evermore delighted to reveal and communicate
Himself by way of Covenant. He might have done good to man before
his fall, as also since his fall, without binding Himself in the bond of
Covenant; Noah, Abraham, and David, Jews, Gentiles, might have had
the blessings intended, without any promise or Covenant. But the Lord's
heart is so full of love (especially to His own) that it cannot be contained
so long within the bounds of secrecy—*viz.* from God's eternal purpose to

the actual accomplishment of good things intended—but it must afore-hand overflow and break out into the many streams of a blessed Covenant. The Lord can never get near enough to His people, and thinks He can never get them near enough unto Himself, and therefore unites and binds and fastens them close to Himself, and Himself unto them, by the bonds of a Covenant. And therefore when we break our Covenant, and that will not hold us, He takes a faster bond and makes a sure and everlasting Covenant, according to Grace, not according to Works; and that shall hold His people firm unto Himself, and hold Himself close and fast unto them, that He may never depart from us.

Oh! the depth of God's grace herein: that when sinful man deserves never to have the least good word from Him, that He should open His whole heart and purpose to him in a Covenant; that when he deserves nothing else but separation from God, and to be driven up and down the world as a vagabond, or as dried leaves fallen from our God, that yet the Almighty God cannot be content with it, but must make Himself to us, and us to Himself, more sure and near than ever before! And is not this Covenant then (Christian reader) worth thy looking into and searching after? Surely never was there a time wherein the Lord calls His people to more serious searching into the nature of the Covenant than in these days.

THE SIMPLE COBBLER OF
AGGAWAM IN AMERICA

NATHANIEL WARD

———◆•◆———

Not all New England Puritans were ministers, but it sometimes seems that way, because they are the ones whose writings have come down to us. They spoke for the colony; in the following excerpt, about worldly matters. Nathaniel Ward (1578–1652) came to Massachusetts in 1634 and was minister at Ipswich (in Indian, Aggawam). He codified the first Massachusetts statutes, The Body of Liberties, *and returned to England in 1645 where his book—which had been written in New England—was published under its full title of* The Simple Cobbler of Aggawam in America. Willing to help 'mind his Native Country, lamentably tattered, both in the upper-Leather and the sole, with all the honest stitches he can take. And as willing never to bee paid for his work, by Old English wonted pay. It is* his Trade to patch all the year long, gratis Therefore I pray Gentlemen keep your purses.

ON THE FRIVOLITIES OF FASHION

SHOULD I not keep promise in speaking a little to Women's fashions, they would take it unkindly. I was loath to pester better matter with such stuff; I rather thought it meet to let them stand by themselves, like the *Quœ Genus* in the grammar, being deficients, or redundants, not to be brought under any rule: I shall therefore make bold for this once, to borrow a little of their loose-tongued Liberty, and misspend a word or two upon their long-waisted, but short-skirted Patience: a little use of my stirrup will do no harm. . . .

It is a more common than convenient saying, that nine tailors make a man: it were well if nineteen could make a woman to her mind. If tailors were men indeed, well furnished but with mere moral principles, they would disdain to be led about like Apes, by such mimic Marmosets. It is a most unworthy thing for men that have bones in them, to spend their lives in making fiddle-cases for futilous women's fancies; which are the very pettitoes of infirmity, the giblets of perquisquilian toys. I am so charitable to think, that most of that mystery would work the cheerfuller while they live, if they might be well discharged of the tiring slavery of mistiring women. It is no little labor to be continually putting up English women, into outlandish casks; who if they be not shifted anew, once in a few months, grow too sour for their husbands. What this trade will answer for themselves when God shall take measure of tailors' consciences is beyond my skill to imagine. There was a time when,

> The joining of the Red Rose with the White,
> Did set our State into a Damask plight.

But now our roses are turned to *flore de lices,* our carnations to tulips, our gillyflowers to daisies, our city dames, to an indenominable quæmalry of overturcased things. He that makes Coats for the Moon, had need take measures every noon: and he that makes for women, as often, to keep them from lunacy.

I have often heard divers ladies vent loud feminine complaints of the wearisome varieties and chargeable changes of fashions: I marvel themselves prefer not a Bill of redress. I would Essex Ladies would lead the Chore, for the honor of their county and persons; or rather the thrice honorable Ladies of the Court, whom it best beseems: who may well presume of a *Le Roy le veult* from our sober King, a *Les Seigneurs ont assentus* from our prudent Peers, and the like *Assentus,* from our considerate, I dare not say Wife-worn commons; who I believe had much rather pass one such Bill, than pay so many tailor's bills as they are forced to do.

Most dear and unparalleled Ladies, be pleased to attempt it: as you have the precellency of the women of the world for beauty and feature; so assume the honor to give, and not take law from any, in matter of attire. If ye can transact so fair a motion among yourselves unanimously, I dare say, they that most renite, will least repent. What greater honor can your Honors desire, than to build a Promontory precedent to all foreign Ladies, to deserve so eminently at the hands of all the English gentry present and to come: and to confute the opinion of all the wise men in the world; who never thought it possible for women to do so good a work.

If any man think I have spoken rather merrily than seriously he is much mistaken, I have written what I write with all the indignation I can, and no more than I ought. . . .

But I address myself to those who can both hear and mend all if they please: I seriously fear, if the Pious Parliament do not find time to state fashions, as ancient Parliaments have done in part, God will hardly find a time to state religion or peace. . . .

It is beyond all account how many gentlemen's and citizens' estates are deplumed by their feather-headed Wives, what useful supplies the pannage of England would afford other countries, what rich returns to itself, if it were not sliced out into male and female fripperies: and what a multitude of misemployed hands might be better improved in some more manly manufactures for the public weal. It is not easily credible, what may be said of the Preterpluralities of tailors in London: I have heard an honest man say, that not long since there were numbered between Temple-bar and Charing-Cross, eight thousand of that trade; let it be conjectured by that proportion how many there are in and about London, and in all England they will appear to be very numerous. If the Parliament would please to mend women, which their husbands dare not do, there need not so many men to make and mend as there are. I hope the present doleful estate of the realm will persuade more strongly to some considerate course herein than I now can.

THE CLEAR SUN-SHINE OF THE GOSPEL BREAKING FORTH UPON THE INDIANS

REV. JOHN ELIOT

---◆◆---

As a child I was told the horrendous story of how Lord Jeffrey Amherst sold the Indians poisoned bread in order that they should in short order become "the only good Indians." In actual fact, the earliest settlers began sending out missionaries to the Indians, and while "missionary" is not necessarily synonymous with "charitable," some of these clergy were kind and helpful, notably the Rev. John Eliot (1604–1690), first to preach to the Indians in their own language. He established fourteen villages of "Praying Indians," which were, however, destroyed in King Philip's War. The following letter to the Rev. Thomas Shepard is taken from a book called The Clear Sun-Shine of the Gospel Breaking Forth Upon the Indians, *published in 1648.*

It is followed here by a short excerpt from A Historical Collection of the Indians in New England *by Daniel Gookin (1612–1687) describing Eliot's work with the Indians. Gookin had been a large landowner in the Virginia colonies but, an ardent Puritan, soon emigrated to Massachusetts, where he was deputy to the General Court for 35 years and major general of the colony's forces.*

ON ADMONISHING THE INDIANS

In my exercise among them (as you know) we attend four things, besides prayer unto God for his presence and blessing upon all we do.

First, I catechise the children and youth; wherein some are very ready and expert; they can readily say all the Commandments, so far as I have communicated them, and all other principles about the creation, the fall, the redemption by Christ, etc., wherein also the aged people are pretty expert, by the frequent repetition thereof to the children, and are able to teach it to their children at home, and do so.

Secondly, I preach unto them out of some texts of Scripture, wherein I study all plainness and brevity, unto which many are very attentive.

Thirdly, if there be any occasion, we in the next place go to admonition

and censure; unto which they submit themselves reverently, and obedi-
ently, and some of them penitently confessing their sins with much
plainness, and without shiftings and excuses. I will instance in two or
three particulars; this was one case, a man named Wampoowas, being in
a passion upon some light occasion, did beat his wife, which was a very
great offence among them now (though in former times it was very usual)
and they had made a Law against it, and set a fine upon it; whereupon he
was publicly brought forth before the Assembly, which was great that
day, for our Governor and many other English were then present. The
man wholly condemned himself without any excuse: and when he was
asked what provocation his wife gave him, he did not in the least measure
blame her but himself, and when the quality of the sin was opened, that
it was cruelty to his own body, and against God's Commandment, and
that passion was a sin, and much aggravated by such effects, yet God was
ready to pardon it in Christ, etc., he turned his face to the wall and wept,
though with modest endeavor to hide it; and such was the modest, peni-
tent, and melting behavior of the man, that it much affected all to see it in
a Barbarian, and all did forgive him, only this remained, that they executed their Law notwithstanding his repentance, and required his fine, to
which he willingly submitted, and paid it.

Another case of admonition was this, Cutshamaquin the Sachem having a son of about fourteen or fifteen years old, he had been drunk, and
had behaved himself disobediently and rebelliously against his father
and mother, for which sin they did blame him, but he despised their admonition. And before I knew of it, I did observe when I catechised him,
when he should say the fifth Commandment, he did not freely say, "Honor
thy father," but wholly left out "mother," and so he did the Lecture day
before, but when this sin of his was produced, he was called forth
before the Assembly, and he confessed that what was said against him was
true, but he fell to accuse his father of sundry evils, as that he would
have killed him in his anger, and that he forced him to drink Sack, and I
know not what else: which behavior we greatly disliked, showed him the
evil of it, and Mr. Wilson being present labored much with him, for he
understood the English, but all in vain, his heart was hard and hopeless
for that time. Therefore using due loving persuasions, we did sharply admonish him of his sin, and required him to answer further the next Lecture day, and so left him; and so stout he was, that when his father
offered to pay his fine of ten shillings for his drunkenness according to
their Law, he would not accept it at his hand. When the next day was
come, and other exercises finished, I called him forth, and he willingly
came, but still in the same mind as before. Then we turned to his father,
and exhorted him to remove that stumbling-block out of his son's way, by
confessing his own sins whereby he had given occasion of hardness of
heart to his son; which thing was not sudden to him, for I had formerly in

private prepared him thereunto, and he was very willing to hearken to that counsel, because his conscience told him he was blameworthy; and accordingly he did, he confessed his main and principal evils of his own accord: and upon this advantage I took occasion to put him upon confession of sundry other vices which I knew he had in former times been guilty of, and all the Indians knew it likewise; and put it after this manner, Are you now sorry for your drunkenness, filthiness, false dealing, lying, etc., which sins you committed before you knew God? unto all which cases he expressed himself sorrowful, and condemned himself for them: which example of the Sachem was profitable for all the Indians. And when he had thus confessed his sins, we turned again to his son and labored with him, requiring him to confess his sin, and entreat God to forgive him for Christ his sake, and to confess his offence against his father and mother, and entreat them to forgive him, but he still refused; and now the other Indians spake unto him soberly and affectionately, to put him on, and divers spake one after another, and some several times. Mr. Wilson again did much labor with him, and at last he did humble himself, confessed all, and entreated his father to forgive him, and took him by the hand, at which his father burst forth into great weeping. He did the same also to his mother, who wept also, and so did divers others; and many English being present, they fell a-weeping, so that the house was filled with weeping on every side; and then we went to prayer, in all which time Cutshamaquin wept, insomuch that when he had done the board he stood upon was all dropped with his tears. . . .

Fourthly, the last exercise, you know, we have among them, is their asking us questions, and very many they have asked, which I have forgotten, but some few that come to my present remembrance I will briefly touch.

One was Wabbakoxet's question, who is reputed an old Powwaw; it was to this purpose, seeing the English had been twenty-seven years (some of them) in this land, why did we never teach them to know God till now? "Had you done it sooner," said he, "we might have known much of God by this time, and much sin might have been prevented, but now some of us are grown old in sin," etc. To whom we answered, that we do repent that we did not long ago, as now we do, yet withal we told them, that they were never willing to hear till now, and that seeing God hath bowed their hearts to be willing to hear, we are desirous to take all the pains we can now to teach them. . . .

Another question was about their children, Whither their little children go when they die, seeing they have not sinned?

Which question gave occasion more fully to teach them original sin, and the damned state of all men. And also, and especially it gave occasion to teach them the Covenant of God, which He hath made with all his people, and with their children, so that when God chooses a man or a woman to be his servant, He chooses all their children to be so also; which doctrine was exceeding grateful unto them.

THE INDIANS IN NEW ENGLAND
Daniel Gookin

The manner practised by these Indians in the worship of God is thus. Upon the Lord's days, fast days, and lecture days, the people assemble together at the sound of a drum,—for bells they yet have not,—twice a day, in the morning and afternoon, on Lord's days, but only once upon lecture days; where one of their teachers, if they have more than one, begins with solemn and affectionate prayer. Then, after a short pause, either himself or some other thereunto appointed readeth a chapter distinctly out of the Old or New Testament. At the conclusion thereof a psalm, or part of a psalm, is appointed, rehearsed, and solemnly sung. Then the minister catechises and prays before his sermon; and so preacheth from some text of Scripture. Then concludeth with prayer, and a psalm, and a blessing pronounced. Sometimes, instead of reading the chapter, some persons do answer some part of the catechism. . . .

Mr. Eliot hath of late years fallen into a practice among the Indians, the better to prepare and furnish them with abilities to explicate and apply the Scriptures, by setting up a lecture among them in logic and theology, once every fortnight, all the summer, at Natick; whereat he is present and ready, and reads and explains to them the principles of those arts. And God hath been pleased graciously so to bless these means, that several of them, especially young men of acute parts, have gained much knowledge, and are able to speak methodically and profitably unto any plain text of Scripture, yea, as well as you can imagine such little means of learning can advantage them unto. From this church and town of Natick hath issued forth, as from a seminary of virtue and piety, divers teachers that are employed in several new praying towns; of which we shall hear more, God willing, hereafter.

GRANDFATHER'S CHAIR

NATHANIEL HAWTHORNE

---◆◆◆---

Before ever he could dream of going to Harvard, a Massachusetts Bay Colony boy was given an essential grounding in the Classics. Boston Latin School was founded in 1635, Roxbury Latin School in 1645, and both institutions are still going strong. The following description of a Puritan schoolroom is taken from Grandfather's Chair, *by Nathaniel Hawthorne (1804–1864).*

"At the death of Sir William Phipps," proceeded Grandfather, "our chair was bequeathed to Mr. Ezekiel Cheever, a famous schoolmaster in Boston. This old gentleman came from London in 1637, and had been teaching school ever since; so that there were now aged men, grandfathers like myself, to whom Master Cheever had taught their alphabet. He was a person of venerable aspect, and wore a long white beard."

"Was the chair placed in his school?" asked Charley.

"Yes, in his school," answered Grandfather; "and we may safely say that it had never before been regarded with such awful reverence,—no, not even when the old governors of Massachusetts sat in it. Even you, Charley, my boy, would have felt some respect for the chair if you had seen it occupied by this famous schoolmaster."

And here grandfather endeavored to give his auditors an idea how matters were managed in schools above a hundred years ago. As this will probably be an interesting subject to our readers, we shall make a separate sketch of it, and call it

THE OLD-FASHIONED SCHOOL

Now, imagine yourselves, my children, in Master Ezekiel Cheever's school-room. It is a large, dingy room, with a sanded floor, and is lighted by windows that turn on hinges and have little diamond-shaped panes of glass. The scholars sit on long benches, with desks before them. At one end of the room is a great fireplace, so very spacious that there is room enough for three or four boys to stand in each of the chimney corners. This was the good old fashion of fireplaces when there was wood enough in the forests to keep people warm without their digging into the bowels of the earth for coal.

It is a winter's day when we take our peep into the school-room. See what great logs of wood have been rolled into the fireplace, and what a broad, bright blaze goes leaping up the chimney! And every few moments a vast cloud of smoke is puffed into the room, which sails slowly over the heads of the scholars, until it gradually settles upon the walls and ceiling. They are blackened with the smoke of many years already.

Next look at our old historic chair! It is placed, you perceive, in the most comfortable part of the room, where the generous glow of the fire is sufficiently felt without being too intensely hot. How stately the old chair looks, as if it remembered its many famous occupants, but yet were conscious that a greater man is sitting in it now! Do you see the venerable schoolmaster, severe in aspect, wth a black skullcap on his head, like an ancient Puritan, and the snow of his white beard drifting down to his very girdle? What boy would dare to play, or whisper, or even glance aside from his book, while Master Cheever is on the lookout behind his spectacles? For such offenders, if any such there be, a rod of birch is hanging over the fireplace, and a heavy ferule lies on the master's desk.

And now school is begun. What a murmur of multitudinous tongues, like the whispering leaves of a wind-stirred oak, as the scholars con over their various tasks! Buzz! buzz! buzz! Amid just such a murmur has Master Cheever spent above sixty years; and long habit has made it as pleasant to him as the hum of a beehive when the insects are busy in the sunshine.

Now a class in Latin is called to recite. Forth steps a row of queer-looking little fellows, wearing square-skirted coats and small-clothes, with buttons at the knee. They look like so many grandfathers in their second childhood. These lads are to be sent to Cambridge and educated for the learned professions. Old Master Cheever has lived so long, and seen so many generations of school-boys grow up to be men, that now he can almost prophesy what sort of a man each boy will be. One urchin shall hereafter be a doctor, and administer pills and potions, and stalk gravely through life, perfumed with assafœtida. Another shall wrangle at the bar, and fight his way to wealth and honors, and, in his declining age, shall be a worshipful member of his Majesty's council. A third—and he is the master's favorite—shall be a worthy successor to the old Puritan ministers now in their graves; he shall preach with great unction and effect, and leave volumes of sermons, in print and manuscript, for the benefit of future generations.

But, as they are merely school-boys now, their business is to construe Virgil. Poor Virgil! whose verses, which he took so much pains to polish, have been misscanned, and misparsed, and misinterpreted by so many generations of idle school-boys. There, sit down, ye Latinists. Two or three of you, I fear, are doomed to feel the master's ferule.

Next comes a class in arithmetic. These boys are to be the merchants, shopkeepers, and mechanics of a future period. Hitherto they have traded only in marbles and apples. Hereafter some will send vessels to England for broadcloths and all sorts of manufactured wares, and to the West Indies for sugar, and rum, and coffee. Others will stand behind counters, and measure tape, and ribbon, and cambric by the yard. Others will upheave the blacksmith's hammer, or drive the plane over the carpenter's bench, or take the lapstone and the awl and learn the trade of shoemaking. Many will follow the sea, and become bold, rough sea-captains.

This class of boys, in short, must supply the world with those active, skilful hands, and clear, sagacious heads, without which the affairs of life would be thrown into confusion by the theories of studious and visionary men. Wherefore, teach them their multiplication-table, good Master Cheever, and whip them well when they deserve it; for much of the country's welfare depends on these boys.

But, alas! while we have been thinking of other matters, Master Cheever's watchful eye has caught two boys at play. Now we shall see awful times. The two malefactors are summoned before the master's chair, wherein he sits with the terror of a judge upon his brow. Our old chair is now a judgment-seat. Ah, Master Cheever has taken down that terrible birch rod! Short is the trial,—the sentence quickly passed,—and now the judge prepares to execute it in person. Thwack! thwack! thwack! In these good old times, a schoolmaster's blows were well laid on.

See, the birch rod has lost several of its twigs, and will hardly serve for another execution. Mercy on us, what a bellowing the urchins make! My ears are almost deafened, though the clamor comes through the far length of a hundred and fifty years. There, go to your seats, poor boys; and do not cry, sweet little Alice, for they have ceased to feel the pain a long time since.

And thus the forenoon passes away. Now it is twelve o'clock. The master looks at his great silver watch, and then, with tiresome deliberation, puts the ferule into his desk. The little multitude await the word of dismissal with almost irrepressible impatience.

"You are dismissed," says Master Cheever.

The boys retire, treading softly until they have passed the threshold; but, fairly out of the school-room, lo, what a joyous shout! what a scampering and trampling of feet! what a sense of recovered freedom expressed in the merry uproar of all their voices! What care they for the ferule and birch rod now? Were boys created merely to study Latin and arithmetic? No; the better purposes of their being are to sport, to leap, to run, to shout, to slide upon the ice, to snowball.

Happy boys! Enjoy your playtime now, and come again to study and to feel the birch rod and the ferule to-morrow; not till to-morrow; for to-day is Thursday lecture; and, ever since the settlement of Massachusetts, there has been no school on Thursday afternoons. Therefore sport, boys, while you may, for the morrow cometh, with the birch rod and the ferule; and after that another morrow, with troubles of its own.

Now the master has set everything to rights, and is ready to go home to dinner. Yet he goes reluctantly. The old man has spent so much of his life in the smoky, noisy, buzzing school-room, that, when he has a holiday, he feels as if his place were lost and himself a stranger in the world. But forth he goes; and there stands our old chair, vacant and solitary, till good Master Cheever resumes his seat in it to-morrow morning.

"Grandfather," said Charley, "I wonder whether the boys did not use to upset the old chair when the schoolmaster was out."

"There is a tradition," replied Grandfather, "that one of its arms was dislocated in some such manner. But I cannot believe that any school-boy would behave so naughtily."

As it was now later than little Alice's usual bedtime, Grandfather broke off his narrative, promising to talk more about Master Cheever and his scholars some other evening.

THE SEPARATION OF
ROGER WILLIAMS

NATHANIEL MORTON

———◆◆———

Roger Williams was the most modern, the most liberal, of the many able men the Massachusetts Bay Colony banished for differing religious views. The following account of him by Nathaniel Morton (1613–1686) of the Plymouth brethren, reflects the outraged reaction to Williams' ideas. Morton's own morals have an interesting history. His book New England's Memoriall, *from which this account is excerpted, was, he admitted, based on the writings of Edward Winslow and his uncle; but in 1855 recovery of the lost manuscript of Bradford's* History of Plimmoth Plantation *revealed that Morton had used great sections of it almost word for word.*

Quakers, too, suffered persecution at the hands of the Puritans for their religious beliefs, and, following Morton's statement, is appended a petition which the Quakers offered in 1661 to the King of England, giving nineteen incidents of cruelty shown them and pleading for mercy. It is taken from Collection of the Sufferings of the People called Quakers, *published a century later.*

In the year 1634, Mr. Roger Williams removed from Plymouth to Salem; he had lived about three years at Plymouth, where he was well accepted as an assistant in the ministry to Mr. Ralph Smith, then pastor of the church there, but by degrees venting of divers of his own singular opinions, and seeking to impose them upon others, he not finding such a concurrence as he expected, he desired his dismission to the church of Salem, which though some were unwilling to, yet through the prudent counsel of Mr. Brewster, the ruling elder there, fearing that his continuance amongst them might cause divisions, and there being many abler men in the bay, they would better deal with him than themselves could, and foreseeing, what he professed he feared concerning Mr. Williams, which afterwards came to pass, that he would run the same course of rigid separation and anabaptistry, which Mr. John Smith, the se-baptist at Amsterdam had done; the church of Plymouth consented to his dismission, and such as did adhere to him were also dismissed, and removed with him, or not long after him, to Salem.

He came to Salem in the time of Mr. Skelton's weakness, who lived not long after Mr. Williams was come, whereupon after some time, the church there called him to office; but he having in one year's time filled that place with principles of rigid separation, and tending to anabaptistry, the prudent magistrates of the Massachusetts jurisdiction sent to the church of Salem, desiring them to forbear calling him to office, which they hearkening to, was a cause of much disturbance; for Mr. Williams had begun, and then being in office, he proceeded more vigorously to vent many dangerous opinions, as amongst many others these were some; that it is not lawful for an unregenerate man to pray, nor to take an oath, and in special, not the oath of fidelity to the civil government; nor was it lawful for a godly man to have communion, either in family prayer, or in an oath, with such as they judged unregenerate; and therefore he himself refused the oath of fidelity, and taught others so to do; also, that it was not lawful so much as to hear the godly ministers of England, when any occasionally went thither, and therefore he admonished any church members that had done so, as for heinous sin; also he spake dangerous words against the patent, which was the foundation of the government of the Massachusetts colony; also he affirmed, that the magistrates had nothing to do in matters of the first table, but only the second; and that there should be a general and unlimited toleration of all religions, and for any man to be punished for any matters of his conscience, was persecution.

And further, he procured the church of Salem's consent unto letters of admonition, which were written and sent by him, in their name, to the churches at Boston, Charlestown, Newtown (now Cambridge), etc., accusing the magistrates, that were members of the respective churches, of sundry heinous offences, which he laid unto their charge; and though divers did acknowledge their error and gave satisfaction, yet Mr. Williams himself, notwithstanding all the pains that was taken with him by Mr. Cotton, Mr. Hooker, and many others, to bring him to a sight of his errors and miscarriages, and, notwithstanding all the court's gentle proceedings with him, he not only persisted, but grew more violent in his way, insomuch as he staying at home in his own house, sent a letter, which was delivered and read in the public church assembly, the scope of which was to give them notice, that if the church of Salem would not separate not only from the churches of Old England, but the churches of New England too, he would separate from them.

The more prudent and sober part of the church, being amazed at his way, could not yield unto him; whereupon he never came to the church assembly more, professing separation from them as antichristian, and not only so, but he withdrew all private religious communion from any that would hold communion with the church there, insomuch as he would not pray nor give thanks at meals with his own wife nor any of his family, because they went to the church assemblies. Divers of the weaker sort of the church members, that had been thoroughly leavened with his opinions, of which number were divers women that were zealous in their way, did by degrees fall off to him, insomuch as he kept a meeting in his own house, unto which a numerous company did resort, both on the Sabbath day and at other times, in way of separation from, and opposition to the church assembly there; which the prudent magistrates understanding, and seeing things grow more and more towards a general division and disturbance, after all other means used in vain, they passed a sentence of banishment against him out of the Massachusetts colony, as against a disturber of the peace, both of the church and commonwealth.

After which Mr. Williams sat down in a place called Providence, out of the Massachusetts jurisdiction, and was followed by many of the members of the church at Salem, who did zealously adhere to him, and who cried out of the persecution that was against him; some others also resorted to him from other parts. They had not been long there together, but from rigid separation they fell to anabaptistry, renouncing the baptism which they had received in their infancy, and taking up another baptism, and so began a church in that way; but Mr. Williams stopped not there long, for after some time he told the people that followed him, and joined with him in a new baptism, that he was out of the way himself, and had misled them, for he did not find that there was any upon earth that could administer baptism, and therefore their last baptism was a nullity, as well as their first; and therefore they must lay down all, and wait for the coming of new apostles; and so they dissolved themselves and turned Seekers, keeping that one principle, that every one should have liberty to worship God according to the light of their own consciences; but otherwise not owning any churches or ordinances of God anywhere upon earth.

THE SUFFERINGS OF THE PEOPLE CALLED QUAKERS

A declaration of some part of the sufferings of the People of God in scorn called Quakers, from the Professors in New England, only for the exercise of their consciences to the Lord, and obeying and confessing to the truth, as in his light he had discovered it to them:

1. Two honest and innocent women stripped stark naked, and searched after an inhuman manner.

2. Twelve strangers in that country, but freeborn of this nation, received twenty-three whippings, the most of them being with a whip of three cords with knots at the ends, and laid on with as much strength as could be by the arm of their executioner, the stripes amounting to three hundred and seventy.

3. Eighteen inhabitants of the country, being freeborn English, received twenty-three whippings, the stripes amounting to two hundred and fifty.

4. Sixty-four imprisonments of the Lord's People, for their obedience to his will, amounting to five hundred and nineteen weeks, much of it being very cold weather, and the inhabitants kept in prison in harvest time, which was very much to their loss; besides many more imprisoned, of which time we cannot give a just account.

5. Two beaten with pitched ropes, the blows amounting to an hundred and thirty-nine, by which one of them was brought near unto death, much of his body being beaten like unto a jelly, and one of their doctors, a member of their church, who saw him, said, it would be a miracle if ever he recovered, he expecting the flesh should rot off the bones, who afterwards was banished upon pain of death. There are many witnesses of this there.

6. Also an innocent man, an inhabitant of Boston, they banished from his wife and children, and put to seek an habitation in the winter, and in case he returned again, he was to be kept prisoner during his life, and for returning again he was put in prison, and hath been now a prisoner above a year.

7. Twenty-five banishments upon the penalties of being whipped, or having their ears cut, or branded in the hand, if they returned.

8. Fines laid upon the inhabitants for meeting together, and edifying one another, as the Saints ever did; and for refusing to swear, it being contrary to Christ's Command, amounting to about a thousand pounds, beside what they have done since that we have not heard of. Many families, in

which there are many children, are almost ruined by their unmerciful proceedings.

9. Five kept fifteen days in all, without food, and fifty-eight days shut up close by the gaoler, and had none that he knew of; and from some of them he stopt up the windows, hindering them from convenient air.

10. One laid neck and heels in irons for sixteen hours.

11. One very deeply burnt in the right hand with the letter (H) after he had been whipt with above thirty stripes.

12. One chained to a log of wood the most part of twenty days, in an open prison, in the winter time.

13. Five appeals to England denied at Boston.

14. Three had their right ears cut by the hangman in the prison, the door being barred, and not a friend suffered to be present while it was doing, though some much desired it.

15. One of the inhabitants of Salem, who since is banished upon pain of death, had one half of his house and land seized on while he was in prison, a month before he knew of it.

16. At a General Court in Boston they made an order, that those who had not wherewithal to answer the fines that were laid upon them for their consciences, should be sold for bondmen and bondwomen to Barbadoes, Virginia, or any of the English plantations.

17. Eighteen of the People of God were at several times banished upon pain of death; six of them were their own inhabitants, two of which being very aged people, and well known among their neighbors to be of honest conversation, being banished from their houses and families, and put upon travelling and other hardships, soon ended their days, whose death we can do no less than charge upon the rulers of Boston, they being the occasion of it.

18. Also three of the servants of the Lord they put to death, all of them for obedience to the truth, in the testimony of it, against the wicked rulers and laws at Boston.

19. And since they have banished four more upon pain of death, and twenty-four of the inhabitants of Salem were presented, and more fines called for, and their goods seized on to the value of forty pounds for meeting together in the fear of God, and some for refusing to swear.

These things, O King! from time to time have we patiently suffered, and not for the transgression of any just or righteous law, either pertaining to the Worship of God, or the Civil Government of England, but simply and barely for our consciences to God, of which we can more at large give thee, or whom thou mayst order, a full account (if thou will let us have admission to thee, who are banished upon pain of death, and have had our ears cut, who are some of us in England attending upon thee) both of the causes of our sufferings, and the manner of their disorderly and illegal proceedings against us; they began with immodesty, went on in inhumanity and cruelty, and were not satisfied until they had the blood of three of the martyrs of Jesus: revenge for all which we do not seek, but lay them before thee, considering thou has been well acquainted with sufferings, and so mayst the better consider them that suffer, and mayst for the future restrain the violence of these rulers of New England, having power in thy hands, they being but the children of the family of which thou art Chief Ruler, who have in divers their proceedings forfeited their Patent, as upon strict inquiry in many particulars will appear.

And this, O King! we are assured of, that in time to come it will not repent thee, if by a close rebuke thou stoppest the bloody proceedings of these bloody persecutors, for in so doing thou wilt engage the hearts of many honest people unto thee both there and here, and for such works of mercy the blessing is obtained; and showing it is the way to prosper: We are witnesses of these things, who

Besides many long imprisonments, and many cruel whippings, had our ears cut,

> JOHN ROUSE,
> JOHN COPELAND.

Besides many long imprisonments, divers cruel whippings, with the seizing on our goods, are banished upon pain of death, and some of us do wait here in England, and desire that we may have an order to return in peace to our families,

> SAMUEL SHATTOCK, JOSIAH SOUTHICK,
> NICHOLAS PHELPS, JOSEPH NICHOLSON, JANE NICHOLSON.

THE DAY OF DOOM

MICHAEL WIGGLESWORTH

———◆•◆———

The testimony of Richard Mather, given earlier, gives the modern reader an idea of the blissful spiritual support the devout Puritan might expect. For those less readily led than pushed toward virtue, there was always fear of divine retribution. Many New Englanders alive today, myself among them, remember grandparents brought up in a terror of hell-fire which haunted them all their days. In the Puritan world hell-fire was taken so for granted that The Day of Doom, *by Michael Wigglesworth, (1631–1705) in 224 stanzas, from which these are excerpted, was written*

in almost cheerful ballad meter. The long poem was published at Cam-
bridge in 1662—the first American best seller. Wigglesworth is a name
that continued to be celebrated in New England.

Rom. 5. 12.
Psal. 51. 5.
Gen. 5. 3.

Since then to share in his welfare,
    you could have been content,
You may with reason share in his treason,
    and in the punishment.
Hence you were born in state forlorn,
    with Natures so depraved:
Death was your due, because that you
    had thus your selves behaved.

Mat. 23. 30, 31.

You think if we had been as he,
    whom God did so betrust,
We to our cost would ne'er have lost
    all for a paltry Lust.
Had you been made in Adam's stead,
    you would like things have wrought,
And so into the self same wo,
    your selves and yours have brought. . . .

Mat. 20. 15.

Am I alone of what's my own,
    no Master or no Lord?
O if I am, how can you claim
    what I to some afford?
Will you demand Grace at my hand,
    and challenge what is mine?
Will you teach me whom to set free,
    and thus my grace confine?

Psl. 58. 3.
Rom. 6. 23.
Gal. 3. 10.
Rom. 8. 29, 30,
& 11. 7.
Rev. 21. 27.

You sinners are, and such a share
    as sinners may expect,
Such you shall have; for I do save
    none but my own Elect. . . .

1 Cor. 6. 2.

Where tender love mens hearts did move
    unto a sympathy,
And bearing part of others smart
    in their anxiety;
Now such compassion is out of fashion,
    and wholly laid aside:
No Friends so near, but Saints to hear
    their Sentence can abide.

Compare
Prov. 1. 26.
with 1 John 3.
2, & 2 Cor. 5.
16.
One natural Brother beholds another
    in his astonied fit,
Yet sorrows not thereat a jot,
    nor pities him a whit.
The godly wife conceives no grief,
    nor can she shed a tear
For the sad state of her dear Mate,
    when she his doom doth hear.

He that was erst a Husband pierc't
    with sense of Wives distress,
Whose tender heart did bear a part
    of all her grievances,
Shall mourn no more as heretofore
    because of her ill plight;
Although he see her now to be
    a damn'd forsaken wight.

Luk. 16. 25.
The tender Mother will own no other
    of all her numerous brood,
But such as stand at Christ's right hand
    acquitted through his Blood.
The pious father had now much rather
    his graceless son should ly
In Hell with Devils, for all his evils,
    burning eternally. . . .

The Judge
pronounceth
the Sentence
of condemna-
tion.
Mat. 25. 41.
Ye sinful wights, and cursed sprights,
    that work iniquity,
Depart together from me for ever
    to endless Misery;
Your portion take in yonder Lake,
    where Fire and Brimstone flameth:
Suffer the smart, which your desert
    as it's due wages claimeth.

The terrour of
it.
Oh piercing words more sharp than swords!
    what, to depart from thee,
Whose face before for evermore
    the best of Pleasures be!
What? to depart (unto our smart)
    from thee Eternally:
To be for aye banish'd away,
    with Devils company!

What? to be sent to Punishment,
　　and flames of Burning Fire,
To be surrounded, and eke confounded
　　with Gods Revengeful ire!
What? to abide, not for a tide
　　these Torments, but for Ever:
To be released, or to be eased,
　　not after years, but Never.

Oh fearful Doom! now there's no room
　　for hope or help at all:
Sentence is past which aye shall last,
　　Christ will not it recall.
There might you hear them rent and tear
　　the Air with their out-cries:
The hideous noise of their sad voice
　　ascendeth to the Skies.

Luke 13. 28.
Prov. 1. 26.

They wring their hands, their caitiff-hands,
　　and gnash their teeth for terrour;
They cry, they roar for anguish sore,
　　and gnaw their tongues for horrour.
But get away without delay,
　　Christ pities not your cry:
Depart to Hell, there may you yell,
　　and roar Eternally. . . .

Rev. 14. 10, 11.

For day and night, in their despight,
　　their torments smoak ascendeth.
Their pain and grief have no relief,
　　their anguish never endeth.
There must they ly, and never dy,
　　though dying every day:
There must they dying ever ly,
　　and not consume away.

Dy fain they would, if dy they could,
　　but death will not be had.
God's direful wrath their bodies hath
　　for ev'r Immortal made.
They live to ly in misery,
　　and bear eternal wo;
And live they must whilst God is just,
　　that he may plague them so.

The insuffer-
able torments
of the damned.
Luk. 16. 24.
Jude 7.

> But who can tell the plagues of Hell,
>   and torments exquisite?
> Who can relate their dismal state,
>   and terrours infinite?
> Who fare the best, and feel the least,
>   yet feel that punishment
> Whereby to nought they should be brought,
>   if God did not prevent.

Isa. 33. 14.
Mark 9. 43, 44.

> The least degree of misery
>   there felt's incomparable,
> The lightest pain they there sustain
>   more than intolerable.
> But God's great pow'r from hour to hour
>   upholds them in the fire,
> That they shall not consume a jot,
>   nor by it's force expire.

UNCLE TRACY'S THANKSGIVING

TRADITIONAL

———◆•◆———

"Uncle Tracy's Thanksgiving" was a great favorite of my childhood, as sung by my father and his father before him. It showed that Puritan life had its convivial side.

In his New England History in Ballads, *E. E. Hale has this to say of it: "There can be no doubt but that this queer song runs back in time to the end of the first century of the colony. It is purely traditional. I heard it as early as 1825, and I do not believe it has ever been printed until now [1903]. I have no doubt as to its antiquity. It belongs before 1689 and after 1661."*

> 'Twas up to Uncle Tracy's
> The Fifth of November
> Last Thanksgiving night
> As I very well remember
>   And there we had a Frolic
>   A Frolic indeed
>   Where we drank good full glasses
>   Of old Anise-seed.

And there was Mr. Holmes
  And there was Peter Drew
And there was Seth Gilbert
  And Seth Thomas too
      And there were too many
        Too many for to name
        And by and by I'll tell you how
          We carried on the Game.

We carried on the Game
  Until late in the night
And one pretty Girl
  Almost lost her Eyesight.
      No wonder, no wonder
        No wonder indeed,
        For she drank good full glasses
          Of old Anise-seed.

1665-1688

LAST WILL AND TESTAMENT

ANDREW HODGES

————◆•◆————

*The following copy of a will made in 1665 by one Andrew Hodges gives
an idea of what sort of a property a Puritan might bequeath. The document is from the records of the Ipswich Quarterly Court of Essex County,
Massachusetts. Note the gift to Harvard.*

WILL of Andrew Hodges, dated Oct. 11, 1665, was proved, 27: 1:
1666, by Dea. Thomas Knowlton and Theophilus Willson: "I give to my
beloued Wife fiue pound a year during hear naturall life to be paid her as
followeth six bushel of wheat and the rest half in molt and the other half
in Indian also I giue her two Cows and a Red heyfer and two sheep
and these are to be maintayned by my ground so long as she liues as hir
own and half of the wool of the rest of my sheep and I giue to my wif the
wool and yarn in the house also I giue her my swine and I giue to my
wife Twenty pound to be at her disposing and my household goods be
for my wiues youse so long as she liues vnles she se cause to take part of
them in payment of the twenty pound I haue giuen her also I giue to my
Wife and her Grandchild three pound to buy them som parrell also my
kinsman Ghiles is to find her Wood as long as she lives my Wif paying hir
for the Cutting of it out in Aples or otherwise and my wif is to haue her
liueing in the house and the youse of the ground about it her life only the
barne to be at liberty for my kinsman and I giue to the poor of this Town
fiue shillings a year after my Wiues death for euer also I giue to the
Colledg of Cambridg hear, fiue pound to be paid after my Wiues death in
fiue year by twenty shillings a year for the good of poore skollers also I
giue to henry Bennit fiue pound and to Edward Walden fourty shillings
and to Mr. Cobbet fourty shillings and to Mary quilter fourty shillings
and to Theophilus Wilson twenty shillings and these legasys to be paid
in thre year after my death, and to my cossen Ghils Berdly I giue my
house and ground about it after my Wiues death, and all my other ground

both meddow and upland and cattle and sheep with my wearing parrell at my death and for the performanc of this my will I bind ouer my house and ground to my two ouerseers and I mak my Cossen Ghiles Berdly my Execcetour and Decon Knowlton and Theophilus Wilson my two ouerseers and giue them powr in case of not performenc of my will to dispose of my hous and ground for the discharging of my will." Andrew Hodges. Wit: Theophi us Wilson and Thomas Knowlton.

Inventory of the estate of Andrew Hodges of Ipswich, lately deceased, taken Jan. 16, 1665, by Robert Lord and Jacob Foster, and allowed, Mar. 27, 1666, in Ipswich court: Wearing apparrell, 10li.; a fether bed, 2 feather boulsters & 2 pillows, an old blankett & ould rug, 7li.; little flock bed, 1li.; one bedstead & cord, 1li. 10s.; a paire of curtaines & valence, 1li. 18s.; trundle bed & cord, 10s.; flockbed, 1li. 15s.; one fether pillow with a new tike, 9s.; one old fether pillow, 3s.; one woole pillow, 3s.; a blankett of trucking cloth, 12s.; 2 old blankets, 3s.; an old darnacle coverlett & curtaine, 4s.; one paire of flaxen sheetes, 1li. 3s. 4d.; one old worne fine sheete, 7s.; 2 paire old corse sheets, 10s.; 3 corse sheetes, 14s.; one corse table cloth, 5s.; a flaxen table cloth, 6s. 8d.; one napkin, 3s. & 4 napkins at 5s., 8s.; one paire of fine old pillow beeres, 5s.; two paire corse pillow beeres, 8s.; 4 corse towells, 3s.; a trunke, 6s. 8d.; a broad box, 3s. 4d.; a desk, 2s. & 3 old boxes, 3s., 5s.; a table & forme, 12s.; 3 darnacle curtaines, old ones, 4s. 6d.; one great chaire, 3s.; two chaires, 3s.; two old cushens, 2s.; a paire of Andiorns, 6s.; fire pan & tongs, 5s. 6d.; a paire of bellows, 2s.; 2 smotheing Irons, 2s.; a lookeing glase, 10s.; a leather case, 6d.; a bible & 2 little bookes, 10s.; one grt. Iron pott, 18s.; a little Iron pot, 6s.; one Iron kettle, 4s. 6d.; a small Iron pott, 2s. 6d.; brase pott, 12s.; two brase kittells, 16s.; a skillet & little kettell, 3s.; chafen dish, 5s.; 2 skimers, 3s. 6d.; brase morter & pestle, 6s.; old warming pan, 5s.; a spitt & bread bowle, 3s.; a frying pan, 2s. 6d.; 3 grter pewter dishes & a plate, 1li. 4s.; 4 smaller dishes of pewter, 10s.; a vearged bassen, 8s.; a peece bassen, 3s.; pewter candlestick, 3s.; pewter salt, 2s. 6d.; wine qurt. pott, 4s. 6d.; an ale qurt. & pint pott, 6s.; 4 poringers, 3s. 4d.; 3 pewter sasers, 2s.; 4 ocumy spoones, 1s. 4d.; a driping pan & puding pan, 3s.; pan, fish plate & tunell, 1s.; earthenware, 4s. 6d.; pewter chamberpot, 2s.; a paire of taylours sheeres, 1s. 6d.; a paire of pincers, 1s.; a broad grat, 8d.; hamer, ager, chissell & old goudg, 3s.; a mortiseing axe and a handsaw, 3s.; 2 sives, 2s. 6d.; cheesepres, 4s.; cubbard, 10s.; 2 little old tables, 3s. 6d.; beetle rings, 2 old axes & 2 wedges, 7s.; old spade, broken pikax, old how, 1s. 6d.; wooden dishes, 2s.; paile & pigin, 2s. 6d.; tramell, 4s.; 3 trayes, bowle, 2 keelars, 8s.; a red rugg, 15s.; a trunck, 6s.; poudereing tub & chirne, 7s.; 2 firkings & salt, 3s. 6d.; 3 beerefirkings, 4s.; about 3 peackes of wheate, 3s. 9d.; tobaco in the leafe, 2s.; pott of butter, 7s.; in pourke, 2li. 10s.; hatchell, 4s.; scales & waites, 1s. 6d.; coslet & pike, 1li. 5s.; sea chest, 8s.; English corne, 4li. 15s. 9d.; Indian corne, 3li. 19s. 6d.; 2 lenen wheeles & a wollen one, 10s.; halfe bushell, 2s.; tub & little ground malt, 3s.; an old cart rope, 2s.; 8li. of fleese woole & 3 of lambes, 14s.; 12li. cotton woole, 12s.; sheepes woole, 7s. 6d.; cotton yarne, 7s. 6d.; woollen yarne, 15s.; paire of pot-hookes & a houre glase, 2s.; 2 bullocks, 11li.; 4 cowes, 18li.; a steere, 4li. 10s.; heifer, 3li.; 2 calves, 2li. 10s.; 9 sheepe, 4li. 10s.; harrow, 3s.; one yoke & one chaine & span shakell, 11s.; halfe the cart & plow, 1li.; tub to scald hoggs, 2s.; 3 piggs, 18s.; laders & forkes, 6s.; sword, 8s.; apples, 6s.; two baggs, 4s.; house, barne and homestead, 50li.; 28 acres of upland & meddow, 112li.; 2 pr. cards, 3s.; cotton woole, 18d.; cheese, 5s.; debts due to the estate, 1li. 10s. total, 228li. 19s. Debts due from the estate, 19li. 6s. 8d.

FAST DAY AND THANKSGIVING PROCLAMATIONS

MASSACHUSETTS BAY COLONY RECORDS

———◆•◆———

Eliza Orne White, a New England writer of stories for children whom I knew when she was a very old lady, says in her enchanting A Little Girl of Long Ago *that by the nineteenth century fast days had come to be days on which a particularly good dinner was served. In the Massachusetts Bay Colony such fast days, or days of humiliation, ordered by the General Court, had a practical theory behind them. Fast days worked (as when the Rev. Mr. Higginson laid storms on the Atlantic crossing). Later on, it was felt necessary to lay less outward perils: hardheartedness, security, sloth, sensuality, lack of zeal among children, formality, hypocrisy, were some of the reasons to proclaim a day of humiliation, when the whole town would gather in church, and a special type of sermon was delivered. Sins were pointed out, divine retribution pictured, and repentance demanded.*

On the other hand, when some piece of good fortune crowned the colonists' efforts, a day of Thanksgiving was proclaimed by the Court, where again people gathered in church to thank God for the favor he had shown and promise to continue obedient to His will. There were many more Days of Humiliation, in early days, than there were Days of Thanksgiving.

A proclamation of each kind of day is given below, taken from the Records of the Massachusetts Bay Colony.

ORDER FOR A DAY OF THANKSGIVINGE,
8 NOVEMBER NEXT

THE Lord hath sajd, He that offereth me prajse glorifyes me, & he that orders his conversation aright shall see the salvation of God, & that prajse is comely for the vpright, & that in Zion especially the Lord is to be exalted; & forasmuch as it must needs be acknouledged that the poore people in these ends of the earth haue had not only diuers former but later experiences of the favour & grace of God to us, & in particcular the yeare past, in the continuance of our civil & spirittual libertjes, in preseruing us from invasion of the comon ennemjes of our nation, in sparing such a portion of the fruites of the earth as may be for necessary sustenance, notw^thstanding the threats of his displeasure against vs the summer past, in the drought, blastings, & mildews, the consideration & sence of these mercjes hath mooued the Generall Court hereby to appoint the 8th day of November next to be kept as a day of solemne thanksgiving to Almighty God for his mercjes in the respects before mentioned, & doe comend it to the ministers, people, & churches w^thin this jurisdiction to keepe the same accordingly.

ORDER FOR A DAY OF HUMILIATION,
22 NOVEMBER NEXT

Forasmuch as there are many causes of deepe humiliation & earnest supplication remayning among us, as well in respect of the growth of sin & prophanes, as pride, oppression, sensuality, carnall security, formality & heresy; as also the Lords hand still inflicted vpon vs in some parts of the country, in respect of the smale pox, blastings, meldews, drought, caterpillars, grashoppers, wth the effects thereof, whereby many of our outward comforts haue binn shortned, together wth the consideration of our nation in respect of warrs & pæstilence, yet continuing in some parts, especially considering the low estate of the true professors of Christian religion in all parts; and, in particular, that the Lord would yet continue our precious libertjes & injoyments, civil & spirituall, & keepe vs from the assaults & invasion of our ennemjes, & that he will please to blesse all good meanes to those ends, or otherwise to prepare us to submitt to his good pleasure, and that the Lord will please to preserve the fleet of ships lately gonne from hence, & giue them a safe arrivall at their desired ports; the sence & consideration of these things hath mooued the Generall Court hereby to appoint the two & twentieth day of November next as a solemne day of humiliation & supplication of the Lord our God, & doe comend it to all the respective churches, people, & miñsters w^thin this jurisdiction, to keepe the same accordingly.

AN ESSAY FOR THE RECORDING OF ILLUSTRIOUS PROVIDENCES

INCREASE MATHER

———◆•◆———

"Providence," to the Puritans, did not mean, as it does to us, something fortunate happening or some peril averted. It meant the judgment of God, for good or ill. This brief excerpt from An Essay for the Recording of Illustrious Providences *by Increase Mather (1639–1723), son of Richard, describes what happened to people rash enough to do wrong. It is partly atavistic belief in this kind of "providence" that is behind the famous New England conscience that is so very much a reality even today.*

CONCERNING REMARKABLE JUDGMENTS

THOSE memorable judgments which the hand of Heaven has executed upon notorious sinners are to be reckoned amongst Remarkable Providences. *Lubricus hic locus et difficilis.* He undertakes a difficult province that shall relate all that might be spoken on such a subject, both in that it cannot but be gravaminous to surviving relations when such things are published, also in that men are apt to misapply the unsearchable judgments of God, which are a great deep, as Job's friends did; and wicked Papists have done the like with respect to the untimely death of famous Zuinglius. We may not judge of men merely by outward accidents which befal them in this world, since all things happen alike unto all, and no man knoweth either love or hatred by all that is before them. We have seen amongst ourselves that the Lord's faithful servants have sometimes been the subjects of very dismal dispensations. There happened a most awful providence at Farmington in Connecticut colony, Dec. 14, 1666, when the house of Serjeant John Hart taking fire in the night, no man knows how (only it is conjectured that it might be occasioned by an oven), he and his wife and six children were all burned to death before the neighbours knew anything of it, so that his whole family had been extinguished by the fatal flames of that unhappy night had not one of his children been providentially from home at that time. This Hart was esteemed a choice Christian, and his wife also a good woman. Such things sometimes fall upon those that are dear unto God, to intimate, "If this be done to the green tree, what shall be done to the dry? that is, fit for nothing but the fire." Nevertheless, a judgment may be so circumstanced as that the displeasure of Heaven is plainly written upon it in legible characters; on which account it is said, "That the wrath of God is revealed from heaven against all ungodliness and unrighteousness of men." . . .

It hath been by many observed, that men addicted to horrid cursings and execrations have pulled down the imprecated vengeance of Heaven upon themselves. Sundry very awful examples of this kind have lately happened: I shall here mention one or two.

The hand of God was very remarkable in that which came to pass in the Narraganset country in New England, not many weeks since; for I have good information, that on August 28, 1683, a man there (viz. Samuel Wilson) having caused his dog to mischief his neighbour's cattle was blamed for his so doing. He denied the fact with imprecations, wishing that he might never stir from that place if he had so done. His neighbour being troubled at his denying the truth, reproved him, and told him he did very ill to deny what his conscience knew to be truth. The atheist thereupon used the name of God in his imprecations, saying, "He wished to God he might never stir out of that place, if he had done that which he was charged with." The words were scarce out of his mouth before he sunk down dead, and never stirred more; a son-in-law of his standing by and catching him as he fell to the ground.

A LOVE LETTER TO HER HUSBAND

ANNE BRADSTREET

———◆•◆———

Edward Everett Hale forebore to include poetry of Anne Bradstreet's in his New England History in Ballads *because, he said, he had hoped he "might find one line which should show that she had ever seen a hepatica, or a wood anemone, or bloodroot, or a ladies' slipper, or a fringed gentian. No! She had only seen violets and primroses and roses—the conventional flowers of English poetry. . . . She had never seen a moccasin, or a dug-out, or a tobaggan, or a squaw, or a papoose."*

Although it is true that Anne Bradstreet (1612–1672), who came to the Colony on the Arbella *and whom Cotton Mather called the "tenth Muse," did not write of her surroundings, her poem, "A Love Letter to Her Husband," follows, because I think it shows how very far from cold and stern Puritan affections were.*

Phœbus make haste, the day's too long, begone,
The silent night's the fittest time for moan;
But stay this once, unto my suit give ear,
And tell my griefs in either Hemisphere:
(And if the whirling of thy wheels do n't drown'd
The woful accents of my doleful sound),
If in thy swift career thou canst make stay,
I crave this boon, this errand by the way:
Commend me to the man more lov'd than life,
Show him the sorrows of his widow'd wife,
My dumpish thoughts, my groans, my brackish tears,
My sobs, my longing hopes, my doubting fears,
And, if he love, how can he there abide?
My interest's more than all the world beside.
He that can tell the stars or Ocean sand,
Or all the grass that in the meads do stand,
The leaves in th' woods, the hail or drops of rain,
Or in a cornfield number every grain,
Or every mote that in the sunshine hops,
May count my sighs and number all my drops.
Tell him, the countless steps that thou dost trace,
That once a day thy spouse thou mayst embrace;
And when thou canst not treat by loving mouth,
Thy rays afar, salute her from the south.
But for one month I see no day (poor soul)
Like those far situate under the pole,
Which day by day long wait for thy arise,
O how they joy when thou dost light the skies.
O Phœbus, hadst thou but thus long from thine
Restrain'd the beams of thy beloved shine,
At thy return, if so thou couldst or durst,
Behold a Chaos blacker than the first.
Tell him here's worse than a confused matter,
His little world's a fathom under water,
Naught but the fervor of his ardent beams
Hath power to dry the torrent of these streams.
Tell him I would say more, but cannot well,
Opressed minds abrupted tales do tell.
Now post with double speed, mark what I say,
By all our loves conjure him not to stay.

UPON WEDLOCK, AND DEATH OF CHILDREN

REV. EDWARD TAYLOR

———◆•◆———

The Puritans, so literate and so articulate, wrote a good deal of verse among them, but little of it can be called real poetry except that of the Rev. Edward Taylor (c. 1644–1729). His is not merely a colonial reflection of the metaphysical poems of Vaughan and Herbert, which it resembles; it has its own flavor—strong, delicate, and aware of his barbarous (from an English point of view) surroundings. Taylor's poetry has only been known to readers since Thomas H. Johnson's editing of the Yale University Library manuscripts, in 1943.

A knot, in the seventeenth century, meant a flower bed. Behind Shakespeare's house at Stratford-on-Avon there is a lovely "knot-garden."

A curious Knot God made in Paradise,
  And drew it out inamled neatly fresh.
It was the True-Love Knot, more sweet than Spice
  And set with all the flowres of Grace's dress.
  Its Wedding's Knot, that ne're can be unti'de,
  No Alexander's Sword can it divide.

The slips here planted, gay and glorious grow:
  Unless an Hellish breath do sindge their Plumes.
Here Primrose, Cowslips, Roses, Lilies blow
  With Violets and Pinkes that voide perfumes,
  Whose beautious leaves ore laid with Hony Dew,
  And chanting birds cherp out sweet Musick true.

When in this Knot I planted was, my Stock
  Soon knotted, and a manly flower out brake;
And after it my branch again did knot,
  Brought out another Flowre, its sweet breathd mate.
  One knot gave one, tother the tother's place.
  Whence checkling smiles fought in each other's face.

But oh! a glorious hand from glory came
  Guarded with Angells, soon did crop this flowre,

Which almost tore the root up of the same
    At that unlookt for, dolesome, darksome houre.
    In Pray're to Christ perfum'de it did ascend,
    And Angells bright did it to heaven tend.

But pausing on't, this sweet perfum'd my thought,
    Christ would in Glory have a Flowre, choice, prime,
And having Choice, chose this my branch forth brought.
    Lord take't. I thanke thee, thou tak'st ought of mine,
    It is my pledg in glory, part of mee
    Is now in it, Lord, glorifi'de with thee.

But praying ore my branch, my branch did sprout
    And bore another manly flower, and gay,
And after that another, sweet brake out,
    The which the former hand soon got away.
    But oh! the tortures, vomit, screechings, groans,
    And six weeks' Fever would pierce hearts like stones.

Griefe ore doth flow: and Nature fault would finde
    Were not thy Will, my Spell, Charm, Joy and Gem:
That as I said, I say, take Lord, they're thine.
    I piecemeale pass to Glory bright in them.
    I joy, may I sweet Flowers for Glory breed,
    Whether thou get'st them green, or let'st them seed.

A FIRSTHAND ACCOUNT OF CAPTIVITY

MARY ROWLANDSON

King Philip's War was touched on only glancingly when I was a child at school. Perhaps the teaching of American history in secondary schools has changed greatly, but in case it has not, I should like to give a tip to teachers who want to catch their pupils' interest: Give plenty of time to the Indians.

This most devastating war in New England's history was a struggle between the Mohawk nation and the English settlers, started by the Indians, who now possessed firearms and were able to work terrible harassment on the colonies from Narragansett far north. In the end the colonies, which were confederated by 1645 as the Mohawks were not, and which in

*addition had many Indian scouts loyal to them, put down the Indians of
southern New England for good. (Indians to the north, with Canadian
assistance, remained on the rampage for a long time.)*

*In the course of the war (1675–1676) many colonists were murdered
and many led away into captivity. There are several firsthand accounts
of these captivities, among them that of Mary Rowlandson (c. 1635–c.
1678), excerpts from which follow. Her story is a good description of the
nightmare that haunts New England dreams.*

*I remember as a child reading and weeping over the death of King
Philip. I append an account of this sad event, taken from* Entertaining
Passages Relating to King Philip's War, *by Thomas Church (1673–1748),
the son of a soldier in the war, Benjamin Church, whose notes Thomas
used in writing his forthright, vivid account of the fighting.*

STORY OF HER CAPTIVITY, SUFFERINGS, AND RESTORATION

THE DOLEFUL ONSLAUGHT OF THE INDIANS

ON the 10th of February, 1675 [o.s.], came the Indians with great
numbers upon Lancaster: their first coming was about sun-rising; hearing the noise of some guns we looked out; several houses were burning,
and the smoke ascending to heaven. There were five persons taken in one
house, the father and mother and a suckling child they knocked on the
head, the other two they took and carried away alive. There were two
others, who, being out of their garrison upon occasion, were set upon,
one was knocked on the head, the other escaped. Another there was who,
running along, was shot and wounded, and fell down; he begged of them
his life, promising them money (as they told me), but they would not
hearken to him, but knocked him on the head, stripped him naked, and
split open his bowels. Another seeing many of the Indians about his barn
ventured and went out, but was quickly shot down. There were three
others belonging to the same garrison who were killed; the Indians, getting up upon the roof of the barn, had advantage to shoot down upon
them over their fortification. Thus these murtherous wretches went on
burning and destroying all before them.

At length they came and beset our house, and quickly it was the dolefulest day that ever mine eyes saw. The house stood upon the edge of
a hill; some of the Indians got behind the hill, others into the barn, and
others behind anything that would shelter them; from all which places
they shot against the house, so that the bullets seemed to fly like hail,
and quickly they wounded one man among us, then another, then a third.
About two hours (according to my observation in that amazing time)

they had been about the house before they prevailed to fire it, (which they did with flax and hemp which they brought out of the barn, and there being no defence about the house, only two flankers at two opposite corners, and one of them not finished) they fired it once, and one ventured out and quenched it, but they quickly fired it again, and that took. Now is the dreadful hour come that I have often heard of (in time of the war, as it was the case of others) but now mine eyes see it. Some in our house were fighting for their lives, others wallowing in blood, the house on fire over our heads, and the bloody heathen ready to knock us on the head if we stirred out. Now might we hear mothers and children crying out for themselves and one another, Lord, what shall we do! Then I took my children (and one of my sisters hers) to go forth and leave the house: but, as soon as we came to the door and appeared, the Indians shot so thick that the bullets rattled against the house as if one had taken a handful of stones and threw them, so that we were forced to give back. We had six stout dogs belonging to our garrison, but none of them would stir, though at another time if an Indian had come to the door, they were ready to fly upon him and tear him down. The Lord hereby would make us the more to acknowledge his hand, and to see that our help is always in him. But out we must go, the fire increasing, and coming along behind us roaring, and the Indians gaping before us with their guns, spears, and hatchets to devour us. No sooner were we out of the house, but my brother-in-law (being before wounded in defending the house, in or near the throat) fell down dead, whereat the Indians scornfully shouted and hallowed, and were presently upon him, stripping off his clothes. The bullets flying thick, one went through my side, and the same (as would seem) through the bowels and hand of my poor child in my arms. One of my elder sister's children (named William) had then his leg broke, which the Indians perceiving they knocked him on the head. Thus were we butchered by those merciless heathens, standing amazed, with the blood running down to our heels. My eldest sister being yet in the house, and seeing those woful sights, the infidels hauling mothers one way and children another, and some wallowing in their blood; and her eldest son telling her that her son William was dead, and myself was wounded, she said, "and Lord, let me die with them;" which was no sooner said, but she was struck with a bullet, and fell down dead over the threshold. I hope she is reaping the fruit of her good labors, being faithful to the service of God in her place. . . .

Oh! the doleful sight that now was to behold at this house! Come, behold the works of the Lord, what desolations he has made in the earth. Of thirty-seven persons who were in this one house, none escaped either present death, or a bitter captivity, save only one, who might say as in Job i. 15: "And I only am escaped alone to tell the news." There were twelve killed, some shot, some stabbed with their spears, some knocked

down with their hatchets. When we are in prosperity, Oh the little that
we think of such dreadful sights, to see our dear friends and relations lie
bleeding out their heart's-blood upon the ground. There was one who was
chopped in the head with a hatchet, and stripped naked, and yet was
crawling up and down. It was a solemn sight to see so many Christians
lying in their blood, some here and some there, like a company of sheep
torn by wolves. All of them stripped naked by a company of hell-hounds,
roaring, singing, ranting, and insulting, as if they would have torn our
very hearts out; yet the Lord, by his almighty power, preserved a number
of us from death, for there were twenty-four of us taken alive and carried
captive.

I had often before this said, that if the Indians should come, I should
choose rather to be killed by them than taken alive, but when it came to
the trial, my mind changed; their glittering weapons so daunted my spirit,
that I chose rather to go along with those (as I may say) ravenous bears,
than that moment to end my days. And that I may the better declare what
happened to me during that grievous captivity, I shall particularly speak
of the several Removes we had up and down the wilderness.

THE FIRST REMOVE

Now away we must go with those barbarous creatures, with our bodies
wounded and bleeding, and our hearts no less than our bodies. About a
mile we went that night, up upon a hill, within sight of the town, where
we intended to lodge. There was hard by a vacant house (deserted by
the English before, for fear of the Indians); I asked them whether I might
not lodge in the house that night? to which they answered, "What, will
you love Englishmen still?" This was the dolefulest night that ever my
eyes saw. Oh, the roaring and singing, and dancing, and yelling of those
black creatures in the night, which made the place a lively resemblance
of hell. And miserable was the waste that was there made, of horses,
cattle, sheep, swine, calves, lambs, roasting pigs, and fowls (which they
had plundered in the town), some roasting, some lying and burning, and
some boiling, to feed our merciless enemies; who were joyful enough,
though we were disconsolate. To add to the dolefulness of the former
day, and the dismalness of the present night, my thoughts ran upon my
losses and sad, bereaved condition. All was gone, my husband gone (at
least separated from me, he being in the Bay; and to add to my grief, the
Indians told me they would kill him as he came homeward), my children
gone, my relations and friends gone, our house and home, and all our
comforts within door and without, all was gone (except my life), and I
knew not but the next moment that might go too.

There remained nothing to me but one poor, wounded babe, and it
seemed at present worse than death, that it was in such a pitiful condi-

tion, bespeaking compassion, and I had no refreshing for it, nor suitable things to revive it. Little do many think, what is the savageness and brutishness of this barbarous enemy, those even that seem to profess more than others among them, when the English have fallen into their hands. . . .

THE EIGHTH REMOVE–A VISIT TO KING PHILIP

On the morrow morning we must go over Connecticut river to meet with King Philip; two canoes full they had carried over, the next turn myself was to go; but as my foot was upon the canoe to step in, there was a sudden out-cry among them, and I must step back; and instead of going over the river, I must go four or five miles up the river farther northward. Some of the Indians ran one way, and some another. The cause of this rout was, as I thought, their espying some English scouts who were thereabouts. In this travel up the river, about noon the company made a stop and sat down, some to eat and others to rest them. . . .

We traveled on till night, and in the morning we must go over the river to Philip's crew. When I was in the canoe, I could not but be amazed at the numerous crew of Pagans that were on the bank on the other side. When I came ashore, they gathered all about me, I sitting alone in the midst: I observed they asked one another questions, and laughed, and rejoiced over their gains and victories. Then my heart began to fail, and I fell a weeping; which was the first time, to my remembrance, that I wept before them; although I had met with so much affliction, and my heart was many times ready to break, yet could I not shed one tear in their sight, but rather had been all this while in a maze, and like one astonished; but now I may say as Psal. cxxxvii. 1: "By the river of Babylon, there we sat down, yea, we wept, when we remembered Zion." There one of them asked me why I wept? I could hardly tell what to say; yet I answered, they would kill me: No, said he, none will hurt you. Then came one of them, and gave me two spoonfuls of meal (to comfort me) and another gave me half a pint of peas, which was worth more than many bushels at another time. Then I went to see King Philip; he bade me come in and sit down, and asked me whether I would smoke it? (a usual compliment now a days, among the saints and sinners), but this no way suited me. For though I had formerly used tobacco, yet I had left it ever since I was first taken. It seems to be a bait the devil lays to make men lose their precious time. I remember with shame how formerly, when I had taken two or three pipes, I was presently ready for another; such a bewitching thing it is: but I thank God, He has now given me power over it; surely there are many who may be better employed than to sit sucking a stinking tobacco-pipe.

Now the Indians gathered their forces to go against Northampton.

Over night one went about yelling and hooting to give notice of the design. Whereupon they went to boiling of ground-nuts, and parching corn (as many as had it) for their provision: and in the morning away they went. During my abode in this place, Philip spake to me to make a shirt for his boy, which I did; for which he gave me a shilling. I offered the money to my mistress, but she bid me keep it, and with it I bought a piece of horse-flesh. Afterward he asked me to make a cap for his boy, for which he invited me to dinner; I went, and he gave me a pancake, about as big as two fingers; it was made of parched wheat, beaten and fried in bear's grease, but I thought I never tasted pleasanter meat in my life. There was a squaw who spake to me to make a shirt for her sannup; for which she gave me a piece of beef. Another asked me to knit a pair of stockings, for which she gave me a quart of peas. I boiled my peas and beef together, and invited my master and mistress to dinner; but the proud gossip, because I served them both in one dish, would eat nothing, except one bit that he gave her upon the point of his knife. . . .

The Indians returning from Northampton brought with them some horses, and sheep, and other things which they had taken; I desired them that they would carry me to Albany upon one of those horses, and sell me for powder; for so they had sometimes discoursed. I was utterly helpless of getting home on foot, the way that I came. I could hardly bear to think of the many weary steps I had taken to this place.

THE DEATH OF KING PHILIP
Thomas Church

Captain Church being now at Plymouth again, weary and worn, would have gone home to his wife and family; but the government being solicitous to engage him in the service until Philip was slain, and promising him satisfaction and redress for some mistreatment that he had met with, he fixes for another expedition.

He had soon volunteers enough to make up the company he desired, and marched through the woods, until he came to Pocasset. And not seeing or hearing of any of the enemy, they went over the ferry to Rhode Island, to refresh themselves. The Captain, with about half a dozen in his company, took horses and rid about eight miles down the island to Mr. Sanford's, where he had left his wife. Who no sooner saw him, but fainted with surprise; and by that time she was a little revived, they spied two horsemen coming a great pace. Captain Church told his company, that "Those men (by their riding) come with tidings." When they came up, they proved to be Major Sanford and Captain Golding. . . . They told him, they had rid hard with some hopes of overtaking him, and were now come on purpose to inform, that there were just now tidings from Mount-hope. An Indian came down from thence (where Philip's camp now was) on to Sandy point, over against Trip's, and hallooed, and made signs to be fetched over. And being fetched over, he reported, that he was fled from Philip, "who (said he) has killed my brother just before I came away, for giving some advice that displeased him." And said, he was fled for fear of meeting with the same his brother had met with. Told them also, that Philip was now in Mount-hope Neck. Captain Church thanked them for their good news, and said he hoped by to-morrow morning to have the rogue's head. . . . They immediately mounted, set spurs to their horses, and away. . . .

And they were soon at Trip's ferry, (with Captain Church's company) where the deserter was. Who was a fellow of good sense, and told his story handsomely. He offered Captain Church, to pilot him to Philip, and to help to kill him, that he might revenge his brother's death. Told him, that Philip was now upon a little spot of upland, that was in the south end of the miry swamp, just at the foot of the mount, which was a spot of ground that Captain Church was well acquainted with.

By that time they were got over the ferry, and came near the ground, half the night was spent. The Captain commands a halt, and bringing the company together, he asked Major Sanford's and Captain Golding's advice, what method was best to take in making the onset; but they declined giving any advice; telling him, that his great experience and success forbid their taking upon them to give advice. Then Captain Church offered Captain Golding that he should have the honor (if he would please accept of it) to beat up Philip's headquarters. He accepted the offer and had his allotted number drawn out to him, and the pilot. Captain Church's instructions to him were, to be very careful in his approach to the enemy, and be sure not to show himself, until by daylight they might see and discern their own men from the enemy; told him also, that his custom in the like cases was, to creep with his company, on their bellies, until they came as near as they could; and that as soon as the enemy discovered them, they would cry out, and that was the word for his men to fire and fall on. He directed him, that when the enemy should start and take into the swamp, they should pursue with speed; every man shouting and making what noise he could; for he would give orders to his ambuscade to fire on any that should come silently.

Captain Church, knowing that it was Philip's custom to be foremost in the flight, went down to the swamp, and gave Captain Williams of Scituate the command of the right wing of the ambush, and placed an Englishman and an Indian together behind such shelters of trees, etc., as he could find, and took care to place them at such distance that none might pass undiscovered between them; charged them to be careful of themselves, and of hurting their friends, and to fire at any that should come silently through the swamp. But it being somewhat farther through the swamp than he was aware of, he wanted men to make up his ambuscade.

Having placed what men he had, he took Major Sanford by the hand, and said, "Sir, I have so placed them that it is scarce possible Philip should escape them." The same moment a shot whistled over their heads, and then the noise of a gun towards Philip's camp. Captain Church, at first, thought it might be some gun fired by accident; but, before he could speak, a whole volley followed, which was earlier than he expected. One of Philip's gang going forth to ease himself, when he had done, looked round him, and Captain Golding thought that the Indian looked right at him, (though probably it was but his conceit); so fired at him; and upon his firing, the whole company that were with him fired upon the enemy's shelter, before the Indians had time to rise from their sleep, and so over-shot them. But their shelter was open on that side next the swamp, built so on purpose for the convenience of flight on occasion. They were soon in the swamp, and Philip the foremost, who, starting at the first gun, threw his *petunk* and powderhorn over his head, catched up his gun, and ran as fast as he could scamper, without any more clothes than his small breeches and stockings; and ran directly upon two of Captain Church's ambush. They let him come fair within shot, and the Englishman's gun missing fire, he bid the Indian fire away, and he did so to the purpose; sent one musket bullet through his heart, and another not above two inches from it. He fell upon his face in the mud and water, with his gun under him. . . .

The man that had shot down Philip ran with all speed to Captain Church, and informed him of his exploit, who commanded him to be silent about it and let no man more know it, until they had driven the swamp clean. But when they had driven the swamp through, and found the enemy had escaped, or, at least, the most of them, and the sun now up, and so the dew gone, that they could not easily track them, the whole company met together at the place where the enemy's night shelter was, and then Captain Church gave them the news of Philip's death. Upon which the whole army gave three loud huzzas.

Captain Church ordered his body to be pulled out of the mire on to the upland. So some of Captain Church's Indians took hold of him by his stockings, and some by his small breeches (being otherwise naked) and drew him through the mud to the upland; and a doleful, great, naked, dirty beast he looked like. Captain Church then said that, forasmuch as he had caused many an Englishman's body to lie unburied, and rot above ground, not one of his bones should be buried. And, calling his old Indian executioner, bid him behead and quarter him. Accordingly he came with his hatchet and stood over him, but before he struck he made a small speech directing it to Philip, and said, "he had been a very great man, and had made many a man afraid of him, but so big as he was, he would now chop him to pieces." And so went to work and did as he was ordered.

Philip, having one very remarkable hand, being much scarred, occasioned by the splitting of a pistol in it formerly, Captain Church gave the head and that hand to Alderman, the Indian who shot him, to show to such gentlemen as would bestow gratuities upon him; and accordingly he got many a penny by it.

This being on the last day of the week, the Captain with his company, returned to the island, tarried there until Tuesday; and then went off and ranged through all the woods to Plymouth, and received their premium, which was thirty shillings per head, for the enemies which they had killed or taken, instead of all wages; and Philip's head went at the same price. Methinks it is scanty reward, and poor encouragement; though it was better than what had been some time before. For this march they received four shillings and sixpence a man, which was all the reward they had, except the honor of killing Philip. This was in the latter end of August, 1676.

INDIAN WARFARE IN NEW HAMPSHIRE

JEREMY BELKNAP

———◆•◆———

A reader of early records might gain the impression that the life of the colonies was concentrated in Massachusetts, Connecticut, and what is now Rhode Island. This is merely the result of their citizens' capacity for getting into print. In actual fact, things were going on at a great rate in New Hampshire, the County of Cornwall (or Maine), and what is now Vermont. Actually I should not speak of citizens of these states since there were so few cities. Up to 1826 there were only four cities in all New England—Boston, Hartford, York in Maine and, of all places, Vergennes, Vermont. (Vergennes was incorporated in 1788 by the legislature of Vermont, which was then an independent nation that did not belong to the new confederation of states or share in their deliberations over a constitution.)

Jeremy Belknap (1744–1798), a Congregational minister, was author of the three-volume History of New Hampshire, *from which the following excerpt is taken. Belknap was one of the founders of the Massachusetts Historical Society—the first such organization in America.*

In that part of the town of Dover which lies about the first falls in the river Cochecho, were five garrisoned houses; three on the north side, viz., Waldron's, Otis' and Heard's; and two on the south side, viz., Peter Coffin's and his son's. These houses were surrounded with timber-walls, the gates of which, as well as the house doors, were secured with bolts and bars. The neighboring families retired to these houses by night; but by an unaccountable negligence, no watch was kept. The Indians who were daily passing through the town visiting and trading with the inhabitants, as usual in time of peace, viewed their situation with an attentive eye. Some hints of a mischievous design had been given out by their squaws; but in such dark and ambiguous terms that no one could comprehend their meaning. Some of the people were uneasy; but Waldron, who from a long course of experience was intimately acquainted with the Indians, and on other occasions had been ready enough to suspect them, was now so thoroughly secure, that when some of the people hinted their fears to him, he merrily bade them go and plant their pumpkins, saying he would tell them when the Indians would break out. The very evening before the mischief was done, being told by a young man that the town was full of Indians and the people were much concerned, he answered that he knew the Indians very well and there was no danger.

The plan which the Indians had preconcerted was, that two squaws should go to each of the garrisoned houses in the evening, and ask leave to lodge by the fire; that in the night when the people were asleep they should open the doors and gates, and give the signal by a whistle; upon which the strange Indians, who were to be within hearing, should rush in, and take their long meditated revenge. This plan being ripe for execution, on the evening of Thursday, the twenty-seventh of June, two squaws applied to each of the garrisons for lodging, as they frequently did in time of peace. They were admitted into all but the younger Coffin's, and the people, at their request, showed them how to open the doors, in case they should have occasion to go out in the night. Mesandowit, one of their chiefs, went to Waldron's garrison, and was kindly entertained, as he had often been before. The squaws told the major, that a number of Indians were coming to trade with him the next day, and Mesandowit while at supper, with his usual familiarity, said, "Brother Waldron, what would you do if the strange Indians should come?" The major carelessly answered, that he could assemble a hundred men, by lifting up his finger. In this unsuspecting confidence the family retired to rest.

When all was quiet, the gates were opened and the signal given. The Indians entered, set a guard at the door, and rushed into the major's apartment, which was an inner room. Awakened by the noise, he jumped out of bed, and though now advanced in life to the age of eighty years, he retained so much vigor as to drive them with his sword through two or three doors; but as he was returning for his other arms, they came behind him, stunned him with a hatchet, drew him into his hall, and seating him in an elbow chair on a long table insultingly asked him, "Who shall judge Indians now?" They then obliged the people in the house to get them some victuals; and when they had done eating, they cut the major across the breast and belly with knives, each one with a stroke, saying, "I cross out my account." They then cut off his nose and ears, forcing them into his mouth; and when spent with the loss of blood, he was falling down from the table, one of them held his own sword under him, which put an end to his misery. They also killed his son-in-law, Abraham Lee; but took his daughter Lee with several others, and having pillaged the house, left it on fire.

Elizabeth Heard, with her three sons and a daughter, and some others, were returning in the night from Portsmouth. They passed up the river in their boat unperceived by the Indians, who were then in possession of the houses; but suspecting danger by the noise which they heard, after they had landed they betook themselves to Waldron's garrison, where they saw lights, which they imagined were set up for direction to those who might be seeking a refuge. They knocked and begged earnestly for admission; but no answer being given, a young man of the company climbed up the wall, and saw, to his inexpressible surprise, an Indian standing in the door of the house, with his gun. The woman was so overcome with the fright that she was unable to fly; but begged her children to shift for themselves; and they, with heavy hearts, left her. When she had a little recovered she crawled into some bushes, and lay there till daylight. She then perceived an Indian coming toward her with a pistol in his hand; he looked at her and went away: returning, he looked at her again; and she asked him what he would have; he made no answer, but ran yelling to the house, and she saw him no more. She kept her place till the house was burned, and the Indians were gone; and then returning home, found her own house safe. Her preservation in these dangerous circumstances was more remarkable, if (as it is supposed) it was an instance of justice and gratitude in the Indians. For at the time when the four or five hundred were seized in 1676, a young Indian escaped and took refuge in her house, where she concealed him; in return for which kindness he promised her that he would never kill her, nor any of her family in any future war, and that he would use his influence with the other Indians to the same purpose. This Indian was one of the party who surprised the place, and she was well known to most of them.

THE NEW ENGLAND PRIMER

ANONYMOUS

———◆•◆———

The seriousness with which education was taken in New England soon evidenced itself in the compiling and publishing of The New England Primer, *a Calvinist schoolbook for children. The alphabet beginning "In Adam's Fall, wee sinned alle" seems to be all most people have ever heard of it. First published in 1683, it sold in its many editions more than five million copies. The text, adapted to the infant Puritan mind, was illustrated with rough woodcuts. The prayer "Now I lay me down to sleep" originated in* The New England Primer. *A less commonly known alphabet from it follows.*

New-England Primer
    Enlarged.
For the more easy attaining
the true Reading of English
    To which is added,
The Assembly of Divines
Catechism.

Boston: Printed by S. Kneeland, & T. Green, Sold by the Booksellers, 1727.

An Alphabet of Lessons for Youth.

A Wise Son makes a glad Father, but a foolish Son is the heaviness of his
    Mother.
B etter is a little with the fear of the Lord, than great treasure and
    trouble therewith.
C ome unto Christ all ye that labour and are heavy laden, and He will
    give you rest.
D o not the abominable thing which I hate, saith the Lord.
E xcept a Man be born again, he cannot see the Kingdom of God.
F oolishness is bound up in the heart of a child, but the rod of Correction
    shall drive it far from him.
G rieve not the Holy Spirit.
H oliness becomes God's House forever.

I t is good for me to draw near unto God.

K eep thy Heart with all Diligence, for out of it are the issues of Life.

L iars shall have their part in the lake which burns with fire and brimstone.

M any are the Afflictions of the Righteous, but the Lord delivers them out of them all.

N ow is the accepted time, now is the day of salvation.

O ut of the abundance of the heart the mouth speaketh.

P ray to thy Father which is in secret, and they Father which sees in secret, shall reward thee openly.

Q uit you like Men, be strong, stand fast in the Faith.

R emember thy Creator in the days of thy Youth.

S alvation belongeth to the Lord.

T rust in God at all times ye people, pour out your hearts before him.

U pon the wicked, God shall rain an horrible Tempest.

W o to the wicked, it shall be ill with him, for the reward of his hands shall be given him.

eX hort one another daily while it is called today, lest any of you be hardened through the deceitfulness of Sin.

Y oung Men ye have overcome the wicked one.

Z eal hath consumed me, because thy enemies have forgotten the words of God.

ELEGIE ON THE DEATH OF
THOMAS SHEPARD

URIAN OAKES

———◆◆◆———

Thomas Shepard, persecutor of Anne Hutchinson and author of The Covenant of Grace, *in the fullness of time died and was gathered to his fathers. Urian Oakes (c. 1631–1681), another minister, wrote the graceful* Elegie *upon Shepard's death in 1677—his only published poetry. The following is an excerpt. Oakes, as acting president of Harvard (1675–1680), has been accused of letting the college come for a time to the brink of extinction.*

Oh! that I were a poet now in grain!
How would I invoke the Muses all

To deign their presence, lend their flowing vein;
And help to grace dear Shepard's funeral!
  How would I paint our griefs, and succours borrow
  from art and fancy, to limn out our sorrow!

  . . . .

Oh! that my head were waters, and mine eyes
A flowing spring of tears, still issuing forth
In streams of bitterness, to solemnize
The obits of this man of matchless worth!
  Next to the tears our sins do need and crave,
  I would bestow my tears on Shepard's grave.

  . . . .

What! must we with our God, and glory part?
Lord! is thy treaty with New-England come
Thus to an end? And is war in thy heart
That this embassadour is called home?
  So earthly Gods (Kings), when they war intend,
  Call home their ministers, and treaties end.

  . . . .

If holy life, and deeds of charity,
If grace illustrious, and virtue tried,
If modest carriage, rare humility,
Could have brib'd Death, good Shepard had not died.
  Oh! but inexorable Death attacks
  The best men, and promiscuous havock makes.

  . . . .

He govern'd well the tongue (that busie thing,
Unruly, lawless and pragmatical),
Gravely reserv'd, in speech not lavishing,
Neither too sparing, nor too liberal.
  His words were few, well season'd, wisely weigh'd,
  And in his tongue the law of kindness sway'd.

Learned he was beyond the common size,
Befriended much by nature in his wit,
And temper (sweet, sedate, ingenious, wise),
And (which crown'd all) he was Heavens favourite;
  On whom the God of all Grace did command,
  And show'r down blessings with a liberal hand.

  . . . .

Zealous in God's cause, but meek in his own;
Modest of nature, bold as any lion
Where conscience was concern'd: and there were none
More constant mourners for afflicted Sion:

So general was his care for th' Churches all,
His spirit seemed apostolical.

. . . .

Cambridge groans under this so heavy cross,
And sympathizes with her Sister dear;
Renews her griefs afresh for her old loss
Of her own Shepard, and drops many a tear.
 Cambridge and Charlstown now joint mourners are,
 And this tremendous loss between them share.

Must Learnings friend (ah! worth us all) go thus?
That great support to Harvard's nursery!
Our Fellow (that no fellow had with us)
Is gone to Heaven's great University.
 Ours now indeed's a lifeless Corporation,
 The soul is fled, that gave it animation!

Poor Harvard's sons are in their mourning dress:
Their sure friend's gone! their hearts have put on mourning;
Within their walls are sighs, tears, pensiveness;
Their new foundations dread an overturning.
 Harvard! where's such a fast friend left to thee?
 Unless thy great friend LEVERET, it be.

. . . .

See what our sins have done! what ruines wrought
And how they have pluck'd out our very eyes!
Our sins have slain our Shepard! we have bought,
And dearly paid for, our enormities.
 Ah, cursed sins! that strike at God and kill
 His servants, and the blood of prophets spill.

. . . .

Farewell, dear Shepard! Thou art gone before,
Made free of Heaven, where thou shalt sing loud hymns
Of high triumphant praises ever more,
In the sweet quire of saints and seraphims.
 Lord! look on us here, clogg'd with sin and clay,
 And we, through grace, shall be as happy as they.

THE REGICIDES IN NEW ENGLAND

THOMAS HUTCHINSON

I always felt the liveliest curiosity about the Regicides, having been told that an ancestress of mine named Octavia Throop was the daughter of a Regicide. The Regicides were those who assisted in the judging and execution of Charles I of England, some of whom fled to this country. There are a number of accounts of their wanderings and their narrow escapes from capture.

The account that follows comes from The History of Massachusetts *by Thomas Hutchinson (1711–1780), the last royal governor of Massachusetts Bay Colony. His insistence on the strict enforcement of the Stamp Act was among the factors that led to the Boston Tea Party, and when his mansion in Boston was burned by the mob, he left forever for England.*

But I am getting ahead of the Regicides, who came to America after Charles was beheaded in 1649. I still don't know which of them was the father of Octavia. Throop must have been her married name, for I can find no mention of a Regicide by that name.

In the ship which arrived from London the 27th of July, there came passengers, Col. Whaley and Col. Goffe, two of the late King's judges. . . . The story of these persons has never yet been published to the world. It has never been known in New England. Their papers after their death were collected, and have remained near an hundred years in a library in Boston. It must give some entertainment to the curious. They left London before the King was proclaimed. It does not appear that they were among the most obnoxious of the judges; but as it was expected vengeance would be taken of some of them, and a great many had fled, they did not think it safe to remain. They did not attempt to conceal their persons or characters when they arrived at Boston, but immediately went to the governor, Mr. Endicott, who received them very courteously. They were visited by the principal persons of the town, and among others they take notice of Col. Crown's coming to see them. He was a noted royalist. Although they did not disguise themselves, yet they chose to reside at Cambridge, a village about four miles distant from the town, where they went the first day they arrived. They went publicly to meetings on the Lord's

days, and to occasional lectures, fasts and thanksgivings, and were admitted to the sacrament, and attended private meetings for devotion,
visited many of the principal towns, and were frequently at Boston, and
once when insulted there the person insulting them was bound to his good
behavior. They appeared grave, serious and devout, and the rank they had
sustained commanded respect. Whaley had been one of Cromwell's lieu-
tenant-generals, and Goffe a major-general. It is not strange that they
should meet with this favorable reception, nor was this reception any
contempt of the authority in England. They were known to have been
two of the King's judges; but King Charles the Second was not proclaimed when the ship that brought them left London; they had the
news of it in the channel. The reports afterward by way of Barbados
were that all the judges would be pardoned but seven. The act of indem-
nity was not brought over until the last of November. When it appeared
that they were not excepted, some of the principal persons in the government were alarmed; pity and compassion prevailed with others. They
had assurances from some that belonged to the general court that they
would stand by them, but were advised by others to think of removing.

The 22d of February the governor summoned a court of assistants to
consult about securing them, but the court did not agree to it. Finding
it unsafe to remain any longer, they left Cambridge the 26th following,
and arrived at New Haven the 7th of March. One Capt. Breedan, who
had seen them at Boston, gave information thereof upon his arrival in
England. A few days after their removal, an hue-and-cry, as they term it
in their diary, was brought by the way of Barbados; and thereupon a
warrant to secured them issued, the 8th of March, from the governor and
assistants, which was sent to Springfield and the other towns in the western parts of the colony; but they were beyond the reach of it. . . .

They were well treated at New Haven by the ministers and some of the
magistrates, and for some days seemed to apprehend themselves out of
danger. But the news of the King's proclamation being brought to New
Haven, they were obliged to abscond. The 27th of March they removed
to Milford, and appeared there in the daytime, and made themselves
known; but at night returned privately to New Haven, and lay concealed
in Mr. Davenport the minister's house, until the 30th of April. About that
time news came to Boston that ten of the judges were executed; and the
governor received a royal mandate, dated March 5, 1660, to cause Whaley
and Goffe to be secured. This greatly alarmed the country, and there is
no doubt that the court were now in earnest in their endeavors to apprehend them; and, to avoid all suspicion, they gave commission and instructions to two young merchants from England, Thomas Kellond and
Thomas Kirk, zealous royalists, to go through the colonies as far as Man-
hadoes in search of them. They had friends who informed them what was
doing, and they removed from Mr. Davenport's to the house of one Jones,

where they lay hid until the 11th of May and then removed to a mill, and from thence on the 13th into the woods, where they met Jones and two of his companions, Sperry and Burrill, who first conducted them to a place called Hatchet harbor where they lay two nights until a cave or hole in the side of a hill was prepared to conceal them. This hill they called Providence hill, and there they continued from the 15th of May to the 11th of June, sometimes in the cave, and in very tempestuous weather in a house near to it.

During this time the messengers went through New Haven to the Dutch settlement, from whence they returned to Boston by water. They made diligent search, and had full proof that the regicides had been seen at Mr. Davenport's, and offered great rewards to English and Indians who should give information that they might be taken; but by the fidelity of their three friends, they remained undiscovered. Mr. Davenport was threatened with being called to an account for concealing and comforting traitors, and might well be alarmed. They had engaged to surrender, rather than the country or any particular persons should suffer upon their account; and upon intimation of Mr. Davenport's danger, they generously resolved to go to New Haven, and deliver themselves up to the authority there. The miseries they had suffered and were still exposed to, and the little chance they had of finally escaping, in a country where every stranger is immediately known to be such, would not have been sufficient to have induced them. They let the deputy governor, Mr. Leete, know where they were, but he took no measures to secure them, and the next day some persons came to them to advise them not to surrender. Having publicly shown themselves at New Haven, they had cleared Mr. Davenport from the suspicion of still concealing them, and the 24th of June went into the woods again to their cave. They continued there, sometimes venturing to a house near the cave, until the 19th of August, when the search for them being pretty well over, they ventured to the house of one Tomkins near Milford, where they remained two years, without so much as going into the orchard.

After that, they took a little more liberty, and made themselves known to several persons in whom they could confide; and each of them frequently prayed and also exercised, as they term it, or preached, at private meetings in their chamber. In 1664 the commissioners from King Charles arrived at Boston. Upon the news of it, they retired to their cave, where they tarried eight or ten days. Soon after, some Indians in their hunting discovered the cave with the bed, etc., and the report being spread abroad, it was not safe to remain near it. On the 13th of October, 1664, they removed to Hadley, near an hundred miles distant, travelling only by night, where Mr. Russell, the minister of the place, had previously agreed to receive them. Here they remained concealed fifteen or sixteen years, very few persons in the colony being privy to it. The last account of Goffe is from a letter, dated Ebenezer (the name they gave their several places of abode), April 2d, 1679. Whaley had been dead some time before. The tradition at Hadley is, that two persons unknown were buried in the minister's cellar. The minister was no sufferer by his boarders. They received more or less remittances every year, for many years together, from their wives in England. Those few persons who knew where they were made them frequent presents. Richard Saltonstall, Esq., who was in the secret, when he left the country and went to England in 1672, made them a present of fifty pounds at his departure; and they take notice of donations from several other friends.

They were in constant terror, though they had reason to hope, after some years, that the inquiry for them was over. They read with pleasure the news of their being killed with other judges in Switzerland. Their diary for six or seven years contains every little occurrence in the town, church and particular families in the neighborhood. These were small affairs. . . . Their lives were miserable and constant burdens. They complain of being banished from all human society. . . .

Whilst they were at Hadley (February 10th, 1664) Dixwell, another of the judges, came to them; but from whence, or in what part of America he first landed, is not known. The first mention of him in their journal is by the name of Col. Dixwell, but ever after they call him Mr. Davids. He continued some years at Hadley, and then removed to New Haven. He was generally supposed to have been one of those who were obnoxious in England, but he never discovered who he was until he was on his death-bed. . . . Col. Dixwell was buried at New Haven. His gravestone still remains, with this inscription: "J. D., Esq., deceased March 18th, in the 82d year of his age, 1688."

It cannot be denied that many of the principal persons in the colony greatly esteemed these persons, for their professions of piety and their grave deportment, who did not approve of their political conduct. Mr. Mitchell, the minister of Cambridge, who showed them great friendship upon their first arrival, says, in a manuscript which he wrote in his own vindication, "Since I have had opportunity by reading and discourse to look a little into that action for which these men suffer, I could never see that it was justifiable."

DIARY

COTTON MATHER

———◆•◆———

In Cotton Mather (1663–1728) Puritanism was compounded, he being the son of Increase Mather and grandson of both Richard Mather and John Cotton. He was much impressed by his own heritage, and thought of himself as destined to lead Massachusetts in church and state. He was a prodigy of mammoth intellect and achievement. (However, his attachment to the past made his ideas seem overconservative to his contemporaries.) Deeply interested in the Salem trials for witchcraft, he privately held the view that witches should be treated by fasting and prayer, not hanged.

The following excerpt from Cotton Mather's vast Diary, published in 1911–12 by the Massachusetts Historical Society, illustrates the workings of the individual Puritan mind to which the modern "New England conscience" owes so much. The outstanding characteristic of both is the impossibility of winning. If Mather thought he had preached well, he berated himself for the sin of pride; if badly, he castigated himself for his misuse of God's gifts.

THE XXIst YEAR OF MY AGE

Horæ plusquam Amœnæ, nunquam redituræ.

12 d. 12 m. [*February*], 1682–83. I am this Day twenty Yeare old. But alas, how little have I done, for the Glory of God all this While!

I would this Day resolve, especially two Things.

I. To bee more diligent in searching of the *Scriptures.*

II. To bee more Concerned, for the Welfare of the *Church* whereto I am related.

19 d. 12 m. A Purpose. There are some *Gentlemen,* and *Merchants,* in whom the Good God, hath given mee an Interest; and shall I not improve that Interest?

I may do well, to engage them, in Agreements, together, to single out some godly, but needy *Ministers* in the Countrey, for the Objects of their Charity; unto whom their *Bounty* may so express itself, that God may bee *glorified* and they themselves gloriously *rewarded.*

4 d. 1 m. [*March.*] 1682–83. *Lord's-Day.* Hearing my Father preach a

Sermon, upon the *Eighth Commandment,* I considered, that I have in my study, two or three small *Books,* which I borrowed of my Schoolfellow, when wee were at School together, and the Promise, to return them when hee should call for them. He afterwards left off Learning, and went out of the Countrey, but I still have the Books: I resolve to lay out, however ten times the Value of them in good Books to give away; not knowing how else to have Peace in my own mind. . . .

August, 1683: This Day, I also made a most explicit Address unto the Lord Jesus Christ, as having all *Keyes* in His Hands, for my *Speech,* that I might have such continual and sufficient Supplies of it, as in my Ministry I had Occasion for. I adored, I confessed, His infinite *Might.* I praised Him for His *Mercy;* I exceedingly bewayled the Sins of my *Tongue.* I declared, I asked for a *Tongue* only to serve Him, and bespeak the Loves and Lives of my Neighbours for Him; and I concluded, with a glorious Assurance, that the ☞ *Tongue of the Stammerer should speak Plainly;* and whereas there are vile Mortals, who have questioned His *Diety,* I should from an happy Experience testify, That *verily Hee is GOD, and His Kingdome ruleth over all.* Whereto I added,

"Only, O Lord, thy Servant herewith, does *vow* unto Thee, that Hee Will endeavour to honour Thee, with His poor *Speech,* more than heretofore; and labour after greater Deliberation, Gravity, Savouriness therein, than hee has yett attended or attained." *Amen,* Lord lett mee do so!

But in the Close of this Day I formed certain *Contrivances,* about my *Walk with God,* which having in them something of *Curiositie,* I shall give a particular Account of them.

I was desirous, not only to entertain *Purposes* of glorifying my glorious Lord Jesus Christ, but also to *honour Him with my Substance,* particularly thro' my being thereby quickened unto Stedfastness in those Purposes.

There now occurr'd unto mee, no way more ingenious, or ingenuous, than for mee to awe myself into *Faithfulness* unto *them,* with *Forfeits* upon *that.*

Such *Penalties,* I also saw, would lay mee under a necessitie to *Do Good* still, one Way or other.

Herein I was very far from any vile Imagination, That I could *buy off* the Guilt of any Omission whatsoever; I knew, I own'd, that only the precious Blood of the *Lamb of God,* signified anything to do that. But I imagined, that for mee to make my Omissions more painful and costly unto my *Flesh* would bee to furnish myself, with effectual *Monitors* of my Duty.

Wherefore, I now purposed, that if I did any Day omitt such or such Exercises of Religion, which I have heretofore prescribed unto myself, I would *forfeit* a certain Piece of Money, (besides and beyond my *Tithes*) to be given unto the *Poor.*

These Usages, I continued for some while, until I found my Disposition unto such Methods of conversing with God, so strengthened, that I had not so much Need of using these *Incitements* any longer.

Thus, I have sometimes laid a *Penalty*, for some while upon myself, that if in joining with the *Prayers* of another, I did lett more than one entire Sentence pass mee at any Time without annexing some Ejaculation pertinent thereunto, I would forfeit a Piece of Money to bee given unto the Poor. And I found this Effect of it, that in a Week or two, I had little Occasion to lay my *Penalty;* for I found, my Distractions in my Duties, which had been my Plague, most wonderfully cured.

Thus also, I have sometimes laid a *Penalty* upon myself, on a *Lord's-Day,* that if thro' the whole Day, I spoke *one Word,* which I could not judge proper to bee spoken on such a Day, I would, in like manner, forfeit. And I found myself marvellously strengthened by this Caution, in keeping the *Lord's-Day* at such a Rate, as was unto mee, a little-Præliba-tion of the *rest remaining for the People of God.* . . .

MANTISSA

February, 1683–84: Having somewhere in these Papers mentioned this, for one of my Methods to do good; "As I walk in the *Street,* or sitt in the *House,* tho' I will not bee so *pharisaical* as to show it, yett I will use frequently to lift up a Cry unto God, for some *suitable Blessing* to bee vouchsafed, unto the Persons that I have before mee:" I am willing to add a more particular Explanation of that passage, for the Instruction of those few Friends, with whom I may leave (if at all I leave!) these *Memorials* of my *sinful Conversation.*

It has been a frequent Thing with mee, to redeem the *silent,* and other-wise, *thoughtless,* Minutes of my Time, in shaping Thousands of *ejacula-tory Prayers* for my Neighbours. And by reciting a *Few* of them, the Way of my shaping the *Rest,* may bee conjectured.

At a *Table,* where, I being the *youngest* of the Company, it was not proper for *mee* to discourse at all, and the Discourses of *others* were too trivial, to bee worthy of my Attention.

Casting my Eye upon,	Ejaculations.
The Gentlewoman that *carved* for us.	*Lord, carve,* of thy Graces and Comforts, a *rich portion,* unto that Person.
A Gentlewoman *stricken in years.*	*Lord,* adorn that Person, with the vertues which thou prescribest unto *aged* women, and præpare her for her approaching *Dissolution.*

A Gentlewoman lately *married*.	*Lord, espouse* and *marry,* the Soul of that Person to thyself, in a Covenant never to be forgotten.
A Gentlewoman very *beautiful*.	*Lord, beautify* the Soul of that Person with *thy Comeliness.*
A Gentlewoman very *gay in her Apparrel.*	*Lord,* give that Person an *humble Mind,* and lett her Mind bee most concern'd for the *Ornaments,* that are *of great Price in thy Sight.* ....

In like Manner, when I have been sitting in a Room full of People, at a *Funeral,* where they take not much Liberty for *Talk,* and where yett much *Time* is most unreasonably lost, I have usually sett my Witts a work, to contrive *agreeable Benedictions,* for each Person in the Company.

In passing along the *Street,* I have sett myself to *bless* thousands of persons, who never knew that I did it; with *secret Wishes,* after this manner sent unto Heaven for them.

Upon the Sight of	Ejaculations.
A Negro.	*Lord, wash* that poor Soul *white* in the *Blood* of thy Son.
Children at *Play.*	*Lord,* lett not these Children always forgett the *Work,* which they came into the World upon.
A Very *little* Man.	*Lord,* bestow *great Blessings* upon that Man, and above all, thy *Christ,* the *greatest of Blessings.*
A Man on *Horseback.*	*Lord,* thy *Creatures* do serve that man; help him to serve his *Maker.*
Young Gentlewomen.	*Lord,* make 'em *wise Virgins,* as the *polish'd Stones of thy Temple.*
A Man, who going by mee took *no Notice* of mee.	*Lord,* help that Man, to take a *due Notice* of the Lord Jesus Christ, I pray thee.

1689-1730

THE REVOLT AGAINST
SIR EDMUND ANDROS

NATHANIEL BYFIELD

———◆◆———

Until 1685 the New England colonies were self-governing and held an-
nual elections. But in that year a royal governor, Sir Edmund Andros, was
appointed by James II to bring under one central government Massachu-
setts, Maine, New Hampshire, Plymouth, King's Province, Rhode Island,
the County of Cornwall (northern Maine), and Connecticut. Andros
proved an autocratic administrator. Revolt was instigated by Increase
Mather and led by his son Cotton. On April 18, 1689, in Boston, a declara-
tion composed by Cotton Mather was read from the balcony of the Town
House to the crowd. One sentence may be quoted as an example of how
to rouse rabble in the seventeenth century:

> *But of all our Oppressors we were chiefly squeez'd by a Crew of*
> *abject Persons fetched from New York [Andros had previously been*
> *governor there] to be Tools of the Adversary, standing at our right*
> *Hand; by these were extraordinary and intollerable Fees extorted*
> *from every one upon all Occasions, without any Rules but those of*
> *their own insatiable Avarice and Beggary; and even the probate of a*
> *Will must now cost as many Pounds perhaps as it did Shillings here-*
> *tofore; nor could a small Volume contain the other Illegalities done*
> *by these Horse-leeches in the two or three Years that they have been*
> *sucking of us; and what Laws they made it was as impossible for*
> *us to know, as dangerous for us to break.*

As they were to do later, during the Revolution, the Boston rebels made
a point of getting their side of the story before the English public before
the royal officials had a chance to state theirs. Deacon Nathaniel Byfield
of Bristol, Rhode Island, wrote The Account of the Late Revolution in
New England, *from which an excerpt follows. By June of 1689 it was*

published in England. Not until the end of 1689 did John Palmer—one of the "abject Persons fetched from New York"—get his defense of Andros into print. In the meantime Andros had been deposed and the New Englanders had gone back to their charter governments.

GENTLEMEN:—Here being an opportunity of sending for London, by a vessel that loaded at Long Island and for want of a wind put in here; and not knowing that there will be the like from this country suddenly, I am willing to give you some brief account of the most remarkable things that have happened here within this fortnight last past; concluding that, till about that time, you will have received, per Carter, a full account of the management of affairs here. Upon the 18th instant, about eight of the clock in the morning, in Boston, it was reported at the south end of the town, that at the north end they were all in arms; and the like report was at the north end, respecting the south end. Whereupon Captain John George was immediately seized, and about nine of the clock the drums beat through the town; and an ensign was set up upon the beacon. Then Mr. Bradstreet, Mr. Danforth, Major Richards, Dr. Cooke, and Mr. Addington, etc., were brought to the council-house by a company of soldiers under the command of Captain Hill. The meanwhile the people in arms did take up and put into jail Justice Bullivant, Justice Foxcroft, Mr. Randolf, Sheriff Sherlock, Captain Ravenscroft, Captain White, Farewel, Broadbent, Crafford, Larkin, Smith, and many more, as also Mercey the then jail-keeper, and put Scates the bricklayer in his place. About noon, in the gallery at the council-house, was read the declaration here inclosed. Then a message was sent to the fort to Sir Edmund Andros, by Mr. Oliver and Mr. Eyres, signed by the Gentlemen then in the council-chamber, . . . to inform him how unsafe he was like to be if he did not deliver up himself, and fort and government forthwith, which he was loath to do. By this time, being about two of the clock (the lecture being put by) the town was generally in arms, and so many of the country came in that there was twenty companies in Boston, besides a great many that appeared at Charlestown that could not get over (some say fifteen hundred). There then came information to the soldiers, that a boat was come from the frigate that made towards the fort, which made them haste thither, and come to the sconce soon after the boat got thither; and 'tis said that Governor Andros and about half a score gentlemen were coming down out of the fort; but the boat being seized, wherein were small arms, hand-grenades, and a quantity of match, the Governor and the rest went in again; whereupon Mr. John Nelson, who was at the head of the soldiers, did demand the fort and the Governor, who was loath to submit to them; but at length did come down, and was with the gentlemen that were with him conveyed to the council-house, where Mr. Bradstreet and the rest of the gentlemen waited to receive him; to whom Mr. Stoughton first spake, telling him, he might thank himself for the present disaster that had befallen him, etc. He was then confined for that night to Mr. John Usher's house under strong guards, and the next day conveyed to the fort (where he yet remains, and with him Lieutenant-Colonel Ledget), which is under the command of Mr. John Nelson; and at the castle, which is under the command of Mr. John Fairweather, is Mr. West, Mr. Graham, Mr. Palmer, and Captain Tryfroye. At that time Mr. Dudley was out upon the circuit, and was holding a court at Southold on Long Island. And on the 21st instant he arrived at Newport, where he heard the news. The next day letters came to him, advising him not to come home; he thereupon went over privately to Major Smith's at Naraganzett, and advice is this day come hither, that yesterday about a dozen young men, most of their own heads, went thither to demand him; and are gone with him down to Boston. We have also advice, that on Friday last towards evening Sir Edmund Andros did attempt to make an escape in woman's apparel, and passed two guards, and was stopped at the third, being discovered by his shoes, not having changed them. We are here ready to blame you sometimes, that we have not to this day received advice concerning the great changes in England, and in particular how it is like to fare with us here; who do hope and believe that all these things will work for our good; and that you will not be wanting to promote the good of a country that stands in such need as New England does at this day. The first day of May, according to former usage, is the election-day at Road Island; and many do say they intend their choice there then. I have not farther to trouble you with at present, but recommending you, and all our affairs with you, to the direction and blessing of our most gracious God, I remain

Gentlemen,

Your most humble servant at command,

NATHANIEL BYFIELD.

BRISTOL, *April* 29, 1689.

Through the goodness of God, there has been no blood shed. Nath. Clark is in Plymouth jail, and John Smith in jail here, all waiting for news from England.

THE COURTING OF
MADAM WINTHROP

SAMUEL SEWALL

*One of the most persistent myths about the Puritans is that they were cold
in matters concerning the opposite sex. Actually, the Biblical injunction to
go forth and multiply was one never long out of their minds, and when
they lost their wives, as they did with fair regularity under the circumstances of harsh conditions and no obstetrics worth mentioning, they
straightway sought others.*

*Samuel Sewall, (1652–1730) graduated from Harvard in 1671, and for
a long time was a tutor there. In 1679 he entered upon a political career;
he aided Increase Mather in appealing to William of Orange to return to
the colonies their charters. Active as a commissioner in the Salem witchcraft trials, Sewall later regretted it and in 1697, on a fast day, recanted
publicly, standing in the Old South Church while the minister read his
confession of guilt aloud. He wrote a number of works, one justifying the
colonies' stand against Andros, one an early antislavery appeal, one an
argument for humane treatment of the Indians, and one which argued in
favor of the notion that woman might possibly aspire to resurrection. This
egalitarian attitute is apparent in the following account of his wooing of
Madam Winthrop excerpted from his Diary.*

MAY 26 [1720]. . . . Went to Bed after Ten: about 11 or before, my dear
Wife was oppress'd with a rising of Flegm that obstructed her Breathing.
I arose and lighted a Candle, made Scipio give me a Bason of Water (he
was asleep by the fire) Call'd Philadelphia, Mr. Cooper, Mayhew. About
midnight my dear wife expired to our great astonishment, especially
mine. May the Sovereign Lord pardon my Sin, and sanctify to me this
very Extraordinary, awfull Dispensation. . . .

8ʳ. [October] 1. Satterday, I dine at Mr. Stoddard's: from thence I
went to Madam Winthrop's just at 3. Spake to her, saying my loving wife
died so soon and suddenly, 'twas hardly convenient for me to think of
Marrying again; however I came to this Resolution, that I would not
make my Court to any person without first Consulting with her. . . .

Octob^r. 3.2. Waited on Madam Winthrop again; 'twas a little while before she came in. Her daughter Noyes being there alone with me, I said, I hoped my Waiting on her Mother would not be disagreeable to her. She answer'd she should not be against that that might be for her Comfort. . . . By and by in came Mr. Airs, Chaplain of the Castle, and hang'd up his Hat, which I was a little startled at, it seeming as if he was to lodge there. At last Madam Winthrop came too. After a considerable time, I went up to her and said, if it might not be inconvenient I desired to speak with her. She assented, and spake of going into another Room; but Mr. Airs and Mrs. Noyes presently rose up, and went out, leaving us there alone. Then I usher'd in Discourse from the names in the Foreseat; at last I pray'd that Katharine [Mrs. Winthrop] might be the person assign'd for me. She instantly took it up in the way of Denyal, as if she had catch'd at an Opportunity to do it, saying she could not do it before she was asked. Said that was her mind unless she should Change it, which she believed she should not; could not leave her Children. I express'd my Sorrow that she should do it so Speedily, pray'd her Consideration, and ask'd her when I should wait on her agen. She setting no time, I mention'd that day Sennight. . . .

8^r. 6th . . . A little after 6 P.M. I went to Madam Winthrop's. . . . Madam seem'd to harp upon the same string. Must take care of her Children; could not leave that House and Neighbourhood where she had dwelt so long. I told her she might doe her children as much or more good by bestowing what she laid out in Hous-keeping, upon them. Said her Son would be of Age the 7th of August. I said it might be inconvenient for her to dwell with her Daughter-in-Law, who must be Mistress of the House. I gave her a piece of Mr. Belcher's Cake and Ginger-Bread wrapped up in a clean sheet of Paper; told her of her Father's kindness to me when Treasurer, and I Constable. My Daughter Judith was gon from me and I was more lonesom—might help to forward one another in our Journey to Canaan. . . . I took leave about 9 aclock. I told [her] I came now to refresh her Memory as to Monday-night; said she had not forgot it. . . .

8^r. 10th. . . . In the Evening I visited Madam Winthrop, who treated me with a great deal of Curtesy; Wine, Marmalade. I gave her a News-Letter about the Thanksgiving; . . .

8^r. 11th. I writ a few Lines to Madam Winthrop to this purpose: "Madam, These wait on you with Mr. Mayhew's Sermon, and Account of the state of the Indians on Martha's Vinyard. I thank you for your Unmerited Favours of yesterday; and hope to have the Happiness of Waiting on you to-morrow before Eight aclock after Noon. I pray GOD to keep you, and give you a joyfull entrance upon the Two Hundred and twenty ninth year of Christopher Columbus his Discovery; and take Leave, who am, Madam, your humble Servt.

8^r. 12. . . . Mrs. Anne Cotton came to door (twas before 8.) said Madam

Winthrop was within, directed me into the little Room, where she was full of work behind a Stand; Mrs. Cotton came in and stood. Madam Winthrop pointed to her to set me a Chair. Madam Winthrop's Countenance was much changed from what 'twas on Monday, look'd dark and lowering. At last, the work, (black stuff or Silk) was taken away, I got my Chair in place, had some Converse, but very Cold and indifferent to what 'twas before. Ask'd her to acquit me of Rudeness if I drew off her Glove. Enquiring the reason, I told her twas great odds between handling a dead Goat, and a living Lady. Got it off. I told her I had one Petition to ask of her, that was, that she would take off the Negative she laid on me the third of October: She readily answer'd she could not, and enlarg'd upon it; She told me of it so soon as she could; could not leave her house, children, neighbours, business. I told her she might do some Good to help and support me. . . . She thank'd me for my Book, (Mr. Mayhew's Sermon), But said not a word of the Letter. When she insisted on the Negative, I pray'd there might be no more Thunder and Lightening, I should not sleep all night. I gave her Dr. Preston, The Church's Marriage and the Church's Carriage, which cost me 6ˢ at the Sale. . . . Sarah fill'd a Glass of Wine, she drank to me, I to her, She sent Juno home with me with a good Lantern, I gave her 6ᵈ. and bid her thank her Mistress. In some of our Discourse, I told her [Madam Winthrop] I had rather go to the Stone-House adjoining to her, than to come to her against her mind. Told her the reason why I came every other night was lest I should drink too deep draughts of Pleasure. She had talk'd of Canary, her Kisses were to me better than the best Canary. Explain'd the expression Concerning Columbus. . . .

8ʳ. 17. . . . In the Evening I visited Madam Winthrop, who Treated me Courteously, but not in Clean Linen as somtimes. She said, she did not know whether I would come again, or no. I ask'd her how she could so impute inconstancy to me. (I had not visited her since Wednesday night being unable to get over the Indisposition received by the Treatment received that night, . . . Gave her this day's Gazett. . . .

8ʳ. 21. Friday, My Son, the Minister, came to me P.M. by appointment and we pray one for another in the Old Chamber; more especially respecting my Courtship. About 6. a-clock I go to Madam Winthrop's; Sarah told me her Mistress was gon out, but did not tell me whither she went. She presently order'd me a Fire; so I went in, having Dr. Sibb's Bowels with me to read. I read the two first sermons, still no body came in: at last about 9. a-clock Mr. Jnº Eyre came in; I took the opportunity to say to him as I had done to Mrs. Noyes before, that I hoped my Visiting his Mother would not be disagreeable to him; He answered me with much Respect. When twas after 9. a-clock He of himself said he would go and call her, she was but at one of his Brothers: A while after I heard Madam Winthrop's voice, enquiring somthing about John. After a good while and

Clapping the Garden door twice or thrice, she came in. I mention'd somthing of the lateness; she banter'd me, and said I was later. She receiv'd
me Courteously. I ask'd when our proceedings should be made publick:
She said They were like to be no more publick than they were already.
Offer'd me no Wine that I remember. I rose up at 11 a-clock to come
away, saying I would put on my Coat, She offer'd not to help me. I pray'd
her that Juno might light me home, she open'd the Shutter, and said twas
pretty light abroad; Juno was weary and gon to bed. So I came hôm by
Star-light as well as I could. . . .

Novr. 2. Midweek, went again, and found Mrs. Alden there, who
quickly went out. Gave her about ½ pound of Sugar Almonds, cost 3^s per
£. Carried them on Monday. She seem'd pleas'd with them, ask'd what
they cost. Spake of giving her a Hundred pounds per annum if I dy'd before her. Ask'd her what sum she would give me, if she should dy first?
Said I would give her time to Consider of it. She said she heard as if I had
given all to my Children by Deeds of Gift. I told her 'twas a mistake.
Point-Judith was mine &c. That in England, I own'd, my Father's desire
was that it should go to my eldest Son; 'twas 20£ per annum; she thought
'twas forty. I think when I seem'd to excuse pressing this, she seem'd to
think twas best to speak of it; a long winter was coming on. Gave me a
Glass or two of Canary.

Novr. 4th. Friday, Went again about 7. a-clock; found there Mr. John
Walley and his wife; sat discoursing pleasantly. . . . About 9. they went
away. I ask'd Madam what fashioned Neck-lace I should present her
with, She said, None at all. I ask'd her Whereabout we left off last time;
mention'd what I had offer'd to give her; Ask'd her what she would give
me; She said she could not Change her Condition: She had said so from
the beginning; could not be so far from her Children, the Lecture. Quoted
the Apostle Paul affirming that a single Life was better than a Married.
I answer'd That for the present Distress. Said she had not pleasure in
things of that nature as formerly: I said, you are the fitter to make me a
Wife. If she held in that mind, I must go home and bewail my Rashness
in making more haste than good Speed. . . . She charg'd me with saying,
that she must put away Juno, if she came to me: I utterly deny'd it, it
never came in my heart; yet she insisted upon it; . . .

Monday, Novr. 7th. My Son pray'd in the Old Chamber. Our time had
been taken up by Son and Daughter Cooper's Visit; so that I only read
the 130th. and 143. Psalm. Twas on the Account of my Courtship. I went
to Mad. Winthrop; found her rocking her little Katee in the Cradle. I ex-
cus'd my Coming so late (near Eight). She set me an arm'd Chair and
Cusheon; and so the Cradle was between her arm'd Chair and mine. Gave
her the remnant of my Almonds; She did not eat of them as before; but
laid them away; I said I came to enquire whether she had alter'd her mind
since Friday, or remained of the same mind still. She said, Thereabouts.

I told her I loved her, and was so fond as to think that she loved me: She said she had a great respect for me. I told her, I had made her an offer, without asking any advice; she had so many to advise with, that twas a hindrance. . . . I think I repeated again that I would go home and bewail my Rashness in making more haste than good Speed. I would endeavour to contain myself, and not go on to solicit her to do that which she could not Consent to. Took leave of her. As came down the steps she bid me have a Care. Treated me Courteously. Told her she had enter'd the 4th year of her Widowhood. I had given her the News-Letter before: I did not bid her draw off her Glove as sometime I had done. Her Dress was not so clean as somtime it had been. Jehovah jireh!

March, 29th [1722]. Samuel Sewall, and Mrs. Mary Gibbs were joined together in Marriage by the Rev^d. Mr. William Cooper.

COURT TRIALS ON WITCHCRAFT

People who have it in for New England always point to the Salem witch trials to justify their aversion. Actually, belief in witchcraft was far from limited to New England, but was characteristic of the still partly medieval spirit of the times both in England and on the European Continent.

On Cape Ann, Massachusetts, stands an ancient dwelling, one of those termed a blockhouse—being built from solid-hewn blocks of wood and not boards. It is called the Witch House because the sons of a woman under suspicion of witchcraft in Salem, twenty miles away, spirited her away to this haven they built for her. The story always seemed romantic to me, as did the family story of how the Rev. John Hale, a great persecutor of witches, saw the error of his views and changed his ways when his own wife was "cried out upon."

Although persons had been hanged in Boston earlier for what was sincerely held to be the sin and crime of witchcraft, in 1692 a form of epilepsy spreading through Salem gave rise to the belief that the sufferers were bewitched. Sermons delivered on the subject resulted in a sort of panic; people came to believe that evil spirits were at large and could afflict anybody. In the first half of that year nineteen people were hanged, one pressed to death, fifty-five had confessions extorted from them, a hundred and fifty were imprisoned, and more than two hundred placed under suspicion. For a time practically no resistance was offered to the hysteria from even the most learned men. It spread to Andover; at least one witch was taken in Maine. By autumn the tide had turned. Evidence the ministers had produced in preaching against witchcraft began to back-fire; as that spectral evidence, much invoked, was actually unreliable. The governor, Sir William Phips, prohibited the arrest of any more persons, forbade further executions and, shortly after, dismissed the witchcraft "Court of Oyer and Terminer." Hysteria of a different sort was to be noted in the way judges who had convicted witches now flocked to make public apologies. As lately as 1957 a Boston court published its finding that the descendants of persons executed for witchcraft were not to be held disgraced.

Following are an excerpt from a sermon by Cotton Mather on witch-craft and the court records of the examination of Sarah Good, together with a statement signed by two officers of the court (John Hawthorne is the ancestor of Nathaniel). A warrant for Sarah's execution was sworn out on Tuesday, July 19, 1692. Next is part of a letter from Cotton Mather to John Richards—a judge who had written asking for Mather's advice on the proper procedure for conducting witch trials—touching on witches' "puppets." Next are the typical bits of testimony introduced into the trial of Bridget Bishop concerning first the finding of "puppets," and next the suspicious behavior of a sow. Bridget was a twice-married woman, keeper of a tavern and gaudy in her dress. With a kind of inevitability the long record of her trial concludes:

> *According to the within Written precept I have taken the body of the within named Bridget Bishop out of their Majesties Jail in Salem and Safely Conveyed her to the place provided for her Execution and caused the above Bridget to be hanged by the neck until she was dead all which was according to the time within Required and So I make Return by me*
>
> GEORGE CORWIN, *Sheriff*

The place where the condemned were hanged is described in the excerpt from Salem Witchcraft *by Charles Wentworth Upham (1802–1875), a Unitarian minister and brother-in-law of Nathaniel Hawthorne's. Finally there follows the confession of one of the accused witches, William Barker. Such confessions as this further confirmed in the minds of the jurors their suspicion that all of Massachusetts was the object of a dia-bolical plot.*

A SERMON BY COTTON MATHER

It should next be proved THAT Witchcraft *is*.

The *Being* of such a thing is denied by many that place a *great part* of their *small wit* in deriding the Stories that are told of it. Their chief Argument is, that they never *saw* any Witches, therefore there are *none*. Just as if you or I should say, we never met with any *Robbers* on the Road, therefore there was never any *Padding* there.

Indeed the *Devils* are loath to have true Notions of *Witches* entertained with us. I have beheld them to put out the Eyes of an Enchanted Child, when a Book that proves, *There is Witchcraft*, was laid before her. But there are especially two Demonstrations that Evince the Being of that Infernal mysterious thing.

First, We have the Testimony of *Scripture* for it. We find *Witchcrafts* often mentioned, sometimes by way of *Assertion*, sometimes by way of *Allusion*, in the Oracles of God. Besides that, We have there the History of divers *Witches* in these infallible and inspired Writings. Particularly, the Instance of the *Witch* at *Endor*, in I *Sam.* 28. 7. is so plain and full that *Witchcraft* itself is not a more amazing thing than any *Dispute* about the Being of it, after this. The Advocates of *Witches* must use more *Tricks* to make Nonsense of the *Bible*, than ever the *Witch* of *Endor* used in her Magical Incantations, if they would Evade the Force of that Famous History. They that will believe no *Witches*, do imagine that *Jugglers* only are meant by them whom the Sacred Writ calleth so. But what do they think of that Law in *Exod.* 22. 18. *Thou shalt not suffer a Witch to live?* Methinks 'tis a little too hard to punish every silly *Juggler* with so great severity.

Secondly, We have the *Testimony* of *Experience* for it. What will those *Incredulous*, who must be the only *Ingenious* Men say to this? Many *Witches* have like those in *Acts* 19. 18. *Confessed and showed their Deeds.* We see those things done, that it is impossible any *Disease*, or any *Deceit* should procure. We see some hideous *Wretches* in hideous *Horrors* confessing, *That they did the Mischiefs.* This Confession is often made by them that are owners of as much Reason as the people that laugh at all *Conceit* of *Witchcraft:* The Exactest Scrutiny of Skillful Physicians cannot find any distraction in their minds. This *Confession* is often made by them that are apart one from another, and yet they *agree* in all the Circumstances of it. This *Confession* is often made by them that at the same time will produce the *Engines* and *Ensigns* of their *Hellish Trade*, and give the standers-by an *Ocular Conviction* of what they do, and how. There can be no Judgment left of any *Human Affairs*, if such *Confessions* must be Ridiculed: all the *Murders*, yea, and all the *Bargains* in the World must be mere *Imaginations* if such *Confessions* are of no Account.

THE EXAMINATION OF SARAH GOOD

The examination of Sarah Good before the worshipful Assistants John Hawthorne Jonathan Corwin

Q. Sarah Good what evil Spirit have you familiarity with

A. None

Q. Have you made no contract with the Devil

Good answered no

Q. Why do you hurt these children

A. I do not hurt them. I scorn it.

Q. Who do you employ then to do it.

A. I employ nobody

Q. What creature do you employ then.

A. no creature but I am falsely accused.

Q. Why did you go away muttering from Mr Parris his house.

A. I did not mutter but I thanked him for what he gave my child.

Q. have you made no contract with the devil.

A. no.

H[awthorne] desired the children all of them to look upon her and see if this were the person that had hurt them and so they all did look upon her, and said this was one of the persons that did torment them—presently they were all tormented.

Q. Sarah Good do you not see now what you have done, why do you not tell us the truth, why do you thus torment these poor children

A. I do not torment them.

Q. who do you employ then.

A. I employ nobody I scorn it.

Q. how came they thus tormented

A. what do I know you bring others here and now you charge me with it.

Q. why who was it.

A. I do not know but it was some you brought into the meeting house with you.

Q. we brought you into the meeting house.

A. but you brought in two more.

Q. who was it then that tormented the children.

A. it was osborne.

Q. what is it you say when you go muttering away from person's houses

A. if I must tell I will tell.

Q. do tell us then

A. if I must tell, I will tell, it is the commandments. I may say my commandments I hope.

Q. what commandment is it.

A. if I must tell I will tell, it is a psalm.

q. what psalm.

after a long time she muttered over some part of a psalm.

q. who do you serve

a. I serve God

q. what God do you serve.

a. the God that made heaven and earth. though she was not willing to mention the word God. her answers were in a very wicked spiteful manner. reflecting and retorting against the authority with base and abusive words and many lies she was taken in it was here said that her husband had said that he was afraid that she either was a witch or would be one very quickly. the worshipful Mr. Hawthorne asked him his reason why he said so of her, whether he had ever seen anything by her, he answered no, not in this nature, but it was her bad carriage to him, and indeed said he I may say with tears that she is an enemy to all good.

Salem Village March the 1st 1691-92

Written by Ezekiel Cheever . . .

Salem Village March the 1st 1691-92

Sarah Good the wife of William Good of Salem Village Laborer Brought before us by George Locker Constable in Salem to Answer, Joseph Hutchinson Thomas Putnam etc. of Salem Village yeomen (Complainants on behalf of their Majesties) against said Sarah Good for Suspicion of witchcraft by her Committed and thereby much Injury done to the Bodies of Elizabeth Parris Abigail Williams Ann Putnam and Elizabeth Hubbard all of Salem Village aforesaid according to their Complaints as per warrants

Dated Salem March 29th 1691-92.

Sarah Good upon Examination denieth the matter of fact (viz) that she ever used any witchcraft or hurt the abovesaid children or any of them.

The above-named Children being all present positively accused her of hurting of them Sundry times within this two months and also that morning.

Sarah Good denied that she had been at their houses in said time or near them, or had done them any hurt. all the abovesaid children then present accused her face to face upon which they were all dreadfully tortured and tormented for a short space of time and the affliction and tortures being over they charged said Sarah Good again that she had then so tortured them, and came to them and did it, although she was personally then kept at a Considerable distance from them.

Sarah Good being Asked if, that she did not then hurt them who did it. And the children being again tortured she looked upon them And said that it was one of them we brought into the house with us. We Asked her who it was, she then Answered and said it was Sarah Osborne, and Sarah Osborne was then under Custody and not in the house; And the children being quickly after recovered out of their fit said that it was Sarah Good and also Sarah Osborne that then did hurt & torment or afflict them—although both of them at the same time at a distance or Remote from them personally—there were also sundry other Questions put to her and Answers given thereunto by her according as is also given in. p[er]. us.

JOHN HAWTHORNE ⎫
JONATHAN CORWIN ⎭ Assistants.

LETTER OF COTTON MATHER TO JOHN RICHARDS. 1692

V. To determine a matter so much in the Dark as to Know the guilty Employers of the Devils in this work of darkness, this is a work, this is a labor. Now first a credible Confession of the guilty wretches is one of the most hopeful ways of coming at them, & I say a credible confession, because even confession itself sometimes is not credible. But a person of a Sagacity many times thirty furlongs less than yours, will Easily perceive what Confession may be Credible, & what may be the result of only a delirious brain, or a discontented heart. All the difficulty is, how to obtain this Confession. For this I am far from urging the un-English method of torture, but instead thereof I propound these three things, first, Who can tell but when the witches come upon their trials, they may be so forsaken, as to confess all. The Almighty God having heard the appeals of our Cries to Heaven, may so thunder strike their souls, as to make them show their Deeds. Moreover the Devils themselves who aim at the entrapping of their own miserable Clients, may treacherously depart from them in their Examinations, which throws them into such toiling vexations they [that] they'll discover all. . . . An unexpected confession, is that whereunto Witches are very often driven. Secondly, I am ready to think, that there is usually some Expression or behavior, whereto the Devils do constantly oblige the Witches, as a Kind of Sacrament, upon their least failure wherein the Witches presently lose the thus forfeited assistances of the Devils, & all comes out. Please then to observe, if you can find any one constant scheme of discourse or action, whereto the suspected seem religiously devoted, & (which may Easily be done by the common policies of conversation) cause them to transgress That, a confession will probably then come on apace. Thirdly, what Ever hath a tendency to put the witches into confusion, is likely to bring them unto Confession too. Here Cross & Swift Questions have their use, but besides them, for my part, I should not be unwilling, that an Experiment be made whether accused parties can repeat the Lord's prayer, or those other Systems of christianity, which it seems, the Devils often make the witches unable to repeat, without ridiculous Depravations or Amputations. The danger of this Experiment will be taken away, if you make no Evidence of it, but only put it to the use I mention, which is that of confounding the lisping Witches to give a reason why they cannot, Even with prompting, repeat those heavenly Composures. the like I would say of some other experiments only we may venture too far before we are aware.

VI. But what if no confession can be obtained, I say yet the case is far from desperate. For if there have been those words uttered by the witches, Either by way of threatening, or of Asking, or of Bragging, which rationally demonstrate such a Knowledge of the woeful circumstances attending the afflicted people, as could not be had, without some Diabolical Communion, the proof of such words is Enough to fix the guilt. . . .

Once more, can there be no puppets found out? & here I would say thus much, I am thinking, that some witches make their own bodies to be their Puppets. If therefore you can find that when the witches do anything Easy, that is not needful (& it is needful that I put in that clause, "not needful," because it is possible that a prestidigital Demon may imitate what we do, though we are none of His) I say if you find the same thing, presently & hurtfully, & more violently done by any unseen hand, unto the bodies of the sufferers, hold them, for you have catched a Witch. I add, why should not Witch-marks be searched for? The properties, the qualities of those marks are described by divers weighty writers. I never saw any of those marks, but it is doubtless not impossible for a chiurgien [surgeon], when he sees them, to say what are magical, & if these become once apparent, it is apparent that these witches have gone so far in their wickedness as to admit most cursed Suckages, whereby the Devils have not only fetched out of them, it may be the Spirits of which they make vehicles, wherein they visit the afflicted, but also they have infused a venom into them which Exalts the malignity of their spirits as well as of their bodies: & it is likely, that by means of this ferment they would be found Buoyant (if the water-Ordeal were made upon them).

TESTIMONY AGAINST BRIDGET BISHOP

Jno Bly Sr. and William Bly v. Bridget Bishop

June 2d 1692. John Bly Senior aged about 57 years and William Bly aged about 15 years both of Salem Testifieth and saith that being Employed by Bridget Bishop Alias Oliver of Salem to help take down the Cellar wall of The Old house she formerly Lived in we the said Deponents in holes in the said old wall belonging to the said Cellar found several puppets made up of Rags And hog's Bristles with headless pins in Them. with the points outward and this was about Seven years Last past.

John Bly Sr. and Rebecca Bly v. Bridget Bishop

John Bly senior and Rebecca Bly his wife of Salem, both Testify and say that said Jno Bly Bought a Sow of Edwd Bishop of Salem Sawyer and by agreement with said Bishop was to pay the price agreed upon unto Lt. Jeremiah Neale of Salem. and Bridget the wife of Said Edward Bishop because she could not have the money or value agreed for paid unto her, she came to the house of the deponents in Salem and Quarrelled with them about it, soon after which the sow having pigged, she was taken with strange fits Jumping up and knocking her head against the fence and seemed blind and deaf and would not Eat neither Let her pigs suck but foamed at the mouth which Goody Henderson hearing of said she believed she was overlooked and that they had their cattle ill in such a manner at the eastward when she lived there and used to cure them by giving of them, Red Okra and Milk which we also gave the sow: Quickly after eating of which she grew Better and then for the space of near two hours together she getting into the street did set off Jumping and running between the house of said deponents and said Bishops as if she were stark mad, and after that was well again and we did then apprehend or Judge and do still that said Bishop had bewitched said sow.

Jurat in Curia.

ON THE PLACE OF EXECUTION

The place selected for the executions is worthy of notice. It was at a considerable distance from the jail, and could be reached only by a circuitous and difficult route. It is a fatiguing enterprise to get at it now, although many passages that approach it from some directions have since been opened. But it was a point where the spectacle would be witnessed by the whole surrounding country far and near, being on the brow of the highest eminence in the vinicity of the town. As it was believed by the people generally that they were engaged in a great battle with Satan, one of whose titles was "the Prince of the Power of the Air," perhaps they chose that spot to execute his confederates, because, in going to that high point, they were flaunting him in his face, celebrating their triumph over him in his own realm. . . .

"Witch Hill" is a part of an elevated ledge of rock on the western side of the city of Salem, broken at intervals; beginning at Legg's Hill, and trending northerly. . . . Its sombre and desolate appearance admits of little variety of delineation. It is mostly a bare and naked ledge. At the top of this cliff, on the southern brow of the eminence, the executions are supposed to have taken place. The outline rises a little towards the north, but soon begins to fall off to the general level of the country. From that direction only can the spot be easily reached. It is hard to climb the western side, impossible to clamber up the southern face. . . . It is, as it were, a platform raised high in air.

A magnificent panorama of ocean, island, headland, bay, river, town, field, and forest spreads out and around to view. On a clear summer day, the picture can scarcely be surpassed. Facing the sun and the sea, and the evidences of the love and bounty of Providence shining over the landscape, the last look of earth must have suggested to the sufferers a wide contrast between the mercy of the Creator and the wrath of his creatures. They beheld the face of the blessed God shining upon them in his works, and they passed with renewed and assured faith into his more immediate presence. The elevated rock, uplifted by the divine hand, will stand while the world stands, in bold relief, and can never be obscured by the encroachments of society or the structures of art,—a fitting memorial of their constancy. When, in some coming day, a sense of justice, appreciation of moral firmness, sympathy for suffering innocence, the diffusion of refined sensibility, a discriminating discernment of what is really worthy of commemoration among men, a rectified taste, a generous public spirit, and gratitude for the light that surrounds and protects us against error, folly, and fanaticism, shall demand the rearing of a suitable monument to the memory of those who in 1692 preferred death to a falsehood, the pedestal for the lofty column will be found ready, reared by the Creator on a foundation that can never be shaken while the globe endures, or worn away by the elements, man, or time—the brow of Witch Hill. On no other spot could such a tribute be more worthily bestowed, or more conspicuously displayed.

CONFESSION OF WILLIAM BARKER

God having called me to Confess my sin and Apostasy in that fall in giving the Devil advantage over me appearing to me like a Black, in the evening to set my hand to his Book, as I have owned to my shame. He told me that I should not want so doing. At Salem Village, there being a little off the Meeting-House, about an hundred five Blades, some with Rapiers by their side, which was called and might be more for aught I know by B[ishop]. and Bu[rroughs]. and the Trumpet sounded, and Bread and Wine which they called the Sacrament, but I had none; being carried over all on a Stick, never being at any other Meeting. I being at Cart a Saturday last, all the day, of Hay and English Corn, the Devil brought my Shape to Salem, and did afflict M. S. and R. F. by clutching my Hand; and a Sabbath day my Shape afflicted A. M. and at night afflicted M. S. and A. M. E. I. and A. F. have been my Enticers to this great abomination, as one have owned and charged her to her Sister with the same. And the design was to Destroy Salem Village, and to begin at the Minister's House, and to destroy the Church of God, and to set up Satan's

Kingdom, and then all will be well. And now I hope God in some measure has made me something sensible of my sin and apostasy, begging pardon of God, and of the Honorable Magistrates and all God's people, hoping and promising by the help of God, to set to my heart and hand to do what in me lieth to destroy such wicked worship, humbly begging the prayers of all God's People for me, I may walk humbly under this great affliction and that I may procure to myself, the sure mercies of David, and the blessing of Abraham.

MAGNALIA CHRISTI AMERICANA

COTTON MATHER

———— ◆◆ ————

It would be impossible, or at least unlikely, for any collection of writings by New Englanders about New England to be made without the inclusion of some part of Cotton Mather's Magnalia Christi Americana.

Mather's Magnalia. *Who has not heard of it? Who, today, has read it? Scholars. It is the ecclesiastical history of New England, written in an ornate style quite different from the "plain style" so precious to the earlier Puritans (although Cotton Mather, too, was quite capable of writing in plain style). The book is in seven parts: 1) the settlement of New England; 2) the lives of the governors; 3) lives of famous ministers; 4) a description of Harvard; 5) a history of the Congregational Church in New England; 6) a record of "providences"—judgments of God—and 7) an account of various disturbances in the church. An appendix gave remarkable occurrences in the wars with the Indians. This huge work—the title, translated, means "The Greatness of Christ in America"—was published in London in 1702. A short excerpt from the Introduction follows.*

A GENERAL INTRODUCTION

Ἐρῶ δὲ τοῦτο, τῆς τῶν ἐντευξαμένων ʼωφελείας ἕνεκα.

Dicam hoc propter utilitatem eorum qui Lecturi sunt hoc opus. Theodorit.

I write the *Wonders* of the CHRISTIAN RELIGION, flying from the Depravations of *Europe,* to the *American Strand:* And, assisted by the

Holy Author of that *Religion,* I do, with all Conscience of *Truth,* required therein by Him, who is the *Truth* it self, Report the *Wonderful Displays* of His Infinite Power, Wisdom, Goodness, and Faithfulness, wherewith His Divine Providence hath *Irradiated* an *Indian Wilderness.*

I Relate the *Considerable Matters,* that produced and attended the First Settlement of COLONIES, which have been Renowned for the Degree of REFORMATION, Professed and Attained by *Evangelical Churches,* erected in those *Ends of the Earth:* And a *Field* being thus prepared, I proceed unto a Relation of the *Considerable Matters* which have been acted thereupon.

I first introduce the *Actors,* that have, in a more exemplary manner served those *Colonies;* and give *Remarkable Occurrences,* in the exemplary LIVES of many *Magistrates,* and of more *Ministers,* who so *Lived,* as to leave unto Posterity, *Examples* worthy of *Everlasting Remembrance.*

I add hereunto, the *Notables* of the only *Protestant University,* that ever *shone* in that Hemisphere of the *New World;* with particular Instances of *Criolians,* in our *Biography,* provoking the *whole World,* with vertuous Objects of Emulation.

I introduce then, the *Actions* of a more Eminent Importance, that have signalized those *Colonies;* Whether the *Establishments,* directed by their *Synods;* with a Rich Variety of *Synodical* and *Ecclesiastical* Determinations; or, the *Disturbances,* with which they have been from all sorts of *Temptations* and *Enemies* Tempestuated; and the *Methods* by which they have still weathered out each *Horrible Tempest.*

And into the midst of these *Actions,* I interpose an entire *Book,* wherein there is, with all possible Veracity, a *Collection* made, of *Memorable Occurrences,* and amazing *Judgments* and *Mercies,* befalling many *particular Persons* among the People of *New-England.*

Let my Readers expect all that I have promised them, in this *Bill of Fare;* and it may be they will find themselves entertained with yet many other Passages, above and beyond their Expectation, deserving likewise a room in *History:* In all which, there will be nothing, but the *Author's* too mean way of preparing so great Entertainments, to Reproach the Invitation.

§ 2. The Reader will doubtless desire to know, what it was that

> ———— *tot Volvere casus*
> *Insignes Pietate Viros, tot adire Labores,*
> *Impulerit.*

And our *History* shall, on many fit Occasions which will be therein offered, endeavour, with all *Historical Fidelity and Simplicity,* and with as little Offence as may be, to satisfy him. The Sum of the Matter is, That from the very Beginning of the REFORMATION in the *English Nation,* there hath always been a Generation of *Godly Men,* desirous to pursue the *Reformation of Religion, according to the Word of God, and the Example of the best Reformed Churches;* and answering the Character of *Good Men,* given by *Josephus,* in his Paraphrase on the words of *Samuel* to *Saul,* μηδὲν ἄλλο πραχθήσεσθαι καλῶς ὑφ᾽ ἑαυτῶν νομίζοντες ἤ ὅτι ἄν ποιήσωσι τοῦ θεοῦ κεκελευκότος. *They think they do nothing Right in the Service of God, but what they do according to the Command of God.* And there hath been another Generation of Men, who have still employed the *Power* which they have generally still had in their Hands, not only to stop the Progress of the Desired *Reformation,* but also, with Innumerable Vexations, to Persecute those that most Heartily wished well unto it. There were many of the *Reformers,* who joyned with the Reverend *JOHN FOX,* in the *Complaints* which he then entred in his *Martyrology,* about the *Baits of Popery* yet left in the Church; and in his *Wishes, God take them away, or ease us from them, for God knows, they be the Cause of much Blindness and Strife amongst Men!* They Zealously decried the *Policy* of complying always with the *Ignorance* and *Vanity* of the *People;* and cried out earnestly for *Purer Administrations* in the House of God, and more *Conformity* to the *Law of Christ,* and *Primitive Christianity:* While others would not hear of going any further than the *First Essay* of *Reformation.* 'Tis very certain, that the *First Reformers* never intended, that what *They* did, should be the *Absolute Boundary* of *Reformation,* so that it should be a Sin to proceed any further; as, by their own going beyond *Wicklift,* and *Changing* and *Growing* in their own *Models* also, and the Confessions of *Cranmer,* with the *Scripta Anglicana* of *Bucer,* and a thousand other things, was abundantly demonstrated. But after a Fruitless Expectation, wherein the truest Friends of the *Reformation* long waited, for to have that which *Heylin* himself owns to have been the Design of the *First Reformers,* followed as it should have been, a Party very unjustly arrogating to themselves, the Venerable Name of, *The Church of* England, by Numberless Oppressions, grievously *Smote those their Fellow-Servants.* Then 'twas that, as our Great *OWEN* hath expressed it, *Multitudes of Pious, Peaceable Protestants, were driven, by their Severities, to leave their Native Country, and seek a Refuge for their Lives and Liberties, with Freedom, for the Worship of God, in a Wilderness, in the Ends of the Earth.*

THE REDEEMED CAPTIVE
RETURNED TO ZION

REV. JOHN WILLIAMS

———◆•◆———

Deerfield, Massachusetts, is the prototype of the many New England villages that were attacked and their inhabitants massacred by Indians. The following account from The Redeemed Captive Returned to Zion *is that of the Rev. John Williams (1664–1729). During the French and Indian Wars, Williams, who was Deerfield's pastor, and all his family were captured. With the help of Cotton Mather, Williams later described his two-year captivity and his resistance to Jesuit attempts to convert him.*

THE DESOLATIONS OF DEERFIELD

On Tuesday, the 29th of February, 1703-4, not long before break of day, the enemy came in like a flood upon us; our watch being unfaithful;—an evil, the awful effects of which, in the surprisal of our fort, should bespeak all watchmen to avoid, as they would not bring the charge of blood upon themselves. They came to my house in the beginning of the onset, and by their violent endeavors to break open doors and windows, with axes and hatchets, awaked me out of sleep; on which I leaped out of bed, and, running towards the door, perceived the enemy making their entrance into the house. I called to awaken two soldiers in the chamber, and returning toward my bedside for my arms, the enemy immediately broke into the room, I judge to the number of twenty, with painted faces, and hideous acclamations. I reached up my hands to the bed-tester for my pistol, uttering a short petition to God, for everlasting mercies for me and mine, on account of the merits of our glorified Redeemer; expecting a present passage through the valley of the shadow of death; saying in myself, as Isa. xxxviii. 10, 11, "I said, in the cutting off of my days, I shall go to the gates of the grave: I am deprived of the residue of my years. I said, I shall not see the Lord, even the Lord, in the land of the living: I shall behold man no more with the inhabitants of the world." Taking down my pistol, I cocked it, and put it to the breast of the first Indian that came up; but my pistol missing fire, I was seized by three Indians who disarmed me, and bound me naked, as I was in my shirt, and so I stood for near the space of an hour. . . .

I cannot relate the distressing care I had for my dear wife, who had lain in but a few weeks before; and for my poor children, family, and Christian neighbors. The enemy fell to rifling the house, and entered in great numbers into every room. I begged of God to remember mercy in the midst of judgment; that he would so far restrain their wrath, as to prevent their murdering of us; that we might have grace to glorify his name, whether in life or death; and, as I was able, committed our state to God. The enemies who entered the house, were all of them Indians and Macquas, and insulted over me awhile, holding up hatchets over my head, threatening to burn all I had; but yet God, beyond expectation, made us in a great measure to be pitied; for, though some were so cruel and barbarous as to take and carry to the door two of my children and murder them, as also a negro woman; yet they gave me liberty to put on my clothes, keeping me bound with a cord on one arm, till I put on my clothes to the other; and then changing my cord, they let me dress myself, and then pinioned me again. Gave liberty to my dear wife to dress herself and our remaining children. About sun an hour high, we were all carried out of the house, for a march, and saw many of the houses of my neighbors in flames, perceiving the whole fort, one house excepted, to be taken. Who can tell what sorrows pierced our souls, when we saw ourselves carried away from God's sanctuary, to go into a strange land, exposed to so many trials; the journey being at least three hundred miles we were to travel; the snow up to the knees, and we never inured to such hardships and fatigues; the place we were to be carried to, a Popish country. Upon my parting from the town, they fired my house and barn. We were carried over the river, to the foot of the mountain, about a mile from my house, where we found a great number of our Christian neighbors, men, women, and children, to the number of an hundred, nineteen of which were afterward murdered by the way, and two starved to death, near Cowass, in a time of great scarcity or famine the savages underwent there. When we came to the foot of the mountain, they took away our shoes, and gave us in the room of them Indian shoes, to prepare us for our travel. Whilst we were there, the English beat out a company that remained in the town, and pursued them to the river, killing and wounding many of them; but the body of the army being alarmed, they repulsed those few English that pursued them.

I am not able to give you an account of the number of the enemy slain, but I observed after this fight no great, insulting mirth, as I expected; and saw many wounded persons, and for several days together they buried of their party, and one of chief note among the Macquas. . . .

After this, we went up to the mountain, and saw the smoke of the fires in the town, and beheld the awful desolations of Deerfield. And before we marched any farther, they killed a sucking child belonging to one of the English. There were slain by the enemy of the inhabitants of Deerfield, to the number of thirty-eight, besides nine of the neighboring towns.

JOURNEY FROM BOSTON
TO NEW YORK

SARAH KEMBLE KNIGHT

————◆•◆————

From our comfortable distance, we often marvel that the early colonists got around at all, such were the difficulties and the rigors of travel. They did, and to a considerable extent, and not only male colonists. Sarah Kemble Knight (1666–1727), a Boston schoolteacher, during the winter of 1704–05 traveled from Boston to New York and back on family business —unaccompanied. The trip took five months. The journal she kept, from which an extract follows, reveals that in high spirits, wit, and gumption, she represents the very best brand of New England traveler.

SATURDAY, October 7th, we set out early in the morning, and being something unacquainted with the way, having asked it of some we met, they told us we must ride a mile or two and turn down a lane on the right hand; and by their direction we rode on, but not yet coming to the turning, we met a young fellow and asked him how far it was to the lane which turned down towards Guilford. He said we must ride a little further, and turn down by the corner of Uncle Sam's lot. My guide vented his spleen at the lubber; and we soon after came into the road and keeping still on, without anything further remarkable, about two o'clock afternoon we arrived at New Haven, where I was received with all possible respects and civility. Here I discharged Mr. Wheeler with a reward to his satisfaction, and took some time to rest after so long and toilsome a journey; and informed myself of the manners and customs of the place, and at the same time employed myself in the affair I went there upon.

They are governed by the same laws as we in Boston (or little differing), throughout this whole colony of Connecticut, and much the same way of Church government, and many of them good, sociable people, and I hope religious too: but a little too much independent in their principles, and, as I have been told, were formerly in their zeal very rigid in their administrations toward such as their laws made offenders, even to a harmless kiss or innocent merriment among young people. Whipping being a frequent and counted an easy punishment, about which as other crimes, the Judges were absolute in their sentences. . . .

Their diversions in this part of the country are on lecture days and training days mostly: on the former there is riding from town to town.

And on training days the youth divert themselves by shooting at the target, as they call it (but it very much resembles a pillory), where he that hits nearest the white has some yards of red ribbon presented him, which being tied to his hat-band, the two ends streaming down his back, he is led away in triumph, with great applause, as the winners of the Olympic games. They generally marry very young: the males oftener, as I am told, under twenty than above: they generally make public weddings, and have a way of something singular (as they say) in some of them, viz., just before joining hands the bridegroom quits the place, who is soon followed by the bridesmen, and as it were dragged back to duty—being the reverse to the former practice among us to steal mistress bride.

There are great plenty of oysters all along by the sea side, as far as I rode in the colony, and those very good. And they generally lived very well and comfortably in their families. But too indulgent (especially the farmers) to their slaves: suffering too great familiarity from them, permitting them to sit at the table and eat with them (as they say to save time), and into the dish goes the black hoof as freely as the white hand. They told me that there was a farmer lived near the town where I lodged who had some difference with his slave, concerning something the master had promised him and did not punctually perform; which caused some hard words between them; but at length they put the matter to arbitration and bound themselves to stand to the award of such as they named—which done, the arbitrators, having heard the allegations of both parties, ordered the master to pay forty shillings to black face, and acknowledge his fault. And so the matter ended: the poor master very honestly standing to the award.

There are everywhere, in the towns as I passed, a number of Indians the natives of the country, and are the most salvage of all the salvages of that kind that I had ever seen: little or no care taken (as I heard upon enquiry) to make them otherwise. They have in some places lands of their own, and governed by laws of their own making;—they marry many wives and at pleasure put them away, and on the least dislike or fickle humor, on either side, saying "Stand away," to one another is a sufficient divorce. And indeed those uncomely "Stand aways" are too much in vogue among the English in this (indulgent) colony, as their records plentifully prove, and that on very trivial matters, of which some have been told me, but are not proper to be related by a female pen, though some of that foolish sex have had too large a share in the story. . . .

They give the title of merchant to every trader; who rate their goods according to the time and specie they pay in, viz., "Pay," "Money," "Pay as money," and "Trusting." "Pay" is grain, pork, beef, etc., at the prices set by the General Court that year; "Money" is pieces of eight, reals, or

Boston or bay shillings (as they call them), or "good hard money," as sometimes silver coin is termed by them; also "Wampum," viz., Indian beads, which serve for change. "Pay as money" is provisions, as aforesaid, one-third cheaper than as the Assembly or General Court sets it; and "Trust" as they and the merchant agree for time.

Now, when the buyer comes to ask for a commodity, sometimes before the merchant answers that he has it, he says, "Is your pay ready?" Perhaps the chap replies, "Yes." "What do you pay in?" says the merchant. The buyer having answered, then the price is set; as suppose he wants a six-penny knife, in pay it is twelve pence—in pay as money, eight pence, and hard money, its own price, viz., six pence. It seems a very intricate way of trade and what *lex mercatoria* had not thought of. . . .

They are generally very plain in their dress, throughout all the colony, as I saw, and follow one another in their modes; that you may know where they belong, especially the women, meet them where you will.

Their chief red letter day is St. Election, which is annually observed according to charter, to choose their governor—a blessing they can never be thankful enough for, as they will find, if ever it be their hard fortune to lose it. The present governor in Connecticut is the Hon. John Winthrop, Esq., a gentleman of an ancient and honorable family, whose father was governor here sometime before, and his grandfather had been governor of the Massachusetts. This gentlemen is a very courteous and affable person, much given to hospitality, and has by his good services gained the affections of the people as much as any who had been before him in that post.

December 6th. Being by this time well recruited and rested after my journey, my business lying unfinished by some concerns at New York depending thereupon, my kinsman, Mr. Thomas Trowbridge, of New Haven, must needs take a journey there before it could be accomplished, I resolved to go there in company with him and a man of the town which I engaged to wait on me there. Accordingly, December 6th, we set out from New Haven, and about eleven same morning came to Stratford ferry; which crossing, about two miles on the other side baited our horses and would have eat a morsel ourselves, but the pumpkin and Indian mixed bread had such an aspect, and the bare-legged punch so awkward or rather awful a sound, that we left both, and proceeded forward, and about seven at night came to Fairfield, where we met with good entertainment and lodged; and early next morning set forward to Norrowalk, from its half Indian name "North-walk," where about twelve at noon we arrived, and had a dinner of fried venison, very savory.

THE BIG SNOW OF 1717

COTTON MATHER

———◆•◆———

Big snows, along with literature, have been a great specialty of New England's from the beginning. This letter from Cotton Mather to Dr. Woodward of Gresham College in London describes one of the worst of them: what we may call the Blizzard of '17, meaning 1717.

TO DR. WOODWARD ABOUT "AN HORRID SNOW"

10d. X m. 1717.
[December 10, 1717]

Sr

Tho' we are gott so far onward at the Beginning of another Winter, yett we have not forgott the Last: which at the Latter End whereof, we were Entertained & overwhelmed with a *Snow*, which was attended with some Things that were uncommon enough, to afford matter for a letter from us. The *Winter* was not so bad as that wherein *Tacitus* tells us that *Corbulo* made his Expedition against the *Parthians.* Nor like that which proved so fatal to the Beasts & Birds, in the Days of the Emperour *Justinian* [nor?] that whercin the very Fishes were killed under the Freezing Sea, when *Phocas* did as much to the men whom Tyrants treat like the Fishes of the Sea. But the Conclusion of our *Winter* was hard enough, & was too formidable to be easily forgotten: and of a peece with what you had in *Europe,* a year before. The *Snow* was the Chief Thing that made it so. For tho' rarely does a *Winter* pass us, wherein we may not say with *Pliny, Ingens Hyeme Nivis apud nos copia;* yett the Last *Winter* brought with it a *Snow* that Excelled them all. A *Snow* tis true, not equal to that which once fell and Lay Twenty Cubits high, about the Beginning of *October,* in the parts about the *Euxine Sea.* Nor to that, which the *French Annals* tell us, kept falling for twenty Nine weeks together. Nor to several mentioned by *Boethius,* wherein vast Numbers of people, and of Cattel, perished; Nor to those that *Strabo* finds upon *Caucasus* and *Rhodiginus* in *Armenia.* But yett such an one, and attended with such Circumstances, as may deserve to be Remembred.

On the Twentieth of the Last *February,* there came on a *Snow,* which being added unto what had covered the ground a few Days before, made

a Thicker Mantle for our Mother than what was usual: And the Storm
with it, was for the following Day so violent, as to make all communication between the Neighbours every where to cease. People for some Hours
could not pass from one side of a Street unto another, and the poor
Women, who happened at this critical time to fall into Travail, were putt
into Hardships which anon produced many odd Stories for us. But on the
Twenty-fourth Day of the Month comes *Pelion* upon Ossa. Another *Snow*
came on, which almost buried the Memory of the former: With a Storm
so furious, that Heaven laid an Interdict on the Religious Assemblies
throughout the countrey on this Lords-day, the like whereunto had never
been seen before. The Indians near an hundred years old, affirm, that
their Fathers never told them of any thing that equall'd it. Vast Numbers
of Cattel were destroy'd in this Calamity; Whereof some that were of the
Stronger Sort, were found standing Dead on their Legs, as if they had
been alive, many weeks after, when the Snow melted away. And others
had their Eyes glazed over with Ice at such a rate, that being not
far from the Sea, they went out of their way, and drowned them there.

One Gentleman, on whose Farms, there were now Lost above eleven
hundred *Sheep,* which with other cattel were Interred (Shall I Say, or
Inniv'd) in the Snow; writes me That there were Two *Sheep* very singularly circumstanced. For no Less than Eight & Twenty Days after the
Storm, the people pulling out the Ruines of above an hundred Sheep, out
of a Snow-bank, which Lay sixteen foot high drifted over them, there
were Two found alive, which had been there all this time, & kept themselves alive by Eating the Wool of their Dead Companions. When they
were taken out, they shed their own Fleeces, but soon gott into good
Case again.

Sheep were not the only creatures, that Lived unaccountably for whole
weeks without their usual Sustenance, entirely buried in the *Snow-drifts.*
The *Swine* had a share with the *Sheep* in Strange Survivals. A man had
a couple of Young *Hogs,* which he gave over for Dead; But on the twenty-
seventh day after their Burial, they made their way out of a *Snow-bank,*
at the bottom of which they had found a Little Tansy to feed upon.

The *Poultry* as unaccountably survived as these. *Hens* were found
alive, after *Seven Days; Turkeys* were found alive, after *five & Twenty
Days;* Buried in the *Snow,* and at a Distance from the Ground; and altogether destitute of any thing to feed them.

The Number of Creatures, that kept a *Rigid Fast,* shutt up in *Snow,*
for several weeks together, & were found Alive after all, have yielded
surprizing stories to us.

The Wild Creatures of the Woods, (the *Outgoings of the Evening*)
made their Descent as well as they could in this Time of Scarcity for them,
towards the Sea-side. A vast multitude of Deer for the Same Cause taking
the Same Course, & the Deep Snow Spoiling them of their only Defence:

which is, *To Run,* they became such a prey to those Devourers, that it is thought, not one in Twenty Escaped.

But here again occurr'd a Curiosity.

These carniverous Sharpers, and especially the *Foxes,* would make their *Nocturnal Visits,* to the Pens, where the people had their *Sheep* defended from them. The poor Ewes big with young were so terrified with the frequent Approaches of the *Foxes,* & the Terror had such Impression on them, that most of the *Lambs* brought forth in the Spring following, were of Monsieur *Reinard's* complexion, when the Dams were all either *White* or *Black.*

It was remarkable, that immediately after the Fall of the Snow, an infinite multitude of *Sparrows,* made their Appearance; but then after a short continuance all disappeared.

It is incredible, how much Damage was done to the *Orchards;* For the Snow freezing to a Crust, as high as the Boughs of the Trees, anon Splitt them to peeces. The Cattle also, walking on the Crusted Snow, a dozen foot from the Ground, so fed upon the Trees as very much to damnify them.

The Ocean was in a prodigious Ferment, and after it was over, Vast Heaps of Little Shells were driven ashore, where they were never seen before. Mighty Shoals of Porpoises, also kept a Play-day in the Disturbed waves of our Harbours.

The odd Accidents befalling many poor people, whose Cottages were totally covered with the Snow, & not the very tops of their Chimneys to be seen, would afford a Story; But there not being any Relacion to philosophy in them, I forbear them. And now, *I am Satis Terris Nivis.*—And here is enough of my Winter-tale. If it serve to no other purpose, yett it will give me an opportunity to tell you, That Nine months ago, I did a thousand times wish myself with you in *Gresham-Colledge,* which is never so horribly Snow'd upon. But instead of so great a satisfaction, all I can attain to, is the pleasure of talking with you in this Epistolary way, and subscribing myself,

Syr, Yours with an Affection that knows no Winter

[Cotton Mather]

Dr Woodward.

AUTOBIOGRAPHY

BENJAMIN FRANKLIN

———◆◆◆———

Benjamin Franklin (1706–1790), although history claims him for Phila-delphia, was born and brought up in Boston. He was a grandson on his mother's side of Peter Folger the pioneer of Nantucket Island. In the following excerpt from his Autobiography, *Franklin tells of his early days. He first worked with his father, a tallow chandler and soap boiler, then for a time as a cutler; and from the age of twelve until he was seventeen was apprenticed to his brother James, publisher of the* New England Courant, *a Yankee version of the English* Spectator. *From 1723 on, the journal was published under Franklin's name.*

A BOSTON BOYHOOD

JOSIAH, my father, married young, and carried his wife with three children into New England about 1682. The conventicles having been forbidden by law and frequently disturbed induced some considerable men of his acquaintance to remove to that country, and he was prevailed with to accompany them thither, where they expected to enjoy their mode of religion with freedom. By the same wife he had four children more born there, and by a second wife ten more, in all seventeen; of which I remember thirteen sitting at one time at his table, who all grew up to be men and women, and married; I was the youngest son, and the youngest child but two, and was born in Boston, New England. My mother, the second wife, was Abiah Folger, a daughter of Peter Folger, one of the first settlers of New England, of whom honorable mention is made by Cotton Mather, in his church history of that country, entitled *Magnalia Christi Americana,* as "a godly, learned Englishman," if I remember the words rightly. I have heard that he wrote sundry small occasional pieces, but only one of them was printed, which I saw now many years since. . . .

My elder brothers were all put apprentices to different trades. I was put to the grammar school at eight years of age, my father intending to devote me, as the tithe of his sons, to the service of the church. My early readiness in learning to read (which must have been very early, as I do not remember when I could not read) and the opinion of all his friends that I should certainly make a good scholar encouraged him in this purpose of his. My uncle Benjamin, too, approved of it, and proposed to give me all his shorthand volumes of sermons, I suppose as a stock to set up with, if I would learn his character. I continued, however, at the grammar school not quite one year, though in that time I had risen gradually from the middle of the class of that year to be the head of it, and farther was removed into the next class above it, in order to go with that into the third at the end of the year. But my father, in the meantime, from a view of the expense of a college education, which having so large a family he could not well afford, and the mean living many so educated were afterwards able to obtain—reasons that he gave to his friends in my hearing—altered his first intention, took me from the grammar school, and sent me to a school for writing and arithmetic, kept by a then famous man, Mr. George Brownell, very successful in his profession generally, and that by mild, encouraging methods. Under him I acquired fair writing pretty soon, but I failed in the arithmetic, and made no progress in it. At ten years old I was taken home to assist my father in his business, which was that of a tallow-chandler and soap-boiler; a business he was not bred to, but had assumed on his arrival in New England, and on finding his dying trade would not maintain his family, being in little request. Accordingly, I was employed in cutting wick for the candles, filling the dipping mold and the molds for cast candles, attending the shop, going of errands, etc.

I disliked the trade, and had a strong inclination for the sea, but my father declared against it; however, living near the water, I was much in and about it, learned early to swim well and to manage boats; and when in a boat or canoe with other boys, I was commonly allowed to govern, especially in any case of difficulty; and upon other occasions I was generally a leader among the boys, and sometimes led them into scrapes, of which I will mention one instance, as it shows an early projecting public spirit, though not then justly conducted.

There was a salt-marsh that bounded part of the mill-pond, on the edge of which, at high water, we used to stand to fish for minnows. By much trampling, we had made it a mere quagmire. My proposal was to build a wharf there fit for us to stand upon, and I showed my comrades a large heap of stones which were intended for a new house near the marsh and which would very well suit our purpose. Accordingly, in the evening, when the workmen were gone, I assembled a number of my playfellows, and, working with them diligently like so many emmets, sometimes two or three to a stone, we brought them all away and built our little wharf. The next morning the workmen were surprised at missing the stones, which were found in our wharf. Inquiry was made after the removers; we were discovered and complained of; several of us were corrected by our fathers; and, though I pleaded the usefulness of the work, mine convinced me that nothing was useful which was not honest.

I think you may like to know something of his person and character. He had an excellent constitution of body, was of middle stature, but well set, and very strong; he was ingenious, could draw prettily, was skilled a little in music, and had a clear pleasing voice, so that when he played psalm tunes on his violin and sung withal, as he sometimes did in an evening after the business of the day was over, it was extremely agreeable to hear. He had a mechanical genius too, and, on occasion, was very handy in the use of other tradesmen's tools; but his great excellence lay in a sound understanding and solid judgment in prudential matters, both in private and public affairs. In the latter, indeed, he was never employed, the numerous family he had to educate and the straitness of his circumstances keeping him close to his trade; but I remember well his being frequently visited by leading people, who consulted him for his opinion in affairs of the town or of the church he belonged to, and showed a good deal of respect for his judgment and advice: he was also much consulted by private persons about their affairs when any difficulty occurred, and frequently chosen an arbitrator between contending parties. At his table he liked to have as often as he could some sensible friend or neighbor to converse with, and always took care to start some ingenious or useful topic for discourse, which might tend to improve the minds of his children. By this means he turned our attention to what was good, just, and prudent in the conduct of life; and little or no notice was ever taken of what related to the victuals on the table, whether it was well or ill dressed, in or out of season, of good or bad flavor, preferable or inferior to this or that other thing of the kind, so that I was brought up in such a perfect inattention to those matters as to be quite indifferent what kind of food was set before me, and so unobservant of it that to this day if I am asked I can scarce tell a few hours after dinner what I dined upon. This has been a convenience to me in traveling, where my companions have been sometimes very unhappy for want of a suitable gratification of their more delicate, because better instructed, tastes and appetites.

My mother had likewise an excellent constitution: she suckled all her ten children. I never knew either my father or mother to have any sickness but that of which they died, he at eighty-nine, and she at eighty-five years of age. They lie buried together at Boston, where I some years since placed a marble stone over their grave. . . .

By my rambling digressions I perceive myself to be grown old. I used to write more methodically. But one does not dress for private company as for a public ball. 'Tis perhaps only negligence.

To return: I continued thus employed in my father's business for two years, that is, till I was twelve years old;—and my brother John, who was bred to that business, having left my father, married, and set up for himself at Rhode Island, there was all appearance that I was destined to supply his place and be a tallow-chandler. But my dislike to the trade continuing, my father was under apprehensions that if he did not find one for me more agreeable, I should break away and get to sea, as his son

Josiah had done, to his great vexation. He therefore sometimes took me to walk with him, and see joiners, bricklayers, turners, braziers, etc., at their work, that he might observe my inclination and endeavor to fix it on some trade or other on land. It has ever since been a pleasure to me to see good workmen handle their tools; and it has been useful to me, having learned so much by it as to be able to do little jobs myself in my house when a workman could not readily be got, and to construct little machines for my experiments, while the intention of making the experiment was fresh and warm in my mind. My father at last fixed upon the cutler's trade, and my uncle Benjamin's son Samuel, who was bred to that business in London, being about that time established in Boston, I was sent to be with him some time, on liking. But his expectations of a fee with me displeasing my father, I was taken home again.

From a child I was fond of reading, and all the little money that came into my hands was ever laid out in books. Pleased with the *Pilgrim's Progress*, my first collection was of John Bunyan's works in separate little volumes. I afterwards sold them to enable me to buy R. Burton's *Historical Collections;* they were small chapman's books, and cheap, forty or fifty in all. My father's little library consisted chiefly of books in polemic divinity, most of which I read and have since often regretted that at a time when I had such a thirst for knowledge, more proper books had not fallen in my way, since it was now resolved I should not be a clergyman. *Plutarch's Lives* there was, in which I read abundantly, and I still think that time spent to great advantage. There was also a book of Defoe's, called an *Essay on Projects*, and another of Dr. Mather's, called *Essays to do Good,* which perhaps gave me a turn of thinking that had an influence on some of the principal future events of my life.

This bookish inclination at length determined my father to make me a printer, though he had already one son (James) of that profession. In 1717 my brother James returned from England with a press and letters to set up his business in Boston. I liked it much better than that of my father, but still had a hankering for the sea. To prevent the apprehended effect of such an inclination, my father was impatient to have me bound to my brother. I stood out some time, but at last was persuaded, and signed the indentures when I was yet but twelve years old. I was to serve as an apprentice till I was twenty-one years of age, only I was to be allowed journeyman's wages during the last year. In a little time I made great proficiency in the business and became a useful hand to my brother. I now had access to better books. An acquaintance with the apprentices of booksellers enabled me sometimes to borrow a small one, which I was careful to return soon and clean. Often I sat up in my room reading the greatest part of the night, when the book was borrowed in the evening and to be returned early in the morning, lest it should be missed or wanted.

LOVEWELL'S FIGHT

ANONYMOUS

———◆•◆———

John Lovewell (1691–1725) was a Massachusetts Indian fighter, a profes-
sional who was granted bounties for every Indian he scalped, by the
General Court. His luck caught up with him in Maine and he was am-
bushed and killed. The following anonymous ballad tells the sad tale.

LOVEWELL'S FIGHT

[A Popular Ballad. Written shortly after the Battle of May 8th, 1725.]

Of worthy Captain LOVEWELL, I purpose now to sing,
How valiantly he served his country and his King;
He and his valiant soldiers did range the woods full wide,
And hardships they endured to quell the Indian's pride.

'Twas nigh unto Pigwacket, on the eighth day of May,
They spied a rebel Indian soon after break of day;
He on a bank was walking, upon a neck of land,
Which leads into a pond as we're made to understand.

Our men resolved to have him, and travelled two miles round,
Until they met the Indian, who boldly stood his ground;
Then up speaks Captain LOVEWELL, "Take you good heed," says he,
"This rogue is to decoy us, I very plainly see.

"The Indians lie in ambush, in some place nigh at hand,
In order to surround us upon this neck of land;
Therefore we'll march in order, and each man leave his pack;
That we may briskly fight them when they make their attack."

They came unto this Indian, who did them thus defy,
As soon as they came nigh him, two guns he did let fly,
Which wounded Captain LOVEWELL, and likewise one man more,
But when this rogue was running, they laid him in his gore.

Then having scalped the Indian, they went back to the spot,
Where they had laid their packs down, but there they found them not,
For the Indians having spied them, when they them down did lay,
Did seize them for their plunder, and carry them away.

These rebels lay in ambush, this very place hard by,
So that an English soldier did one of them espy,
And cried out, "Here's an Indian;" with that they started out,
As fiercely as old lions, and hideously did shout.

With that our valiant English all gave a loud huzza,
To show the rebel Indians they feared them not a straw:
So now the fight began, and as fiercely as could be,
The Indians ran up to them, but soon were forced to flee.

Then spake up Captain LOVEWELL, when first the fight began,
"Fight on my valiant heroes! you see they fall like rain."
For as we are informed, the Indians were so thick,
A man could scarcely fire a gun and not some of them hit.

Then did the rebels try their best our soldiers to surround,
But they could not accomplish it, because there was a pond,
To which our men retreated and covered all the rear,
The rogues were forced to flee them, although they skulked for fear.

Two logs there were behind them that close together lay,
Without being discovered, they could not get away;
Therefore our valiant English they travelled in a row,
And at a handsome distance as they were wont to go.

'Twas ten o'clock in the morning when first the fight begun,
And fiercely did continue until the setting sun;
Excepting that the Indians some hours before 'twas night,
Drew off into the bushes and ceased a while to fight.

But soon again returned, in fierce and furious mood,
Shouting as in the morning, but yet not half so loud;
For as we are informed, so thick and fast they fell,
Scarce twenty of their number at night did get home well.

And that our valiant English till midnight there did stay,
To see whether the rebels would have another fray;
But they no more returning, they made off towards their home,
And brought away their wounded as far as they could come.

Of all our valiant English there were but thirty-four,
And of the rebel Indians there were about fourscore.
And sixteen of our English did safely home return,
The rest were killed and wounded, for which we all must mourn.

Our worthy Captain LOVEWELL among them there did die,
They killed Lieut. ROBBINS, and wounded good young FRYE,

Who was our English Chaplain; he many Indians slew,
And some of them he scalped when bullets round him flew.

Young FULLAM too I'll mention, because he fought so well,
Endeavoring to save a man, a sacrifice he fell:
But yet our valiant Englishmen in fight were ne'er dismayed,
But still they kept their motion, and WYMAN's Captain made,

Who shot the old chief PAUGUS, which did the foe defeat,
Then set his men in order, and brought off the retreat;
And braving many dangers and hardships in the way,
They safe arrived at Dunstable, the thirteenth day of May.

THE PURITAN STATE AND PURITAN SOCIETY

PERRY MILLER

———◆•◆———

The source of men's actions may be found in their minds; but what changes their minds often appears a mystery. How, for instance, did New England shift its tight, organized Puritan orthodoxy over to the eager, liberty-loving fervor which preceded the Revolution?

Perry Miller, present-day Professor of American Literature at Harvard, in his many books on the seventeenth century in New England demonstrates a broad and brilliant understanding of the Puritan mind. The following paper, from his collection of essays published under the title Errand into the Wilderness, *makes clear the involuted process of change from a Puritan society to the liberalism of the Age of Reason.*

IT has often been said that the end of the seventeenth and the beginning of the eighteenth century mark the first real break with the Middle Ages in the history of European thought. Even though the Renaissance and Reformation transformed many aspects of the Western intellect, still it was not until the time of Newton that the modern scientific era began; only then could men commence to regard life in this world as something more than preparation for life beyond the grave. Certainly if the eighteenth century inaugurated the modern epoch in natural sciences, so also did it in the political and social sciences. For the first time since the fall of the Roman Empire religion could be separated from politics, doctrinal orthodoxy divorced from loyalty to the state, and the citizens of a nation be permitted to worship in diverse churches and to believe different creeds without endangering the public peace. Various factors contributed to effecting this revolution; the triumph of scientific method and of rationalism made impossible the older belief that government was of divine origin; the rise of capitalism, of the middle class, and eventually of democracy, necessitated new conceptions of the role of the state. Social leadership in England and America was assumed by a group of gentlemen who were, by and large, deists or skeptics, and to them all religious issues had become supremely boring. At the same time the churches themselves, particularly the newer evangelical denominations, were swinging round to a theology that made religious belief the subjective experience of individual men, entirely unrelated to any particular political philosophy or social theory.

In order to understand Puritanism we must go behind these eighteenth-century developments to an age when the unity of religion and politics was so axiomatic that very few men would even have grasped the idea that church and state could be distinct. For the Puritan mind it was not possible to segregate a man's spiritual life from his communal life. Massachusetts was settled for religious reasons, but as John Winthrop announced, religious reasons included "a due forme of Government both ciuill and ecclesiasticall," and the civil was quite as important in his eyes as the ecclesiastical. Only in recent years has it become possible for us to view the political aspects of Puritanism with something like comprehension and justice. For two centuries our social thinking has been dominated by ideas that were generated in the course of a sweeping revolt against everything for which the Puritans stood; the political beliefs of the Puritans were forgotten, or, if remembered at all, either deplored or condemned as unfortunate remnants of medievalism. Puritanism has been viewed mainly as a religious and ethical movement. But of late years the standards of the eighteenth century have for the first time come under serious criticism and in many quarters are showing the strain. In these circumstances the social philosophy of Puritanism takes on a new interest, and quite possibly becomes for us the most instructive and valuable portion of the Puritan heritage.

The Puritan theory of the state began with the hypothesis of original sin. Had Adam transmitted undiminished to his descendants the image of God in which he had been created, no government would ever have been necessary among men; they would all then have done justice to each other without the supervision of a judge, they would have respected each other's rights without the intervention of a policeman. But the Bible said—and experience proved—that since the Fall, without the policeman, the judge, the jail, the law, and the magistrate, men will rob, murder, and fight among themselves; without a coercive state to restrain evil impulses and administer punishments, no life will be safe, no property secure, no honor observed. Therefore, upon Adam's apostasy, God Himself instituted governments among men. He left the particular form to be determined by circumstance—this was one important human art on which the Puritans said the Bible was *not* an absolute and imperious lawgiver—but He enacted that all men should be under some sort of corporate rule, that they should all submit to the sway of their superiors, that no man should live apart from his fellows, that the government should have full power to enforce obedience and to inflict every punishment that the crimes of men deserved.

There was, it is true, a strong element of individualism in the Puritan creed; every man had to work out his own salvation, each soul had to face his maker alone. But at the same time, the Puritan philosophy demanded that in society all men, at least all regenerate men, be marshaled into one united array. The lone horseman, the single trapper, the solitary hunter was not a figure of the Puritan frontier; Puritans moved in groups and towns, settled in whole communities, and maintained firm government over all units. Neither were the individualistic business man, the shopkeeper who seized every opportunity to enlarge his profits, the speculator who contrived to gain wealth at the expense of his fellows, neither were these typical figures of the original Puritan society. Puritan opinion was at the opposite pole from Jefferson's feeling that the best government governs as little as possible. The theorists of New England thought of society as a unit, bound together by inviolable ties; they thought of it not as an aggregation of individuals but as an organism, functioning for a definite purpose, with all parts subordinate to the whole, all members contributing a definite share, every person occupying a particular status. "Society in all sorts of humane affaires is better than Solitariness," said John Cotton. The society of early New England was decidedly "regimented." Puritans did not think that the state was merely an umpire, standing on the side lines of a contest, limited to checking egregious fouls but otherwise allowing men free play according to their abilities and the breaks of the game. They would have expected *laissez faire* to result in a reign of rapine and horror. The state to them was an active instrument of leadership, discipline, and, wherever necessary, of coercion; it legislated over any or all aspects of human behavior, it not merely regulated misconduct but undertook to inspire and direct all conduct. The commanders were not to trim their policies by the desires of the people, but to drive ahead upon the predetermined course; the people were all to turn out as they were ordered, and together they were to crowd sail to the full capacity of the vessel. The officers were above the common men, as the quarter-deck is above the forecastle. There was no idea of the equality of all men. There was no questioning that men who would not serve the purposes of the

society should be whipped into line. The objectives were clear and un-
mistakable; any one's disinclination to dedicate himself to them was
obviously so much recalcitrancy and depravity. The government of Massachusetts, and of Connecticut as well, was a dictatorship, and never pretended to be anything else; it was a dictatorship, not of a single tyrant,
or of an economic class, or of a political faction, but of the holy and
regenerate. Those who did not hold with the ideals entertained by the
righteous, or who believed God had preached other principles, or who
desired that in religious belief, morality, and ecclesiastical preferences all
men should be left at liberty to do as they wished—such persons had
every liberty, as Nathaniel Ward said, to stay away from New England.
If they did come, they were expected to keep their opinions to themselves;
if they discussed them in public or attempted to act upon them, they were
exiled; if they persisted in returning, they were cast out again; if they still
came back, as did four Quakers, they were hanged on Boston Common.
And from the Puritan point of view, it was good riddance.

These views of the nature and function of the state were not peculiar to
the Puritans of New England; they were the heritage of the past, the
ideals, if not always the actuality, of the previous centuries. That government was established by God in order to save depraved men from their
own depravity had been orthodox Christian teaching for centuries; that
men should be arranged in serried ranks, inferiors obeying superiors, was
the essence of feudalism; that men should live a social life, that profit-
making should be restrained within the limits of the "just price," that the
welfare of the whole took precedence over any individual advantage, was
the doctrine of the medieval church, and of the Church of England in the
early seventeenth century. Furthermore, in addition to these general
principles, there were two or three more doctrines in the New England
philosophy which also were common to the age and the background: all
the world at that moment believed with them that the church was to be
maintained and protected by the civil authority, and a certain part of the
world was contending that government must be limited by fundamental
law and that it takes its origin from the consent of the people.

Every respectable state in the Western world assumed that it could
allow only one church to exist within its borders, that every citizen should
be compelled to attend it and conform to its requirements, and that all
inhabitants should pay taxes for its support. When the Puritans came to
New England the idea had not yet dawned that a government could
safely permit several creeds to exist side by side within the confines of a
single nation. They had not been fighting in England for any milk-and-
water toleration, and had they been offered such religious freedom as dissenters now enjoy in Great Britain they would have scorned to accept the
terms. Only a hypocrite, a person who did not really believe what he
professed, would be content to practice his religion under those condi-

tions. The Puritans were assured that they alone knew the exact truth, as it was contained in the written word of God, and they were fighting to enthrone it in England and to extirpate utterly and mercilessly all other pretended versions of Christianity. When they could not succeed at home, they came to America, where they could establish a society in which the one and only truth should reign forever. There is nothing so idle as to praise the Puritans for being in any sense conscious or deliberate pioneers of religious liberty—unless, indeed, it is still more idle to berate them because in America they persecuted dissenters for their beliefs after themselves had undergone persecution for differing with the bishops. To allow no dissent from the truth was exactly the reason they had come to America. They maintained here precisely what they had maintained in England, and if they exiled, fined, jailed, whipped, or hanged those who disagreed with them in New England, they would have done the same thing in England could they have secured the power. It is almost pathetic to trace the puzzlement of New England leaders at the end of the seventeenth century, when the idea of toleration was becoming more and more respectable in European thought. They could hardly understand what was happening in the world, and they could not for a long time be persuaded that they had any reason to be ashamed of their record of so many Quakers whipped, blasphemers punished by the amputation of ears, Antinomians exiled, Anabaptists fined, or witches executed. By all the lights which had prevailed in Europe at the time the Puritans had left, these were achievements to which any government could point with pride. In 1681 a congregation of Anabaptists, who led a stormy and precarious existence for several years in Charlestown, published an attack upon the government of Massachusetts Bay; they justified themselves by appealing to the example of the first settlers, claiming that like themselves the founders had been nonconformists and had fled to New England to establish a refuge for persecuted consciences. When Samuel Willard, minister of the Third Church in Boston, read this, he could hardly believe his eyes; he hastened to assure the authors that they did not know what they were talking about:

> I perceive they are mistaken in the design of our first Planters, whose business was not Toleration; but were professed Enemies of it, and could leave the World professing they *died no Libertines*. Their business was to settle, and (as much as in them lay) secure Religion to Posterity, according to that way which they believed was of God.

For the pamphlet in which Willard penned these lines Increase Mather wrote an approving preface. Forty years later, he and his son Cotton participated in the ordination of a Baptist minister in Boston, and he then preached on the need for harmony between differing sects. But by that

The Honorable Josiah Quincy (1772–1864), by Gilbert Stuart (1755–1828). He was a Federalist Congressman, Mayor of Boston, President of Harvard, a Unitarian, an historian, and a cousin of the Adamses.

Portrait of John Adams, second President of the United States, by a distinguished figure in the contemporary field of art, John Singleton Copley (1738?–1815), Boston painter.

General Nathanael Greene of Rhode Island (1742–1786), quarter-master-general in the Revolution, here painted by Charles Willson

Mrs. John Winthrop (Hannah Fayerweather, 1727–1790), wife of the contemporary bearer of an old, often-repeated

Harriet Beecher Stowe, author of the inflammatory novel *Uncle Tom's Cabin*, wrote it partly while in the kitchen with her numerous children under foot.

Courtesy Massachusetts Historical Society

This mild-faced old gentleman is William Lloyd Garrison, spearhead of the New England Abolitionist movement and editor of the radical abolitionist magazine *The Liberator* for thirty-four years.

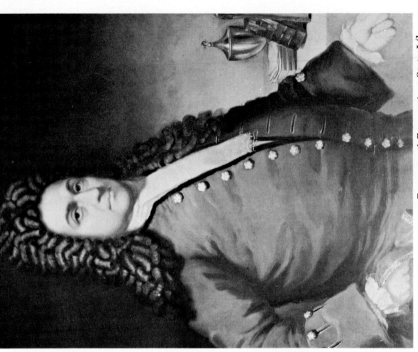

A painting by George F. Wright of Gurdon Saltonstall, Governor of Connecticut from 1708 to 1724, who aided in the founding of Yale College and its establishment at New Haven

A face once familiar to every American school child, Henry Wadsworth Longfellow was the most popular poet of the

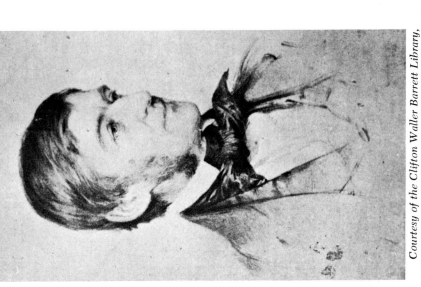

Ralph Waldo Emerson, sage of Concord, transcendentalist philosopher and poet whose angular Yankee lines have a peculiar appeal to our time.

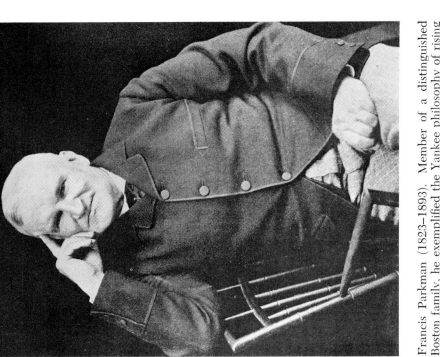

Francis Parkman (1823–1893). Member of a distinguished Boston family, he exemplified the Yankee philosophy of rising above one's weaknesses. In frail health, nearly blind, he produced a series of major historical works. From a photograph by Benjamin Kimball.

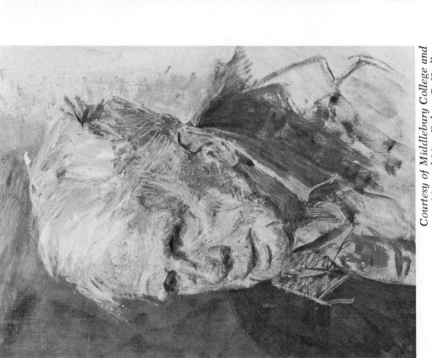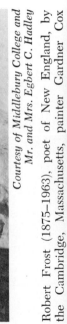

Robert Frost (1875–1963), poet of New England, by
the Cambridge, Massachusetts, painter Gardner Cox

Leverett Saltonstall, Governor of Massachusetts from 1939
to 1944, since then U.S. Senator from Massachusetts. A
great-nephew in the ninth generation of Gurdon Salton-

A Southworth and Hawes daguerreotype of John Quincy
Adams, sixth President of the United States, as he appeared
in old age.

Bronson Alcott, educator and father of Louisa May, photo-
graphed in the doorway to the study, in his barn at Concord,
Massachusetts.

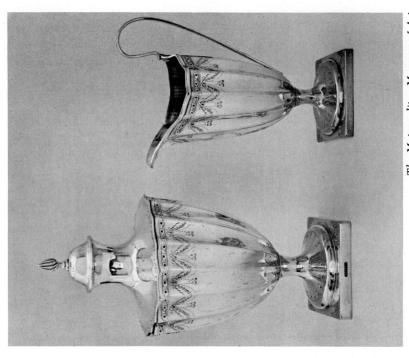

*The Metropolitan Museum of Art
Bequest of A. J. Clearwater, 1933*

Examples of fine silver designed and executed by silversmith
Paul Revere, Revolutionary equestrian and patriot.

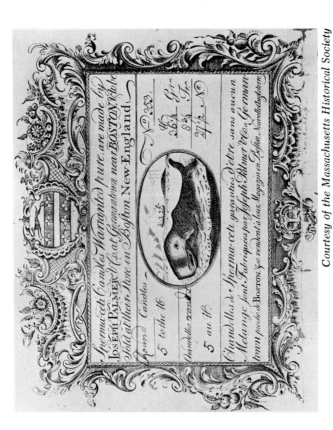

Courtesy of the Massachusetts Historical Society

A "trade card" engraved by Nathaniel Hurd about 1752 for Joseph
Palmer, merchant, and later, Revolutionary soldier.

This Harvard-owned house on Brattle Street, Cambridge, was General Washington's headquarters in the Revolution and later the home of Henry Wadsworth Longfellow, by whose name it is generally called.

A room from the Samuel Wentworth house in Portsmouth, New Hampshire, built in 1671 and panelled about 1710, now in the American Wing of the Metropolitan Museum.

Photograph by the Pictorial Studio, Newcastle, Maine

The Nickels-Sortwell house in Wiscasset, Maine. The arch motif used throughout is typical of northern New England.

Courtesy of the Essex Institute

The Peirce-Nichols house in Salem, Massachusetts, designed by Samuel McIntyre in 1782. Note the "widow's walk" that surmounts each of the port-town houses.

Typical of Newburyport sea-captain houses, this is the mansion of "Lord" Timothy Dexter, a New England eccentric. John P. Marquand wrote his biography.

Built in 1823, the Lyman Mower house is one of many elegantly designed houses in Woodstock, Vermont.

The Puritans of New England did not prettify death. In these Cambridge, Massachusetts, gravestones may be noted devils, skulls, and some most unpuritanical anatomy.

Joseph Tapping's gravestone in King's Chapel, Boston, is one of the few true allegorical stones preserved from the seventeenth century. Here Time attempts to retard the hand of Death which hovers over the burning candle of Life.

Harvard College, founded in 1636 at Newe Towne (Cambridge), Massachusetts, as it appeared about a century later.

Founded in 1701 as the Collegiate School, the college at New Haven, Connecticut, was renamed in 1718 in honor of Elihu Yale. It became a University in 1887.

Founded as Rhode Island College in 1764, the college in Providence did not become Brown University until 1804.

Dartmouth College, founded in 1769 under a charter from George III on the basis of Eleazor Wheelock's school for the Indians.

Williams College, Williamstown, Massachusetts, chartered in 1785, shown as it appeared in 1839–1840.

Amherst College, Massachusetts, a few years after its founding in 1821.

time much water had gone under the bridge, the old charter had been revoked, there was danger that the Church of England might be made the established church of the colonies, theology had come to be of less importance in men's minds than morality, the tone of the eighteenth century was beginning to influence opinion—even in Boston. Increase was old and weary. Puritanism, in the true sense of the word, was dead.

Of course, the whole Puritan philosophy of church and state rested upon the assumption that the Word of God was clear and explicit, that the divines had interpreted it correctly, and that no one who was not either a knave or a fool could deny their demonstrations. *Ergo*, it seemed plain, those who did deny them should be punished for being obstinate. John Cotton said that offenders should not be disciplined for their wrong opinions, but for persisting in them; he said that Roger Williams was turned out of Massachusetts not for his conscience but for sinning against his own conscience. Roger Williams and John Cotton debated the question of "persecution" through several hundred pages; after they had finished, I think it is very doubtful whether Cotton had even begun to see his adversary's point. And still today it is hard to make clear the exact grounds upon which Roger Williams became the great apostle of religious liberty. Williams was not, like Thomas Jefferson, a man to whom theology and divine grace had become stuff and nonsense; on the contrary he was pious with a fervor and passion that went beyond most of his contemporaries. So exalted was his conception of the spiritual life that he could not bear to have it polluted with earthly considerations. He did not believe that any man could determine the precise intention of Scripture with such dreadful certainty as the New England clergy claimed to possess. Furthermore, it seemed to him that even if their version were true, submission to truth itself was worth nothing at all when forced upon men by the sword. Williams evolved from an orthodox Puritan into the champion of religious liberty because he came to see spiritual truth as so rare, so elevated, so supernal a loveliness that it could not be chained to a worldly establishment and a vested interest. He was a libertarian because he contemned the world, and he wanted to separate church and state so that the church would not be contaminated by the state; Thomas Jefferson loved the world and was dubious about the spirit, and he sought to separate church and state so that the state would not be contaminated by the church. But John Cotton believed that the state and church were partners in furthering the cause of truth; he knew that the truth was clear, definite, reasonable, and undeniable; he expected all good men to live by it voluntarily, and he was sure that all men who did not do so were obviously bad men. Bad men were criminals, whether their offense was theft or a belief in the "inner light," and they should be punished. Moses and Aaron, the priest and the statesman, were equally the vice-regents of God, and the notion that one could contaminate the other was utter insanity.

The two other ideas derived from the background of the age, rule by fundamental law and the social compact, were also special tenets of English Puritanism. For three decades before the settlement of Massachusetts the Puritan party in England had been working hand in glove with the Parliament against the King. The absolutist Stuarts were allied with the bishops, and the Puritan agitator and the Parliamentary leader made common cause against them both. As a result of this combination, the Puritan theorists had taken over the essentials of the Parliamentary conception of society, the contention that the power of the ruler should be exercised in accordance with established fundamental law, and that the government should owe its existence to a compact of the governed. Because these ideas were strategically invaluable in England, they became ingrained in the Puritan consciousness; they were carried to the New England wilderness and were preached from every pulpit in the land.

The Puritans did not see any conflict between them and their religious intentions. In New England the fundamental law was the Bible. The magistrates were to have full power to rule men for the specific purposes to which the society was dedicated; but they as well as their subordinates were tied to the specific purposes, and could not go beyond the prescribed limits. The Bible was clear and definite on the form of the church, on the code of punishments for crimes, on the general purposes of social existence; its specifications were binding on all, magistrates, ministers, and citizens. Consequently, the Puritans did not find it difficult to conclude that in those matters upon which the Bible left men free to follow their own discretion, the society itself should establish basic rules. The New England leaders and the people frequently disagreed about what these rules were, or how detailed they should be made, but neither side ever doubted that the community must abide by whatever laws had been enacted, either by God or by the state. The government of New England was, as I have said, a dictatorship, but the dictators were not absolute and irresponsible. John Cotton was the clerical spokesman for the Massachusetts rulers, but he stoutly demanded "that all power that is on earth be limited."

The belief that government originated in the consent of the governed was equally congenial to the Puritan creed. The theology is often enough described as deterministic, because it held that men were predestined to Heaven or Hell; but we are always in danger of forgetting that the life of the Puritan was completely voluntaristic. The natural man was indeed bound in slavery to sin and unable to make exertions toward his own salvation; but the man into whose soul grace has been infused was liberated from that bondage and made free to undertake the responsibilities and obligations of virtue and decency. The holy society was erected upon the belief that the right sort of men could of their own free will and choice carry through the creation and administration of the right sort of community. The churches of New England were made up of "saints," who came into the church because they wanted membership, not because they were born in it, or were forced into it, or joined because of policy and convention. Though every resident was obliged to attend and to pay taxes for the support of the churches, no one became an actual member who did not signify his strong desire to be one. The saints were expected to act positively because they had in them a spirit of God that made them capable of every exertion. No doubt the Puritans maintained that government originated in the consent of the people because that theory was an implement for chastening the absolutism of the Stuarts; but they maintained it also because they did not believe that any society, civil or ecclesiastical, into which men did not enter of themselves was worthy of the name.

Consequently, the social theory of Puritanism, based upon the law of God, was posited also upon the voluntary submission of the citizens. As men exist in nature, said Thomas Hooker, no one person has any power over another; "there must of necessity be a mutuall ingagement, each of the other, by their free consent, before by any rule of God they have any right or power, or can exercise either, each towards the other." This truth appears, he argues, from all relations among men, that of husband and wife, master and servant; there must be a compact drawn up and sealed between them.

> From *mutuall acts* of consenting and ingaging each of other, there is an impression of *ingagement* results, as a *relative bond,* betwixt the contractours and confederatours, wherein the *formalis ratio,* or *specificall nature* of the covenant lieth, in all the former instances especially *that of* corporations. So that however it is true, the rule bindes such to the duties of their places and relations, yet it is certain, it requires that they should *first freely ingage* themselves in such covenants, and *then* be carefull to fullfill such duties. A man is allowed freely to make choice of his wife, and she of her husband, before they need or should perform the duties of husband and wife one towards another.

The rules and regulations of society, the objectives and the duties, are erected by God; but in a healthy state the citizens must first agree to abide by those regulations, must first create the society by willing consent and active participation.

These ideas, of a uniform church supported by the civil authority, of rule by explicit law, of the derivation of the state from the consent of the people, were transported to the wilderness because they were the stock ideas of the time and place. What the New England Puritans added of their own was the unique fashion in which they combined them into one coherent and rounded theory. The classic expression of this theory is the

speech on liberty delivered by John Winthrop to the General Court in
1645. In that year Winthrop was serving as lieutenant governor, and as
such was a justice of the peace; a squabble broke out in the town of Hing-
ham over the election of a militia officer; Winthrop intervened, committing one faction for contempt of court when they would not give bond to
appear peaceably before the legislature and let the affair be adjudicated.
Some of the citizens were enraged, and the lower house of the General
Court impeached Winthrop for exceeding his commission and going beyond the basic law of the land. He was tried and acquitted; thereupon
he pronounced his magnificent oration, setting before the people the uni-
fied theory of the Puritan commonwealth.

As he expounds it, the political doctrine becomes part and parcel of the
theological, and the cord that binds all ideas together is the covenant.
Winthrop argues that individuals, in a natural state, before grace has been
given them, are at absolute liberty to do anything they can, to lie, steal,
murder; obviously he is certain that natural men, being what they are,
will do exactly these things unless prevented. But when men become
regenerate they are then at "liberty" to do only what God commands.
And God commands certain things for the group as a whole as well as for
each individual. Regenerate men, therefore, by the very fact of being
regenerate, come together, form churches and a state upon explicit agreements, in which they all promise to live with one another according to the
laws and for the purposes of God. Thus the government is brought into
being by the act of the people; but the people do not create just any sort
of government, but the one kind of government which God has outlined.
The governors are elected by the people, but elected into an office which
has been established by God. God engenders the society by acting
through the people, as in nature He secures His effects by guiding secondary causes; the collective will of regenerate men, bound together by
the social compact, projects and continues the will of God into the state.
As John Davenport expressed it, "In regular actings of the creature, God
is the first Agent; there are not two several and distinct actings, one of
God, another of the People: but in one and the same action, God, by the
Peoples suffrages, makes such an one Governour, or Magistrate, and not
another." So, when men have made a covenant with God they have
thereby promised Him, in the very terms of that agreement, to compact
among themselves in order to form a holy state in which His discipline
will be practiced. As one of the ministers phrased it:

> Where the Lord sets himselfe over a people, he frames them unto a
> willing and voluntary subjection unto him, that they desire nothing
> more then to be under his government . . . . When the Lord is in
> Covenant with a people, they follow him not forcedly, but as farre
> as they are sanctified by grace, they submit willingly to his regiment.

When men have entered these covenants, first with God, then with each other in the church and again in the state, they have thrice committed themselves to the rule of law and the control of authority. Winthrop can thus insist that though the government of Massachusetts is bound by fundamental law, and though it takes its rise from the people, and though the people elect the officials, still the people's liberty in Massachusetts consists in a "liberty to that only which is good, just and honest." By entering the covenant with God, and the covenant with each other, the citizens renounce all natural liberty, surrender the right to seek for anything that they themselves might lust after, and retain only the freedom that "is maintained and exercised in a way of subjection to authority."

The theory furnishes an excellent illustration of the intellectual ideal toward which all Puritan thought aspired; in the realm of government as of nature, the Puritan thinker strove to harmonize the determination of God with the exertion of men, the edicts of revelation with the counsels of reason and experience. On one side, this account exhibits the creation of society as flowing from the promptings and coaction of God; on the other side it attributes the origination to the teachings of nature and necessity. The social compact may be engineered by God, but it is also an eminently reasonable method of bringing a state into being. Delimitation of the ruler's power by basic law may be a divine ordinance to restrain the innate sinfulness of men, but it is also a very natural device to avoid oppression and despotism; the constitution may be promulgated to men from on high, but it is in fact very much the sort which, had they been left to their own devices, they might have contrived in the interests of efficiency and practicality. Men might conceivably have come upon the erection of governments through explicit compacts, in which they incorporated certain inviolable regulations and a guarantee of rights, quite as much by their own intelligence as by divine instruction. As always in Puritan thought, there was no intention to discredit either source, but rather to integrate the divine and the natural, revelation and reason, into a single inspiration. "Power of Civil Rule, by men orderly chosen, is Gods Ordinance," said John Davenport, even if "It is from the Light and Law of Nature," because "the Law of Nature is God's Law." The Puritan state was thus from one point of view purely and simply a "theocracy"; God was the sovereign; His fiats were law and His wishes took precedence over all other considerations; the magistrates and ministers were His viceroys. But from another point of view, the Puritan state was built upon reason and the law of nature; it was set up by the covenant of the people, the scope of its power was determined by the compact, and the magistrates and ministers were the commissioned servants of the people.

As this theory stands on paper it is, like so many edifices of the Puritan mind, almost perfect. When it was realized in practice, however, there were at least two difficulties that soon became apparent. For one, not all

the people, even in New England, were regenerate; in fact, the provable
elect were a minority, probably no more than one-fifth of the total population. But this did not dismay the original theorists, for they had never
thought that mere numerical majorities proved anything. Consequently,
though the social compact furnished the theoretical basis of society in
New England, nevertheless it was confined to the special few; the election
of officers and the passing of laws was given to those only who could
demonstrate their justification and sanctification. The congregational system, with its membership limited to those who had proved before the
church that they possessed the signs of grace, offered a ready machinery
for winnowing the wheat from the chaff. Therefore, under the first charter
the suffrage in Massachusetts was limited to the church members. In
Connecticut the franchise was not officially restrained in this fashion, but
other means served as well to keep the electorate pure and orthodox. The
"citizens," as they were called, elected delegates to the General Court,
chose judges, and passed laws. The others, the "inhabitants," had equality
before the law, property rights, police protection; they were taxed no
more than the citizens or submitted to no indignities, but they were
allowed no voice in the government or in the choice of ministers, and only
by the mere force of numbers gained any influence in town meetings.

The restriction of the franchise to church membership seemed to solve
the first difficulty confronted by the Puritan theorists. But in time it only
brought them face to face with the second and more serious problem: the
whole structure of theory which Winthrop outlined in his speech, and
which the sermons of the 1660's and 1670's reiterated, fell apart the moment the "citizens" were no longer really and ardently holy. Just as soon
as the early zeal began to die down, and the distinction between the
citizens and the inhabitants became difficult to discern, then the purely
naturalistic, rational, practical aspect of the political theory became detached from the theological, began to stand alone and by itself. As the
religious inspiration waned, there remained no reason why all the people
should not be held partners to the social compact; the idea that God
worked His ends through the covenant of the people grew vague and
obscure, while the notion that all the people made the covenant for their
own reasons and created the state for their own purposes took on more
and more definite outlines. As toleration was forced upon the colonies by
royal command, or became more estimable as religious passions abated,
the necessity for the social bond being considered a commitment of the
nation to the will of God disappeared. Instead, men perceived the charms
and usefulness of claiming that the compact had been an agreement of
the people, not to God's terms, but to their own terms. The divine ordinance and the spirit of God, which were supposed to have presided over
the political process, vanished, leaving a government founded on the
self-evident truths of the law of nature, brought into being by social com-

pact, instituted not for the glory of God, but to secure men's "inalienable rights" of life, liberty, and the pursuit of happiness. Except that, until Jefferson rewrote the phrase, the sacred trinity of interests which government could not tamper with were more candidly summarized as life, liberty—and property.

After the new charter of 1691—which Increase Mather negotiated and which for him was a diplomatic triumph, but which nevertheless was an imposition upon Massachusetts from the outside—leaders of the colony made various efforts to accommodate the original conception of social purpose to the constitutional requirements of the document. I have elsewhere described their flounderings (*The New England Mind: From Colony to Province*, 1953), and the literature of the eighteenth century clearly yields up the evolution of a political philosophy which, by the time of the revolution, was entirely perfected (see Alice M. Baldwin, *The New England Clergy and the American Revolution*, Durham, North Carolina, 1928). Historians now agree that the first clear break with the seventeenth-century complex was John Wise's *Vindication of the Government of the New England Churches* in 1717. Though actually this book had little or no effect on colonial thinking, and does not appear to have been cited even in the revolutionary debates, still it was far ahead of its own time in proclaiming that a contractual system of government, with inalienable rights preserved in society from the original state of nature, was the dictate of aboriginal reason, that it could be said to have only subsequently obtained "the Royal Approbation" of the Creator. The transformation of the doctrine of the founders into a weapon for burgeoning nationalism was virtually completed in 1750 when Jonathan Mayhew, preaching on the anniversary of the day on which the Puritans had decapitated Charles I, delivered "A Discourse Concerning Unlimited Subjection." To this enlightened Puritan it now appeared that the purposes of society are not at all those of the deity but of the subjects. The advantage to be derived from corporate existence is no longer the salvation but the well-being of the citizen. The power even of the Puritan God—and therefore, naturally, that of an English king—is bound by the terms of compact. New England's errand into the wilderness—having set out from the federal theology—had now developed into an assurance that God Himself would respect the laws we have agreed upon. As for King George, if he imposes a tax to which we do not ourselves consent, and if we thereupon resist him, "even to the dethroning him," we are not criminals: we have only taken "a reasonable way" of vindicating our natural rights.

In 1750 Mayhew's boldness still dismayed most of his contemporaries, as did also his theological liberalism, but it was only a matter of time before the community caught up with at least his political argument. Hence he is the most obvious link between Puritan and revolutionary ideas. However, in the excitement of embracing Mayhew's radicalism, few at the time of war had the leisure or inclination to look back to Winthrop or to inquire how they had managed to travel the tortuous road from his doctrine of federal liberty to their constitutionalism. There ceased to survive even the faintest memory of an era when the social contract had incorporated absolute subjection to the ontological realities of the good, just, and honest—those anterior verities which existed from eternity, long before any peoples anywhere were gathered into societies and which no mere convention of the citizens could alter or redefine.

1737-1770

A NARRATIVE OF SURPRISING CONVERSIONS

REV. JONATHAN EDWARDS

———————◆•◆———————

The Rev. Jonathan Edwards (1703–1758), that figure whom Perry Miller cites as marking the change away from a purely Puritan philosophy, evolved a system of theology which has been called neo-Calvinism. (It will be remembered that the Massachusetts Bay colonists, for all their Calvinistic notions, never separated from the Church of England.) At the same time, Edwards was one of those responsible for a new religious spirit in the land which has since been called the Great Awakening—a spirit which held the illumined relation between the individual and his God all-important, whereas Puritanism had been a collective concern based on covenants between God and his people. This new, emotional spirit exactly suited the mass of the people; the intellectual sermons of the Puritans had been over their heads anyway. The movement led to excesses of revivalism to which Edwards never fully lent himself. In the following excerpt from his famous description of the revival movement, entitled A Faithful Narration of the Surprising Work of God in the Conversion of Many Hundred Souls in Northampton, *Edwards tells of the kind of experience desired. The new spirit was not so popular but what, after Edwards attempted to limit church membership to those who had experienced direct supernatural intervention (shades of Mrs. Hutchinson!), he was dismissed from his Northampton pulpit.*

Edwards constitutes an intellectual stepping-stone in still another way. His view of God as an infinite being, instead of the Hebraic concept the earlier Puritans held, developed gradually into nineteenth-century Transcendentalism.

[143]

A FOUR-YEAR-OLD CONVERT

. . . I now proceed to the other instance that I would give an account of, which is of the little child forementioned. Her name is Phebe Bartlet, daughter of William Bartlet. I shall give the account as I took it from the mouths of her parents, whose veracity, none that knows them doubt of.

She was born in March, in the year 1731. About the latter end of April, or beginning of May, 1735, she was greatly affected by the talk of her brother, who had been hopefully converted a little before, at about eleven years of age, and then seriously talked to her about the great things of religion. Her parents did not know of it at that time, and were not wont, in the counsels they gave to their children, particularly to direct themselves to her, by reason of her being so young, and, as they supposed her not capable of understanding; but after her brother had talked to her, they observed her very earnestly to listen to the advice they gave to the other children, and she was observed very constantly to retire, several times in a day, as was concluded, for secret prayer, and grew more and more engaged in religion, and was more frequent in her closet, till at last she was wont to visit it five or six times in a day, and was so engaged in it, that nothing would, at any time divert her from her stated closet exercises. Her mother often observed and watched her, when such things occurred, as she thought most likely to divert her, either by putting it out of her thoughts, or otherwise engaging her inclinations, but never could observe her to fail. She mentioned some very remarkable instances.

She once, of her own accord, spake of her unsuccessfulness, in that she could not find God, or to that purpose. But on Thursday, the last of July, about the middle of the day, the child being in the closet, where it used to retire, its mother heard it speaking aloud, which was unusual, and never had been observed before; and her voice seemed to be as of one exceeding importunate and engaged, but her mother could distinctly hear only these words, (spoken in her childish manner, but seemed to be spoken with extraordinary earnestness, and out of distress of soul) Pray BLESSED LORD, give me salvation! I PRAY, BEG, pardon all my sins! When the child had done prayer, she came out of the closet, and came and sat down by her mother, and cried out aloud. Her mother very earnestly asked her several times, what the matter was, before she would make any answer, but she continued exceedingly crying, and wreathing her body to and fro, like one in anguish of spirit. Her mother then asked her whether she was afraid that God would not give her salvation. She then answered yes, I am afraid I shall go to hell! Her mother than endeavored to quiet her, and told her she would not have her cry . . . she must be a good girl, and pray every day, and she hoped God would give her salvation. But this did not quiet her at all . . . but she continued thus earnestly crying and taking on for some time, till at length she suddenly ceased crying and began to smile, and presently said with a smiling countenance . . . Mother, the kingdom of heaven is come to me! Her mother was surprised at the sudden alteration, and at the speech, and knew not what to make of it, but at first said nothing to her. The child presently spake again, and said, there is another come to me, and there is another . . . there is three; and being asked what she meant, she answered . . . One is, thy will be done, and there is another . . . enjoy him forever; by which it seems that when the child said there is three come to me, she meant three passages of its catechism that came to her mind.

After the child had said this, she retired again into her closet; and her mother went over to her brother's, who was next neighbor; and when she came back, the child being come out of the closet, meets her mother with this cheerful speech . . . I can find God now! Referring to what she had before complained of, that she could not find God. Then the child spoke again, and said . . . I love God! Her mother asked her how well she loved God, whether she loved God better than her father and mother, she said, yes. Then she asked her whether she loved God better than her little sister Rachel, she answered yes, better than any thing! Then her eldest sister, referring to her saying she could find God now, asked her where she could find God; she answered, in heaven: Why, said she, have you been in heaven? No, said the child. By this it seems not to have been any imagination of any thing seen with bodily eyes that she called God, when she said I can find God now. Her mother asked her whether she was afraid of going to hell, and that had made her cry. She answered, yes, I was; but now I shall not. Her mother asked her whether she thought that God had given her salvation; she answered yes. Her mother asked her, when; she answered, to day. She appeared all that afternoon exceeding cheerful and joyful. One of the neighbors asked her how she felt herself? She answered, I feel better than I did. The neighbor asked her what made her feel better; she answered, God makes me. That evening as she lay a bed, she called one of her little cousins to her, that was present in the room, as having something to say to him; and when he came, she told him that heaven was better than earth. The next day being Friday, her mother asking her her catechism, asked her what God made her for; she answered, to serve him; and added, every body should serve God, and get an interest in Christ. . . .

From this time there has appeared a very remarkable abiding change in the child: She has been very strict upon the Sabbath, and seems to long for the sabbath day before it comes, and will often in the week time be inquiring how long it is to the sabbath day, and must have the days particularly counted over that are between, before she will be contented. And she seems to love God's house . . . is very eager to go thither. Her mother once asked her why she had such a mind to go? Whether it was not to see the fine folks? She said no, it was to hear Mr. Edwards preach.

When she is in the place of worship, she is very far from spending her time there as children at her age usually do, but appears with an attention that is very extraordinary for such a child. She also appears, very desirous at all opportunities, to go to private religious meetings, and is very still and attentive at home, in prayer time, and has appeared affected in time of family prayer. She seems to delight much in hearing religious conversation. When I once was there with some others that were strangers, and talked to her something of religion, she seemed more than ordinarily attentive; and when we were gone, she looked out very wistly after us, and said . . . I wish they would come again! Her mother asked her why: Said she, I love to hear them talk! . . .

At some time about the middle of winter, very late in the night, when all were in bed, her mother perceived that she was awake, and heard her as though she was weeping. She called to her, and asked her what was the matter. She answered with a low voice, so that her mother could not hear what she said; but thinking it might be occasioned by some spiritual affection, said no more to her; but perceived her to lie awake, and to continue in the same frame for a considerable time. The next morning she asked her whether she did not cry the last night: The child answered yes, I did cry a little, for I was thinking about God and Christ, and they loved me. Her mother asked her, whether to think of God and Christ's loving her made her cry: She answered yes, it does sometimes. . . .

She has discovered an uncommon degree of a spirit of charity, particularly on the following occasion: A poor man that lives in the woods, had lately lost a cow that the family much depended on, and being at the house, he was relating his misfortune, and telling of the straits and difficulties they were reduced to by it. She took much notice of it, and it wrought exceedingly on her compassions; and after she had attentively heard him a while, she went away to her father, who was in the shop, and intreated him to give that man a cow; and told him that the poor man had no cow! That the hunters or something else had killed his cow! And intreated him to give him one of theirs. Her father told her that they could not spare one. Then she intreated him to let him and his family come and live at his house; and had much talk of the same nature, whereby she manifested bowels of compassion to the poor.

She has manifested great love to her minister; particularly when I returned from my long journey for my health, the last fall, when she heard of it, she appeared very joyful at the news, and told the children of it with an elevated voice, as the most joyful tidings, repeating it over and over, Mr. Edwards is come home! Mr. Edwards is come home! She still continues very constant in secret prayer, so far as can be observed, (for she seems to have no desire that others should observe her when she retires, but seems to be a child of a reserved temper) and every night before she goes to bed will say her catechism, and will by no means miss of it: She never forgot it but once, and then after she was a bed, thought of it and cried out in tears . . . I have not said my catechism! And would not be quieted till her mother asked her the catechism as she lay in bed. She sometimes appears to be in doubt about the condition of her soul, and when asked whether she thinks that she is prepared for death, speaks something doubtfully about it: At other times seems to have no doubt, but when asked, replies yes, without hesitation.

A WITCH STORY OF OLDEN TIME

FRANCIS CHASE

———◆•◆———

There were no more hangings of witches after 1692, but witches in New England throve still, as will be seen from the following incident from Francis Chase's Gathered Sketches of New Hampshire and Vermont, *published at Claremont, New Hampshire, in 1856.*

It is sometimes curious to recall to mind stories which were believed and currently reported a hundred and more years ago by the sturdy founders of our nation, who, though men fit to grapple with all earthly dangers, to fight the bloody Indians, or the wild beasts of the forest, were, notwithstanding, affected with many little weaknesses. Among these may be mentioned particularly a fear of the supernatural, to which agency they ascribed every strange or unusual occurrence.

The following incident was related to the writer by a descendant of the principal actor in the affair.

About the year 1740, a certain man by the name of Jones built a house for himself and family in a clearing he had cultivated in the middle of the State of New Hampshire. The family having moved into the house, a single week sufficed to prove that the house was haunted. Strange noises were heard throughout the house, and whenever any one dared to open his eyes at the "still and witching hour of midnight," startling and inexplicable sights were seen. The family naturally became much alarmed, and dared not remain longer in the house. These facts, being noised abroad, excited a great deal of remark and wonderment. Some proposed to have the spirits exorcised; but a man named Turner finally offered his services to quell the disturbance, and clear the house of its ghastly visitants. He declared that he cared for nothing earthly or unearthly; so, both for the purpose of proving his bravery and of ascertaining the cause of the disturbance, it was determined that he should sleep in the house, and see the matter through.

The family of Mr. Jones departed on a visit to their friends, and in came Turner to sleep as agreed. The house was of one story, consisting of a kitchen, sitting room, and bed room on the ground floor, and an unfurnished loft above, reached by a ladder. On the night in question, Turner, having replenished the fire in the enormous fireplace—one of those comfortable fireplaces which an old-fashioned kitchen always contained, and which occupied nearly the whole of one side of the room—Turner, I say, having rolled on some logs, sat a while in the chimney corner, his elbows resting on his knees, as he gazed at the burning brands. Tongues of flame leaped from the smoking logs, and whirled away up the chimney; and their roaring, as they disappeared, seemed changed to unearthly tones— now soft and musical, now hoarse and low, like distant thunder. The roaring of the wind among the pines near by mingled with that of the fire, and increased the excitement of Turner's imagination. Strange shapes appeared to rise from the flames, and nod and brandish their arms around, then sink, only to be succeeded by others still more fearful. The fitful gleams cast a ghastly light over the remoter parts of the room. The shadows on the wall joined hands, and moved around in solemn silence.

Turner sat in his lonely revery until the sticks he had thrown upon the fire were nearly consumed, and the flames were just dying away; then, rousing up, he bethought himself of his old reputation for courage. Rather than be exposed to the sneers of his neighbors, he was ready to meet ten thousand ghosts. He threw on some fresh fuel, and went to bed.

The bedroom opened immediately out of the kitchen, where he had been sitting. Leaving the door open, he lay down to sleep, and remained undisturbed till about midnight, when a slight noise caused him to open his eyes. Looking through the open door into the kitchen, he beheld, with momentary horror, a cat sitting on the hearth and gazing direfully at him with eyes like two balls of fire, as large as a man's fist. Turner was really a brave man. He quickly expelled from his bosom the first trace of terror, and prepared as quickly to expel his unwelcome guest.

Creeping carefully from the bed to the fireplace,—the cat turning all the while so as to face him,—he snatched a huge fire shovel, with a handle four feet in length, and aiming a blow at the horrid beast before him, struck it with force sufficient to kill any thing of earthly mould. Strange to say, however, the shovel rebounded from the cat in a wonderful manner, almost flying from Turner's hands. It was like beating a large mass of India rubber. Nothing daunted, he laid on still harder, until by dint of oft-repeated blows the monster was pushed near the outer door, when one more tremendous stroke sent the animal straight through the middle of the oaken planks, which closed up as before. Turner instantly sprang to the latch and opened the door; but, wonderful to relate, nothing was in sight. He looked to the right and he looked to the left; but nothing could be seen or heard save the tall pine trees waving and roaring in the stormy blast.

Going to the barn before breakfast, to attend to the stock of the farm, he was surprised to find that a promising calf was missing. The barn was constructed tight and secure, and all the doors were closed. No mode of egress could be discovered. However, as a forlorn hope, he searched the pasture near by, where he soon heard the faint bleating of a calf. He followed the sound, and was led to a log, to all appearance sound and solid. This puzzled him; but he quickly brought an axe and wedges, and with their aid the log was forced to reveal its secrets. The calf was found nicely packed in a cavity the size of its body. Out it jumped, glad to be released from captivity. On a minute examination, Turner discovered a knot hole in the side of the barn, lined with hair, through which it was evident to all the neighbors—who came in crowds to examine the place— that the animal was drawn. We may remark that the unfortunate calf never thrived afterwards, but died soon after, in great pain.

But we have not finished our story yet. In the course of the forenoon, having occasion to go to mill, about five miles distant, Turner set off with horse and sleigh. When he had passed about half this distance, he reached the house of a neighbor, whom he saw standing in the door. The man begged Turner to step in and see his grandmother, who, he said, was taken suddenly ill in the night. On going in, what was his amazement to find the old lady black and blue from head to foot, as if severely bruised in some unusual manner.

The mystery was here solved. No doubt the old woman was the witch who abstracted the calf, and shut it up by her wonderful art in the log. No doubt it was she also who, in the form of a cat, disturbed the house of Mr. Jones, and was driven out by Turner with such vigor.

The old woman died the same day. After this night we may conclude nothing ever again disturbed the haunted house.

THE BALLAD OF THE FRENCH FLEET

HENRY WADSWORTH LONGFELLOW

———◆•◆———

Henry Wadsworth Longfellow (1807–1882), for all that his verses jingle, was a great poet, if greatness includes the power of recapturing the spirit of one's subject. "The Ballad of the French Fleet," which follows, tells the

story of the armada sent in 1746 by Louis XV to avenge the loss of Louis-
burg, Cape Breton Island, to the New Englanders under Pepperell. Bos-
ton was totally unprepared for the attack and her salvation was, seemingly,
a miracle.

My father, who was—perhaps because a minister's son—slightly anti-
clerical, used to say that the clergyman-narrator's impassioned prayer was
typical of the ecclesiastical mentality: "Lord, we would not advise; *but if,*
in thy Providence, a tempest should *arise . . . we should be satisfied."*

There is an old legend that if, on a clear day off Cape Sable, you look
down into smooth waters, you may see the wrecks of the French fleet ly-
ing on the bottom.

> A fleet with flags arrayed
>   Sailed from the port of Brest,
> And the Admiral's ship displayed
>   The signal: "Steer southwest."
> For this Admiral D'Anville
>   Had sworn by cross and crown
> To ravage with fire and steel
>   Our helpless Boston Town.
>
> There were rumors in the street,
>   In the houses there was fear
> Of the coming of the fleet,
>   And the danger hovering near.
> And while from mouth to mouth
>   Spread the tidings of dismay,
> I stood in the Old South,
>   Saying humbly: "Let us pray!
>
> "O Lord! we would not advise;
>   But if in thy Providence
> A tempest should arise
>   To drive the French Fleet hence,
> And scatter it far and wide,
>   Or sink it in the sea,
> We should be satisfied,
>   And thine the glory be."
>
> This was the prayer I made,
>   For my soul was all on flame,
> And even as I prayed
>   The answering tempest came;

It came with a mighty power,
　　Shaking the windows and walls,
And tolling the bell in the tower,
　　As it tolls at funerals.

The lightning suddenly
　　Unsheathed its flaming sword,
And I cried: "Stand still, and see
　　The salvation of the Lord!"
The heavens were black with cloud,
　　The sea was white with hail,
And evermore fierce and loud
　　Blew the October gale.

The fleet it overtook,
　　And the broad sails in the van
Like the tents of Cushan shook,
　　Or the curtains of Midian.
Down on the reeling decks
　　Crashed the o'erwhelming seas;
Ah, never were there wrecks
　　So pitiful as these!

Like a potter's vessel broke
　　The great ships of the line;
They were carried away as a smoke,
　　Or sank like lead in the brine.
O Lord! before thy path
　　They vanished and ceased to be,
When thou didst walk in wrath
　　With thine horses through the sea!

ON THE RIGHTEOUSNESS
OF REBELLION

JONATHAN MAYHEW

———◆•◆———

*Jonathan Mayhew (1720–1766), a friend of John and Sam Adams, James
Otis, and the other liberal leaders of his day, was author in 1750 of the
following discourse. It was one of the earliest important documents to*

justify popular disobedience when civil commands went contrary to divine ordinance.

Most of such antidivine commands seemed to concern taxation. By the close of the French and Indian War, a considerable military establishment was considered necessary on the American continent, and taxation required to support it. Landowners in England, by 1763, were taxed at a rate of 20 percent; it was thought not unreasonable that Americans should be, too. The Sugar Act of 1764 and the Stamp Act of 1765 were introduced to raise the necessary funds. But Americans had become accustomed to smuggling and otherwise evading customs; with the Sugar Act the issue of taxation without representation began to rear its head. Wrote James Otis: "One single Act of Parliament has set people a-thinking in six months more than they had done in their whole lives before." One reaction to the Stamp Act of 1765 was the calling of a colonial Congress in New York to consider the menace, which may be regarded as the first move toward revolution.

A DISCOURSE CONCERNING UNLIMITED SUBMISSION AND NON-RESISTANCE TO THE HIGHER POWERS. 1750

IF we calmly consider the nature of the thing itself, nothing can well be imagined more directly contrary to common sense than to suppose that millions of people should be subjected to the arbitrary, precarious pleasure of one single man,—who has naturally no superiority over them in point of authority,—so that their estates, and everything that is valuable in life, and even their lives also, shall be absolutely at his disposal, if he happens to be wanton and capricious enough to demand them. What unprejudiced man can think that God made all to be thus subservient to the lawless pleasure and frenzy of one, so that it shall always be a sin to resist him? Nothing but the most plain and express revelation from heaven could make a sober, impartial man believe such a monstrous, unaccountable doctrine; and, indeed, the thing itself appears so shocking, so out of all proportion, that it may be questioned whether all the miracles that ever were wrought could make it credible that this doctrine really came from God. . . .

We may very safely assert these two things in general, without undermining government: One is, that no civil rulers are to be obeyed when they enjoin things that are inconsistent with the commands of God. All such disobedience is lawful and glorious; particularly if persons refuse to comply with any legal establishment of religion, because it is a gross perversion and corruption—as to doctrine, worship, and discipline—of a pure and divine religion, brought from heaven to earth by the Son of

God,—the only King and Head of the Christian Church,—and propagated through the world by his inspired apostles. All commands running counter to the declared will of the Supreme Legislator of heaven and earth are null and void, and therefore disobedience to them is a duty, not a crime. Another thing that may be asserted with equal truth and safety is, that no government is to be submitted to at the expense of that which is the sole end of all government—the common good and safety of society. Because to submit in this case, if it should ever happen, would evidently be to set up the means as more valuable and above the end, than which there cannot be a great solecism and contradiction. The only reason of the institution of civil government, and the only rational ground of submission to it, is the common safety and utility. . . .

Whoever considers the nature of civil government, must indeed be sensible that a great degree of implicit confidence must unavoidably be placed in those that bear rule: this is implied in the very notion of authority's being originally a trust committed by the people to those who are vested with it,—as all just and righteous authority is. All besides is mere lawless force and usurpation; neither God nor nature having given any man a right of dominion over any society independently of that society's approbation and consent to be governed by him. Now, as all men are fallible, it cannot be supposed that the public affairs of any state should be always administered in the best manner possible, even by persons of the greatest wisdom and integrity. . . . But it is equally evident, upon the other hand, that those in authority may abuse their trust and power to such a degree, that neither the law of reason nor of religion requires that any obedience or submission should be paid to them; but, on the contrary, that they should be totally discarded, and the authority which they were before vested with transferred to others, who may exercise it more to those good purposes for which it is given. Nor is this principle, that resistance to the higher powers is in some extraordinary cases justifiable, so liable to abuse as many persons seem to apprehend it. For, although there will be always some petulant, querulous men in every state,—men of factious, turbulent, and carping dispositions, glad to lay hold of any trifle to justify and legitimate their caballing against their rulers, and other seditious practices,—yet there are, comparatively speaking, but few men of this contemptible character. It does not appear but that mankind in general have a disposition to be as submissive and passive and tame under government as they ought to be. Witness a great, if not the greatest, part of the known world, who are now groaning, but not murmuring, under the heavy yoke of tyranny! While those who govern do it with any tolerable degree of moderation and justice, and in any good measure act up to their office and character by being public benefactors, the people will generally be easy and peaceable, and be rather inclined to flatter and adore than to insult and resist them. Nor was there ever any general complaint against any administration, which lasted long, but what there was good reason for. Till people find themselves greatly abused and oppressed by their governors, they are not apt to complain; and whenever they do, in fact, find themselves thus abused and oppressed, they must be stupid not to complain. To say that subjects in general are not proper judges when their governors oppress them and play the tyrant, and when they defend their rights, administer justice impartially, and promote the public welfare, is as great treason as ever man uttered. 'Tis treason, not against one single man, but the state—against the whole body politic; 'tis treason against mankind, 'tis treason against common sense, 'tis treason against God. And this impious principle lays the foundation for justifying all the tyranny and oppression that ever any prince was guilty of. The people know for what end they set up and maintain their governors, and they are the proper judges when they execute their trust as they ought to do it;—when their prince exercises an equitable and paternal authority over them; when from a prince and common father he exalts himself into a tyrant; when from subjects and children he degrades them into the classes of slaves, plunders them, makes them his prey, and unnaturally sports himself with their lives and fortunes.

CONSIDERATIONS ON BEHALF OF THE COLONISTS

JAMES OTIS

————◆◆————

Between the years 1763 and 1783 no less than two thousand political pamphlets were published in America. Very gradually their tenor tended toward war with England. Of the great pamphleteers, like Adams and Joseph Warren, none was more energetic and none seems as picturesque as James Otis of Boston—"their patriot, Jimmy Otis." His grave, which can be spied by any passer-by today in the Old Granary Burying Ground behind Park Street Church in Boston, is an oddly moving momento of this lively, vocal agitator for "natural law." Born in 1725, he died, after years of being half off his head, by being struck by a bolt of lightning in 1783.

The following pamphlet was written in the form of a "Letter to a Noble Lord," in rebuttal of the English writer Soame Jenyns. It stresses the profound dependence of the colonies on Britain—although it has plenty of bite and zing in it too. Something I never realized about American history as it was taught to me as a child, is that even up to July 4, 1776, the American colonies were fighting, not for independence, but for a free status in the British Empire.

LETTER TO A NOBLE LORD

MY LORD,

I have read the *opusculum* of the celebrated Mr. J———s, called "Objections to the Taxation of the Colonies by the Legislature of Great Britain briefly considered." In obedience to your Lordship's commands, I have thrown a few thoughts on paper; all, indeed, that I have patience on this melancholy occasion to collect. The gentleman thinks it "absurd and insolent" to question the expediency and utility of a public measure. He seems to be an utter enemy to the freedom of inquiry after truth, justice, and equity. He is not only a zealous advocate for pusillanimous and passive obedience, but for the most implicit faith in the dictatorial mandates of power. . . .

No good reason can, however, be given in any country why every man of a sound mind should not have his vote in the election of a representative. If a man has but little property to protect and defend, yet his life and liberty are things of some importance. Mr. J———s argues only from the vile abuses of power, to the continuance and increase of such abuses. This, it must be confessed, is the common logic of modern politicians and vote-sellers. To what purpose is it to ring everlasting changes to the colonists on the cases of Manchester, Birmingham, and Sheffield, which return no members? If those, now so considerable, places are not represented, they ought to be. Besides, the counties in which those respectable abodes of tinkers, tinmen, and pedlers lie, return members; so do all the neighboring cities and boroughs. In the choice of the former, if they have no vote, they must naturally and necessarily have a great influence. I believe every gentleman of a landed estate near a flourishing manufactory will be careful enough of its interests. Though the great India company, as such, returns no members, yet many of the company are returned, and their interests have been ever very carefully attended to. . . .

Should the British empire one day be extended round the whole world, would it be reasonable that all mankind should have their concerns managed by the electors of Old Sarum and the "occupants of the Cornish barns and alehouses" we sometimes read of? We, who are in the colonies, are by common law, and by act of parliament, declared entitled to all the privileges of the subjects within the realm. Yet we are heavily taxed, without being, in fact, represented. In all trials here relating to the revenue, the admiralty courts have jurisdiction given them, and the subject may, at the pleasure of the informer, be deprived of a trial by his peers. To do as one would be done by is a divine rule. Remember, Britons, when you shall be taxed without your consent, and tried without a Jury, and have an army quartered in private families, you will have little to hope or to fear! But I must not lose sight of any man who sagaciously asks "if the colonists are Englishmen when they solicit protection, but not Englishmen when taxes are required to enable this country to protect them?" I ask, in my turn: When did the colonies solicit protection? They have had no occasion to solicit for protection since the happy accession of our gracious sovereign's illustrious family to the British diadem. His majesty, the father of all his people, protects all his loyal subjects, of every complexion and language, without any particular solicitation. But before the ever-memorable Revolution, the northern colonists were so far from receiving protection from Britain that everything was done, from the throne to the footstool, to cramp, betray, and ruin them; yet against the combined power of France, Indian savages, and the corrupt administration of those times, they carried on their settlements, and under a mild government, for these eighty years past, have made them the wonder and envy of the world. . . .

But Mr. J———s will scribble about *"our American colonies."* Whose colonies can the creature mean? The ministers' colonies? No, surely. Whose then; his own? I never heard he had any colonies. . . . He must mean his majesty's American colonies. His majesty's colonies they are, and I hope and trust ever will be, and that the true native inhabitants, as they ever have been, will continue to be his majesty's most dutiful and loyal subjects. Every garretteer, from the environs of Grub street to the purlieus of St. James's, has lately talked of *his* and *my* and *our* colonies, and of the *rascally colonists,* and of *yoking* and *curbing* the *cattle,* as they are by some politely called, at "this present now and very nascent crisis." I cannot see why the American peasants may not with as much propriety speak of their cities of London and Westminster, of their Isles of Britain, Ireland, Jersey, Guernsey, Sark, and the Orcades, and of the "rivulets and runlets thereof," and consider them all but as appendages to their sheep-cots and goose-pens. But land is land, and men should be men. The property of the farmer, God hath given to the possessor. These are either *sui juris,* or slaves and vassals; there neither is nor can be any medium. . . .

The national debt is confessed on all hands to be a terrible evil, and may, in time, ruin the state. But it should be remembered that the colonists never occasioned its increase, nor ever reaped any of the sweet fruits of involving the finest kingdom in the world in the sad calamity of an enormous, overgrown mortgage, to state and stockjobbers. No places, nor pensions, of thousands and tens of thousands sterling have been laid out to purchase the votes and influence of the colonists. They have gone on with their settlements in spite of the most horrid difficulties and dangers; they have ever supported, to the utmost of their ability, his majesty's provincial government over them; and, I believe, are to a man, and ever will be, ready to make grants for so valuable a purpose. But we cannot see the equity of our being obliged to pay off a score that has been much enhanced by bribes and pensions to keep those to their duty who ought to have been bound by honor and conscience. We have ever been from principle attached to his majesty and his illustrious house. We never asked any pay; the heartfelt satisfaction of having served our King and country has been always enough for us. I cannot see why it would not be well enough to go a-nabob-hunting on this occasion. Why should not the great Mogul be obliged to contribute toward, if not to pay, the national debt, as some have proposed? He is a pagan, an East Indian, and of a dark complexion, which are full as good reasons for laying him under contribution as any I have found abroad in the pamphlets and coffee-house conferences for taxing the colonists. . . .

The gentleman has made himself quite merry with the modest proposal some have made, though I find it generally much disliked in the colonies, and thought impracticable, namely, an American representation in parliament. But, if he is now sober, I would humbly ask him if there be, really and naturally, any greater absurdity in this plan than in a Welsh and Scotch representation? I would by no means, at any time, be understood to intend by an American representation the return of half a score ignorant, worthless, persons, who, like some colony agents, might be induced to sell their country and their God for a golden calf. An American representation, in my sense of the terms, and as I ever used them, implies a thorough beneficial union of these colonies to the realm, or mother country, so that all the parts of the empire may be compacted and consolidated, and the constitution flourish with new vigor, and the national strength, power, and importance shine with far greater splendor than ever yet hath been seen by the sons of men. An American representation implies every real advantage to the subject abroad as well as at home. . . .

It may perhaps sound strangely to some, but it is in my most humble opinion as good law, and as good sense too, to affirm that all the plebeians of Great Britain are in fact, or virtually, represented in the assembly of the Tuskaroras as that all the colonists are in fact or virtually represented in the honorable House of Commons of Great Britain, separately considered as one branch of the supreme and universal legislature of the whole empire. These considerations, I hope, will in due time have weight enough to induce your Lordship to use your great influence for the repeal of the Stamp Act.

JOHN ADAMS' GRADUATION FROM HARVARD

CATHERINE DRINKER BOWEN

———◆◆◆———

A commencement at Harvard is still a glad and glorious occasion. The picture that follows of the graduation of young John Adams (1735–1826), from Catherine Drinker Bowen's John Adams and the American Revolution, *shows that in 1755 it was even gladder, and far more uproarious. The entire Adams connection arriving on the great day displayed the pride and satisfaction that the whole of New England took in Harvard.*

The mention, in the Bowen account, of an Election Day sermon in Boston requires comment. The first charter of Massachusetts appointed the "last Wednesday in Easter term yearly" as the day "the Governor, deputy governor . . . and all other officers shall be in the General Court duly chosen." The same election date was retained after the Revolution when, in 1779, the constitution of the state was drawn up. On that day the legislature always met and, under escort of the governor's guard, marched to the Old South Meeting-House to hear an election sermon.

The occasion sounds staid, and it may have been in the beginning, but by the end of the century the day was one of festivity, when hucksters of every kind set up tents on both sides of Tremont Street mall. To prepare for these wonders, every child in Boston expected " 'Lection money." Family retainers expected it as well. There were families of black children who turned up for a tip only on that day. Ninepence was the traditional 'Lection money given—ninepence of the old Massachusetts standard, that is, which based itself on the Spanish dollar. (The "pieces of eight" in Treasure Island *were dollar pieces, amounting to eight American ninepences.)*

COMMENCEMENT week approached, the days rushed forward. Senior recitations were finished; John was entitled now to the baccalaureate "Sir." Nobody used it except one or two Freshmen. The word, when it came, made John smile. He wished mightily that Treadwell had heard the Freshman from Barnstable address him as "Sir Adams." But Treadwell was gone, graduated last year and far away.

The final examinations were oral and not very difficult. John actually enjoyed himself. Professor Wigglesworth especially was entirely informal, kept John overtime and remarked, with his hand to his ear in the old gesture John knew so well, that it was a relief to question someone with a good loud answering voice. As Commencement approached, Mrs. Adams showed much anxiety about John's clothes, and was highly relieved when he told her a new law had been passed by the Harvard Corporation, forbidding gold-laced coats or brocaded vests for Seniors. All his mother need do, said John, was mend the tear in his scholar's gown and supply a clean shirt. It was far more important to see that Peter and Elihu appeared in something respectable. And would somebody, John added pleadingly, please take Mr. Adams's wig to the barber before July 16? The hair hung down in strings; there was a worn patch at the back where he leaned his head against the kitchen settle. . . .

Mr. Adams, overhearing this exordium, remarked that Sir Adams need have no fear. His family would appear at Commencement strong in numbers and strong in finery; Mrs. Adams had been working over it for months. Uncle Joseph Adams was coming from Newington, New Hampshire. The Braintree uncles were to appear in force, including Ebenezer, who since Briant's death had shown a complete change of heart and desired greatly to be reinstated in the family affections. Ebenezer had gone to Boston and ordered a new hat for Commencement, three-cornered, with a bright purple cockade that looked, said Mr. Adams, like mourning for an emperor. When Mr. Adams asked what the cockade was for, Ebenezer replied that he didn't know, but he thought Johnny deserved it.

Mr. Marsh of course was coming, together with his two sisters and his mother. The old lady was tremendously taken up with the affair, said Mr. Adams. She had an ancient green satin gown and bonnet for the occasion. One day she had called him in to look at it, taken the bonnet from a box and put it on. It was stupendous. More like a tent than a lady's headdress, Mr. Adams added, what with ribbons and streamers and flaps and contraptions. He pitied the man that sat behind it. . . . Or did they seat ladies in the gallery at First Church?—he asked hopefully of John. . . . Anyway, old Mrs. Marsh had got into a habit lately of talking to herself when excited, letting out great deep-chested groans. He had heard her do it in Sabbath Meeting. So had the boys here.

"If she does it at Commencement," young Elihu broke in, "if she grunts out while John is making his Latin responses, Peter and I have a plan. We are going to cough very loud, both together, and drown her out. . . . Like this!" Elihu emitted a strangled roar.

John looked imploringly at his mother. Mrs. Adams, tossing her head, said she never heard such nonsense. Besides, she knew how to deal with old Madam Marsh. She would sit next to her, hold a hand over her mouth if necessary. "What bothers me," Mrs. Adams finished, suddenly serious, "is what is to become of you, John, after Commencement. Are you still thinking of teaching school for a year, before taking orders as a minister? And have you any immediate prospects of a place?"

John's heart sank. *What was he to do when he got out of college?* It was the question he dreaded above all questions. He had not the slightest idea what he was to do. He knew only that he must earn his living. He could not for another week, another day, remain dependent upon his family. The entire tribe of Adamses looked to him to distinguish himself, prove the worth of this long, expensive Harvard investment. When Mrs. Adams spoke, they all gazed at John expectantly. Peter and Elihu looked actually respectful.

"I have received no direct offers," John replied. In spite of himself he blushed, having received no offers direct or indirect. "But I hear they are looking for a schoolmaster in Worcester. The Reverend Thaddeus Maccarty of that town preached the Election Sermon in Boston this June. He is in Cambridge, looking over prospects."

Mr. Adams, whose good-natured pride in his son had never permitted him to share his wife's worries as to John's future, broke in delightedly at the mention of Maccarty's sermon. He had read part of it, he said, in the newspaper. *Scatter thou the People that delight in War. . . .* Meaning, of course, the French. . . . "Now *I*," said Mr. Adams, "fear greatly that it will be the *English* who are scattered, out on the *Ohio.*"

Mrs. Adams gave an exclamation of impatience and moved away. Why could not men keep to the matter in hand? Why must they be always turning the talk to war or politics?

A day later, John returned to College.

Shortly before Commencement, an eloquent letter appeared in the Boston *Gazette*, addressed to the printers and signed with the initials of an unidentified citizen. It was dated July 14, 1755:

MESSIEURS EDES AND GILL,

There is no one of our Red Letter Days that I spend with so great Satisfaction, as that at the Commencement in Cambridge. To see our Youth bringing up to learning, to meet with an old Acquaintance and Friend—to see the universal Joy that is in every Countenance—to take a Pipe in the Cool of the Day—and to ride to the Ferry in a *Charlestown Hack*, is what strikes me with peculiar Pleasure.

But! When I come to the Ferry, the crowded Boats make me uneasy, and solicitous for their safe Passage. The Disorder at the Ferry-Wayes, more especiallay on the Boston side, is shocking. The last Commencement, I landed between 7 and 8 o'clock, but before I could get up on the Wayes (which was so crowded as to render the passing unsafe) two Gentlemen's Servants were thrown over, and not less than 20 of our poor Slaves (Male and Female) were thus injuriously served that Evening. The most astonishing Cursing and Swearing was continually sounding in my Ears. Women as they left the Boat, were indecently talk'd to, and some of them were immodestly handled.

That Part of the Town was in the utmost Disorder, and this effected by a Rabble that consisted of at least 200. Such Disorder! Such Confusion! is at no other Time to be perceived in the Town; No! not on Pope night.

The worthy Gentlemen, whose peculiar Business it is, to preserve Peace and good Order in the Town, will, I hope, bestir themselves; and some of them find their personal Attendance at the Ferry. For notwithstanding the two Constables that placed themselves there, the last Year, all this Confusion happened! I also hope they will not be offended at this modest Hint, for I have only in view, that we may in this particular be reformed.

Yours,

W.K.

The "modest Hint" was wholly futile; the gentleman might have spared himself the pains. Disorder was as much a part of Commencement as the tents on Cambridge Common, the sawdust in the grass, the broken jugs that lay behind the hedges next day. The Harvard Corporation did its best. Commencement came always on the second Wednesday in July. The Corporation had tried to transfer it to Friday, so people would go home and sober up for Sunday instead of prancing all over Cambridge for three frolicsome, fearsome days. But Massachusetts found this edict intolerable and said so in a loud concerted shout. The Corporation sighed, shrugged, and went back to glorious and traditional Wednesday.

The whole of Cambridge was transformed into one vast delightful pleasance, with booths, tents, acrobats, jugglers, drinking, fighting, dancing, love-making and general joy. Long before John Adams's time, poets had celebrated it:

> Each successive Day
>> *Venus* and *Bacchus* bear alternate sway.
> The raking Tribe their lawless Games repeat,
>> Nor can three Days their Baccanals compleat. . . .
> Thus the loose Croud forbidden Pleasures seek,
>> Drink HARVARD dry, and so conclude the Week.

The crowd began drifting into town on Monday. . . . There were Indians with bows and arrows to shoot for coins; Negroes and beggars; children in hordes, scattering across the grass like bits of paper before arriving coaches and horseback riders; merchants and members of the

Governor's Council, splendid in brocades and the gold-laced coats forbidden to Seniors. The roads leading to Cambridge were a cloud of dust, the Charlestown ferrymen at their wit's end with the boats from Boston piled water-deep. People fell in and were fished out, only to be knocked down again at the landing by the crowd. Everybody laughed, joshing the pair of constables on the pier who struggled hopelessly for order.

Visitors from far away lodged at inn or boardinghouse or out under a tree; they slept on three chairs when three chairs were available. They drank ale and rum and flip and negus and Madeira; they made innumerable speeches interlarded with innumerable bad puns. The old boys, wigged, powdered, limping with gout, compared Harvard of their day with Harvard of the moment, to the great disadvantage of the latter, when boys—mere fops it seemed—lacked the virility of their fathers who had rolled cannon balls off the roof of Old Harvard and painted red the face of the clock on Massachusetts Hall.

The college authorities were forever publishing new sets of rules to curb this riot and extravagance. They prohibited plum cake, prohibited treating. Nobody paid the slightest attention. Windows were broken, chairs were broken, heads were broken. Money ran like water from the pockets of rich graduates to whom the Corporation had applied in vain for scholarships or maintenance. In short, a Puritan community, lusty, hard-working, repressed for fifty-one weeks, on the fifty-second simply rolled over Cambridge in a tide of riotous joy.

The Adams family arrived early, coming from Braintree by way of Milton Hill and Roxbury Crossing, avoiding the crowds at the Charlestown Ferry. Dusty, hot and happy, they debouched on the Common, ten or twelve strong, counting the uncles, Joseph and Ebenezer, their wives, sons and daughters. The whole of Braintree seemed to be in Cambridge. The Quincys drove up a little before eleven o'clock, two families of them. The Webbs were there (Cousin Jonathan was to receive his Master's degree), and of course the four Marshes, the younger ladies totally eclipsed by their mother. Mrs. Marsh's green gown swept the earth; she had topped the bonnet with a plume. The effect was breath-taking, prodigious. Mr. Adams conceded he had done her wrong altogether; the old lady looked a very empress. She was in splendid fettle. Mr. Marsh had brought a stool for her; she sat on it outside the church, regally erect, waving gaily to friends and acquaintances.

Uncle Ebenezer came with Mr. Adams. His new cocked hat was too big for him; it kept slipping over his forehead, obscuring his eyebrows. Strangely agitated, talking continually, Ebenezer expressed himself as disapproving this noise and extravagance. All the same, he drank innumerable bumpers, and before nightfall was to be heard singing a song that amazed his brother. Young Peter and Elihu, aged sixteen and fourteen respectively, pleaded to remove their heavy homespun coats, were peremptorily refused, caught sight of the tents, heard the fiddles tuning and forgot instantly that it was hot and their backs itched.

Mrs. Adams wore light gray, her bonnet was lined with pink; she carried a pink silk fan. She looked prim—and very pretty, her sons told her. Mr. Adams was magnificent in a new broadcloth coat, full-skirted, brass-buttoned, which swept back to show his embroidered waistcoat (stitched by Mrs. Adams with infinite pains). His starched shirt frill stuck out, "like a frozen waterfall," he said, complaining that it tickled his chin. All this folderol, he grumbled repeatedly, was too much for a plain farmer like himself. But the family noted, when they reached Cambridge and finally got rid of the horses, that Mr. Adams never walked past a window without glancing in and adjusting his shirt frill with a look of vast satisfaction.

Commencement exercises were scheduled for eleven o'clock, in the old Meeting-house on the Common. They would last four hours or more; after that would come the feasting and festivities. Outside the church a hilarious crowd awaited the arrival of the Governor and his mounted escort; the Cambridge troops were lined up to greet him, with flags and music. Mr. Adams, by arrangement, met Anthony Wibird on the church steps. Wibird was the new Braintree pastor, a Harvard graduate and a friendly young man. He had offered to look after the Adams family and find seats for them. Mrs. Adams, grasping old Mrs. Marsh tightly by an elbow, climbed to the gallery with the ladies. Peter and Elihu squeezed in with their cousin, Nathan Webb (Harvard, '54).

At last the church was filled. The bell in the steeple, which had been ringing for a full ten minutes, suddenly stopped. There was a stir at the door, delighted cheers from the crowd outside. Heads turned as at a wedding, and the procession marched slowly in.

The Seniors came first, two by two in their black gowns. They wore no hats, but one and all were handsomely pig-tailed and powdered. Nathan Webb whispered their names to the Adams boys as the procession moved forward: Cushing and Appleton, leading the march. William Browne next, walking with John Wentworth—David Sewall . . . Tristram Dalton . . . Sam Dana . . . Locke . . . Hemmenway. . . . And toward the end, shorter than his partner, standing very straight, his gown a little open and swinging with his step, his face flushed and solemn, was brother John.

Mrs. Adams in the gallery drew a long breath and clutched the hand of her sister sitting on her left. Old Mrs. Marsh said, "Where is he?" in a loud voice. "*Where? Eh? I don't see Johnny.*" Behind the Seniors marched the Masters of Arts. Next came President Holyoke, tall and imposing, walking by himself. Then Professors Wigglesworth and Winthrop, followed by the four tutors. Last of all, in a blaze of red coats, swords and military boots, walked Governor Shirley with the Lieutenant-Governor and the Royal Council.

The important personages found seats on the platform; President
Holyoke nodded pleasantly to the Seniors below the stage. There were
prayers, a sermon. The first Latin orator walked up the steps, bowed to
the *Honorandi*, the *Venerabilis* and the *Spectatissimi*, and began. Nobody
but the professors understood more than an occasional word, but everyone smiled and nudged his neighbor. As orator succeeded orator, the
whisper, "That's my son!" ran through the Meeting-house like a sigh.
When John Adams mounted the stage the whole Adams family stiffened
to fascinated horror and leaned forward, holding its breath. President
Holyoke, looking genial, rose and addressed him:

"*An libertas politica, in absentia restrictionis, consistat?*"

John bowed. "No, Sir," he replied in Latin. "Political liberty does not
consist in the absence of restrictions. Law is necessary to government."
Holyoke put another question and another; John's voice, answering, was
clear and confident. A dozen Adamses let out their breath like stuck bal-
loons. Mr. Adams, hearing this Latin emerge smooth and easy from his
Johnny's lips in the presence of two governors, His Excellency's Council
and most of the wealth, beauty and ecclesiastical dignity of the Province,
was unable to believe his ears. It was for this he had sold the Stony Acres,
for this he had prayed and worked and waited. In Mr. Adams's eyes the
tears welled, flowed hot and unheeded down his cheeks. Up in the gallery, his wife sobbed happily behind her fan.

John stepped from the platform. Mr. Adams blew his nose, leaned
heavily against the pew back. A tall, dark gentleman in the pew ahead, in
a clerical bib, turned to him and smiled, nodding toward the platform. It
was the Reverend Dr. Maccarty from Worcester, who by order of the
selectmen had been looking for a new schoolteacher, and who had just
decided he had found one.

THE OTHER ADAMS

CATHERINE DRINKER BOWEN

*Another of the great Boston figures of Revolutionary days was Sam Adams
(1722–1803), second cousin of John. The following portrait of him, from
Catherine Drinker Bowen's* John Adams and the American Revolution,
*shows him leading the opposition to the Stamp Act of 1765—the royal
revenue measure which required stamps, on which a tax had been paid,*

to be affixed to all legal documents, commercial papers, pamphlets, newspapers, almanacs, cards, and dice.

WITH a close bond of blood and background—a New England Puritan ancestry—Sam and John Adams were profoundly different in character and outlook. Sam was a town man to his toes, bred by his father to city politics and the manipulation of men to a political end. He had been active on the radical side ever since the day he emerged from Harvard with his dissertation in hand: "Whether it be Lawful to Resist the Supreme Magistrate, if the Commonwealth Cannot Be Otherwise Preserved." At forty-two, he was a pleasant-looking man of slightly above medium height, with light blue eyes and fair complexion, a straight, high-bridged nose and bushy dark eyebrows. He was inveterately and hopelessly untidy about his dress. On his old brown coat the same spot appeared for weeks; his wife complained that if she sewed a button on his sleeve, he plucked it off deliberately before nightfall. When he consented to wear a wig, it looked as if he had slept in it; on warm days he left it off and his straight brown hair, already streaked with gray, was tucked behind his ears. He was never in a hurry, always had time to stop on King Street and hold converse with his friends. Yet his walk was quick and he held himself very straight; all Boston knew his red winter cloak. He had inherited a constitutional tremor of the head and hands; it came with agitation and was somehow shocking in a man whose face seldom betrayed annoyance or anger. When the tremor seized him, Sam was suddenly like an old man.

But in spite of spotted coat and rumpled wig, there was a dignity about Sam Adams. He was poor, with none of the sharp financial acumen traditional with Yankees. (Three times, the sheriff, a Court party man, had put the family estate up for auction. And three times, the town had refused to buy it away from Sam.) When his friends desired to lend him money, they had to approach the subject tactfully; Sam replied cheerfully that he had more than enough for his wants. Widowed in his thirties, he had lately married an agreeable young woman of good family who everyone said would look after him capably. With Surry, a freed slave girl of his mother's, and Queue, the big shaggy dog, Samuel Adams and his bride lived at the South End of Boston in the old residential section down by the docks. The property reached a hundred and fifty feet along the bay front. It had belonged to Sam's father and was flanked, by now, with ropewalks; Sam was in the very midst of his friends. The house itself was rambling and dilapidated; the brown paint peeled off in flakes. There was a long garden full of fruit trees, and a dock and various outbuildings that went with the malt house, now disused and sagging by the roof. Young people liked to go to the Adamses'; they were hospitable, particularly to all such as needed help or shelter.

Not one of the radical leaders, from Otis to Thacher, knew the people as Sam Adams knew them; he was an invaluable ambassador from high to low. From South Battery to Gibbons's shipyard, among the artisans and mechanics, the riggers and carpenters, Sam had a thousand friends, could command a thousand votes. Sam's very shabbiness, his one and only ancient rusty coat, the fact that he never had money in his pocket, were all in his favor. Having no regular employment (Sam had failed at enough business ventures to convince himself and the town that he had better keep his hands out of trade), he was to be found in the mornings sitting on somebody's dock in conversation with the men while they took their eleven o'clock draught of ale. He was a witty talker when he chose to be; laughter followed him on the wharves and in the workmen's taverns. Yet he himself took only an occasional glass of ale and was a strict churchgoer, never missing Sunday meeting, morning or afternoon. His piety was deep and genuine; he was known among the more frivolous as "one of your narrow old Boston Puritans."

Yet somehow, people loved him the better for it; Sam did not ram his piety down other folks' throats. And because he was an essentially serious man, his smile, when it came, carried something flattering. He had a clear, remarkably sweet singing voice and was fond of music; among the workers he had formed a singing society that met regularly under his direction. He belonged to every political club and caucus in town; some of them had indeed been founded by his father.

In the year 1748, Sam Adams, writing to the *Independent Advertiser*, had protested England's part in the peace at Aix-la-Chapelle. Now he wrote for the *Advertiser's* spiritual successor, the Boston *Gazette*. And his output was amazing; he could not invent synonyms fast enough. He was A PURITAN; he was POPULUS, SINCERUS, DETERMINATUS, A BOSTONIAN—or, when he wished to be particularly sarcastic, A TORY. His pieces were instantly recognizable; they had a little turn to them, even at their most venomous, that made people laugh. James Otis himself, whose pen was considered "hasty and rough," took all his writings to Sam Adams before publication. "To *que hew* them," Otis said. "To pour a little oil in them."

Lieutenant Governor Hutchinson had long known that the Adamses, first father then son, were his enemies. At the time of the Land Bank, Hutchinson's policy had ruined Sam's father financially; the son had not forgotten. Sam Adams, moreover, had a natural aversion for men of aristocratic tendency and appearance. Thomas Hutchinson was elegance itself.

But for all Sam's activity, it was not until the Stamp Act threatened that he found real ammunition for his guns. In the spring of 1764, Boston chose him as draftsman for the customary annual Instructions to the town's Representatives in the House. The four men were instructed to oppose the Stamp Tax in every way they could. And—here lay the sting for Hutchinson—they were urged to pass a law unseating any member of House or Council who accepted a post from the crown, also to refuse a salary to any judge who held another post beside his judgeship. Considering that Hutchinson, a member of the Council, was himself both Lieutenant Governor and Chief Justice by crown appointment, considering also that his brothers and cousins occupied like positions, Sam Adams's Instructions were the insult direct. They might as well have named Hutchinson outright and been done with it.

Sam Adams was not a member of the Legislature. Yet his power, indubitably, was growing; it could not be overlooked. In town meeting especially, he ruled supreme. And town meeting was taking on a significance it had not used to possess. A raffishly democratical organization, the Court party called it. At Faneuil Hall on town meeting day, the doorkeeper let men slip in to vote without asking if they had the required twenty pounds sterling behind their names. Court circles no longer dared persuade themselves that Sam Adams's poverty made him negligible politically, although it seemed absurd that men would trust the affairs of government to the hands of a bankrupt! For some eight years, Sam had been constable for Boston—the most popular tax collector the town had ever voted into office. Going from house to house with his worn black collector's pouch hanging from his shoulder, Sam lingered on many an insolvent doorstep to discuss the deplorable state of affairs in the Province since Britain had threatened a stamp tax. Outrageous to the principles of British freedom! Sam said indignantly. He hoped the citizen would use his best efforts to combat the tax when election day came round.

Somehow, when Sam got home, the black pouch weighed no more than when he set out. The city fathers were alarmed. Looking into the public coffers they discovered Samuel Adams was seven thousand pounds in arrears with his returns. He was summoned before town meeting to explain this stunning default, summoned not once but repeatedly. Yet somehow, when the vote was called, Sam was always re-elected. The man seemed to have no pride, his enemies complained. He was willing to serve the town in any capacity—as chimney warden, fire inspector, committeeman for schools and for guarding against the spread of epidemics. For what he did, he expected, apparently, no reward. His very disregard of money held defiance in it, as though the man denied values his betters adored. Against such a creature, what weapons existed? Uneasily, with irritation, the Massachusetts Royal Government eyed this middle-aged insurgent, this maker of trouble—bankrupt, shabby, incorruptible and beloved of thousands.

Such was Mr. Samuel Adams, and such were the parties and factions in Massachusetts at the opening of 1765, that year which was to see John Adams's entrance on the political scene.

THE SNARE BROKEN

JONATHAN MAYHEW

In 1766 the repeal of the Stamp Act occasioned a general feeling of relief and thanksgiving in the colonies, reflected in the following excerpt from Jonathan Mayhew's sermon, "The Snare Broken: A Thanksgiving Discourse, occasioned by the Repeal of the Stamp Act," May 23, 1766.

WE have never known so quick and general a transition from the depth of sorrow to the height of joy, as on this occasion; nor, indeed, so great and universal a flow of either on any other occasion whatever. It is very true, we have heretofore seen times of great adversity. We have known seasons of drought, dearth, and spreading mortal diseases; the pestilence walking in darkness, and the destruction wasting at noonday. We have seen wide devastations made by fire; and amazing tempests, the heavens on flame, the winds and the waves roaring. We have known repeated earthquakes, threatening us with speedy destruction. We have been under great apprehensions by reason of formidable fleets of an enemy on our coasts, menacing fire and sword to all our maritime towns. We have known times when the French and savage armies made terrible havoc on our frontiers, carrying all before them for awhile; when we were not without fear that some capital towns in the colonies would fall into their merciless hands. . . . But never have we known a season of such universal consternation and anxiety among people of all ranks and ages, in these colonies, as was occasioned by that parliamentary procedure which threatened us and our posterity with perpetual bondage and slavery. For they, as we generally suppose, are really slaves to all intents and purposes, who are obliged to labor and toil only for the benefit of others; or, which comes to the same thing, the fruit of whose labor and industry may be lawfully taken from them without their consent, and they justly punished if they refuse to surrender it on demand, or apply it to other purposes than those which their masters, of their mere grace and pleasure, see fit to allow. Nor are there many *American* understandings acute enough to distinguish any material difference between this being done by a *single* person, under the title of absolute monarch, and done by a far-distant legislature, consisting of *many* persons, in which they are not represented; and the members whereof, instead of feeling and sharing equally with them in the burden thus imposed, are eased of their own in proportion to the greatness and weight of it. . . .

The repeal, the repeal, has at once, in good measure, restored things to order, and composed our minds by removing the chief ground of our fears. The course of justice between man and man is no longer obstructed; commerce lifts up her head, adorned with golden tresses, pearls, and precious stones. All things that went on right before are returning gradually to their former course; those that did not we have reason to hope will go on better now; almost every person you meet wears the smiles of contentment and joy; and even our slaves rejoice as though they had received their manumission. Indeed, all lovers of liberty in Europe, in the world, have reason to rejoice; the cause is, in some measure common to them and us. Blessed revolution! glorious change! How great are our obligations for it to the Supreme Governor of the world!

THE BOSTON MASSACRE

THE TOWN OF BOSTON COMMITTEE

———◆•◆———

In my father's study when I was a child there hung a copy of the Paul Revere engraving of the Boston Massacre—so battered that one could not be sure what was damage to the picture and what gunsmoke and confusion in the scene. In any case, it all seemed a fearful outrage—redcoats firing on innocent Boston citizens! Enough to make anybody start a revolution! Even today, reference books on the American Revolution speak of the Boston Massacre as "provoked by British troops."

The fact is, however, that the shoe was on the other foot. A soldier of the British troops quartered on Boston to protect the Commission of Customs did fire first, but only after the most extreme provocation by agitators among the colonials, itching to start a fight. The following "Short Narrative of the horrid Massacre in Boston . . . Printed by order of the Town of Boston, 1770" is an excerpt from the official report of the affair, put together by a committee headed by James Bowdoin and including Joseph Warren. To the everlasting glory of the colony, the British soldiers involved in the Massacre were defended in court by young John Adams and Josiah Quincy.

THERE are depositions in this affair which mention, that several guns were fired at the same time from the Custom-House; before which this shocking scene was exhibited. Into this matter inquisition is now making. —In the mean time it may be proper to insert here the substance of some of those depositions.

Benjamin Frizell, on the evening of the 5th of March, having taken his station near the west corner of the Custom-House in Kingstreet, before and at the time of the soldiers firing their guns, declares (among other things) that the first discharge was only of one gun, the next of two guns, upon which he the deponent thinks he saw a man stumble: the third discharge was of three guns, upon which he thinks he saw two men fall, and immediately after were discharged five guns, two of which were by soldiers on his right hand, *the other three, as appeared to the deponent, were discharged from the balcony, or the chamber window of the* CUSTOM-HOUSE, *the flashes appearing on the left hand, and higher than the right hand flashes appeared to be, and of which the deponent was very sensible,* altho' his eyes were much turned to the soldiers, who were all on his right hand.

Gillam Bass, being in King-street at the same time, declares that they (the party of soldiers from the main guard) posted themselves between the custom-house door, and the west corner of it; and in a few minutes began to fire upon the people: *Two or three of the flashes so high above the rest, that he the deponent verily believes they must have come from the* CUSTOM-HOUSE *windows.* . . . .

George Coster being in King-street at the time above mentioned, declares that in five or six minutes after he stopped, he heard the word of command given to the soldiers *fire,* upon which one gun was fired, which did no execution, as the deponent observed, about half a minute after two guns, one of which killed one Samuel Gray a ropemaker, the other a molatto man, between which two men the deponent stood, after this the deponent heard the discharge of four or five guns more, by the soldiers; immediately after which *the deponent heard the discharge of two guns or pistols, from an open window of the middle story of the* CUSTOM-HOUSE, near to the place where the centry box is placed, and being but a small distance from the window, he heard the people from within speak and laugh, and soon after saw the casement lowered down; after which the deponent assisted others in carrying off one of the corps.

Cato, a Negro man, servant to Tuthill Hubbart, Esq; declares, that on Monday evening the fifth of March current, on hearing the cry of fire, he ran into Kingstreet, where he saw a number of people assembled before the Custom-House, that he stood near the centry-box and saw the soldiers fire on the people, who stood in the middle of said street; directly after which *he saw, two flashes of guns, one quick upon the other, from the chamber window of the* CUSTOM-HOUSE; and that after the firing was all over, while the people were carrying away the dead and wounded, *he saw the Custom-House door opened, and several soldiers (one of whom had a cutlass) go into the Custom-House* and shut the door after them.

Benjamin Andrews declares, that being desired by the committee of enquiry to take the ranges of the holes made by musquet balls, in two houses near opposite to the Custom-House, he finds the bullet hole in the entry door post of Mr. Payne's house (and which graz'd the edge of the door, before it enter'd the post, where it lodged, two and a half inches deep) *ranges just under the stool of the westernmost lower chamber window of the* Custom-House.

Samuel Drowne, towards the end of his deposition (which contains a pretty full account of the proceedings of the soldiers on the evening of the 5th instant) declares, that *he saw the flashes of two guns fired from the* Custom-House, *one of which was out of a window of the chamber westward of the balcony, and the other from the balcony; the gun (which he clearly discerned) being pointed through the ballisters, and the person who held the gun, in a stooping posture withdrew himself into the house, having a handkerchief or some kind of cloth over his face.*

These depositions shew clearly that a number of guns were fired from the Custom-House.

THE FUTURE GLORY OF AMERICA

JONATHAN TRUMBULL

———◆•◆———

The new nationalistic spirit of New England, war aside, was sanguine, hopeful, full of aspiration. The following enthusiastic prophecy in verse is by Jonathan Trumbull (1710–1785), chief justice of the Connecticut Supreme Court, governor of the colony and afterwards of the state. He was the only colonial governor to champion the cause of revolution, and was a friend and advisor of Washington's.

BEING THE CONCLUSION OF AN ORATION, DELIVERED
AT THE PUBLIC COMMENCEMENT OF YALE COLLEGE,
SEPTEMBER 12, 1770

> For pleasing Arts behold her matchless charms
> The first in letters, as the first in arms.
> See bolder genius quit the narrow shore,

And realms of science, yet untraced, explore,
Hiding in brightness of superior day,
The fainting gleam of Europe's setting ray.

   Sublime the Muse shall lift her eagle wing;
Of heavenly themes the sacred bards shall sing,
Tell how the blest Redeemer, man to save,
Thro' the deep mansions of the gloomy grave,
Sought the low shades of night, then rising high
Vanquish'd the powers of hell, and soar'd above the sky;
Or paint the scenes of that funereal day,
When earth's last fires shall mark their dreadful way,
In solemn pomp th' eternal Judge descend,
Doom the wide world and give to nature, end;
Or ope heaven's glories to th' astonish'd eye,
And bid their lays with lofty Milton vie;
Or wake from nature's themes the moral song,
And shine with Pope, with Thomson and with Young.

   This land her Swift and Addison shall view
The former honors equall'd by the new;
Here shall some Shakespeare charm the rising age,
And hold in magic chains the listening stage;
A second Watts shall string the heavenly lyre,
And other muses other bards inspire.

   Her daughters too the happy land shall grace
With powers of genius, as with charms of face;
Blest with the softness of the female mind,
With fancy blooming and with taste refined,
Some Rowe shall rise, and wrest with daring pen
The pride of science from assuming men;
While each bright line a polish'd beauty wears,
For every muse and every grace are theirs.

1773-1775

THE BOSTON TEA PARTY

JOHN ANDREWS

————◆◆◆————

The Townshend duties on English paint, lead, paper, and tea (named for Charles Townshend, "Champagne Charley was his name . . .") were resented bitterly by the colonies. Men used homemade paper, houses were left unpainted, and in New England in particular, violence attended efforts to collect duties. It was the British troops stationed in Boston to quell this very violence that brought about the Boston Massacre. Following that debacle, the ministry of Lord North repealed all the Townshend duties except that on tea. A tax of threepence per pound was retained on this commodity, as an assertion of Parliamentary authority.

In 1773 Bostonians, further enraged by the principle of monopoly on the export of tea held by the East India Company, formed a party that masqueraded as Mohawk Indians, boarded three vessels loaded with monopoly tea, and dumped the tea into the water wholesale. I always visualize the scene in terms of a picture book I had as a child—with beautiful huge boxes covered with Chinese tea paper tossed overboard by men in war paint. The following letter from John Andrews to a friend in Philadelphia was written the day after the Tea Party. I have selected, to follow it, "The Recollections of George Hewes," and the "Rallying Song of the Tea Party," sung in Boston in 1773.

John Andrews to William Barrell, merchant of Philadelphia.

Boston, December 18, 1773

However precarious our situation may be, yet *such* is the present calm composure of the people that a stranger would hardly think that ten thousand pounds sterling of the East India Company's tea was destroyed the night, or rather the evening before last, yet it's a serious truth; and if

[173]

yours, together with the other Southern provinces, should rest satisfied with *their* quota being stored, poor Boston will feel the whole weight of ministerial vengeance. However, it's the opinion of most people that we stand an equal chance now whether troops are sent in consequence of it or not; whereas, had it been stored, we should inevitably have had them to enforce the sale of it.

The affair was transacted with greatest regularity and despatch. Mr. Rotch, finding he exposed himself not only to the loss of his ship but for the value of the tea, in case he sent her back with it *without a clearance from the custom house,* as the Admiral kept a ship in readiness to make a seizure of it whenever it should sail under *those circumstances,* therefore declined complying with his former promises and absolutely declared his vessel should not carry it without a *proper* clearance could be procured or he to be indemnified for the value of her: when a general muster was assembled, from this and all the neighboring towns, to the number of five or six thousand, at 10 o'clock Thursday morning in the Old South Meeting House, where they passed a *unanimous* vote that the tea should go out of the harbour that afternoon, and sent a committee with Mr. Rotch to the Custom house to *demand* a clearance, which the collector told them was not in his power to give, without the duties being first paid. They then sent Mr. Rotch to Milton to ask a pass from the Governor, who sent for answer that "consistent with the rules of government and his duty to the King he could not grant one without they produced a previous clearance from the office."

By the time he returned with this message the candles were light in the house, and upon reading it, such prodigious shouts were made that induced me, while drinking tea at home, to go out and know the cause of it. The house was so crowded I could get no farther than the porch, when I found the moderator was just declaring the meeting to be *dissolved,* which caused another general shout, out doors and in, and three cheers. What with that, and the consequent noise of breaking up the meeting, you'd thought that the inhabitants of the infernal regions had broke loose. For my part, I went contentedly home and finished my tea, but was soon informed what was going forward: but still not crediting it without ocular demonstration, I went and was *satisfied.*

They mustered, I'm told, upon Fort Hill, to the number of about two hundred, and proceeded, two by two, to Griffin's wharf, where Hall, Bruce and Coffin lay, each with 114 chests of the *ill-fated* article on board; the two former with *only* that article, but the latter, arrived at the wharf only the day before, was freighted with a large quantity of other goods, which they took the *greatest* care not to injure in the least, and before *nine* o'clock in the evening, every chest from on board the three vessels was knocked to pieces and flung over the sides. They say the actors were *Indians* from *Narragansett.* Whether they were or not, to a transient observer they appeared as *such,* being cloathed in blankets with the heads muffled, and copper-colored countenances, being each armed with a hatchet or axe, and pair pistols, nor was their *dialect* different from what I conceive these geniusses to speak, as their jargon was unintelligible to all but themselves. . . .

[1834]

RECOLLECTIONS OF GEORGE HEWES

The tea destroyed was contained in three ships, lying near each other at what was called at that time Griffin's wharf, and were surrounded by armed ships of war, the commanders of which had publicly declared that if the rebels, as they were pleased to style the Bostonians, should not withdraw their opposition to the landing of the tea before a certain day, the 17th day of December, 1773, they should on that day force it on shore, under the cover of their cannon's mouth. On the day preceding the seventeenth, there was a meeting of the citizens of the county of Suffolk, convened at one of the churches in Boston, for the purpose of consulting on what measures might be considered expedient to prevent the landing of the tea, or secure the people from the collection of the duty. At that meeting a committee was appointed to wait on Governor Hutchinson, and request him to inform them whether he would take any measures to satisfy the people on the object of the meeting. To the first application of this committee, the Governor told them he would give them a definite answer by five o'clock in the afternoon. At the hour appointed, the committee again repaired to the Governor's house, and on inquiry found he had gone to his country seat at Milton, a distance of about six miles. When the committee returned and informed the meeting of the absence of the Governor, there was a confused murmur among the members, and the meeting was immediately dissolved, many of them crying out, "Let every man do his duty, and be true to his country"; and there was a general huzza for Griffin's wharf.

It was now evening, and I immediately dressed myself in the costume of an Indian, equipped with a small hatchet, which I and my associates denominated the tomahawk, with which, and a club, after having painted my face and hands with coal dust in the shop of a blacksmith, I repaired to Griffin's wharf, where the ships lay that contained the tea. When I first appeared in the street after being thus disguised, I fell in with many who were dressed, equipped and painted as I was, and who fell in with me and marched in order to the place of our destination.

When we arrived at the wharf, there were three of our number who assumed an authority to direct our operations, to which we readily submitted. They divided us into three parties, for the purpose of boarding the three ships which contained the tea at the same time. The name of him who commanded the division to which I was assigned was Leonard Pitt.

The names of the other commanders I never knew. We were immediately ordered by the respective commanders to board all the ships at the same time, which we promptly obeyed. The commander of the division to which I belonged, as soon as we were on board the ship, appointed me boatswain, and ordered me to go to the captain and demand of him the keys to the hatches and a dozen candles. I made the demand accordingly, and the captain promptly replied, and delivered the articles; but requested me at the same time to do no damage to the ship or rigging. We then were ordered by our commander to open the hatches and take out all the chests of tea and throw them overboard, and we immediately proceeded to execute his orders, first cutting and splitting the chests with our tomahawks, so as thoroughly to expose them to the effects of the water.

In about three hours from the time we went on board, we had thus broken and thrown overboard every tea chest to be found in the ship, while those in the other ships were disposing of the tea in the same way, at the same time. We were surrounded by British armed ships, but no attempt was made to resist us.

We then quietly retired to our several places of residence, without having any conversation with each other, or taking any measures to discover who were our associates; nor do I recollect of our having had the knowledge of the name of a single individual concerned in that affair, except that of Leonard Pitt, the commander of my division, whom I have mentioned. There appeared to be an understanding that each individual should volunteer his services, keep his own secret, and risk the consequence for himself. No disorder took place during that transaction, and it was observed at that time that the stillest night ensued that Boston had enjoyed for many months.

During the time we were throwing the tea overboard, there were several attempts made by some of the citizens of Boston and its vicinity to carry off small quantities of it for their family use. To effect that object, they would watch their opportunity to snatch up a handful from the deck, where it became plentifully scattered, and put it into their pockets. One Captain O'Connor, whom I well knew, came on board for that purpose, and when he supposed he was not noticed, filled his pockets, and also the lining of his coat. But I had detected him and gave information to the captain of what he was doing. We were ordered to take him into custody, and just as he was stepping from the vessel, I seized him by the skirt of his coat, and in attempting to pull him back, I tore it off; but, springing forward, by a rapid effort he made his escape. He had, however, to run a gauntlet through the crowd upon the wharf, each one, as he passed, giving him a kick or a stroke.

Another attempt was made to save a little tea from the ruins of the cargo by a tall, aged man who wore a large cocked hat and white wig, which was fashionable at that time. He had slightly slipped a little into his pocket, but being detected, they seized him and, taking his hat and wig from his head, threw them, together with the tea, of which they had emptied his pockets, into the water. In consideration of his advanced age, he was permitted to escape, with now and then a slight kick.

The next morning, after we had cleared the ships of the tea, it was discovered that very considerable quantities of it were floating upon the surface of the water; and to prevent the possibility of any of its being saved for use, a number of small boats were manned by sailors and citizens, who rowed them into those parts of the harbor wherever the tea was visible, and by beating it with oars and paddles so thoroughly drenched it as to render its entire destruction inevitable.

RALLYING SONG OF THE TEA PARTY
1773

Rally, Mohawks! bring out your axes,
And tell King George we'll pay no taxes
    On his foreign tea;
His threats are vain, and vain to think
To force our girls and wives to drink
    His vile Bohea!
Then rally, boys, and hasten on
To meet our chiefs at the Green Dragon.

Our Warren's there and bold Revere,
With hands to do, and words to cheer,
    For liberty and laws;
Our country's "braves" and firm defenders
Shall ne'er be left by true North-Enders
    Fighting Freedom's cause!
Then rally, boys, and hasten on
To meet our chiefs at the Green Dragon.

POEM BY A SLAVE

PHYLLIS WHEATLEY PETERS

———◆•◆———

Meanwhile, through all the agitation for freedom, slavery and the slave trade were humming along as usual. As in the tract by Samuel Sewall of witchcraft fame, antislavery sentiment had gone along side by side with the institution from the beginning.

What of the sentiments of the stock-in-trade? Art is one of the more interesting psychological manifestations of the slave condition, and there are many early evidences of it, mostly of a high-flown nature, as was only to be expected under the influence of the times. In Virginia, some slaves were taught to draw, after a fashion, and there are extant a number of portraits of members of great families, painted "on the place."

The following poem, composed during the Revolution, is the work of Phyllis Wheatley Peters, born in Africa about 1754, brought to America, and sold, about 1761, into slavery to Mr. John Wheatley of Boston, who encouraged her talent. Her volume, Poems on Various Subjects, Religious and Moral, *was published in 1773. When the authenticity of the book's authorship was questioned in London, many American intellectuals rose to defend it, among them Thomas Jefferson who, nevertheless, added that Phyllis Peters' poetry was beneath the dignity of criticism. She died in 1784.*

ON IMAGINATION

Imagination! who can sing thy source,
Or who describe the swiftness of thy course?
Soaring through air to find the bright abode,
The empyreal palace of the thundering God,
We on thy pinions can surpass the wind
And leave the rolling universe behind.
From star to star the mental optics rove,
Measure the skies, and range the realms above;
There in one view we grasp the mighty whole,
Or with new worlds amaze the unbounded soul.

BOSTON BELEAGURED AND HELP SENT

PETER FORCE

————◆◆◆————

Peter Force (1790–1868) was a Washington printer who performed the inestimable service of collecting and publishing a number of rare official and private manuscripts of Revolutionary times under the title American Archives. *It ran to nine volumes, and Force planned at least thirty-six*

*more, but was refused permission to continue publishing by the Depart-
ment of State.*

*The following account of the resistance shown in the town of Farming-
ton, Connecticut, to the Port Bill, which Parliament passed in 1774 in
retaliation for the Boston Tea Party, shows the spirit that united the
colonies at this crucial time. The bill provided that the port of Boston be
closed until the town paid the East India Company for all the tea destroyed. Note, in the resolutions passed, that the king's person is still
revered; it is his ministry only that is called "pimps and parasites."*

*Following the Farmington account is a letter from American Archives
out of the many addressed to Boston by other New England towns.*

Proceedings of Farmington, Connecticut, on the Boston Port Act,
May 19, 1774.

Early in the morning was found the following handbill, posted up in
various parts of the town, viz:

> To pass through the fire at six o'clock this evening, in honour to the
> immortal goddess of Liberty, the late infamous Act of the British
> Parliament for farther distressing the American Colonies; the place
> of execution will be the public parade, where all Sons of Liberty
> are desired to attend.

Accordingly, a very numerous and respectable body were assembled of
near one thousand people, when a huge pole, just forty-five feet high,
was erected and consecrated to the shrine of liberty; after which the Act
of Parliament for blocking up the Boston harbour was read aloud, sentenced to the flames and executed by the hands of the common hangman;
then the following resolves were passed, *nem. con.:*

1ST. That it is the greatest dignity, interest and happiness of every
American to be united with our parent State, while our liberties are duly
secured, maintained and supported by our rightful Sovereign, whose person we greatly revere; whose government, while duly administered, we
are ready with our lives and properties to support.

2D. That the present ministry, being instigated by the devil and led on
by their wicked and corrupt hearts, have a design to take away our liberties and properties and to enslave us forever.

3D. That the late Act which their malice hath caused to be passed in
Parliament, for blocking up the port of Boston, is unjust, illegal and op-
pressive; and that we and every American are sharers in the insults
offered to the town of Boston.

4TH. That those pimps and parasites who dared to advise their master
to such detestable measures be held in utter abhorrence by us and every

American, and their names loaded with the curses of all succeeding generations.

5TH. That we scorn the chains of slavery; we despise every attempt to rivet them upon us; we are the sons of freedom and resolved that, till time shall be no more, godlike virtue shall blazon our hemisphere.

To the Overseers of the Town of Boston.

Sept. 14th., 1774

Gentlemen,

The inhabitants of Kingston, in the Province of New Hampshire, see with deep concern the unhappy misunderstanding and disagreement that now subsists between Great Britain and these American Colonies, being fully sensible the happiness of both countries depend on an union, harmony and agreement to be established between them on a just, equitable and permanent foundation. But when we consider the new, arbitrary and unjust claims of our brethren in Great Britain to levy taxes upon us at their sovereign will and pleasure, and to make laws to bind us in all cases whatsoever, we view and consider ourselves and our posterity under the operations of these claims as absolute slaves; for what is a slave but one who is bound in all cases whatsoever by the will and command of another? And we look on the late unjust, cruel, hostile and tyrannical Acts of the British Parliament, respecting the Massachusetts Bay in general, and the Town of Boston in particular, as consequences of these unrighteous claims, and from them clearly see what the whole continent has to expect under their operation. . . .

We wish the Town of Boston wisdom and prudence to conduct them in these trying and critical times, and that their struggle for liberty may be crowned with abundant success. We look on the cause in which you are engaged as a common cause, and that we and our posterity are equally interested with you in the event. We beg leave to assure that this Town will readily assist the Town of Boston to the utmost of their ability, in every prudent measure that may be taken for regaining their just rights and privileges from all unjust invaders. We heartily sympathize with the poor of the Town of Boston under their present distress, and as an earnest of our readiness to assist you, this Town have contributed and sent by the bearers hereof, one hundred sheep as a present for their relief, to be disposed of for their use in such way and manner as you shall think best.

We are, in behalf of the donors, Your most obedient humble servants,

JACOB HOOKE,[et al.]

FREE AMERICA

DR. JOSEPH WARREN

———◆·◆———

Dr. Joseph Warren was another radical among the colonists, like Sam Adams his fellow Bostonian, Patrick Henry of Virginia, and Christopher Gadsden in South Carolina. The following highly political song, ascribed to Warren, is a sample of his sentiments in the year 1774. He later lost his life at the Battle of Bunker Hill.

Incidentally, this is one of dozens of songs written at the period to be sung to the tune of "The British Grenadiers." It adds to one's enjoyment of them to do so. One burlesque verse of purely Boston origin gives the Tory angle on James Otis, another of Warren's friends:

> *Their patriot, Jimmy Otis,*
>   *That bully in disguise,*
> *That well-known tyke of Yorkshire*
>   *That magazine of lies,*
> *And he will mount the rostrum*
>   *And loudly he will bray*
> *Rebel! Rebel! Rebel! Rebel!*
>   *Rebel America!*

FREE AMERICA

That seat of science, Athens,
  And earth's proud mistress, Rome;
Where now are all their glories?
  We scarce can find a tomb.
Then guard your rights, Americans,
  Nor stoop to lawless sway;
Oppose, oppose, oppose, oppose,
  For North America.

We led fair Freedom hither,
  And lo, the desert smiled!
A paradise of pleasure
  Was opened in the wild!

Your harvest, bold Americans,
　　No power shall snatch away!
Huzza, huzza, huzza, huzza,
　　For free America.

Torn from a world of tyrants,
　　Beneath this western sky,
We formed a new dominion,
　　A land of liberty:
The world shall own we're masters here;
　　Then hasten on the day:
Huzza, huzza, huzza, huzza,
　　For free America. . . .

Lift up your hands, ye heroes,
　　And swear with proud disdain,
The wretch that would ensnare you
　　Shall lay his snares in vain:
Should Europe empty all her force,
　　We'll meet her in array,
And fight and shout, and shout and fight
　　For North America.

Some future day shall crown us
　　The masters of the main,
Our fleets shall speak in thunder
　　To England, France and Spain;
And the nations over the ocean spread
　　Shall tremble and obey
The sons, the sons, the sons, the sons
　　Of brave America. . . .

PAUL REVERE'S OWN ACCOUNT
OF HIS RIDE

◆·◆

*The Port Bill and other Coercion Acts, far from isolating Massachusetts
as they had been intended to do, united the other twelve colonies in a
bond of sympathy with their suffering sister.*

General Thomas Gage—a pleasant man, too, with an American wife—

commanded the garrison at Boston. On February 20, 1775, the radical Dr.
Warren wrote to an English friend:

> ... I am of the opinion that if once General Gage should lead his
> troops into the country with the design to enforce the late Acts of
> Parliament, Great Britain may take her leave, at least of the New
> England colonies, and if I mistake not, of all America. . . . Every day,
> every hour widens the breach. A Richmond, a Chatham, a Shelburne,
> a Camden, with their noble associates, may yet repair it; it is a
> work which none but the greatest of men can conduct.

Gage's duty was, after all, to enforce the Coercive Acts. News that the
colonists were collecting powder and military stores at Concord reached
him, and on the night of April 18 he sent troops to confiscate these
munitions.

Every child knows what happened next. (The name of Will Daws is not
as well known outside New England as that of Paul Revere, but when I
was a child a neighbor of ours had a cat named Mr. Daws.) I append Paul
Revere's own account—the source of Longfellow's—of the great doings on
"the eighteenth of April in 'Seventy-five."

Paul Revere to Dr. Jeremy Belknap.

[1798]

   In the fall of 1774 and winter of 1775, I was one of upwards of thirty,
chiefly mechanics, who formed ourselves into a committee for the purpose
of watching the movements of the British soldiers, and gaining every intelligence of the movements of the Tories. We held our meetings at the
Green Dragon tavern. We were so careful that our meetings should be
kept secret that every time we met, every person swore upon the Bible
that they would not discover any of our transactions but to Messrs. Hancock, Adams, Doctors Warren, Church and one or two more.
   ... In the winter, towards the spring, we frequently took turns, two and
two, to watch the soldiers by patrolling the streets all night. The Saturday
night preceding the 19th of April, about 12 o'clock at night, the boats belonging to the transports were all launched and carried under the sterns
of the men-of-war. (They had been previously hauled up and repaired.)
We likewise found that the grenadiers and light infantry were all taken
off duty.
   From these movements we expected something serious was to be transacted. On Tuesday evening, the 18th, it was observed that a number of
soldiers were marching towards the bottom of the Common. About 10
o'clock, Dr. Warren sent in great haste for me and begged that I would
immediately set off for Lexington, where Messrs. Hancock and Adams

were, and acquaint them of the movement, and that it was thought they were the objects.

When I got to Dr. Warren's house, I found he had sent an express by land to Lexington—a Mr. William Daws. The Sunday before, by desire of Dr. Warren, I had been to Lexington, to Messrs. Hancock and Adams, who were at the Rev. Mr. Clark's. I returned at night through Charlestown; there I agreed with a Colonel Conant and some other gentlemen that if the British went out by water, we would show two lanthorns in the North Church steeple; and if by land, one, as a signal; for we were apprehensive it would be difficult to cross the Charles River or get over Boston Neck. I left Dr. Warren, called upon a friend and desired him to make the signals.

I then went home, took my boots and surtout, went to the north part of the town, where I had kept a boat; two friends rowed me across Charles River, a little to the eastward where the *Somerset* man-of-war lay. It was then young flood, the ship was winding, and the moon was rising. They landed me on the Charlestown side. When I got into town, I met Colonel Conant and several others; they said they had seen our signals. I told them what was acting, and went to get me a horse; I got a horse of Deacon Larkin. While the horse was preparing, Richard Devens, Esq., who was one of the Committee of Safety, came to me and told me that he came down the road from Lexington after sundown that evening; that he met ten British officers, all well mounted, and armed, going up the road.

I set off upon a very good horse; it was then about eleven o'clock and very pleasant. After I had passed Charlestown Neck . . . I saw two men on horseback under a tree. When I got near them, I discovered they were British officers. One tried to get ahead of me, and the other to take me. I turned my horse very quick and galloped towards Charlestown Neck, and then pushed for the Medford Road. The one who chased me, endeavoring to cut me off, got into a clay pond near where Mr. Russell's Tavern is now built. I got clear of him, and went through Medford, over the bridge and up to Menotomy. In Medford, I awaked the captain of the minute men; and after that, I alarmed almost every house, till I got to Lexington. I found Messrs. Hancock and Adams at the Rev. Mr. Clark's; I told them my errand and enquired for Mr. Daws; they said he had not been there; I related the story of the two officers, and supposed that he must have been stopped, as he ought to have been there before me.

After I had been there about half an hour, Mr. Daws came; we refreshed ourselves, and set off for Concord. We were overtaken by a young Dr. Prescott, whom we found to be a high Son of Liberty. . . .

We had got nearly half way. Mr. Daws and the doctor stopped to alarm the people of a house. I was about one hundred rods ahead when I saw two men in nearly the same situation as those officers were near Charlestown. I called for the doctor and Mr. Daws to come up. In an instant I was surrounded by four. They had placed themselves in a straight road that inclined each way; they had taken down a pair of bars on the north side of the road, and two of them were under a tree in the pasture. The doctor being foremost, he came up and we tried to get past them; but they being armed with pistols and swords, they forced us into the pasture. The doctor jumped his horse over a low stone wall and got to Concord.

I observed a wood at a small distance and made for that. When I got there, out started six officers on horseback and ordered me to dismount. One of them, who appeared to have the command, examined me, where I came from and what my name was. I told him. He asked me if I was an express. I answered in the affirmative. He demanded what time I left Boston. I told him, and added that their troops had catched aground in passing the river, and that there would be five hundred Americans there in a short time, for I had alarmed the country all the way up. He immediately rode towards those who stopped us, when all five of them came down upon a full gallop. One of them, whom I afterwards found to be a Major Mitchel, of the 5th Regiment, clapped his pistol to my head, called me by name and told me he was going to ask me some questions, and if I did not give him true answers, he would blow my brains out. He then asked me similar questions to those above. He then ordered me to mount my horse, after searching me for arms. He then ordered them to advance and to lead me in front. When we got to the road, they turned down towards Lexington. When we had got about one mile, the major rode up to the officer that was leading me, and told him to give me to the sergeant. As soon as he took me, the major ordered him, if I attempted to run, or anybody insulted them, to blow my brains out.

We rode till we got near Lexington meeting-house, when the militia fired a volley of guns, which appeared to alarm them very much. The major inquired of me how far it was to Cambridge, and if there were any other road. After some consultation, the major rode up to the sergeant and asked if his horse was tired. He answered him he was—he was a sergeant of grenadiers and had a small horse. "Then," said he, "take that man's horse." I dismounted, and the sergeant mounted my horse, when they all rode towards Lexington meeting-house.

I went across the burying-ground and some pastures and came to the Rev. Mr. Clark's house, where I found Messrs. Hancock and Adams. I told them of my treatment, and they concluded to go from that house towards Woburn. I went with them and a Mr. Lowell, who was a clerk to Mr. Hancock.

When we got to the house where they intended to stop, Mr. Lowell and myself returned to Mr. Clark's, to find what was going on. When we got there, an elderly man came in; he said he had just come from the tavern, that a man had come from Boston who said there were no British troops coming. Mr. Lowell and myself went towards the tavern, when we met a man on a full gallop, who told us the troops were coming up the rocks. We afterwards met another, who said they were close by. Mr. Lowell asked me to go to the tavern with him, to get a trunk of papers belonging to Mr. Hancock. We went up chamber, and while we were getting the trunk, we saw the British very near, upon a full march. We hurried towards Mr. Clark's house. In our way we passed through the militia. There were about fifty. When we had got about one hundred yards from the meeting-house, the British troops appeared on both sides of the meeting-house. In their front was an officer on horseback. They made a short halt; *when I saw, and heard, a gun fired,* which appeared to be a pistol. Then I could distinguish two guns, and then a continual roar of musketry; when we made off with the trunk.

BATTLE OF LEXINGTON

GEORGE BANCROFT

The following description of the Battle of Lexington is that of George Bancroft (1800–1891), Secretary of the Navy, Secretary of War, and Minister to Great Britain, as well as a great historian, from whose History of the United States *it is excerpted. The account closes with the stirring words of Sam Adams as he looked about the battlefield, "Oh, what a glorious morning is this!"*

AT two in the morning, under the eye of the minister, and of Hancock and Adams, Lexington common was alive with the minutemen; and not with them only, but with the old men, who were exempts, except in case of immediate danger to the town. The roll was called, and, of militia and alarm men, about one hundred and thirty answered to their names. The captain, John Parker, ordered every one to load with powder and ball, but to take care not to be the first to fire. Messengers, sent to look for the British regulars, reported that there were no signs of their approach. A watch was therefore set, and the company dismissed with orders to come together at beat of drum. Some went to their own homes; some to the tavern, near the south-east corner of the common. Samuel Adams and Hancock, whose seizure was believed to be intended, were persuaded to retire toward Woburn.

The last stars were vanishing from night, when the foremost party, led by Pitcairn, a major of marines, was discovered, advancing quickly and in silence. Alarm guns were fired, and the drums beat, not a call to village husbandmen only, but the reveille to humanity. Less than seventy, perhaps less than sixty, obeyed the summons, and, in sight of half as many boys and unarmed men, were paraded in two ranks, a few rods north of the meeting-house.

How often in that building had they, with renewed professions of their faith, looked up to God as the stay of their fathers and the protector of their privileges! How often on that green, hard by the burial-place of their forefathers, had they pledged themselves to each other to combat manfully for their birthright inheritance of liberty! There they now stood side by side, under the provincial banner, with arms in their hands, silent and fearless, willing to shed their blood for their rights, scrupulous not to begin civil war. The ground on which they trod was the altar of freedom, and they were to furnish the victims.

The British van, hearing the drum and the alarm guns, halted to load; the remaining companies came up; and, at half an hour before sunrise, the advance party hurried forward at double quick time, almost upon a run, closely followed by the grenadiers. Pitcairn rode in front, and, when within five or six rods of the minute-men, cried out: "Disperse, ye villains! ye rebels, disperse! lay down your arms! why don't you lay down your arms and disperse?" The main part of the countrymen stood motionless in the ranks, witnesses against aggression; too few to resist, too brave to fly. At this, Pitcairn discharged a pistol, and with a loud voice cried, "Fire!" The order was followed first by a few guns, which did no execution, and then by a close and deadly discharge of musketry.

In the disparity of numbers, Parker ordered his men to disperse. Then, and not till then, did a few of them, on their own impulse, return the British fire. These random shots of fugitives or dying men did no harm, except that Pitcairn's horse was perhaps grazed, and a private of the tenth light infantry was touched slightly in the leg.

Jonas Parker, the strongest and best wrestler in Lexington, had promised never to run from British troops; and he kept his vow. A wound brought him on his knees. Having discharged his gun, he was preparing to load it again, when he was stabbed by a bayonet, and lay on the post which he took at the morning's drum-beat. So fell Isaac Muzzey, and so died the aged Robert Munroe, who in 1758 had been an ensign at Louisburg. Jonathan Harrington, junior, was struck in front of his own house on the north of the common. His wife was at the window as he fell. With blood gushing from his breast, he rose in her sight, tottered, fell again, then crawled on hands and knees toward his dwelling; she ran to meet him, but only reached him as he expired on their threshold. Caleb Harrington, who had gone into the meeting-house for powder, was shot as he came out. Samuel Hadley and John Brown were pursued, and killed after they had left the green. Asahel Porter, of Woburn, who had been taken prisoner by the British on the march, endeavoring to escape, was shot within a few rods of the common. Seven men of Lexington were killed, nine wounded; a quarter part of all who stood in arms on the green.

Day came in all the beauty of an early spring. The trees were budding; the grass growing rankly a full month before its time; the blue-bird and the robin gladdening the genial season, and calling forth the beams of the sun which on that morning shone with the warmth of summer; but distress and horror gathered over the inhabitants of the peaceful town. There on the green lay in death the gray-haired and the young; the grassy field was red "with the innocent blood of their brethren slain," crying unto God for vengeance from the ground.

These are the village heroes, who were more than of noble blood, proving by their spirit that they were of a race divine. They gave their lives in testimony to the rights of mankind, bequeathing to their country an assurance of success in the mighty struggle which they began. The expanding millions of their countrymen renew and multiply their praise from generation to generation. They fulfilled their duty not from an accidental impulse of the moment; their action was the ripened fruit of Providence and of time. The light that led them on was combined of rays from the whole history of the race; from the traditions of the Hebrews in the gray of the world's morning; from the heroes and sages of republican Greece and Rome; from the example of Him who died on the cross for the life of humanity; from the religious creed which proclaimed the divine presence in man, and on this truth, as in a life-boat, floated the liberties of nations over the dark flood of the middle ages; from the customs of the Germans transmitted out of their forests to the councils of Saxon England; from the burning faith and courage of Martin Luther; from trust in the inevitable universality of God's sovereignty as taught by Paul of Tarsus and Augustine, through Calvin and the divines of New England; from the avenging fierceness of the Puritans, who dashed the mitre on the ruins of the throne; from the bold dissent and creative self-assertion of the earliest emigrants to Massachusetts; from the statesmen who made, and the philosophers who expounded, the revolution of England; from the liberal spirit and analyzing inquisitiveness of the eighteenth century; from the cloud of witnesses of all the ages to the reality and the rightfulness of human freedom. All the centuries bowed themselves from the recesses of the past to cheer in their sacrifice the lowly men who proved themselves worthy of their forerunners, and whose children rise up and call them blessed.

Heedless of his own danger, Samuel Adams, with the voice of a prophet, exclaimed: "Oh, what a glorious morning is this!" for he saw his country's independence hastening on, and, like Columbus in the tempest, knew that the storm bore him more swiftly toward the undiscovered world.

ON LEXINGTON

JOHN ADAMS

————◆•◆————

John Adams is one of the finest and soundest characters to emerge from the decades that surround the Revolution; his name is interwoven with every event of significance. The following letter, written the day after Lexington and Concord, gives an account as balanced as Adams himself. It ends in a very different, more thoughtful vein than the reaction of the other Adams in the account preceding.

My grandfather's ballad, "New England's Chevy Chase," got its title from an old story that, as Lord Percy rode out with the music of fife and drum to the relief of the British at Lexington, he passed a small Boston boy sitting on a fence, jeering at the redcoats. Percy sent someone to reprove the boy, who replied with the following allusion to the noble house of Percy: "You're marching out to 'Yankee Doodle' but you'll come home to 'Chevy Chase.'" The repartee is said to have stuck to Percy throughout the fighting. And Horace Walpole refers to "the hunting of that day" in speaking of the Battle of Lexington.

Another story is that one of the veterans of Lexington told his recollections of it to Edward Everett, who said, "You've never regretted that day, I'm sure." The old man replied, in true New England vein, "Well, I'd rather have spent it so than to hum."

John Adams to William Barrell.

April 19, [1775]

Yesterday produced a scene the most shocking New England ever beheld. Last Saturday P.M. orders were sent to the several regiments quartered here not to let their Grenadiers or Light Infantry do any duty till further orders, upon which the inhabitants conjectured that some secret expedition was on foot, and being on the look out, they observed those bodies upon the move between ten and eleven o'clock the evening before last, observing a perfect silence in their march towards a point opposite Phip's farm, where [boats?] were in waiting that conveyed 'em over.

The men appointed to alarm the country upon such occasions got over by stealth as early as they [could] and took their different routs. The first advice we had was about eight o'clock in the morning, when it was reported that the troops had fired upon and killed five men in Lexington—

previous to which an officer came express to his Excellency Governor
Gage, when between eight and nine o'clock a brigade marched out under
the command of Earl Piercy, consisting of the Marines, the Welch
Fusileers, the 4th Regiment, the 47th, and two field pieces.

About twelve o'clock it was gave out by the general's aide camps that
no person was killed, and that a single gun had not been fired, which report was variously believed—but between one and two, certain accounts
came that eight were killed outright and fourteen wounded of the inhabitants of Lexington—who had about forty men drawn out early in the
morning near the meeting house to exercise. The party of the Light Infantry and Grenadiers, to the number of about eight hundred, came up
to them and ordered them to disperse. The commander of 'em replied that
they were only innocently amusing themselves with exercise, that they
had not any ammunition with 'em, and therefore should not molest or
disturb them. Which answer not satisfying, the troops fired upon and
killed three or four, the others took to their heels and the troops continued
to fire. A few took refuge in the meeting, when the soldiers shoved up the
windows and pointed their guns in and killed three there. Thus much is
best account I can learn of the beginning of this fatal day.

You must naturally suppose that such a piece would rouse the country
(allowed the report to be true). The troops continued their march to
Concord, entered the town, and refreshed themselves in the meeting and
town house. In the latter place they found some ammunition and stores
belonging to the country, which they found they could not bring away by
reason that the country people had occupied all the posts around 'em.
They therefore set fire to the house, which the people extinguished. They
set fire a second time, which brought on a general engagement at about
eleven o'clock. The troops took two pieces [of] cannon from the peasants,
but their numbers increasing they soon regained 'em, and the troops were
obliged to retreat towards town.

About noon they were joined by the other brigade under Earl Piercy,
when another very *warm* engagement came on at Lexington, which the
troops could not stand; therefore were obliged to continue their retreat,
which they did with the bravery becoming British soldiers—but the
country were in a manner desperate, not regarding their cannon (any
more) in the least, and followed 'em till seven in the evening, by which
time they got into Charlestown, when they left off the pursuit, least they
might injure the inhabitants.

I stood upon the hills in town and saw the engagement very plain. It
was very bloody for seven hours. It's conjectured that one half the soldiers
at least were killed. . . .

When I reflect and consider that the fight was between those whose
parents but a few generations ago were brothers, I shudder at the thought,
and there's no knowing where our calamities will end.

A PARDON TO THE LEXINGTON REBELS

GENERAL GAGE

———◆◆◆———

The stirring events of April, 1775, were followed in June by the issuance of a general pardon by General Gage—excerpted here—to all the rebels involved, excepting Samuel Adams and John Hancock. Far from offering themselves up to any "condign punishment," however, these gentlemen went merrily off to the Second Continental Congress in Philadelphia, where Hancock was later chosen President.

For all the country was still ringing with Lexington and Concord, and for all the presence at it of radical patriots, the ostensible purpose of this Congress was still—like that of the first Congress—to get the Coercive Acts repealed, restore imperial relations to what they were before 1763, and to avert both war and independence. As late as autumn 1775, North Carolina, Pennsylvania, New Jersey, New York, and Maryland went on official record as against independence. Liberty, not independence, was what they wanted, and the "unprincipled hirelings of a venal ministry," not the king, were whom they were against. As late as January, 1776, the king's toast was drunk at the officers' mess presided over by General Washington.

June 12, 1775

Whereas, the infatuated multitude, who have long suffered themselves to be conducted by certain well known incendiaries and traitors, in a fatal progression of crimes against the constitutional authority of the State, have at length proceeded to avowed Rebellion; and the good effects which were expected to arise from the patience and lenity of the King's Government have been often frustrated, and are now rendered hopeless, by the influence of the same evil counsels; it only remains for those who are invested with supreme rule, as well for the punishment of the guilty, as the protection of the well-affected, to prove they do not bear the sword in vain.

. . . A number of armed persons, to the amount of many thousands, assembled on the 19th of April last, and from behind walls and lurking holes, attacked a detachment of the King's Troops, who, not suspecting so consummate an act of frenzy, unprepared for vengeance, and willing to decline it, made use of their arms only in their own defence. Since that period, the rebels, deriving confidence from impunity, have added insult to outrage; have repeatedly fired upon the King's ships and subjects with cannon and small-arms; have possessed the roads and other communications by which the Town of Boston was supplied with provisions; and with a preposterous parade of military arrangement they affected to hold the army besieged; while part of their body made daily and indiscriminate invasions upon private property, and, with a wantonness of cruelty ever incident to lawless tumult, carry depredation and distress wherever they turn their steps. The actions of the 19th of April are of such notoriety as must baffle all attempts to contradict them, and the flames of buildings and other property from the islands and adjacent country, for some weeks past, spread a melancholy confirmation of the subsequent assertions.

In this exigency of complicated calamities, I avail myself of the last effort within the bounds of my duty to spare the effusion of blood; to offer, and I do hereby, in His Majesty's name, offer and promise his most gracious pardon to all persons who shall forthwith lay down their arms and return to their duties of peaceable subjects, excepting only from the benefit of such pardon *Samuel Adams* and *John Hancock,* whose offences are of too flagitious a nature to admit of any other consideration than that of condign punishment.

DIARY OF AN AMERICAN SOLDIER

SIMEON LYMAN

———◆◆———

From all over New England companies of men marched to the relief of Boston. "Let us march immediately," Nathan Hale said in New London, "and never lay down our arms until we obtain our independence." Connecticut made her first call for volunteers soon after the 19th of April, and organized six regiments to go to war.

The siege of Boston presented no thrilling or desperate episodes. By December the terms of most of the troops were expiring, and for these freedom-minded farmers the pull of home was great. In meeting the crisis, it was determined to recruit new regiments as far as possible from existing troops. Washington's anxiety over this problem of re-enlistment is expressed in his letters of this date.

The following excerpt from the diary of a Connecticut soldier gives a picture of how re-enlistment looked from the point of view of the ranks.

Wednesday, November 29th, [1775]. In the morning the whole regiment was ordered to parade before the genera[l's] door, and they formed a hollow square, and the general came in and made a speech to us, and then those that would stay till January must follow the fifers and colors, and the captains turned out and they marched round the company several times, and there was about a 100 soldiers turned out. The most of them had listed to stay another year, and they was led down to the colonel's and treated, and the rest was dismissed to return to their tents again, and I washed my clothes, and about sunset we went out and chose 2 corporals, and then they brought 2 bottles of brandy and they drinked it, and then they was dismissed. . . .

December, Friday, 1st. We was ordered to parade before the general's door, the whole regiment, and General Lee and General Solivan came out, and those that would not stay 4 days longer after their enlistments was out they was ordered to turn out, and there was about 3 quarters turned out, and we was ordered to form a hollow square, and General Lee came in and the first words was "Men, I do not know what to call you; [you] are the worst of all creatures," and flung and curst and swore at us, and said if we would not stay he would order us to go on Bunker Hill and if we would not go he would order the riflemen to fire at us, and they talked they would take our guns and take our names down, and our lieutenants begged of us to stay and we went and joined the rest, and they got about 10 of their guns, and the men was marched off, and the general said that they should go to the work house and be confined, and they agreed to stay the four days, and they gave them a dram, and the colonel told us that he would give us another the next morning, and we was dismissed. There was one that was a mind to have one of his mates turn out with him, and the general see him and he catched his gun out of his hands and struck him on the head and ordered him to be put under guard.

Saturday, 2d. I was on quarter guard in the morning. They was paraded before the colonel's door and he gave us a dram, and then they read some new orders to us and they said that we must not go out of our brigade without a written pass from our captain, and before night there was a paper set up on the general's door not to let the soldiers have any victual if they would not stay 3 weeks longer, and they said that they was 50 miles in the country, and some was mad and said they would not stay the 4 days, and the paper was took down as soon as it was dark, and another put up that General Lee was a fool and if he had not come here we should not know it. The sentries fired at each other all day by spells, and at night our guard took 4 of their horses, and the mortar piece that our men took from the regulars was brought to Cambridge. It was 13 inches across. They brought several chests of small arms, and General Put[nam] dashed a bottle on it and called it the royal congress.

Sunday, 3d. It was my turn to cook, and at night we had orders that if we would stay till 10th we should have a written pass, and we felt a good deal better for it. . . .

Saturday, 9th. The whole regiment was ordered out on the parade, and we was ordered to stand three deep, and the captains was in the front and the luten and the sergeants in the rear, and the general came round the whole, and we all made a salute to him, and then we was ordered to march down before the general's door, and those that was agoing to stay another year should march out and front the regiments, and they was dismissed to go to their tents, and the officers was ordered to view our arms, and then we was dismissed and we came home, and then we was ordered to turn [in] our guns and ammunition and our guns was to be priced, and orders was that all that was not well might march off, and those that had sent for horses and hey (no others) sot off, and when it came night we had orders to go on Plowd Hill and handle the lances all night, and they all said they would not go, and they did not get one.

1775-1798

BUNKER HILL

AMOS FARNSWORTH

————◆◆————

The Congress at Philadelphia took the New England militia besieging Boston into Continental service and appointed George Washington Commander in Chief. On the 23rd of June, 1775, Washington rode away from Philadelphia to take charge of his army, and was met by the exciting news of the Battle of Bunker Hill. The account of the battle that follows here, by a Massachusetts militiaman, gives a picture of a fight that, while technically a defeat for the rebels, rallied their spirits by showing what they could do in battle in the open. After all, they would not even have had to surrender had not their powder run out!

Friday June 16. Nothing done in the forenoon; in the afternoon we had orders to be redy to march. At six agreable to orders our regiment preadid and about sun-set we was drawn up and herd prayers; and about dusk marched for Bunkers Hill under command of our own Col Prescott. Just before we turned out of the rode to go up Bunkers-Hill, Charlestown, we was halted; and about sixty men was taken out of our batallion to go into Charlestown, I being one of them. Capt Nutten heded us down to the town house; we sot our centres by the waterside; the most of us got in the town house but had orders not to shut our eyes. Our men marched to Bunker-Hill and begun thair intrenchment and careed it on with the utmost viger all night. Early in the morning I joined them.

Saturday June 17. The enemy appeared to be much alarmed on Saturday morning when thay discovered our operations and immediately began a heavy cannonading from a batery on Corps-Hill, Boston, and from the ships in the harbour. We with little loss continued to carry on our works till 1 o'clock when we discovered a large body of the enemy crossing Charles-River from Boston. Thay landed on a point of land about a mile eastward of our intrenchment and immediately disposed thair army for an attack, previous to which thay set fire to the town of Charlestown. It is supposed that the enemy intended to attack us under the cover of the smoke from the burning houses, the wind favouring them in such a design; while on the other side their army was extending northward towards Mistick-River with an apparant design of surrounding our men in the works, and of cutting of[f] any assistance intended for our relief. Thay ware however in some measure counteracted in this design, and drew their army into closer order.

As the enemy approached, our men was not only exposed to the attack of a very numerous musketry, but to the heavy fire of the battery on Corps-Hill, 4 or 5 men of war, several armed boats or floating batteries in Mistick-River, and a number of field pieces. Notwithstanding we within the intrenchment, and at a breast work without, sustained the enemy's attacks with great bravery and resolution, kiled and wounded great numbers, and repulsed them several times, and after bearing, for about 2 hours, as sever and heavy a fire as perhaps ever was known, and many having fired away all their ammunition, and having no reinforsement, althoe thare was a great boddy of men nie by, we ware over-powered by numbers and obliged to leave the intrenchment, retreating about sunset to a small distance over Charlestown Neck.

N.B. I did not leave the intrenchment untill the enemy got in. I then retreated ten or fifteen rods; then I receved a wound in my rite arm, the bawl gowing through a little below my elbow breaking the little shel bone. Another bawl struk my back, taking a piece of skin about as big as a penny. But I got to Cambridge that night. The town of Charlestown supposed to contain about 300 dwelling-houses, a great number of which ware large and elegant, besides 150 or 200 other buildings, are almost laid in ashes by the barbarity and wanton cruelty of that infernal villain Thomas Gage.

Oh, the goodness of God in preserving my life althoe thay fell on my right hand and on my left! O, may this act of deliverance of thine, Oh God, lead me never to distrust the[e]; but may I ever trust in the[e] and put confodence in no arm of flesh! I was in great pane the first night with my wound.

TORY VIEWS OF THE AMERICAN SOLDIERS

BENJAMIN THOMPSON

———◆•◆———

The Tory view of events is reflected in the following description of the American soldiers at Boston from an account by Benjamin Thompson. A Massachusetts-born Loyalist soldier in the Revolution, after the war he went to England and was knighted. Thompson later joined the army of the Elector of Bavaria, who ennobled him in the Holy Roman Empire. It is by this latter title of Count Rumford that he is most generally known.

Boston, November 4, 1775

... The army in general is not very badly accoutered, but most wretchedly clothed, and as dirty a set of mortals as ever disgraced the name of a soldier. They have had no clothes of any sort provided for them by the Congress (except the detachment of 1,133 that are gone to Canada under Col. Arnold, who had each of them a new coat and a linen frock served out to them before they set out), tho' the army in general, and the Massachusetts forces in particular, had encouragement of having coats given them by way of bounty for inlisting. And the neglect of the Congress to fulfill their promise in this respect has been the source of not a little uneasiness among the soldiers.

They have no women in the camp to do washing for the men, and they in general not being used to doing things of this sort, and thinking it rather a disparagement to them, choose rather to let their linen, etc., rot upon their backs than to be at the trouble of cleaning 'em themselves. And to this nasty way of life, and to the change of their diet from milk, vegetables, etc., to living almost intirely upon flesh, must be attributed those putrid, malignant and infectious disorders which broke out among them soon after their taking the field, and which have prevailed with unabating fury during the whole summer.

The leading men among them (with their usual art and cunning) have been indefatigable in their endeavors to conceal the real state of the army in this respect, and to convince the world that the soldiers were tolerably healthy. But the contrary has been apparent, even to a demonstration, to every person that had but the smallest acquaintance with their camp. And so great was the prevalence of these disorders in the month of July that out of 4,207 men who were stationed upon Prospect Hill no more than 2,227 were returned fit for duty. . . .

The soldiers in general are most heartily sick of the service, and I believe it would be with the utmost difficulty that they could be prevailed upon to serve another campaign. The Continental Congress are very sensible of this, and have lately sent a committee to the camp to consult with the general officers upon some method of raising the necessary forces to serve during the winter season, as the greatest part of the army that is now in the field is to be disbanded upon the last day of December.

Whether they will be successful in their endeavours to persuade the soldiers to re-inlist or not, I cannot say, but am rather inclined to think that they will. For as they are men possessed of every species of cunning and artifice, and as their political existence depends upon the existence of the army, they will leave no stone unturned to accomplish their designs.

Notwithstanding the indefatigable indeavours of Mr. Washington and the other generals, and particularly of Adjutant General Gates, to arrange and discipline the army, yet any tolerable degree of order and subordination is what they are totally unacquainted with in the rebel camp. And the doctrines of independence and levellism have been so effectually sown throughout the country, and so universally imbibed by all ranks of men, that I apprehend it will be with the greatest difficulty that the inferior officers and soldiers will be ever brought to any tolerable degree of subjection to the commands of their superiors.

Many of their leading men are not insensible of this, and I have often heard them lament that the existence of that very spirit which induced the common people to take up arms and resist the authority of Great Britain, should induce them to resist the authority of their own officers, and by that means effectually prevent their ever making good soldiers.

Another great reason why it is impossible to introduce a proper degree of subordination in the rebel army is the great degree of equality as to birth, fortune and education that universally prevails among them. For men cannot bear to be commanded by others that are their superiors in nothing but in having had the good fortune to get a superior commission, for which perhaps they stood equally fair. And in addition to this, the officers and men are not only in general very nearly upon a par as to birth, fortune, etc., but in particular regiments are most commonly neighbours and acquaintances, and as such can with less patience submit to that degree of absolute submission and subordination which is necessary to form a well-disciplined corps.

Another reason why the army can never be well united and regulated is the disagreement and jealousies between the different troops from the different Colonies; which must never fail to create disaffection and uneasiness among them. The Massachusetts forces already complain very loudly of the partiality of the General to the Virginians, and have even gone so far as to tax him with taking pleasure in bringing their officers to court martials, and having them cashiered that he may fill their places with his friends from that quarter. The gentlemen from the Southern Colonies, in their turn, complain of the enormous proportion of New England officers in the army, and particularly of those belonging to the province of Massachusetts Bay, and say, as the cause is now become a common one, and the experience is general, they ought to have an equal chance for command with their neighbours.

Thus have these jealousies and uneasiness already begun which I think cannot fail to increase and grow every day more and more interesting, and if they do not finally destroy the very existence of the army (which I think they bid very fair to do), yet must unavoidably render it much less formidable than it otherways might have been.

THE CAPTURE OF TICONDEROGA

ETHAN ALLEN

————◆•◆————

The fort at Ticonderoga, near the foot of Lake Champlain and on the route to Canada, had been the scene of a number of battles of the French and Indian Wars. In May, 1775, it was once again a battleground, this time between the British and the Americans led by Benedict Arnold—of yet untarnished name—with Ethan Allen. The Americans won. Allen (1738–1789) was rather vain, certainly a show-off, but fundamentally a thorough Yankee—than which, of course, there can be no higher praise. This is an account of the capture of Ticonderoga from Allen's Narrative of Captivity, *first published in 1779.*

EVER since I arrived at the state of manhood, and acquainted myself with the general history of mankind, I have felt a sincere passion for liberty. The history of nations, doomed to perpetual slavery, in consequence of yielding up to tyrants their natural-born liberties, I read with a sort of philosophical horror; so that the first systematical and bloody attempt, at Lexington, to enslave America, thoroughly electrified my mind, and fully determined me to take part with my country. And, while I was wishing for an opportunity to signalize myself in its behalf, directions were privately sent to me from the then colony (now State) of Connecticut, to raise the Green-Mountain Boys, and, if possible, with them to surprise and take the fortress of Ticonderoga. This enterprise I cheerfully undertook; and, after first guarding all the several passes that led thither, to cut off all intelligence between the garrison and the country, made a forced march from Bennington, and arrived at the lake opposite to Ticonderoga, on the evening of the ninth day of May, 1775, with two hundred and thirty valiant Green-Mountain Boys; and it was with the utmost difficulty that I procured boats to cross the lake. However, I landed eighty-three men near the garrison, and sent the boats back for the rear guard, commanded by Col. Seth Warner; but the day began to dawn, and I found myself under the necessity to attack the fort, before the rear could cross the lake; and, as it was viewed hazardous, I harangued the officers and soldiers in the manner following:

"Friends and fellow-soldiers, You have, for a number of years past been a scourge and terror to arbitrary power. Your valor has been famed abroad, and acknowledged, as appears by the advice and orders to me, from the General Assembly of Connecticut, to surprise and take the garrison now before us. I now propose to advance before you, and, in person, conduct you through the wicket-gate; for we must this morning either quit our pretensions to valor, or possess ourselves of this fortress in a few minutes; and, inasmuch as it is a desperate attempt, which none but the bravest of men dare undertake, I do not urge it on any contrary to his will. You that will undertake voluntarily, poise your firelocks."

The men being, at this time, drawn up in three ranks, each poised his firelock. I ordered them to face to the right, and, at the head of the centre-file, marched them immediately to the wicket-gate aforesaid, where I found a sentry posted, who instantly snapped his fusee at me; I ran immediately toward him, and he retreated through the covered way into the parade within the garrison, gave a halloo, and ran under a bomb-proof. My party, who followed me into the fort, I formed on the parade in such a manner as to face the two barracks which faced each other.

The garrison being asleep, except the sentries, we gave three huzzas which greatly surprised them. One of the sentries made a pass at one of my officers with a charged bayonet, and slightly wounded him. My first thought was to kill him with my sword; but, in an instant, I altered the design and fury of the blow to a slight cut on the side of the head, upon which he dropped his gun, and asked quarter, which I readily granted him, and demanded of him the place where the commanding officer kept; he showed me a pair of stairs in the front of a barrack, on the west part of the garrison, which led up to a second story in said barrack, to which I immediately repaired, and ordered the commander, Capt. De la Place, to come forth instantly, or I would sacrifice the whole garrison; at which the Captain came immediately to the door, with his breeches in his hand; when I ordered him to deliver me the fort instantly; he asked me by what authority I demanded it: I answered him, *"In the name of the great Jehovah, and the Continental Congress."* The authority of the Congress being very little known at that time, he began to speak again; but I interrupted him, and with my drawn sword over his head, again demanded an immediate surrender of the garrison; with which he then complied, and ordered his men to be forthwith paraded without arms, as he had given up the garrison. In the mean time some of my officers had given orders, and in consequence thereof, sundry of the barrack doors were beat down, and about one-third of the garrison imprisoned, which consisted of the said commander, a Lieut. Feltham, a conductor of artillery, a gunner, two sergeants, and forty-four rank and file; about one hundred pieces of cannon, one thirteen-inch mortar, and a number of swivels. This surprise was carried into execution in the gray of the morning of the tenth of May, 1775. The sun seemed to rise that morning with a superior lustre; and Ticonderoga and its dependencies smiled to its conquerors, who tossed about the flowing bowl, and wished success to Congress, and the liberty and freedom of America.

THE BALLAD OF NATHAN HALE

TRADITIONAL

———◆•◆———

The following popular ballad of the Revolution is not by a member of my family, only about one. Hale, born in 1755, never had time to write anything more than a few letters, for he was only twenty-one when he was hanged as a spy by the British. The scene was Turtle Bay, on Manhattan; Hale had been caught serving as a spy on Long Island. His last words, as readers may remember, were somewhat other than those given in the ballad.

    I have always liked the following story about him: Hale had been engaged to marry a Miss Alicia Adams, who lived on after him, married someone else, had children and grandchildren. But when she was dying, as an old, old lady, her last words are supposed to have been "Where is Nathan?"

The breezes went steadily through the tall pines,
  A-saying "oh! hu-ush!" a-saying "oh! hu-ush!"

As stilly stole by a bold legion of horse,
   For Hale in the bush, for Hale in the bush.

"Keep still!" said the thrush as she nestled her young,
   In a nest by the road; in a nest by the road.
"For the tyrants are near, and with them appear
   What bodes us no good, what bodes us no good."

The brave captain heard it, and thought of his home
   In a cot by the brook; in a cot by the brook.
With mother and sister and memories dear,
   He so gayly forsook; he so gayly forsook.

Cooling shades of the night were coming apace,
   The tattoo had beat; the tattoo had beat.
The noble one sprang from his dark lurking-place,
   To make his retreat; to make his retreat.

He warily trod on the dry rustling leaves,
   As he passed through the wood; as he passed through the wood;
And silently gained his rude launch on the shore,
   As she played with the flood; as she played with the flood.

The guards of the camp, on that dark, dreary night,
   Had a murderous will; had a murderous will.
They took him and bore him afar from the shore,
   To a hut on the hill; to a hut on the hill.

No mother was there, nor a friend who could cheer,
   In that little stone cell; in that little stone cell.
But he trusted in love, from his Father above.
   In his heart, all was well; in his heart, all was well.

An ominous owl, with his solemn bass voice,
   Sat moaning hard by; sat moaning hard by:
"The tyrant's proud minions most gladly rejoice,
   For he must soon die; for he must soon die."

The brave fellow told them, no thing he restrained,—
   The cruel general! the cruel general!—
His errand from camp, of the ends to be gained,
   And said that was all; and said that was all.

They took him and bound him and bore him away,
   Down the hill's grassy side; down the hill's grassy side.
'Twas there the base hirelings, in royal array,
   His cause did deride; his cause did deride.

Five minutes were given, short moments, no more,
  For him to repent; for him to repent.
He prayed for his mother, he asked not another,
  To Heaven he went; to Heaven he went.

The faith of a martyr the tragedy showed,
  As he trod the last stage; as he trod the last stage.
And Britons will shudder at gallant Hale's blood,
  As his words do presage, as his words do presage.

"Thou pale king of terrors, thou life's gloomy foe,
  Go frighten the slave, go frighten the slave;
Tell tryants, to you their allegiance they owe.
  No fears for the brave; no fears for the brave."

BOSTON EVACUATED

TIMOTHY NEWELL

*After Washington had besieged Boston for eight months, he decided to
finish up. Seizing and fortifying Dorchester Heights, from them he bom-
barded the enemy out of Boston. General Sir William Howe led his troops
out of the city on St. Patrick's Day, 1776 (a date which has since
fitted in very nicely with parade plans of the Boston politicos).*

The following account of the evacuation comes from the Journal *of
Timothy Newell, a Boston selectman. The "crow feet" he mentions as
being scattered in the streets were devices having several sharp metal
points which, placed on the ground, hindered cavalry.*

[*March*] *17th Lord's day*. This morning at 3 o'clock, the troops began to
move—guards, chevaux de freze, crow feet strewed in the streets to prevent being pursued. They all embarked at about 9 oclock and the whole
fleet came to sail. Every vessel which they did not carry off, they rendered
unfit for use. Not even a boat left to cross the river.

Thus was this unhappy distressed town (through a manifest interposi-
tion of divine providence) relieved from a set of men whose unparalleled
wickedness, profanity, debauchery and cruelty is inexpressible, enduring
a siege from the 19th April 1775 to the 17th March 1776. Immediately
upon the fleet's sailing the Select Men set off through the lines to Roxbury

to acquaint General Washington of the evacuation of the town. After sending a message Major Ward, aid to General Ward, came to us at the lines and soon after the General himself, who received us in the most polite and affectionate manner, and permitted us to pass to Watertown to acquaint the Council of this happy event. The General immediately ordered a detachment of 2000 troops to take possession of the town under the command of General Putnam who the next day began their works in fortifying Forthill, etc., for the better security of the town. A number of loaded shells with trains of powder covered with straw were found in houses left by the Regulars near the fortifycation.

JOHN ADAMS AND ABIGAIL ADAMS

JOHN ADAMS

The following famous letter from John Adams in Philadelphia, to his wife Abigail in Boston, announces the great news of the independence resolution and presages the impending Declaration. (Adams thought it was going to be read on July 2.) It is interesting to note how his prophecy of a celebration suitable to the Declaration of Independence did come true— "pomp, parades, shows, games, sports, guns, bells, bonfires, and illuminations" have been the order of the day, at least up until lately.

YESTERDAY, the greatest question was decided, which ever was debated in America, and a greater, perhaps, never was nor will be decided among men. A resolution was passed without one dissenting colony, "that these United Colonies are, and of right ought to be, free and independent States, and as such they have, and of right ought to have, full power to make war, conclude peace, establish commerce, and to do all other acts and things which other States may rightfully do." You will see in a few days a Declaration setting forth the causes which have impelled us to this mighty revolution, and the reasons which will justify it in the sight of God and man. A plan of confederation will be taken up in a few days.

When I look back to the the year 1761, and recollect the argument concerning writs of assistance in the superior court, which I have hitherto considered as the commencement of this controversy between Great Britain and America, and run through the whole period, from that time to this, and recollect the series of political events, the chain of causes and effects,

I am surprised at the suddenness as well as greatness of this revolution. Britain has been filled with folly, and America with wisdom. At least, this is my judgment. Time must determine. It is the will of Heaven that the two countries should be sundered forever. It may be the will of Heaven that America shall suffer calamities still more wasting, and distresses yet more dreadful. If this is to be the case, it will have this good effect at least. It will inspire us with many virtues, which we have not, and correct many errors, follies and vices which threaten to disturb, dishonor, and destroy us. The furnace of affliction produces refinement, in States as well as individuals. And the new governments we are assuming in every part will require a purification from our vices, and an augmentation of our virtues, or they will be no blessings. The people will have unbounded power, and the people are extremely addicted to corruption and venality, as well as the great. But I must submit all my hopes and fears to an overruling Providence, in which, unfashionable as the faith may be, I firmly believe.

Had a Declaration of Independency been made seven months ago, it would have been attended with many great and glorious effects. We might, before this hour, have formed alliances with foreign States. We should have mastered Quebec, and been in possession of Canada. You will perhaps wonder how such a declaration would have influenced our affairs in Canada, but if I could write with freedom, I could easily convince you that it would, and explain to you the manner how. Many gentlemen in high stations and of great influence had been duped by the ministerial bubble of commissioners to treat. And in real, sincere expectation of this event, which they so fondly wished, they have been slow and languid in promoting measures for the reduction of that province. Others there are in the colonies who really wished that our enterprise in Canada would be defeated, that the colonies might be brought into danger and distress between two fires, and be thus induced to submit. Others really wished to defeat the expedition to Canada, lest the conquest of it should elevate the minds of the people too much to hearken to those terms of reconciliation, which, they believed, would be offered us. These jarring views, wishes, and designs, occasioned an opposition to many salutary measures, which were proposed for the support of that expedition, and caused obstructions, embarrassments, and studied delays, which have finally lost us the province.

All these causes, however, in conjunction, would not have disappointed us, if it had not been for a misfortune which could not be foreseen, and, perhaps, could not have been prevented—I mean the prevalence of the small-pox among our troops. This fatal pestilence completed our destruction. It is a frown of Providence upon us, which we ought to lay to heart.

But, on the other hand, the delay of this declaration to this time has many great advantages attending it. The hopes of reconciliation, which were fondly entertained by multitudes of honest and well-meaning, though weak and mistaken people, have been gradually and, at last, totally extinguished. Time has been given for the whole people maturely to consider the great question of independence, and to ripen their judgment, dissipate their fears, and allure their hopes, by discussing it in newspapers and pamphlets, by debating it in assemblies, conventions, committees of safety and inspection, in town and county meetings, as well as in private conversations, so that the whole people, in every colony of the thirteen, have now adopted it is as their own act. This will cement the union, and avoid those heats, and perhaps convulsions, which might have been occasioned by such a declaration six months ago.

But the day is past. The second day of July, 1776, will be the most memorable epocha in the history of America. I am apt to believe that it will be celebrated by succeeding generations as the great anniversary festival. It ought to be commemorated, as the day of deliverance, by solemn acts of devotion to God Almighty. It ought to be solemnized with pomp and parade, with shows, games, sports, guns, bells, bonfires, and illuminations, from one end of this continent to the other, from this time forward, forevermore.

You will think me transported with enthusiasm, but I am not. I am well aware of the toil, and blood, and treasure, that it will cost us to maintain this declaration, and support and defend these States. Yet, through all the gloom, I can see the rays of ravishing light and glory. I can see that the end is more than worth all the means, and that posterity will triumph in that day's transaction, even although we should rue it, which I trust in God we shall not.

PHILADELPHIA, 3 *July*, 1776.

A NEW ENGLAND MINISTER
ON SLAVERY

SAMUEL HOPKINS

———◆◆———

In writing his deathless Declaration, Jefferson did not mean to include slaves as men when he stated that all men are created equal. However, public opinion, as we know, soon came to regard slavery as inconsistent with the Declaration.

The following imaginary dialogue about the slavery question was composed in 1776 by Samuel Hopkins (1721–1803), a Congregational minister. Although theology was no longer a burning topic of the times, the

New England clergy yet had much to do with forming public opinion. They were called "the black regiment" of the Revolution, for their sermons were largely responsible for the sentiment and actions summed up in the phrase "The Spirit of '76."

B. I HOPE you will not appeal to the Holy Scripture in support of a practice which you and every one else must allow to be so inexpressibly unjust, inhuman, and cruel as is the slave trade, and, consequently, so glaringly contrary to the whole tenor of divine revelation; and if the slave trade is such a gross violation of every divine precept, it is impossible to vindicate the slavery to which the Africans have been reduced by this trade from the Holy Scripture. . . . However, I am willing to hear what you can produce from Scripture in favor of any kind of slavery.

A. You know that a curse was pronounced on the posterity of Ham for his wickedness, in the following words: "A servant of servants shall he be unto his brethren." He could not be a servant unto his brethren unless they made him so, or at least held him in servitude. The curse could not take place unless they executed it, and they seem to be by God appointed to do this; therefore, while we, the children of Japheth, are making such abject slaves of the blacks, the children of Ham, we are only executing the righteous curse denounced upon them; which is so far from being wrong in us, that it would be a sin, even disobedience to the revealed will of God, to refuse to make slaves of them, and attempt to set them at liberty.

B. Do you think, my good sir, it was the duty of Pharaoh to make the Israelites serve him and the Egyptians, and afflict them by ruling over them with rigor, and holding them in hard and cruel bondage, because God has expressly told this, and said it should be done? And was the Assyrian king blameless while he executed the judgment which God had threatened to inflict on his professing people? Did God's threatening them with those evils warrant this king to distress, captivate, and destroy them as he did? And will you say the Jews did right in crucifying our Lord, because by this they fulfilled the Scriptures, declaring that thus it must be? Your argument, if it is of any force, will assert and justify all this, and, therefore, I hope will be renounced by you, and by all who have the least regard for the Holy Scripture, with proper abhorrence. But if this argument were not so fraught with absurdity and impiety as it really is, and it were granted to be forcible with respect to all upon whom the mentioned curse was denounced, yet it would not justify our enslaving the Africans, for they are not the posterity of Canaan, who was the only son of Ham that was doomed to be a servant of servants. The other sons of Ham and their posterity are no more affected with this curse than the other sons of Noah and their posterity. Therefore, this prediction is as much of a warrant for the Africans' enslaving us, as it is for us to make slaves of them. The truth is, it gives not the least shadow of a right to any one of the children of Noah to make slaves of any of their brethren.

A. The people of Israel were allowed by God to buy and make slaves from the nations that were round about them, and the strangers that lived among them,—which could not have been the case if this was wrong and unjust,—and why have not we an equal right to do the same?

B. And why have not we an equal right to invade any nation and land, as they did the land of Canaan, and destroy them all, men, women, and children, and beasts, without saving so much as one alive? It was right for the Israelites to do this, because they had a divine permission and direction to do it, as the God of Israel had a right to destroy the seven nations of Canaan in what way he thought best, and to direct whom he pleased to do it. And it was right for them to make bond-servants of the nations round them, they having an express permission to do it from him who has a right to dispose of all men as he pleases. God saw fit, for wise reasons, to allow the people of Israel thus to make and possess slaves; but is this any license to us to enslave any of our fellow-men, any more than their being allowed to kill the seven nations in Canaan is a license to us to kill any of our fellow-men whom we please and are able to destroy, and take possession of their estates?

This must be answered in the negative by every one who will allow himself a moment's reflection. God gave many directions and laws to the Jews which had no respect to mankind in general; and this under consideration has all the marks of such a one. There is not any thing in it or relating to it, from whence can be deduced the least evidence that it was designed to be a regulation for all nations through every age of the world, but everything to the contrary. The children of Israel were then distinguished from all other nations on earth; they were God's peculiar people, and favored on many accounts above others, and had many things in their constitution and laws that were designed to keep up their separation and distinction from other nations, and to make the special favor of Heaven toward them more apparent to all who had any knowledge of them; and this law respecting bondage is suited to answer these ends. This distinction is now at an end, and all nations are put upon a level; and Christ, who has taken down the wall of separation, has taught us to look on all nations as our neighbors and brethren, without any respect of persons, and to love all men as ourselves, and to do to others as we would they should treat us; by which he has most effectually abolished this permission given to the Jews, as well as many other institutions which were peculiar to them. Besides, that this permission was not designed for all nations and ages will be very evident if we consider what such a supposition implies; for if this be so, then all other nations had a right to make slaves of the Jews. The Egyptians had a right to buy and sell them, and keep them all in bondage forever, and the nations round about Canaan had a right to bring them into bondage, as they sometimes did, and the Babylonians and Romans had a good warrant to reduce them to a state of captivity and servitude. And the Africans had a good right to make slaves of us and our children: the inhabitants of Great Britain may lawfully make slaves of all the Americans, and transport us to England, and buy and sell us in open market, as they do their cattle and horses, and perpetuate our bondage to the latest generation; and the Turks have a good right to all the Christian slaves they have among them, and to make as many more slaves of us and our children as shall be in their power, and to hold them and their children in bondage to the latest posterity. According to this every man has a warrant to make a bondslave of his neighbor whenever it lies in his power, and no one has any right to his own freedom any longer than he can keep himself out of the power of others. For instance: if the blacks now among us should, by some remarkable providence, have the power in their hands to reduce us, they have a right to make us and our children their slaves, and we should have no reason to complain.

This would put mankind into such a state of perpetual war and confusion, and is so contrary to our loving our neighbor as ourselves, that he who has the least regard for his fellow-men, or the divine law, must reject it, and the principle from which it flows, with the greatest abhorrence. Let no Christian, then, plead this permission to the Jews to make bondslaves of their neighbors as a warrant to hold the slaves he has made, and, consequently, for universal slavery.

CONCERNING BENEDICT ARNOLD

GENERAL NATHANAEL GREENE

In the following Order of the Day for September 26, 1780, General Nathanael Greene reveals the news of Benedict Arnold's treason, and his plot to surrender West Point to the British. Major André, to whom he had been about to deliver the fort, was taken prisoner and executed, some say in revenge for Nathan Hale.

Greene is one of the great New England names—a Rhode Island one, still flourishing. The general was later responsible for the British evacuation of Charleston.

Treason of the blackest dye was yesterday discovered. General Arnold, who commanded at West Point, lost to every sentiment of honor, of public and private obligation, was about to deliver up that important fort into the hands of the enemy. Such an event must have given the American cause a deadly wound if not a fatal stab. Happily the scheme was timely discovered to prevent the final misfortune. The providential train of circumstances which led to it affords the most convincing proofs that the liberties of America are the object of divine protection. At the same time the treason is so regretted the General cannot help congratulating the army on the happy discovery.

Our enemies, despairing of carrying their point by force, are practising every base art to effect, by bribery and corruption, what they cannot accomplish in a manly way. Great honor is due to the American army that this is the first instance of treason of this kind, where many were to be expected from the nature of the dispute, and nothing is so high an ornament to the characters of the American soldiers as their withstanding all the arts and seductions of an insidious enemy.

Arnold the traitor has made his escape to the enemy, but Mr. André, Adjutant-General to the British army, who came out as a spy to negotiate the business, is our prisoner.

His Excellency the Commander-in-Chief has arrived at West Point from Hartford, and is now doubtless taking proper steps to unravel fully so hellish a plot.

THE YORKTOWN SURRENDER

JAMES THACHER

———◆◆◆———

James Thacher (1754–1844), a Massachusetts surgeon in the Continental Army, in 1823 published his Military Journal During the American Revolutionary War, *from which the following account of the British surrender at Yorktown is taken. The General Lincoln he speaks of as having capitulated at Charleston was forced to do so when his troops were trapped there by the British General Clinton.*

The "British march" to which Thacher refers was a popular air of the day, wildly apropriate—"The World Turned Upside Down."

[October] 19th.—This is to us a most glorious day, but to the English, one of bitter chagrin and disappointment. Preparations are now making to receive as captives that vindictive, haughty commander and that victorious army, who, by their robberies and murders, have so long been a scourge to our brethren of the Southern states. Being on horseback, I anticipate a full share of satisfaction in viewing the various movements in the interesting scene.

The stipulated terms of capitulation are similar to those granted to General Lincoln at Charleston the last year. The captive troops are to march out with shouldered arms, colors cased and drums beating a British or German march, and to ground their arms at a place assigned for the purpose. The officers are allowed their side-arms and private property, and the generals and such officers as desire it are to go on parole to England or New York. The marines and seamen of the king's ships are prisoners of war to the navy of France; and the land forces to the United States. All military and artillery stores to be delivered up unimpaired. The royal prisoners to be sent into the interior of Virginia, Maryland and Pennsylvania in regiments, to have rations allowed them equal to the American soldiers, and to have their officers near them. Lord Cornwallis to man and despatch the *Bonetta* sloop-of-war with despatches to Sir Henry Clinton at New York without being searched, the vessel to be returned and the hands accounted for.

At about twelve o'clock, the combined army was arranged and drawn up in two lines extending more than a mile in length. The Americans were drawn up in a line on the right side of the road, and the French occupied the left. At the head of the former, the great American commander, mounted on his noble courser, took his station, attended by his aids. At the head of the latter was posted the excellent Count Rochambeau and his suite. The French troops, in complete uniform, displayed a martial and noble appearance; their bands of music, of which the timbrel formed a part, is a delightful novelty and produced while marching to the ground a most enchanting effect. The Americans, though not all in uniform, nor their dress so neat, yet exhibited an erect, soldierly air, and every countenance beamed with satisfaction and joy. The concourse of spectators from the country was prodigious, in point of numbers was probably equal to the military, but universal silence and order prevailed.

It was about two o'clock when the captive army advanced through the line formed for their reception. Every eye was prepared to gaze on Lord Cornwallis, the object of peculiar interest and solicitude; but he disappointed our anxious expectations; pretending indisposition, he made General O'Hara his substitute as the leader of his army. This officer was followed by the conquered troops in a slow and solemn step, with shouldered arms, colors cased and drums beating a British march. Having arrived at the head of the line, General O'Hara, elegantly mounted, advanced to his excellency the commander-in-chief, taking off his hat, and apologized for the non-appearance of Earl Cornwallis. With his usual dignity and politeness, his excellency pointed to Major-General Lincoln for directions, by whom the British army was conducted into a spacious field, where it was intended they should ground their arms.

The royal troops, while marching through the line formed by the allied army, exhibited a decent and neat appearance, as respects arms and clothing, for their commander opened his store and directed every soldier to be furnished with a new suit complete, prior to the capitulation. But in their line of march we remarked a disorderly and unsoldierly conduct, their step was irregular, and their ranks frequently broken.

But it was in the field, when they came to the last act of the drama, that the spirit and pride of the British soldier was put to the severest test: here their mortification could not be concealed. Some of the platoon officers appeared to be exceedingly chagrined when giving the word "*ground arms*," and I am a witness that they performed this duty in a very unofficer-like manner; and that many of the soldiers manifested a *sullen temper*, throwing their arms on the pile with violence, as if determined to render them useless. This irregularity, however, was checked by the authority of General Lincoln. After having grounded their arms and divested themselves of their accoutrements, the captive troops were conducted back to Yorktown and guarded by our troops till they could be removed to the place of their destination.

The British troops that were stationed at Gloucester surrendered at the same time and in the same manner to the command of the Duke de Luzerne [Lauzun].

This must be a very interesting and gratifying transaction to General Lincoln, who, having himself been obliged to surrender an army to a haughty foe the last year, has now assigned him the pleasing duty of giving laws to a conquered army in return, and of reflecting that the terms which were imposed on him are adopted as a basis of the surrender in the present instance.

PRESIDENT STILES OF YALE

ABIEL HOLMES

The New Englanders returned from battle not only to the plow but to the desk. Ezra Stiles (1727–1795), a president of Yale, was one of the most learned Americans of his time. Also, he possessed a universality of interests that ranged in scope from the establishing of silk manufacture in

New England to the founding of Brown University. Grandson of Rev. Edward Taylor the poet, Stiles was himself a Congregational minister. The following account of him is that of Abiel Holmes, Stiles's son-in-law and the father of the older Oliver Wendell Holmes.

THE LIFE OF EZRA STILES, D.D., LL.D. 1798

PRESIDENT Stiles was a man of low and small stature; of a very delicate structure; and of a well-proportioned form. His eyes were of a dark gray color; and, in the moment of contemplation, singularly penetrating. His voice was clear and energetic. His countenance, especially in conversation, was expressive of mildness and benignity; but, if occasion required, it became the index of majesty and authority.

The delicacy of his frame requiring a special care of his health, he was prudently attentive, amidst his multiplied studies and labors, to its preservation. Always temperate, he found it easy, when necessary, to be abstemious. Having carefully studied his own constitution, he was generally his own physician. By regulating his diet, exercising daily in the open air, and using occasionally a few simple medicines, he was, by the divine blessing, enabled, with but very small interruptions, to apply himself assiduously to study, and to discharge the various duties of public and domestic life. . . . He accustomed himself to the exercise of walking in the open air; and often walked within-doors, in a very comtemplative manner, especially on Saturday evenings, and on the Lord's-day.

His passions were naturally strong and impetuous; but he attained an habitual government of them, by prayerful and pious influence. Proofs of this are derived from his particular conduct, when put to the test of temptation, as well as from the general equability of his deportment. On the reception of injuries, he was patient and placable; and took peculiar pains to effect a reconciliation with those, who, having done him an injury, were disposed to alienation. When assaulted with virulence, as he was in some instances from the press, he made it an inflexible rule to offer no public reply; and his private behavior, in such instances, evinced a superiority to insult, and the divine temper of Christian forgiveness. Sometimes he briefly recorded the injury in his Diary, and, without one acrimonious reflection, made it subservient to new improvement in knowledge and virtue; observing, with one of the ancients: *Fas est et ab hoste doceri* —"It is lawful to be taught, even by an enemy."

With a rare felicity, he united, in his address and manners, familiarity with dignity. While an ornament to the highest, he was accessible to the lowest, classes of mankind. Communicative, hospitable, and polite to strangers, entertaining and instructive to all, none left his company without delightful impressions. . . .

For his extensive acquisitions of knowledge, he was indebted to a mind at once active and comprehensive; to a memory quick to receive, and faithful to retain; and to a diligence patient and indefatigable. . . . Though he read with rapidity, he read with heedful attention; and made himself master of the subject. If the book was not his own, and especially if rare and valuable, he copied its most interesting passages into his literary diary. If his own, he wrote in the margin such remarks as occurred to him in the perusal. . . . He always carried a pencil in his pocket, and a small quarto sheet of blank paper, doubled lengthwise, on which he minuted every noticeable occurrence, and useful information. . . . When these memoranda formed materials sufficient for a volume, he had them bound; and they, collectively, compose four curious volumes of Itineraries, preserved in his cabinet of manuscripts. . . .

Though it was peculiarly the province of the Tutors to visit the scholars at their chambers—a practice which, from the experience of its numerous advantages, was uniformly maintained—yet he often made such visits in person. He made choice of the hours of study, for this purpose, that he might detect and admonish the negligent or vicious; applaud the studious; assist and encourage all. . . .

It was his early resolution to receive no gifts, directly or indirectly, from the students. In many instances their parents sent him articles of provision, as gratuities, for which, as appears by his account-books, he uniformly gave credit in their quarterly bills. He manifested a paternal concern for such of his pupils as found it difficult to defray the expenses of their education; inquired and ascertained their exigencies; and in numerous instances gratuitously discharged their bills for quarterly tuition. The best scholars are, not unfrequently, to be found among the most indigent. Knowing that their future fortunes are suspended on their present diligence, they learn to estimate their collegiate privileges more justly than many others, who, through the indiscretion of their parents, are furnished with the means of dissipation; or, in the expectation of an ample patrimony, seek nothing more than the honor of a diploma. The President coming, one day, out of the Library, and seeing a student, of bright parts and of studious application, walking pensively alone in the college yard, called him, and made some inquiry about his situation. Having encouraged his perseverance, he put a guinea into his hand, and dismissed him with renovated spirits and a brightened countenance. It was done with his usual delicacy. "Make a good improvement of it," said he; "ask no questions; and say nothing."

1798-1812

ADVICE TO THE PRIVILEGED
ORDERS

JOEL BARLOW

———◆•◆———

*Even before the new nation had adopted its Constitution, an ardently
nationalistic school of American writers came into being—the Hartford
Wits. The revolutionary view of America as a future artistic Utopia, expressed in Jonathan Trumbull's poem (page 171) now sought to express
itself in reality. It must be borne in mind that in the eighteenth century
wit meant something a little different than what it means now. A "wit,"
now, is somebody being skillfully funny; then, being a wit meant the
same as being a "brain" means now.*

*Joel Barlow (1754–1812) lived in France long enough to be converted
from a conservative Connecticut Puritan into a cosmopolitan democrat.
His* Advice to the Privileged Orders, *from which the following is excerpted, was inspired by his friend Tom Paine, the famous pamphleteer.*

IT is a truth, I believe, not to be called in question, that every man is
born with an imprescriptible claim to a portion of the elements; which
portion is termed his *birth-right*. Society may vary this right, as to its
form, but never can destroy it in substance. She has no control over the
man, till he is born; and the right being born with him, and being necessary to his existence, she can no more annihilate the one than the other,
though she has the power of new-modelling both. But on coming into the
world, he finds that the ground which nature had promised him is taken
up, and in the occupancy of others; society has changed the form of his
birth-right; the general stock of elements, from which the lives of men
are to be supported, has undergone a new modification; and his portion
among the rest. He is told that he cannot claim it in its present form, as
an independent inheritance; that he must draw on the stock of society,

instead of the stock of nature; that he is banished from the mother and must cleave to the nurse. In this unexpected occurrence he is unprepared to act; but *knowledge* is a part of the stock of society; and an indispensable part to be allotted in the portion of the claimant is *instruction* relative to the new arrangement of natural right. To withhold this instruction therefore would be, not merely the omission of a duty, but the commission of a crime; and society in this case would sin against the man, before the man could sin against society.

I should hope to meet the assent of all unprejudiced readers, in carrying this idea still farther. In cases where a person is born of poor parents, or finds himself brought into the community of men without the means of subsistence, society is bound to furnish him the means. She ought not only to instruct him in the artificial laws by which property is secured, but in the artificial industry by which it is obtained. She is bound, in *justice* as well as policy, to give him some art or trade. For the reason of his incapacity is, that *she* has usurped his birth-right; and this is restoring it to him in another form, more convenient for both parties. The failure of society in this branch of her duty is the occasion of much the greater part of the evils that call for criminal jurisprudence. The individual feels that he is robbed of his natural right; he cannot bring his process to reclaim it from the great community, by which he is overpowered; he therefore feels authorized in reprisal; in taking another's goods to replace his own. And it must be confessed, that in numberless instances the conduct of society justifies him in this proceeding; she has seized upon his property, and commenced the war against him.

Some, who perceive these truths, say that it is unsafe for society to publish them; but I say it is unsafe not to publish them. For the party from which the mischief is expected to arise has the knowledge of them already, and has acted upon them in all ages. It is the wise who are ignorant of these things, and not the foolish. They are truths of nature; and in them the teachers of mankind are the only party that remains to be taught. It is a subject on which the logic of indigence is much clearer than that of opulence. The latter reasons from contrivance, the former from feeling; and God has not endowed us with false feelings, in things that so weightily concern our happiness.

None can deny that the obligation is much stronger on me, to support my life, than to support the claim that my neighbour has to his property. Nature commands the first, society the second:—in one I obey the laws of God, which are universal and eternal; in the other, the laws of man, which are local and temporary.

It has been the folly of all governments, to begin every thing at the wrong end, and to erect their institutions on an inversion of principle. This is more sadly the case in their systems of jurisprudence, than is commonly imagined. *Compelling* justice is always mistaken for *rendering* justice. But this important branch of administration consists not merely in compelling men to be just to each other, and individuals to society,—this is not the whole, nor is it the principal part, nor even the beginning, of the operation. The source of power is said to be the source of justice; but it does not answer to this description, as long as it contents itself with *compulsion.* Justice must begin by flowing from its source; and the first as well as the most important object is, to open its channels from society to all the individual members. This part of the administration being well devised and diligently executed, the other parts would lessen away by degrees to matters of inferior consideration.

It is an undoubted truth, that our duty is inseparably connected with our happiness. And why should we despair of convincing every member of society of a truth so important for him to know? Should any person object, by saying, that nothing like this has ever yet been done; I answer, that nothing like this has ever yet been tried. Society has hitherto been curst with governments, whose existence depended on the extinction of truth. Every moral light has been smothered under the bushel of perpetual imposition; from whence it emits but faint and glimmering rays, always insufficient to form any luminous system on any of the civil concerns of men. But these covers are crumbling to the dust, with the governments which they support; and the probability becomes more apparent, the more it is considered, that society is capable of curing all the evils to which it has given birth.

A NEW ENGLAND FROLIC

JOHN NEAL

————◆•◆————

A description of the lighter side of life in Maine in the late eighteenth century comes from The Yankee, *a literary journal founded by John Neal (1793–1876). Neal was born a Quaker in Portland and was simultaneously shrewd Yankee and man of the world. Most of all he was a prophet of Americanism in literature. Enthusiastic and tempestuous (they read him out of the Friends for knocking a man down), he may not have been a great writer but he seems a very American one. His most famous novel, which older readers may still remember, was* Brother Jonathan. *The picture which follows here of cold winter nights and the kissing games that warmed them is a fair sample of Neal's liveliness.*

THE state of society in the country, was rapidly improving at this time; or perhaps I should say it had very much improved within the last few years. The difficulties which ever oppose improvement in a new country, were disappearing. The increase of wealth enabled them to provide more efficient instructors for their children, to supply them with useful books, and to extend their intercourse with the more improved parts of the country. It should be remarked, that in purchasing books in those days, they selected such only as were calculated to inform the mind, or improve the heart; and after purchasing, *they read them.* Hence the honest freedom and stern virtues of the first settlers had received the first and most useful polish of refinement, without being either destroyed or impaired by it.

The education of young females, was both useful and respectable. With every part of house-work and domestic economy, they were perfectly familiar; they were taught the solid branches of education, and their minds unincumbered with the frippery, and nonsense of a town education, were improved, and enlightened by much useful reading. And there was more kindly good feeling in the community; more of that unrestrained friendly intercourse, which unites man to man, and convinces him that he is a social being,—that he lives not for himself alone, than can be found in the most refined societies of the present age.

The long winters, and long winter-evenings had much influence in producing this state of society. Sleigh-riding presented an easy and pleasant mode of travelling over roads that were barely passable in summer; the long evenings afforded ample time for making social visits through a large neighbourhood; and the time and the means thus happily united, were seldom allowed to pass unimproved. The young men who were employed in taking care of the stock of the farm, preparing firewood and tools for summer; and the girls, who were employed in spinning, and weaving the wool and flax raised on the farm, & preparing clothes and furniture for the family the coming year, frequently finished their day's work by early candle-light, or before; and all parties were then prepared to jump into a sleigh, and be off to a frolic.

The word frolic, so far as the meeting of a large number of acquaintances at the house of a neighbour is concerned, meant what the word party means now; but otherwise it was quite a different thing. It was not a place where young ladies, with false curls stuck full of turtle-shell, met to talk nonsense and retail scandal. But as I may have occasion to speak of parties hereafter, I will now confine myself to a frolic.

A meeting at a friend's house having been previously agreed upon, the double-sleigh was brought to the door; and if there were not boys and girls enough in the family to fill it, they called at the neighbours and took in one or more until it was full. Then crack! went the whip, and away went a sleigh-load of laughing, frolicing girls and boys, some five, six, or perhaps ten miles, to a friend's house; their hearts as light, and their spirits as pure as the mountain-air that was whistling by them. There they met other sleigh-loads, all of whom received an unceremonious, but hearty welcome; and the house was soon filled with innocent hearts and happy eyes. The dress of the girls on these occasions was a gown with long sleeves, brought tight round the breast, a little below the arms; with a collar, or sometimes a frilled vandyke of the same. Their long hair was combed back and secured just below the neck with a steel-clasp, some six inches long (called a hair spring) thence falling in rich waves, it floated below the waist. And on a beautiful girl, this was indeed a beautiful dress —forcibly reminding one of Tom Moore's Norah.

> Och, my Norah's gown for me,
> That floats as wild as mountain breezes;
> Leaving every beauty free,
> To sink, or swell, as nature pleases.

The evening would pass away with free and rational conversation; subjects and talents for which were never wanting. Not unfrequently plays were introduced. Blind-man's-buff was at this time going out of fashion, and Break-the-Pope's-neck, or Who's got the button? for the purpose of obtaining and redeeming pawns or pledges, had each become a favorite, particularly with the girls; for there was always more or less—kissing, (its out!) hitched in to it.

To break the Pope's neck, chairs were placed round the room, for all the company save one; one person stood in the centre of the room, with a plate in his hand; the whole company forming a circle round him, taking hold of hands, and passing rapidly round. He placed the edge of the plate upon the floor, gave it a whirl, saying "I've broke the Pope's neck," and calling some one by name to set it. The one called on sprang for the plate, and the rest made a rush for the seats; and the one who failed in obtaining a seat, as one certainly must, was obliged to deposit a pledge for redemption. The scrabble, and sometimes half-scuffling, and tumbling, that occurred in the endeavour to obtain a seat, was by no means an uninteresting scene. But it was a slow way of procuring pledges. Who's got the button? was much better. When a sufficient number of pledges were obtained, preparation was made to redeem them. One person, generally a female, presided as judge in the affair; and was always blinded, to preclude the possibility of a partial decree—an idea worthy of imitation. It was common to hold up two articles over the head of the judge, one belonging to a person of each sex at the same time; to redeem which they were not unfrequently ordered to kiss each other "wheelbarrow fashion." You would then see a fine, well formed young man, and a beautiful, half blushing—half laughing girl, with "long loose hair" meet on the floor; close their right and left hands, on both sides; and with a whirl as quick, and mysterious as the lightning's flash—almost—turn through their arms, bring the back part of their shoulders in contact—each with the head resting upon the other's right shoulder, their mouths meeting with as much precision as the points of a pair of scissors. It was considered very ungenteel to err in the performance of the manœuvre, either in time or point.

And again, ever and anon, the malicious creature would doom a poor wight to kiss all the girls in the room—by way of redeeming a pair of gloves, or a pocket handkerchief, not worth a four-penny-happeny—the poor fellow's lips wouldn't get cold again for a week.

Thus merrily and happily passed the time, until the hour of separation arrived; when a momentary bustle for coats, and cloaks, and the crowding of sleighs about the door ensued: And a sigh escaped them, and a kind feeling was expressed, as they took leave of each other, and made their arrangements for another meeting.

by A YANKEE

AN OLD HOUSE IN BOSTON

EDMUND QUINCY

———◆•◆———

Among the fallacies that abound about what old New England was like, none is more prevalent than that all New England houses were pinched and mean, sparsely furnished, and uncomfortable. Catherine Sedgwick's novel reconstructed Governor Winthrop's elegant house in the seventeenth century; here is a first-person account of an old Boston house of the late eighteenth century. Its author, Edmund Quincy (1808–1877), was a grandson of the Josiah Quincy who, together with John Adams, defended the British soldiers after the Boston Massacre, and son of the Josiah Quincy who was a Unitarian and president of Harvard. Edmund Quincy became an ardent Abolitionist and editor of The Liberator. *The following excerpt is from* The Haunted Adjutant, *a collection of his short stories.*

THE good old class of "garden-houses," in which it is recorded that Milton always chose to live, is now almost as entirely extinct here as in London itself. How well do I remember one of these, in which some of my happiest days and merriest nights were spent! It stood with its end to the street, overshadowed by a magnificent elm of aboriginal growth, which made strange and solemn music in my boyish ears when the autumn winds called forth its hidden harmonies at midnight. Entering the gate, you proceeded on a flagged walk, having the house close to you on your left, and on your right the courtyard, filled with "flowers of all hues," and fragrant shrubs, each forming the mathematical centre of an exact circle cut in the velvet greensward. When within the front door, you had on your left hand the best parlor, opened only on high solemnities, and which used to excite in my young mind a mysterious feeling of mingled curiosity and awe whenever I stole a glance at its darkened interior, with its curiously carved mahogany chairs black as ebony with age, its blue damask curtains, the rare piece of tapestry which served as a carpet —all reflected in the tall mirror, with its crown and sceptred top, between the windows. I remember it used to put me in mind of the fatal blue chamber in Bluebeard. I am not sure now that there was not something supernatural about it.

But it was the parlor opposite that was the very quintessence of snugness and comfort, worth half a hundred fantastic boudoirs and modern drawing-rooms bedizened with French finery. On your right hand as you entered were two windows opening upon the courtyard above commemorated, with their convenient window-seats—an accommodation which I sadly miss—with their appropriate green velvet cushions, a little the worse for wear. On the opposite side of the room to the windows was a glass door opening into the garden,—a pleasant sight to see, with its rectangular box-lined gravel walks, its abundant vegetables, its luxuriant fruit-trees, its vine trained over the stable-wall. As you returned to the house through the garden-door, you had on your right the door of a closet with a window looking into the garden, which was entitled the study, having been appropriated to that purpose by the deceased master of the house. This recess possessed substantial charms to my infant imagination as the perennial fountain of cakes and apples, which my good aunt—of whom presently —conducted in a never-failing stream to the never-satisfied mouth of an urchin of six years old. I thought they grew there by some spontaneous process of reproduction.

A little farther on, nearer to the study-door than the one by which we entered, was the fireplace, fit shrine for the Penates of such a household; its ample circumference adorned with Dutch tiles, where stout shepherdesses in hoops and high-heeled shoes gave sidelong looks of love to kneeling swains in cocked hats and trunk-hose; while their dogs and sheep had grown so much alike from long intimacy as to be scarcely distinguishable. How I loved those little glimpses into pastoral life! I have one of them now, which I rescued from the wreck of matter when the house came down. Within the ample jaws of the chimney, which might have swallowed up at a mouthful a century of patent grates, crackled and roared the merry wood fire,—fed with massy logs which it would take two men to lift, as men are now,—casting its cheerful light as evening drew in on the panelled walls, bringing out the curious "egg-and-anchor" carvings, which were my special pride and wonder, and flashing back from the mirror globe which depended from the beam which divided the comfortable low ceiling into two unequal parts. And let me not forget the mantelpiece, adorned with grotesque heads in wood and clusters of fruit and flowers, of which Grinling Gibbons him self need not have been ashamed. And then the Turkey carpet, covering the breadth, but not the length, of the room; and the books,—the "Spectator's" short face in his title-page, the original "Tatler," the first editions of Pope. But time would fail me were I to record all the well-remembered contents of that dear old room,—the sofa or settee, of narrow capacity, looking as if three single chairs had been rolled into one; the card-table, with its corners for candles, and its pools for fish scooped out of the verdant champaign of green broadcloth. But enough: let us now approach the divinity whose penetralia we have entered, and who well befits such a shrine.

SKETCHES OF A NEW ENGLAND VILLAGE

ELIZA BUCKMINSTER LEE

Eliza Buckminster Lee (c. 1788–1864) was a New Hampshire author and translator. The "large, dark, unpainted house" she describes as the parsonage in the following passage from Sketches of a New England Village *is typical of the older New England houses; they turned almost black with weather and, I suppose, oiling. In Ipswich, Massachusetts, alone, there are over forty seventeenth-century houses that still stand, many of them of this type.*

You request me, my dear friend, to give you a written account of that period in my early life which has interested you so much in the recital. It can only be from the contrast those early days present to your own elevated station in society, that scenes of remote retirement and humble obscurity can afford you interest. In looking back on them myself, they seem to have passed in another and earlier world. It has been beautifully said, that "the actions and events of our childhood lie like fair pictures in the air; always in memory, they are objects of beauty, however base their origin and neighborhood." In looking back, therefore, I am grateful that my early life was passed in remote obscurity, amid scenes of humble virtue, of peace and beauty.

You have seen, I think, W——, the distant village in New England, where I spent nearly the last half of the last century. Perhaps, however, you have merely looked at it as a passing traveller, and did not remark its simple beauty. To memory, every tree, every green pasture and humble dwelling, are as familiar as the room I sit in. It was distant about two miles from the ocean, and scattered on both sides of a small but tranquil and beautiful river, which was crossed by a wooden bridge in the centre of the village. On the north side rose gentle hills gracefully from the river, and on the south spread out level meadows, dotted with buttonwood trees and weeping elms. The meeting-house and parsonage were on the north side, overlooking on the south the village, whose houses were scattered about the bridge, and ascended, at least the better sort, towards the church. Beyond the hills on the north, stretched out, as if to shelter us, the protecting forest. The meeting-house was the square, barn-like structure, common at that period to all New England. Ours, however, was adorned with a steeple and belfry, and graced with a most sweet sounding bell.

You must remember my often-repeated descriptions of the dear old parsonage. It was a tolerably large, dark, unpainted house, two stories in front, full of windows, to admit all the genial influences of the south, while on the north it sloped down so that one might lay his hand on the roof. These old fashioned houses are fast disappearing from our country. They were admirably calculated to protect us from the severe winters of our climate. The front always turned to the sun, and the long sloping roof, on which the deep snows rested, afforded from that very circumstance, a protecting warmth. Almost the only picturesque object in our unpoetical county, the long well-pole, with its "mossy, iron-bound bucket," is disappearing with them.

Our house was rather irregular in form, and on the outside of a most venerable blackness, stained here and there with spots of moss and decay. We entered a sort of low, wide hall, which had been originally built of logs, by a low portal. A block of unhewn granite, worn smooth and even hollow on the surface by the weary feet of many pilgrims, was the door-step. The rest of the house had been added at a later period. On the right of this low hall a door led to my father's study, and on the opposite side to our little parlor. At the back part were the kitchen, dairy, etc. In the hall stood the spinning-wheels, and it was hung all around with skeins of linen and woollen yarn, and with other productions of rural and domestic labor. This humble dwelling was overshadowed by two giant sycamore trees, while its only ornament, the double white rose, grew profusely about its doors and windows.

I cannot but look back with gratitude to Heaven for the charm of solitude and beauty that environed my home. "A piteous lot it were to flee from man and not rejoice in nature." I loved, and I love still the glorious ocean, the gentle, quiet river, the sheltered valley, and the protecting forest of my native village.

My father, as you remember, was the pastor of this parish. It was a wide and scattered one, although the immediate village was small. The inhabitants of the village were poor; the richer portion of the parishioners living on distant farms. Owing to its proximity to the ocean, I suppose, there was a great proportion of poor widows in the parish—the men probably going to sea, or on fishing voyages, where many of them perished.

It was long before any sectarians had invaded our parishes, and when the influence of the clergy was very great. Perhaps at that time they exercised a more extended and absolute influence than should ever be granted to any class of men in a free country. Their counsel was asked and taken in all temporal as well as spiritual affairs, and they were looked up to with unbounded reverence. But never was this influence lodged in purer hands, and never exercised with more disinterested and beneficent effect than in the case of my father.

The death of my mother happened about my fifteenth year, and left him a mourner with eight children, of which I was the eldest but one, and the youngest an infant of a day old. . . .

From that moment the care of the younger children, under his direction, devolved on my sister and myself. The influence he exercised over us all was gentle, but it was absolute and unbounded. It was the influence of religious principle and devoted tenderness. To oppose his mild authority was as little thought of as it would have been to break through the wall of the house, when there was an open door to go out. Yet he was not unwisely indulgent. The extreme frugality of our manner of life allowed us few desires. Our remoteness from cities and all factitious pleasures limited so much our action, that there were few occasions that called for discipline. Our employments were of the simplest and most natural kind. A walk on the beach to gather shells, or in the woods to gather berries, the care of birds and animals, the repeated study of our few books—these were our pleasures.

A NEW LANGUAGE PROPOSED

WILLIAM SMITH SHAW

———◆·◆———

If we, today, think of the eighteenth century in New England as intellectual to an awesome degree, they at the time feared that, brainwise, they were not doing so well. I append two excerpts from The Monthly Anthology and Boston Review *for April, 1806.*

THE office of the Remarker is not confined to speculations on morals and literature, but will occasionally be extended to the delineation of schemes for the whole country. Objects of national concern ought to employ the most active exertions of every individual, and the labours of our statesmen ought to be diminished by the assistance of every citizen who possesses leisure and ingenuity to devise means of publick safety and private repose.

Since the liberation of our countrymen from the tuition of a cruel stepdame, who fondly hoped that in the decrepitude of age she should be nourished and sustained by our labour and love, our citizens while engaged in lawful commerce have been exposed to violence and impressment. The licensed buccaneers and royal robbers of the ocean have divorced our citizens from their friends and families, and compelled them to exert, in the service of a king, every muscle not palsied by fear of the thong and scourge. Remonstrance only admonishes them of their power of inflicting still greater injuries, and the specious plea of justification is that *similarity of language prevents discrimination between Englishmen and Americans.* It is now proposed to strike at the root of the evil, and to construct a language entirely novel. This language must be composed of five-parts, viz. one part Indian, another Irish, and three fifths Negro tongue. These ingredients well mixed will constitute a language unintelligible by any human nation from Gades to Ganges. As drivers of herds of cattle sometimes bind a spat across the horns of a fierce bullock to prevent his escape in the thickets of the forest, so will this language debar us from all intercourse with other nations, and will erect a strong wall of partition between us and our adversaries.

Without doubt this plan will be strenuously opposed by those who are continually declaiming against the subversion of ancient institutions and the destruction of ancient principles. But it is reasonable that man would pursue a course analogical to that of nature, which is a process of continual change, of decay and revival. . . . Besides, a virtuous republican government induces modes of thought and action so different from those produced by a monarchy that many of the terms of the English language are in this country as insignificant and destitute of meaning as the representatives of old Sarum are of constituents, and the bold and original thoughts of Americans perish as would giants in this pigmy land, because they could not be cooped in our cabins, or covered by our garments. On account of this paucity of terms, adapted to our ideas, most of our authors and holiday orators have been compelled to invent new words, and make our language as various as the face of our country.

It will be perceived, that this new language is the result of a spirit of compromise and conciliation, and that those classes of citizens which are most numerous contribute most to its formation. If we inspect the American court calendar, we shall immediately ascertain that in selecting materials for this language due attention has been paid to the origin and descent of those who guide the destinies of our nation: the most eminent of whom are of Irish or Indian blood. We need not the aid of the college of heralds to trace the lineage of our greatest orator, Randolph, to the renowned Pocahontas, for no sachem among the aboriginals could hurl the tomahawk with more unerring aim, or could, with more adroitness, mangle, and scalp, and lacerate the trembling victims of his wrath. His eloquence is of the whooping kind, and his words, "like bullets chewed, rankled where they entered, and, like melted lead, blistered where they lighted. . . ." The fame and glory of our orators in Congress must be attributed wholly to their knowledge of Indian dialects. Those who utter English are fortunately few; otherwise the circumstance of their receiving their tone and language from a foreign court would subject them to punishment, as it now does to suspicion and disgrace.

The excellencies of the proposed dialect will be numerous; it will not possess the quality of harmony, so that it may be congenial to the nature of our government; and as it will be difficult to be uttered, it will counteract tumults and seditions, which are usually the effect of sudden and inconsiderate expressions of anger and indignation. Our countrymen, like the wing-footed horses of Phoebus, need restraint, rather than impulse. . . .

The adoption of this new language will operate very favourably on our foreign relations, and will erect a barrier more powerful than navies, and proclamations, and non-intercourse bills. The policy of our government is not to exhaust the bowels of our country to afford protection to commerce, which infects the manners of republicans with a thirst for lucre and love of luxuries; which imports the elegancies of the East, and yellow fever of the West Indies, and supplies silks for our ladies; and slaves for our lords. Though our ports are thronged with merchantmen, richly laden, they receive no other protection than one gun-boat to each port, "ut unoculus inter caecos."

When this language shall have become common and universal in our country, we shall be a world by ourselves; and will surround our territory by an impregnable wall of brass, and all sit down, each in his whirligig chair, and philosophize. Then our oaks shall not be ravished from our mountains, and compelled to sport in the ocean with mermaids and monsters of the deep; but they shall be permitted still to wear their green honours, and their foliage, instead of quivering through fear of the axe of the shipwright, shall dance and dally with Zephyrus. Our citizens will then enjoy all the happiness of hermits, and all the tranquillity of monks.

THE DEGENERACY OF MODERN SCHOLARS
ANONYMOUS

There is hardly a surer mark of the degeneracy of modern literature than the inordinate attention which is now paid to bibliography. The knowledge of title pages has succeeded to the knowledge of subjects, and to ascertain the year of an *editio princeps* is now thought of as much importance and divides the learned as seriously as to settle the true year of the birth of Christ. *Scire ubi aliquid posses invenire, magna pars eruditionis est;* but to know where a thing may be found is very consistent with ignorance of what may be found there. It is well worth inquiry whether the innumerable literary journals of the present age have promoted the cause of real learning. Certain it is that the race of laborious scholars is nearly extinct. Boehart may perhaps be said to have been revived in Bryant; Walton and Castell in Kennicott, Bentley in Wakefield, and more than one scholar of the old school in Sir William Jones. But these men are now dead! Where now are the universal scholars, who can boast of being the legitimate successors of Selden, Grotius, Le Clerc, Vossius, and Bayle? What wonderfully crowded and comprehensive minds! Alas, we are hardly competent to the republications of their words. *Damnosa quid non imminuit dies!*

THE CAPTURE OF THE GUERRIÈRE

ANONYMOUS

———◆•◆———

The War of 1812 has been called a futile and unnecessary war. But 1812 had its great moments. The American frigate Constitution sailed from Boston in June of that year to fight the British Guerrière. Legitimate commerce at sea had come to a stop, there were many out-of-work seamen eager to fight, and every man of Constitution's crew at the time she whipped Guerrière was a well-trained skipper who could have commanded the vessel himself. A contemporary ballad about the battle follows.

Edward Everett Hale writes of another, more famous ballad, "By the combination of the new western states with the southern oligarchies, General Jackson was chosen President [in 1828]. The new dynasty, well in the saddle, as a neat bit of bravado gave orders to break up the New

England frigate Constitution. *She had been built under the older Adams.*
They had now turned out the younger Adams, and the plan for her de-
struction was rather an ingenious insult to the North. The ship . . . was
not more than thirty years old at the time.

"*The insult was received with more spirit than was expected. . . . It*
roused Oliver Wendell Holmes, then scarcely more than a boy, and he
himself has told how he retired to his attic room . . . and wrote the
verses which 'fired the northern heart.' The order for the destruction of
the ship was withdrawn, and we still preserve her under the shadow of
Bunker Hill as the Athenians preserved the Galley of Theseus. Dr. Holmes
might well claim the credit of saving 'Old Ironsides,' and the poem,
printed everywhere in the northern states, won for him at once his na-
tional reputation."

Long, the tyrant of our coast,
    Reigned the famous *Guerriere:*
Our little navy she defied,
    Public ship and privateer;
On her sails, in letters red,
To our captains were displayed
Words of warning, words of dread,
"All who meet me, have a care!
I am England's *Guerriere.*"

On the wide Atlantic deep
    (Not her equal for the fight)
The *Constitution,* on her way,
    Chanced to meet these men of might:
On her sails was nothing said:
But her waist the teeth displayed
That a deal of blood could shed,
Which, if she would venture near,
Would stain the decks of the *Guerriere.*

Now our gallant ship they met,
    And, to struggle with John Bull,
Who had come they little thought,
    Strangers, yet, to Isaac Hull.
Better, soon, to be acquainted,
Isaac hailed the Lord's anointed,
While the crew the cannon pointed,
And the balls were so directed
With a blaze so unexpected,—

Isaac did so maul and rake her,
That the decks of Captain Dacres
Were in such a woful pickle,
As if death, with scythe and sickle,
With his sling or with his shaft
Had cut his harvest fore and aft.
Thus, in thirty minutes, ended
Mischiefs that could not be mended:
Masts, and yards, and ship descended,
All to David Jones's locker—
Such a ship in such a pucker!

Drink about to the *Constitution!*
She performed some execution,
Did some share of retribution
   For the insults of the year,
   When she took the *Guerriere.*
May success again await her,
   Let who will again command her,
Bainbridge, Rodgers, or Decatur:
   Nothing like her can withstand her
With a crew like that on board her
Who so boldly called "to order"
One bold crew of English sailors,
Long, too long, our seamen's jailers—
   Dacres and the *Guerriere!*

THE FEDERALISTS

HENRY ADAMS

———◆•◆———

I had always assumed that secession and State rights, as issues, were limited to the Southern states and for the most part to the years before 1861. On the contrary. It is a surprise to find today, when Jefferson is everywhere idolized, how, to the Federalists in New England, he was almost the incarnation of the devil. The purchase of Louisiana, thrust on Jefferson by Napoleon, felt to them like the last straw. "To the clergy and party leaders of New England," one modern history states, "Jefferson's victory was the triumph of democracy, which to them was but

*another name for terror, atheism, and free love. It meant just what
Communism does to many respectable Americans today." In 1803 Senator
Pickering of Massachusetts had written, "Must we with folded hands wait
the result? The principles of our Revolution point to the remedy—a
separation."*

*The annexation of Louisiana absolved New England, it was felt, from
any allegiance to the Union; a confederacy was planned, and the doctrine
of State rights invoked. During the whole nineteenth century, a large and
vocal segment of New England continued to consider that Jefferson had
been the ruination of the country.*

*A fair picture of Federalist New England may be drawn from the fol-
lowing excerpt from* The History of the United States during the Administration of Jefferson and Madison *by Henry Adams (1838–1918). Grandson
of John Quincy Adams, son of the Charles Francis Adams who edited his
father's works, Adams is a saturnine and enigmatic New Englander whose*
Education of Henry Adams *did much to rid provincial New England of
its naïveté.*

THE power of the Congregational clergy, which had lasted unbroken
until the Revolution, was originally minute and inquisitory, equivalent to
a police authority. During the last quarter of the century the clergy
themselves were glad to lay aside the more odious watchfulness over their
parishes, and to welcome social freedom within limits conventionally
fixed; but their old authority had not wholly disappeared. In country
parishes they were still autocratic. Did an individual defy their authority,
the minister put his three-cornered hat on his head, took his silver-topped
cane in his hand, and walked down the village street, knocking at one
door and another of his best parishioners, to warn them that a spirit of
license and of French infidelity was abroad, which could be repressed
only by a strenuous and combined effort. Any man once placed under this
ban fared badly if he afterward came before a bench of magistrates. The
temporal arm vigorously supported the ecclesiastical will. Nothing tended
so directly to make respectability conservative, and conversatism a fetich
of respectability, as this union of bench and pulpit. The democrat had no
caste; he was not respectable; he was a Jacobin,—and no such character
was admitted into a Federalist house. Every dissolute intriguer, loose-
liver, forger, false-coiner, and prison-bird; every hair-brained, loud-talk-
ing demagogue; every speculator, scoffer, and atheist,—was a follower of
Jefferson; and Jefferson was himself the incarnation of their theories.

A literature belonging to this subject exists,—stacks of newspapers and
sermons, mostly dull, and wanting literary merit. In a few of them Jefferson figured under the well-remembered disguises of Puritan politics: he

was Ephraim, and had mixed himself among the people; had apostatized from his God and religion; gone to Assyria, and mingled himself among the heathen; "gray hairs are here and there upon him, yet he knoweth not;" or he was Jeroboam, who drave Israel from following the Lord, and made them sin a great sin. He had doubted the authority of revelation, and ventured to suggest that petrified shells found embedded in rocks fifteen thousand feet above sea-level could hardly have been left there by the Deluge, because if the whole atmosphere were condensed as water, its weight showed that the seas would be raised only fifty-two and a half feet. Sceptic as he was, he could not accept the scientific theory that the ocean-bed had been uplifted by natural forces; but although he had thus instantly deserted this battery raised against revelation, he had still expressed the opinion that a universal deluge was *equally* unsatisfactory as an explanation, and had avowed preference for a profession of ignorance rather than a belief in error. He had said, "It does me no injury for my neighbors to say there are twenty gods, or no god," and that all the many forms of religious faith in the Middle States were "good enough, and sufficient to preserve peace and order." He was notoriously a deist; he probably ridiculed the doctrine of total depravity; and he certainly would never have part or portion in the blessings of the New Covenant, or be saved because of grace.

No abler or more estimable clergyman lived than Joseph Buckminster, the minister of Portsmouth, in New Hampshire, and in his opinion Jefferson was bringing a judgment upon the people.

> "I would not be understood to insinuate," said he in his sermon on Washington's death, "that contemners of religious duties, and even men void of religious principle, may not have an attachment to their country and a desire for its civil and political prosperity,—nay, that they may not even expose themselves to great dangers, and make great sacrifices to accomplish this object; but by their impiety . . . they take away the heavenly defence and security of a people, and render it necessary for him who ruleth among the nations in judgment to testify his displeasure against those who despise his laws and contemn his ordinances."

Yet the congregational clergy, though still greatly respected, had ceased to be leaders of thought. Theological literature no longer held the prominence it had enjoyed in the days of Edwards and Hopkins. The popular reaction against Calvinism, felt rather than avowed, stopped the development of doctrinal theology; and the clergy, always poor as a class, with no weapons but their intelligence and purity of character, commonly sought rather to avoid than to challenge hostility. Such literary activity as existed was not clerical but secular. Its field was the Boston press, and its recognized literary champion was Fisher Ames. . . .

The bitterness against democrats became intense after the month of May, 1800, when the approaching victory of Jefferson was seen to be inevitable. Then for the first time the clergy and nearly all the educated and respectable citizens of New England began to extend to the national government the hatred which they bore to democracy. The expressions of this mixed antipathy filled volumes. "Our country," wrote Fisher Ames in 1803, "is too big for union, too sordid for patriotism, too democratic for liberty. What is to become of it, he who made it best knows. Its vice will govern it, by practising upon its folly. This is ordained for democracies." He explained why this inevitable fate awaited it. "A democracy cannot last. Its nature ordains that its next change shall be into a military despotism,—of all known governments perhaps the most prone to shift its head, and the slowest to mend its vices. The reason is that the tyranny of what is called the people, and that by the sword, both operate alike to debase and corrupt, till there are neither men left with the spirit to desire liberty, nor morals with the power to sustain justice. Like the burning pestilence that destroys the human body, nothing can subsist by its dissolution but vermin." George Cabot, whose political opinions were law to the wise and good, held the same convictions. "Even in New England," wrote Cabot in 1840, "where there is among the body of the people more wisdom and virtue than in any other part of the United States, we are full of errors which no reasoning could eradicate, if there were a Lycurgus in every village. We are democratic altogether, and I hold democracy in its natural operation to be the government of the worst."

Had these expressions of opinion been kept to the privacy of correspondence, the public could have ignored them; but so strong were the wise and good in their popular following, that every newspaper seemed to exult in denouncing the people. They urged the use of force as the protection of wisdom and virtue. A paragraph from Dennie's "Portfolio," reprinted by all the Federalist newspapers in 1803, offered one example among a thousand of the infatuation which possessed the Federalist press, neither more extravagant nor more treasonable than the rest:—

"A democracy is scarcely tolerable at any period of national history. Its omens are always sinister, and its powers are unpropitious. It is on its trial here, and the issue will be civil war, desolation, and anarchy. No wise man but discerns its imperfections, no good man but shudders at its miseries, no honest man but proclaims its fraud, and no brave man but draws his sword against its force. The institution of a scheme of policy so radically contemptible and vicious is a memorable example of what the villany of some men can devise, the folly of others receive, and both establish in spite of reason, reflection, and sensation."

The Philadelphia grand jury indicted Dennie for this paragraph as a seditious libel, but it was not more expressive than the single word uttered by Alexander Hamilton, who owed no small part of his supremacy to the faculty of expressing the prejudices of his followers more tersely than they themselves could do. Compressing the idea into one syllable, Hamilton, at a New York dinner, replied to some democratic sentiment by striking his hand sharply on the table and saying, "Your people, sir,—your people is a great *beast!*" ...

Even Boston, the most cosmopolitan part of New England, showed no tendency in its educated classes to become American in thought or feeling. Many of the ablest Federalists, and among the rest George Cabot, Theophilus Parsons, and Fisher Ames, shared few of the narrower theological prejudices of their time, but were conservatives of the English type, whose alliance with the clergy betrayed as much policy as religion, and whose intellectual life was wholly English. Boston made no strong claim to intellectual prominence. Neither clergy, lawyers, physicians, nor literary men were much known beyond the State. Fisher Ames enjoyed a wider fame; but Ames's best political writing was saturated with the despair of the tomb to which his wasting body was condemned. . . . The number of his thorough-going admirers was small, if his own estimate was correct. "There are," he said, "not many, perhaps not five hundred, even among the Federalists, who yet allow themselves to view the progress of licentiousness as so speedy, so sure, and so fatal as the deplorable experience of our country shows that it is, and the evidence of history and the constitution of human nature demonstrate that it must be." These five hundred, few as they were, comprised most of the clergy and the State officials, and overawed large numbers more. . . .

Nevertheless, the reign of old-fashioned conservatism was near its end. The New England Church was apparently sound; even Unitarians and Baptists were recognized as parts of one fraternity. Except a few Roman and Anglican bodies, all joined in the same worship, and said little on points of doctrinal difference. No one had yet dared to throw a firebrand into the temple; but Unitarians were strong among the educated and wealthy class, while the tendencies of a less doctrinal religious feeling were shaping themselves in Harvard College. William Ellery Channing took his degree in 1798, and in 1800 was a private tutor in Virginia. Joseph Stevens Buckminster, thought by his admirers a better leader than Channing, graduated in 1800, and was teaching boys to construe their Latin exercises at Exeter Academy. Only the shell of orthodoxy was left, but respectable society believed this shell to be necessary as an example of Christian unity and a safeguard against more serious innovations. No one could fail to see that the public had lately become restive under its antiquated discipline. The pulpits still fulminated against the fatal tolerance which within a few years had allowed theatres to be opened in Boston, and which scandalized God-fearing men by permitting public advertisements that "Hamlet" and "Othello" were to be performed in the town founded to protest against worldly pageants. Another innovation was more strenuously resisted. Only within the last thirty years had Sunday travel been allowed even in England; in Massachusetts and Connecticut it was still forbidden by law, and the law was enforced. Yet not only travellers, but inn-keepers and large numbers of citizens connived at Sunday travel, and it could not long be prevented. The clergy saw their police authority weakening year by year, and understood, without need of many words, the tacit warning of the city congregations that in this world they must be allowed to amuse themselves, even though they were to suffer for it in the next.

The longing for amusement and freedom was a reasonable and a modest want. Even the young theologians, the Buckminsters and Channings, were hungry for new food. Boston was little changed in appearance, habits, and style from what it had been under its old king. When young Dr. J. C. Warren returned from Europe about the year 1800, to begin practice in Boston, he found gentlemen still dressed in colored coats and figured waistcoats, short breeches buttoning at the knee, long boots with white tops, ruffled shirts and wristbands, a white cravat filled with what was called a "pudding," and for the elderly, cocked hats, and wigs which once every week were sent to the barber's to be dressed,—so that every Saturday night the barbers' boys were seen carrying home piles of wig-boxes in readiness for Sunday's church. At evening parties gentlemen appeared in white small-clothes, silk stockings and pumps, with a colored or white waistcoat. There were few hackney-coaches, and ladies walked to evening entertainments. The ancient minuet was danced as late as 1806. The waltz was not yet tolerated.

Fashionable society was not without charm. In summer Southern visitors appeared, and admired the town, with its fashionable houses perched on the hillsides, each in its own garden, and each looking seaward over harbor and islands. Boston was then what Newport afterward became, and its only rival as a summer watering-place in the North was Ballston, whither society was beginning to seek health before finding it a little farther away at Saratoga. Of intellectual amusement there was little more at one place than at the other, except that the Bostonians devoted themselves more seriously to church-going and to literature. The social instinct took shape in varied forms, but was highly educated in none; while the typical entertainment in Boston, as in New York, Philadelphia, and Charleston, was the state dinner,—not the light, feminine triviality which Franco introduced into an amusement-loving world, but the serious dinner of Sir Robert Walpole and Lord North, where gout and plethora waited behind the chairs; an effort of animal endurance.

There was the arena of intellectual combat, if that could be called combat where disagreement in principle was not tolerated. The talk of Samuel Johnson and Edmund Burke was the standard of excellence to all American society that claimed intellectual rank, and each city possessed its own circle of Federalist talkers. Democrats rarely figured in these entertainments, at least in fashionable private houses. "There was no exclusiveness," said a lady who long outlived the time; "but I should as soon have expected to see a cow in a drawing-room as a Jacobin." In New York, indeed, Colonel Burr and the Livingstons may have held their own, and the active-minded Dr. Mitchill there, like Dr. Eustis in Boston, was an agreeable companion. Philadelphia was comparatively cosmopolitan; in Baltimore the Smiths were a social power; and Charleston, after deserting Federal principles in 1800, could hardly ignore Democrats; but Boston society was still pure. The clergy took a prominent part in conversation, but Fisher Ames was the favorite of every intelligent company; and when Gouverneur Morris, another brilliant talker, visited Boston, Ames was pitted against him.

The intellectual wants of the community grew with the growing prosperity; but the names of half-a-dozen persons could hardly be mentioned whose memories survived by intellectual work made public in Massachusetts between 1783 and 1800. . . .

The city was still poorer in science. Excepting the medical profession, which represented nearly all scientific activity, hardly a man in Boston got his living either by science or art. When in the year 1793 the directors of the new Middlesex Canal Corporation, wishing to bring the Merrimac River to Boston Harbor, required a survey of an easy route not thirty miles long, they could find no competent civil engineer in Boston, and sent to Philadelphia for an Englishman named Weston, engaged on the Delaware and Schuylkill Canal.

Possibly a few Bostonians could read and even speak French; but Germany was nearly as unknown as China, until Madame de Staël published her famous work in 1814. Even then young George Ticknor, incited by its account of German university education, could find neither a good teacher nor a dictionary, nor a German book in the shops or public libraries of the city or at the college in Cambridge. He had discovered a new world.

Pope, Addison, Akenside, Beattie, and Young were still the reigning poets. Burns was accepted by a few; and copies of a volume were advertised by book-sellers, written by a new poet called Wordsworth. America offered a fair demand for new books, and anything of a light nature published in England was sure to cross the ocean. Wordsworth crossed with the rest, and his "Lyrical Ballads" were reprinted in 1802, not in Boston or New York, but in Philadelphia, where they were read and praised. In default of other amusements, men read what no one could have endured had a choice of amusements been open. Neither music, painting, science, the lecture-room, nor even magazines offered resources that could rival what was looked upon as classical literature. Men had not the alternative of listening to political discussions, for stump-speaking was a Southern practice not yet introduced into New England, where such a political canvass would have terrified society with dreams of Jacobin license. The clergy and the bar took charge of politics; the tavern was the club and the forum of political discussion; but for those who sought other haunts, and especially for women, no intellectual amusement other than what was called "belles-lettres" existed to give a sense of occupation to an active mind. This keen and innovating people, hungry for the feast that was almost served, the Walter Scotts and Byrons so near at hand, tried meanwhile to nourish themselves with husks. . . .

Meanwhile Connecticut was a province by itself, a part of New England rather than of the United States. The exuberant patriotism of the Revolution was chilled by the steady progress of democratic principles in the Southern and Middle States, until at the election of Jefferson in 1800 Connecticut stood almost alone with no intellectual companion except Massachusetts, while the breach between them and the Middle States seemed to widen day by day. That the separation was only superficial was true; but the connection itself was not yet deep. An extreme Federalist partisan like Noah Webster did not cease working for his American language and literature because of the triumph of Jeffersonian principles elsewhere; Barlow became more American when his friends gained power; the work of the colleges went on unbroken; but prejudices, habits, theories, and laws remained what they had been in the past, and in Connecticut the influence of nationality was less active than ten, twenty, or even thirty years before. Yale College was but a reproduction of Harvard with stricter orthodoxy, turning out every year about thirty graduates, of whom nearly one fourth went into the Church. For the last ten years the number tended rather to diminish than to increase.

Evidently an intellectual condition like that of New England could not long continue. The thoughts and methods of the eighteenth century held possession of men's minds only because the movement of society was delayed by political passions. Massachusetts, and especially Boston, already contained a younger generation eager to strike into new paths, while forcibly held in the old ones. The more decidedly the college graduates of 1800 disliked democracy and its habits of thought, the more certain they were to compensate for political narrowness by freedom in fields not political. The future direction of the New England intellect seemed already suggested by the impossibility of going further in the line of President Dwight and Fisher Ames. Met by a barren negation on that side, thought was driven to some new channel; and the United States were the more concerned in the result because, with the training and literary habits of New Englanders and the new models already established in Europe for their guidance, they were likely again to produce something that would command respect.

THE LIFE OF
OLIVER HAZARD PERRY

JOHN M. NILES

———◆◆◆———

The joke out sailing, when I was a girl visiting in Rhode Island in the summer, was: "Rhode Island waters are full of Hazards." So is dry land, and so have both always been since the founding.

The most famous figure to bear Hazard as one of his names was Commodore Oliver Hazard Perry (1794–1819), who served the young American navy in the War of 1812. His defeat of the British at the Battle of Lake Erie made his reputation, and the following excerpt from The Life of Oliver Hazard Perry, *by John M. Niles, gives us Perry's immortal lines following that occasion.*

THERE is one circumstance which was related by Perry, that deserves particular mention. It has something in it which does not belong to common life, and which has the appearance of inspiration.

"When in the sweeping havoc which was sometimes made, a number of men were shot away from around a gun, the survivors *looked silently around to Perry*—and then stepped into their places. When he looked at the poor fellows that lay wounded and weltering on the deck, he always found *their faces turned towards him, and their eyes fixed on his countenance.* It is impossible for words to heighten the simple and affecting eloquence of this anecdote. It speakes volumes in praise of the heroism of the commander, and the confidence and affection of his men."

During this dreadful conflict, which thickened with perils, and was characterised by a carnage unexampled, there was but a single moment when the cool intrepidity and the self command of Perry, experienced any thing like a shock. This was on seeing his brother, a youth of but thirteen, who served on board as a midshipman, knocked down by a hammock, which was driven by a cannon ball. The first impression of the Commodore was, that he was killed, which gave him a momentary agony, that disconcerted the calmness of his mind. But the sprightly youth immediately rising up unhurt and undismayed, relieved the mind of the Commodore, which, being occupied with the engagement, and intent on victory, no more thought of the danger to which the youth was exposed.

This splendid victory, so complete and honourable in its character, and so important in its consequences, was announced by Commodore Perry, in a spirit of humility and moderation, which always accompany real merit and true greatness. In his first letter * to the Secretary of the navy, he keeps himself, and, in a measure, the squadron under his command, out of view; his language being, that "it has pleased the Almighty to give to *the arms of the United States,* a signal victory over their enemies on this lake." But his laconic letter † to General Harrison, on the occasion, is perhaps, a more striking evidence of a mind capable of great and heroic achievements.

The emphatic language, "WE HAVE MET THE ENEMY AND THEY ARE OURS," could only have proceeded from the hero of Erie.

* The following is a transcript of this letter:

> U. S. brig Niagara, off the western Lister, head of ⎱
> Lake Erie, Sept. 10th, 1813, 4 o'clock, P. M. ⎰

Sir—It has pleased the Almighty to give to the arms of the United States a signal victory over their enemies on this lake. The British squadron, consisting of two ships, two brigs, one schooner, and one sloop, have this moment surrendered to the force under my command, after a sharp conflict.

> I have the honour to be, sir,
> Your obedient servant,
>
> O. H. PERRY.

The Hon. William Jones, ⎱
Secretary of the Navy. ⎰

† The following is a copy of this letter:

> U. S. brig Niagara, off the western Lister, head of ⎱
> Lake Erie, Sept. 10th, 1813, 4 o'clock, P. M. ⎰

Dear General—We have met the enemy, and they are ours. Two ships, two brigs, one schooner, and one sloop.

> Yours, with great respect and esteem,
>
> O. H. PERRY.

1812-1824

THE ADAMS-JEFFERSON LETTERS

*Surely one of the pleasantest exchanges of letters on record is that be-
tween the aged John Adams and the aged Jefferson. In their active political lives they had disagreed bitterly; each had been President of a United
States which each had played a major part in bringing into being. Now
they were sages, elder statesmen, philosophers, and, as such, reconciled. In
the following excerpts from the* Adams-Jefferson Letters *the old signers
exchange their views on life, death, fear, hope and immortality. It is always worth recalling the somehow splendid fact that both were to breathe
their last on Independence Day, July 4, 1826.*

ADAMS TO JEFFERSON

QUINCY, *2 March, 1816.*

I cannot be serious! I am about to write you the most frivolous letter
you ever read. Would you go back to your cradle, and live over again
your seventy years? I believe you would return me a New England answer, by asking me another question, "Would you live your eighty years
over again?" If I am prepared to give you an explicit answer, the question
involves so many considerations of metaphysics and physics, of theology
and ethics, of philosophy and history, of experience and romance, of tragedy, comedy, and farce, that I would not give my opinion without writing
a volume to justify it. . . .

JEFFERSON TO ADAMS

April 8, 1816.

You ask if I would agree to live my seventy or rather seventy-three
years over again? To which I say, yea. I think with you, that it is a good

world on the whole; that it has been framed on a principle of benevolence, and more pleasure than pain dealt out to us. There are, indeed, (who might say nay) gloomy and hypochondriac minds, inhabitants of diseased bodies, disgusted with the present, and despairing of the future; always counting that the worst will happen, because it may happen. To these I say, how much pain have cost us the evils which have never happened! My temperament is sanguine. I steer my bark with Hope in the head, leaving Fear astern. My hopes, indeed, sometimes fail; but not oftener than the forebodings of the gloomy. There are, I acknowledge, even in the happiest life, some terrible convulsions, heavy set-offs against the opposite page of the account. . . .

ADAMS TO JEFFERSON

QUINCY, *3 May, 1816.*

Yours of April 8th has long since been received.

J. Would you agree to live your eighty years over again?

A. Aye, and *sans phrase.*

J. Would you agree to live your eighty years over again forever?

A. I once heard our acquaintance, Chew, of Philadelphia, say, he should like to go back to twenty-five to all eternity. But I own my soul would start and shrink back on itself at the prospect of an endless succession of *boules de savon,* almost as much as at the certainty of annihilation. For what is human life? I can speak only for one. I have had more comfort than distress, more pleasure than pain, ten to one; nay, if you please, a hundred to one. A pretty large dose, however, of distress and pain. But, after all, what is human life? A vapor, a fog, a dew, a cloud, a blossom, a flower, a rose, a blade of grass, a glass bubble, a tale told by an idiot, a *boule de savon,* vanity of vanities, an eternal succession of which would terrify me almost as much as annihilation.

J. Would you prefer to live over again rather than accept the offer of a better life in the future?

A. Certainly not.

J. Would you live again, rather than change for the worse in a future state, for the sake of trying something new?

A. Certainly, yes.

J. Would you live over again once or forever rather than run the risk of annihilation, or a better or worst state at or after death?

A. Most certainly I would not.

J. How valiant you are!

A. Aye, at this moment and at all other moments of my life that I can recollect; but who can tell what will become of his bravery, when his

flesh and his philosophy were not sufficient to support him in his last hours?
D'Alembert said, Happy are they who have courage, but I have none.
Voltaire, the greatest genius of them all, behaved like the greatest coward
of them all, at his death, as he had like the wisest fool of them all in his
lifetime. Hume awkwardly affects to sport away all sober thoughts. Who
can answer for his last feelings and reflections, especially as the priests are
in possession of the custom of making the great engines of their craft,
procul este profani.

J. How shall we, how can we, estimate the value of human life?

A. I know not; I cannot weigh sensations and reflections, pleasures
and pains, hopes and fears in money scales. But I can tell you how I have
heard it estimated by some philosophers. One of my old friends and
clients, a *mandamus* counsellor against his will, a man of letters and
virtues, without one vice that I ever knew or suspected, except garrulity,
William Vassal, asserted to me, and strenuously maintained, that pleasure
is no compensation for pain. A hundred years of the keenest delights of
human life, could not atone for one hour of bilious colic that he had felt.
The sublimity of this philosophy my dull genius could not reach, I was
willing to state a fair account between pleasure and pain, and give credit
for the balance, which I found very great in my favor. Another philosopher, who, as we say, believed nothing, ridiculed the notion of a future
state. One of the company asked, "Why are you an enemy to a future
state? Are you wearied of life? Do you detest existence? "Weary of
life! Detest existence!" said the philosopher, "no, I love life so well and am
so attached to existence, that to be sure of immortality, I would consent
to be pitched about with forks by the devils among flames of fire and
brimstone to all eternity." I find no resources in my courage for this exalted philosophy. I would rather be blotted out. *Il faut trancher le mot.*
What is there in life to attach us to it, but the hope of a future and a better? It is a cracker, a bouquet, a firework, at best.

I admire your navigation, and should like to sail with you either in
your bark or in my own, alongside with yours. Hope, with her gay ensigns displayed at the prow; Fear, with her hobgoblins behind the stern.
Hope remains. What pleasure? I mean, take away fear, and what pain remains? Ninety-nine hundredths of the pleasures and pains of life are
nothing but hopes and fears. All nations known in history or in travels
have hoped, believed, and expected a future and a better state. The
Maker of the universe, the cause of all things, whether we call it *fate,* or
chance, or *God,* has inspired this hope. If it is a fraud, we shall never
know it; we shall never resent the imposition, be grateful for the illusion,
nor grieve for the disappointment; we shall be no more. . . .

Suppose the cause of the universe should reveal to all mankind at once
a certainty, that they must all die within a century, and that death is an
external extinction of all living powers, of all sensation and reflection.

What would be the effect? Would there be one man, woman, or child existing on this globe twenty years hence? Would every human being be a Madame Deffand, Voltaire's *"aveugle clairvoyante,"* all her lifetime regretting her existence, bewailing that she had ever been born; grieving that she had ever been dragged without her consent into being? Who would bear the gout, the stone, the colic, for the sake of a *boule de savon,* when a pistol, a cord, a pond, a phial of laudanum, was at hand? What would men say to their Maker? Would they thank him? No; they would reproach him, they would curse him to his face.

Voilà, a sillier letter than my last! For a wonder, I have filled a sheet, and a greater wonder, I have read fifteen volumes of Grimm. *Digito compesce labellum.* I hope to write you more upon this and other topics of your letter. I have read also a history of the Jesuits, in four volumes. Can you tell me the author, or any thing of this work?

ADAMS TO JEFFERSON

QUINCY, *23 February, 1819.*

If these letters [of Madamoiselle de l'Espinasse] and the fifteen volumes of De Grimm are to give me an idea of the amelioration of society, and government, and manners in France, I should think the age of reason had produced nothing much better than Mahometans, the Mamelukes, or the Hindoos, or the North American Indians have produced, in different parts of the world.

Festina lente, my friend, in all your projects of reformation. Abolish polytheism, however, in every shape, if you can, and unfrock every priest who teaches it, if you can.

JEFFERSON TO ADAMS

MONTICELLO, *October 12, 1823.*

DEAR SIR,—I do not write with the ease which your letter of September 18th supposes. Crippled wrists and fingers make writing slow and laborious. But while writing to you, I lose the sense of these things in the recollection of ancient times, when youth and health made happiness out of everything. I forget for a while the hoary winter of age, when we can think of nothing but how to keep ourselves warm, and how to get rid of the heavy hours until the friendly hand of death shall rid us of all at once. Against this *tedium vitæ,* however, I am fortunately mounted on a hobby, which, indeed, I should have better managed some thirty or forty years ago; but whose easy amble is still sufficient to give exercise and amusement to an octogenary rider. This is the establishment of a University, on a scale more comprehensive, and in a country more healthy and central than our old William and Mary, which these obstacles have long kept in a state of languor and inefficiency. But the tardiness with which such works proceed, may render it doubtful whether I shall live to see it go into action.

Putting aside these things, however, for the present, I write this letter as due to a friendship coeval with our government, and now attempted to be poisoned, when too late in life to be replaced by new affections. I had for some time observed in the public papers, dark hints and mysterious innuendos of a correspondence of yours with a friend, to whom you had opened your bosom without reserve, and which was to be made public by that friend or his representative. And now, it is said to be actually published. It has not yet reached us, but extracts have been given, and such as seemed most likely to draw a curtain of separation between you and myself. Were there no other motive than that of indignation against the author of this outrage on private confidence, whose shaft seems to have been aimed at yourself more particularly, this would make it the duty of every honorable mind to disappoint that aim, by opposing to its impression a seven-fold shield of apathy and insensibility. With me, however, no such armor is needed. The circumstances of the times in which we have happened to live, and the partiality of our friends at a particular period, placed us in a state of apparent opposition, which some might suppose to be personal also; and there might not be wanting those who wished to make it so, by filling our ears with malignant falsehoods, by dressing up hideous phantoms of their own creation, presenting them to you under my name, to me under yours, and endeavoring to instill into our minds things concerning each other the most destitute of truth. And if there had been at any time, a moment when we were off our guard, and in a temper to let the whispers of these people make us forget that we had known of each other for so many years, and years of so much trial, yet all men who have attended to the workings of the human mind, who have seen the false colors under which passion sometimes dresses the actions and motives of others, have seen also those passions subsiding with time and reflection, dissipating like mists before the rising sun, and restoring to us the sight of all things in their true shape and colors. It would be strange indeed, if, at our years, we were to go back an age to hunt up imaginary or forgotten facts, to disturb the repose of affections so sweetening to the evening of our lives. Be assured, my dear Sir, that I am incapable of receiving the slightest impression from the effort now made to plant thorns on the pillow of age, worth and wisdom, and to sow tares between friends who have been such for near half a century. Beseeching you then, not to suffer your mind to be disquieted by this wicked attempt to poison its peace, and praying you to throw it by among the things which have never happened, I add sincere assurances of my unabated and constant attachment, friendship and respect.

JEFFERSON TO ADAMS

March 25, 1826.

My grandson, Thomas J. Randolph, the bearer of this letter, being on a visit to Boston, would think he had seen nothing were he to leave without seeing you. Although I truly sympathize with you in the trouble these interruptions give, yet I must ask for him permission to pay you his personal respects. Like other young people, he wishes to be able in the winter nights of old age, to recount to those around him, what he has heard and learnt of the heroic age preceding his birth, and which of the Argonauts individually he was in time to have seen.

It was the lot of our early years to witness nothing but the dull monotony of a colonial subservience; and of our riper years, to breast the labors and perils of working out of it. Theirs are the Halcyon calms succeeding the storm which our Argosy had so stoutly weathered. Gratify his ambition then, by receiving his best bow; and my solicitude for your health, by enabling him to bring me a favorable account of it. Mine is but indifferent, but not so my friendship and respect for you.

ADAMS TO JEFFERSON

April 17, 1826.

Your letter of March 25th has been a cordial to me, and the more consoling as it was brought by your grandsons, Mr. Randolph and Mr. Coolidge. Everybody connected with you is snatched up, so that I cannot get any of them to dine with me. They are always engaged.—How happens it that you Virginians are all sons of Anak? We New Englanders are but pygmies by the side of Mr. Randolph; I was much gratified with Mr. Randolph and his conversation. Your letter is one of the most beautiful and delightful I have ever received.

Public affairs go on pretty much as usual, perpetual chicanery and rather more personal abuse than there used to be; . . . My love to all your family and best wishes for your health.

THANATOPSIS

WILLIAM CULLEN BRYANT

————◆•◆————

In the days when it was the custom for young people to memorize long passages of poetry, many learned by heart "Thanatopsis" (which means "a view of or musing upon death") by William Cullen Bryant. But I fear it is no longer true that every literate New England person would recognize the opening lines: "To him who in the love of Nature holds/Communion with her visible forms she speaks/A various language. . . ."

Bryant (1794–1878) wrote "Thanatopsis" at the age of seventeen. Its consideration of how death is to be faced is interesting to compare with John Adams' views on the same subject in the preceding excerpt: Adams the venerable, eighteenth-century, reasonable man; Bryant the young offshoot of grandparental Puritanism and the Unitarianism of his doctor father.

The boy hid the poem from his grandfather, but in 1817 his father submitted it to The North American Review, *one of whose editors, the anglophile Richard Henry Dana, suspected that the magazine had been imposed upon. "No one on this side of the Atlantic," he protested, "is capable of writing such verse!" With the poem's publication, Bryant's long and fruitful career as a writer began.*

> To him who in the love of Nature holds
> Communion with her visible forms, she speaks
> A various language; for his gayer hours
> She has a voice of gladness, and a smile
> And eloquence of beauty, and she glides
> Into his darker musings, with a mild
> And healing sympathy, that steals away
> Their sharpness, ere he is aware. When thoughts
> Of the last bitter hour come like a blight
> Over thy spirit, and sad images
> Of the stern agony, and shroud, and pall,
> And breathless darkness, and the narrow house,
> Make thee to shudder, and grow sick at heart;—
> Go forth, under the open sky, and list

To Nature's teachings, while from all around—
Earth and her waters, and the depths of air—
Comes a still voice.—

                    Yet a few days, and thee
The all-beholding sun shall see no more
In all his course; nor yet in the cold ground,
Where thy pale form was laid, with many tears,
Nor in the embrace of ocean, shall exist
Thy image. Earth, that nourished thee, shall claim
Thy growth, to be resolved to earth again,
And, lost each human trace, surrendering up
Thine individual being, shalt thou go
To mix forever with the elements,
To be a brother to the insensible rock
And to the sluggish clod, which the rude swain
Turns with his share, and treads upon. The oak
Shall send his roots abroad, and pierce thy mould.

   Yet not to thine eternal resting-place
Shalt thou retire alone, nor could'st thou wish
Couch more magnificent. Thou shalt lie down
With patriarchs of the infant world—with kings,
The powerful of the earth—the wise, the good,
Fair forms, and hoary seers of ages past,
All in one mighty sepulchre. The hills
Rock-ribbed and ancient as the sun,—the vales
Stretching in pensive quietness between;
The venerable woods—rivers that move
In majesty, and the complaining brooks
That make the meadows green; and, poured round all,
Old Ocean's gray and melancholy waste,—
Are but the solemn decorations all
Of the great tomb of man. The golden sun,
The planets, all the infinite host of heaven,
Are shining on the sad abodes of death,
Through the still lapse of ages. All that tread
The globe are but a handful to the tribes
That slumber in its bosom.—Take the wings
Of morning, pierce the Barcan wilderness,
Or lose thyself in the continuous woods
Where rolls the Oregon, and hears no sound,
Save his own dashings—yet the dead are there:
And millions in those solitudes, since first

The flight of years began, have laid them down
In their last sleep—the dead reign there alone.
So shalt thou rest, and what if thou withdraw
In silence from the living, and no friend
Take note of thy departure? All that breathe
Will share thy destiny. The gay will laugh
When thou art gone, the solemn brood of care
Plod on, and each one as before will chase
His favorite phantom; yet all these shall leave
Their mirth and their employments, and shall come
And make their bed with thee. As the long train
Of ages glides away, the sons of men,
The youth in life's fresh spring, and he who goes
In the full strength of years, matron and maid,
The speechless babe, and the gray-headed man—
Shall one by one be gathered to thy side,
By those, who in their turn shall follow them.

So live, that when thy summons comes to join
The innumerable caravan, which moves
To that mysterious realm, where each shall take
His chamber in the silent halls of death,
Thou go not, like the quarry-slave at night,
Scourged to his dungeon, but, sustained and soothed
By an unfaltering trust, approach thy grave,
Like one who wraps the drapery of his couch
About him, and lies down to pleasant dreams.

CHARGE TO A GRAND JURY ON SLAVERY

JOSEPH STORY

———◆•◆———

*Joseph Story (1779–1845) was a Justice of the Supreme Court of the
United States from 1811 to the end of his life. The following, from a
charge to a grand jury at Portland, Maine, in 1820, gives a vivid picture
of the realities of slave-dealing days.*

AT length the ship arrives at her destined port, and the unhappy Africans, who have survived the voyage, are prepared for sale. Some are consigned to brokers, who sell them for the ships at private sale. With this view, they are examined by the planters, who want them for their farms; and in the selection of them, friends and relations are parted without any hesitation; and when they part with mutual embraces, they are severed by a lash. Others are sold at public auction, and become the property of the highest bidder. Others are sold by what is denominated a "scramble." In this case the main and quarter decks of the ship are darkened by sails hung over them at a convenient height. The slaves are then brought out of the hold and made to stand in the darkened area. The purchasers, who are furnished with long ropes, rush at a given signal within the awning, and endeavor to encircle as many of them as they can. Nothing can exceed the terror which the wretched Africans exhibit on these occasions. A universal shriek is immediately heard—all is consternation and dismay—the men tremble—the women cling together in each other's arms—some of them faint away, and others are known to expire.

About twenty thousand, or one-fifth part of those who are annually imported, die during the "seasoning," which seasoning is said to expire, when the two first years of the servitude are completed; so that of the whole number about one-half perish within two years from their first captivity. I forbear to trace the subsequent scenes of their miserable lives,— worn out in toils, from which they can receive no profit, and oppressed with wrongs, from which they can hope for no relief. . . .

Let it be considered, that this wretchedness does not arise from the awful visitations of Providence, in the shape of plagues, famines, or earthquakes, the natural scourges of mankind; but it is inflicted by man on man, from the accursed love of gold. May we not justly dread the displeasure of that Almighty Being, who is the common Father of us all, if we do not by all means within our power endeavor to suppress such infamous cruelties? If we cannot, like the good Samaritan, bind up the wounds and soothe the miseries of the friendless Africans, let us not, like the Levite, pass with sullen indifference on the other side. What sight can be more acceptable in the eyes of Heaven than that of good men struggling in the cause of oppressed humanity? What consolation can be more sweet in a dying hour, than the recollection, that at least one human being may have been saved from sacrifice by our vigilance in enforcing the laws? . . .

In vain shall we expend our wealth in missions abroad for the promotion of Christianity; in vain shall we rear at home magnificent temples to the service of the Most High. If we tolerate this traffic, our charity is but a name, and our religion little more than a faint and delusive shadow.

THE MORAL ARGUMENT
AGAINST CALVINISM

WILLIAM ELLERY CHANNING

———◆•◆———

The religious tradition of the Puritans had always had two sides. One side was spiritual, which allowed for the thrilling experience of the soul's regeneration. The other was the decorous, cautious, sober, law-abiding, self-controlled side. Over the decades the latter half gradually became apotheosized in Unitarianism, which had its roots in the Arian heresy that holds that Jesus was not of the same substance as God but only the best of created beings. Unitarianism for many decades represented the most characteristic mode of thought of enlightened New England. Mrs. Edward Everett Hale, granddaughter of the Calvinist Lyman Beecher, told a daughter-in-law in 1902, "At the time when I was married (1852) there was no other church one could consider but the Unitarian."

The other half of the Puritan tradition found expression, for the time being, in the almost mystical spiritual feeling of Jonathan Edwards, who tried to revitalize Calvinism. Unitarianism, having rejected the Westminster Confession, liberated its followers—and indeed many who were not consciously Unitarians—from the concept of original sin.

The following passage, giving the Unitarian view, is part of an essay by William Ellery Channing (1780–1842), the finest Unitarian thinker of his time. Today, curiously enough, his writings are often read responsively in Unitarian churches, as modern gospel. A highly intellectual "convert" from Congregationalism, Channing had widely varied literary interests, and did much to prepare New England for the next spiritual movement— toward Transcendentalism.

. . . Calvinism teaches, that in consequence of Adam's sin in eating the forbidden fruit. God brings into life all his posterity with a nature wholly corrupt, so that they are utterly indisposed, disabled, and made opposite to all that is spiritually good, and wholly inclined to all evil, and that continually. It teaches, that all mankind, having fallen in Adam, are under God's wrath and curse, and so made liable to all miseries in this life, to death itself, and to the pains of hell for ever. It teaches, that from this ruined race God out of his mere good pleasure has elected a certain number to be saved by Christ, not induced to this choice by any foresight of their faith or good works, but wholly by his free grace and love; and that having thus predestinated them to eternal life, he renews and sanctifies them by his almighty and special agency, and brings them into a state of grace, from which they cannot fall and perish. It teaches, that the rest of mankind he is pleased to pass over, and to ordain them to dishonour and wrath for their sins, to the honour of his justice and power; in other words, he leaves the rest to the corruption in which they were born, withholds the grace which is necessary to their recovery, and condemns them to "most grievous torments in soul and body without intermission in hell fire forever." Such is Calvinism, as gathered from the most authentic records of the doctrine. Whoever will consult the famous Assembly's Catechisms and Confession, will see the peculiarities of the system in all their length and breadth of deformity. A man of plain sense, whose spirit had not been broken to this creed by education or terror, will think that it is not necessary for us to travel to heathen countries, to learn how mournfully the human mind may misrepresent the Deity. . . .

We shall conclude this discussion with an important inquiry. If God's justice and goodness are consistent with those operations and modes of government, which Calvinism ascribes to him, of what use is our belief in these perfections? What expectations can we found upon them? If it consist with divine rectitude to consign to everlasting misery, beings who have come guilty and impotent from his hand, we beg to know what interest we have in this rectitude, what pledge of good it contains, or what evil can be imagined which may not be its natural result? If justice and goodness, when stretched to infinity, take such strange forms and appear in such unexpected and apparently inconsistent operations, how are we sure, that they will not give up the best men to ruin, and leave the universe to the powers of darkness? Such results indeed seem incompatible with these attributes, but not more so than the acts attributed to God by Calvinism. It is said, that the divine faithfulness is pledged in the Scriptures to a happier issue of things? But why should not divine faithfulness transcend our poor understandings as much as divine goodness and justice, and why may not God, consistently with this attribute, crush every hope which his Word has raised? Thus all the divine perfections are lost to us as grounds of encouragement and consolation, if we maintain, that their infinity places them beyond our judgment, and that we must expect from them measures and operations entirely opposed to what seems to us most accordant with their nature.

We have thus endeavoured to show that the testimony of our rational and moral faculties against Calvinism is worthy of trust. We know that this reasoning will be met by the question, What then becomes of Christianity? for this religion plainly teaches the doctrines you have condemned. Our answer is ready. Christianity contains no such doctrines. Christianity, reason, and conscience, are perfectly harmonious on the subject under discussion. Our religion, fairly construed, gives no countenance to that system, which has arrogated to itself the distinction of Evangelical. We cannot, however, enter this field at present. We will only say, that the general spirit of Christianity affords a very strong presumption, that its records teach no such doctrines as we have opposed. This spirit is love, charity, benevolence. Christianity, we all agree, is designed to manifest God as perfect benevolence, and to bring men to love and imitate him. . . .

Calvinism, we are persuaded, is giving place to better views. It has passed its meridian, and is sinking, to rise no more. It has to contend with foes more formidable than theologians, with foes from whom it cannot shield itself in mystery and metaphysical subtleties, we mean with the progress of the human mind, and with the progress of the spirit of the Gospel. Society is going forward in intelligence and charity, and of course is leaving the theology of the sixteenth century behind it. We hail this revolution of opinion as a most auspicious event to the Christian cause. We hear much at present of efforts to spread the Gospel. But Christianity is gaining more by the removal of degrading errors, than it would by armies of missionaries who should carry with them a corrupted form of the religion. We think the decline of Calvinism one of the most encouraging facts in our passing history; for this system, by outraging conscience and reason, tends to array these high faculties against revelation. Its errors are peculiarly mournful, because they relate to the character of God. It darkens and stains his pure nature; spoils his character of its sacredness, loveliness, glory; and thus quenches the central light of the universe, makes existence a curse, and the extinction of it a consummation devoutly to be wished. . . .

WEBSTER AT BUNKER HILL

SAMUEL GRISWOLD GOODRICH

Today the name of Daniel Webster (1782–1852) is venerated, possibly, but the legend of his personal powers is fast passing away. There was a time when he was the Paul Bunyan of New England. For a glimpse of this folk figure the reader is recommended to Stephen Vincent Benét's short story "The Devil and Daniel Webster." ". . . He never got to be President, but he was the biggest man. There were thousands that trusted in him

right next to God Almighty, and they told stories about him. . . . They
said when he stood up to speak, stars and stripes came right out in the
sky, and once he spoke against a river and made it sink into the ground.
They said, when he walked the woods with his fishing-rod, Killall, the
trout would jump out of the streams right into his pocket, for they knew
it was no use putting up a fight against him. . . . His big farm up at
Marshfield was suitable to him. The chickens he raised were all white
meat down through the drumsticks, the cows were tended like children,
and the big ram he called Goliath . . . had horns with a curl like a morn-
ing-glory vine and could butt through an iron door. A man with a mouth
like a mastiff, a brow like a mountain and eyes like burning anthracite—
that was Dan'l Webster in his prime."

For a real-life account of the great man as orator I append a mov-
ing account of Webster's address, delivered fifty years after the battle
of Bunker Hill at the ceremonies where Lafayette laid the cornerstone of
the Monument, by Samuel Griswold Goodrich, Boston publisher and
author.

THE first time I ever saw Mr. Webster was on the 17th of June, 1825,
at the laying of the corner-stone of the Bunker Hill Monument. I shall
never forget his appearance as he strode across the open area, encircled
by some fifty thousand persons—men and women—waiting for the "Orator
of the Day," nor the shout that simultaneously burst forth, as he was recognized, carrying up to the skies the name of "Webster!" "Webster!"
"Webster!"

It was one of those lovely days in June, when the sun is bright, the air
clear, and the breath of nature so sweet and pure as to fill every bosom
with a grateful joy in the mere consciousness of existence. There were
present long files of soldiers in their holiday attire; there were many
associations, with their mottoed banners; there were lodges and grand
lodges, in white aprons and blue scarfs; there were miles of citizens from
the towns and the country round about; there were two hundred gray-
haired men, remnants of the days of the Revolution; there was among
them a stranger, of great mildness and dignity of appearance, on whom
all eyes rested, and when his name was known, the air echoed with the
cry—"Welcome, welcome, Lafayette!" Around all this scene, was a rainbow of beauty such as New England alone can furnish.

I have seen many public festivities and ceremonials, but never one,
taken all together, of more general interest than this. Everything was
fortunate: all were gratified; but the address was that which seemed up-
permost in all minds and hearts. Mr. Webster was in the very zenith of his

fame and of his powers. I have looked on many mighty men—King George, the "first gentleman in England;" Sir Astley Cooper, the Apollo of his generation; Peel, O'Connell, Palmerston, Lyndhurst—all nature's noblemen; I have seen Cuvier, Guizot, Arago, Lamartine—marked in their persons by the genius which has carried their names over the world; I have seen Clay, and Calhoun, and Pinkney, and King, and Dwight, and Daggett, who stand as high examples of personal endowment, in our annals, and yet not one of these approached Mr. Webster in the commanding power of their personal presence. There was a grandeur in his form, an intelligence in his deep dark eye, a loftiness in his expansive brow, a significance in his arched lip, altogether beyond those of any other human being I ever saw. And these, on the occasion to which I allude, had their full expression and interpretation.

In general, the oration was serious, full of weighty thought and deep reflection. Occasionally there were flashes of fine imagination, and several passages of deep, overwhelming emotion. I was near the speaker, and not only heard every word, but I saw every movement of his countenance. When he came to address the few scarred and time-worn veterans—some forty in number—who had shared in the bloody scene which all had now gathered to commemorate, he paused a moment, and, as he uttered the words "Venerable men," his voice trembled, and I could see a cloud pass over the sea of faces that turned upon the speaker. When at last, alluding to the death of Warren, he said—

"But ah, Him!—the first great martyr of this great cause. Him, the patriotic victim of his own self-devoting heart. Him, cut off by Providence in the hour of overwhelming anxiety and thick gloom: falling ere he saw the star of his country rise—how shall I struggle with the emotions that stifle the utterance of thy name!" Here the eyes of the veterans around, little accustomed to tears, were filled to the brim, and some of them "sobbed aloud in their fulness of heart." The orator went on:

"Our poor work may perish, but thine shall endure: this monument may moulder away, the solid ground it rests upon may sink down to the level of the sea; but thy memory shall not fail. Wherever among men a heart shall be found that beats to the transports of patriotism and liberty, its aspirations shall claim kindred with thy spirit!"

I have never seen such an effect, from a single passage: a moment before, every bosom bent, every brow was clouded, every eye was dim. Lifted as by inspiration, every breast seemed now to expand, every gaze to turn above, every face to beam with a holy yet exulting enthusiasm. It was the omnipotence of eloquence, which, like the agitated sea, carries a host upon its waves, sinking and swelling with its irresistible undulations.

THE FROG CATCHER

HENRY J. FINN

————————◆•◆————————

New England back-country humor is a special version of American folk humor, as in the following story of Timothy Drew of Vermont. What the New England touch consists of, it seems to me, is the emphasis the characters in the tale put on outsmarting each other.

Henry J. Finn, the author, was born in Sydney, Cape Breton, in 1785. He died in the burning of the steamship Lexington *off Long Island Sound in 1840.*

ONCE upon a time, there lived in a town in Vermont, a little whipper-snapper of a fellow, named Timothy Drew. Timmy was not more than five feet one, in this thick-soled boots. When standing by the side of his tall neighbors, he appeared like a dwarf among giants. Tall people are too apt to look down on those of less dimensions. Thus did the long-legged Yankees hector poor Timmy for not being a greater man. But, what our hero wanted in bulk, he made up in spirit. This is generally the case with small men. As for Timmy, he was "all pluck and gristle!" No steel-trap was smarter!

How such a little one grew on the Green Mountains, was always a mystery. Whether he was actually raised there, is, indeed, uncertain. Some say he was of Canadian descent, and was brought to the States by a Vermont peddler, who took him in barter for wooden cucumber-seeds. But Timmy was above following the cart. He disliked trade as too precarious a calling, and preferred a mechanic art. Though small, Timmy always knew which side of his bread had butter on it. Let it not be supposed that Timothy Drew always put up with coarse jibes at his size. On necessary occasions he was "chock-full of fight." To be sure, he could not strike higher than the abdomen of his associates; but his blows were so rapid that he beat out the daylights of a ten-footer, before one could say "Jack Robinson." A threat from Timmy was enough. How many belligerents have been quelled by this expressive admonition;—"If you say that 'ere again, I'll knock you into the middle of next week!" This occurred in Timmy's younger days. Age cooled his transports, and taught him to endure. He thought it beneath the dignity of an old man to quarrel with idle striplings.

Timmy Drew was a natural shoemaker. No man could hammer out a piece of sole-leather with such expedition. He used his knee for a lap-stone, and by dint of thumping, it became as hard and stiff as an iron hinge. Timmy's shop was situated near the foot of a pleasant valley on the edge of a pond, above which thousands of water-lilies lifted their snowy heads. In the spring it was a fashionable watering-place for bull-frogs, who gathered there from all parts, to spend the warm season. Many of these were of extraordinary size, and they drew near his shop, raised their heads, and swelled out their throats like bladders, until the welkin rung with their music. Timmy, engaged at his work, beat time for them with his hammer, and the hours passed away as pleasantly as the day is long.

Timmy Drew was not one of those shoemakers that eternally stick to their bench like a ball of wax. It was always his rule to carry his work to the dwellings of his customers, to make sure of the fit. On his way home, he usually stopped at the tavern to inquire the news, and take a drop of something to drink. Here it was that the wags fastened upon him with their jokes, and often made him feel as uncomfortable as a short-tailed horse in fly-time. Still Timmy loved to sit in the bar, and talk with the company, which generally consisted of jolly peddlers, recruiting from the fatigues of the last cruise. With such society much was to be learned, and Timmy listened with intense curiosity to their long-spun tales of the wonderful and wild. There is no person that can describe an incredible fact with greater plausibility than a Yankee peddler. His difficult profession teaches him to preserve an iron gravity in expatiating on his wares, which in few cases can be said to recommend themselves. Thus, narratives, sufficient to embarrass the speech of any other relater, carry with them conviction, when soberly received from such a respectable source. . . . It would be impossible to repeat all the jokes played off on the poor shoemaker. The standing jest, however, was on his diminutive stature, which never was more conspicuous than in their company, for most of them were as tall as bean-poles. On this subject Timmy once gave them a memorable retort. Half a dozen of the party were sitting by the fire, when our hero entered the room. He sat down, but they affected to over-look him. This goaded Timmy, and he preserved a moody silence. Presently one of them spoke: "I wonder what has become of little Timmy Drew? I hav'n't seen that are fellow for a week. By gosh! the frogs must have chawed him up." "If he was sitting here before your eyes, you wouldn't see him," said another, "he's so darnation small." . . . A general roar of laughter brought Timmy on his legs. His dander was raised. "You boast of your bulk," said he, straining up to his full height, and looking contemptuously around; "why, I am like a fourpenny-bit among *six cents*—worth the whole of ye!"

I shall now describe a melancholy joke, which they played off on the unfortunate shoemaker;—I say melancholy, for so it proved to him. A fashionable tailor in a neighboring village came out with a flaming advertisement, which was pasted up in the bar-room of the tavern, and excited general attention. He purported to have for sale a splendid assortment of coats, pantaloons, and waistcoats, of all colors and fashions; also, a great variety of trimmings, such as tape, thread, buckram, *frogs*, buttonmoulds, and all the endless small articles that make up a tailor's stock.

The next time Timmy made his appearance, they pointed out to him the advertisement. They especially called his attention to the article of "*frogs*," and reminded him of the great quantity to be caught in Lily Pond. "Why, Timmy," said they, "if you would give up shoemaking, and take to frog-catching, you would make your 'tarnal fortune!" "Yes, Timmy," said another, "you might bag a thousand in a half a day, and folks say they will bring a dollar a hundred." "*Two* for a cent apiece, they brought in New York, when I was there last," said a cross-eyed fellow, tipping the wink. "There's frogs enough in Lily Pond," said Timmy; "but it's darnation hard work to catch 'em. I swaggers, I chased one nearly half a day before I took him—he jumped like a grasshopper. I wanted him for bait. They're plaguey slippery fellows." "Never mind, Timmy, take a fish-net, and scoop 'em up. You must have 'em alive, and fresh. A lot at this time would fetch a great price." "I'll tell you what, Timmy," said one of them, taking him aside, "I'll go you shares. Say nothing about it to nobody. To-morrow night I'll come and help you catch 'em, and we'll divide the gain." Timmy was in raptures.

As Timmy walked home that night, one of those lucky thoughts came into his head, which are always the offspring of solitude and reflection. Thought he, "These 'ere frogs in a manner belong to me, since my shop stands nearest the pond. Why should I make two bites at a cherry, and divide profits with Jo Gawky? By gravy! I'll get up early to-morrow morning, catch the frogs, and be off with them to the tailor's before sunrise, and so keep all the money myself."

Timmy was awake with the lark. Never before was there such a stir amongst the frogs of Lily Pond. But they were taken by surprise. With infinite difficulty he filled his bag, and departed on his journey.

Mr. Buckram, the tailor, was an elderly gentleman, very nervous and very peevish. He was extremely nice in his dress, and prided himself on keeping his shop as neat as wax-work. In his manner he was grave and abrupt, and in countenance severe. I can see him now, handling his shears with all the solemnity of a magistrate, with spectacles on nose, and prodigious ruffles puffing from his bosom.

He was thus engaged one pleasant spring morning, when a short, stubbed fellow, with a bag on his shoulder, entered the shop. The old gentleman was absorbed in his employment, and did not notice his visitor. But his inattention was ascribed by Timmy to deafness, and he approached and applied his mouth to the tailor's ear, exclaiming—"I say, mister! do you want any frogs to-day?" The old gentleman dropped his shears, and sprung back in astonishment and alarm.—"Do you want any frogs this morning?" shouted Timmy, at the top of his voice. "No!" said the tailor, eying him over his spectacles, as if doubting whether he was a fool or a madman. "I have got a fine lot here," rejoined Timmy, shaking his bag. "They are jest from the pond, and as lively as kittens." "Don't bellow in my ears," said the old man pettishly, "I am not deaf. Tell me what you want, and begone!" "I want to sell you these 'ere frogs, old gentleman. You shall have them at a bargain. Only one dollar a hundred. I won't take a cent less. Do you want them?" The old man now got a glance at the frogs, and was sensible it was an attempt at imposition. He trembled with passion. "No!" exclaimed he, "get out of my shop, you rascal!" "I say you do want 'em," said Timmy, bristling up. "I *know* you want 'em; but you're playing offish like, to beat down the price. I won't take a mill less. Will you have them, or not, old man?" "Scoundrel!" shouted the enraged tailor, "get out of my shop this minute!"

Puzzled, mortified, and angry, Timmy slowly turned on his heel, and withdrew. "He won't buy them," thought he, "for what they are worth, and as for taking *nothing* for them, I won't. And yet I don't want to lug them back again; but if I ever plague myself by catching frogs again, may I be buttered! Curse the old curmudgeon! I'll try him once more"— and he again entered the shop.

"I say, Mr. Buckram, are you willing to give me anything for these 'ere frogs?" The old man was now goaded past endurance. Stamping with rage, he seized his great shears to beat out the speaker's brains. "Well, then," said Timmy, bitterly, "take 'em among ye for nothing,"—at the same time emptying the contents of his bag on the floor and marching out.

Imagine the scene that followed! One hundred live bull-frogs emptied upon the floor of a tailor's shop! It was a subject for the pencil of Cruikshanks. Some jumped this way and some that way, some under the bench and some upon it, some into the fireplace and some behind the door. Every nook and corner of the shop was occupied in an instant. Such a spectacle was never seen before. The old man was nearly distracted. He rent his hair, and stamped in a paroxysm of rage. Then seizing a broom, he made vain endeavors to sweep them out at the door. But they were as contrary as hogs, and when he swept one away, they jumped another. He tried to catch them with his hands, but they were as slippery as eels, and passed through his fingers. It was enough to exhaust the patience of Job. The neighbors, seeing Mr. Buckram sweeping frogs out of his shop, gathered around in amazement, to inquire if they were about to be beset with the plagues of Egypt. But old Buckram was in such a passion that he could not answer a word, and they were afraid to venture within the reach of his broom. It is astonishing what talk the incident made in the village. Not even the far-famed frogs of Windham excited more.

Thus were the golden visions of the frog-catcher resolved into thin air. How many speculators have been equally disappointed!

After this affair Timothy Drew could never endure the sight of a bull-frog. Whether he discovered the joke that had been played upon him, is uncertain. He was unwilling to converse on the subject. His irritability when it was mentioned only provoked inquiry. People were continually vexing him with questions. "Well, Timmy, how goes the frog market?" "How do you sell frogs?" Even the children would call after him as he passed—"There goes the frog-catcher!" Some mischievous person went so far as to disfigure his sign, so that it read—

> SHOES MENDED,
>
> AND FROGS CAUGHT,
>
> BY T. DREW.

AN EVENING IN NEW ENGLAND

LYDIA MARIA CHILD

Lydia Maria Child (1802–1880), leading Massachusetts Abolitionist, was the author of much fiction, including a collection of tales entitled Evenings in New England, Intended for Juvenile Amusement and Instruction *and signed "By An American Lady." The tales are highly didactic as, it must be remembered, was the fashion of the day. An aunt and some children are the characters, and the tales are told through their questions and her answers. The following example gives the tenor of the philosophy and displays a characteristic view of the institution of slavery.*

THE LITTLE MASTER AND HIS LITTLE SLAVE

Robert. It seems to me the people at the southward must be very cruel, or they would not keep slaves as they do.

Aunt. Your opinion is very unjust, my child. Every man who possesses any national pride must indeed regret that the indelible stain of slavery is fastened upon our country; and every one that has a single particle of human kindness could not but rejoice to see the Africans released from a state of servitude and oppression. But it is not right to conclude that our southern brethren have not as good feelings as ourselves, merely because they keep slaves. I am certain that no part of our country is more rich in overflowing kindness and genuine hospitality; and I must acknowledge that I regard slavery rather as their misfortune than their fault. Many of their best men would gladly be rid of it; and, some time or other, I have no doubt they will. Slaves were sent to those states when they were British colonies, and, with the true feelings of free-born Englishmen, they petitioned government to have the evil removed; but the British ministry considered slaves as necessary in order to carry on the plantations, and unwilling to give up the prospect of wealth, for the sake of justice or kindness, they refused to grant the petition. Now it has become such a fixed habit that it cannot be changed suddenly. It is like some inveterate sickness which must be slowly and carefully cured. The negroes are very numerous, and they have been so unused to liberty, that they would become licentious and abandoned if left to themselves. Therefore, all that a good man can do, at present, is to make all the slaves in his power as comfortable as possible, to instruct their children, to give freedom to those who deserve it, to use all his personal influence to remove the evil, and to wait patiently till the curse of slavery can be entirely and safely removed from the land. I believe that kind masters and grateful slaves are very numerous at the South. I will read one instance of this from "The Winter in Washington." The little girl is telling a story of her father when he was a small boy, which it seems she heard from an old negro, called Daddy Steevy.

"I love Daddy Steevy," said Emily, "he is so good; and I love to sit on his knee, and hear him tell about grandpapa and grandmama, and all about the great house, and about dear papa—when he was born, and what grand doings there were when he was christened; how all the servants had new clothes, and all the slaves had such a frolic, and the bells in the old church were rung,—and all about it, mama."

"Indeed, mama," said Louisa, "I think you would like to hear him tell of old times too,—particularly about what a sweet, good boy, papa was, and how all the house servants, and field negroes, and the poor people loved him. When any one who had done wrong, was going to be whipped, he would go and beg and cry, till their old master would forgive them."

"And once," continued Emily, when her sister stopped,—"and once, mama, there was one very careless, mischievous boy, who was always galloping the horses so fast that he almost killed them, and he would climb over the garden wall and steal the fruit, and would leave open the gates, and let all the cattle get into the cornfields, and would set the dogs on the cows to see them run, just for play; and grandpapa said he must be sold, he was so bad; but papa cried, and begged grandpapa not to sell him; and so, mama, one day when he had done something very bad; the overseers had him tied up to whip him; and so, mama, his mother ran to the house and told papa, who was a little boy, only eight years old; and he ran as fast as he could, though his tutor called to him to come back: but he ran till he came to the place where Ned was tied up; and his back was all bare, and the overseer was standing over him with a great whip, and was whipping him; and so little Edward, that is papa, I mean, ran and jumped right upon Ned's back, and caught him round the neck, and the overseer, before he knew who it was, gave him a lash too. The other slaves that were standing by, ran up, and daddy Steevy caught the overseer's arm, and cried, 'Stop; stop; don't you see it is master Edward?' 'Take him away, take him away then,' said the overseer, and he was in such a passion, mama, that he did not know what he was doing. 'Take him away,' said he, 'I tell you Ned shall have his thirty-nine lashes—why that child will ruin all the negroes on the plantation.' But little Edward, papa, I mean, wouldn't let go his hold; and he clasped his arms so tight round Ned's back, that the overseer couldn't pull him away, and none of the people would so much as touch him—and then the overseer was so furious that he began whipping again; but struck Ned on the legs; and then Ned's mother, and daddy Steevy, ran to the house, calling as loud as they could, 'Master, master, come down to the quarters!' And master, I mean grandpapa, came,—and when he heard what was the matter, he walked very fast, and saw with his own eyes the overseer whipping away as hard as he could—and sometimes, though he didn't mean it, he struck little Edward. Then grandpapa ran and snatched the whip out of the overseer's hand, and threw it on the ground, and caught little Edward in his arms, and hugged and kissed him; and then papa jumped down, and ran and tried to untie Ned; but it was such a big rope he couldn't; and then he asked daddy Steevy, but he didn't dare to, but looked at his master. Then grandpapa turned to the overseer and said, 'Unloose that boy, sir.' But the overseer wouldn't. He looked sullen and proud, and said, 'No, sir, I cannot unloose him. I was only doing my duty.' Then grandpapa said, 'That's true—Stephen, untie the rope.' And then papa ran and helped him, and took a knife out of daddy Stephen's hand, and cut the rope in two. I have seen the very knife, mama; and daddy Steevy says, he never will part with it so long as he lives. Well, when all this was done, Ned turned round and kneeled down before grandpapa, without speaking a word; and old master, grandpapa I mean, stood considering, and every one was as still, as still could be. The old master said, at last—'Well, Edward, we must sell this boy, after all!' 'Oh, no, no, dear papa, don't sell him, dear papa!' 'What then shall I do with him, said grandpapa, for he is a very wicked, mischievous boy?' 'Give him to me, papa, and I will make him good," said little Edward. 'That will be a difficult matter, my child,' said old master—mama, I can't help saying *old master* and *little Edward*, because daddy Stephen tells me it so."

"No matter, my dear,—tell it like Stephen; it will do very well."

"Oh, I remember all he said; he was so particular, and would tell just how grandpapa looked; and sometimes, mama, he almost acts it and makes brother Edward do like papa, and makes Joe do like Ned."

"Indeed! and do the boys love to listen to the old man's stories?"

"Oh, yes; dearly, mama; but they like best to hear about the war, and about the battles, and about General Washington, and"—

"But, Emily, finish this story first; I really wish to know what became of poor Ned. Your father never told any stories about himself; but I wonder you never told this before."

Emily hung down her head, coloured up to the eyes, and looked very conscious.

"Why, Emily, what ails you? I only inquired why you had not told me before."

Emily burst into tears, and said, "Indeed, mama, I was very naughty. I did what you forbade me. Dear mama, pray forgive me."

"My dear," said her mother, "you never, in your whole life, have told me an untruth; therefore, whatever you now tell me, I shall believe it, and, I am sure, forgive you too."

"Why then, mama, I did not tell you, because I used to go into the kitchen, and make daddy Steevy tell me all about old times, as he calls it. It was when you were out a visiting, mama, and while sister was in New-York. But I never went after sister came home, because she told me I must not do any thing contrary to your orders. When I told her about old times, and papa, she wanted to hear too, and she asked the housekeeper to let daddy Stephen come in to her room, and tell us stories about old times; and so, mama, Flora let him come; and of evenings, last winter, when you sent us all to play, because you liked to be alone at twilight, then we used to get daddy Stephen into the housekeeper's room, and there Louisa and the boys used to sit and listen to him, till you rang the bell for tea."

"I will forgive you, Emily, for two reasons; because you were so young, and because the stories were about your father. But now you are a big girl, I am sure you will never go into the kitchen any more, and never talk with the servants, except old mammy nurse, old daddy Stephen, and our good old Flora. I scarcely deem them servants; they seem more like near relatives and tender friends. They were the faithful servants of your grand-parents, and nursed and attended on your father from the time of his birth to the present day, and, I am sure, love his children as fondly as if they were their own."

"Oh, mama, my heart feels lighter now, I am so glad I have told you."

"But now, Emily, for our story; I forget where you left off."

"Just where papa asked grandpapa to give him Ned, and said he would make him good, and grandpapa said that it would be a difficult matter. And then Ned, who had been kneeling on the ground, without saying a word, or looking up, then Ned cried, 'Oh, master, pray give me to young master Edward, and I will never be wicked again; indeed I will be a good boy.'

"Old master shook his head, as much as to say, 'I fear not.' Then said Ned, 'Don't be afraid, master. I swear by my master in heaven, I will always be a faithful, and dutiful, and bounden slave to my young master. I will go between him and death, and will give my life to save his life, as he has done this day for me.'

"Poor Ned's hands were held up; the big tears rolled down his cheeks, and little master, sweet soul, held his father's hand between his, and looked, oh, how pitiful he looked in his face. Old master couldn't stand this; he snatched little Edward up in his arms, and hugging him close, he said, 'Give me a hundred kisses, my darling, and you shall have him. He shall be your own for all his life.' Master Edward began giving his father the hundred kisses, while Ned jumped up, and danced, and capered, and clapped his hands as if he was out of his senses. So papa took him to the house with him, and would not let him live at the quarters any more, and grandmamma gave him a livery-suit, and let him wait on his young master, and ride with him. And before Ned went to bed he sent to ask little Edward to come out in the entry to him; and when he went, he handed him the rope he had been tied with, and said, 'Now, young master, this rope ties me to you, as fast as it tied me to the whipping-post.' So, mamma, there is the end; for Ned has lived with papa ever since."

"But where is he now?"

"Why, mamma, don't you know he is Eddy?"

"What, is Eddy, your father's body servant, the Ned you have been telling me of?"

"Yes, mamma, the very same."

"Well, this is very strange; but one thing is certain, he loves mischief still; and I recollect when I was once urging your father to send him to the plantation, he said he could never part with him; for, although heedless and inattentive, he was a most attached and faithful slave, and devoted to him from a principle of gratitude, ever since he once saved him from a severe whipping. Your story, my little darling, has served to beguile an anxious hour."

Robert. The little girl's papa and grandpapa seem to have been very good indeed; but, after all, I cannot bear the idea of keeping slaves.

Aunt. And I am very glad you cannot. It certainly is the greatest evil that we have to complain of in this happy country; and he who is the means of adding one to the number of slaves is guilty of an enormous crime, and so is the man who abuses the poor creatures already in his power. What I have said was only to prove to you that our Southern brethren have an abundance of kind and generous feeling; though the system of slavery no doubt makes many of them proud, indolent, and tyrannical. I have already told you, that it is dangerous to cure some kinds of sickness too suddenly. It is so with slavery. It has become such a fixed habit, that it is very difficult to do it away. Therefore, let us not condemn the Southerners as cruel, because they continue in this practice; but since there is so much to admire and love in their characters, let us hope that the time will soon come when they will scorn to receive any other services than such as freemen render to freemen for honourable hire.

Robert. I know what I would do if I had a little slave. I would teach him to read, and write, and cypher, and then I would send him to the island of Hayti, where he might be as free and happy as I am.

AN ADDRESS

EDWARD EVERETT

———◆•◆———

Edward Everett (1794–1865) was another celebrated orator, in a day when Clay, Calhoun, Webster and Parker flourished. Among other offices he held those of Governor of Massachusetts, Minister to the Court of St. James's, President of Harvard, and Secretary of State. Everett's sister, Sarah Preston Everett, married Nathan Hale, nephew of the patriot. There is a family story about her which conveys a sense of the smallness and intimacy of Boston in the early years of the nineteenth century. Soon after Sarah's marriage and removal to Boston, one of her girlhood friends from Dorchester came up to town and walked along Tremont Street inquiring of all she passed, "Can you tell me where she that was Sally Everett lives?" She is said to have received correct directions on the third try.

I append three passages. The first is from Everett's Phi Beta Kappa address in 1824, "The Circumstances Favorable to the Progress of Literature in America." He was one of the first to point out the special influence of America on the mind, and to distinguish an inherent group of "American scholars."

The second passage is from John Quincy Adams' Diary, written after he had heard Everett preach a sermon (Everett began life as a Unitarian minister, and was professor of Greek at Harvard) in 1820, at the Capitol in

*Washington. It is amusing to note the critical reaction of the Southerners
Adams quotes, in view of the third excerpt concerning Everett that I give
here, from a lecture the aged Emerson gave, in 1880, before the Concord
Lyceum, on his recollections of the earlier part of the century.*

*Everett is too often remembered solely as the orator at Gettysburg who
delivered a two-hour address, after which "the President rose and said
a few words." On the day of delivery, the speech was a great success and
it seems unfair to laugh at him for talking as long as the period he had
been scheduled to fill.*

THIS condition of things is, evidently, substantially new, and renders
it impossible to foresee what garments our native muses will weave to
themselves. To foretell our literature would be to create it. There was
a time, before an epic poem, a tragedy, an historical composition, or a
forensic harangue, had ever been produced by the wit of man. It was
a time of vast and powerful empires, and of populous and wealthy cities.
We have no reason to think that any work, in either of those departments of literature, (with the exception, perhaps, of some meagre
chronicle, which might be called history,) was produced by the early
Ethiopians, the Egyptians, or the Assyrians. Greece herself had been
settled a thousand years, before the golden age of her literature. At
length, the new and beautiful forms, in which human thought and passion expressed themselves in that favored region, sprang up, and under
the excitement of free political institutions. Before the epos, the drama,
the oration, the history, appeared, it would, of course, have been idle for
the philosopher to form conjectures as to the paths which would be struck
out by the kindling genius of the age. He who could form such an anticipation could and would realize it, and it would be anticipation no longer.
The critic is ages behind the poet. Epic poetry was first conceived of,
when the gorgeous vision of the Iliad, not, indeed, in its full detail of
circumstances, but in the dim fancy of its leading scenes and bolder
features, burst upon the soul of Homer.

It would be equally impossible to mark out, beforehand, the probable
direction in which the intellect of this country will move, under the influence of institutions as new and peculiar as those of Greece, and so
organized as to secure the best blessings of popular government, without
the evils of anarchy. But if, as no one will deny, our political system
brings more minds into action, on equal terms, and extends the advantages of education, more equally, throughout the community; if it provides a prompter and wider circulation of thought; if, by raising the
character of the masses, it swells to tens of thousands and millions those
"sons of emulation, who crowd the narrow strait where honor travels," it

would seem not too much to anticipate new varieties and peculiar power in the literature, which is but the voice and utterance of all this mental action. The instrument of communication may receive improvement; the written and spoken language acquire new vigor; possibly, forms of address wholly new will be devised. Where great interests are at stake, great concerns rapidly succeeding each other, depending on almost innumerable wills, and yet requiring to be apprehended in a glance, and explained in a word; where movements are to be given to a vast population, not so much by transmitting orders as by diffusing opinions, exciting feelings, and touching the electric chord of sympathy; there language and expression will become intense, and the old processes of communication must put on a vigor and a directness adapted to the condition of things.

Our country is called, as it is, practical; but this is the element for intellectual action. No strongly-marked and high-toned literature, poetry, eloquence, or philosophy, ever appeared, but under the pressure of great interests, great enterprises, perilous risks, and dazzling rewards. Statesmen, and warriors, and poets, and orators, and artists, start up under one and the same excitement. They are all branches of one stock. They form, and cheer, and stimulate, and, what is worth all the rest, understand, each other; and it is as truly the sentiment of the student, in the recesses of his cell, as of the soldier in the ranks, which breathes in the exclamation,

> "To all the sons of sense proclaim,
> One glorious hour of *crowded life*
> Is worth an age without a name;"

crowded with emotion, thought, utterance, and achievement.

EDWARD EVERETT IN 1820

John Quincy Adams

Attended the divine service at the Capitol, and heard Mr. Edward Everett, the Professor of the Greek language at Harvard University, a young man of shining talents and of illustrious promise. His text was from I. Cor. vii. 29: "Brethren, the time is short;" and it was without comparison the most splendid composition as a sermon that I ever heard delivered. He had preached it last Sunday evening, where my sons had heard him, and George had written to me that it was the finest sermon he had ever heard, and foretelling that he would preach it again here. Hackneyed as this subject, the shortness of time, is, I never before saw so forcibly exemplified the truth that nothing is stale or trite in the hands of genius. His composition is more rich, more varied, more copious, more

magnificent, than was that of Buckminster. There were passages that reminded me perhaps too much of Massillon, but the whole sermon was
equal to any of the best that Massillon ever wrote. It abounded in
splendid imagery, in deep pathos, in cutting satire, in profound reflections
of morals, in coruscations of wit, in thunder-bolts of feeling. His manner
of speaking was slow, and his articulation distinct, perhaps to excess.
There was some want of simplicity both in the matter and manner. A
still greater defect was a want of unity in his subject. He gave as one
sermon a cento of extracts from two or more. There was a description of
the destructive operations of time, absolutely terrific—and a portrait of
the blessings and future glories of this country, wrought up like a work
of enchantment. The house was full, but not crowded. The New England
hearers were rapt in enthusiasm. Mr. King told me he had never heard
anything like it. The Southern auditors approved more coolly. Mr. Clay,
with whom I walked, after the service, to call upon Chief-Justice Marshall,
told me that although Everett had a fine fancy and a chaste style of composition, his manner was too theatrical, and he liked Mr. Holley's manner
better. . . .

RECOLLECTIONS OF EVERETT
Ralph Waldo Emerson

Germany had created criticism in vain for us until 1820, when Edward
Everett returned from his five years in Europe, and brought to Cambridge
his rich results, which no one was so fitted by natural grace and the
splendor of his rhetoric to introduce and recommend. He made us for
the first time acquainted with Wolff's theory of the Homeric writings,
with the criticism of Heyne. The novelty of the learning lost nothing in
the skill and genius of his relation, and the rudest undergraduate found a
new morning opened to him in the lecture-room of Harvard Hall.

There was an influence on the young people from the genius of Everett
which was almost comparable to that of Pericles in Athens. He had an
inspiration which did not go beyond his head, but which made him the
master of elegance. If any of my readers were at that period in Boston or
Cambridge, they will easily remember his radiant beauty of person, of a
classic style, his heavy large eye, marble lids, which gave the impression
of mass which the slightness of his form needed; sculptured lips; a voice
of such rich tones, such precise and perfect utterance, that, although
slightly nasal, it was the most mellow and beautiful and correct of all the
instruments of the time. The word that he spoke, in the manner in which
he spoke it, became current and classical in New England. He had a great
talent for collecting facts, and for bringing those he had to bear with
ingenious felicity on the topic of the moment. Let him rise to speak on
what occasion soever, a fact had always just transpired which composed,

with some other fact well known to the audience, the most pregnant and happy coincidence. It was remarked that for a man who threw out so many facts he was seldom convicted of a blunder. He had a good deal of special learning, and all his learning was available for purposes of the hour. It was all new learning, that wonderfully took and stimulated the young men. It was so coldly and weightily communicated from so commanding a platform, as if in the consciousness and consideration of all history and all learning—adorned with so many simple and austere beauties of expression, and enriched with so many excellent digressions and significant quotations, that, though nothing could be conceived beforehand less attractive or indeed less fit for green boys from Connecticut, New Hampshire and Massachusetts, with their unripe Latin and Greek reading, than exegetical discourses in the style of Voss and Wolff and Ruhnken, on the Orphic and Ante-Homeric remains—yet this learning instantly took the highest place to our imagination in our unoccupied American Parnassus. All his auditors felt the extreme beauty and dignity of the manner, and even the coarsest were contented to go punctually to listen, for the manner, when they had found out that the subject-matter was not for them. In the lecture-room, he abstained from all ornament, and pleased himself with the play of detailing erudition in a style of perfect simplicity. In the pulpit (for he was then a clergyman) he made amends to himself and his auditor for the self-denial of the professor's chair, and, with an infantine simplicity still, of manner, he gave the reins to his florid, quaint and affluent fancy.

Then was exhibited all the richness of a rhetoric which we have never seen rivalled in this country. Wonderful how memorable were words made which were only pleasing pictures, and covered no new or valid thoughts. He abounded in sentences, in wit, in satire, in splendid allusion, in quotation impossible to forget, in daring imagery, in parable and even in a sort of defying experiment of his own wit and skill in giving an oracular weight to Hebrew or Rabbinical words—feats which no man could better accomplish, such was his self-command and the security of his manner. All his speech was music, and with such variety and invention that the ear was never tired. Especially beautiful were his poetic quotations. He delighted in quoting Milton, and with such sweet modulation that he seemed to give as much beauty as he borrowed; and whatever he has quoted will be remembered by any who heard him, with inseparable association with his voice and genius. He had nothing in common with vulgarity and infirmity, but, speaking, walking, sitting, was as much aloof and uncommon as a star. The smallest anecdote of his behavior or conversation was eagerly caught and repeated, and every young scholar could recite brilliant sentences from his sermons, with mimicry, good or bad, of his voice. This influence went much farther, for he who was heard with such throbbing hearts and sparkling eyes in the lighted and crowded churches, did not let go his hearers when the church was dismissed, but the bright image of that eloquent form followed the boy home to his bed-chamber; and not a sentence was written in academic exercises, not a declamation attempted in the college chapel, but showed the omnipres-ence of his genius to youthful heads. This made every youth his defender, and boys filled their mouths with arguments to prove that the orator had a heart. This was a triumph of Rhetoric. It was not the intellectual or the moral principles which he had to teach. It was not thoughts. When Massa-chusetts was full of his fame it was not contended that he had thrown any truths into circulation. But his power lay in the magic of form; it was in the graces of manner; in a new perception of Grecian beauty, to which he had opened our eyes. There was that finish about this person which is about women, and which distinguishes every piece of genius from the works of talent—that these last are more or less matured in every degree of completeness according to the time bestowed on them, but works of genius in their first and slightest form are still wholes. In every public discourse there was nothing left for the indulgence of his hearer, no marks of late hours and anxious, unfinished study, but the goddess of grace had breathed on the work a last fragrancy and glitter.

By a series of lectures largely and fashionably attended for two winters in Boston he made a beginning of popular literary and miscellaneous lec-turing, which in that region at least had important results. It is acquiring greater importance every day, and becoming a national institution. I am quite certain that this purely literary influence was of the first importance to the American mind.

THE BOSTON LECTURE—
ITS ORIGIN AND EVOLUTION

SAMUEL GARDNER DRAKE

————◆•◆————

E. E. Hale writes, "The Thursday lecture was a regular function, in which one of the Congregational ministers of Boston addressed such audi-ences as came together on Thursday. . . . The congregation consisted [by the 1820's, when schools kept Thursday afternoon a holiday, even al-though the Thursday lecture occurred at 11 A.M.] of the ministers of the town and such ladies, generally past youth, as liked to go to hear the city clerk read the intentions of marriage. The law then required that these intentions should be read three times before some public assembly. . . .

*But in older times the lecture had been much more important. . . . The
restrictions in England on weekday addresses by distinguished preachers,
drove the particular thorn in the side of the Puritan which did most to
drive him to his new home in the West. Cotton and the other preachers
had all been imprisoned, or threatened with being imprisoned, because
they would deliver these weekday lectures. The people who emigrated
were absolutely determined that they would hear them, and that is
probably the reason why the reader and I are in this country—because
our ancestors chose to go to church in the middle of the week."*

*An example of one of the effects of this ancient institution is set forth
in the following essay by Samuel Gardner Drake (1798–1875) from* The
History and Antiquities of Boston, *published in 1856.*

THE Thursday Lecture, which had its beginning in Boston, soon after
the arrival of Mr. Cotton, has, with some intermissions, been kept up
until the present generation. It was an excellent institution, and early exercised a good influence. Many of the discourses at this lecture were
printed during the last century, and constitute a valuable portion of its
literary history. At these lectures subjects were sometimes discussed
which were of too secular a nature, as was then thought, for the pulpit on
Sundays. Thus, Mr. Cotton took occasion at one of these early lectures to
discuss the propriety of women's wearing veils. Mr. Endicott being present, he spoke in opposition to Mr. Cotton's views; and, "after some debate,
the Governor, perceiving it to grow to some earnestness, interposed, and
so it brake off." What effect, if any, the lecture had to bring the veil into
disuse here at that time, no mention is made. But about this time, whether
before or after, is not quite certain, but probably before, Mr. Cotton
lectured at Salem on the same grave question, with great effect. His arguments against veils were so conclusive to the females of the congregation,
that, though they all wore them in the forenoon, in the afternoon they
all came without them. This may have taken Governor Endicott by surprise, and he may have come up to Boston to counteract this wholesale,
and, as he believed, unscriptural denunciation of a necessary appendage
to the attire of all modest women, especially, as Mr. Williams and Mr.
Skelton had proved conclusively from Scripture, that it ought to be worn
in public assemblies. For females to wear veils, they maintained, was no
badge of superstition, while the Cross in the King's colors was evidently
of that character; or so Mr. Endicott considered it, and he forthwith proceeded to cut it out. Roger Williams is accused of agitating this matter,
and therefore accountable for the trouble that it occasioned; and as it was
done in accordance with his views, it was of course condemned by all
those who had denounced him as promulgating heretical doctrines. Upon

this Mr. Hubbard sarcastically adds, "What that good man would have done with the Cross upon his coin, if he had any left that bore that sign of superstition, is uncertain." Mr. Endicott cut out the red Cross from an entirely conscientious conviction, that it was idolatrous to let it remain; arguing, and truly, that it had been given to the King of England by the Pope; and that it was a relic of Antichrist. Mr. Richard Browne, Ruling Elder of the church of Watertown, complained of the act to the Court of Assistants, as a high-handed proceeding, which might be construed, in England, into one of rebellion. To conclude the account of this matter by anticipating the order of events, it may be briefly stated, that the Court issued an attachment against Ensign Richard Davenport, then the ensign-bearer of Salem, whose Colors had been mutilated, to appear at the next Court. When that Court came together, which was a year after the Cross was cut out, "Endicott was judged to be guilty of a great offence;" inasmuch as he had, "with rash indiscretion, and by his sole authority," committed an act, "thereby giving occasion to the Court of England to think ill of them;" that, therefore, "he was worthy of admonition, and should be disabled from bearing any public office for one year."

This affair of the Cross would hardly have been noticed, probably, but for the opportunity it afforded the people of Boston to punish those of Salem for their adherence to Roger Williams. And thus early is seen that spirit of dictation, which has ever since been conspicuous in this metropolis; and though it has, in a measure, made it what it is, it also shows that, what Boston undertakes, Boston will do.

1824-1841

THE ASSOCIATION MAN

WILLIAM CHANNING

———◆◆———

William Ellery Channing (1780–1842), Unitarian divine, speaks, in the excerpt given below from an article, "The Disposition Which Now Prevails to Form Associations and to Accomplish All Objects by Organized Masses," on a subject as pertinent today as ever—the "organization man."

WE have prefixed to this article the titles of several reports of Societies, not so much for the purpose of discussing the merits of the several institutions whose labours they celebrate, as with the more general design of offering some remarks on the disposition, which now prevails, to form Associations, and to accomplish all objects by organized masses. A difference of opinion on this point has begun to manifest itself, and murmurs against the countless Societies which modestly solicit, or authoritatively claim our aid, which now assail us with fair promises of the good which they purpose, and now with rhetorical encomiums on the good they have done, begin to break forth from the judicious and well disposed, as well as from the querulous and selfish. These doubts and complaints, however, are most frequently excited by particular cases of unfair or injurious operations in Societies. As yet, no general principles have been established, by which the value of this mode of action may be determined, or the relative claims of different Associations may be weighed. We will not promise to supply the deficiency, but we hope to furnish some help to a sounder judgement than yet prevails on the subject.

That the subject deserves attention, no man who observes the signs of the times, can doubt. Its importance forces itself on the reflecting. In truth, one of the most remarkable circumstances or features of our age, is the energy with which the principle of combination, or of action by joint forces, by associated numbers, is manifesting itself. It may be said, without much exaggeration, that everything is done now by Societies. Men have learned what wonders can be accomplished in certain cases by union, and seem to think that union is competent to everything. You can scarcely name an object for which some institution has not been formed. Would men spread one set of opinions, or crush another? They make a Society. Would they improve the penal code, or relieve poor debtors? They make Societies. Would they encourage agriculture, or manufactures, or science? They make Societies. Would one class encourage horse-racing, and another discourage travelling on Sunday? They form Societies. We have immense institutions spreading over the country, combining hosts for particular objects. We have minute ramifications of these Societies, penetrating everywhere except through the poor-house, and conveying resources from the domestic, the labourer, and even the child, to the central treasury. This principle of association is worthy of the attention of the philosopher, who simply aims to understand society, and its most powerful springs. To the philanthropist and the Christian it is exceedingly interesting, for it is a mighty engine, and must act, either for good or for evil, to an extent which no man can foresee or comprehend.

It is very easy, we conceive, to explain this great development of the principle of cooperation. The main cause is, the immense facility given to intercourse by modern improvements, by increased commerce and travelling, by the post-office, by the steam-boat, and especially by the press, by newspapers, periodicals, tracts, and other publications. Through these means, men of one mind, through a whole country, easily understand one another, and easily act together. The grand manoeuvre to which Napoleon owed his victories, we mean the concentration of great numbers, on a single point, is now placed within the reach of all parties and sects. It may be said, that by facilities of intercourse, men are brought within one another's attraction, and become arranged according to their respective affinities. Those who have one great object, find one another out through a vast extent of country, join their forces, settle their mode of operation, and act together with the uniformity of a disciplined army. So extensive have coalitions become, through the facilities now described, and so various and rapid are the means of communication, that when a few leaders have agreed on an object, an impulse may be given in a month to the whole country. Whole States may be deluged with tracts and other publications, and a voice like that of many waters be called forth from immense and widely separated multitudes. Here is a new power brought to bear on society; and it is a great moral question, how it ought to be viewed, and what duties it imposes. . . .

Associations often injure free action by a very plain and obvious operation. They accumulate power in a few hands, and this takes place just in proportion to the surface over which they spread. In a large institution, a few men rule, a few do everything; and if the institution happens to be directed to objects about which conflict and controversy exist, a few are able to excite in the mass strong and bitter passions, and by these to obtain an immense ascendancy. Through such an Association, widely spread, yet closely connected by party feeling, a few leaders can send their voices and spirit far and wide, and, where great funds are accumulated, can league a host of instruments, and by menace and appeals to interest, can silence opposition. Accordingly, we fear that in this country, an influence is growing up through widely spread Societies, altogether at war with the spirit of our institutions, and which, unless jealously watched, will gradually but surely encroach on freedom of thought, of speech, and of the press. It is very striking to observe, how, by such combinations, the very means of encouraging a free action of men's minds, may be turned against it. We all esteem the press as the safeguard of our liberties, as the power which is to quicken intellect by giving to all minds an opportunity to act on all. Now by means of Tract Societies, spread over a whole community, and acting under a central body, a few individuals, perhaps not more than twenty, may determine the chief reading for a great part of the children of the community, and for a majority of the adults, and may deluge our country with worthless sectarian writings, fitted only to pervert its taste, degrade its intellect, and madden it with intolerance. Let Associations devoted to any objects which excite the passions, be everywhere spread and leagued together for mutual support, and nothing is easier than to establish a control over newspapers. We are persuaded that by an artful multiplication of Societies, devoted apparently to different objects, but all swayed by the same leaders, and all intended to bear against a hated party, as cruel a persecution may be carried on in a free country as in a despotism. Public opinion may be so combined, and inflamed, and brought to bear on odious individuals or opinions, that it will be as perilous to think and speak with manly freedom, as if an Inquistion were open before us. . . .

Individual action is the great point to be secured. That man alone understands the true use of society, who learns from it to act more and more from his own deliberate conviction, to think more for himself, to be less swayed by numbers, to rely more on his own powers. One good action, springing from our own minds, performed from a principle within, performed without the excitement of an urging and approving voice from abroad, is worth more than hundreds which grow from mechanical imitation, or from the heat and impulse which numbers give us. In truth, all great actions are solitary ones. All the great works of genius come from deep, lonely thought. The writings which have quickened, electrified, regenerated the human mind, did not spring from Associations. That is most valuable which is individual; which is marked by what is peculiar and characteristic in him who accomplishes it. In truth, Associations are chiefly useful by giving means and opportunities to gifted individuals to act out their own minds. A Missionary Society achieves little good, except when it can send forth an individual who wants no teaching or training from the Society, but who carries his commission and chief power in his own soul. We urge this, for we feel that we are all in danger of sacrificing our individuality and independence to our social connections. We dread new social trammels. They are too numerous already. From these views we learn, that there is cause to fear and to withstand great Associations, as far as they interfere with, or restrain individual action, personal independence, private judgement, free, self-originated effort. We do fear, from not a few Associations which exist, that power is to be accumulated in the hands of a few, and a servile, tame dependent spirit, to be generated in the many. Such is the danger of our times, and we are bound as Christians and freemen to withstand it.

KEYNOTE OF ABOLITION

WILLIAM LLOYD GARRISON

Uneasiness of conscience about slavery had always been felt in New England—and rightly, since New England ships played a large part in the slave trade up until the ban on it in 1794. Yet moral action against the institution lay dormant until January 1, 1831, when the first issue of The Liberator *appeared in Boston. Its editor, William Lloyd Garrison (1805–1879), made no bones about the purpose of his magazine: "I shall strenuously contend for the immediate enfranchisement of our slave population," he stated on page one of the first issue. "On this subject I do not wish to think, or speak, or write with moderation. . . . I am in earnest—I will not equivocate—I will not excuse—I will not retreat a single inch—AND I WILL BE HEARD." The journal's policy continued to be one of righteous sensationalism, without, however, proposing any solution to the problem. It picked the most gruesome examples, the most extreme cases, to put over its point: that a monstrous injustice was abroad in the Land of Liberty.*

The Northern reaction against Garrison's magazine was very nearly as strong as the Southern reaction. A "broadcloth mob" of businessmen forced Garrison, on one occasion, to seek refuge in a Boston jail. Garrison wrote that he found opposition in New England "more stubborn, and apathy more frozen" than among the slaveholders themselves. Yet gradually his following grew. It seemed to thrive on opposition. Garrison did not equivocate, he did not excuse, he did not retreat an inch, and he was heard. He was the antislavery cause's major inspiration.

The following is an editorial from The Liberator.

THERE is much declamation about the sacredness of the compact which was formed between the free and slave States, on the adoption of the Constitution. A sacred compact, forsooth! We pronounce it the most bloody and heaven-daring arrangement ever made by men for the continuance and protection of a system of the most atrocious villany ever exhibited on earth. Yes—we recognize the compact, but with feelings of shame and indignation; and it will be held in everlasting infamy by the friends of justice and humanity throughout the world. It was a compact formed at the sacrifice of the bodies and souls of millions of our race, for the sake of achieving a political object—an unblushing and monstrous coalition to do evil that good might come. Such a compact was, in the nature of things and according to the law of God, null and void from the beginning. No body of men ever had the right to guarantee the holding of human beings in bondage.

Who or what were the framers of our Government that they should dare confirm and authorize such high-handed villany—such a flagrant robbery of the inalienable rights of man—such a glaring violation of all the precepts and injunctions of the Gospel—such a savage war upon a sixth part of our whole population? They were men, like ourselves—as fallible, as sinful, as weak, as ourselves. By the infamous bargain which they made between themselves, they virtually dethroned the Most High God, and trampled beneath their feet their own solemn and heaven-attested Declaration, that all men are created equal, and endowed by their Creator with certain inalienable rights—among which are life, liberty, and the pursuit of happiness. They had no lawful power to bind themselves or their posterity for one hour—for one moment—by such an unholy alliance. It was not valid then—it is not valid now. Still they persisted in maintaining it—and still do their successors, the people of Massachusetts, of New England, and of the twelve free States, persist in maintaining it. A sacred compact! a sacred compact! What, then, is wicked and ignominious?

It is said that if you agitate this question you will divide the Union. Believe it or not; but should disunion follow, the fault will not be yours. You must perform your duty, faithfully, fearlessly and promptly, and leave the consequences to God: that duty clearly is, to cease from giving countenance and protection to Southern kidnappers. Let them separate, if they can muster courage enough—and the liberation of their slaves is certain. Be assured that slavery will very speedily destroy this Union *if it be let alone;* but even if the Union can be preserved by treading upon the necks, spilling the blood, and destroying the souls of millions of your race, we say it is not worth a price like this, and that it is in the highest degree criminal for you to continue the present compact. Let the pillars thereof fall—let the superstructure crumble into dust—if it must be up-held by robbery and oppression.

A NEW ENGLAND BOYHOOD

EDWARD EVERETT HALE

————◆•◆————

Edward Everett Hale was born in 1822 and died in 1911. In 1893 he was asked by the editor of the Atlantic Monthly *to write his recollections of growing up in Boston. He did so, and titled it after a little book Lucy Larcom published a few years earlier,* A New England Girlhood.

"It was a good place to be born," Hale says, "and a good place in which to grow to manhood." The following is an excerpt from A New England Boyhood. *Hale's father was Nathan Hale, nephew of the patriot; his mother, Sarah Preston Everett, sister of Edward Everett.*

Many of the family traditions of life at home of which Hale speaks persisted into my own generation. In particular I think of the newspaper the Hale children edited, the hand press they printed it on, and of their making drawings in the evening in the family circle. I was given a little hand press when I was eight; my family paper was called The Society Cat, *and was illustrated (after a fashion) by its editor.*

I AM certainly not writing my autobiography; but I cannot give any idea of how boys lived in the decade when I was a boy—that is, in the years between 1826 and 1836—without giving a chapter to home life as I saw it. . . .

I was the youngest of four children who made the older half of a large family. By a gap between me and my brother Alexander,—who afterwards was lost in the government service in Pensacola,—"we four" were sepa-rated from the "three little ones." It is necessary to explain this in advance, in a history which is rather a history of young life in Boston than of mine alone.

My father, as I have said, was an experienced teacher in young life, and he never lost his interest in the business of education. My mother had a genius for education, and it is a pity that, at an epoch in her life when she wanted to open a girls' school, she was not permitted to do so. They had read enough of the standard books on education to know how much sense there was in them, and how much nonsense. Such books were about in the house, more or less commented on by us young critics as we grew big enough to dip into them.

At the moment I had no idea that any science or skill was expended on our training. I supposed I was left to the great American proverb which I have already cited: "Go as you please." But I have seen since that the hands were strong which directed this gay team of youngsters, though there was no stimulus we knew of, and though the touch was velvet. An illustration of this was in that wisdom of my father in sending me for four years to school to a simpleton.

The genius of the whole, shown by both my father and mother, came out in the skill which made home the happiest place of all, so that we simply hated any engagement which took us elsewhere, unless we were in the open air. I have said that I disliked school, and that I did not want to go down on the wharves, even with that doubtful bribe of the molasses casks. At home we had an infinite variety of amusements. At home we might have all the other boys, if we wished. At home, in our two stories, we were supreme. The scorn of toys which is reflected in the Edgeworth books had, to a certain extent, its effect on the household. But we had almost everything we wanted for purposes of manufacture or invention. Whalebone, spiral springs, pulleys, and catgut, for perpetual motion or locomotive carriages; rollers and planks for floats—what they were I will explain—all were obtainable. In the yard we had parallel bars and a high cross-pole for climbing. When we became chemists we might have sulphuric acid, nitric acid, litmus paper, or whatever we desired, so our allowance would stand it. I was not more than seven years old when I burned off my eyebrows by igniting gunpowder with my burning-glass. My hair was then so light that nobody missed a little, more or less, above the eyelids. I thought it was wisest not to tell my mother, because it might shock her nerves, and I was a man, thirty years old, before she heard of it. Such playthings as these, with very careful restrictions on the amount of powder, with good blocks for building, quite an assortment of carpenter's tools, a work-bench good enough, printing materials *ad libitum* from my father's printing-office, furnished endless occupation.

Before I attempt any account of the home life which grew out of such conditions I must make a little excursus to describe the domestic service of those days, quite different from ours. I wish particularly to describe Fullum, who outlived the class to which he belonged, and had, when he died, in 1886, long been its last representative. . . .

Fullum . . . had been a country lad, who came down from Worcester

County to make his fortune. I do not know when, but it was before the time of the short war with England. He expected to be, and was, the hired boy and hired man in one and another Boston family. Early in the business he was in Mr. William Sullivan's service. . . . Afterward he was in Daniel Webster's service, and here also he took care of horses and carriages. He was a born tyrant, and it was always intimated that Mr. Webster did not fancy his rule. Anyway he came from the Websters to us, I suppose when Mr. Webster went to Congress, in the autumn of 1820. And, in one fashion or another, he lived with our family, as a most faithful vassal or tyrant, for sixty-six years from that time. I say "vassal or tyrant," for this was a pure piece of feudalism; and in the feudal system, as I have often had to say, the vassal is often a tyrant, while the master is almost always a slave. So it is that the memories of my boyhood are all mixed up with memories of Fullum.

I have spoken of him in connection with Miss Whitney's school. Here was a faithful man Friday, who would have died for any of us, so strong was his love for us, yet who insisted on rendering his service very much in his own way. If my father designed a wooden horse for me, to be run on four wheels, after the fashion of what were called velocipedes in those days, he would make the drawings, but it would be Fullum's business to take them to the carpenter's and see the horse made. If we were to have heavy hoops from water-casks, Fullum was the person who conducted the negotiation for them. There was no harm in the tutorship to which we were thus intrusted. He never used a profane or impure word while he was with us children; and as he was to us an authority in all matters of gardening, of carpentry, of driving and the care of horses, we came to regard him as, in certain lines, omniscient and omnipotent. If now the reader will bear in mind that this omniscient and omnipotent person, at once the Hercules and the Apollo of our boyhood, could not read, write, or spell so well as any child four years old who had been twelve months at Miss Whitney's school, that reader may understand why a certain scorn of book-learning sometimes stains these pages, otherwise so pure. And if the same reader should know that this same Fullum always spoke in superlatives, and multiplied every figure with which he had to do by hundreds or by thousands, he may have a key to a certain habit of exaggeration which has been detected in the present writer. "They was ten thousand men tryin' to git in. But old Reed, he wouldn't let um." This would be his way of describing the effort of four or five men to enter some place from which Reed, the one constable of Boston, meant to keep them out. . . .

The oldest child of "us four" was but four years and nine months older than the youngest. She had, as I have said, received, and deserved, at Miss Whitney's a medal given to the "most amiable." Next to her came a boy, then another girl, and then this writer. The movements of "us four" had much in common; but at school and in most plays the boys made one unit and the girls another, to report every evening to one another. It is to the boyhood experiences that these pages belong.

But it was a Persian and Median rule of that household, which I recommend to all other households, that after tea there were to be no noisy games. The children must sit down at the table—there was but one—and occupy themselves there till bedtime. . . .

Everybody of whom we knew anything dined at one or two o'clock in Boston then. After dinner men went back to their places of business. At six, or possibly as late as seven in the summer, came "tea." After tea, as I have said, the children of this household gathered round the table. Fullum came in and took away the tea things, folded the cloth and put it away. Our mother then drew up her chair to the drawer of the table, probably with a baby in her arms awaiting the return of its nurse. We four drew up our chairs on the other sides. Then we might do as we chose—teetotum games, cards of all sorts, books, drawing, or evening lessons, if there were any such awful penalty resulting from the sin of Adam and Eve. But nobody might disturb anyone else.

Drawing was the most popular of the occupations, and took the most of our time and thought. The provisions for it were very simple, and there was only the faintest pretence at instruction. There was one particular brand of lead pencils, sold by one particular grocer in West Street at twelve cents a dozen. These were bought by us at this wholesale rate, and kept in the drawer. One piece of India rubber was also kept there for the crowd. As we gathered at the table, a quarter-sheet of foolscap was given to each child and to each guest—as regularly as a bit of butter had been given half an hour before—and one pencil. . . .

Perhaps two of us put together our paper, folded it and pinned it in the fold, and then made a magazine. Of magazines there were two—*The New England Herald,* composed and edited by the two elders of the group, and *The Public Informer,* by my sister Lucretia and me. I am afraid that the name "Public Informer" was suggested wickedly to us little ones, when we did not know that those words carry a disagreeable meaning. But when we learned this, afterwards, we did not care. I think some of the Everetts, my uncles, had had a boy newspaper with the same name. When things ran with perfect regularity *The New England Herald* was read at the breakfast-table one Monday morning, and *The Public Informer* the next Monday morning. But this was just as it might happen. They were published when the editors pleased, as all journals should be, and months might go by without a number. And there was but one copy of each issue. It would be better if this could be said of some other journals.

Once a year prizes were offered at school for translations or original compositions. We always competed, not to say were made to compete, by the unwritten law of the family. This law was simply that we could certainly do anything if we wanted to and tried. I remember a long rhythmical version I made of the story of the flood, in Ovid, and another of Phaeton. . . . I stinted myself in this translation to four lines before dinner and four lines after tea; and by writing eight lines thus, in fifty days I accomplished the enterprise. I would come home from the swimming school ten minutes earlier because this translation was to be made; and, while Fullum was setting the table for dinner, I would stand at the sideboard. There was always an inkstand on it, with two or three quill pens. I took out the poem from the upper drawer of the sideboard, which I never see to this moment without thinking of Ovid. Then I wrote my four lines, such as they were, put the manuscript away again, and proceeded to dinner.

Other boys and girls liked to come in to such an evening congress as I have described, but nothing was changed in the least because the visitor came, excepting that room was made at the table. He or she had a quarter-sheet of foolscap, like the others. . . .

I must not give the idea, however, by speaking of these evenings thus that our lives were specially artistic or literary. They were devoted to play, pure and simple, with no object but having a good time. The principal part of the attics—or, as we called them, garrets—in every house we lived in was surrendered to us boys. In Tremont Place we had the valuable addition of a dark cockloft over the garret chambers. It had no windows, but was all the better place to sit and tell stories in. Then we controlled the stairs to the roof, and we spent a good deal of time, in the summer days, on the ridge-pole. There were not twenty houses in Boston on higher land, so that from this point we commanded a good view of the harbor. I was amused the other day when an infantile correspondent of a New York newspaper asked how Napoleon could have used a telegraph before what is called Mr. Morse's invention, for as early as 1831 we read all the telegraphic signals of all the vessels arriving in Boston harbor, and the occasional semaphoric signals on the lookout on Central Wharf.

About the year 1830, under the pressure of the "march of intellect," were published some books for young children from which the present generation is profiting largely. There were "The Boy's Own Book," "The Girl's Own Book," "The American Girl's Own Book," and "The Young Lady's Own Book," each of them excellent in its way. I think "The Boy's Own Book," which has since been published with the double title "An Encyclopædia for Boys," led the way in this affair; and I still regard it as rather the best of the series. It had subdivisions for indoor games, outdoor games, gymnastics, chemistry, chess, riddles, riding, walking, and I think driving, boxing, and fencing. Perhaps there were more heads, but these were those which occupied our attention most. Somebody made

me a New Year's present of this book in the year 1830 or 1831, and from
that moment it was the text-book of the attic. Professor Andrews and
President Eliot would feel their hair growing gray, if for five minutes
they were obliged to read the chemistry which soaked into us from this
book. Whoever wrote it still used the old nomenclature a good deal. We
knew nothing of HO, and little of the proportions in which they go into
the constitution of things. We read of "oil of vitriol" and "muriatic acid,"
and had other antiquarian names for agents and reagents. All the same,
the book gave us experiments which we could try—taught us how to
manufacture fireworks in a fashion, and even suggested to us the painting of our own magic lantern slides. Our apparatus was of the most
limited kind. It was a high festival day when one went down to Gibbens's
grocer's shop and bought for three cents an empty Florence flask; this was
the retort of that simple chemistry. In connection with this, like all other
boys of that time known to me, we made what were called electrical
machines, which gave us good sparks and Leyden jar shocks quite sufficient to satisfy the guests who visited us.

It is in connection with one of these machines that I remember one
of my mother's gospels. I was trying to catch a fly, to give him an electric
shock, and she would not permit me. I pleaded in vain that it would
not hurt him, but she said: "It would certainly not give him pleasure,
and it might give him pain."

My father was a civil engineer, somewhat in advance of his time. He
was the first person to propose the railroad system of Massachusetts; and
that system would not be what it is, but for his work for it, in season
and out of season. I cannot remember the time when we did not have
a model railway in the house; in earlier years it was in the parlor, so that
he might explain to visitors what was meant by a car running upon
rails. I can still see the sad, incredulous look, which I understood then
as well as I should now, with which some intelligent person listened
kindly, and only in manner implied that it was a pity that so intelligent
a man as he should go crazy. His craziness, fortunately, led his associates,
and in the year 1831, after endless reverses, a charter was given for the
incorporation of the Boston and Worcester Railway. In the earlier
proposals for such work it was always suggested that horses should be
the moving power. In point of fact the first railway, which carried the
Quincy granite from Quincy to the sea, was operated by the weight of
the descending trains, which pulled up the empty cars. I was with him,
as a little boy, sitting on a box in the chaise, when he drove out once to
see the newly laid Quincy track, and I perfectly remember his trying
with his foot the steadiness of the rail where it crosses the road to Quincy.
His tastes, of course, led ours. There was a lathe in the house, which we
were permitted to run under severe conditions; and we very early made
our own locomotives, which were propelled by whalebone springs. . . .

I have stated already the absolute rule that we must report at home before we went anywhere to play after school. I think this rule affected our lives a great deal more than my mother meant it should in laying it down. She simply wanted to know at certain stages of the day where her children were. I do not recollect that she ever forbade our going anywhere, where we wanted to. But practically the rule worked thus: We rushed home from school, very likely with a plan on foot for the Common, or for some combined movement with the other boys. We went into the house to report. There was invariably gingerbread ready for us, which was made in immense quantities for the purpose. This luncheon was ready not only for us, but for any boys we might bring with us. When once arrived at home the home attractions asserted themselves. There was some chemical experiment to be continued, or there was some locomotive to be displayed to another boy, or there had come in a new number of the *Juvenile Miscellany*. In a word, we were seduced up into the attic, and up in the attic we were very apt to stay. . . .

My father was editor of the *Daily Advertiser;* and in that day this meant that he owned the whole printing plant, engaged all the printers, and printed his own newspaper. He was never a practical printer, but, with his taste for mechanics, he understood all the processes of the business. Not unnaturally this grew into his establishing a book printing-office, which did as good work in its time as was done anywhere. The first American edition of Cicero's "Republic," after the discovery of that book in a Pompeian manuscript by Mai, was printed by him. Naturally he went forward into the study of power-press printing, and, at his suggestion, Daniel Treadwell made the first power presses which worked to advantage in this country. In the years between 1820 and 1825 the Boston Mill-dam was constructed, for the purpose of making a water power out of the tide power of the Back Bay. My father then introduced power-press printing there, and that printing-office was maintained until the year 1836. When the time came he was president of the first type foundry in New England, perhaps in America. All the arrangements for these contrivances were, of course, interesting to his sons. So, as I have said, we had type from the printing-office, and we all learned to set type and to arrange it. When, in 1834, my brother went to college, and I was left alone, I used to repair every day to the book office for my printing, and there learned the case and all the processes of imposing scientifically. I used to work off my own books on a hand press. I have never lost the memories of the case, and am rather fond of saying now that, if it were necessary, I could support my family as a compositor.

I would not have gone into this detail but that I am always urging people to let their boys have printing apparatus in early life, because I think it is such a good educator. The absolute accuracy that is necessary is good for a boy. The solid fact that 144 ems will go into a certain space, and will require that space, and that no prayers nor tears, hopes nor fears, will change that solid fact—this is most important. I do not mean the mere convenience to an author of being able to talk familiarly with the compositor who has his book in hand: that is a good thing. But I mean that human life in general has lessons to teach which every compositor requires which few other experiences of life teach so well. I think also that, as a study of English style, the school of Franklin and Horace Greeley is a good one.

NATURE

RALPH WALDO EMERSON

———◆•◆———

The side of the New England Puritan tradition that was not cautious and sober, decorous and self-controlled, the side that did not find its expression in Unitarianism, was the spiritual side. The old Puritans staked their hopes on a personal experience of the Deity; they yearned for the soul's supernatural regeneration, for a living sense of the divine sovereignty.

Unitarianism freed the New England mind from dogma, but, for men who were born with the mystic crave, Unitarianism seemed prosaic and rationalistic. These were the men who instituted the Transcendentalist movement. Ralph Waldo Emerson (1803–1882) Perry Miller calls a "Jonathan Edwards in whom the concept of original sin has evaporated." Edwards, Miller says, sought "the images or shadows of divine things" in nature, but could not trust his discoveries; he believed man to be cut off from full communion with nature because of his inherent depravity; but Emerson, who started out as a Unitarian minister, "announced that there is no inherent separation between the mind and the thing, that in reality they leap to embrace each other."

Emerson stated this principle of Transcendentalism in his first book, Nature—the manifesto of the Transcendentalists, published in 1836, from which the following passage is an excerpt. I have appended to it two of Emerson's best-known short poems, "The Rhodora," and "The Concord Hymn," which, a generation ago, every New England child knew by heart. The slight clumsiness of Emerson's poetry made it less appealing to readers of his day than that of Longfellow, but makes it much more appealing to our own. In addition, I have added a passage from Emerson's

*longer poem, "Monadnoc," because it evokes the bare-topped peak
(Monadnock means mountain, in the Indian tongue) which unforgettably
dominates an expanse of southern New Hampshire.*

*In spite of his esoteric erudition, Emerson was pre-eminently a New
Englander—not a Bostonian, but a Yankee. He would stand in front of the
post office in Concord talking politics with the farmers; practical, shrewd,
down-to-earth. When a friend told him of how, in the Irish famine, a poor
Irish family threw out of the window the cornmeal he had sent to them,
Emerson replied, "You should have sent them hot cakes."*

To go into solitude, a man needs to retire as much from his chamber
as from society. I am not solitary whilst I read and write, though nobody
is with me. But if a man would be alone, let him look at the stars. The
rays that come from those heavenly worlds will separate between him and
what he touches. One might think the atmosphere was made transparent
with this design, to give man, in the heavenly bodies, the perpetual presence of the sublime. Seen in the streets of cities, how great they are! If
the stars should appear one night in a thousand years, how would men
believe and adore; and preserve for many generations the remembrance
of the city of God which had been shown! But every night come out
these envoys of beauty, and light the universe with their admonishing
smile.

The stars awaken a certain reverence, because though always present,
they are inaccessible; but all natural objects make a kindred impression,
when the mind is open to their influence. Nature never wears a mean
appearance. Neither does the wisest man extort her secret, and lose his
curiosity by finding out all her perfection. Nature never became a toy to
a wise spirit. The flowers, the animals, the mountains, reflected the wisdom of his best hour, as much as they had delighted the simplicity of his
childhood.

When we speak of nature in this manner, we have a distinct but most
poetical sense in the mind. We mean the integrity of impression made
by manifold natural objects. It is this which distinguishes the stick of
timber of the wood-cutter, from the tree of the poet. The charming landscape which I saw this morning is indubitably made up of some twenty
or thirty farms. Miller owns this field, Locke that, and Manning the
woodland beyond. But none of them owns the landscape. There is a property in the horizon which no man has but he whose eye can integrate all
the parts, that is, the poet. This is the best part of these men's farms, yet
to this their warranty-deeds give no title.

To speak truly, few adult persons can see nature. Most persons do not
see the sun. At least they have a very superficial seeing. The sun illumi-

nates only the eye of the man, but shines into the eye and the heart of the child. The lover of nature is he whose inward and outward senses are still truly adjusted to each other; who has retained the spirit of infancy even into the era of manhood. His intercourse with heaven and earth, becomes part of his daily food. In the presence of nature, a wild delight runs through the man, in spite of real sorrows. Nature says,—he is my creature, and maugre all his impertinent griefs, he shall be glad with me. Not the sun or the summer alone, but every hour and season yields its tribute of delight; for every hour and change corresponds to and authorizes a different state of the mind, from breathless noon to grimmest midnight. Nature is a setting that fits equally well a comic or a mourning piece. In good health, the air is a cordial of incredible virtue. Crossing a bare common, in snow puddles, at twilight, under a clouded sky, without having in my thoughts any occurrence of special good fortune, I have enjoyed a perfect exhilaration. I am glad to the brink of fear. In the woods too, a man casts off his years, as the snake his slough, and at what period soever of life, is always a child. In the woods, is perpetual youth. Within these plantations of God, a decorum and sanctity reign, a perennial festival is dressed, and the guest sees not how he should tire of them in a thousand years. In the woods, we return to reason and faith. There I feel that nothing can befall me in life,—no disgrace, no calamity (leaving me my eyes), which nature cannot repair. Standing on the bare ground,—my head bathed by the blithe air, and uplifted into infinite space,—all mean egotism vanishes. I become a transparent eyeball; I am nothing; I see all; the currents of the Universal Being circulate through me; I am part or particle of God. The name of the nearest friend sounds then foreign and accidental: to be brothers, to be acquaintances,—master or servant, is then a trifle and a disturbance. I am the lover of uncontained and immortal beauty. In the wilderness, I find something more dear and connate than in streets and villages. In the tranquil landscape, and especially in the distant line of the horizon, man beholds somewhat as beautiful as his own nature.

The greatest delight which the fields and woods minister, is the suggestion of an occult relation between man and the vegetable. I am not alone and unacknowledged. They nod to me, and I to them. The waving of the boughs in the storm, is new to me and old. It takes me by surprise, and yet is not unknown. Its effect is like that of a higher thought or a better emotion coming over me, when I deemed I was thinking justly or doing right.

Yet it is certain that the power to produce this delight does not reside in nature, but in man, or in a harmony of both. It is necessary to use these pleasures with great temperance. For, nature is not always tricked in holiday attire, but the same scene which yesterday breathed perfume and glittered as for the frolic of the nymphs, is overspread with melancholy

to-day. Nature always wears the colors of the spirit. To a man laboring
under calamity, the heat of his own fire hath sadness in it. Then, there is a
kind of contempt of the landscape felt by him who has just lost by death
a dear friend. The sky is less grand as it shuts down over less worth in
the population.

THE RHODORA:
ON BEING ASKED, WHENCE IS THE FLOWER?

In May, when sea-winds pierced our solitudes
I found the fresh Rhodora in the woods,
Spreading its leafless blooms in a damp nook,
To please the desert and the sluggish brook.
The purple petals, fallen in the pool,
Made the black water with their beauty gay;
Here might the red-bird come his plumes to cool,
And court the flower that cheapens his array.
Rhodora! if the sages ask thee why
This charm is wasted on the earth and sky,
Tell them, dear, that if eyes were made for seeing,
Then Beauty is its own excuse for being:
Why thou wert there, O rival of the rose!
I never thought to ask, I never knew:
But, in my simple ignorance, suppose
The self-same Power that brought me there brought you.

CONCORD HYMN:
SUNG AT THE COMPLETION OF THE BATTLE MONUMENT, APRIL 19, 1836

By the rude bridge that arched the flood,
    Their flag to April's breeze unfurled,
Here once the embattled farmers stood,
    And fired the shot heard round the world.

The foe long since in silence slept;
    Alike the conqueror silent sleeps;
And Time the ruined bridge has swept
    Down the dark stream which seaward creeps.

On this green bank, by this soft stream,
    We set to-day a votive stone;
That memory may their deed redeem,
    When, like our sires, our sons are gone.

Spirit, that made those heroes dare
    To die, and leave their children free,

> Bid Time and Nature gently spare
> The shaft we raise to them and thee.

MONADNOC

... Hither we sing
Our insect miseries to thy rocks;
And the whole flight, with folded wing,
Vanish, and end their murmuring,—
Vanish beside these dedicated blocks,
Which who can tell what mason laid?
Spoils of a front none need restore,
Replacing frieze and architrave;—
Where flowers each stone rosette and metope brave;
Still is the haughty pile erect
Of the old building Intellect.

Complement of human kind,
Holding us at vantage still,
Our sumptuous indigence,
O barren mound, thy plenties fill!
We fool and prate;
Thou art silent and sedate.
To myriad kinds and times one sense
The constant mountain doth dispense;
Shedding on all its snows and leaves,
One joy it joys, one grief it grieves.
Thou seest, O watchman tall,
Our towns and races grow and fall,
And imagest the stable good
For which we all our lifetime grope,
In shifting form the formless mind,
And though the substance us elude,
We in thee the shadow find.
Thou, in our astronomy
An opaker star,
Seen haply from afar,
Above the horizon's hoop,
A moment, by the railway troop,
As o'er some bolder height they speed,—
By circumspect ambition,
By errant gain,
By feasters and the frivolous,—
Recallest us,

And makest sane.
Mute orator! well skilled to plead,
And send conviction without phrase,
Thou dost succor and remede
The shortness of our days,
And promise, on thy Founder's truth,
Long morrow to this mortal youth.

SELECTIONS

HENRY DAVID THOREAU

Of the Concord group—Emerson, Alcott, Hawthorne, Thoreau, that ex-plosion of intellect heard around the world—none was so wholly a local product as Thoreau (1817–1862). He was the apotheosis of the Yankee. He called himself "a mystic, a transcendentalist, and a natural philosopher to boot"; yet that universality which makes him live for our day more than any of his great contemporaries truly was transcendental. He was universal in his head only. As he put it, "I have travelled a good deal in Concord." What he saw on those travels he saw with a seemingly modern eye. No one else has put so much meaning into nature, or so much nature into meaning.

A selection from Thoreau's Journal follows; then his poems "Con-science" and "Independence" on subjects ever close to a New England heart, and a passage from A Week on the Concord and Merrimack Rivers. *I urge the reader to go to* Walden *for himself, as perhaps the most suc-cessful adjustment to the Industrial Revolution any Victorian writer made —a simple rejection of it.*

APRIL 2 [1852]. It appears to me that, to one standing on the heights of philosophy, mankind and the works of man will have sunk out of sight altogether; that man is altogether too much insisted on. The poet says the proper study of mankind is man. I say, study to forget all that; take wider views of the universe. That is the egotism of the race. What is this our childish, gossiping, social literature, mainly in the hands of the pub-lishers? When another poet says the world is too much with us, he means, of course, that man is too much with us. In the promulgated views of man, in institutions, in the common sense, there is narrowness and delusion. It is our weakness that so exaggerates the virtues of philanthropy and charity and makes it the highest human attribute. The world will sooner or later tire of philanthropy and all religions based on it mainly. They cannot long sustain my spirit. In order to avoid delusions, I would fain let man go by and behold a universe in which man is but as a grain of sand. I am sure that those of my thoughts which consist, or are contemporaneous, with social personal connections, however humane, are not the wisest and widest, most universal. What is the village, city, State, nation, aye the civilized world, that it should concern a man so much? The thought of them affects me in my wisest hours as when I pass a woodchuck's hole. It is a comfortable place to nestle, no doubt, and we have friends, some sympathizing ones, it may be, and a hearth, there; but I have only to get up at midnight, to find them all slumbering. Look at our literature. What a poor, puny, social thing, seeking sympathy! The author troubles himself about his readers—would fain have one before he dies. He stands too near his printer; he corrects the proofs. Not satisfied with defiling one another in this world, we would all go to heaven together. To be a good man, that is, a good neighbor in the widest sense, is but little more than to be a good citizen. Mankind is a gigantic institution; it is a community to which most men belong. It is a test I would apply to my companion—can he forget man? Can he see this world slumbering?

I do not value any view of the universe into which man and the institutions of man enter very largely and absorb much of the attention. Man is but the place where I stand, and the prospect hence is infinite. It is not a chamber of mirrors which reflect me. When I reflect, I find that there is other than me. Man is a past phenomenon to philosophy. The universe is larger than enough for man's abode. Some rarely go outdoors, most are always home at night, very few indeed have stayed out all night once in their lives, fewer still have gone behind the world of humanity, seen its institutions like toadstools by the wayside.

Landed on Tall's Island. It is not cold or windy enough, perchance, for the meadow to make its most serious impression. The staddles, from which the hay has been removed, rise a foot or two above the water. Large white gulls are circling over the water. The shore of this meadow lake is quite wild, and in most places low and rather inaccessible to walkers. On the rocky point of this island, where the wind is felt, the waves are breaking merrily, and now for half an hour our dog has been standing in the water under the small swamp white oaks, and ceaselessly snapping at each wave as it broke, as if it were a living creature. He, regardless of cold and wet, thrusts his head into each wave to gripe it. A dog snapping at the waves as they break on a rocky shore. He then rolls himself in the leaves for a napkin. We hardly set out to return, when the water looked sober and rainy. There was more appearance of rain in the water than in the sky—April weather look. And soon we saw the dimples of drops on the surface. I forgot to mention before the cranberries seen on the bottom, as we pushed over the meadows, and the red beds of pitcher-plants.

We landed near a corn-field in the bay on the west side, below Sherman's Bridge, in order to ascend Round Hill, it still raining gently or with drops far apart. From the top we see smoke rising from the green pine hill in the southern part of Lincoln. The steam of the engine looked very white this morning against the oak-clad hillsides. The clouds, the showers, and the breaking away now in the west, all belong to the summer side of the year and remind me of long-past days. The prospect is often best from two thirds the way up a hill, where, looking directly down at the parts of the landscape—the fields and barns—nearest the base, you get the sense of height best, and see how the land slopes up to where you stand. From the top, commonly, you overlook all this, and get a sense of *distance* merely, with a break in the landscape by which the most interesting point is concealed. This hill with its adjuncts is now almost an island, surrounded by broad lakes. The south lakes reflect the most light at present, but the sober surface of the northern is yet more interesting to me.

How novel and original must be each new man's view of the universe! For though the world is so old, and so many books have been written, each object appears wholly undescribed to our experience, each field of thought wholly unexplored. The whole world is an America, a *New World*. The fathers lived in a dark age and throw no light on any of our subjects. The sun climbs to the zenith daily, high over all literature and science. Astronomy, even, concerns us worldlings only, but the sun of poetry and of each new child born into the planet has never been astronomized, nor brought nearer by a telescope. So it will be to the end of time. The end of the world is not yet. Science is young by the ruins of Luxor, unearthing the Sphinx, or Nineveh, or between the Pyramids. The parts of the meadows nearly surrounded by water form interesting peninsulas and promontories.

Return to our boat. We have to go ashore and upset it every half-hour, it leaks so fast, for the leak increases as it sinks in the water in geometrical progression. I see, among the phenomena of spring, here and there a dead sucker floating on the surface, perhaps dropped by a fish hawk or a gull, for the gulls are circling this way overhead to reconnoitre us. They will come sailing overhead to observe us. On making the eastward curve in the river, we find a strong wind against us. Pushing slowly across the meadow in front of the Pantry, the waves beat against the bows and sprinkle the water half the length of the boat. The froth is in long white streaks before the wind, as usual striping the surface.

We land in a steady rain and walk inland by R. Rice's barn, regardless of the storm, toward White Pond. Overtaken by an Irishman in search of work. Discovered some new oaks and pine groves and more New England fields. At last the drops fall wider apart, and we pause in a sandy field near the Great Road of the Corner, where it was agreeably retired and sandy, drinking up the rain. The rain was soothing, so still and sober, gently beating against and amusing our thoughts, swelling the brooks. The robin now peeps with scared note in the heavy overcast air, among the apple trees. The hour is favorable to thought. Such a day I like a sandy road, snows that melt and leave bare the corn and grain fields, with Indian relics shining on them, and prepare the ground for the farmer. Saw a cow or ox in a hollow in the woods, which had been skinned and looked red and striped, like those Italian anatomical preparations. It scared the dog. Went through a reddish andromeda swamp, where still a little icy stiffness in the crust under the woods keeps us from slumping. The rain now turns to snow with large flakes, so soft many cohere in the air as they fall. They make us white as millers and wet us through, yet it is clear gain. I hear a solitary hyla for the first time. At Hubbard's Bridge, count eight ducks going over. Had seen one with outstretched neck over the Great Meadows in Sudbury. Looking up, the flakes are black against the sky. And now the ground begins to whiten. Got home at 5:30 P.M.

CONSCIENCE

Conscience is instinct bred in the house,
Feeling and Thinking propagate the sin
By an unnatural breeding in and in.
I say, Turn it out doors,
Into the moors.
I love a life whose plot is simple,
And does not thicken with every pimple,
A soul so sound no sickly conscience binds it,
That makes the universe no worse than't finds it.
I love an earnest soul,
Whose mighty joy and sorrow
Are not drowned in a bowl,
And brought to life to-morrow;
That lives one tragedy,
And not seventy;
A conscience worth keeping,
Laughing not weeping;
A conscience wise and steady,
And for ever ready;
Not changing with events,

Dealing in compliments;
A conscience exercised about
Large things, where one *may* doubt.
I love a soul not all of wood,
Predestinated to be good,
But true to the backbone
Unto itself alone,
And false to none;
Born to its own affairs,
Its own joys and own cares;
By whom the work which God begun
Is finished, and not undone;
Taken up where he left off,
Whether to worship or to scoff;
If not good, why then evil,
If not good god, good devil.
Goodness—you hypocrite, come out of that,
Live your life, do your work, then take your hat.
I have no patience towards
Such conscientious cowards.
Give me simple laboring folk,
Who love their work,
Whose virtue is a song
To cheer God along.

INDEPENDENCE

My life more civil is and free
Than any civil polity.

Ye princes keep your realms
And circumscribed power,
Not wide as are my dreams,
Nor rich as is this hour.

What can he give which I have not?
What can ye take which I have got?
Can ye defend the dangerless?
Can ye inherit nakedness?

To all true wants time's ear is deaf,
Penurious states lend no relief
Out of their pelf—
But a free soul—thank God—
Can help itself.

Be sure your fate
Doth keep apart its state—
Not linked with any band—
Even the nobles of the land

In tented fields with cloth of gold—
No place doth hold
But is more chivalrous than they are.
And sigheth for a nobler war.
A finer strain its trumpet rings—
A brighter gleam its armor flings.

The life that I aspire to live
No man proposeth me—
No trade upon the street
Wears its emblazonry.

A WEEK ON THE CONCORD AND MERRIMACK RIVERS

We were thus entering the State of New Hampshire on the bosom of the flood formed by the tribute of its innumerable valleys. The river was the only key which could unlock its maze, presenting its hills and valleys, its lakes and streams, in their natural order and position. The MERRIMACK, or Sturgeon River, is formed by the confluence of the Pemigewasset, which rises near the Notch of the White Mountains, and the Winnepisiogee, which drains the lake of the same name, signifying "The Smile of the Great Spirit." From their junction it runs south seventy-eight miles to Massachusetts, and thence east thirty-five miles to the sea. I have traced its stream from where it bubbles out of the rocks of the White Mountains above the clouds, to where it is lost amid the salt billows of the ocean on Plum Island beach. At first it comes on murmuring to itself by the base of stately and retired mountains, through moist primitive woods whose juices it receives, where the bear still drinks it, and the cabins of settlers are far between, and there are few to cross its stream; enjoying in solitude its cascades still unknown to fame; by long ranges of mountains of Sandwich and Squam, slumbering like tumuli of Titans, with the peaks of Mossehillock, the Haystack, and Kearsarge reflected in its waters; where the maple and the raspberry, those lovers of the hills, flourish amid temperate dews;—flowing long and full of meaning, but untranslatable as its name Pemigewasset, by many a pastured Pelion and Ossa, where unnamed muses haunt, tended by Oreads, Dryads, Naiads, and receiving the tribute of many an untasted Hippocrene. There are earth, air, fire, and water,—very well, this is water, and down it comes.

> Such water do the gods distil,
> And pour down every hill
>   For their New England men;
> A draught of this wild nectar bring,
> And I'll not taste the spring
>   Of Helicon again.

Falling all the way, and yet not discouraged by the lowest fall. By the law of its birth never to become stagnant, for it has come out of the clouds, and down the sides of precipices worn in the flood, through beaver dams broke loose, not splitting but splicing and mending itself, until it found a breathing place in this low land. There is no danger now that the sun will steal it back to heaven again before it reach the sea, for it has a warrant even to recover its own dews into its bosom again with interest at every eve.

It was already the water of Squam and Newfound Lake and Winnepisiogee, and White Mountain snow dissolved, on which we were floating, and Smith's and Baker's and Mad rivers, and Nashua and Souhegan and Piscataquoag, and Suncook and Soucook and Contoocook, mingled in incalculable proportions, still fluid, yellowish, restless all, with an ancient, ineradicable inclination to the sea.

So it flows on down by Lowell and Haverhill, at which last place it first suffers a sea change, and a few masts betray the vicinity of the ocean. Between the towns of Amesbury and Newbury it is a broad commercial river, from a third to half a mile in width, no longer skirted with yellow and crumbling banks, but backed by high green hills and pastures, with frequent white beaches on which the fishermen draw up their nets. I have passed down this portion of the river in a steamboat, and it was a pleasant sight to watch from its deck the fishermen dragging their seines on the distant shore, as in pictures of a foreign strand. At intervals you may meet with a schooner laden with lumber, standing up to Haverhill, or else lying at anchor or aground, waiting for wind or tide; until, at last, you glide under the famous Chain Bridge, and are landed at Newburyport. Thus she who at first was "poore of waters, naked of renowne," having received so many fair tributaries, as was said of the Forth,

> "Doth grow the greater still, the further downe;
> Till that abounding both in power and fame,
> She long doth strive to give the sea her name;"

or if not her name, in this case, at least the impulse of her stream. From the steeples of Newburyport, you may review this river stretching far up into the country, with many a white sail glancing over it like an inland sea, and behold, as one wrote who was born on its head-waters, "Down out at its mouth, the dark inky main blending with the blue above. Plum Island, its sand ridges scolloping along the horizon like the sea serpent, and the distant outline broken by many a tall ship, leaning, *still*, against the sky."

Rising at an equal height with the Connecticut, the Merrimack reaches the sea by a course only half as long, and hence has no leisure to form broad and fertile meadows like the former, but is hurried along rapids, and down numerous falls without long delay. The banks are generally steep and high, with a narrow interval reaching back to the hills, which is only occasionally and partially overflown at present, and is much valued by the farmers. Between Chelmsford and Concord in New Hampshire, it varies from twenty to seventy-five rods in width. It is probably wider than it was formerly, in many places, owing to the trees having been cut down, and the consequent wasting away of its banks. The influence of the Pawtucket dam is felt as far up as Cromwell's Falls, and many think that the banks are being abraded and the river filled up again by this cause. Like all our rivers, it is liable to freshets, and the Pemigewasset has been known to rise twenty-five feet in a few hours. It is navigable for vessels of burden about twenty miles, for canal boats by means of locks as far as Concord in New Hampshire, about seventy-five miles from its mouth, and for smaller boats to Plymouth, one hundred and thirteen miles. A small steamboat once plied between Lowell and Nashua, before the railroad was built, and one now runs from Newburyport to Haverhill.

SPEECH ON ABOLITION AND FREEDOM OF THE PRESS

WENDELL PHILLIPS

———◆◆◆———

Wendell Phillips (1811–1884) was a prominent Boston lawyer and supporter of William Lloyd Garrison's policies. The following speech of his has an interesting history. An abolitionist clergyman, Rev. E. P. Lovejoy, had been shot by a mob in Illinois while attempting to protect his printing press from destruction. A meeting in sympathy with Lovejoy was called by William Ellery Channing at Faneuil Hall in Boston. The meeting was orderly until a speech "of the utmost bitterness" by Hon. J. T. Austin, Attorney General of the Commonwealth, compared slaves to a

menagerie of wild beasts, the Illinois mob to the participants in the Bos-
ton Tea Party, and called Lovejoy "presumptuous and imprudent." Austin
said a clergyman with a gun in his hand—as Lovejoy had been—or one
"mingling in the debates of a popular assembly, was marvellously out of
place."

You could not say that to a Boston audience with impunity. Wendell
Phillips, who had not expected to speak, then rose.

I should like to add a note about the pronunciation of Faneuil Hall.
To modern tourists (and even Bostonians) it is Fan-you-well, to Bos-
tonians of my generation it is Fannel, but to the old Bostonians who were
already dying out when I was a child, it was Funnel Hall.

MR. CHAIRMAN:—We have met for the freest discussion of these resolutions, and the events which give rise to them. [Cries of "Question,"
"Hear him," "Go on," "No gagging," etc.] I hope I shall be permitted to
express my surprise at the sentiments of the last speaker,—surprise not
only at such sentiments from such a man, but at the applause they have
received within these walls. A comparison has been drawn between the
events of the Revolution and the tragedy at Alton. We have heard it
asserted here, in Faneuil Hall, that Great Britain had a right to tax the
Colonies, and we have heard the mob at Alton, the drunken murderers
of Lovejoy, compared to those patriot fathers who threw the tea overboard! [Great applause.] Fellow-citizens, is this Faneuil Hall doctrine?
["No, no."] The mob at Alton were met to wrest from a citizen his just
rights,—met to resist the laws. We have been told that our fathers did the
same; and the glorious mantle of Revolutionary precedent has been
thrown over the mobs of our day. To make out their title to such defence, the gentleman says that the British Parliament had a *right* to tax
these Colonies. It is manifest that, without this, his parallel falls to the
ground; for Lovejoy had stationed himself within constitutional bulwarks.
He was not only defending the freedom of the press, but he was under
his own roof, in arms with the sanction of the civil authority. The men
who assailed him went against and over the laws. The *mob*, as the gentleman terms it,—mob, forsooth! certainly we sons of the tea-spillers are
a marvellously patient generation!—the "orderly mob" which assembled
in the Old South to destroy the tea were met to resist, not the laws, but
illegal exactions. Shame on the American who calls the tea-tax and
stamp-act *laws!* Our fathers resisted, not the King's prerogative, but the
King's usurpation. To find any other account, you must read our Revolutionary history upside down. Our State archives are loaded with arguments of John Adams to prove the taxes laid by the British Parliament
unconstitutional,—beyond its power. It was not till this was made out that

the men of New England rushed to arms. The arguments of the Council Chamber and the House of Representatives preceded and sanctioned the contest. To draw the conduct of our ancestors into a precedent for mobs, for a right to resist laws we ourselves have enacted, is an insult to their memory. The difference between the excitements of those days and our own, which the gentleman in kindness to the latter has overlooked, is simply this: the men of that day went for the right, as secured by the laws. They were the people rising to sustain the laws and constitution of the Province. The rioters of our day go for their own wills, right or wrong. Sir, when I heard the gentleman lay down principles which place the murderers of Alton side by side with Otis and Hancock, with Quincy and Adams, I thought those pictured lips [pointing to the portraits in the Hall] would have broken into voice to rebuke the recreant American,— the slanderer of the dead. [Great applause and counter applause.] The gentleman said that he should sink into insignificance if he dared to gainsay the principles of these resolutions. Sir, for the sentiments he has uttered, on soil consecrated by the prayers of Puritans and the blood of patriots, the earth should have yawned and swallowed him up.

[Applause and hisses, with cries of "Take that back." The uproar became so great that for a long time no one could be heard. At length the Hon. William Sturgis came to Mr. Phillips's side at the front of the platform. He was met with cries of "Phillips or nobody," "Make him take back 'recreant,'" "He sha'n't go on till he takes it back." When it was understood that Mr. Sturgis meant to sustain, not to interrupt, Mr. Phillips, he was listened to, and said: "I did not come here to take any part in this discussion, nor do I intend to; but I do entreat you, fellow-citizens, by everything you hold sacred,—I conjure you by every association connected with this Hall, consecrated by our fathers to freedom of discussion,—that you listen to every man who addresses you in a decorous manner." Mr. Phillips resumed.]

. . . I must find some fault with the statement which has been made of the events at Alton. It has been asked why Lovejoy and his friends did not appeal to the executive,—trust their defence to the police of the city. It has been hinted that, from hasty and ill-judged excitement, the men within the building provoked a quarrel, and that he fell in the course of it, one mob resisting another. Recollect, Sir, that they did act with the approbation and sanction of the Mayor. In strict truth, there was no executive to appeal to for protection. The Mayor acknowledged that he could not protect them. They asked him if it was lawful for them to defend themselves. He told them it was, and sanctioned their assembling in arms to do so. They were not, then, a mob; they were not merely citizens defending their own property; they were in some sense the *posse comitatus,* adopted for the occasion into the police of the city, acting under the order of a magistrate. It was civil authority resisting lawless violence. Where, then, was the imprudence? Is the doctrine to be sustained here, that it is *imprudent* for men to aid magistrates in executing the laws? . . .

Sir, as I understand this affair, it was not an individual protecting his property; it was not one body of armed men resisting another, and making the streets of a peaceful city run blood with their contentions. It did not bring back the scenes in some old Italian cities, where family met family, and faction met faction, and mutually trampled the laws under foot. No; the men in that house were regularly *enrolled*, under the sanction of the Mayor. There being no militia in Alton, about seventy men were enrolled with the approbation of the Mayor. These relieved each other every other night. About thirty men were in arms on the night of the sixth, when the press was landed. The next evening, it was not thought necessary to summon more than half that number; among these was Lovejoy. It was, therefore, you perceive, Sir, the police of the city resisting rioters,—civil government breasting itself to the shock of lawless men.

Here is no question about the right of self-defence. It is in fact simply this: Has the civil magistrate a right to put down a riot?

Some persons seem to imagine that anarchy existed at Alton from the commencement of these disputes. Not at all. "No one of us," says an eye-witness and a comrade of Lovejoy, "has taken up arms during these disturbances but at the command of the Mayor." Anarchy did not settle down on that devoted city till Lovejoy breathed his last. Till then the law, represented in his person, sustained itself against its foes. When he fell, civil authority was trampled under foot. He had "planted himself on his constitutional rights,"—appealed to the laws,—claimed the protection of the civil authority,—taken refuge under "the broad shield of the Constitution. When through that he was pierced and fell, he fell but one sufferer in a common catastrophe." He took refuge under the banner of liberty,—amid its folds; and when he fell, its glorious stars and stripes, the emblem of free institutions, around which cluster so many heart-stirring memories, were blotted out in the martyr's blood.

It has been stated, perhaps inadvertently, that Lovejoy or his comrades fired first. This is denied by those who have the best means of knowing. Guns were first fired by the mob. After being twice fired on, those within the building consulted together and deliberately returned the fire. But suppose they did fire first. They had a right so to do; not only the right which every citizen has to defend himself, but the further right which every civil officer has to resist violence. Even if Lovejoy fired the first gun, it would not lessen his claim to our sympathy, or destroy his title to be considered a martyr in defence of a free press. The question now is, Did he act within the Constitution and the laws? The men who fell in State

Street on the 5th of March, 1770, did more than Lovejoy is charged with. They were the *first* assailants. Upon some slight quarrel they pelted the troops with every missile within reach. Did this bate one jot of the eulogy with which Hancock and Warren hallowed their memory, hailing them as the first martyrs in the cause of American liberty?

If, Sir, I had adopted what are called Peace Principles, I might lament the circumstances of this case. But all you who believe, as I do, in the right and duty of magistrates to execute the laws, join with me and brand as base hypocrisy the conduct of those who assemble year after year on the 4th of July, to fight over the battles of the Revolution, and yet "damn with faint praise," or load with obloquy, the memory of this man, who shed his blood in defence of life, liberty, property, and the freedom of the press! ...

Imprudent to defend the liberty of the press! Why? Because the defence was unsuccessful? Does success gild crime into patriotism, and the want of it change heroic self-devotion to imprudence? ...

Imagine yourself present when the first news of Bunker Hill battle reached a New England town. The tale would have run thus: "The patriots are routed,—the redcoats victorious,—Warren lies dead upon the field." With what scorn would that *Tory* have been received, who should have charged Warren with *imprudence!* who should have said that, bred a physician, he was "out of place" in that battle, and "died as the *fool dieth*"! [Great applause.] ...

The question that stirred the Revolution touched our civil interests. *This* concerns us not only as citizens, but as immortal beings. Wrapped up in its fate, saved or lost with it, are not only the voice of the statesman, but the instructions of the pulpit, and the progress of our faith. . . .

Mr. Chairman, from the bottom of my heart I thank that brave little band at Alton for resisting. We must remember that Lovejoy had fled from city to city,—suffered the destruction of three presses patiently. At length he took counsel with friends, men of character, of tried integrity, of wide views, of Christian principle. They thought the crisis had come: it was full time to assert the laws. They saw around them, not a community like our own, of fixed habits, of character moulded and settled, but one "in the gristle, not yet hardened into the bone of manhood." The people there, children of our older States, seem to have forgotten the blood-tried principles of their fathers the moment they lost sight of our New England hills. Something was to be done to show them the priceless value of the freedom of the press, to bring back and set right their wandering and confused ideas. He and his advisers looked out on a community, staggering like a drunken man, indifferent to their rights and confused in their feelings. Deaf to argument, haply they might be stunned into sobriety. They saw that of which we cannot judge, the *necessity* of resistance. Insulted law called for it. Public opinion, fast hastening on the downward course, must be arrested.

Does not the event show they judged rightly? Absorbed in a thousand trifles, how has the nation all at once come to a stand? Men begin, as in 1776 and 1640, to discuss principles, to weigh characters, to find out where they are. Haply we may awake before we are borne over the precipice.

I am glad, Sir, to see this crowded house. It is good for us to be here. When Liberty is in danger, Faneuil Hall has the right, it is her duty, to strike the key-note for these United States. I am glad, for one reason, that remarks such as those to which I have alluded have been uttered here. The passage of these resolutions, in spite of this opposition, led by the Attorney-General of the Commonwealth, will show more clearly, more decisively, the deep indignation with which Boston regards this outrage.

BACKGROUND FOR
"THE WRECK OF THE HESPERUS"

HENRY WADSWORTH LONGFELLOW

Even today that poem of Henry Wadsworth Longfellow's called "The Wreck of the Hesperus" is familiar to most Americans. When I was young, school children learned it by heart as much as a matter of course as the multiplication table. Instead of reprinting the poem here, I thought I would give the notes in Longfellow's Journal which give the poem's genesis in his mind.

Longfellow seems to have been slightly mixed up about where the wreck occurred. The following is an excerpt from the Boston Evening Transcript of December 16, 1839.

> *During the gale yesterday ... Sch. Hesperus, at anchor in the stream, parted chains and drove against ship Wm. Badger, N side Rowe's wharf [Boston harbor] parted her fasts, and both drove up across the dock; sch. carried away her bow sprit and stove her bow, The ship was badly chafed, and stove end of gib boom through the upper window of the four story store opposite.*

But the poet got what mattered. Hesperus is a lovely name, for a ship, and Norman's Woe direful, for a reef. Longfellow could hardly have written "It was the schooner William Badger, drove up against Rowe's Wharf...."

December 7, 1839. Wrote letters. Dined on rice. Then walked to town with Felton. Took tea with Mrs. E., then went to Mr. Ticknor's. Saw the folio edition of Stapfer's Faust with engravings; large, coarse and very expressive. I like them better than Retzsch's. Ticknor thinks them worthless. . . .

December 12, 1839. A drenching rain. Read Jean Paul. Drowsy, dull, desoeuvré, not having a book in press, and having given up smoking. It cleared up and I went to town. Bought a handsome edition of Minot's Poems,—I believe the only edition of an English bard before Chaucer and Gower, though of the fourteenth century. . . .

December 14, 1839. Highly commendatory notice of Poems (Voices of the Night) in the Mercantile Journal and Morning Post, papers which abused Hyperion.

December 17, 1839. News of shipwrecks horrible on the coast. Twenty bodies washed ashore near Gloucester, one lashed to a piece of the wreck. There is a reef called Norman's Woe where many of these took place; among others the schooner Hesperus. Also the Sea-flower on Black Rock. I must write a ballad upon this; also two others,—"The Skeleton In Armor," and "Sir Humphrey Gilbert."

December 30, 1839. I wrote last evening a notice of Allston's poems. After which I sat till twelve o'clock by my fire, smoking, when suddenly it came into my mind to write the "Ballad of the Schooner Hesperus"; which I accordingly did. Then I went to bed, but could not sleep. New thoughts were running in my mind and I got up to add them to the ballad. It was three by the clock. I then went to bed and fell asleep. I feel pleased with the ballad. It hardly cost me an effort. It did not come into my mind by lines but by stanzas.

MARGARET FULLER'S CONVERSATIONS

THOMAS HIGGINSON

———◆•◆———

The period dominated by Transcendentalism in New England is roughly 1820 to 1860. Historically, it was the function of Unitarianism to prepare the way for Transcendentalism; in it the New England sense of freedom of the mind found a new dimension—freedom to feel. In Emerson, Thoreau, Hawthorne and Margaret Fuller (1810–1850) New England reached

its intellectual peak. After them, immigration and industrialism sullied the
flavor of what had been a very rare distillation.

Margaret Fuller was a real "Boston baby," a prodigy—she read Ovid at
eight. As a young woman she made enduring friendships with the great
Transcendentalist men, who accepted her as their equal. From 1839 to
1844 she held a series of conversational classes at the house of Elizabeth
Peabody, sister-in-law of Hawthorne, and through them exerted a great
influence on Boston society.

Later she went to Italy and became an ardent adherent of Mazzini the
revolutionist. She married another of his followers, the Marchese Ossoli,
but the ship bringing them back to the United States was wrecked and
she was drowned.

What follows is an account of Miss Fuller's conversations, from the
biography of her by Thomas Wentworth Higginson (1823–1911), Uni-
tarian minister, writer, and discoverer of Emily Dickinson.

THE conversations began November 6, 1839, at Miss Peabody's rooms in
West Street—those rooms where many young men and women found,
both then and at a later day, the companionship of cultivated people,
and the best of French, German, Italian, and English literature. The
conversations continued for five winters, closing in April, 1844. Their
theory was not high-flown but eminently sensible, being based expressly
on the ground stated in the circular, that the chief disadvantage of
women in regard to study was in not being called upon, like men, to re-
produce in some way what they had learned. As a substitute for this she
proposed to try the uses of conversation, to be conducted in a somewhat
systematic way, under efficient leadership. Accordingly these meetings,
although taking a wide range, were always concentrated, and with a good
deal of effect, on certain specified subjects; the most prominent of these
being, perhaps, that of Mythology, or the reappearance of religious ideas
under varying forms. It is a theme which has since assumed great importance and commanded a literature of its own; but it was then new,
and had to be studied at great disadvantage. Through early versions of
the "Bhagvat Geeta" and the "Desatir," Margaret Fuller had made ad-
vances into this realm: and for her, as for her early companion and
life-long friend, Lydia Maria Child, it had great fascinations. She writes
in her journal, for instance (February 21, 1841):—

> "This Hindoo mythology is like an Indian jungle. The growth is
> too luxuriant for beauty and leaves a lair for monsters. Being cleared
> away, here is an aftergrowth of fair proportioned trees, and beau-
> teous flowers, the Greek myths.

"Oh, Nature—History of man, last birth of Nature,—how I see the fibres of God woven all through every part as far as the eye can stretch!"

While Mrs. Child was making preparations to develop this new thought in her "Progress of Religious Ideas," Margaret Fuller made it a frequent theme of her conversations; beginning with the Greek mythology, and following up with illustrations from other sources, the rich materials for which are scattered everywhere in her note-books. In later years, however, following the constant current which led her toward life and action, she had for her themes a variety of points in ethics and education.

The usual hour for these conversations was eleven in the morning. The persons present were usually twenty-five or thirty in number, rarely less, sometimes more; and they were among the most alert and active-minded women in Boston. Ten or a dozen, besides Miss Fuller, usually took actual part in the talk. Her method was to begin each subject with a short introduction, giving the outline of the subject, and suggesting the most effective points of view. This done, she invited questions or criticisms: if these lagged, she put questions herself, using persuasion for the timid, kindly raillery for the indifferent. There was always a theme, and a thread. One whole winter was devoted—through thirteen conversations—to the Fine Arts; another to Ethics, in different applications; another to Educaion, in various respects; another to the proper influence of women on family, school, church, society, and literature. On some of these subjects she had, in her circle, undoubted experts, who knew on certain particular points more than she did. Of these she availed herself, but kept the reins in her own hands. We all know that the best-planned talk is a lottery; to-day blanks, to-morrow prizes; and there were times when the leader could bring out no coöperation, and had to fall back on monologue. But this was not common, and even the imperfect fragments in the way of report given by Mr. Emerson in the "Memoirs" are enough to show the general success of these occasions. When the subject was "Life," and she called upon one of her favorite pupils to answer, "What is life?" the lively girl replied, "It is to laugh or cry, according to our constitution." In such a repartee, we can see that the most philosophic teacher met her match and had original minds to deal with. Yet, after all, reports of conversation are failures; and in this case their defects can only be supplied by more general reminiscences from pupils or friends, trying to give the secret of her acknowledged power. [Of] two of these testimonials I shall cite the first, from one of her lifelong intimates,—an artist by profession and a woman of singularly clear and dispassionate nature,—Miss Sarah Freeman Clarke:—

"In looking for the causes of the great influence possessed by Margaret Fuller over her pupils, companions, and friends, I find something in the fact of her unusual truth-speaking power. She not only did not speak lies after our foolish social customs, but she met you fairly. She broke her lance upon your shield. Encountering her glance, something like an electric shock was felt. Her eye pierced through your disguises. Your outworks fell before her first assault, and you were at her mercy. And then began the delight of true intercourse. Though she spoke rudely searching words, and told you startling truths, though she broke down your little shams and defenses, you felt exhilarated by the compliment of being found out, and even that she had cared to find you out. I think this was what attracted or bound us to her. We expected good from such a new condition of our relations, and good usually came of it.

"No woman ever had more true lovers among those of her own sex, and as many men she also numbered among her friends. She had an immense appetite for social intercourse. When she met a new person she met him courageously, sincerely, and intimately. She did not study him to see beforehand how he might bear the shock of truth, but offered her best direct speech at once. Some could not or would not hear it, and turned away; but often came back for more, and some of these became her fast friends.

"Many of us recoiled from her at first; we feared her too powerful dominion over us, but as she was powerful, so she was tender; as she was exacting, she was generous. She demanded our best, and she gave us her best. To be with her was the most powerful stimulus, intellectual and moral. It was like the sun shining upon plants and causing buds to open into flowers. This was her gift, and she could no more help exercising it than the sun can help shining. This gift, acting with a powerful understanding and a generous imagination, you can perceive would make an educational force of great power. Few or none could escape on whom she chose to exercise it. Of her methods of education she speaks thus simply:—

"'I have immediate and invariable power over the minds of my pupils; my wish has been more and more to purify my own conscience when near them, to give clear views of the aims of this life, to show them where the magazines of knowledge lie, and to leave the rest to themselves and the spirit that must teach and help them to self impulse.'

"'The best that we receive from anything can never be written. For it is not the positive amount of thought that we have received, but the virtue that has flowed into us, *and is now us,* that is precious. If we can tell no one thought, yet are higher, larger, wiser, the work is done. The best part of life is too spiritual to bear recording.'"

THE WELL BRED BOY

T. H. CARTER

———◆◆◆———

In the house by the sea where I spend my summers are the remnants of
my grandfather's and great-grandfather's libraries—thick black works of
theology, many Greek and Latin classics bound in calf, and an assortment
of old books for children I grew up reading. Kingsley's Heroes, Miss
Edgeworth's Harry and Lucy *in three red morocco volumes, the* Fables of
La Fontaine, Sock Stories by Aunt Fanny's Daughter, Anna Ross, Flowers
For Children—*they are all very tiny, and bound, generally, in crumbling*
paper with leather spine.

As a sample of the hortatory style in which nineteenth-century chil-
dren's books were written, I append the first chapter of The Well Bred
Boy, or, *New School of Good Manners. It was copyrighted by T. H.*
Carter in 1839, published in Boston that year by William Crosby and
Co. and printed by Philip A. Kirk, 9 Devonshire Street.

ALFRED had now reached the age of ten years. He was no longer
obliged to sleep in a room under the care of some one older than himself, but his mother had caused a chamber to be fitted up for his own use,
and furnished with every thing necessary for his comfort and convenience. He had drawers for his clothes, and these he was expected to keep
in nice order. He had shelves for his little library, and on these his books
were always found neatly placed and never lying in disorder about the
room. There was a place prepared for every thing, and he had been so
well taught that it was more easy for him to keep every thing in its place
than to allow his articles of dress or his playthings to remain in disorder
about his room.

He was a very careful boy, and his parents having found by his constant good conduct that they might depend upon him, had entrusted to
his care a neat watch, which he wore in the day time, and placed under
his pillow at night. This enabled him to know exactly the time when
he was to get up, go to school and do all that his friends expected and
desired him to do. Although he was at an age when some boys would
forget to wind up a watch, or would toss it about in play, and ruin it,
yet he was so very well bred and of such an excellent disposition and

character, that he never forgot to wind it up at a proper hour, and never made a foolish display of it, by taking it out of his pocket unnecessarily, to show to other boys, and never took pride to himself for being allowed to wear a watch.

In the morning as soon as he awoke he looked at his darling watch, for though he was not proud of it, he was very fond of it, and finding it was the proper hour for him to get up, he did not allow himself to lie a few moments longer to stretch himself and perhaps fall asleep again, but jumped immediately out of bed, and dressed himself quickly, though not carelessly. He did not stop while he was dressing, to look at any book, or handle any of his playthings, but went on steadily, washing himself with great care, cleaning his teeth and nails nicely, brushing his hair and his clothes with great exactness. There was a furnace in the cellar of his father's house, by means of which hot air was carried round into all the apartments so that even in winter his room was so warm that he could do all this with comfort. But little boys who do not enjoy this luxury, if they do not stop to play, but dress themselves as quick as they can, having taken care the night before to place all their things so that they can find them easily, can do all that is necessary and proper, to enable them to look neat when they enter the breakfast room, without suffering from cold. Their teeth may chatter a little, and their fingers be rather stiff before they get through their morning labour, but it will do them no hurt, and if they rub and brush away smartly, they will find it very good exercise.

After Alfred had finished dressing himself and placed his night clothes in the place which was prepared for them, he sat down to read a portion of the Bible. His mother had marked several passages which she thought might be useful to him, and the one he turned to, on the morning of the day which I am going to describe, was in the third chapter of Kings, the 5th verse. . . .

After Alfred had finished reading this passage he sat and thought about it for a few moments. . . .

He thought that this passage was a lesson to him, to teach him what he should pray for, and when after a few moments he knelt down to say his morning prayers, he did not do it in a careless, thoughtless manner, merely saying over the words of a prayer, but he begged with his whole heart that God would give him wisdom to know what was his duty, and that he would give him strength to do it, and help him to become not only as good as Solomon, but to follow as far as it was possible for a weak child to do so, the example of Jesus Christ.

Having finished his morning devotion, Alfred walked to the window. It had snowed during the night, and the ground was all over white with snow. It was the first snow of the winter and Alfred was very glad to see it. . . .

Alfred ran quickly down stairs, he was about to hasten into the parlor and tell all the family how glad he was to see the snow, and how he should get out his new sled, but as he reached the door, he remembered that it was very rude to burst noisily into the room, and perhaps interrupt some one who might be speaking. He therefore opened the door gently, and shut it carefully after him, and did not say a word until he found there was no one speaking. The family were all glad to see Alfred so bright and happy, and his older brother William promised to help him make a coast as soon as school was over in the morning.

Alfred went to the closet and took down and put on the apron he was accustomed to wear when he ate his meals. He was not ashamed of it as some silly boys are, for he knew very well he was apt to soil his clothes in eating, and he thought it was much more like a man to appear neat after breakfast was over, than to wear a spotted and dirty jacket, which he could not help doing if he ate his breakfast without an apron. Alfred's usual seat was very near his father, and he liked very much to sit there, and usually he took his place there when the rest of the family seated themselves at table. But on the morning of which I am speaking, a friend of Alfred's mother was to breakfast with them, and he found, that when the family seated themselves at the table some one else was in his place. He waited a moment until he saw those who were older and those who were younger than himself fixed, and then he took the place which seemed most proper for him. . . . He did not say much at table but listened to the conversation of those who were older. It was quite entertaining this morning, for the lady who was visiting his mother described some amusing things she had seen at a fancy ball, the night before. . . .

Some children when they are at table are whispering to each other or talking over some little matters of their own all the time, and do not pay attention to what older people are saying. Perhaps by their noisy chatter they prevent older people from talking at all, but if they would be quiet, they would frequently find the conversation very entertaining, because at table it is generally of a light and amusing kind such as any one can understand.

After he had finished his breakfast, Alfred observed by the clock in the room that the hour had come when it was time for him to go to school. He was sorry to leave the agreeable conversation which was going on in the parlor, but he was always very punctual, and never allowed himself to be a moment behind the time. He had prepared all the books he was to take to school and placed them, before breakfast, in a place where he could take them without a moment's delay, and he now went quietly out of the room, without making any bustle. He spoke in a low voice to his mother before he left the apartment, and told her he was going to school, he then shut the door after him without noise and proceeded to prepare himself for school, this he did, carefully tying on his tippet and buttoning

up his coat, for though he had not been brought up to be delicate and
afraid of the cold, he had been told to dress himself in a proper manner,
in the clothes his mother had provided for him, when he was to go out
in very severe weather. Having dressed himself properly, he took his
books and proceeded on his way to school.

A TEMPERANCE MANIFESTO

J. W. GOODRICH

*The sublime language of Thomas Jefferson's Declaration of Independence
made a profound dent in the minds and memories of Americans. For
decades afterwards whenever people wanted to declare anything, they
tended to do so in Jefferson's words. In 1841 a body of temperance societies convened at Worcester, Massachusetts, and on July 4th issued its
manifesto—the deadly serious parody of the Declaration that follows
here. (Nothing daunted, when, in 1848, Women's Rights organizations in
convention at Seneca Falls wanted to declare their views, they did so in
just such another sober parody, called "The Declaration of Sentiments.")*

A SECOND DECLARATION OF INDEPENDENCE:
THE MANIFESTO OF ALL THE WASHINGTON
TOTAL ABSTINENCE SOCIETIES

WHEN from the depths of human misery, it becomes possible for a portion of the infatuated victims of appetite to arise, and dissolve the vicious
and habitual bonds which have connected them with *inebriety* and degradation, and to assume among the temperate and industrious of the
community, the useful, respectable and appropriate stations, to which the
laws of Nature, and of Nature's God entitle them, an anxious regard for
the safety of their former companions, and the welfare of society requires,
that they should declare the causes that impel them to such a *Reformation!*

We hold these truths to be self-evident; that all men are created *temperate;* that they are endowed by their Creator with certain natural and
innocent desires; that among these are the appetite for COLD WATER
and the pursuit of happiness! that to secure the gratification of these
propensities fountains and streams are gushing and meandering from
the hills and vales, benignly and abundantly abroad among men, deriving
their just powers from their beneficial adaptation to the natures of all the

varieties of animal organization; that whenever any form of substituted artificial beverage becomes destructive of these natures, it is the right of the recipients to proscribe—to alter, or to abolish it and to return to the use of that crystal element, which alone of all that has come to us from Eden, still retains all its primitive purity and sweetness, demonstrating its benefits on such principles, and testing its powers in such quantities, and under such circumstances, as to them shall seem most likely to effect their safety and happiness. . . .

We, therefore, the Reformed Inebriates of the United States of America, for the celebration of the 4th of July, 1841, throughout the Union assembled, appealing to the Supreme Judge of the world for support in the maintenance of our pledges, do, in the name, and by the authority of all the *Washington Total Abstinence Societies* of these States, solemnly publish and declare, that the members of these blessed and blessing Washingtonian Fraternities, are, and of right ought to be, temperate, free, and independent citizens; that they are absolved from all allegiance to the ALCOHOLIC CROWN, and that all social intercourse, or connection, or fellowship, between them and any and all of the numerous branches of the *Alcoholic Family,* is, and ought to be totally dissolved; and that as free, temperate, reformed, and independent citizens, they have full power to levy war against all the Alcoholic Legions—conclude peace when the same are vanquished and exterminated—contract alliances for the accomplishment of their objects—establish commerce in the deeds of benevolence and charity, and to do all other acts and things which reformed, temperate, free, and independent citizens may of right do.

And for the support of this Declaration, with a firm reliance on the protection of Divine Providence, we mutually pledge to each other our adhesion to PURE WATER, TOTAL ABSTINENCE, and the CAUSE OF HUMANITY.

BROOK FARM

NATHANIEL HAWTHORNE

———◆•◆———

The social dislocations following on the Industrial Revolution in the nineteenth century were so varied and so extreme that they could not at once be solved—if, indeed, they ever have been. One response was to escape from the new machine age into one or another utopian, socialized community for the betterment of mankind. Of these, Brook Farm is the most celebrated, although it was only one of forty such cooperative communities in the North. By virtue of having Nathaniel Hawthorne to visit and to celebrate it, as well as Emerson, Margaret Fuller, Elizabeth Peabody and Charles A. Dana, its name endures. Its buildings, too, endure—gray, forlorn and barrackslike—just off the Veterans' Parkway from Boston, near Dedham.

The following passage is from Hawthorne's Blithedale Romance, *a novel about Brook Farm; the character of Zenobia is based on Margaret Fuller.*

A MODERN ARCADIA

MAY-DAY—I forget whether by Zenobia's sole decree, or by the unanimous vote of our Community—had been declared a movable festival. It was deferred until the sun should have had a reasonable time to clear away the snow-drifts along the lee of the stone walls, and bring out a few of the readiest wild-flowers. On the forenoon of the substituted day, after admitting some of the balmy air into my chamber, I decided that it was nonsense and effeminacy to keep myself a prisoner any longer. So I descended to the sitting-room, and finding nobody there, proceeded to the barn, whence I had already heard Zenobia's voice, and along with it a girlish laugh, which was not so certainly recognizable. Arriving at the spot, it a little surprised me to discover that these merry outbreaks came from Priscilla.

The two had been a Maying together. They had found anemones in abundance, housatonias by the handful, some columbines, a few long-stalked violets, and a quantity of white everlasting-flowers, and had filled up their basket with the delicate spray of shrubs and trees. None were prettier than the maple-twigs, the leaf of which looks like a scarlet bud in May, and like a plate of vegetable gold in October. Zenobia, who showed no conscience in such matters, had also rifled a cherry-tree of one of its blossomed boughs, and, with all this variety of sylvan ornament, had been decking out Priscilla. Being done with a good deal of taste, it made her look more charming than I should have thought possible, with my recollection of the wan, frost-nipt girl, as heretofore described. Nevertheless, among those fragrant blossoms, and conspicuously, too, had been stuck a weed of evil odor and ugly aspect, which, as soon as I detected it, destroyed the effect of all the rest. There was a gleam of latent mischief—not to call it deviltry—in Zenobia's eye, which seemed to indicate a slightly malicious purpose in the arrangement.

As for herself, she scorned the rural buds and leaflets, and wore nothing but her invariable flower of the tropics.

"What do you think of Priscilla now, Mr. Coverdale?" asked she, surveying her as a child does its doll. "Is not she worth a verse or two?"

"There is only one thing amiss," answered I.

Zenobia laughed, and flung the malignant weed away.

"Yes; she deserves some verses now," said I, "and from a better poet than myself. She is the very picture of the New England spring; subdued in tint, and rather cool, but with a capacity of sunshine, and bringing us a few Alpine blossoms, as earnest of something richer, though hardly more beautiful, hereafter. The best type of her is one of those anemones."

"What I find most singular in Priscilla, as her heath improves," observed Zenobia, "is her wildness. Such a quiet little body as she seemed, one would not have expected that. Why, as we strolled the woods together, I could hardly keep her from scrambling up the trees, like a squirrel? She has never before known what it is to live in the free air, and so it intoxicates her as if she were sipping wine. And she thinks it such a paradise here, and all of us, particularly Mr. Hollingsworth and myself, such angels! It is quite ridiculous, and provokes one's malice almost, to see a creature so happy,—especially a feminine creature."

"They are always happier than male creatures," said I.

"You must correct that opinion, Mr. Coverdale," replied Zenobia, contemptuously, "or I shall think you lack the poetic insight. Did you ever see a happy woman in your life? Of course, I do not mean a girl, like Priscilla, and a thousand others,—for they are all alike, while on the sunny side of experience,—but a grown woman. How can she be happy, after discovering that fate has assigned her but one single event, which she must contrive to make the substance of her whole life? A man has his choice of innumerable events."

"A woman, I suppose," answered I, "by constant repetition of her one event, may compensate for the lack of variety."

"Indeed!" said Zenobia.

While we were talking, Priscilla caught sight of Hollingsworth, at a distance, in a blue frock, and with a hoe over his shoulder, returning from the field. She immediately set out to meet him, running and skipping, with spirits as light as the breeze of the May morning, but with limbs too little exercised to be quite responsive; she clapped her hands, too, with great exuberance of gesture, as is the custom of young girls when their electricity overcharges them. But, all at once, midway to Hollingsworth, she paused, looked round about her, towards the river, the road, the woods, and back towards us, appearing to listen, as if she heard some one calling her name, and knew not precisely in what direction.

"Have you bewitched her?" I exclaimed.

"It is no sorcery of mine," said Zenobia; "but I have seen the girl do that identical thing once or twice before. Can you imagine what is the matter with her?"

"No; unless," said I, "she has the gift of hearing those 'airy tongues that syllable men's names,' which Milton tells about."

From whatever cause, Priscilla's animation seemed entirely to have deserted her. She seated herself on a rock, and remained there until Hollingsworth came up; and when he took her hand and led her back to us, she rather resembled my original image of the wan and spiritless Priscilla than the flowery May-queen of a few moments ago. These sudden transformations, only to be accounted for by an extreme nervous susceptibility, always continued to characterize the girl, though with diminished frequency as her heath progressively grew more robust.

I was now on my legs again. My fit of illness had been an avenue between two existences; the low-arched and darksome doorway, through which I crept out of a life of old conventionalisms, on my hands and knees, as it were, and gained admittance into the freer region that lay beyond. In this respect, it was like death. And, as with death, too, it was good to have gone through it. No otherwise could I have rid myself of a thousand follies, fripperies, prejudices, habits, and other such worldly dust as inevitably settles upon the crowd along the broad highway, giving them all one sordid aspect before noontime, however freshly they may have begun their pilgrimage in the dewy morning. The very substance upon my bones had not been fit to live with in any better, truer, or more energetic mode than that to which I was accustomed. So it was taken off me and flung aside, like any other worn-out or unseasonable garment; and, after shivering a little while in my skeleton, I began to be clothed anew, and much more satisfactorily than in my previous suit. In literal and physical truth, I was quite another man. I had a lively sense of the exultation with which the spirit will enter on the next stage of its eternal progress, after leaving the heavy burthen of its mortality in an earthly grave, with as little concern for what may become of it as now affected me for the flesh which I had lost. . . .

In the interval of my seclusion, there had been a number of recruits to our little army of saints and martyrs. They were mostly individuals who had gone through such an experience as to disgust them with ordinary pursuits, but who were not yet so old, nor had suffered so deeply, as to lose their faith in the better time to come. On comparing their minds one with another, they often discovered that this idea of a Community had been growing up, in silent and unknown sympathy, for years. Thoughtful, strongly-lined faces were among them; sombre brows, but eyes that did not require spectacles, unless prematurely dimmed by the student's lamplight, and hair that seldom showed a thread of silver. Age, wedded to the past, incrusted over with a stony layer of habits, and retaining nothing fluid in its possibilities, would have been absurdly out of place in an enterprise like this. Youth, too, in its early dawn, was hardly more adapted to our purpose; for it would behold the morning radiance of its own spirit beaming over the very same spots of withered grass and barren sand whence most of us had seen it vanish. We had very young people with us, it is true,—downy lads, rosy girls in their first teens, and children of all heights above one's knee;—but these had chiefly been sent hither for education, which it was one of the objects and methods of our institution to supply. Then we had boarders, from town and elsewhere, who lived with us in a familiar way, sympathized more or less in our theories, and sometimes shared in our labors.

On the whole, it was a society such as has seldom met together; nor, perhaps, could it reasonably be expected to hold together long. Persons of marked individuality—crooked sticks, as some of us might be called— are not exactly the easiest to bind up into a fagot. But, so long as our union should subsist, a man of intellect and feeling, with a free nature in him, might have sought far and near without finding so many points of attraction as would allure him hitherward. We were of all creeds and opinions, and generally tolerant of all, on every imaginable subject. Our bond, it seems to me, was not affirmative, but negative. We had individually found one thing or another to quarrel with in our past life, and were pretty well agreed as to the inexpediency of lumbering along with the old system any further. As to what should be substituted, there was much less unanimity. We did not greatly care—at least, I never did—for the written constitution under which our millennium had commenced. My hope was, that, between theory and practice, a true and available mode of life might be struck out; and that, even should we ultimately fail, the months or years spent in the trial would not have been wasted, either as regarded passing enjoyment, or the experience which makes men wise.

Arcadians though we were, our costume bore no resemblance to the be-ribboned doublets, silk breeches and stockings, and slippers fastened with artificial roses, that distinguish the pastoral people of poetry and the stage. In outward show, I humbly conceive, we looked rather like a gang of beggars, or banditti, than either a company of honest laboring men, or a conclave of philosophers. Whatever might be our points of difference, we all of us seemed to have come to Blithedale with the one thrifty and laudable idea of wearing out our old clothes. Such garments as had an airing, whenever we strode a-field! Coats with high collars and with no collars, broad-skirted or swallow-tailed, and with the waist at every point between the hip and armpit; pantaloons of a dozen successive epochs, and greatly defaced at the knees by the humiliations of the wearer before his lady-love;—in short, we were a living epitome of defunct fashions, and the very raggedest presentment of men who had seen better days. It was gentility in tatters. . . . So we gradually flung them all aside, and took to honest homespun and linsey-woolsey, as preferable, on the whole, to the plan recommended, I think, by Virgil,—"*Ara nudus; sere nudus,*"—which, as Silas Foster remarked, when I translated the maxim, would be apt to astonish the women-folks.

After a reasonable training, the yeoman life throve well with us. Our faces took the sunburn kindly; our chests gained in compass, and our shoulders in breadth and squareness; our great brown fists looked as if they had never been capable of kid gloves. The plough, the hoe, the scythe, and the hay-fork, grew familiar to our grasp. The oxen responded to our voices. We could do almost as fair a day's work as Silas Foster himself, sleep dreamlessly after it, and awake at daybreak with only a little stiffness of the joints, which was usually quite gone by breakfast-time.

To be sure, our next neighbors pretended to be incredulous as to our real proficiency in the business which we had taken in hand. They told slanderous fables about our inability to yoke our own oxen, or to drive them a-field when yoked, or to release the poor brutes from their conjugal bond at night-fall. They had the face to say, too, that the cows laughed at our awkwardness at milking-time, and invariably kicked over the pails; partly in consequence of our putting the stool on the wrong side, and partly because, taking offence at the whisking of their tails, we were in the habit of holding these natural fly-flappers with one hand, and milking with the other. They further averred that we hoed up whole acres of Indian corn and other crops, and drew the earth carefully about the weeds; and that we raised five hundred tufts of burdock, mistaking them for cabbages; and that, by dint of unskilful planting, few of our seeds ever came up at all, or, if they did come up, it was stern-foremost; and that we spent the better part of the month of June in reversing a field of beans, which had thrust themselves out of the ground in this unseemly way. They quoted it as nothing more than an ordinary occurrence for one or other of us to crop off two or three fingers, of a morning, by our clumsy use of the hay-cutter. Finally, and as an ultimate catastrophe, these mendacious rogues circulated a report that we communitarians were exterminated, to the last man, by severing ourselves asunder with the sweep of our own scythes!—and that the world had lost nothing by this little accident.

But this was pure envy and malice on the part of the neighboring farmers. The peril of our new way of life was not lest we should fail in becoming practical agriculturists, but that we should probably cease to be anything else. While our enterprise lay all in theory, we had pleased ourselves with delectable visions of the spiritualization of labor. It was to be our form of prayer and ceremonial of worship. Each stroke of the hoe was to uncover some aromatic root of wisdom, heretofore hidden from the sun. Pausing in the field, to let the wind exhale the moisture from our foreheads, we were to look upward, and catch glimpses into the far-off soul of truth. In this point of view, matters did not turn out quite so well as we anticipated. It is very true that, sometimes, gazing casually around me, out of the midst of my toil, I used to discern a richer picturesqueness in the visible scene of earth and sky. There was, at such moments, a novelty, an unwonted aspect, on the face of Nature, as if she had been taken by surprise and seen at unawares, with no opportunity to put off her real look, and assume the mask with which she mysteriously hides herself from mortals. But this was all. The clods of earth, which we so constantly belabored and turned over and over, were never etherealized into thought. Our thoughts, on the contrary, were fast becoming cloddish. Our labor symbolized nothing, and left us mentally sluggish in the dusk of the evening. Intellectual activity is incompatible with any large amount of bodily exercise. The yeoman and the scholar—the yeoman and the man of finest moral culture, though not the man of sturdiest sense and integrity—are two distinct individuals, and can never be melted or welded into one substance.

SONNETS

BRONSON ALCOTT

———◆•◆———

After Emerson left the Unitarian ministry in 1829 he settled down as "lay preacher to the world" at Concord, Massachusetts, where over the years he was joined by some of the finest minds of Transcendentalism. One such was Bronson Alcott (1799–1888). Alcott, who wrote prose and poetry, was primarily an educator. His theories were so ahead of his time that they lost him many pupils whose parents considered his ideas—such as a conversational method of instruction, giving study the aspect of recreation, and organized play—dangerous and improper. In 1859, however, after an attempt at founding a community at Fruitlands, Alcott did become superintendent of the Concord schools, where he introduced the teaching of singing, dancing, and reading aloud.

There seem to have been two sides to Alcott. Many profoundly admired him. Emerson said, "As pure intellect, I have never seen his equal," and Thoreau agreed he was "the sanest man I ever knew." Yet Carlyle, meeting him in England, found him tiresome and added he was "bent on saving the world by a return to acorns and the golden age." I remember my father making fun of Alcott's method of punishing his pupils by having them whip his hand. It was supposed to shame them, I suppose, but my father claimed the boys simply loved it.

Following are four sonnets of Alcott's in praise of his Transcendental friends.

CHANNING

Channing! my Mentor whilst my thought was young,
And I the votary of fair liberty,—
How hung I then upon thy glowing tongue,
And thought of love and truth as one with thee!
Thou wast the inspirer of a nobler life,
When I with error waged unequal strife,
And from its coils thy teaching set me free.
Be ye, his followers, to his leading true,
Nor privilege covet, nor the wider sway;
But hold right onward in his loftier way,
As best becomes, and is his rightful due.
If learning's yours,—gifts God doth least esteem,—
Beyond all gifts was his transcendent view;
O realize his Pentecostal dream!

EMERSON

Misfortune to have lived not knowing thee!
'T were not high living, nor to noblest end,
Who, dwelling near, learned not sincerity,
Rich friendship's ornament that still doth lend
To life its consequence and propriety.
Thy fellowship was my culture, noble friend:
By the hand thou took'st me, and did'st condescend
To bring me straightway into thy fair guild;
And life-long hath it been high compliment
By that to have been known, and thy friend styled,
Given to rare thought and to good learning bent;
Whilst in my straits an angel on me smiled.
Permit me, then, thus honored, still to be
A scholar in thy university.

MARGARET FULLER

Thou, Sibyl rapt! whose sympathetic soul
Infused the myst'ries thy tongue failed to tell;
Though from thy lips the marvellous accents fell,
And weird wise meanings o'er the senses stole,
Through those rare cadences, with winsome spell;
Yet, even in such refrainings of thy voice,
There struggled up a wailing undertone,
That spoke thee victim of the Sisters' choice,—

Charming all others, dwelling still alone.
They left thee thus disconsolate to roam,
And scorned thy dear, devoted life to spare.
Around the storm-tost vessel sinking there
The wild waves chant thy dirge and welcome home;
Survives alone thy sex's valiant plea,
And the great heart that loved the brave and free.

THOREAU

Who nearer Nature's life would truly come
Must nearest come to him of whom I speak;
He all kinds knew,—the vocal and the dumb;
Masterful in genius was he, and unique,
Patient, sagacious, tender, frolicsome.
This Concord Pan would oft his whistle take,
And forth from wood and fen, field, hill, and lake,
Trooping around him, in their several guise,
The shy inhabitants their haunts forsake:
Then he, like Esop, man would satirize,
Hold up the image wild to clearest view
Of undiscerning manhood's puzzled eyes,
And mocking say, "Lo! mirrors here for you:
Be true as these, if ye would be more wise."

THE TRANSIENT AND THE
PERMANENT IN CHRISTIANITY

REV. THEODORE PARKER

———◆◆◆———

It seems odd to think of Unitarianism as an orthodoxy. Yet the Transcendentalists, who became more and more convinced that all nature is divine and that the New Testament miracles were figures of speech, found the Unitarian acceptance of Christ's miracles as literal events unbearable, and called Andrews Norton, author of a tome on the miracles, a "Unitarian Pope." Emerson wrote that Christ "spoke of miracles, for he felt that man's life was a miracle, and all that man doth. . . . But the Miracle, as pronounced by Christian churches, gives a false impression; it is Monster."

An attack from within on Unitarian orthodoxy was led by the Rev. The-
odore Parker (1810–1860). By 1840 Parker was virtually ostracized by
other Unitarian ministers for his stand against "the Miracle." A young
admirer asked Parker to preach at his ordination in 1841. Parker's sermon
on the meaning of the miracles, an excerpt from which follows, caused an
uproar that shook Boston as badly as ever Anne Hutchinson did. Yet
today Parker is another whose writings are read responsively in many
Unitarian churches as modern gospel.

DOUBTLESS the time will come when men shall see Christ also as he is. Well might he still say, "Have I been so long with you, and yet hast thou not known me?" No! we have made him an idol, have bowed the knee before him, saying, "Hail, king of the Jews!" called him "Lord, Lord!" but done not the things which he said. The history of the Christian world might well be summed up in one word of the evangelist—"and there they crucified him;" for there has never been an age when man did not crucify the Son of God afresh. But if error prevail for a time and grow old in the world, truth will triumph at the last, and then we shall see the Son of God as he is. Lifted up, he shall draw all nations unto him. Then will men understand the word of Jesus, which shall not pass away. Then shall we see and love the divine life that he lived. How vast has his influence been! How his spirit wrought in the hearts of his disciples, rude, selfish, bigoted, as at first they were! How it has wrought in the world! His words judge the nations. The wisest son of man has not measured their height. They speak to what is deepest in profound men, what is holiest in good men, what is divinest in religious men. They kindle anew the flame of devotion in hearts long cold. They are spirit and life. His truth was not derived from Moses and Solomon; but the light of God shone through him, not colored, not bent aside. His life is the perpetual rebuke of all time since. It condemns ancient civilization; it condemns modern civiliza- tion. Wise men we have since had, and good men; but this Galilean youth strode before the world whole thousands of years, so much of divinity was in him. His words solve the questions of this present age. In him the Godlike and the human met and embraced, and a divine life was born. Measure him by the world's greatest sons—how poor they are! Try him by the best of men—how little and low they appear! Exalt him as much as we may, we shall yet perhaps come short of the mark. But still was he not our brother; the son of man, as we are; the son of God, like ourselves? His excellence—was it not human excellence? His wisdom, love, piety—sweet and celestial as they were—are they not what we also may attain? In him, as in a mirror, we may see the image of God, and go on from glory to glory, till we are changed into the same image, led by the spirit which enlightens the humble. Viewed in this way, how beautiful is the life of Jesus! Heaven has come down to earth, or, rather, earth has become heaven. The Son of God, come of age, has taken possession of his birthright. The brightest revelation is this of what is possible for all men—if not now, at least hereafter. How pure is his spirit, and how encouraging its words! "Lowly sufferer," he seems to say, "see how I bore the cross. Patient laborer, be strong; see how I toiled for the unthankful and the merciless. Mistaken sinner, see of what thou art capable. Rise up, and be blessed."

But if, as some early Christians began to do, you take a heathen view, and make him a God, the Son of God in a peculiar and exclusive sense, much of the significance of his character is gone. His virtue has no merit, his love no feeling, his cross no burthen, his agony no pain. His death is an illusion, his resurrection but a show. For if he were not a man, but a god, what are all these things? what his words, his life, his excellence of achievement? It is all nothing, weighed against the illimitable greatness of Him who created the worlds and fills up all time and space! Then his resignation is no lesson, his life no model, his death no triumph to you or me, who are not gods, but mortal men, that know not what a day shall bring forth, and walk by faith "dim sounding on our perilous way." Alas! we have despaired of man, and so cut off his brightest hope.

In respect of doctrines as well as forms, we see all is transitory. "Everywhere is instability and insecurity." Opinions have changed most on points deemed most vital. Could we bring up a Christian teacher of any age, from the sixth to the fourteenth century, for example, though a teacher of undoubted soundness of faith, whose word filled the churches of Christendom, clergymen would scarce allow him to kneel at their altar, or sit down with them at the Lord's table. His notions of Christianity could not be expressed in our forms, nor could our notions be made intelligible to his ears. The questions of his age, those on which Christianity was thought to depend—questions which perplexed and divided the subtle doctors—are no questions to us. The quarrels which then drove wise men mad now only excite a smile or a tear, as we are disposed to laugh or weep at the frailty of man. We have other straws of our own to quarrel for. Their ancient books of devotion do not speak to us; their theology is a vain word. To look back but a short period—the theological speculations of our fathers during the last two centuries, their "practical divinity," even the sermons written by genius and piety, are, with rare exceptions, found unreadable; such a change is there in the doctrines.

1841-1854

SONNET TO EMERSON

ELLEN HOOPER

———◆•◆———

Ellen Sturgis Hooper (1812–1848) wrote poetry for The Dial, *the maga-*
zine which Emerson and Margaret Fuller founded (1840) after Unitarian
journals had been closed against the writings of the Transcendentalists.
The following poem shrewdly assesses Emerson's great limitation, a cer-
tain aridity.

TO R.W.E.

Dry lighted soul, the ray that shines in thee,
  Shot without reflex from primeval sun,
We twine the laurel for the victories
  Which thou on thought's broad, bloodless field has won.

Thou art the mountain where we climb to see
  The land our feet have trod this many a year.
Thou art the deep and crystal winter sky,
  Where noiseless, one by one, bright stars appear.

It may be Bacchus, at thy birth, forgot
  That drop from out the purple grape to press
Which is his gift to man, and so thy blood
  Doth miss the heat which ofttimes breeds excess.

QUESTIONINGS

FREDERIC HEDGE

―――◆◆―――

Another Unitarian Transcendentalist was Frederic Henry Hedge (1805–1890) who wrote essays for Unitarian journals that were of great importance in shaping the Transcendental philosophy. In 1835 Hedge accepted a call to Bangor, Maine; thereafter his trips to Boston were made the occasion for assembling the Transcendental group in sessions called "the Hedge Club." He was primarily a scholar; the following poem only came into his mind after a sleepless night on a stagecoach. It was considered to sum up Transcendental thought.

Hath this world, without me wrought,
Other substance than my thought?
Lives it by my sense alone,
Or by essence of its own?
Will its life, with mine begun,
Cease to be when that is done,
Or another consciousness
With the self-same forms impress?

Doth yon fireball, poised in air,
Hang by my permission there?
Are the clouds that wander by,
But the offspring of mine eye,
Born with every glance I cast,
Perishing when that is past?
And those thousand, thousand eyes,
Scattered through the twinkling skies,
Do they draw their life from mine,
Or, of their own beauty shine?

Now I close my eyes, my ears,
And creation disappears;
Yet if I but speak the word,
All creation is restored.
Or—more wonderful—within,
New creations do begin;

Hues more bright and forms more rare,
Than reality doth wear,
Flash across my inward sense,
Born of the mind's omnipotence.

Soul! that all informest, say!
Shall these glories pass away?
Will those planets cease to blaze,
When these eyes no longer gaze?
And the life of things be o'er
When these pulses beat no more?

Thought! that in me works and lives—
Life to all things living gives—
Art thou not thyself, perchance,
But the universe in trance?
A reflection inly flung
By that world thou fanciedst sprung
From thyself—thyself a dream—
Of the world's thinking thou the theme.

Be it thus, or be thy birth
From a source above the earth—
Be thou matter, be thou mind,
In thee alone myself I find,
And through thee alone, for me,
Hath this world reality.
Therefore, in thee will I live,
To thee all myself will give,
Losing still, that I may find,
This bounded self in boundless Mind.

THE LOWELL MILLS

LUCY LARCOM

———◆◆◆———

One attempted solution to problems the Industrial Revolution brought about was the model factories at Lowell, Massachusetts, which were showcases of good employer-employee relations and displayed the most humanitarian attitude toward labor of its time. Dickens gives them high praise in his not always flattering American Notes. The following passage from the delightful New England Girlhood *by Lucy Larcom (1824–1893) gives the firsthand view of one of the high-minded, literary young mill-workers.*

Yet even the Lowell factory girls—who, after improved machinery had speeded up their work, petitioned the Massachusetts legislature to reduce their twelve-hour working day to ten—found it was to no avail.

AND, indeed, what we wrote was not remarkable,—perhaps no more so than the usual school compositions of intelligent girls. It would hardly be worth while to refer to it particularly, had not the Lowell girls and their magazines been so frequently spoken of as something phenomenal. But it was a perfectly natural outgrowth of those girls' previous life. For what were we? Girls who were working in a factory for the time, to be sure; but none of us had the least idea of continuing at that kind of work permanently. Our composite photograph, had it been taken, would have been the representative New England girlhood of those days. We had all been fairly educated at public or private schools, and many of us were resolutely bent upon obtaining a better education. Very few were among us without some distinct plan for bettering the condition of themselves and those they loved. For the first time, our young women had come forth from their home retirement in a throng, each with her own individual purpose. For twenty years or so, Lowell might have been looked upon as a rather select industrial school for young people. The girls there were just such girls as are knocking at the doors of young women's colleges to-day. They had come to work with their hands, but they could not hinder the working of their minds also. Their mental activity was overflowing at every possible outlet.

Many of them were supporting themselves at schools like Bradford Academy or Ipswich Seminary half the year, by working in the mills the other half. Mount Holyoke Seminary broke upon the thoughts of many of them as a vision of hope,—I remember being dazzled by it myself for a while,—and Mary Lyon's name was honored nowhere more than among the Lowell mill-girls. Meanwhile they were improving themselves and preparing for their future in every possible way, by purchasing and reading standard books, by attending lectures and evening classes of their own getting up, and by meeting each other for reading and conversation.

That they should write was no more strange than that they should study, or read, or think. And yet there were those to whom it seemed incredible that a girl could, in the pauses of her work, put together words with her pen that it would do to print; and after a while the assertion was circulated, through some distant newspaper, that our magazine was not written by ourselves at all, but by "Lowell lawyers." This seemed almost too foolish a suggestion to contradict, but the editor of the "Offering" thought it best to give the name and occupation of some of the writers by way of refutation. It was for this reason (much against my own wish) that my real name was first attached to anything I wrote. I was then book-keeper in the cloth-room of the Lawrence Mills. We had all used any fanciful signature we chose, varying it as we pleased. After I began to read and love Wordsworth, my favorite *nom de plume* was "Rotha." In the later numbers of the magazine, the editor more frequently made use of my initials. One day I was surprised by seeing my name in full in Griswold's "Female Poets;"—no great distinction, however, since there were a hundred names or so, besides.

It has seemed necessary to give these gossip items about myself; but the real interest of every separate life-story is involved in the larger life-history which is going on around it. We do not know ourselves without our companions and surroundings. I cannot narrate my workmates' separate experiences, but I know that because of having lived among them, and because of having felt the beauty and power of their lives, I am different from what I should otherwise have been, and it is my own fault if I am not better for my life with them.

In recalling those years of my girlhood at Lowell, I often think that I knew then what real society is better perhaps than ever since. For in that large gathering together of young womanhood there were many choice natures—some of the choicest in all our excellent New England, and there were no false social standards to hold them apart. It is the best society when people meet sincerely, on the ground of their deepest sympathies and highest aspirations, without conventionality or cliques or affectation; and it was in that way that these young girls met and became acquainted with each other, almost of necessity.

There were all varieties of woman-nature among them, all degrees of refinement and cultivation, and, of course, many sharp contrasts of agreeable and disagreeable. It was not always the most cultivated, however, who were the most companionable. There were gentle, untaught girls, as fresh and simple as wild flowers, whose unpretending goodness of heart was better to have than bookishness; girls who loved everybody, and were loved by everybody. Those are the girls that I remember best, and their memory is sweet as a breeze from the clover fields.

As I recall the throngs of unknown girlish forms that used to pass and repass me on the familiar road to the mill-gates, and also the few that I knew so well, those with whom I worked, thought, read, wrote, studied, and worshiped, my thoughts send a heartfelt greeting to them all, wherever in God's beautiful, busy universe they may now be scattered:—

"I am glad I have lived in the world with you!"

DEACON GILES'S DISTILLERY

GEORGE CHEEVER

◆•◆

*The nineteenth century was a century of great reforms, though, of course,
it had great wrongs to reform. Imprisonment for debt was abolished,
whipping outlawed in most states, and flogging in the navy was done
away with in 1850, owing to the influence of R. H. Dana's* Two Years
Before the Mast *and Melville's* White Jacket. *Reformers like Dorothea
Dix rescued the insane from jails and put them in asylums; Samuel
Gridley Howe, husband of Julia Ward Howe who was to write "The
Battle Hymn of the Republic," started the wonderful Massachusetts
School for the Blind outside of Boston. No reform was more popular
than the crusade toward total abstinence—not such a preposterous cause
as it sounds, in view of the saloon habits of those days.*

*Much fictional effort was expended on arousing popular emotion
against the Demon Rum. The following story, "Deacon Giles's Distillery," is by George B. Cheever, a writer from the state of Maine.*

SOME time ago the writer's notice was arrested by an advertisement
in one of the newspapers, which closed with words similar to the following: "INQUIRE AT AMOS GILES'S DISTILLERY." The reader may suppose,
if he choose, that the following story was a dream, suggested by that
phrase.

Deacon Giles was a man who loved money, and was never troubled
with tenderness of conscience. His father and his grandfather before
him had been distillers, and the same occupation had come to him as
an heirloom in the family. The still-house was black with age, as well as
with the smoke of furnaces that never went out, and the fumes of tortured ingredients, ceaselessly converted into alcohol. It looked like one of
Vulcan's Stithies, translated from the infernal regions into this world. Its
stench filled the atmosphere, and it seemed as if drops of poisonous alcoholic perspiration might be made to ooze out from any one of its timbers
or clapboards on a slight pressure. Its owner was a treasurer to a Bible
Society; and he had a little counting-room in one corner of the distillery
where he sold Bibles.

"He that is greedy of gain troubleth his own house." Any one of those

Bibles would have told him this, but he chose to learn it from experience. It was said that the Worm of the Still lay coiled in the bosom of his family, and certain it is that one of its members had drowned himself in the vat of hot liquor, in the bottom of which a skeleton was some time after found, with heavy weights tied to the ankle-bones. Moreover, Deacon Giles's temper was none of the sweetest, naturally; and the liquor he drank, and the fires and spirituous fumes among which he lived, did nothing to soften it. If his workmen sometimes fell into his vats, he himself oftener fell out with his workmen. This was not to be wondered at, considering the nature of their wages, which, according to no unfrequent stipulation, would be as much raw rum as they could drink.

Deacon Giles worked on the Sabbath. He would neither suffer the fires of the distillery to go out, nor to burn while he was idle; so he kept as busy as they. One Saturday afternoon his workmen had quarrelled, and all went off in anger. He was in much perplexity for want of hands to do the work of the devil on the Lord's day. In the dusk of the evening a gang of singular-looking fellows entered the door of the distillery. Their dress was wild and uncouth, their eyes glared, and their language had a tone that was awful. They offered to work for the Deacon; and he, on his part, was overjoyed; for he thought within himself that as they had probably been turned out of employment elsewhere, he could engage them on his own terms.

He made them his accustomed offer; as much rum every day, when work was done, as they could drink; but they would not take it. Some of them broke out and told him that they had enough of hot things where they came from, without drinking damnation in the distillery. And when they said that, it seemed to the Deacon as if their breath burned blue; but he was not certain, and could not tell what to make of it. Then he offered them a pittance of money; but they set up such a laugh, that he thought the roof of the building would fall in. They demanded a sum which the Deacon said he could not give, and would not, to the best set of workmen that ever lived, much less to such piratical looking scape-jails as they. Finally, he said, he would give half what they asked if they would take two-thirds of that in Bibles. When he mentioned the word Bibles, they all looked towards the door, and made a step backwards, and the Deacon thought they trembled; but whether it was with anger or delirium tremens or something else, he could not tell. However, they winked, and made signs to each other, and then one of them, who seemed to be the head man, agreed with the Deacon, that if he would let them work by night instead of day, they would stay with him awhile, and work on his own terms. To this he agreed, and they immediately went to work.

The Deacon had a fresh cargo of molasses to be worked up, and a great many hogsheads then in from his country customers, to be filled with liquor. When he went home, he locked up the doors, leaving the distillery to his new workmen. As soon as he was gone, you would have thought that one of the chambers of hell had been transported to earth, with all its inmates. The distillery glowed with fires that burned hotter than ever before; and the figures of the demons passing to and fro, and leaping and yelling in the midst of their work, made it look like the entrance to the bottomless pit.

Some of them sat astride the rafters, over the heads of the others, and amused themselves with blowing flames out of their mouths. The work of distilling seemed play to them, and they carried it on with super-natural rapidity. It was hot enough to have boiled the molasses in any part of the distillery; but they did not seem to mind it at all. Some lifted the hogsheads as easily as you would raise a teacup, and turned their contents into the proper receptacles; some scummed the boiling liquids; some, with huge ladles, dipped the smoking fluid from the different vats, and raising it high in the air, seemed to take great delight in watching the fiery stream, as they spouted it back again; some drafted the distilled liquor into empty casks and hogsheads; some stirred the fire; all were boisterous and horribly profane, and seemed to engage in their work with such familiar and malignant satisfaction, that I concluded the busi-ness of distilling was as natural as hell, and must have originated there.

I gathered from their talk that they were going to play a trick upon the Deacon, that should cure him of offering rum and Bibles to his work-men; and I soon found out from their conversation and movements what it was. They were going to write certain inscriptions on all his rum casks, that should remain invisible until they were sold by the Deacon, but should flame out in characters of fire as soon as they were broached by his retailers, or exposed for the use of the drunkards.

When they had filled a few casks with liquor, one of them took a great coal of fire, and having quenched it in a mixture of rum and molasses, proceeded to write, apparently by way of experiment, upon the heads of the different vessels. Just as it was dawn, they left off work, and all vanished together.

In the morning the Deacon was puzzled to know how the workmen got out of the distillery, which he found fast locked as he had left it. He was still more amazed to find that they had done more work in one night than could have been accomplished, in the ordinary way, in three weeks. He pondered the thing not a little, and almost concluded that it was the work of supernatural agents. At any rate they had done so much that he thought he could afford to attend meeting that day, as it was the Sabbath. Accordingly he went to church, and heard his minister say that God could pardon sin without an atonement, and that the words hell and devils were mere figures of speech, and that all men would certainly be saved. He was much pleased, and inwardly resolved he would send his minister a half cask of wine; and, as it happened to be communion Sabbath, he attended meeting all day.

In the evening the men came again, and again the Deacon locked them in to themselves, and they went to work. They finished all his molasses, and filled all his rum barrels, and kegs, and hogsheads, with liquor, and marked them all, as on the preceding night, with invisible inscriptions. Most of the titles ran thus:—

"CONSUMPTION SOLD HERE. *Inquire at Deacon Giles's Distillery.*"
"CONVULSIONS AND EPILEPSIES. *Inquire at Amos Giles's Distillery.*"
"INSANITY AND MURDER. *Inquire at Deacon Giles's Distillery.*"
"DROPSY AND RHEUMATISM." "PUTRID FEVER, AND CHOLERA IN THE COLLAPSE. *Inquire at Amos Giles's Distillery.*"
"DELIRIUM TREMENS. *Inquire at Deacon Giles's Distillery.*"
"A POTION FROM THE LAKE OF FIRE AND BRIMSTONE. *Inquire at Deacon Giles's Distillery.*"

All these inscriptions burned, when visible, a "still and awful red." One of the most terrible in its appearance was as follows:—

"WEEPING AND WAILING AND GNASHING OF TEETH. *Inquire at Deacon Giles's Distillery.*"

In the morning the workmen vanished as before, just as it was dawn; but in the dusk of the evening they came again, and told the Deacon it was against their principles to take any wages for work done between Saturday night and Monday morning, and as they could not stay with him any longer, he was welcome to what they had done. The Deacon was very urgent to have them remain, and offered to hire them for the season at any wages, but they would not. So he thanked them and they went away, and he saw them no more.

In the course of the week most of the casks were sent into the country, and duly hoisted on their stoups, in conspicuous situations, in the taverns and groceries, and rum-shops. But no sooner had the first glass been drawn from any of them, than the invisible inscriptions flamed out on the cask-head to every beholder. "CONSUMPTION SOLD HERE. DELIRIUM TREMENS, DAMNATION AND HELL-FIRE." The drunkards were terrified from the dram-shops; the bar-rooms were emptied of their customers; but in their place a gaping crowd filled every store that possessed a cask of the Deacon's devil-distilled liquor, to wonder and be affrighted at the spectacle. For no art could efface the inscriptions. And even when the liquor was drawn into new casks, the same deadly letters broke out in blue and red flame all over the surface.

The rumsellers, and grocers, and tavern-keepers were full of fury. They

loaded their teams with the accursed liquor, and drove it back to the distillery. All around and before the door of the Deacon's establishment the
returned casks were piled one upon another, and it seemed as if the
inscriptions burned brighter than ever. Consumption, Damnation, Death
and Hell, mingled together in frightful confusion; and in equal prominence, in every case, flamed out the direction, "INQUIRE AT DEACON
GILES'S DISTILLERY." One would have thought that the bare sight would
have been enough to terrify every drunkard from his cups, and every
trader from the dreadful traffic in ardent spirits. Indeed it had some
effect for a time, but it was not lasting, and the demons knew it would not
be, when they played the trick; for they knew the Deacon would continue to make rum, and that as long as he continued to make it, there
would be people to buy and drink it. And so it proved.

The Deacon had to turn a vast quantity of liquor into the streets, and
burn up the hogsheads; and his distillery has smelled of brimstone ever
since; but he would not give up the trade. He carries it on still, and
every time I see his advertisement, *"Inquire at Amos Giles's Distillery,"*
I think I see Hell and Damnation, and he, the proprietor.

MOBY DICK

HERMAN MELVILLE

*Herman Melville (1801–1891) could be called a twentieth-century writer
born into the nineteenth century. The fame he won in his day was moderate. It remained for our own time to find in his books, and particularly
in* Moby Dick—*that tale of Captain Ahab who tries to "draw out Leviathan with a hook"—the key to our own struggles to reconcile the warring
sides of the human psyche.*

The greatness of Moby Dick *defies anthologizing, but the early chapter
which follows gives a picture of a New England seaport town and inn in
mid-century. New Bedford, today, has little of that look; it is neat and
shining clean, its waters filled, not with dark whalers at anchor, but
with white pleasure craft.*

CHAPTER II

The Carpet-bag

I stuffed a shirt or two into my old carpet-bag, tucked it under my arm, and started for Cape Horn and the Pacific. Quitting the good city of old Manhatto, I duly arrived in New Bedford. It was on a Saturday night in December. Much was I disappointed upon learning that the little packet for Nantucket had already sailed, and that no way of reaching that place would offer, till the following Monday.

As most young candidates for the pains and penalties of whaling stop at this same New Bedford, thence to embark on their voyage, it may as well be related that I, for one, had no idea of so doing. For my mind was made up to sail in no other than a Nantucket craft, because there was a fine, boisterous something about everything connected with that famous old island, which amazingly pleased me. Besides though New Bedford has of late been gradually monopolizing the business of whaling, and though in this matter poor old Nantucket is now much behind her, yet Nantucket was her great original—the Tyre of this Carthage;—the place where the first dead American whale was stranded. Where else but from Nantucket did those aboriginal whalemen, the Red-Men, first sally out in canoes to give chase to the Leviathan? And where but from Nantucket, too, did that first adventurous little sloop put forth, partly laden with imported cobble-stones—so goes the story—to throw at the whales, in order to discover when they were nigh enough to risk a harpoon from the bowsprit?

Now having a night, a day, and still another night following before me in New Bedford, ere I could embark for my destined port, it became a matter of concernment where I was to eat and sleep meanwhile. It was a very dubious-looking, nay, a very dark and dismal night, bitingly cold and cheerless. I knew no one in the place. With anxious grapnels I had sounded my pocket, and only brought up a few pieces of silver,—So, wherever you go, Ishmael, said I to myself, as I stood in the middle of a dreary street shouldering my bag, and comparing the gloom towards the north with the darkness towards the south—wherever in your wisdom you may conclude to lodge for the night, my dear Ishmael, be sure to inquire the price, and don't be too particular.

With halting steps I paced the streets, and passed the sign of "The Crossed Harpoons"—but it looked too expensive and jolly there. Further on, from the bright red windows of the "Sword-Fish Inn," there came such fervent rays, that it seemed to have melted the packed snow and ice from before the house, for everywhere else the congealed frost lay ten inches thick in a hard, asphaltic pavement,—rather weary for me, when I struck my foot against the flinty projections, because from hard, remorseless service the soles of my boots were in a most miserable plight. Too expensive and jolly, again thought I, pausing one moment to watch the broad glare in the street, and hear the sounds of the tinkling glasses within. But go on, Ishmael, said I at last; don't you hear? get away from before the door; your patched boots are stopping the way. So on I went. I now by instinct followed the streets that took me waterward, for there, doubtless, were the cheapest, if not the cheeriest inns.

Such dreary streets! blocks of blackness, not houses, on either hand, and here and there a candle, like a candle moving about in a tomb. At this hour of the night, of the last day of the week, that quarter of the town proved all but deserted. But presently I came to a smoky light proceeding from a low, wide building, the door of which stood invitingly open. It had a careless look, as if it were meant for the uses of the public; so, entering, the first thing I did was to stumble over an ash-box in the porch. Ha! thought I, ha, as the flying particles almost choked me, are these ashes from that destroyed city, Gomorrah? But "The Crossed Harpoons," and "The Sword-Fish?"—this, then, must needs be the sign of "The Trap." However, I picked myself up and hearing a loud voice within, pushed on and opened a second, interior door.

It seemed the great Black Parliament sitting in Tophet. A hundred black faces turned round in their rows to peer; and beyond, a black Angel of Doom was beating a book in a pulpit. It was a negro church; and the preacher's text was about the blackness of darkness, and the weeping and wailing and teeth-gnashing there. Ha, Ishmael, muttered I, backing out, Wretched entertainment at the sign of "The Trap!"

Moving on, I at last came to a dim sort of light not far from the docks, and heard a forlorn creaking in the air; and looking up, saw a swinging sign over the door with a white painting upon it, faintly representing a tall straight jet of misty spray, and these words underneath—"The Spouter-Inn:—Peter Coffin."

Coffin?—Spouter?—Rather ominous in that particular connexion, thought I. But it is a common name in Nantucket, they say, and I suppose this Peter here is an emigrant from there. As the light looked so dim, and the place, for the time, looked quiet enough, and the dilapidated little wooden house itself looked as if it might have been carted here from the ruins of some burnt district, and as the swinging sign had a poverty-stricken sort of creak to it, I thought that here was the very spot for cheap lodgings, and the best of pea coffee.

It was a queer sort of place—a gable-ended old house, one side palsied as it were, and leaning over sadly. It stood on a sharp bleak corner, where that tempestuous wind Euroclydon kept up a worse howling than ever it did about poor Paul's tossed craft. Euroclydon, nevertheless, is a mighty pleasant zephyr to any one in-doors, with his feet on the hob quietly toasting for bed. "In judging of that tempestuous wind called Euroclydon," says an old writer—of whose works I possess the only copy extant—"it maketh a marvellous difference, whether thou lookest out at it from a glass window where the frost is all on the outside, or whether thou observest it from that sashless window, where the frost is on both sides, and of which the wight Death is the only glazier." True enough, thought I, as this passage occurred to my mind—old black-letter, thou reasonest well. Yes, these eyes are windows, and this body of mine is the house. What a pity they didn't stop up the chinks and the crannies though, and thrust in a little lint here and there. But it's too late to make any improvements now. The universe is finished; the copestone is on, and the chips were carted off a million years ago. Poor Lazarus there, chattering his teeth against the curbstone for his pillow, and shaking off his tatters with his shiverings, he might plug up both ears with rags, and put a corn-cob into his mouth, and yet that would not keep out the tempestuous Euroclydon. Euroclydon! says old Dives, in his red silken wrapper—(he had a redder one afterwards) pooh, pooh! What a fine frosty night; how Orion glitters; what northern lights! Let them talk of their oriental summer climes of everlasting conservatories; give me the privilege of making my own summer with my own coals.

But what thinks Lazarus? Can he warm his blue hands by holding them up to the grand northern lights? Would not Lazarus rather be in Sumatra than here? Would he not far rather lay him down lengthwise along the line of the equator; yea, ye gods! go down to the fiery pit itself, in order to keep out this frost?

Now, that Lazarus should lie stranded there on the curbstone before the door of Dives, this is more wonderful than that an iceberg should be moored to one of the Moluccas. Yet Dives himself, he too lives like a Czar in an ice palace made of frozen sighs, and being a president of a temperance society, he only drinks the tepid tears of orphans.

But no more of this blubbering now, we are going a-whaling, and there is plenty of that yet to come. Let us scrape the ice from our frosted feet, and see what sort of a place this "Spouter" may be.

RICHARD EDNEY AND THE GOVERNOR'S FAMILY

SYLVESTER JUDD

————◆◆————

More congenial to the average Victorian New England mind than Melville's tortured Ahab would have been the adventures of Richard Edney, hero of the novel Richard Edney and the Governor's Family *by Sylvester*

Judd (1813–1853), a Unitarian minister and reformer. In its idealism
Judd's work is not unreminiscent of Hawthorne and Melville, but in the
telling of his tales he seems too concerned with religious and philan-
thropic ideas—temperance, opposition to capital punishment, antislavery
—to suit our action-whetted literary taste. Yet they are acute pictures
Edney gives, one of which is excerpted here, of a side of Boston not often
written about.

DURING the year, there arose in Woodylin a movement, which ultimately embodied itself in what was called the Knuckle Lane Club. Its
object was to remove degradation from the city; and no person was
deemed fit to join it who was not willing to spend an evening in Knuckle
Lane. This precinct, extending along a deep gorge, was sinuous, jagged,
damp and dark. It was a result of the city. Its waste measured the improvement of the city. It was the slag and dross of the city refinement.
Its houses were the old city houses, that had been replaced by better
ones; and they looked as if they had been brought to the edge of the
gully, and one after another pitched into the receptacle below, where
they lay, in all shapes, at all angles, and in all predicaments.

This Club did not, however, confine itself to that locality; it had a more
comprehensive aim. It was a sort of subterranean method of doing good
in general. It proposed to look at vice from beneath. Like the sewers of
London, there are moral sewers in all our cities, extending many miles, in
the labyrinthine passages of which one may travel days. It would go into
these.

The Club resolved, not merely to berate vice, but to follow it home,—
see its bed and board; talk with it, and find out what was on its mind; listen to its arguments; make a stethoscopic examination of it, and trace to
their source some of its streams. . . .

The plan had been for some time maturing. There was no secrecy
about it, nor were there any attempts at publicity. There was no desire
to provoke opposition, or to be impeded by prejudice; therefore, those
were chiefly spoken to who, it was thought, would be interested in the
matter. Richard and Nefon were particularly interested.

In the course of this business, Richard made new acquaintances, and,
as he thought, with nice people. Among these was Augustus Mangil, one
of the Brokers. No one dreamed of Augustus Mangil in such a connection.
At his capacious office window lay all day long piles of gold and silver,
and passers by, seeing the man through the window, and, as it were,
breast-high in the precious stuff, supposed him a sort of monster,—half a
knave, half a fool. He was reputed to shave notes, get up panics, disturb
the street; and, with a shark-like voracity, devour railroads and factories,

and orphan patrimonies. He had a pleasant, smiling face,—but that was to win your money. He played on the flute,—that was to decoy the unwary; his head was partly bald, and some said the widow's tears scalded it; yet he was fat and sleek;—still, there were hundreds who knew where his marrow and oil flowed from.

But Nefon, who prided himself on his insight into human nature, knew his man, and knew this man. He looked him in the eye, somewhat as Klumpp would, and said, "Gus,"—he called him Gus,—"you must go with us." "Go? go? go where?" "Knuckle Lane." "I know Knuckle Lane. I have just sold some Knuckle Lane stock." "Don't speak of it. We must try to improve the stock."

"Not speak of it?" exclaimed the Broker. "I have saved five dollars for the poor dog. He put all he had in a railroad share, because they told him it would help his trucking. Frightened, horse dead, wife confined, and all that,—would sacrifice. I never stand about such things; cashed the bond, divide the profits; and five dollars is his,—that goes into Knuckle Lane."

"Come along!" said Nefon; "you are a man, and the man, and our man."

In addition, Richard was introduced to a worthy lady, of whom he had heard, a sister-in-law of the Broker's, Mrs. Helen Mangil; and as there was another lady in Woodylin of the same name, and whose husband bore the same name with that of the first, this one, in certain circles, was called Helen the Good.

This Knuckle Lane became a cause; it counted its friends and supporters,—it grew into a spirit and a feeling. . . .

It will be recollected the condition of membership was willingness to spend an evening in Knuckle Lane; and this, in the estimation of many good people of Woodylin, was narrow and exclusive. It savored of bigotry; it was a reflection on excellence. . . .

There must be first a reconnoissance, and a report. Richard, Mr. Mangil, Elder Jabson, and Nefon, were commissioned to this task. It was a thick and misty night when they sallied forth. From the height that overlooked Knuckle Lane, that region, with its pent lights, appeared like a gully cut through Hades by some deluge, along the hideousness of which a dim phosphorescence luridly gleamed. . . . It was the rendezvous of theft, the resort of bawdery, and a creek into which whatever is unfortunate in human condition, or depraved in human nature, daily set, like the tide.

"There are children there!" ejaculated Richard. "There are souls there," said Elder Jabson, with pious eagerness. "I have a customer there," answered the oily, laughing Broker, "and I think we had better corner him."

They entered the house of the truckman, where they found a sick wife, and a sorrowful looking man vainly attempting to fill the office of nurse, and keep his infant child alive. "Where was the Lady Caroline?" bethought Richard. It had not been deemed safe or prudent for the ladies to come out that night. Mr. Mangil had in his hands a balance of money due the truckman. This was opportune. It enabled the man to buy a horse; a horse would restore him to his business,—his business would support his family. "A transaction," said the Broker. "I negotiated his share, and put five dollars into my own pocket; if he has any more dealings of the sort, I should be happy to act for him." . . .

They visited a washerwoman, who cared more for others than herself, and seemed to absorb in her own family all the dirt she took from the world at large. . . .

Slaver's, they attempted to inventory, but it was an endless task; it stood plus nothing, and minus everything. Yet there were cats, and a pig, broken stools, smoked walls, unseemly beds, and some of Elder Jabson's "souls," staring out, wild and savage, through uncut hair, bronzed cheeks, and shaking about in rags and dirt.

No. 6 was a rookery,—music and dancing, drinking and swearing, the Satyrism and Bacchantism of modern civilization.

Our Heroes stood their ground at all points, patiently investigated, kindly counselled, and carefully remembered. Sometimes the Elder prayed. Nefon had with him tracts, little picture-books, and embellished cards, which he distributed.

They made due report of proceedings. The Club was surprised, horrified; they inquired, What shall be done? They passed resolutions; they adopted plans; and all with an honest purpose at the bottom.

Committees were sent out by twos; not Knuckle Lane alone, but other similar spots were visited. They explored the shores of the River, picking their way through driftwood, hulks of boats, drag-nets, hog-styes, hen-coops, and went up the bank to tenements that hang down from many stories above, where the freshet and the cholera sometimes enter, —where squalidness and destitution are always entering,—where children, like bank-swallows, are seen entering,—inhabited by Canadian French, and Connaught Irish. They traversed the Pebbles. They searched the purlieus of hotels and stables. Eating-houses on the wharves, and boarding-houses in the same vicinity, were remembered. They risked the most in the rum-shops. It was voted that two members of the sacred band should sit out an evening in these retreats. The thing was done. They entered the curtained door, took chairs in the midst of *that* congregation, saw what was done, heard what was said,—staid from eight o'clock till midnight. . . .

Not that this was done at once. Summer hardly sufficed, and winter was upon them before even their preliminary operations were concluded.

But Knuckle Lane flourished. . . .

It was a rule of Knuckle Lane to give no offensive publicity to discoveries they might make. As the historian of the society, we are bound by the same reserve, and cannot relate all that fell under the observation of our friend [Richard], albeit they were matters of interest and moment, both to him and his co-laborers.

We shall briefly advert to one or two results. The Club had gathered facts and statistics enough,—the map of the thing was definitely drawn and pretty deeply colored before their eyes. Some where overwhelmed,— some disheartened,—but the majority seemed to derive illumination from afar, and clearness, on the whole, came to the relief of obscurity.

Knuckle Lane, having disentangled itself from Phumbics, came near falling out with Polemics. What was the Church to it, and it to the Church?—that was the question. One or two Clergymen said it interfered with their labors,—usurped the prerogative of the Church, and drew off communicants. But Clergy and Laity, on the whole, favored it. Still, among the adherents of the cause, the inquiry arose, Shall the Church go to Knuckle Lane, or Knuckle Lane come to the Church? But Knuckle Lane was too dirty and too ragged to go to the Church. Shall the Church wash and clothe it? It may not stay washed and clothed. Shall the Church support external Knuckle Lane organizations? Not agreed. Prosecute the rum-shops? General shaking of heads. Knuckle Lane itself would take it in dudgeon. Furthermore, the Church is represented partly in Victoria Square, and La Fayette-street. What have these to do with Knuckle Lane? Shall these streets go down to Knuckle Lane? Shall Knuckle Lane, the Docks, the Stables, the Islands, go up to Victoria Square? . . .

Why should not Victoria Square deputize its interest in Knuckle Lane? . . . Create deputy almoners of its bread, deputy carriers of its compliments, deputy communicators of its instruction? But who shall bring back the thanks, the love, and the evidences of good, from Knuckle Lane to Victoria Square? Shall Knuckle Lane have its deputies, too? Shall the whole business of Christian intercourse and human duty be a matter of delegation? . . . How shall the rich and poor meet together, and the Lord be the Maker of them all? "That is *the* question," said Nefon. "That points to the ring-bolt, I tell *you!*"

A plan was proposed and achieved somewhat in this wise.

A building was erected, called The Griped Hand, from a device of that sort, cut in stone, over the entrance. It was a three-story house, and divided into a Coffee-room, a Reading-room, and an Assembly-room. It was a large building, of freestone, tastefully designed, and standing in a convenient spot. It was a contribution of the Church, Victoria Square, and other parts of the city, or of various individuals in the city,—or, more systematically, of Religion, Wealth, and Common Sense,—to Knuckle Lane. The Coffee-room supplied cheap refreshments of various kinds; the Reading-room was well stocked with newspapers, magazines, and comprised also a library; the Assembly-room was devoted to miscellaneous gatherings, collations, reünions, lectures, etc., etc. . . .

At the dedication, Dr. Broadwell preached an eloquent discourse, and the combined Church choirs added excellent music.

The people of Woodylin were invited to unite freely in the Griped Hand, and what it could afford. Members of the holy brotherhood visited Knuckle Lane, and other places, and extended the graciousness of the Griped Hand to those people.

Would Fuzzle enjoy his evenings as well at the Griped Hand as in Quiet Arbor? He did. Sailors, stevedores, river-drivers, teamsters, came to the Griped Hand for their cups of tea and coffee. Victoria Square and Knuckle Lane did meet in the Assembly-room of the Griped Hand. . . .

The Church lost nothing. Indeed, the whole world belongs to the Church, through Christ Jesus, and has been bought with a great price, and paid for; but how many briers and thorns, how much sour bog, how much gravelly drift, there is on the farm! The Church gained in the improvement of Knuckle Lane. It was so much muck, and decayed vegetation, and corrupted life, hauled out and mixed with Gospel lime and sunlight, and Woodylin culture; and it became excellent soil—and it was all clear gain to the Church. . . .

Well, in process of time it was found the rum-shops were a good deal thinned out. The Coffee-room, and kindness, and cordiality, had superior attractions. . . .

The Theatre lost some of its charms, and much of its perniciousness. The Griped Hand furnished cheap amusements for the poor. . . .

Popular lectures were had in the Assembly-room, and singing concerts; panoramas and wax-work were exhibited; that large class of people who itinerate through the country with their wisdom and their shows found it for their interest to employ the same Hall, where indeed Knuckle Lane was admitted *ad valorem,* while Victoria Square paid enough to keep the revenue good.

Did this redeem Knuckle Lane? It went some ways towards redeeming what was redemptible in it. Would any one refuse the blessings of the Griped Hand? He must indeed be reprobate. Did it Christianize the Church and Victoria Square? It helped their Christianization.

Were there no drawbacks? Yes, a plenty. One or two of the Clergy and their people drew back. They said there was no religion in it,—that to introduce the subject of Knuckle Lane and the Griped Hand into their pulpits was a desecration,—that they ought to preach the Gospel, and not exciting topics, etc., etc. I need not enumerate all they said. . . .

But why recount expressions and feelings that would fill a volume, and which would reduce Richard Edney and the Governor's Family to a very small space in their own book, and which, in truth, gave Richard and his friends trouble enough, without being employed to obscure the narration of events in his story.

What did the Knuckle Lane adventure determine? Not whether the

Knights Templar were guilty, nor who wrote Ossian, nor whether mankind have more than one origin. It did determine this to the mind of Richard, and others,—that by resolutely undertaking to do good, something might be done.

SLAVERY AND SECESSION

DANIEL WEBSTER

———◆◆———

Secession of the Southern states from the Union over the question of slavery was in the air long before it came to a head. The following speech by Daniel Webster delivered before the Senate on March 7, 1850, shows how secession was regarded a decade before the great conflict.

MR. PRESIDENT, I should much prefer to have heard from every member on this floor declarations of opinion that this Union could never be dissolved, than the declaration of opinion by anybody, that, in any case, under the pressure of any circumstances, such a dissolution was possible. I hear with distress and anguish the word "secession," especially when it falls from the lips of those who are patriotic, and known to the country, and known all over the world, for their political services. Secession! Peaceable secession! Sir, your eyes and mine are never destined to see that miracle. The dismemberment of this vast country without convulsion! The breaking up of the fountains of the great deep without ruffling the surface! Who is so foolish, I beg everybody's pardon, as to expect to see any such thing? Sir, he who sees these States, now revolving in harmony around a common centre, and expects to see them quit their places and fly off without convulsion, may look the next hour to see the heavenly bodies rush from their spheres, and jostle against each other in the realms of space, without causing the wreck of the universe. There can be no such thing as a peaceable secession. Peaceable secession is an utter impossibility. Is the great Constitution under which we live, covering this whole country, is it to be thawed and melted away by secession, as the snows on the mountain melt under the influence of a vernal sun, disappear almost unobserved, and run off? No, sir! No, sir! I will not state what might produce the disruption of the Union; but, sir, I see as plainly as I see the sun in heaven what that disruption itself must produce; I see that it must produce war, and such a war as I will not describe, *in its twofold character.*

Peaceable secession! Peaceable secession! The concurrent agreement of all the members of this great republic to separate! A voluntary separation, with alimony on one side and on the other. Why, what would be the result? Where is the line to be drawn? What States are to secede? What is to remain American? What am I to be? An American no longer? Am I to become a sectional man, a local man, a separatist, with no country in common with the gentlemen who sit around me here, or who fill the other house of Congress? Heaven forbid! Where is the flag of the republic to remain? Where is the eagle still to tower? or is he to cower, and shrink, and fall to the ground? Why, sir, our ancestors, our fathers and our grandfathers, those of them that are yet living amongst us with prolonged lives, would rebuke and reproach us; and our children and our grandchildren would cry out shame upon us, if we of this generation should dishonor these ensigns of the power of the government and the harmony of that Union which is every day felt among us with so much joy and gratitude. What is to become of the army? What is to become of the navy? What is to become of the public lands? How is each of the thirty States to defend itself? I know, although the idea has not been stated distinctly, there is to be, or it is supposed possible that there will be, a Southern Confederacy. I do not mean, when I allude to this statement, that any one seriously contemplates such a state of things. I do not mean to say that it is true, but I have heard it suggested elsewhere, that the idea has been entertained, that, after the dissolution of this Union, a Southern Confederacy might be formed. I am sorry, sir, that it has ever been thought of, talked of, or dreamed of, in the wildest flights of human imagination. But the idea, so far as it exists, must be of a separation, assigning the slave States to one side and the free States to the other. Sir, I may express myself too strongly, perhaps, but there are impossibilities in the natural as well as in the physical world, and I hold the idea of a separation of these States, those that are free to form one government, and those that are slave-holding to form another, as such an impossibility. We could not separate the States by any such line, if we were to draw it. We could not sit down here to-day and draw a line of separation that would satisfy any five men in the country. There are natural causes that would keep and tie us together, and there are social and domestic relations which we could not break if we would, and which we should not if we could.

Sir, nobody can look over the face of this country at the present moment, nobody can see where its population is the most dense and growing, without being ready to admit, and compelled to admit, that ere long the strength of America will be in the Valley of the Mississippi. Well, now, sir, I beg to inquire what the wildest enthusiast has to say on the possibility of cutting that river in two, and leaving free States at its source and on its branches, and slave States down near its mouth, each forming a separate government? Pray, sir, let me say to the people of this country, that these things are worthy of their pondering and of their consideration. Here, sir, are five millions of freemen in the free States north of the river Ohio. Can anybody suppose that this population can be severed, by a line that divides them from the territory of a foreign and an alien government, down somewhere, the Lord knows where, upon the lower banks of the Mississippi? What would become of Missouri? Will she join the *arrondissement* of the slave States? Shall the man from the Yellowstone and the Platte be connected, in the new republic, with the man who lives on the southern extremity of the Cape of Florida? Sir, I am ashamed to pursue this line of remark. I dislike it, I have an utter disgust for it. I would rather hear of natural blasts and mildews, war, pestilence, and famine, than to hear gentlemen talk of secession. To break up this great government! to dismember this glorious country! to astonish Europe with an act of folly such as Europe for two centuries has never beheld in any government or any people! No, sir! no, sir! There will be no secession! Gentlemen are not serious when they talk of secession.

THANKSGIVING

HARRIET BEECHER STOWE

———◆•◆———

The scene of Uncle Tom's Cabin *is laid in the South, not New England, so, to represent Harriet Beecher Stowe (1811–1896) in this volume, I have chosen an excerpt from her novel* Oldtown Folks, *an evocation of bygone ways of life in a New England village.*

Harriet was one of the talented children of the Calvinist minister, Lyman Beecher, of Connecticut. She married another Calvinist clergyman, Charles Stowe, and it was while they were living at the parsonage in Cincinnati, Ohio, across the river from slave-owning Kentucky, that she gathered the material she used for Uncle Tom's Cabin. *When asked later how she had managed to write a novel that aroused such vast social upheaval, she replied, "God wrote it." I, and I expect most people, always assumed she must have been an abolitionist. But she was not; her famous book was merely embraced by the abolitionists.*

The following selection from Oldtown Folks *shows Mrs. Stowe to have been gifted as a realist and gives a picture of an old-fashioned New*

England Thanksgiving. I have appended to it a recipe for Marlborough pie—once a Thanksgiving dinner staple; now unknown even in New England. Edward Everett Hale says, in his New England Boyhood, *"In any old and well-regulated family, you will find there is a traditional method of making the Marlborough pie, which is a sort of lemon pie, and each good housekeeper thinks that her grandmother left a better receipt for Marlborough pie than anybody else did. We had Marlborough pies at other times, but we were sure to have them on Thanksgiving Day; and it ought to be said that there was no other day on which we had four kinds of pies on the table and plum pudding beside. . . . In those early days ice creams or sherbets or any other kickshaws of that variety would have been spurned from a Thanksgiving dinner." I have selected a recipe for Marlborough pie that comes, not from Boston, but Deerfield, Massachusetts.*

WELL, at last, when all the chopping and pounding and baking and brewing, preparatory to the festival, were gone through with, the eventful day dawned. All the tribes of the Badger family were to come back home to the old house, with all the relations of every degree, to eat the Thanksgiving dinner. And it was understood that in the evening the minister and his lady would look in upon us, together with some of the select aristocracy of Oldtown.

Great as the preparations were for the dinner, everything was so contrived that not a soul in the house should be kept from the morning service of Thanksgiving in the church, and from listening to the Thanksgiving sermon, in which the minister was expected to express his views freely concerning the politics of the country, and the state of things in society generally, in a somewhat more secular vein of thought than was deemed exactly appropriate to the Lord's day. But it is to be confessed, that, when the good man got carried away by the enthusiasm of his subject to extend these exercises beyond a certain length, anxious glances, exchanged between good wives, sometimes indicated a weakness of the flesh, having a tender reference to the turkeys and chickens and chicken pies, which might possibly be over-doing in the ovens at home. But your old brick oven was a true Puritan institution, and backed up the devotional habits of good housewives, by the capital care which he took of whatever was committed to his capacious bosom. A truly well-bred oven would have been ashamed of himself all his days, and blushed redder than his own fires, if a God-fearing house-matron, away at the temple of the Lord, should come home and find her piecrust either burned or underdone by his over or under zeal; so the old fellow generally managed to brings things out exactly right.

When sermons and prayers were all over, we children rushed home to see the great feast of the year spread.

What chitterings and chatterings there were all over the house, as all the aunties and uncles and cousins came pouring in, taking off their things, looking at one another's bonnets and dresses, and mingling their comments on the morning sermon with various opinions on the new millinery outfits, and with bits of home news, and kindly neighborhood gossip.

Uncle Bill, whom the Cambridge college authorities released, as they did all the other youngsters of the land, for Thanksgiving day, made a breezy stir among them all, especially with the young cousins of the feminine gender.

The best room on this occasion was thrown wide open, and its habitual coldness had been warmed by the burning down of a great stack of hickory logs, which had been heaped up unsparingly since morning. It takes some hours to get a room warm where a family never sits, and which therefore has not in its walls one particle of the genial vitality which comes from the indwelling of human beings. But on Thanksgiving day, at least, every year, this marvel was effected in our best room.

Although all servile labor and vain recreation on this day were by law forbidden, according to the terms of the proclamation, it was not held to be a violation of the precept, that all the nice old aunties should bring their knitting-work and sit gently trotting their needles around the fire; nor that Uncle Bill should start a full-fledged romp among the girls and children, while the dinner was being set on the long table in the neighboring kitchen. Certain of the good elderly female relatives, of serious and discreet demeanor, assisted at this operation.

But who shall do justice to the dinner, and describe the turkey, and chickens, and chicken pies, with all that endless variety of vegetables which the American soil and climate have contributed to the table, and which, without regard to the French doctrine of courses, were all piled together in jovial abundance upon the smoking board? There was much carving and laughing and talking and eating, and all showed that cheerful ability to dispatch the provisions which was the ruling spirit of the hour. After the meat came the plum-puddings, and then the endless array of pies, till human nature was actually bewildered and overpowered by the tempting variety; and even we children turned from the profusion offered to us, and wondered what was the matter that we could eat no more.

When all was over, my grandfather rose at the head of the table, and a fine venerable picture he made as he stood there, his silver hair flowing in curls down each side of his clear, calm face, while, in conformity to the old Puritan custom, he called their attention to a recital of the mercies of God in his dealings with their family.

It was a sort of family history, going over and touching upon the various events which had happened. He spoke of my father's death, and gave a tribute to his memory; and closed all with the application of a time-honored text, expressing the hope that as years passed by we might "so number our days as to apply our hearts unto wisdom." ...

And now, the dinner being cleared away, we youngsters, already excited to a tumult of laughter, tumbled into the best room, under the supervision of Uncle Bill, to relieve ourselves with a game of "blind-man's-buff," while the elderly women washed up the dishes and got the house in order, and the men-folks went out to the barn to look at the cattle, and walked over the farm and talked of the crops.

In the evening the house was all open and lighted with the best of tallow candles, which Aunt Lois herself had made with especial care for this illumination. It was understood that we were to have a dance, and black Cæsar, full of turkey and pumpkin pie, and giggling in the very jollity of his heart, had that afternoon rosined his bow, and tuned his fiddle, and practiced jigs and Virginia reels, in a way that made us children think him a perfect Orpheus.

As soon as the candles were lighted came in Miss Mehitable with her brother Jonathan, and Tina, like a gay little tassel, hanging on her withered arm. Mr. Jonathan Rossiter was a tall, well-made man, with a clear-cut, aquiline profile, and high round forehead, from which his powdered hair was brushed smoothly back and hung down behind in a long cue. His eyes were of a piercing dark gray, with that peculiar expression of depth and intensity which marks a melancholy temperament. He had a large mouth, which he kept shut with an air of firmness that suggested something even hard and dictatorial in his nature. He was quick and alert in all his movements, and his eyes had a searching quickness of observation, which seemed to lose nothing of what took place around him. There was an air of breeding and self-command about him; and in all his involuntary ways he bore the appearance of a man more interested to make up a judgment of others than concerned as to what their judgment might be about himself. Miss Mehitable hung upon his arm with an evident admiration and pride, which showed that when he came he made summer at least for her.

After them soon arrived the minister and his lady,—she in a grand brocade satin dress, open in front to display a petticoat brocaded with silver flowers. With her well-formed hands shining out of a shimmer of costly lace, and her feet propped on high-heeled shoes, Lady Lothrop justified the prestige of good society which always hung about her. Her lord and master, in the spotless whiteness of his ruffles on wrist and bosom, and in the immaculate keeping and neatness of all his clerical black, and the perfect *pose* of his grand full-bottomed clerical wig, did honor to her conjugal cares. They moved through the room like a royal prince and princess, with an appropriate, gracious, well-considered word for each and every one. They even returned, with punctilious civility, the awestruck obeisance of black Cæsar, who giggled over straightway with joy and exultation at the honor.

But conceive of my Aunt Lois's pride of heart, when, following in the train of these august persons, actually came Ellery Davenport, bringing upon his arm Miss Deborah Kittery. Here was a situation! Had the whole island of Great Britain waded across the Atlantic Ocean to call on Bunker Hill, the circumstance could scarcely have seemed to her more critical.

"Mercy on us!" she thought to herself, "all these Episcopalians coming! I do hope mother'll be careful; I hope she won't feel it necessary to give them a piece of her mind, as she's always doing."

Miss Deborah Kittery, however, knew her soundings, and was too genuine an Englishwoman not to know that "every man's house is his castle," and that one must respect one's neighbor's opinions on his own ground.

As to my grandmother, her broad and buxom heart on this evening was so full of motherliness, that she could have patted the very King of England on the head, if he had been there, and comforted his soul with the assurance that she supposed he meant well, though he didn't exactly know how to manage; so, although she had a full consciousness that Miss Deborah Kittery had turned all America over to uncovenanted mercies, she nevertheless shook her warmly by the hand, and told her she hoped she'd make herself at home. And I think she would have done exactly the same by the Pope of Rome himself, if that poor heathen sinner had presented himself on Thanksgiving evening. . . .

You may imagine the astounding wassail among the young people, when two such spirits as Ellery Davenport and my Uncle Bill were pushing each other on, in one house. My Uncle Bill related the story of "the Wrymouth Family," with such twists and contortions and killing extremes of the ludicrous as perfectly overcame even the minister; and he was to be seen, at one period of the evening, with a face purple with laughter, and the tears actually rolling down over his well-formed cheeks, while some of the more excitable young people almost fell in trances, and rolled on the floor in the extreme of their merriment. In fact, the assemblage was becoming so tumultuous, that the scrape of Cæsar's violin, and the forming of sets for a dance, seemed necessary to restore the peace.

Whenever or wherever it was that the idea of the sinfulness of dancing arose in New England, I know not; it is a certain fact that at Oldtown, at this time, the presence of the minister and his lady was held not to be in the slightest degree incompatible with this amusement. I appeal to many of my readers, if they or their parents could not recall a time in New England when in all the large towns dancing assemblies used to be statedly held, at which the minister and his lady, though never uniting in the dance, always gave an approving attendance, and where all the decorous, respectable old church-members brought their children, and stayed to watch an amusement in which they no longer actively partook. No one looked on with a more placid and patronizing smile than Dr. Lothrop and his lady, as one after another began joining the exercise, which, commencing first with the children and young people, crept gradually upwards among the elders. . . .

Of course the dances in those days were of a strictly moral nature. The very thought of one of the round dances of modern times would have sent Lady Lothrop behind her big fan in helpless confusion, and exploded my grandmother like a full-charged arsenal of indignation. As it was, she stood, her broad, pleased face radiant with satisfaction, as the wave of joyousness crept up higher and higher round her, till the elders, who stood keeping time with their heads and feet, began to tell one another how they had danced with their sweethearts in good old days gone by, and the elder women began to blush and bridle, and boast of steps that they could take in their youth, till the music finally subdued them, and into the dance they went.

"Well, well!" quoth my grandmother; "they're all at it so hearty, I don't see why I shouldn't try it myself." And into the Virginia reel she went, amid screams of laughter from all the younger members of the company.

But I assure you my grandmother was not a woman to be laughed at; for whatever she once set on foot, she "put through," with a sturdy energy befitting a daughter of the Puritans. . . .

As nine o'clock struck, the whole scene dissolved and melted; for what well-regulated village would think of carrying festivities beyond that hour?

And so ended our Thanksgiving at Oldtown.

DEERFIELD MARLBOROUGH PIE

6 large tart apples (2 cups sauce)
3 tablespoons butter
½ teaspoon salt
1 cup sugar
3 tablespoons lemon juice
1 teaspoon grated lemon rind
4 eggs, slightly beaten
1 9-inch unbaked pie shell (deep)

Peel, core, and slice apples; steam until tender and strain. Stir in butter, add salt, sugar, and cool. Add lemon juice and rind to eggs and stir into sauce. Stir until blended and pour into unbaked pastry shell. Bake in a 450° oven for 15 minutes; reduce heat to 275° and bake 1 hour or longer. The pie should be a golden brown and cut like a custard pie.

1854-1862

AN AUTOBIOGRAPHY

LYMAN BEECHER

————◆◆————

Lyman Beecher (1775–1863), the father of Harriet, of my great-grand-mother Mary, of Catherine who ran a young ladies academy in Litchfield, Connecticut, and founded a women's college in Cincinnati, and of six clergyman sons including Henry Ward Beecher, was a Calvinist minister of the Edwards orthodoxy, and remained so. Edward Everett Hale referred to his wife's grandfather's theology as "the religion of Connecticut." For Calvinism was by no means done for in the reaches of New England beyond the Unitarian rays emanating from the Hub of the Universe and, as a matter of fact, Beecher brought his Connecticut religion into the Hanover Street Church in Boston, in the 1820's.

His pulpit for many years before that had been in the beautiful old church at Litchfield, Connecticut, and there is a family story about some most unorthodox assistance Beecher used to receive there. His congregation included—as most congregations do—a harmless old crazy woman. This lady used to seat herself on the steps winding up to the pulpit, while Beecher was preaching, with a bag of apples in her lap; she would throw an apple at anybody who went to sleep during the sermon. "That's right, Dr. Beecher!" she would cry. "You preach to 'em and I'll keep 'em awake!"

The following excerpt from his Autobiography renders the experience of "awakening" as Beecher encountered it when a young man. The Dwight he sketches in the early paragraphs is Timothy Dwight, president of Yale at the time Beecher graduated in 1797.

THAT was the day of the infidelity of the Tom Paine school. Boys that dressed flax in the barn, as I used to, read Tom Paine and believed him;

[347]

I read, and fought him all the way. Never had any propensity to infidelity. But most of the class before me were infidels, and called each other Voltaire, Rousseau, D'Alembert, etc., etc. They thought the Faculty were afraid of free discussion. But when they handed Dr. Dwight a list of subjects for class disputation, to their surprise he selected this: "Is the Bible the word of God?" and told them to do their best.

He heard all they had to say, answered them, and there was an end. He preached incessantly for six months on the subject, and all infidelity skulked and hid its head.

He elaborated his theological system in a series of forenoon sermons in the chapel; the afternoon discourses were practical. The original design of Yale College was to found a divinity school. To a mind appreciative like mine, his preaching was a continual course of education and a continual feast. He was copious and polished in style, though disciplined and logical. There was a pith and power of doctrine there that has not been since surpassed, if equalled. I took notes of all his discourses, condensing and forming skeletons. He was of noble form, with a noble head and body, and had one of the sweetest smiles that ever you saw. He always met me with a smile. Oh, how I loved him! I loved him as my own soul, and he loved me as a son. And once at Litchfield I told him that all I had I owed to him. "Then," said he, "I have done a great and soul-satisfying work. I consider myself amply rewarded."

He was universally revered and loved. I never knew but one student undertake to frustrate his wishes.

It was not, however, before the middle of my Junior year that I was really awakened. It is curious, but when I entered college I had a sort of purpose to be a preacher. I was naturally fitted to be a lawyer. But, though I had heard the first at the bar—Pierpont Edwards and David Daggett—the little quirks, and turns, and janglings disgusted me. My purpose was as fully made up—"I'll preach"—as afterward. Yet I had only a traditionary knowledge; alive without the law; sense of sin all outward; ignorant as a beast of the state of my heart, and its voluntary spiritual state toward God.

One day, as we were sitting at home, mother looked out of the window, and saw a drunkard passing. "Poor man," said she, "I hope he'll receive all his punishment in this life. He was under conviction once, and thought he had religion; but he's nothing but a poor drunkard now." There was no perceptible effect from these words, only, after she left the room, I felt a sudden impulse to pray. It was but a breath across the surface of my soul. I was not in the habit of prayer. I rose to pray, and had not spoken five words before I was under as deep conviction as ever I was in my life. The sinking of the shaft was instantaneous. I understood the law and my heart as well as I do now, or shall in the day of judgment, I believe.

The commandment came, sin revived, and I died, quick as a flash of lightning.

"Well," I thought, "it's all over with me. I'm gone. There's no hope for such a sinner." Despair followed the inward revelation of what I had read, but never felt. I had never had any feeling of love to God, and all my affections were selfish and worldly.

After a while that entireness of despair (for I was sure I was lost, as I deserved) lessened so that I could pray without weeping; and then I began to hope I was growing good. Then my motives in praying came up before me, and I saw there was no true love in them. I then tried reformation, but seemed no better. God let down light into the dark places, and showed me there was no change of character. I turned away from this self-righteousness, and turned in, and laid hold of my heart like a giant to bring it round so as to pray aright, but could not. Couldn't make a right prayer with a wrong heart. Worked away at that till I gave up. Then Election tormented me. I fell into a dark, sullen, unfeeling state that finally affected my health.

I can see now that if I had had the instruction I give to inquirers, I should have come out bright in a few days. Mine was what I should now call a hopeful, promising case. Old Dr. Hopkins had just such an awakening, and was tormented a great while. The fact is, the law and doctrines, without any explanation, is a cruel way to get souls into the kingdom. It entails great suffering, especially on thinking minds.

During all this struggle I had no guidance but the sermons of Dr. Dwight. When I heard him preach on "The harvest is past, the summer is ended, and we are not saved," a whole avalanche rolled down on my mind. I went home weeping every step. One reason I was so long in the dark was, I was *under law,* was stumbling in the doctrines, and had no views of Christ. They gave me other books to read besides the Bible—a thing I have done practising long since. For cases like mine, Brainerd's Life is a most undesirable thing. It gave me a tinge for years. So Edwards on the Affections—a most overwhelming thing, and to common minds the most entangling. The impressions left by such books were not spiritual, but a state of permanent hypochondria—the horrors of a mind without guidance, motive, or ability to do anything. They are a bad generation of books, on the whole. Divine sovereignty does the whole in spite of them. I was converted in spite of such books. I wish I could give you my clinical theology. I have used my evangelical philosophy all my lifetime, and relieved people without number out of the sloughs of high Calvinism.

It was many months that I suffered; and, finally, the light did not come in a sudden blaze, but by degrees. I began to see more into the doctrines of the Bible. Election and decrees were less a stumbling-block. I came in by that door.

SKIPPER IRESON'S RIDE

JOHN GREENLEAF WHITTIER

All the while that life was going on in New England's cities and towns, its countryside and forests, another life was going on at sea—life on the New England fishing schooners and whalers and clipper ships which depended, as life at sea must, upon the complete reliance upon each other of seafaring men. John Greenleaf Whittier's "Skipper Ireson's Ride"—another of the poems every New England child used to be required to learn by heart, complete with dialect—is concerned with the breach of one of these mortal reliances.

Of all the rides since the birth of time,
Told in story or sung in rhyme,—
On Apuleius's Golden Ass,
Or one-eyed Calendar's horse of brass,
Witch astride of a human hack,
Islam's prophet on Al-Borák,—
The strangest ride that ever was sped
Was Ireson's, out from Marblehead!
   Old Floyd Ireson, for his hard heart,
      Tarred and feathered and carried in a cart
         By the women of Marblehead!

Body of turkey, head of owl,
Wings adroop like a rained-on fowl,
Feathered and ruffled in every part,
Skipper Ireson stood in the cart.
Scores of women, old and young,
Strong of muscle, and glib of tongue,
Pushed and pulled up the rocky lane,
Shouting and singing the shrill refrain:
   "Here's Flud Oirson, fur his horrd horrt,
      Torr'd an' futherr'd an' corr'd in a corrt
         By the women o' Morble'ead!"

Wrinkled scolds with hands on hips,
Girls in bloom of cheek and lips,

Wild-eyed, free-limbed, such as chase
Bacchus round some antique vase,
Brief of skirt, with ankles bare,
Loose of kerchief and loose of hair,
With conch-shells blowing and fish-horns' twang,
Over and over the Mænads sang:
   "Here's Flud Oirson, fur his horrd horrt,
   Torr'd an' futherr'd an' corr'd in a corrt
     By the women o' Morble'ead!"

Small pity for him!—He sailed away
From a leaking ship, in Chaleur Bay,—
Sailed away from a sinking wreck,
With his own town's-people on her deck!
"Lay by! lay by!" they called to him.
Back he answered, "Sink or swim!
Brag of your catch of fish again!"
And off he sailed through the fog and rain!
   Old Floyd Ireson, for his hard heart,
   Tarred and feathered and carried in a cart
     By the women of Marblehead!

Fathoms deep in dark Chaleur
That wreck shall lie forevermore.
Mother and sister, wife and maid,
Looked from the rocks of Marblehead
Over the moaning and rainy sea,—
Looked for the coming that might not be!
What did the winds and the sea-birds say
Of the cruel captain who sailed away?—
   Old Floyd Ireson, for his hard heart,
   Tarred and feathered and carried in a cart
     By the women of Marblehead!

Through the street, on either side,
Up flew windows, doors swung wide;
Sharp-tongued spinsters, old wives gray,
Treble lent the fish-horn's bray.
Sea-worn grandsires, cripple-bound,
Hulks of old sailors run aground,
Shook head, and fist, and hat, and cane,
And cracked with curses the hoarse refrain:
   "Here's Flud Oirson, fur his horrd horrt,
   Torr'd an' futherr'd an' corr'd in a corrt
     By the women o' Morble'ead!"

Sweetly along the Salem road
Bloom of orchard and lilac showed.
Little the wicked skipper knew
Of the fields so green and the sky so blue.
Riding there in his sorry trim,
Like an Indian idol glum and grim,
Scarcely he seemed the sound to hear
Of voices shouting, far and near:
   "Here's Flud Oirson, fur his horrd horrt,
   Torr'd an' futherr'd an' corr'd in a corrt
    By the women o' Morble'ead!"

"Hear me, neighbors!" at last he cried,—
"What to me is this noisy ride?
What is the shame that clothes the skin
To the nameless horror that lives within?
Waking or sleeping, I see a wreck,
And hear a cry from a reeling deck!
Hate me and curse me,—I only dread
The hand of God and the face of the dead!"
   Said old Floyd Ireson, for his hard heart,
   Tarred and feathered and carried in a cart
    By the women of Marblehead!

Then the wife of the skipper lost at sea
Said, "God has touched him!—why should we?"
Said an old wife mourning her only son,
"Cut the rogue's tether and let him run!"
So with soft relentings and rude excuse,
Half scorn, half pity, they cut him loose,
And gave him a cloak to hide him in,
And left him alone with his shame and sin.
   Poor Floyd Ireson, for his hard heart,
   Tarred and feathered and carried in a cart
    By the women of Marblehead!

THE RIVEN OAK—JOHN BROWN

DANIEL RICKETSON

————◆•◆————

*The flowering of New England, that literary outpouring, kertreed every-
where, not only in Boston and Concord. Daniel Ricketson (1813–1898)
was a New Bedford poet whose verse displayed his sympathy with the
working class. He was a friend of the Transcendentalists and knew Thoreau well. The poem that follows concerns the tragic event which occasioned so much literature, from Thoreau's "Last Days of John Brown," to
Whittier's "John Brown of Osawatomie," to Benét's John Brown's Body.*

Firm the oak upon the hill-top,
  Though its branches may be torn,
Standeth in its solemn glory,
  Standeth solemn and forlorn.

Though the lightning rend asunder
  And prostrate the noble bole,
Acorns that have fallen under
  Shall increase a thousand fold.

So old Brown of Osawatomie,
  With his sons in blood and death,
Like the dragon's teeth when planted,
  Serried armies shall bequeath.

Nov. 22, 1859.

LITERARY FRIENDS AND
ACQUAINTANCES

WILLIAM DEAN HOWELLS

————◆•◆————

*William Dean Howells (1837–1920) was born in Ohio, but no writer ever
embraced New England more fondly as his spiritual home. A part of
Boston's golden age of literature throughout its prime, the prescient*

Howells felt the chill wind of its decline in 1889, and moved to New York, the coming capital of letters.

No one but scholars read his books today, but, to his time, he spoke for his time, both of democratic egalitarianism and of the "higher things of life." He wrote dozens of novels and short stories, thirty-one plays, eleven travel books, several works of autobiography and a few volumes of verse. It seems in an eerie way significant that his summer house on Cape Ann, which I pass often on vacation, should now belong to Russel Crouse, the New York playwright.

The following excerpt from Howells' Literary Friends and Acquaintances, published in 1900, tells of his joyful arrival in and acceptance by literary Boston.

As it fell out, I lived without farther difficulty to the day and hour of the dinner Lowell made for me; and I really think, looking at myself impersonally, and remembering the sort of young fellow I was, that it would have been a great pity if I had not. The dinner was at the old-fashioned Boston hour of two, and the table was laid for four people in some little upper room at Parker's, which I was never afterwards able to make sure of. Lowell was already there when I came, and he presented me, to my inexpressible delight and surprise, to Dr. Holmes, who was there with him.

Holmes was in the most brilliant hour of that wonderful second youth which his fame flowered into long after the world thought he had completed the cycle of his literary life. He had already received full recognition as a poet of delicate wit, nimble humor, airy imagination, and exquisite grace, when the Autocrat papers advanced his name indefinitely beyond the bounds which most immortals would have found range enough. The marvel of his invention was still fresh in the minds of men, and time had not dulled in any measure the sense of its novelty. His readers all fondly identified him with his work; and I fully expected to find myself in the Autocrat's presence when I met Dr. Holmes. But the fascination was none the less for that reason; and the winning smile, the wise and humorous glance, the whole genial manner was as important to me as if I had foreboded something altogether different. I found him physically of the Napoleonic height which spiritually overtops the Alps, and I could look into his face without that unpleasant effort which giants of inferior mind so often cost the man of five feet four.

A little while after, Fields came in, and then our number and my pleasure were complete.

Nothing else so richly satisfactory, indeed, as the whole affair could have happened to a like youth at such a point in his career; and when I sat down with Doctor Holmes and Mr. Fields, on Lowell's right, I felt through and through the dramatic perfection of the event. The kindly Autocrat recognized some such quality of it in terms which were not the less precious and gracious for their humorous excess. I have no reason to think that he had yet read any of my poor verses, or had me otherwise than wholly on trust from Lowell; but he leaned over towards his host, and said, with a laughing look at me, "Well, James, this is something like the apostolic succession; this is the laying on of hands." I took his sweet and caressing irony as he meant it; but the charm of it went to my head long before any drop of wine, together with the charm of hearing him and Lowell calling each other James and Wendell, and of finding them still cordially boys together.

I would gladly have glimmered before those great lights in the talk that followed, if I could have thought of anything brilliant to say, but I could not, and so I let them shine without a ray of reflected splendor from me. It was such talk as I had, of course, never heard before, and it is not saying enough to say that I have never heard such talk since except from these two men. It was as light and kind as it was deep and true, and it ranged over a hundred things, with a perpetual sparkle of Doctor Holmes's wit, and the constant glow of Lowell's incandescent sense. From time to time Fields came in with one of his delightful stories (sketches of character they were, which he sometimes did not mind caricaturing), or with some criticism of the literary situation from his stand-point of both lover and publisher of books. I heard fames that I had accepted as proofs of power treated as factitious, and witnessed a frankness concerning authorship, far and near, that I had not dreamed of authors using. When Doctor Holmes understood that I wrote for the *Saturday Press*, which was running amuck among some Bostonian immortalities of the day, he seemed willing that I should know they were not thought so very undying in Boston, and that I should not take the notion of a Mutual Admiration Society too seriously, or accept the New York bohemian view of Boston as true. For the most part the talk did not address itself to me, but became an exchange of thoughts and fancies between himself and Lowell. They touched, I remember, on certain matters of technique, and the doctor confessed that he had a prejudice against some words that he could not overcome; for instance, he said, nothing could induce him to use 'neath for *beneath*, no exigency of versification or stress of rhyme. Lowell contended that he would use any word that carried his meaning; and I think he did this to the hurt of some of his earlier things. He was then probably in the revolt against too much literature in literature, which every one is destined sooner or later to share; there was a certain roughness, very like crudeness, which he indulged before his thought and phrase mellowed to one music in his later work. I tacitly agreed rather with the doctor, though I did not swerve from my allegiance to Lowell, and if I had spoken I should have sided with him: I would have given that or any other proof of my devotion. Fields casually mentioned that he thought "The Dandelion" was the most popularly liked of Lowell's briefer poems, and I made haste to say that I thought so too, though I did not really think anything about it; and then I was sorry, for I could see that the poet did not like it, quite; and I felt that I was duly punished for my dishonesty.

Hawthorne was named among other authors, probably by Fields, whose house had just published his "Marble Faun," and who had recently come home on the same steamer with him. Doctor Holmes asked if I had met Hawthorne yet, and when I confessed that I had hardly yet even hoped for such a thing, he smiled his winning smile, and said: "Ah, well! I don't know that you will ever feel you have really met him. He is like a dim room with a little taper of personality burning on the corner of the mantel."

They all spoke of Hawthorne, and with the same affection, but the same sense of something mystical and remote in him; and every word was priceless to me. But these masters of the craft I was 'prentice to probably could not have said anything that I should not have found wise and well, and I am sure now I should have been the loser if the talk had shunned any of the phases of human nature which it touched. It is best to find that all men are of the same make, and that there are certain universal things which interest them as much as the supernal things, and amuse them even more. There was a saying of Lowell's which he was fond of repeating at the menace of any form of the transcendental, and he liked to warn himself and others with his homely, "Remember the dinner-bell." What I recall of the whole effect of a time so happy for me is that in all that was said, however high, however fine, we were never out of hearing of the dinner-bell; and perhaps this is the best effect I can leave with the reader. It was the first dinner served in courses that I had sat down to, and I felt that this service gave it a romantic importance which the older fashion of the West still wanted. Even at Governor Chase's table in Columbus the Governor carved; I knew of the dinner à la Russe, as it was then called, only from books; and it was a sort of literary flavor that I tasted in the successive dishes. When it came to the black coffee, and then to the *petits verres* of cognac, with lumps of sugar set fire to atop, it was something that so far transcended my home-kept experience that it began to seem altogether visionary.

Neither Fields nor Doctor Holmes smoked, and I had to confess that I did not; but Lowell smoked enough for all three, and the spark of his cigar began to show in the waning light before we rose from the table. The time that never had, nor can ever have, its fellow for me, had to come to an end, as all times must, and when I shook hands with Lowell in parting, he overwhelmed me by saying that if I thought of going to Concord he would send me a letter to Hawthorne. I was not to see Lowell again during my stay in Boston; but Doctor Holmes asked me to tea for the next evening, and Fields said I must come to breakfast with him in the morning. . . .

We breakfasted in the pretty room whose windows look out through leaves and flowers upon the river's coming and going tides, and whose walls were covered with the faces and the autographs of all the contemporary poets and novelists. The Fieldses had spent some days with Tennyson in their recent English sojourn, and Mrs. Fields had much to tell of him, how he looked, how he smoked, how he read aloud, and how he said, when he asked her to go with him to the tower of his house, "Come up and see the sad English sunset!" which had an instant value to me such as some rich verse of his might have had. I was very new to it all, how new I could not very well say, but I flattered myself that I breathed in that atmosphere as if in the return from life-long exile. Still I patriotically bragged of the West a little, and I told them proudly that in Columbus no book since *Uncle Tom's Cabin* had sold so well as *The Marble Faun.* This made the effect that I wished, but whether it was true or not, heaven knows; I only know that I heard it from our leading bookseller, and I made no question of it myself.

After breakfast, Fields went away to the office, and I lingered, while Mrs. Fields showed me from shelf to shelf in the library, and dazzled me with the sight of authors' copies, and volumes invaluable with the autographs and the pencilled notes of the men whose names were dear to me from my love of their work. Everywhere was some souvenir of the living celebrities my hosts had met; and whom had they not met in that English sojourn in days before England embittered herself to us during our civil war? Not Tennyson only, but Thackeray, but Dickens, but Charles Reade, but Carlyle, but many a minor fame was in my ears from converse so recent with them that it was as if I heard their voices in their echoed words.

I do not remember how long I stayed; I remember I was afraid of staying too long, and so I am sure I did not stay as long as I should have liked. But I have not the least notion how I got away, and I am not certain where I spent the rest of a day that began in the clouds, but had to be ended on the common earth. I suppose I gave it mostly to wandering about the city, and partly to recording my impressions of it for that newspaper which never published them. The summer weather in Boston, with its sunny heat struck through and through with the coolness of the sea, and its clear air untainted with a breath of smoke, I have always loved, but it had then a zest unknown before; and I should have thought it enough simply to be alive in it. But everywhere I came upon something that fed my famine for the old, the quaint, the picturesque, and however the day passed it was a banquet, a festival. I can only recall my breathless first sight of the Public Library and of the Athenæum Gallery: great sights then, which the Vatican and the Pitti hardly afterwards eclipsed for mere emotion. In fact I did not see these elder treasuries of literature and art between breakfasting with the Autocrat's publisher in the morning, and taking tea with the Autocrat himself in the evening, and that made a whole world's difference.

THE AUTOCRAT AND THE BRAHMIN

OLIVER WENDELL HOLMES

Oliver Wendell Holmes (1809–1894) was a Bostonian par excellence. He adored Boston, and took every opportunity of celebrating her. Trained as a doctor, it is said of him that he felt about science as the Puritans did about religion. His own religion was Unitarianism, and he once said his beliefs could be summed up in the first two words of the Lord's Prayer. He wrote a number of spirited poems as a college boy, among them "Old Ironsides."

He was fond of saying that it was James Russell Lowell who dragged him back into literature, when Holmes was more than forty and a distinguished professor of anatomy. Back when Holmes was a young man, he had written a column entitled "The Autocrat of the Breakfast-Table" for a paper called The New England Magazine, *which died a premature death. Twenty years later, when Lowell asked him to write for the first issue of the new* Atlantic Monthly, *Holmes picked up his pen and wrote, "I was just going to say, when I was interrupted." That began the first number of a column that was to become world-famous.*

Also, I have chosen here a chapter from Holmes's novel, Elsie Venner, *which makes a contribution to understanding of what is meant by the so-called Brahmin caste of Boston, to which Holmes belonged.*

THE AUTOCRAT OF THE BREAKFAST-TABLE

I WAS just going to say, when I was interrupted, that one of the many ways of classifying minds is under the heads of arithmetical and algebraical intellects. All economical and practical wisdom is an extension or variation of the following arithmetical formula: $2 + 2 = 4$. Every philosophical proposition has the more general character of the expression

White Island, among the Isles of Shoals in Maine, "where burning Celia loved and sung," is a resort for Unitarian ministers and laiety in summer.

New England summer "cottages" range from stark simplicity to Cornelius Vanderbilt's "The Breakers," above, at Newport, Rhode Island. It was rebuilt for $3,000,000 after the original "cottage" burned in 1893.

The Sacred Cod, said to have been constructed of wood in the 1760's, hangs above the Speaker's desk at the Boston State House, symbolizing what was for centuries the core of New England's economy. A decade ago some Harvard students stole it away in a florist's box, but like the Stone of Scone, it was found and restored to its place.

Painting by G. P. A. Healy of Daniel Webster in the United States Senate in 1830 replying to Senator Hayne of South Carolina, who, in a debate on Western land sale, impugned the patriotism of New England. Webster's has been called the greatest recorded American oration.

A Connecticut Yankee faced with some distasteful prospect is likely to exclaim, "I'd sooner cut down the Charter Oak!" Near Hartford, Connecticut, this tree, which no longer stands, was the hiding-place for the colonial charter in 1687 when it was demanded by the royal governor-general, Sir Edmund Andros.

A train arrival—until far later than the period of this painting by Edward Lamson Henry, *The 9:45 Accommodation, Stratford, Connecticut*—was an exciting occasion. The passing of New England passenger trains and railroad stations is a real loss to gaiety.

Courtesy Paul B. Victorius, Charlottesville, Va.

The name, ubiquitous in Boston, of "Tremont" means, of course, three hills; and the above early engraving shows two of them. That furthest to the right is Bunker Hill, surmounted by the Bunker Hill Monument. But the battle was fought on Breed's Hill, not visible here.

Courtesy of the Clifton Waller Barrett Library, University of Virginia Library

This nineteenth century drawing represents the memorial reconstruction of "the rude bridge that arched the flood" at Concord, Massachusetts. "Here once the embattled farmers stood, And fired the shot heard round the world" on April 19, 1775.

ICE CUTTING AT SPY POND, WEST CAMBRIDGE, MASS.

Courtesy Paul B. Victorius, Charlottesville, Va.

In the days before refrigeration, ice in ponds was cut in neat rectangles, as here at Spy Pond, West Cambridge, Massachusetts, and stored in deep wells between layers of sawdust.

This central block of the State House in Boston was designed by Charles Bulfinch (1763–1844), first professional architect in the United States, who did his best work in Boston.

This early view of Boston's Faneuil Hall (center, in background) shows it in relation to the waterfront, lost sight of in today's crowded construction. Originally designed by John Smibert in 1740, it was reconstructed after a fire and in 1806 enlarged by the architect Charles Bulfinch.

The inscription under this early engraving of Nathan Hale's execution for spying, in the Revolution, reads in part: "Stung by Hale's words the infuriated officer exclaimed 'Swing the Rebel up!' . . . This tragedy was enacted on a calm Sabbath morning in early autumn, 1776." The British officer was a Major Cunningham.

Photo by Harry T. Holbrook

The first Northern Negro regiment in the Civil War was raised and commanded by Colonel Robert Gould Shaw. This memorial to him by Augustus St. Gaudens (1848–1907) is opposite the Boston State House. Many Bostonians wanted its inscription to quote, ironically, the command of the South Carolina officer when Shaw fell, outside Charleston—"Bury him with his niggers."

The Gloucester Fisherman, by Cape Ann sculptor Leonard Craske, looks straight out through Gloucester Harbor to the ocean as a memorial to three centuries of fishing—most ancient industry in the Commonwealth of Massachusetts.

Photo by Gloucester Camera and Photo, Inc.

Photograph by George M. Cushing, Jr.

Anyone strolling along Boston's Tremont Street can look in at the Old Granary Burying Ground behind Park Street Church and see, not ten feet away, the grave of James Otis, Revolutionary patriot.

Courtesy of the House of Seven Gables Settlement Association

The House of the Seven Gables in Salem, Massachusetts, scene of Nathaniel Hawthorne's novel by that name. On view today, it is an enchanting seventeenth century "black house" with a secret passage that encircles the huge chimney.

Courtesy of the Mariners Museum, Newport News, Va.

Oil painting by Robert Salmon of the full-rigged ship *Aristides*, shown off Liverpool, possibly on her maiden voyage. She was built at Newcastle, Maine, in 1806, and may have been sunk or captured during the War of 1812.

Courtesy of the Mariners Museum, Newport News, Va.

Oil painting by D. McFarlane of the full-rigged ship *Frank Pierce*, built in 1852 in Portsmouth, New Hampshire, as, in 1848, was the *Peter Marcy*, behind and to the right. *Peter Marcy* made the trip from New Orleans to Liverpool, in 1850, taking 26 days for a passage ordinarily requiring 40 to 50 days.

Oil painting by Frank Vining Smith of the clipper ship *Sovereign of the Seas*, built in East Boston in 1852 and lost in the Straits of Malacca in 1859.

Oil painting, artist unknown, of the whaler *James Arnold*, built in New Bedford in 1852. In 1896 she was sold to Chilean ownership, and continued operating as a whaling vessel under the same name until 1927—a remarkable record for a wooden ship.

Courtesy of the Mariners Museum, Newport News, Va.

Oil painting by Frank Vining Smith of the bark *Andrew Hicks*, built at Fair Haven, Massachusetts, as a whaling vessel, in 1867. She foundered off Cape Henry, Virginia, in 1917.

Courtesy of the Mariners Museum, Newport News, Va.

Oil painting by Montague Dawson of the clipper ship *Glory of the Seas*, built at East Boston by Donald McKay in 1869 and operated as a sailing vessel until 1908, when she became a floating salmon cannery until burned for her metal in 1923.

The Fog Warning by Winslow Homer (1836–1910) shows a dory far from its schooner base, on board which a horn would be blown to warn of the rising fog bank.

Cape Ann by Leon Kroll (1884–   ) shows the typical granite boulder formations in northern Massachusetts, which are glacial in origin.

Toilers of the Sea by Albert Pinkham Ryder (1847–1917) is typical of the many marine paintings of this New Bedford artist.

The Metropolitan Museum of Art, George A. Hearn Fund, 1915

op *Berkeley's Rock, New-*
by John La Farge (1835–
), one of the painting,
ng, and priestly family
iated with Rhode Island,
cts an American haunt
e Irish idealistic philoso-

The Metropolitan Museum of Art, Gift of Frank Jewett Nather, Jr., 1949

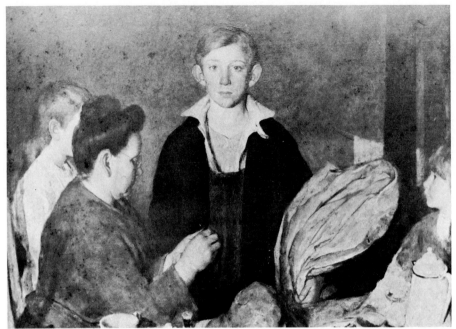

The First Voyage, a poignant example of the work of Charles W. Hawthorne (1872–1930), Provincetown painter who caught the spirit of the New England fishermen.

First Snow is one of the New England water-colors of Dodge McKnight (1860–1950), whose home base was on Cape Cod.

A Victorian sketch of Bar Harbor, the Maine summer resort on Mount Desert
Island which has had a wide appeal to Southerners since before the Civil War.

A Victorian view of Provincetown, Massachusetts. The artists and players for which
the Cape Cod town is famous began summering there toward the end of the last
century.

The wild mountain scenery of N
Hampshire gave it a romantic
peal to Victorians as a summer
sort.

An early nineteenth century print of Lenox, Massachusetts. Later in the century
Lenox, amid the Berkshire Hills, was fashionable as a summer resort.

$a + b = c$. We are mere operatives, empirics, and egotists, until we learn to think in letters instead of figures.

They all stared. There is a divinity student lately come among us to whom I commonly address remarks like the above, allowing him to take a certain share in the conversation, so far as assent or pertinent questions are involved. He abused his liberty on this occasion by presuming to say that Leibnitz had the same observation.—No, sir, I replied, he has not. But he said a mighty good thing about mathematics, that sounds something like it, and you found it, *not in the original,* but quoted by Dr. Thomas Reid. I will tell the company what he did say, one of these days.

—If I belong to a Society of Mutual Admiration?—I blush to say that I do not at this present moment. I once did, however. It was the first association to which I ever heard the term applied; a body of scientific young men in a great foreign city who admired their teacher, and to some extent each other. Many of them deserved it; they have become famous since. It amuses me to hear the talk of one of those things described by Thackeray—

"Letters four do form his name"—

about a social development which belongs to the very noblest stage of civilization. All generous companies of artists, authors, philanthropists, men of science, are, or ought to be, Societies of Mutual Admiration. A man of genius, or any kind of superiority, is not debarred from admiring the same quality in another, nor the other from returning his admiration. They may even associate together and continue to think highly of each other. And so of a dozen such men, if any one place is fortunate enough to hold so many. The being referred to above assumes several false premises. First, that men of talent necessarily hate each other. Secondly, that intimate knowledge or habitual association destroys our admiration of persons whom we esteemed highly at a distance. Thirdly, that a circle of clever fellows, who meet together to dine and have a good time, have signed a constitutional compact to glorify themselves and to put down him and the fraction of the human race not belonging to their number. Fourthly, that it is an outrage that he is not asked to join them.

Here the company laughed a good deal, and the old gentleman who sits opposite said: "That's it! that's it!"

I continued, for I was in the talking vein. As to clever people's hating each other, I think *a little* extra talent does sometimes make people jealous. They become irritated by perpetual attempts and failures, and it hurts their tempers and dispositions. Unpretending mediocrity is good, and genius is glorious; but a weak flavor of genius in an essentially common person is detestable. It spoils the grand neutrality of a commonplace character, as the rinsings of an unwashed wine-glass spoil a draught of fair water. No wonder the poor fellow we spoke of, who always belongs to this class of slightly flavored mediocrities, is puzzled and vexed by the strange sight of a dozen men of capacity working and playing together in harmony. He and his fellows are always fighting. With them familiarity naturally breeds contempt. If they ever praise each other's bad drawings, or broken-winded novels, or spavined verses, nobody ever supposed it was from admiration; it was simply a contract between themselves and a pubisher or dealer.

If the Mutuals have really nothing among them worth admiring, that alters the question. But if they are men with noble powers and qualities, let me tell you that, next to youthful love and family affections, there is no human sentiment better than that which unites the Societies of Mutual Admiration. And what would literature or art be without such associations? Who can tell what we owe to the Mutual Admiration Society of which Shakespeare, and Ben Jonson, and Beaumont and Fletcher were members? Or to that of which Addison and Steele formed the centre, and which gave us the Spectator? Or to that where Johnson, and Goldsmith, and Burke, and Reynolds, and Beauclerk, and Boswell, most admiring among all admirers, met together? Was there any great harm in the fact that the Irvings and Paulding wrote in company? or any unpardonable cabal in the literary union of Verplanck and Bryant and Sands, and as many more as they chose to associate with them?

The poor creature does not know what he is talking about when he abuses this noblest of institutions. Let him inspect its mysteries through the knot-hole he has secured, but not use that orifice as a medium for his popgun. Such a society is the crown of a literary metropolis; if a town has not material for it, and spirit and good feeling enough to organize it, it is a mere caravansary, fit for a man of genius to lodge in, but not to live in. Foolish people hate and dread and envy such an association of men of varied powers and influence, because it is lofty, serene, impregnable, and, by the necessity of the case, exclusive. Wise ones are prouder of the title M. S. M. A. than of all their other honors put together.

—All generous minds have a horror of what are commonly called "facts." They are the brute beasts of the intellectual domain. Who does not know fellows that always have an ill-conditioned fact or two which they lead after them into decent company like so many bulldogs, ready to let them slip at every ingenious suggestion, or convenient generalization, or pleasant fancy? I allow no "facts" at this table. What! Because bread is good and wholesome, and necessary and nourishing, shall you thrust a crumb into my windpipe while I am talking? Do not these muscles of mine represent a hundred loaves of bread? and is not my thought the abstract of ten thousand of these crumbs of truth with which you would choke off my speech?

[The above remark must be conditioned and qualified for the vulgar mind. The reader will, of course, understand the precise amount of seasoning which must be added to it before he adopts it as one of the axioms of his life. The speaker disclaims all responsibility for its abuse in incompetent hands.]

This business of conversation is a very serious matter. There are men whom it weakens one to talk with an hour more than a day's fasting would do. Mark this which I am going to say, for it is as good as a working professional man's advice, and costs you nothing: It is better to lose a pint of blood from your veins than to have a nerve tapped. Nobody measures your nervous force as it runs away, nor bandages your brain and marrow after the operation.

There are men of *esprit* who are excessively exhausting to some people. They are the talkers who have what may be called *jerky* minds. Their thoughts do not run in the natural order of sequence. They say bright things on all possible subjects, but their zigzags rack you to death. After a jolting half-hour with one of these jerky companions, talking with a dull friend affords great relief. It is like taking the cat in your lap after holding a squirrel.

What a comfort a dull but kindly person is, to be sure, at times! A ground-glass shade over a gas-lamp does not bring more solace to our dazzled eyes than such a one to our minds.

"Do not dull people bore you?" said one of the lady-boarders,—the same who sent me her autograph-book last week with a request for a few original stanzas, not remembering that "The Pactolian" pays me five dollars a line for every thing I write in its columns.

"Madam," said I (she and the century were in their teens together), "all men are bores, except when we want them. There never was but one man whom I would trust with my latch-key."

"Who might that favored person be?"

"Zimmermann."

—The men of genius that I fancy most, have erectile heads like the cobra-di-capello. You remember what they tell of William Pinkney, the great pleader; how in his eloquent paroxysms the veins of his neck would swell and his face flush and his eyes glitter, until he seemed on the verge of apoplexy. The hydraulic arrangements for supplying the brain with blood are only second in importance to its own organization. The bulbous-headed fellows who steam well when they are at work are the men that draw big audiences and give us marrowy books and pictures. It is a good sign to have one's feet grow cold when he is writing. A great writer and speaker once told me that he often wrote with his feet in hot water; but for this, *all* his blood would have run into his head, as the mercury sometimes withdraws into the ball of a thermometer.

—You don't suppose that my remarks made at this table are like so many postage-stamps, do you,—each to be only once uttered? If you do, you are mistaken. He must be a poor creature who does not often repeat himself. Imagine the author of the excellent piece of advice, "Know thyself," never alluding to that sentiment again during the course of a protracted existence! Why, the truths a man carries about with him are his tools; and do you think a carpenter is bound to use the same plane but once to smooth a knotty board with, or to hang up his hammer after it has driven its first nail? I shall never repeat a conversation, but an idea often. I shall use the same types when I like, but not commonly the same stereotypes. A thought is often original, though you have uttered it a hundred times. It has come to you over a new route, by a new and express train of associations.

Sometimes, but rarely, one may be caught making the same speech twice over, and yet be held blameless. Thus, a certain lecturer, after performing in an inland city, where dwells a *Littératrice* of note, was invited to meet her and others over the social teacup. She pleasantly referred to his many wanderings in his new occupation. "Yes," he replied, "I am like the Huma, the bird that never lights, being always in the cars, as he is always on the wing."—Years elapsed. The lecturer visited the same place once more for the same purpose. Another social cup after the lecture, and a second meeting with the distinguished lady. "You are constantly going from place to place," she said.—"Yes," he answered, "I am like the Huma," —and finished the sentence as before.

What horrors, when it flashed over him that he had made this fine speech, word for word, twice over! Yet it was not true, as the lady might perhaps have fairly inferred, that he had embellished his conversation with the Huma daily during that whole interval of years. On the contrary, he had never once thought of the odious fowl until the recurrence of precisely the same circumstances brought up precisely the same idea. He ought to have been proud of the accuracy of his mental adjustments. Given certain factors, and a sound brain should always evolve the same fixed product with the certainty of Babbage's calculating machine.

—What a satire, by the way, is that machine on the mere mathematician! A Frankenstein-monster, a thing without brains and without heart, too stupid to make a blunder; which turns out results like a corn-sheller, and never grows any wiser or better, though it grind a thousand bushels of them!

I have an immense respect for a man of talents *plus* "the mathematics." But the calculating power alone should seem to be the least human of qualities, and to have the smallest amount of reason in it; since a machine can be made to do the work of three or four calculators, and better than any one of them. Sometimes I have been troubled that I had not a deeper intuitive apprehension of the relations of numbers. But the triumph of the ciphering hand-organ has consoled me. I always fancy I can hear the wheels clicking in a calculator's brain. The power of dealing with numbers is a kind of "detached lever" arrangement, which may be put into a mighty poor watch. I suppose it is about as common as the power of moving the ears voluntarily, which is a moderately rare endowment.

—Little localized powers, and little narrow streaks of specialized knowledge, are things men are very apt to be conceited about. Nature is very wise; but for this encouraging principle how many small talents and little accomplishments would be neglected! Talk about conceit as much as you like, it is to human character what salt is to the ocean; it keeps it sweet, and renders it endurable. Say rather it is like the natural unguent of the sea-fowl's plumage, which enables him to shed the rain that falls on him and the wave in which he dips. When one has had *all* his conceit taken out of him, when he has lost *all* his illusions, his feathers will soon soak through, and he will fly no more.

"So you admire conceited people, do you?" said the young lady who has come to the city to be finished off for—the duties of life.

I am afraid you do not study logic at your school, my dear. It does not follow that I wish to be pickled in brine because I like a salt-water plunge at Nahant. I say that conceit is just as natural a thing to human minds as a centre is to a circle. But little-minded people's thoughts move in such small circles that five minutes' conversation gives you an arc long enough to determine their whole curve. An arc in the movement of a large intellect does not sensibly differ from a straight line. Even if it have the third vowel as its centre, it does not soon betray it. The highest thought, that is, is the most seemingly impersonal; it does not obviously imply any individual centre.

Audacious self-esteem, with good ground for it, is always imposing. What resplendent beauty that must have been which could have authorized Phyrne to "peel" in the way she did! What fine speeches are those two: "*Non omnis moriar*," and "I have taken all knowledge to be my province"! Even in common people, conceit has the virtue of making them cheerful; the man who thinks his wife, his baby, his house, his horse, his dog, and himself severally unequalled, is almost sure to be a good-humored person, though liable to be tedious at times.

—What are the great faults of conversation? Want of ideas, want of words, want of manners, are the principal ones, I suppose you think. I don't doubt it, but I will tell you what I have found spoil more good talks than anything else;—long arguments on special points between people who differ on the fundamental principles upon which these points depend. No men can have satisfactory relations with each other until they have agreed on certain *ultimata* of belief not to be disturbed in ordinary conversation, and unless they have sense enough to trace the secondary questions depending upon these ultimate beliefs to their source. In short, just as a written constitution is essential to the best social order, so a code of finalities is a necessary condition of profitable talk between two persons. Talking is like playing on the harp; there is as much in laying the hand on the strings to stop their vibrations as in twanging them to bring out their music.

—Do you mean to say the pun-question is not clearly settled in your minds? Let me lay down the law upon the subject. Life and language are alike sacred. Homicide and *verbicide*—that is, violent treatment of a word with fatal results to its legitimate meaning, which is its life—are alike forbidden. Manslaughter, which is the meaning of the one, is the same as man's laughter, which is the end of the other. A pun is *primâ facie* an insult to the person you are talking with. It implies utter indifference to or sublime contempt for his remarks, no matter how serious. I speak of total depravity, and one says all that is written on the subject is deep raving. I have committed my self-respect by talking with such a person. I should like to commit him, but cannot, because he is a nuisance. Or I speak of geological convulsions, and he asks me what was the cosine of Noah's ark; also, whether the Deluge was not a deal huger than any modern inundation.

A pun does not commonly justify a blow in return. But if a blow were given for such a cause, and death ensued, the jury would be judges both of the facts and of the pun, and might, if the latter were of an aggravated character, return a verdict of justifiable homicide. Thus, in a case lately decided before Miller, J., Doe presented Roe a subscription paper, and urged the claims of suffering humanity. Roe replied by asking, When charity was like a top? It was in evidence that Doe preserved a dignified silence. Roe then said, "When it begins to hum." Doe then—and not till then—struck Roe, and his head happening to hit a bound volume of the Monthly Rag-Bag and Stolen Miscellany, intense mortification ensued with a fatal result. The chief laid down his notions of the law to his brother justices, who unanimously replied, "Jest so." The chief rejoined, that no man should jest so without being punished for it, and charged for the prisoner, who was acquitted, and the pun ordered to be burned by the sheriff. The bound volume was forfeited as a deodand, but not claimed.

People that make puns are like wanton boys that put coppers on the railroad tracks. They amuse themselves and other children, but their little trick may upset a freight train of conversation for the sake of a battered witticism.

I will thank you, B. F., to bring down two books, of which I will mark the places on this slip of paper. (While he is gone, I may say that this boy, our landlady's youngest, is called BENJAMIN FRANKLIN, after the celebrated philosopher of that name. A highly merited compliment.)

I wished to refer to two eminent authorities. Now be so good as to listen. The great moralist says: "To trifle with the vocabulary which is the vehicle of social intercourse is to tamper with the currency of human intelligence. He who would violate the sanctities of his mother tongue would invade the recesses of the paternal till without remorse, and repeat the banquet of Saturn without an indigestion."

And, once more, listen to the historian. "The Puritans hated puns. The Bishops were notoriously addicted to them. The Lords Temporal carried them to the verge of license. Majesty itself must have its Royal quibble. 'Ye be burly, my Lord of Burleigh,' said Queen Elizabeth, 'but ye shall make less stir in our realm than my Lord of Leicester.' The gravest wisdom and the highest breeding lent their sanction to the practice. Lord Bacon playfully declared himself a descendant of 'Og, the King of Bashan. Sir Philip Sidney, with his last breath, reproached the soldier who brought him water, for wasting a casque full upon a dying man. A courtier, who saw Othello performed at the Globe Theatre, remarked, that the blackamoor was a brute, and not a man. 'Thou hast reason,' replied a great Lord, 'according to Plato his saying; for this be a two-legged animal *with* feathers.' The fatal habit became universal. The language was corrupted. The infection spread to the national conscience. Political double-dealings naturally grew out of verbal double meanings. The teeth of the new dragon were sown by the Cadmus who introduced the alphabet of equivocation. What was levity in the time of the Tudors grew to regicide and revolution in the age of the Stuarts."

Who was that boarder that just whispered something about the Macaulay-flowers of literature?—There was a dead silence.—I said calmly, I shall henceforth consider any interruption by a pun as a hint to change my boarding-house. Do not plead my example. If *I* have used any such, it has been only as a Spartan father would show up a drunken helot. We have done with them.

—If a logical mind ever found out anything with its logic?—I should say that its most frequent work was to build a *pons asinorum* over chasms which shrewd people can bestride without such a structure. You can hire logic, in the shape of a lawyer, to prove anything that you want to prove. You can buy treatises to show that Napoleon never lived, and that no battle of Bunker-hill was ever fought. The great minds are those with a wide span, which couple truths related to, but far removed from, each other. Logicians carry the surveyor's chain over the track of which these are the true explorers. I value a man mainly for his primary relations with truth, as I understand truth,—not for any secondary artifice in handling his ideas. Some of the sharpest men in argument are notoriously unsound in judgment. I should not trust the counsel of a clever debater, any more than that of a good chess-player. Either may of course advise wisely, but not necessarily because he wrangles or plays well.

The old gentleman who sits opposite got his hand up, as a pointer lifts his forefoot, at the expression, "his relations with truth, as I understand truth," and when I had done, sniffed audibly, and said I talked like a transcendentalist. For his part, common sense was good enough for him.

Precisely so, my dear sir, I replied; common sense, *as you understand it*. We all have to assume a standard of judgment in our own minds, either of things or persons. A man who is willing to take another's opinion has to exercise his judgment in the choice of whom to follow, which is often as nice a matter as to judge of things for one's self. On the whole, I had rather judge men's minds by comparing their thoughts with my own, than judge of thoughts by knowing who utter them. I must do one or the other. It does not follow, of course, that I may not recognize another man's thoughts as broader and deeper than my own; but that does not necessarily change my opinion, otherwise this would be at the mercy of every superior mind that held a different one. How many of our most cherished beliefs are like those drinking-glasses of the ancient pattern, that serve us well so long as we keep them in our hand, but spill all if we attempt to set them down! I have sometimes compared conversation to the Italian game of *mora*, in which one player lifts his hand with so many fingers extended, and the other gives the number if he can. I show my thought, another his; if they agree, well; if they differ, we find the largest common factor, if we can, but at any rate avoid disputing about remainders and fractions, which is to real talk what tuning an instrument is to playing on it.

THE BRAHMIN CASTE OF NEW ENGLAND

THERE is nothing in New England corresponding at all to the feudal aristocracies of the Old World. Whether it be owing to the stock from which we were derived, or to the practical working of our institutions, or to the abrogation of the technical "law of honor," which draws a sharp line between the personally responsible class of "gentlemen" and the unnamed multitude of those who are not expected to risk their lives for an abstraction,—whatever be the cause, we have no such aristocracy here as that which grew up out of the military systems of the Middle Ages.

What we mean by "aristocracy" is merely the richer part of the community, that live in the tallest houses, drive real carriages, (not "kerridges,") kid-glove their hands, and French-bonnet their ladies' heads, give parties where the persons who call them by the above title are not invited, and have a provokingly easy way of dressing, walking, talking, and nodding to people, as if they felt entirely at home, and would not be embarrassed in the least, if they met the Governor, or even the President of the United States, face to face. Some of these great folks are really well-bred, some of them are only purse-proud and assuming,—but they form a class, and are named as above in the common speech.

It is in the nature of large fortunes to diminish rapidly, when subdivided and distributed. A million is the unit of wealth, now and here in

America. It splits into four handsome properties; each of these into four good inheritances; these, again, into scanty competences for four ancient maidens,—with whom it is best the family should die out, unless it can begin again as its great-grandfather did. Now a million is a kind of golden cheese, which represents in a compendious form the summer's growth of a fat meadow of craft or commerce; and as this kind of meadow rarely bears more than one crop, it is pretty certain that sons and grandsons will not get another golden cheese out of it, whether they milk the same cows or turn in new ones. In other words, the millionocracy, considered in a large way, is not at all an affair of persons and families, but a perpetual fact of money with a variable human element, which a philosopher might leave out of consideration without falling into serious error. Of course, this trivial and fugitive fact of personal wealth does not create a permanent class, unless some special means are taken to arrest the process of disintegration in the third generation. This is so rarely done, at least successfully, that one need not live a very long life to see most of the rich families he knew in childhood more or less reduced, and the millions shifted into the hands of the country-boys who were sweeping stores and carrying parcels when the now decayed gentry were driving their chariots, eating their venison over silver chafing-dishes, drinking Madeira chilled in embossed coolers, wearing their hair in powder, and casing their legs in long boots with silken tassels.

There is, however, in New England, an aristocracy, if you choose to call it so, which has a far greater character of permanence. It has grown to be a *caste*,—not in any odious sense,—but, by the repetition of the same influences, generation after generation, it has acquired a distinct organization and physiognomy, which not to recognize is mere stupidity, and not to be willing to describe would show a distrust of the good-nature and intelligence of our readers, who like to have us see all we can and tell all we see.

If you will look carefully at any class of students in one of our colleges, you will have no difficulty in selecting specimens of two different aspects of youthful manhood. Of course I shall choose extreme cases to illustrate the contrast between them. In the first, the figure is perhaps robust, but often otherwise,—inelegant, partly from careless attitudes, partly from ill-dressing,—the face is uncouth in feature, or at least common,—the mouth coarse and unformed,—the eye unsympathetic, even if bright,—the movements of the face are clumsy, like those of the limbs,—the voice is unmusical,—and the enunciation as if the words were coarse castings, instead of fine carvings. The youth of the other aspect is commonly slender,—his face is smooth, and apt to be pallid,—his features are regular and of a certain delicacy,—his eye is bright and quick,—his lips play over the thought he utters as a pianist's fingers dance over their music,—and his whole air, though it may be timid, and even awkward, has nothing clownish. If you

are a teacher, you know what to expect from each of these young men.
With equal willingness, the first will be slow at learning; the second will
take his books as a pointer or a setter to his field-work.

The first youth is the common country-boy, whose race has been bred
to bodily labor. Nature has adapted the family organization to the kind of
life it has lived. The hands and feet by constant use have got more than
their share of development,—the organs of thought and expression less
than their share. The finer instincts are latent and must be developed. A
youth of this kind is raw material in its first stage of elaboration. You must
not expect too much of any such. Many of them have force of will and
character, and become distinguished in practical life; but very few of
them ever become great scholars. A scholar is, in a large proportion of
cases, the son of scholars or scholarly persons.

That is exactly what the other young man is. He comes of the *Brahmin
caste of New England*. This is the harmless, inoffensive, untitled aristocracy
referred to, and which many readers will at once acknowledge. There are
races of scholars among us, in which aptitude for learning, and all these
marks of it I have spoken of, are congenital and hereditary. Their names
are always on some college catalogue or other. They break out every
generation or two in some learned labor which calls them up after they
seem to have died out. At last some newer name takes their place, it may
be,—but you inquire a little and you find it is the blood of the Edwardses
or the Chauncys or the Ellerys or some of the old historic scholars, disguised under the altered name of a female descendant.

There probably is not an experienced instructor anywhere in our
Northern States who will not recognize at once the truth of this general
distinction. But the reader who has never been a teacher will very probably object, that some of our most illustrious public men have come direct from the homespun-clad class of the people,—and he may, perhaps,
even find a noted scholar or two whose parents were masters of the
English alphabet, but of no other.

It is not fair to pit a few chosen families against the great multitude of
those who are continually working their way up into the intellectual
classes. The results which are habitually reached by hereditary training
are occasionally brought about without it. There are natural filters as
well as artificial ones; and though the great rivers are commonly more
or less turbid, if you will look long enough, you may find a spring that
sparkles as no water does which drips through your apparatus of sands
and sponges. So there are families which refine themselves into intellectual aptitude without having had much opportunity for intellectual
acquirements. A series of felicitous crosses develops an improved strain
of blood, and reaches its maximum perfection at last in the large un-
combed youth who goes to college and startles the hereditary class-lead-
ers by striding past them all. That is Nature's republicanism; thank God

for it, but do not let it make you illogical. The race of the hereditary
scholar has exchanged a certain portion of its animal vigor for its new instincts, and it is hard to lead men without a good deal of animal vigor.
The scholar who comes by Nature's special grace from an unworn stock
of broad-chested sires and deep-bosomed mothers must always overmatch
an equal intelligence with a compromised and lowered vitality. A man's
breathing and digestive apparatus (one is tempted to add *muscular*) are
just as important to him on the floor of the Senate as his thinking organs.
You broke down in your great speech, did you? Yes, your grandfather had
an attack of dyspepsia in '82, after working too hard on his famous
Election Sermon. All this does not touch the main fact: our scholars come
chiefly from a privileged order, just as our best fruits come from well-
known grafts,—though now and then a seedling apple, like the Northern
Spy, or a seedling pear, like the Seckel, springs from a nameless ancestry
and grows to be the pride of all the gardens in the land.

TAKE THE LOAN

EDWARD EVERETT HALE

————— ◆•◆ —————

*On April 12, 1861, at 4:30 in the morning, the first shot of the Civil War
was fired, on Fort Sumter—the Federal fort off Charleston which had thus
far resisted surrendering to the new Confederacy. This body had seceded
from the Union, following the election of Abraham Lincoln as President
instead of Breckinridge of Kentucky—the secession candidate running
on a platform of slavery extension and annexation of Cuba. A. H. Stephens
of Georgia predicted at the time of the election that secession would be
sheerest folly, since Southerners in combination with Democrats would
have commanded a majority in both houses of Congress.*

*It is worthy of note that when ordered to surrender, Major Anderson,
commander of Sumter, agreed to do so if it might be done with honor—
in two days, when his food supply would run out. This condition was instantly rejected. One of the four officers who gave the order to open fire
admitted in later life that it was because they feared Jefferson Davis
would be reconciled with Secretary of State Seward, and the chance of
war be lost.*

*Thus commenced the long, bitter and bloody conflict that split not only
section from section, but friend from friend, down even to fissures within*

families. For the issues were not simple. Society in many Northern cities was aligned behind the Confederate cause, for that way of life was more appealing. Where General Robert E. Lee chose his native Virginia over his country, General G. H. Thomas, also a noble Virginian, chose the Union cause. Another Virginian, Senator James M. Mason, summed up the meaning of the struggle thus: "I look upon it then, Sir, as a war of sentiment and opinion by one form of society against another form of society." Perhaps more than anywhere else New England represented the other form of society.

I append some verses by Edward Everett Hale dated May, 1861. His note on them is: "Written when people had to be persuaded as patriots to subscribe for a 7.30 loan! [A war bond issue.] Those who did so are today's millionaires (October, 1903)."

"TAKE THE LOAN"

Come, freemen of the land,
Come meet the great demand,
True heart and open hand,—
    Take the loan!
For the hopes the prophets saw,
For the swords your brothers draw,
For liberty and law,
    Take the loan!

Ye ladies of the land,
As ye love the gallant band
Who have drawn a soldier's brand,
    Take the loan!
Who would bring them what she could,
Who would give the soldier food,
Who would staunch her brothers' blood,
    Take the loan!

All who saw our hosts pass by,
All who joined the parting cry,
When we bade them do or die,
    Take the loan!
As ye wished their triumph then,
As ye hope to meet again,
And to meet their gaze like men,
    Take the loan!

Who would press the great appeal
Of our ranks of serried steel,
Put your shoulders to the wheel,
   Take the loan!
That our prayers in truth may rise,
Which we press with streaming eyes
On the Lord of earth and skies,
   Take the loan!

LINCOLN IN WARTIME

NATHANIEL HAWTHORNE

————◆•◆————

In the Atlantic Monthly *for July, 1862, appeared the following sketch of the wartime Lincoln in the White House. It was signed "A Peaceable Man," but even then most people knew or suspected the article was by Nathaniel Hawthorne. Later it appeared in a collection entitled* Chiefly About War Matters.

OF course, there was one other personage, in the class of statesmen, whom I should have been truly mortified to leave Washington without seeing; since (temporarily, at least, and by force of circumstances) he was the man of men. But a private grief had built up a barrier about him, impeding the customary free intercourse of Americans with their chief magistrate; so that I might have come away without a glimpse of his very remarkable physiognomy, save for a semi-official opportunity of which I was glad to take advantage. The fact is, we were invited to annex ourselves, as supernumeraries, to a deputation that was about to wait upon the President, from a Massachusetts whip-factory, with a present of a splendid whip. . . .

Nine o'clock had been appointed as the time for receiving the deputation, and we were punctual to the moment; but not so the President, who sent us word that he was eating his breakfast, and would come as soon as he could. His appetite, we were glad to think, must have been a pretty fair one; for we waited about half an hour in one of the antechambers, and then were ushered into a reception-room, in one corner of which sat the Secretaries of War and of the Treasury, expecting, like ourselves, the termination of the Presidential breakfast. . . .

By and by there was a little stir on the staircase and in the passage-way, and in lounged a tall, loose-jointed figure, of an exaggerated Yankee port and demeanor, whom (as being about the homeliest man I ever saw, yet by no means repulsive or disagreeable) it was impossible not to recognize as Uncle Abe.

Unquestionably, Western man though he be, and Kentuckian by birth, President Lincoln is the essential representative of all Yankees, and the veritable specimen, physically, of what the world seems determined to regard as our characteristic qualities. It is the strangest and yet the fittest thing in the jumble of human vicissitudes, that he, out of so many millions, unlooked for, unselected by any intelligible process that could be based upon his genuine qualities, unknown to those who chose him, and unsuspected of what endowments may adapt him for his tremendous responsibility, should have found the way open for him to fling his lank personality into the chair of state,—where, I presume, it was his first impulse to throw his legs on the council-table, and tell the Cabinet Ministers a story. There is no describing his lengthy awkwardness, nor the uncouthness of his movement; and yet it seemed as if I had been in the habit of seeing him daily, and had shaken hands with him a thousand times in some village street; so true was he to the aspect of the pattern American, though with a certain extravagance which, possibly, I exaggerated still further by the delighted eagerness with which I took it in. If put to guess his calling and livelihood, I should have taken him for a country schoolmaster as soon as anything else. He was dressed in a rusty black frock-coat and pantaloons, unbrushed, and worn so faithfully that the suit had adapted itself to the curves and angularities of his figure, and had grown to be an outer skin of the man. He had shabby slippers on his feet. His hair was black, still unmixed with gray, stiff, somewhat bushy, and had apparently been acquainted with neither brush nor comb that morning, after the disarrangement of the pillow; and as to a night-cap, Uncle Abe probably knows nothing of such effeminacies. His complexion is dark and sallow, betokening, I fear, an insalubrious atmosphere around the White House; he has thick black eyebrows and an impending brow; his nose is large, and the lines about his mouth are very strongly defined.

The whole physiognomy is as coarse a one as you would meet anywhere in the length and breadth of the States; but, withal, it is redeemed, illuminated, softened, and brightened by a kindly though serious look out of his eyes, and an expression of homely sagacity, that seems weighted with rich results of village experience. A great deal of native sense; no bookish cultivation, no refinement; honest at heart, and thoroughly so, and yet, in some sort, sly,—at least, endowed with a sort of tact and wisdom that are akin to craft, and would impel him, I think, to take an antagonist in flank, rather than to make a bull-run at him right in front.

But, on the whole, I like this sallow, queer, sagacious visage, with the homely human sympathies that warmed it; and, for my small share in the matter, would as lief have Uncle Abe for a ruler as any man whom it would have been practicable to put in his place.

Immediately on his entrance the President accosted our member of Congress, who had us in charge, and, with a comical twist of his face, made some jocular remark about the length of his breakfast. He then greeted us all round, not waiting for an introduction, but shaking and squeezing everybody's hand with the utmost cordiality, whether the individual's name was announced to him or not. His manner towards us was wholly without pretence, but yet had a kind of natural dignity, quite sufficient to keep the forwardest of us from clapping him on the shoulder and asking him for a story. A mutual acquaintance being established, our leader took the whip out of its case, and began to read the address of presentation. The whip was an exceedingly long one, its handle wrought in ivory (by some artist in the Massachusetts State Prison, I believe), and ornamented with a medallion of the President, and other equally beautiful devices; and along its whole length there was a succession of golden bands and ferrules. The address was shorter than the whip, but equally well made, consisting chiefly of an explanatory description of these artistic designs, and closing with a hint that the gift was a suggestive and emblematic one, and that the President would recognize the use to which such an instrument should be put.

This suggestion gave Uncle Abe rather a delicate task in his reply, because, slight as the matter seemed, it apparently called for some declaration, or intimation, or faint foreshadowing of policy in reference to the conduct of the war, and the final treatment of the Rebels. But the President's Yankee aptness and not-to-be-caughtness stood him in good stead, and he jerked or wiggled himself out of the dilemma with an uncouth dexterity that was entirely in character; although, without his gesticulation of eye and mouth,—and especially the flourish of the whip, with which he imagined himself touching up a pair of fat horses,—I doubt whether his words would be worth recording, even if I could remember them. The gist of the reply was, that he accepted the whip as an emblem of peace, not punishment; and, this great affair over, we retired out of the presence in high good-humor, only regretting that we could not have seen the President sit down and fold up his legs (which is said to be a most extraordinary spectacle), or have heard him tell one of those delectable stories for which he is so celebrated. A good many of them are afloat upon the common talk of Washington, and are certainly the aptest, pithiest, and funniest little things imaginable; though, to be sure, they smack of the frontier freedom, and would not always bear repetition in a drawing-room, or on the immaculate page of the Atlantic.

Good Heavens! what liberties have I been taking with one of the potentates of the earth, and the man on whose conduct more important consequences depend than on that of any other historical personage of the century! But with whom is an American citizen entitled to take a liberty, if not with his own chief magistrate? However, lest the above allusions to President Lincoln's little peculiarities (already well known to the country and to the world) should be misinterpreted, I deem it proper to say a word or two in regard to him, of unfeigned respect and measurable confidence. He is evidently a man of keen faculties, and, what is still more to the purpose, of powerful character. As to his integrity, the people have that intuition of it which is never deceived. Before he actually entered upon his great office, and for a considerable time afterwards, there is no reason to suppose that he adequately estimated the gigantic task about to be imposed on him, or, at least, had any distinct idea how it was to be managed; and I presume there may have been more than one veteran politician who proposed to himself to take the power out of President Lincoln's hands into his own, leaving our honest friend only the public responsibility for the good or ill success of the career. The extremely imperfect development of his statesmanly qualities, at that period, may have justified such designs. But the President is teachable by events, and has now spent a year in a very arduous course of education; he has a flexible mind, capable of much expansion, and convertible towards far loftier studies and activities than those of his early life; and if he came to Washington a backwoods humorist, he has already transformed himself into as good a statesman (to speak moderately) as his prime-minister.

A CIVIL WAR DIARY

CHARLES E. DAVIS

—◆◆—

Driving through Gettysburg, one is repeatedly touched by Victorian stone monuments lining the edge of the battlefield, each erected by the folks back home to honor some regiment in the great engagement. 12TH NEW HAMPSHIRE VOLUNTEERS *a tablet will read, and one is haunted by the thought of those awkward, rangy country boys, so far from home, shot down in their prime.*

    Charles E. Davis might serve as a prototype for the New England soldier in the Civil War. He kept a singularly complete diary. Born in Boston, he entered the 13th Massachusetts Regiment at eighteen as a private in Company B, and was wounded and taken prisoner at Bull Run (or, as the Southerners would say, Manassas) on August 30, 1862. In 1892, in Boston, he was chosen historian of the regiment, so that his published diary is a compilation of government records, the recollections of other soldiers, plus his own memories.

His regiment was under the command of Samuel H. Leonard (whom I hope, but am not sure, was the presumably one-legged "Old Festive" mentioned in the excerpt from Davis's diary which follows). The first four companies of the regiment's thirteen were raised in Boston, the rest from towns nearby such as Roxbury. Company D was plagued by so many volunteers they had to limit enlistment to men who got voted in and could pay $12.50. The money was spent for uniforms.

On July 16, 1861, the regiment was mustered into United States service for three years and soon after left for the seat of war, going from Fort Independence to Boston and thence to Framingham, Worcester, New York, Philadelphia and so to Virginia. On July 4, 1862, it reached Manassas Junction.

TUESDAY, July 22: In passing through towns and villages, and even on the high-roads, we naturally attracted a good deal of attention. We frequently noticed among the crowds so gathered, the scowling faces of women, who, upon learning we were from Massachusetts, saluted us as "Nigger-lovers," and other opprobrious epithets, while it occasionally happened that by grimaces only could they express the intensity of their feelings. . . .

The remarks we heard from the bystanders as we marched along often became by-words in the regiment. We were no exception to the generality of mankind, of liking to see a pretty face, even if it did belong to a woman of "secesh" sentiments. When the boys at the head of the column discovered a pretty girl, if she was on the right side of the road, *"guide right"* would be passed along the line; and *"guide left"* if on the left side of the road. By this ingenious device we were enabled to direct our eyes where we would receive the largest return for our admiration. . . .

Various were the devices adopted by the boys to relieve the monotony of weary marches. On these occasions, as conversation was allowed, stories were told, gossip repeated, discussions carried on, and criticisms made on the acts of public men, as well as on the merits of our commanders. An occasional silence would be broken by the starting of a familiar song, and very soon the whole regiment would join in the singing. Sometimes it would be a whistling chorus, when all would be whistling. Toward the end of a day, however, so tired we were all, that it was difficult to muster courage for these diversions, then our only reliance for music would be the band. When a temporary halt was granted, it was curious to see how quickly the boys would dump themselves over on their backs at the side of the road as soon as the word was given, looking like so many dead men. There was one thing we were thankful to the colonel for, and that was his freedom from nonsense on such occasions. No "right-facing," no "right-dressing," no "stacking arms," to waste valuable minutes, but "get all the rest you can, boys," and when the order was given to "forward," each man took his place in line without confusion or delay. . . .

It would often occur, when we were tired and dusty from a long day's march, "Old Festive" would ride by, when suddenly you would hear sung:

> "Saw my leg off,
> Saw my leg off,
> Saw my leg off—
> SHORT! ! !"

There was another man in the regiment who contributed a large share of fun for the amusement of others, and that was the "Medicine man"—the man who honored the doctor's sight-drafts for salts, castor-oil, etc., delicacies intended for the sick, but greatly in demand by those who wished to rid themselves of unpleasant duties. He was the *basso profundo* of the glee club, and could gaze without a tremor at the misery of a man struggling with castor-oil, while at the same time encouraging him to show his gratitude at the generosity of the Government by drinking the last drop. "Down with it, my boy, the more you take the less I carry."

Saturday, Aug. 9: The last place to look for a stock company would be among a regiment of soldiers. After being deprived of camp kettles, mess pans, etc., each man was obliged to do his own cooking, as already stated, in his tin dipper, which held about a pint. Whether it was coffee, beans, pork, or anything depending on the services of a fire to make it palatable, it was accomplished by the aid of the dipper only. Therefore any utensil like a frying-pan was of incalculable service in preparing a meal. There were so few of these in the regiment, that only men of large means, men who could raise a dollar thirty days after a paymaster's visit, could afford such a luxury.

In one instance the difficulty was overcome by the formation of a joint-stock company, composed of five stockholders, each paying the sum of twenty cents toward the purchase of a frying-pan, which cost the sum of one dollar. The par value of each share was therefore twenty cents. It was understood that each stockholder should take his turn at carrying the frying-pan when on a march, which responsibility entitled him to its first use in halting for the night. While in camp, it passed from one to the other each day in order of turn. It was frequently loaned for a consideration,

thereby affording means for an occasional dividend among the stockholders. The stock advanced in value until it reached as high as forty cents
per share, so that a stockholder in the "Joint Stock Frying Pan Company"
was looked upon as a man of consequence. Being treated with kindness
and civility by his comrades, life assumed a roseate hue to the sharehold-
ers in this great company, in spite of their deprivations. It was flattering to
hear one's self mentioned in terms of praise by some impecunious comrade who wished to occupy one side of it while you were cooking.

On this particular morning, when we started out, expecting shortly to
be in a fight, the stock went rapidly down, until it could be bought for
almost nothing. As the day progressed, however, there was a slight rise,
though the market was not strong. When the order was given to leave
knapsacks, it necessarily included this utensil, and so the "Joint Stock
Frying Pan Company" was wiped out.

1862-1885

A HOSPITAL SKETCH

LOUISA MAY ALCOTT

*Louisa May Alcott (1832–1888), even now, needs no introduction to
young girls or to anyone who has ever been a young girl.* Little Women
*is the girl's-book classic of this country. Daughter of Bronson Alcott,
learner at the knees of Emerson, Thoreau, Theodore Parker, Miss Alcott
spent most of her early life in Boston and Concord. In the Civil War she
served as a nurse in a Union hospital until her health failed. It is from*
Hospital Sketches *that the following excerpt is taken.*

I FOUND a lately emptied bed occupied by a large, fair man, with a fine
face, and the serenest eyes I ever met. One of the earlier comers had
often spoken of a friend, who had remained behind, that those apparently
worse wounded than himself might reach a shelter first. It seemed a
David and Jonathan sort of friendship. The man fretted for his mate, and
was never tired of praising John—his courage, sobriety, self-denial, and
unfailing kindliness of heart; always winding up with: "He's an out an'
out fine feller, ma'am; you see if he aint."

I had some curiosity to behold this piece of excellence, and when he
came, watched him for a night or two, before I made friends with him;
for, to tell the truth, I was a little afraid of the stately looking man, whose
bed had to be lengthened to accommodate his commanding stature; who
seldom spoke, uttered no complaint, asked no sympathy, but tranquilly
observed what went on about him; and, as he lay high upon his pillows,
no picture of dying statesman or warrior was ever fuller of real dignity
than this Virginia blacksmith. A most attractive face he had, framed in
brown hair and beard, comely featured and full of vigor, as yet unsub-
dued by pain; thoughtful and often beautifully mild while watching the
afflictions of others, as if entirely forgetful of his own. His mouth was

grave and firm, with plenty of will and courage in its lines, but a smile could make it as sweet as any woman's; and his eyes were child's eyes, looking one fairly in the face, with a clear, straightforward glance, which promised well for such as placed their faith in him. He seemed to cling to life, as if it were rich in duties and delights, and he had learned the secret of content. The only time I saw his composure disturbed was when my surgeon brought another to examine John, who scrutinized their faces with an anxious look, asking of the elder: "Do you think I shall pull through, sir?" "I hope so, my man." And, as the two passed on, John's eye still followed them, with an intentness which would have won a truer answer from them, had they seen it. A momentary shadow flitted over his face; then came the usual serenity, as if, in that brief eclipse, he had acknowledged the existence of some hard possibility, and, asking nothing yet hoping all things, left the issue in God's hands, with that submission which is true piety.

The next night, as I went my rounds with Dr. P., I happened to ask which man in the room probably suffered most; and, to my great surprise, he glanced at John:

"Every breath he draws is like a stab; for the ball pierced the left lung, broke a rib, and did no end of damage here and there; so the poor lad can find neither forgetfulness nor ease, because he must lie on his wounded back or suffocate. It will be a hard struggle, and a long one, for he possesses great vitality; but even his temperate life can't save him; I wish it could."

"You don't mean he must die, doctor?"

"Bless you, there's not the slightest hope for him; and you'd better tell him so before long; women have a way of doing such things comfortably, so I leave it to you. He won't last more than a day or two, at furthest."

I could have sat down on the spot and cried heartily, if I had not learned the wisdom of bottling up one's tears for leisure moments. Such an end seemed very hard for such a man, when half a dozen worn out, worthless bodies round him were gathering up the remnants of wasted lives, to linger on for years perhaps, burdens to others, daily reproaches to themselves. The army needed men like John, earnest, brave, and faithful; fighting for liberty and justice with both heart and hand, true soldiers of the Lord. I could not give him up so soon, or think with any patience of so excellent a nature robbed of its fulfilment, and blundered into eternity by the rashness or stupidity of those at whose hands so many lives may be required. It was an easy thing for Dr. P. to say "Tell him he must die," but a cruelly hard thing to do, and by no means as "comfortable" as he politely suggested. I had not the heart to do it then, and privately indulged the hope that some change for the better might take place, in spite of gloomy prophesies; so rendering my task unnecessary.

A few minutes later, as I came in again, with fresh rollers, I saw John sitting erect, with no one to support him, while the surgeon dressed his back. I had never hitherto seen it done; for, having simpler wounds to attend to, and knowing the fidelity of the attendant, I had left John to him, thinking it might be more agreeable and safe; for both strength and experience were needed in his case. I had forgotten that the strong man might long for the gentle tendance of a woman's hands, the sympathetic magnetism of a woman's presence, as well as the feebler souls about him. The doctor's words caused me to reproach myself with neglect, not of any real duty perhaps, but of those little cares and kindnesses that solace homesick spirits and make the heavy hours pass easier. John looked lonely and forsaken just then, as he sat with bent head, hands folded on his knee, and no outward sign of suffering, till, looking nearer, I saw great tears roll down and drop upon the floor. It was a new sight there; for, though I had seen many suffer, some swore, some groaned, most endured silently, but none wept. Yet it did not seem weak, only very touching, and straightway my fear vanished, my heart opened wide and took him in, as, gathering the bent head in my arms, as freely as if he had been a little child, I said: "Let me help you bear it, John."

Never, on any human countenance, have I seen so swift and beautiful a look of gratitude, surprise, and comfort as that which answered me more eloquently than the whispered—

"Thank you, ma'am; this is right good! this is what I wanted!"

"Then why not ask for it before?"

"I didn't like to be a trouble; you seemed so busy, and I could manage to get on alone."

"You shall not want it any more, John."

Nor did he: for now I understood the wistful look that sometimes followed me, as I went out, after a brief pause beside his bed, or merely a passing nod, while busied with those who seemed to need me more than he, because more urgent in their demands. Now I knew that to him, as to so many, I was the poor substitute for mother, wife, or sister, and in his eyes no stranger, but a friend who hitherto had seemed neglectful; for, in his modesty, he had never guessed the truth. This was changed now; and, through the tedious operation of probing, bathing, and dressing his wounds, he leaned against me, holding my hand fast, and, if pain wrung further tears from him, no one saw them fall but me. When he was laid down again, I hovered about him, in a remorseful state of mind that would not let me rest till I had bathed his face, brushed his bonny brown hair, set all things smooth about him, and laid a knot of heath and heliotrope on his clean pillow. While doing this, he watched me with the satisfied expression I so liked to see; and when I offered the little nosegay, held it carefully in his great hand, smoothed a ruffled leaf or two, surveyed and smelt it with an air of genuine delight, and lay contentedly

regarding the glimmer of the sunshine on the green. Although the man-
liest man among my forty, he said, "Yes, ma'am" like a little boy;
received suggestions for his comfort with the quick smile that brightened
his whole face; and now and then, as I stood tidying the table by his
bed, I felt him softly touch my gown, as if to assure himself that I was
there. Anything more natural and frank I never saw, and found this brave
John as bashful as brave, yet full of excellencies and fine aspirations,
which, having no power to express themselves in words, seemed to have
bloomed into his character and made him what he was.

After that night, an hour of each evening that remained to him was
devoted to his ease or pleasure. He could not talk much, for breath was
precious, and he spoke in whispers; but from occasional conversations, I
gleaned scraps of private history which only added to the affection and
respect I felt for him. Once he asked me to write a letter, and as I settled
pen and paper, I said, with an irrepressible glimmer of feminine curiosity: "Shall it be addressed to wife, or mother, John?"

"Neither, ma'am; I've got no wife, and will write to mother myself
when I get better. Did you think I was married because of this?" he
asked, touching a plain ring he wore, and often turned thoughtfully on his
finger when he lay alone.

"Partly that, but more from a settled sort of look you have; a look
which young men seldom get until they marry."

"I didn't know that; but I'm not so very young, ma'am; thirty in May,
and have been what you might call settled this ten years. Mother's a
widow, I'm the oldest child she has, and it wouldn't do for me to marry
until Lizzy has a home of her own, and Jack's learned his trade; for we're
not rich, and I must be father to the children and husband to the dear
old woman, if I can."

"No doubt but you are both, John; yet how came you to go to war,
if you felt so? Wasn't enlisting as bad as marrying?"

"No, ma'am, not as I see it; for one is helping my neighbor, the other
pleasing myself. I went because I couldn't help it. I didn't want the glory
or the pay; I wanted the right thing done, and people kept saying the
men who were in earnest ought to fight. I was in earnest, the Lord
knows! but I held off as long as I could, not knowing which was my duty.
Mother saw the case, gave me her ring to keep me steady, and said 'Go':
so I went."

A short story and a simple one, but the man and the mother were
portrayed better than pages of fine writing could have done it.

"Do you ever regret that you came, when you lie here suffering so
much?"

"Never, ma'am; I haven't helped a great deal, but I've shown I was
willing to give my life, and perhaps I've got to; but I don't blame anybody, and if it was to do over again, I'd do it. I'm a little sorry I wasn't

wounded in front; it looks cowardly to be hit in the back, but I obeyed orders, and it don't matter in the end, I know."

Poor John! it did not matter now, except that a shot in front might have spared the long agony in store for him. He seemed to read the thought that troubled me, as he spoke so hopefully when there was no hope, for he suddenly added:

"This is my first battle; do they think it's going to be my last?"

"I'm afraid they do, John."

It was the hardest question I had ever been called upon to answer; doubly hard with those clear eyes fixed on mine, forcing a truthful answer by their own truth. He seemed a little startled at first, pondered over the fateful fact a moment, then shook his head, with a glance at the broad chest and muscular limbs stretched out before him:

"I'm not afraid, but it's difficult to believe all at once. I'm so strong it don't seem possible for such a little wound to kill me."

Merry Mercutio's dying words glanced through my memory as he spoke: " 'Tis not so deep as a well, nor so wide as a church door, but 'tis enough." And John would have said the same could he have seen the ominous black holes between his shoulders; he never had, but, seeing the ghastly sights about him, could not believe his own wound more fatal than these, for all the suffering it caused him.

"Shall I write to your mother, now?" I asked, thinking that these sudden tidings might change all plans and purposes. But they did not; for the man received the order of the Divine Commander to march with the same unquestioning obedience with which the soldier had received that of the human one; doubtless remembering that the first led him to life, and the last to death.

"No, ma'am; to Jack just the same; he'll break it to her best, and I'll add a line to her myself when you get done."

So I wrote the letter which he dictated, finding it better than any I had sent; for, though here and there a little ungrammatical or inelegant, each sentence came to me briefly worded, but most expressive; full of excellent counsel to the boy, tenderly bequeathing "mother and Lizzie" to his care, and bidding him good-bye in words the sadder for their simplicity. He added a few lines, with steady hand, and, as I sealed it, said, with a patient sort of sigh: "I hope the answer will come in time for me to see it"; then, turning away his face, laid the flowers against his lips, as if to hide some quiver of emotion at the thought of such a sudden sundering of all the dear home ties.

These things had happened two days before; now John was dying, and the letter had not come. I had been summoned to many death-beds in my life, but to none that made my heart ache as it did then, since my mother called me to watch the departure of a spirit akin to this in its gentleness and patient strength. As I went in, John stretched out both hands:

"I knew you'd come! I guess I'm moving on, ma'am."

He was; and so rapidly that, even while he spoke, over his face I saw the gray veil falling that no human hand can lift. I sat down by him, wiped the drops from his forehead, stirred the air about him with the slow wave of a fan, and waited to help him die. He stood in sore need of help—and I could do so little; for, as the doctor had foretold, the strong body rebelled against death, and fought every inch of the way, forcing him to draw each breath with a spasm, and clench his hands with an imploring look, as if he asked: "How long must I endure this, and be still!" For hours he suffered dumbly, without a moment's respite, or a moment's murmuring; his limbs grew cold, his face damp, his lips white, and, again and again, he tore the covering off his breast, as if the lightest weight added to his agony; yet through it all, his eyes never lost their perfect serenity, and the man's soul seemed to sit therein, undaunted by the ills that vexed his flesh.

One by one, the men woke, and round the room appeared a circle of pale faces and watchful eyes, full of awe and pity; for, though a stranger, John was beloved by all. Each man there had wondered at his patience, respected his piety, admired his fortitude, and now lamented his hard death; for the influence of an upright nature had made itself deeply felt, even in one little week. Presently the Jonathan who so loved this comely David came creeping from his bed for a last look and word. The kind soul was full of trouble, as the choke in his voice, the grasp of his hand, betrayed; but there were no tears, and the farewell of the friends was the more touching for its brevity.

"Old boy, how are you?" faltered the one.

"Most through, thank heaven!" whispered the other.

"Can I say or do anything for you anywheres?"

"Take my things home, and tell them that I did my best."

"I will! I will!"

"Good-bye, Ned."

"Good-bye, John, good-bye!"

They kissed each other, tenderly as women, and so parted, for poor Ned could not stay to see his comrade die. For a little while, there was no sound in the room but the drip of water, from a stump or two, and John's distressful gasps, as he slowly breathed his life away. I thought him nearly gone, and had just laid down the fan, believing its help to be no longer needed, when suddenly he rose up in his bed, and cried out with a bitter cry that broke the silence, sharply startling every one with its agonized appeal:

"For God's sake, give me air!"

It was the only cry pain or death had wrung from him, the only boon he had asked; and none of us could grant it, for all the airs that blew were useless now. Dan flung up the window. The first red streak of dawn was warming the gray east, a herald of the coming sun; John saw it, and with the love of light which lingers in us to the end, seemed to read in it a sign of hope of help, for over his whole face there broke that mysterious expression, brighter than any smile, which often comes to eyes that look their last. He laid himself gently down; and, stretching out his strong right arm, as if to grasp and bring the blessed air to his lips in a fuller flow, lapsed into a merciful unconsciousness, which assured us that for him suffering was forever past. He died then; for, though the heavy breaths still tore their way up for a little longer, they were but the waves of an ebbing tide that beat unfelt against the wreck which an immortal voyager had deserted with a smile. He never spoke again, but to the end held my hand close, so close that when he was asleep at last, I could not draw it away. Dan helped me, warning me as he did so that it was unsafe for dead and living flesh to lie so long together; but though my hand was strangely cold and stiff, and four white marks remained across its back, even when warmth and color had returned elsewhere, I could not but be glad that, through its touch, the presence of human sympathy, perhaps, had lightened that hard hour.

When they had made him ready for the grave, John lay in state for half an hour, a thing which seldom happened in that busy place; but a universal sentiment of reverence and affection seemed to fill the hearts of all who had known or heard of him; and when the rumor of his death went through the house, always astir, many came to see him, and I felt a tender sort of pride in my lost patient; for he looked a most heroic figure, lying there stately and still as the statue of some young knight asleep upon his tomb. The lovely expression which so often beautifies dead faces soon replaced the marks of pain, and I longed for those who loved him best to see him when half an hour's acquaintance with Death had made them friends. As we stood looking at him, the ward-master handed me a letter, saying it had been forgotten the night before. It was John's letter, come just an hour too late to gladden the eyes that had longed and looked for it so eagerly! but he had it; for, after I had cut some brown locks for his mother, and taken off the ring to send her, telling how well the talisman had done its work, I kissed this good son for her sake, and laid the letter in his hand, still folded as when I drew my own away, feeling that its place was there, and making myself happy with the thought, that, even in his solitary grave in the "Government Lot," he would not be without some token of the love which makes life beautiful and outlives death. Then I left him, glad to have known so genuine a man, and carrying with me an enduring memory of the brave Virginia blacksmith, as he lay serenely waiting for the dawn of that long day which knows no night.

THE GENESIS OF "THE BATTLE HYMN OF THE REPUBLIC"

JULIA WARD HOWE

————— ◆•◆ —————

There is no one who does not know the song, or hymn, "Mine Eyes Have Seen the Glory," by Julia Ward Howe (1819–1910). She was the wife of Samuel Gridley Howe, who founded the Massachusetts School for the Blind (Perkins Institution). Together, they had founded the antislavery journal Commonwealth, *published in Boston. The following excerpt from Mrs. Howe's* Reminiscences *gives the genesis of her great battle song.*

AMONG my recollections of this period I especially cherish that of an interview with President Abraham Lincoln, arranged for us by our kind friend, Governor Andrew. The President was laboring at this time under a terrible pressure of doubt and anxiety. He received us in one of the drawing-rooms of the White House, where we were invited to take seats, in full view of Stuart's portrait of Washington. The conversation took place mostly between the President and Governor Andrew. I remember well the sad expression of Mr. Lincoln's deep blue eyes, the only feature of his face which could be called other than plain. Mrs. Andrew, being of the company, inquired when we could have the pleasure of seeing Mrs. Lincoln, and Mr. Lincoln named to us the day of her reception. He said to Governor Andrew, apropos of I know not what, "I once heerd George Sumner tell a story." The unusual pronunciation fixed in my memory this one unimportant sentence. The talk, indeed, ran mostly on indifferent topics.

When we had taken leave, and were out of hearing, Mr. Clarke said of Mr. Lincoln, "We have seen it in his face; hopeless honesty; that is all." He said it as if he felt that it was far from enough.

None of us knew then—how could we have known?—how deeply God's wisdom had touched and inspired that devout and patient soul. At the moment few people praised or trusted him. "Why did he not do this, or that, or the other? He a President, indeed! Look at this war, dragging on so slowly! Look at our many defeats and rare victories!" Such was the talk that one constantly heard regarding him. The most charitable held that he meant well. Governor Andrew was one of the few whose faith in him never wavered.

Meanwhile, through evil and good report, he was listening for the mandate which comes to one alone, bringing with it the decision of a mind convinced and of a conscience resolved. When the right moment came, he issued the proclamation of emancipation to the slaves. He sent his generals into the enemy's country. He lived to welcome them back as victors, to electrify the civilized world with his simple, sincere speech, to fall by the hand of an assassin, to bequeath to his country the most tragical and sacred of her memories.

It would be impossible for me to say how many times I have been called upon to rehearse the circumstances under which I wrote the "Battle Hymn of the Republic." I have also had occasion more than once to state the simple story in writing. As this oft-told tale has no unimportant part in the story of my life, I will briefly add it to these records. I distinctly remember that a feeling of discouragement came over me as I drew near the city of Washington at the time already mentioned. I thought of the women of my acquaintance whose sons or husbands were fighting our great battle; the women themselves serving in the hospitals, or busying themselves with the work of the Sanitary Commission. My husband, as already said, was beyond the age of military service, my eldest son but a stripling; my youngest was a child of not more than two years. I could not leave my nursery to follow the march of our armies, neither had I the practical deftness which the preparing and packing of sanitary stores demanded. Something seemed to say to me, "You would be glad to serve, but you cannot help any one; you have nothing to give, and there is nothing for you to do." Yet, because of my sincere desire, a word was given me to say, which did strengthen the hearts of those who fought in the field and of those who languished in the prison.

We were invited, one day, to attend a review of troops at some distance from the town. While we were engaged in watching the manœuvres, a sudden movement of the enemy necessitated immediate action. The review was discontinued, and we saw a detachment of soldiers gallop to the assistance of a small body of our men who were in imminent danger of being surrounded and cut off from retreat. The regiments remaining on the field were ordered to march to their cantonments. We returned to the city very slowly, of necessity, for the troops nearly filled the road. My dear minister was in the carriage with me, as were several other friends. To beguile the rather tedious drive, we sang from time to time snatches of the army songs so popular at that time, concluding, I think, with

> "John Brown's body lies a-mouldering in the ground;
>   His soul is marching on."

The soldiers seemed to like this, and answered back, "Good for you!" Mr. Clarke said, "Mrs. Howe, why do you not write some good words for that stirring tune?" I replied that I had often wished to do this, but had not as yet found in my mind any leading toward it.

I went to bed that night as usual, and slept, according to my wont, quite soundly. I awoke in the gray of the morning twilight; and as I lay waiting for the dawn, the long lines of the desired poem began to twine themselves in my mind. Having thought out all the stanzas, I said to myself, "I must get up and write these verses down, lest I fall asleep again and forget them." So, with a sudden effort, I sprang out of bed, and found in the dimness an old stump of a pen which I remembered to have used the day before. I scrawled the verses almost without looking at the paper. I had learned to do this when, on previous occasions, attacks of versification had visited me in the night, and I feared to have recourse to a light lest I should wake the baby, who slept near me. I was always obliged to decipher my scrawl before another night should intervene, as it was only legible while the matter was fresh in my mind. At this time, having completed my writing, I returned to bed and fell asleep, saying to myself, "I like this better than most things that I have written."

The poem, which was soon after published in the "Atlantic Monthly," was somewhat praised on its appearance, but the vicissitudes of the war so engrossed public attention that small heed was taken of literary matters. I knew, and was content to know, that the poem soon found its way to the camps, as I heard from time to time of its being sung in chorus by the soldiers.

As the war went on, it came to pass that Chaplain McCabe, newly released from Libby Prison, gave a public lecture in Washington, and recounted some of his recent experiences. Among them was the following: He and the other Union prisoners occupied one large, comfortless room, in which the floor was their only bed. An official in charge of them told them, one evening, that the Union arms had just sustained a terrible defeat. While they sat together in great sorrow, the negro who waited upon them whispered to one man that the officer had given them false information, and that the Union soldiers had, on the contrary, achieved an important victory. At this good news they all rejoiced, and presently made the walls ring with my Battle Hymn, which they sang in chorus, Chaplain McCabe leading. The lecturer recited the poem with such effect that those present began to inquire, "Who wrote this Battle Hymn?" It now became one of the leading lyrics of the war. In view of its success, one of my good friends said, "Mrs. Howe ought to die now, for she has done the best that she will ever do." I was not of this opinion, feeling myself still "full of days' works," although I did not guess at the new experiences which then lay before me.

A FAREWELL TO AGASSIZ

OLIVER WENDELL HOLMES

———◆◆◆———

A Swiss who became an integral part of the New England scene was Louis Agassiz—Jean Louis Rodolphe Agassiz (1807–1873). Brought to Boston to lecture at the Lowell Institute, it was said that "American natural history . . . found its leader" in him. More than any other one man he stimulated interest in the natural sciences; for many years he held the chair of Zoology and Geology at Harvard, and from it exerted great influence as a teacher. Dr. Holmes wrote the following poem of farewell to Agassiz on his departure on one of his many explorations, the Thayer Expedition to Brazil in 1865. Elizabeth Cary Agassiz, his wife, was a founder and president of Radcliffe College.

How the mountains talked together,
Looking down upon the weather,
When they heard our friend had planned his
Little trip among the Andes!
How they'll bare their snowy scalps
To the climber of the Alps
When the cry goes through their passes,
"Here comes the great Agassiz!"
"Yes, I'm tall," says Chimborazo,
"But I wait for him to say so,—
That's the only thing that lacks,—he
Must see me, Cotopaxi!"
"Ay! ay!" the fire-peak thunders,
"And he must view my wonders!
I'm but a lonely crater
Till I have him for spectator!"
The mountain hearts are yearning,
The lava-torches burning,
The rivers bend to meet him,
The forests bow to greet him,
It thrills the spinal column
Of fossil fishes solemn,
And glaciers crawl the faster

To the feet of their old master!
Heaven keep him well and hearty,
Both him and all his party!
From the sun that broils and smites,
From the centipede that bites,
From the hail-storm and the thunder,
From the vampire and the condor,
From the gust upon the river,
From the sudden earthquake shiver,
From the trip of mule or donkey,
From the midnight howling monkey,
From the stroke of knife or dagger,
From the puma and the jaguar,
From the horrid boa-constrictor
That has scared us in the pictur',
From the Indians of the Pampas
Who would dine upon their grampas,
From every beast and vermin
That to think of sets us squirmin',
From every snake that tries on
The traveller his p'ison,
From every pest of Natur',
Likewise the alligator,
And from two things left behind him,—
(Be sure they'll try to find him,)
The tax-bill and assessor,—
Heaven keep the great Professor!
May he find, with his apostles,
That the land is full of fossils,
That the waters swarm with fishes
Shaped according to his wishes,
That every pool is fertile
In fancy kinds of turtle,
New birds around him singing,
New insects, never stinging,
With a million novel data
About the articulata,
And facts that strip off all husks
From the history of mollusks.

And when, with loud Te Deum,
He returns to his Museum,
May he find the monstrous reptile
That so long the land has kept ill

By Grant and Sherman throttled,
And by Father Abraham bottled,
(All specked and streaked and mottled
With the scars of murderous battles,
Where he clashed the iron rattles
That gods and men he shook at,)
For all the world to look at!
God bless the great Professor!
And Madam, too, God bless her!
Bless him and all his band,
On the sea and on the land,
Bless them head and heart and hand,
Till their glorious raid is o'er,
And they touch our ransomed shore!
Then the welcome of a nation,
With its shout of exultation,
Shall awake the dumb creation,
And the shapes of buried æons
Join the living creature's pæans,
Till the fossil echoes roar;
While the mighty megalosaurus
Leads the palæozoic chorus,—
God bless the great Professor,
And the land his proud possessor,—
Bless them now and evermore!

THE LADY WHO PUT SALT
IN HER COFFEE

LUCRETIA P. HALE

————◆◆————

My father used to say, "Boston lost her character when she stopped be-
ing provincial." One of the myriad effects of the Civil War was the dele-
terious one of opening New England up to a sort of false cosmopolitanism.
The day of her great poets—who were simple, sensuous, passionate, but
above all simple—declined. The only poet of real quality to emerge in the
later century was Emily Dickinson, who as much as possible hid herself
from this world.

However, on the positive side, the growing worldliness made New

*England capable of laughing at itself. Jokes on Boston have flown fast
and furious ever since.* The Peterkin Papers, *by Lucretia P. Hale (1820–
1900), which caricature the intellectual Bostonian approach to life, were
greeted with cries of delight when the first of them, reprinted here, appeared in 1866 in the magazine* Our Young Folks *(which was to become*
St. Nicholas).

THIS was Mrs. Peterkin. It was a mistake. She had poured out a delicious cup of coffee, and, just as she was helping herself to cream, she
found she had put in salt instead of sugar! It tasted bad. What should
she do? Of course she couldn't drink the coffee; so she called in the
family, for she was sitting at a late breakfast all alone. The family came
in; they all tasted, and looked, and wondered what should be done, and
all sat down to think.

At last Agamemnon, who had been to college, said, "Why don't we go
over and ask the advice of the chemist?" (For the chemist lived over the
way, and was a very wise man.)

Mrs. Peterkin said, "Yes," and Mr. Peterkin said, "Very well," and all
the children said they would go too. So the little boys put on their india-
rubber boots, and over they went.

Now the chemist was just trying to find out something which should
turn everything it touched into gold; and he had a large glass bottle into
which he put all kinds of gold and silver, and many other valuable things,
and melted them all up over the fire, till he had almost found what he
wanted. He could turn things into almost gold. But just now he had used
up all the gold that he had round the house, and gold was high. He had
used up his wife's gold thimble and his great-grandfather's gold-bowed
spectacles; and he had melted up the gold head of his great-great-grandfather's cane; and, just as the Peterkin family came in, he was down on
his knees before his wife, asking her to let him have her wedding-ring to
melt up with all the rest, because this time he should succeed, and
should be able to turn everything into gold; and then she could have a
new wedding-ring of diamonds, all set in emeralds and rubies and to-
pazes, and all the furniture could be turned into the finest of gold.

Now his wife was just consenting when the Peterkin family burst in.
You can imagine how mad the chemist was! He came near throwing his
crucible—that was the name of his melting-pot—at their heads. But he
didn't. He listened as calmly as he could to the story of how Mrs. Peterkin had put salt in her coffee.

At first he said he couldn't do anything about it; but when Agamemnon
said they would pay in gold if he would only go, he packed up his bottles
in a leather case, and went back with them all.

First he looked at the coffee, and then stirred it. Then he put in a little chlorate of potassium, and the family tried it all round; but it tasted no better. Then he stirred in a little bichlorate of magnesia. But Mrs. Peterkin didn't like that. Then he added some tartaric acid and some hypersulphate of lime. But no; it was no better. "I have it!" exclaimed the chemist,—"a little ammonia is just the thing!" No, it wasn't the thing at all.

Then he tried, each in turn, some oxalic, cyanic, acetic, phosphoric, chloric, hyperchloric, sulphuric, boracic, silicic, nitric, formic, nitrous nitric, and carbonic acids. Mrs. Peterkin tasted each, and said the flavor was pleasant, but not precisely that of coffee. So then he tried a little calcium, aluminum, barium, and strontium, a little clear bitumen, and a half of a third of a sixteenth of a grain of arsenic. This gave rather a pretty color; but still Mrs. Peterkin ungratefully said it tasted of anything but coffee. The chemist was not discouraged. He put in a little belladonna and atropine, some granulated hydrogen, some potash, and a very little antimony, finishing off with a little pure carbon. But still Mrs. Peterkin was not satisfied.

The chemist said all that he had done ought to have taken out the salt. The theory remained the same, although the experiment had failed. Perhaps a little starch would have effect. If not, that was all the time he could give. He should like to be paid, and go. They were all much obliged to him, and willing to give him $1.37½ in gold. Gold was now 2.69¾, so Mr. Peterkin found in the newspaper. This gave Agamemnon a pretty little sum. He sat himself down to do it. But there was the coffee! All sat and thought awhile, till Elizabeth Eliza said, "Why don't we go to the herb-woman?" Elizabeth Eliza was the only daughter. She was named after her two aunts,—Elizabeth, from the sister of her father; Eliza, from her mother's sister. Now, the herb-woman was an old woman who came round to sell herbs, and knew a great deal. They all shouted with joy at the idea of asking her, and Solomon John and the younger children agreed to go and find her too. The herb-woman lived down at the very end of the street; so the boys put on their india-rubber boots again, and they set off. It was a long walk through the village, but they came at last to the herb-woman's house, at the foot of a high hill. They went through her little garden. Here she had marigolds and hollyhocks, and old maids and tall sunflowers, and all kinds of sweet-smelling herbs, so that the air was full of tansy-tea and elder-blow. Over the porch grew a hop-vine, and a brandy-cherry tree shaded the door, and a luxuriant cranberry-vine flung its delicious fruit across the window. They went into a small parlor, which smelt very spicy. All around hung little bags full of catnip, and peppermint, and all kinds of herbs; and dried stalks hung from the ceiling; and on the shelves were jars of rhubarb, senna, manna, and the like.

But there was no little old woman. She had gone up into the woods to get some more wild herbs, so they all thought they would follow her,—

Elizabeth Eliza, Solomon John, and the little boys. They had to climb up over high rocks, and in among huckleberry-bushes and blackberry-vine. But the little boys had their india-rubber boots. At last they discovered the little old woman. They knew her by her hat. It was steeple-crowned, without any vane. They saw her digging with her trowel round a sassafras bush. They told her their story,—how their mother had put salt in her coffee, and how the chemist had made it worse instead of better, and how their mother couldn't drink it, and wouldn't she come and see what she could do? And she said she would, and took up her little old apron, with pockets all round, all filled with everlasting and pennyroyal, and went back to her house.

There she stopped, and stuffed her huge pockets with some of all the kinds of herbs. She took some tansy and peppermint, and caraway-seed and dill, spearmint and cloves, pennyroyal and sweet marjoram, basil and rosemary, wild thyme and some of the other time,—such as you have in clocks,—sappermint and oppermint, catnip, valerian, and hop; indeed, there isn't any kind of herb you can think of that the little old woman didn't have done up in her little paper bags, that had all been dried in her little Dutch-oven. She packed these all up, and then went back with the children, taking her stick.

Meanwhile Mrs. Peterkin was getting quite impatient for her coffee.

As soon as the little old woman came she had it set over the fire, and began to stir in the different herbs. First she put in a little hop for the bitter. Mrs. Peterkin said it tasted like hop-tea, and not at all like coffee. Then she tried a little flagroot and snakeroot, then some spruce gum, and some caraway and some dill, some rue and rosemary, some sweet marjoram and sour, some oppermint and sappermint, a little spearmint and peppermint, some wild thyme, and some of the other tame time, some tansy and basil, and catnip and valerian, and sassafras, ginger, and pennyroyal. The children tasted after each mixture, but made up dreadful faces. Mrs. Peterkin tasted, and did the same. The more the old woman stirred, and the more she put in, the worse it all seemed to taste.

So the old woman shook her head, and muttered a few words, and said she must go. She believed the coffee was bewitched. She bundled up her packets of herbs, and took her trowel, and her basket, and her stick, and went back to her root of sassafras, that she had left half in the air and half out. And all she would take for pay was five cents in currency.

Then the family were in despair, and all sat and thought a great while. It was growing late in the day, and Mrs. Peterkin hadn't had her cup of coffee. At last Elizabeth Eliza said, "They say that the lady from Philadelphia, who is staying in town, is very wise. Suppose I go and ask her what is best to be done." To this they all agreed, it was a great thought, and off Elizabeth Eliza went.

She told the lady from Philadelphia the whole story,—how her mother had put salt in the coffee; how the chemist had been called in; how he tried everything but could make it no better; and how they went for the little old herb-woman, and how she had tried in vain, for her mother couldn't drink the coffee. The lady from Philadelphia listened very attentively and then said, "Why doesn't your mother make a fresh cup of coffee?" Elizabeth Eliza started with surprise. Solomon John shouted with joy; so did Agamemnon, who had just finished his sum; so did the little boys, who had followed on. "Why didn't we think of that?" said Elizabeth Eliza; and they all went back to their mother, and she had her cup of coffee.

STORY OF A BAD BOY

THOMAS BAILEY ALDRICH

———◆◆◆———

As a poet, Thomas Bailey Aldrich (1836–1917) was one of what Van Wyck Brooks *calls "the idle singers of empty days" in the later nineteenth century in New England, when the Civil War and the spread of science had "killed the imagination." He is best remembered for his* Story of a Bad Boy, *a fictional autobiography of his boyhood in Portsmouth, New Hampshire. (Old-line Yankees pronounced it "Porchmouth.") An excerpt follows.*

The parlor wallpaper which Aldrich describes sounds characteristic of similar wallpapers (not all so funny) in similar old New England houses. A friend of mine bought and moved into an old house in Dedham, Massachusetts, and started to peel the rather ordinary paper off the walls of the hall only to find, underneath, the original paper, magnificent with scenes of the Palio at Siena. The furnishings of New England houses often possessed great sophistication owing to the world travels of their shipmaster owners, and to the China Trade.

Also note the beloved Irish maid in Aldrich's story. Almost every New England household, by that time, had one or more such—all, like her, "descended in a direct line from an extensive family of kings who formerly ruled over Ireland." The old-time Yankee servant, as an institution, was already becoming a figure of the past.

THE Nutter House—all the more prominent dwellings in Rivermouth are named after somebody; for instance, there is the Walford House, the

Venner House, the Trefethen House, etc., though it by no means follows that they are inhabited by the persons whose names they bear—the Nutter House, to resume, has been in our family nearly a hundred years, and is an honor to the builder (an ancestor of ours, I believe), supposing durability to be a merit. If our ancestor *was* a carpenter, he knew his trade. I wish I knew mine as well. Such timber and such workmanship do not often come together in houses built nowadays.

Imagine a low-studded structure, with a wide hall running through the middle. At your right hand, as you enter, stands a tall black mahogany clock, looking like an Egyptian mummy set up on end. On each side of the hall are doors (whose knobs, it must be confessed, do not turn very easily), opening into large rooms wainscoted and rich in wood-carvings about the mantelpieces and cornices. The walls are covered with pictured paper, representing landscapes and sea-views. In the parlor, for example, this enlivening figure is repeated all over the room: A group of English peasants, wearing Italian hats, are dancing on a lawn that abruptly resolves itself into a sea-beach, upon which stands a flabby fisherman (nationality unknown), quietly hauling in what appears to be a small whale, and totally regardless of the dreadful naval combat going on just beyond the end of his fishing-rod. On the other side of the ships is the mainland again, with the same peasants dancing. Our ancestors were very worthy people, but their wall-papers were abominable.

There are neither grates nor stoves in these quaint chambers, but splendid open chimney-places, with room enough for the corpulent backlog to turn over comfortably on the polished andirons. A wide staircase leads from the hall to the second story, which is arranged much like the first. Over this is the garret. I need not tell a New England boy what a museum of curiosities is the garret of a well-regulated New England house of fifty or sixty years' standing. Here meet together, as if by some preconcerted arrangement, all the broken-down chairs of the household, all the spavined tables, all the seedy hats, all the intoxicated-looking boots, all the split walking-sticks that have retired from business, "weary with the march of life." The pots, the pans, the trunks, the bottles—who may hope to make an inventory of the numberless odds and ends collected in this bewildering lumber-room? But what a place it is to sit of an afternoon with the rain pattering on the roof! what a place in which to read Gulliver's Travels, or the famous adventures of Rinaldo Rinaldini!

My grandfather's house stood a little back from the main street, in the shadow of two handsome elms, whose overgrown boughs would dash themselves against the gables whenever the wind blew hard. In the rear was a pleasant garden, covering perhaps a quarter of an acre, full of plumtrees and gooseberry-bushes. These trees were old settlers, and are all dead now, excepting one, which bears a purple plum as big as an egg. This tree, as I remark, is still standing, and a more beautiful tree to tumble out of never grew anywhere. In the northwestern corner of the garden were the stables and carriage-house, opening upon a narrow lane. You may imagine that I made an early visit to that locality to inspect Gypsy. Indeed, I paid her a visit every half-hour during the first day of my arrival. At the twenty-fourth visit she trod on my foot rather heavily, as a reminder, probably, that I was wearing out my welcome. She was a knowing little pony, that Gypsy, and I shall have much to say of her in the course of these pages.

Gypsy's quarters were all that could be wished, but nothing among my new surroundings gave me more satisfaction than the cosey sleeping apartment that had been prepared for myself. It was the hall room over the front door.

I had never before had a chamber all to myself, and this one, about twice the size of our stateroom on board the Typhoon, was a marvel of neatness and comfort. Pretty chintz curtains hung at the window, and a patch quilt of more colors than were in Joseph's coat covered the little truckle-bed. The pattern of the wall-paper left nothing to be desired in that line. On a gray background were small bunches of leaves, unlike any that ever grew in this world; and on every other bunch perched a yellow-bird, pitted with crimson spots, as if it had just recovered from a severe attack of the small-pox. That no such bird ever existed did not detract from my admiration of each one. There were two hundred and sixty-eight of these birds in all, not counting those split in two where the paper was badly joined. I counted them once when I was laid up with a fine black eye, and falling asleep immediately dreamed that the whole flock suddenly took wing and flew out of the window. From that time I was never able to regard them as merely inanimate objects.

A wash-stand in the corner, a chest of carved mahogany drawers, a looking-glass in a filigreed frame, and a high-backed chair studded with brass nails like a coffin, constituted the furniture. Over the head of the bed were two oak shelves, holding perhaps a dozen books—among which were Theodore, or The Peruvians; Robinson Crusoe; an odd volume of Tristram Shandy; Baxter's Saint's Rest, and a fine English edition of the Arabian Nights, with six hundred wood-cuts by Harvey.

Shall I ever forget the hour when I first overhauled these books? I do not allude especially to Baxter's Saint's Rest, which is far from being a lively work for the young, but to the Arabian Nights, and particularly to Robinson Crusoe. The thrill that ran into my fingers' ends then has not run out yet. Many a time did I steal up to this nest of a room, and, taking the dog's-eared volume from its shelf, glide off into an enchanted realm, where there were no lessons to get and no boys to smash my kite. In a lidless trunk in the garret I subsequently unearthed another motley collection of novels and romances, embracing the adventures of Baron Trenck,

Jack Sheppard, Don Quixote, Gil Blas, and Charlotte Temple—all of which I fed upon like a bookworm.

I never come across a copy of any of those works without feeling a certain tenderness for the yellow-haired little rascal who used to lean above the magic pages hour after hour, religiously believing every word he read, and no more doubting the reality of Sindbad the Sailor, or the Knight of the Sorrowful Countenance, than he did the existence of his own grandfather.

Against the wall at the foot of the bed hung a single-barrelled shot-gun —placed there by Grandfather Nutter, who knew what a boy loved, if ever a grandfather did. As the trigger of the gun had been accidentally twisted off, it was not, perhaps, the most dangerous weapon that could be placed in the hands of youth. In this maimed condition its bump of destructiveness was much less than that of my small brass pocket-pistol, which I at once proceeded to suspend from one of the nails supporting the fowling-piece, for my vagaries concerning the red men had been entirely dispelled.

Having introduced the reader to the Nutter House, a presentation to the Nutter family naturally follows. The family consisted of my grandfather; his sister, Miss Abigail Nutter; and Kitty Collins, the maid-of-all-work.

Grandfather Nutter was a hale, cheery old gentleman, as straight and as bald as an arrow. He had been a sailor in early life; that is to say, at the age of ten years he fled from the multiplication-table, and ran away to sea. A single voyage satisfied him. There was but one of our family who did not run away to sea, and this one died at his birth. My grandfather had also been a soldier—a captain of militia in 1812. If I owe the British nation anything, I owe thanks to that particular British soldier who put a musket-ball into the fleshy part of Captain Nutter's leg, causing that noble warrior a slight permanent limp, but offsetting the injury by furnishing him with material for a story which the old gentleman was never weary of telling and I never weary of listening to. The story, in brief, was as follows—

At the breaking out of the war, an English frigate lay for several days off the coast near Rivermouth. A strong fort defended the harbor, and a regiment of minute-men, scattered at various points alongshore, stood ready to repel the boats, should the enemy try to effect a landing. Captain Nutter had charge of a slight earthwork just outside the mouth of the river. Late one thick night the sound of oars was heard; the sentinel tried to fire off his gun at half-cock, and could not, when Captain Nutter sprang upon the parapet in the pitch darkness, and shouted, "Boat ahoy!" A musket-shot immediately embedded itself in the calf of his leg. The Captain tumbled into the fort, and the boat, which had probably come in search of water, pulled back to the frigate.

This was my grandfather's only exploit during the war. That his prompt and bold conduct was instrumental in teaching the enemy the hopelessness of attempting to conquer such a people was among the firm beliefs of my boyhood.

At the time I came to Rivermouth my grandfather had retired from active pursuits, and was living at ease on his money, invested principally in shipping. He had been a widower many years; a maiden sister, the aforesaid Miss Abigail, managing his household. Miss Abigail also managed her brother, and her brother's servant, and the visitor at her brother's gate—not in a tyrannical spirit, but from a philanthropic desire to be useful to everybody. In person she was tall and angular; she had a gray complexion, gray eyes, gray eyebrows, and generally wore a gray dress. Her strongest weak point was a belief in the efficacy of "hot-drops" as a cure for all known diseases.

If there were ever two persons who seemed to dislike each other, Miss Abigail and Kitty Collins were those persons. If ever two persons really loved each other, Miss Abigail and Kitty Collins were those persons also. They were always either skirmishing or having a cup of tea lovingly together.

Miss Abigail was very fond of me, and so was Kitty; and in the course of their disagreements each let me into the private history of the other.

According to Kitty, it was not originally my grandfather's intention to have Miss Abigail at the head of his domestic establishment. She had swooped down on him (Kitty's own words), with a band-box in one hand and a faded blue cotton umbrella, still in existence, in the other. Clad in this singular garb—I do not remember that Kitty alluded to any additional peculiarity of dress—Miss Abigail had made her appearance at the door of the Nutter House on the morning of my grandmother's funeral. The small amount of baggage which the lady brought with her would have led the superficial observer to infer that Miss Abigail's visit was limited to a few days. I run ahead of my story in saying she remained seventeen years! How much longer she would have remained can never be definitely known now, as she died at the expiration of that period.

Whether or not my grandfather was quite pleased by this unlooked-for addition to his family is a problem. He was very kind always to Miss Abigail, and seldom opposed her; though I think she must have tried his patience sometimes, especially when she interfered with Kitty.

Kitty Collins, or Mrs. Catherine, as she preferred to be called, was descended in a direct line from an extensive family of kings who formerly ruled over Ireland. In consequence of various calamities, among which the failure of the potato-crop may be mentioned, Miss Kitty Collins, in company with several hundred of her countrymen and countrywomen— also descended from kings—came over to America in an emigrant ship, in the year eighteen hundred and something.

I do not know what freak of fortune caused the royal exile to turn up
at Rivermouth; but turn up she did, a few months after arriving in this
country, and was hired by my grandmother to do "general housework"
for the modest sum of four shillings and sixpence a week.

Kitty had been living about seven years in my grandfather's family
when she unburdened her heart of a secret which had been weighing
upon it all that time. It may be said of persons, as it is said of nations,
"Happy are they that have no history." Kitty had a history, and a pathetic
one, I think.

On board the emigrant ship that brought her to America, she became
acquainted with a sailor, who, being touched by Kitty's forlorn condition,
was very good to her. Long before the end of the voyage, which had been
tedious and perilous, she was heart-broken at the thought of separating
from her kindly protector; but they were not to part just yet, for the
sailor returned Kitty's affection, and the two were married on their
arrival at port. Kitty's husband—she would never mention his name, but
kept it locked in her bosom like some precious relic—had a considerable
sum of money when the crew were paid off; and the young couple—for
Kitty was young then—lived very happily in a lodging-house on South
Street, near the docks. This was in New York.

The days flew by like hours, and the stocking in which the little bride
kept the funds shrunk and shrunk, until at last there were only three or
four dollars left in the toe of it. Then Kitty was troubled; for she knew
her sailor would have to go to sea again unless he could get employment
on shore. This he endeavored to do, but not with much success. One
morning as usual he kissed her good-day, and set out in search of work

"Kissed me good-by, and called me his little Irish lass," sobbed Kitty,
telling the story—"kissed me good-by, and, Heaven help me! I niver set oi
on him nor on the likes of him again."

He never came back. Day after day dragged on, night after night, and
then the weary weeks. What had become of him? Had he been murdered?
had he fallen into the docks? had he—*deserted her?* No! she could not
believe that; he was too brave and tender and true. She could not believe
that. He was dead, dead, or he would come back to her.

Meanwhile the landlord of the lodging-house turned Kitty into the
streets, now that "her man" was gone, and the payment of the rent doubtful. She got a place as a servant. The family she lived with shortly moved
to Boston, and she accompanied them; then they went abroad, but Kitty
would not leave America. Somehow she drifted to Rivermouth, and for
seven long years never gave speech to her sorrow, until the kindness of
strangers, who had become friends to her, unsealed the heroic lips.

Kitty's story, you may be sure, made my grandparents treat her more
kindly than ever. In time she grew to be regarded less as a servant than as
a friend in the home circle, sharing its joys and sorrows—a faithful nurse,

a willing slave, a happy spirit in spite of all. I fancy I hear her singing over her work in the kitchen, pausing from time to time to make some witty reply to Miss Abigail—for Kitty, like all her race, had a vein of unconscious humor. Her bright honest face comes to me out from the past, the light and life of the Nutter House when I was a boy at Rivermouth.

AMONG THE ISLES OF SHOALS

CELIA THAXTER

Celia Thaxter (1835–1894) lived almost her entire life on the Isles of Shoals off the Maine coast, where she had grown up as a child of the lighthouse keeper on White Island. The islands were later to become a resort for artists and writers, among them Childe Hassam (who illustrated her books), Hawthorne, Thoreau, Lowell and Whittier. Every New England child used to be able to repeat, at the very least, Mrs. Thaxter's poem, "Across the narrow beach we flit, One little sandpiper and I . . ."

As a prose writer, her qualities of keen observation and acute feeling wear well. The following is an excerpt from her Among the Isles of Shoals.

IN the long, covered walk that bridged the gorge between the lighthouse and the house, we played in stormy days; and every evening it was a fresh excitement to watch the lighting of the lamps, and think how far the lighthouse sent its rays, and how many hearts it gladdened with assurance of safety. As I grew older I was allowed to kindle the lamps sometimes myself. That was indeed a pleasure. So little a creature as I might do that much for the great world! But by the fireside our best pleasure lay,—with plants and singing birds and books and playthings and loving care and kindness the cold and stormy season wore itself at last away, and died into the summer calm. We hardly saw a human face beside our own all winter; but with the spring came manifold life to our lonely dwelling,—human life among other forms. Our neighbors from Star rowed across; the pilot-boat from Portsmouth steered over, and brought us letters, newspapers, magazines, and told us the news of months. The faint echoes from the far-off world hardly touched us little ones. We listened to the talk of our elders. "Winfield Scott and Santa Anna!" "The war in Mexico!" "The famine in Ireland!" It all meant nothing to us. We heard the reading aloud of details of the famine, and saw tears in the eyes of the reader, and were vaguely sorry; but the fate of Red Riding-Hood was much more near and dreadful to us. We waited for the spring with an eager longing; the advent of the growing grass, the birds and flowers and insect life, the soft skies and softer winds, the everlasting beauty of the thousand tender tints that clothed the world,—these things brought us unspeakable bliss. To the heart of Nature one must needs be drawn in such a life; and very soon I learned how richly she repays in deep re-freshment the reverent love of her worshipper. With the first warm days we built our little mountains of wet gravel on the beach, and danced after the sandpipers at the edge of the foam, shouted to the gossiping kittiwakes that fluttered above, or watched the pranks of the burgomaster gull, or cried to the crying loons. The gannet's long, white wings stretched overhead, perhaps, or the dusky shag made a sudden shadow in mid-air, or we startled on some lonely ledge the great blue heron that flew off, trailing legs and wings, stork-like, against the clouds. Or, in the sunshine on the bare rocks, we cut from the broad, brown leaves of the slippery, varnished kelps, grotesque shapes of man and bird and beast that with-ered in the wind and blew away; or we fashioned rude boats from bits of driftwood, manned them with a weird crew of kelpies, and set them adrift on the great deep, to float we cared not whither. . . .

Often, in pleasant days, the head of the family sailed away to visit the other islands, sometimes taking the children with him, oftener going alone, frequently not returning till after dark. The landing at White Is-land is so dangerous that the greatest care is requisite, if there is any sea running, to get ashore in safety. Two long and very solid timbers about three feet apart are laid from the boat-house to low-water mark, and between those timbers the boat's bow must be accurately steered; if she goes to the right or the left, woe to her crew unless the sea is calm! Safely lodged in the slip, as it is called, she is drawn up into the boat-house by a capstan, and fastened securely. The lighthouse gave no ray to the dark rock below it; sending its beams far out to sea, it left us at its foot in greater darkness for its lofty light. So when the boat was out late, in soft, moonless summer nights, I used to light a lantern, and, go-ing down to the water's edge, take my station between the timbers of the slip, and, with the lantern at my feet, sit waiting in the darkness, quite content, knowing my little star was watched for, and that the safety of the boat depended in a great measure upon it. How sweet the summer wind blew, how softly plashed the water round me, how refreshing was the odor of the sparkling brine! High above, the lighthouse rays streamed out into the humid dark, and the cottage windows were ruddy from the glow within. I felt so much a part of the Lord's universe, I was no more afraid of the dark than the waves or winds; but I was glad to hear at last the creaking of the mast and the rattling of the row-locks as the boat approached; and, while yet she was far off, the lighthouse touched her one large sail into sight, so that I knew she was nearing me, and shouted, listening for the reply that came so blithely back to me over the water.

Unafraid, too, we watched the summer tempests, and listened to the deep, melodious thunder rolling away over the rain-calmed ocean. The lightning played over the iron rods that ran from the lighthouse-top down into the sea. Where it lay on the sharp ridgepole of the long, covered walk that spanned the gorge, the strange fire ran up the spikes that were set at equal distances, and burnt like pale flame from their tips. It was fine indeed from the lighthouse itself to watch the storm come rushing over the sea and ingulf us in our helplessness. How the rain weltered down over the great panes of plate glass,—floods of sweet, fresh water that poured off the rocks and mingled with the bitter brine. I wondered why the fresh floods never made the salt sea any sweeter. Those pale flames that we beheld burning from the spikes of the lightning-rod, I suppose were identical with the St. Elmo's fire that I have since seen described as haunting the spars of ships in thunder-storms. And here I am reminded of a story told by some gentlemen visiting Appledore sixteen or eighteen years ago. They started from Portsmouth for the Shoals in a whaleboat, one evening in summer, with a native Star-Islander, Richard Randall by name, to manage the boat. They had sailed about half the distance, when they were surprised at seeing a large ball of fire, like a rising moon, rolling toward them over the sea from the south. They watched it eagerly as it bore down upon them, and, veering off, went east of them at some little distance, and then passed astern, and there, of course, they expected to lose sight of it; but while they were marvelling and speculating, it altered its course, and suddenly began to near them, coming back upon its track against the wind and steadily following in their wake. This was too much for the native Shoaler. He took off his jacket and turned it inside out to exorcise the fiend, and lo, the apparition most certainly disappeared! We heard the excited account of the strange gentlemen and witnessed the holy horror of the boatman on the occasion; but no one could imagine what had set the globe of fire rolling across the sea. Some one suggested that it might be an exhalation, a phosphorescent light, from the decaying body of some dead fish; but in that case it must have been taken in tow by some living finny creature, else how could it have sailed straight "into the teeth of the wind"? It was never satisfactorily accounted for, and must remain a mystery.

One autumn at White Island our little boat had been to Portsmouth for provisions, etc. With the spy-glass we watched her returning, beating against the head wind. The day was bright, but there had been a storm at sea, and the breakers rolled and roared about us. The process of "beating" is so tedious that, though the boat had started in the morning, the sun was sending long yellow light from the west before it reached the island. There was no cessation in those resistless billows that rolled

from the Devil's Rock upon the slip; but still the little craft sailed on,
striving to reach the landing. The hand at the tiller was firm, but a huge
wave swept suddenly in, swerving the boat to the left of the slip, and in
a moment she was overturned and flung upon the rocks, and her only
occupant tossed high upon the beach, safe except for a few bruises; but
what a moment of terror it was for us all, who saw and could not save! All
the freight was lost except a roll of iron wire and a barrel of walnuts.
These were spread on the floor of an unoccupied eastern chamber in the
cottage to dry. And they did dry; but before they were gathered up came
a terrible storm from the southeast. It raved and tore at lighthouse and
cottage; the sea broke into the windows of that eastern chamber where
the walnuts lay, and washed them out till they came dancing down the
stairs in briny foam! The sea broke the windows of the house several
times during our stay at the lighthouse. Everything shook so violently
from the concussion of the breakers, that dishes on the closet shelves fell
to the floor, and one member of the family was at first always made sea-
sick in storms, by the tremor and deafening confusion. One night when,
from the southeast, the very soul of chaos seemed to have been let loose
upon the world, the whole ponderous "walk" (the covered bridge that
connected the house and lighthouse) was carried thundering down the
gorge and dragged out into the raging sea.

It was a distressing situation for us,—cut off from the precious light
that must be kept alive; for the breakers were tearing through the gorge so
that no living thing could climb across. But the tide could not resist the
mighty impulse that drew it down; it was forced to obey the still voice
that bade it ebb; all swollen and raging and towering as it was, slowly
and surely, at the appointed time, it sank away from our rock, so that,
between the billows that still strove to clutch at the white, silent, golden-
crowned tower, one could creep across, and scale the height, and wind up
the machinery that kept the great clustered light revolving till the gray
daylight broke to extinguish it.

I often wondered how it was possible for the sea-birds to live through
such storms as these. But, when one could see at all, the gulls were always
soaring, in the wildest tumult, and the stormy petrels half flying, half
swimming in the hollows of the waves.

Would it were possible to describe the beauty of the calm that followed
such tempests! The long lines of silver foam that streaked the tranquil
blue, the "tender-curving lines of creamy spray" along the shore, the clear-
washed sky, the peaceful yellow light, the mellow breakers murmuring
slumberously!

Of all the storms our childish eyes watched with delighted awe, one
thunder-storm remains fixed in my memory. Late in an August afternoon
it rolled its awful clouds to the zenith, and, after the tumult had subsided,
spread its lightened vapors in an under-roof of gray over all the sky.

Presently this solemn gray lid was lifted at its western edge, and an insufferable splendor streamed across the world from the sinking sun. The whole heaven was in a blaze of scarlet, across which sprang a rainbow unbroken to the topmost clouds, "with its seven perfect colors chorded in a triumph" against the flaming background; the sea answered the sky's rich blush, and the gray rocks lay drowned in melancholy purple. I hid my face from the glory,—it was too much to bear. Ever I longed to *speak* these things that made life so sweet, to speak the wind, the cloud, the bird's flight, the sea's murmur. A vain longing! I might as well have sighed for the mighty pencil of Michael Angelo to wield in my impotent child's hand. Better to "hush and bless one's self with silence"; but ever the wish grew. Facing the July sunsets, deep red and golden through and through, or watching the summer northern lights,—battalions of brilliant streamers advancing and retreating, shooting upward to the zenith, and glowing like fiery veils before the stars; or when the fog-bow spanned the silver mist of morning, or the earth and sea lay shimmering in a golden haze of noon; in storm or calm, by day or night, the manifold aspects of Nature held me and swayed all my thoughts until it was impossible to be silent any longer, and I was fain to mingle my voice with her myriad voices, only aspiring to be in accord with the Infinite harmony, however feeble and broken the notes might be.

PERSONS AND PLACES

GEORGE SANTAYANA

———◆•◆———

George Santayana (1863–1952), born in Spain, was primarily a philosopher and writer of the present century, but I have placed the following excerpt from his Persons and Places *here because of the picture it gives of two famous Boston schools, Brimmer and Boston Latin, at the time when Santayana was attending them.*

THE Brimmer School, where I went during the next winter, 1873–1874, was the public grammar school of our city district, although more than a mile from our house, in the depths of the South End. I had to walk the whole level length of Beacon Street, cross the Common, and go some distance downhill in Tremont Street to Common Street, where the school was situated, looking like a police station. It was a poor boys' free school, the roughest I was ever in, where the rattan played an important part, although usually behind the scenes, and where there was an atmosphere of rowdiness and ill-will, requiring all sorts of minor punishments, such as standing in the corner or being detained after school. I don't know what lessons we had, except that there were oral spelling-matches, in which naturally I didn't shine. A word spelt aloud (as some Americans like to do facetiously, instead of pronouncing it) still puzzles me and leaves me dumb. Nevertheless, partly because I was older and bigger than most of the boys, I soon became "monitor," and had my little desk beside the teacher's, a woman, facing the whole class. This distinction was invidious, and there were attempts at chasing me or hooting at me when we got out of school. Only once did it come to blows; and inexpert as I was at fisticuffs, or rather wrestling, I was taller, and managed to hold my own, and make my nasty little enemy sneak away sullenly. And I was not friendless. There was another boy from the West End, Bob Upham by name, with whom I usually crossed the Common; this was the danger-zone, since in the streets there were policemen who understood these things and would stop hostilities. On that occasion Bob Upham behaved according to the strictest rules of honor, standing by me sympathetically, but without interfering, and he afterwards said that the other boy had "Very nearly got me." But I hadn't been at all hurt, and never have had another opportunity to try my hand at the manly art, in which no doubt I should have been a miserable failure.

By a happy chance it was possible to transfer me the next year to a much better school, the historic Latin School, where from the earliest times until my day at least, all well-educated Bostonians had been prepared for College. The School Committee in the City government had that year decided to try an experiment, and establish a preparatory course of two years, to precede the six traditional classes. The experiment was not long continued, but I profited by it, and passed eight full years in the Latin School, thus being more of a Latin School boy than almost anybody else. We were not lodged during those preliminary years in the regular Schoolhouse, but at first in Harrison Avenue, and later in Mason Street. Both these places, as well as the Schoolhouse in Bedford Street, were in a central quarter of the town. I still had to cross the Common, but now to West Street, whence it was but a step to those school-houses....

Certain detached images, with the crude spectral coloring of a child's picture-book, remain from this first somnambulist season. At the school in Harrison Avenue I can see the yellow wainscoting of the schoolroom, and the yellow desks; and especially I can see the converging leaden sides of the sink, where on one winter morning the teacher—now a man—sent me to thaw out my ears, frozen stiff on the way to school. I was to bathe them in cold water; there was sharp pain and subsequently enormous blisters; but the accident never recurred, although I resolutely refused all scarves, pads, or ridiculous cloth rosettes, such as the women recommended to protect those asinine organs. I found that a little pressure, applied at the right moment, at once brought the warm blood coursing back, and prevented trouble. Cold, rain, and wind, unless there were dust, never spoilt my pleasure in the open air when I was young; on the contrary, I liked them.

I remember also my first Headmaster at the Latin School, Mr. Gardner by name: a tall, gaunt figure in some sort of flowing long coat—of course not a gown—with a diminutive head like the knob of a mannikin. The insignificant occiput was enlarged, however, as if by a halo, by a great crop of dusty brown hair. Was it a wig? That suspicion seemed to my mocking young mind curiously comic and exciting. What if it were a wig and should fall off? What if we hung a hook on an invisible wire over the door, to catch it as he sailed out? One day on his rounds of inspection the Headmaster found us having our French lesson. A headmaster has to pretend to know everything, and the pretense soon becomes a conviction. Mr. Gardner at once took over the duty of teaching us his super-French. "The French word *bonne*," he said, "is pronounced in Paris—I have been in Paris myself—exactly as the English word *bun*." Now, I had heard a good deal of French out of school. There had been the French *bonne* Justine, the Alsatian tutor who loved *avec rage*, and the Catholic families in Boston who chatted in French together. . . . If *bonne* sounds exactly like bun, would Mr. Gardner maintain that *couronne*, save for that first letter, sounds exactly like *you run*? I was sure that it was as ridiculous to call a *bonne* a bun as to call a bun a *bonne*. But apparently headmasters were like that; and I kept my phonetic science to myself with the immense satisfaction of feeling that I knew better than my teacher.

I may add that at that time our French master was not a Frenchman, but a Yankee farmer named Mr. Capen, whom we called Old Cudjo, and who had a physiological method of acquiring a Parisian accent without needing to accompany the Headmaster to Paris. He would open his mouth wide, like the hippopotamus at the Zoo, and would insert a pencil, to point out exactly what parts of the tongue, lips, palate or larynx we should contract or relax in order to emit the pure French sounds of *u, an, en, in, un,* and *on.* Nobody laughed. I think the boys were rather impressed for the moment by the depth of Mr. Capen's science, and the hopelessness of profiting by it. He was not a man to be trifled with. He had a most thunderous way of playing what he called Voluntaries on the piano; and rumor had it that he had stolen a march, under a heavy handicap of years, on his own son, by marrying the girl his son was engaged to.

Scraps of rude, quaint, grotesque humanity: bits of that Dickensian bohemia still surviving in my day in certain old-fashioned places, of which I shall have occasion to speak again. But the image that for me sets the key to them all appeared when we moved to the Bedford Street school-house. It seemed a vast, rattling old shell of a building, bare, shabby, and forlorn to the point of squalor; not exactly dirty, but worn, shaky, and stained deeply in every part by time, weather, and merciless usage. The dingy red brick—and everything in that world was dingy red brick—had none of that plastic irregularity, those soft pink lights and mossy patina that make some old brick walls so beautiful: here all the surfaces re-mained stark and unyielding, thin and sharp, like impoverished old maids. This house was too modern to be as solid as the Hollis and Stoughton Halls that I afterwards lived in at Harvard; it had been built in a hurry, and not to last long. The windows were much larger, but blank and somber; their cold, glassy expanse with its slender divisions looked comfortless and insecure. When up three or four worn granite steps you entered the door, the interior seemed musty and ill-lighted, but spacious, even mysterious. Each room had four great windows, but the street and the courts at the side and rear were narrow, and overshadowed by ware-houses or office-buildings. No blackboard was black; all were indelibly clouded with ingrained layers of old chalk; the more you rubbed it out, the more you rubbed it in. Every desk was stained with generations of ink-spots, cut deeply with initials and scratched drawings. What idle thoughts had been wandering for years through all those empty heads in all those tedious school hours! In the best schools, almost all schooltime is wasted. Now and then something is learned that sticks fast; for the rest the boys are merely given time to grow and are kept from too much mischief.

A ramshackle wooden staircase wound up through the heart of the building to the fourth story, where the Hall was; and down those steep and dangerous curves the avalanche of nail-hoofed boys would come thundering, forty or eighty or two hundred together. However short their legs might be, it was simpler and safer, if not altogether inevitable, to rush down spontaneously with the herd rather than to hold back and be pushed or fall out, or be tramped upon or deserted.

And the teachers, though it is not possible for me now to distinguish them all in memory, were surely not out of keeping with their surround-ings: disappointed, shabby-genteel, picturesque old Yankees, with a little bitter humor breaking through their constitutional fatigue. I daresay that for them as for me, and for all the boys who were at all sensitive, the school was a familiar symbol of fatality. They hadn't chosen it, they hadn't wanted it, they didn't particularly like it; they knew no reason why it should be the sort of school it was: but there it stood, there they somehow found themselves entangled; and there was nothing else practicable but to go on there, doing what was expected and imposed upon them. . . .

Those teachers were stray individuals; they had not yet been standard-ized by educational departments and pedagogy. Some were like village schoolmasters or drudges; elderly men, like Mr. Capen, with crotchets, but good teachers, knowing their particular book and knowing how to keep order, and neither lax nor cruel. Others, especially Mr. Fiske, afterwards headmaster, and Mr. Groce, were younger, with a more modern education. They might have been college professors; they loved their subjects, Greek and English, and allowed them to color their minds out of school hours. In a word, they were *cultivated* men. I was an unprofitable though not unappreciative pupil to Mr. Fiske, because I didn't learn my Greek properly. That was not his fault. If I could have had him for a private tutor I should have become a good Grecian: it would have added immensely to my life and to my philosophy. But I was only one of forty; I was expected to study dryly, mechanically, without the side-lights and the stimulus of non-verbal interest attached to the words. In Latin, I could supply these side-lights and non-verbal interests out of my own store. Latin was the language of the Church, it was old Spanish. The roots were all my roots. But Greek roots were more often foreign and at first unmeaning; they had to be learned by hammering, to which my indolence was not inclined....

Even as it was, however, I learned a little Greek at school after my fashion, and one day surprised Mr. Fiske by reciting a long speech out of *Œdipus Tyrannus* for my ordinary declamation. He couldn't believe his ears, and afterwards privately congratulated me on my pronunciation of the *o*'s. But that didn't make me master of the Greek vocabulary or the Greek inflections. I didn't *study* enough. I learned and remembered well what I could learn from Mr. Fiske without studying. He was an exceedingly nervous, shy man; evidently suffered at having to address any one, or having to find words in which to express his feelings. His whole body would become tense, he would stand almost on tiptoe, with two or three fingers in the side pocket of his trousers, and the other two or three moving outside, as if reaching for the next word. These extreme mannerisms occasioned no ridicule: the boys all saw that there was a clear mind and a goodwill behind them; and Mr. Fiske was universally liked and admired. This, although his language was as contorted as his gestures. He always seemed to be translating literally and laboriously from the Greek or the German. When he wished to fix in our minds the meaning of a Greek word he would say, for instance: "χἄράδρα, a ravine, from which our word *character*, the deeply graven result of long-continued habit." Or "χἄταρρέω, to flow down, whence our word *catarrh*, copious down-flowings from the upper regions of the head." We didn't laugh, and we remembered.

Very different was dapper Mr. Groce, our teacher of English composition and literature, a little plump man, with a keen, dry, cheerful, yet irritable disposition, a sparkling bird-like eye, and a little black mustache and diminutive chin-beard. I suspect that he was too intelligent to put up patiently with all the conventions. Had he not been a public-school

teacher, dependent on the democratic hypocrisies of a government committee, he might have said unconventional things. This inner rebellion
kept him from being sentimental, moralistic, or religious in respect to
poetry; yet he *understood* perfectly the penumbra of emotion that good
and bad poetry alike may drag after them in an untrained mind. He knew
how to rescue the structural and rational beauties of a poem from that
bog of private feeling. To me this was a timely lesson, for it was precisely
sadness and religiosity and grandiloquence that first attracted me in
poetry; and perhaps I owe to Mr. Groce the beginnings of a capacity to
distinguish the musical and expressive charm of poetry from its moral
appeal. At any rate, at sixteen, I composed my first longish poem, in
Spenser's measure, after *Childe Harold* and *Adonais,* full of pessimistic,
languid, Byronic sentiments, describing the various kinds of superiority
that Night has over Day. It got the prize. . . .

That prize-day in June, 1880, in the old Boston Music Hall, marked my
emergence into public notice. It abolished, or seemed to abolish, my shy-
ness and love of solitude. I could now face any public and speak before
it; and this assurance never forsook me afterwards, except when sometimes, in my unwritten lectures or speeches, I found myself out of my
element, had nothing to say, or was weary of saying it. . . .

My lachrymose prize poem about the beauties of darkness was not my
only effusion. The habit of scribbling mocking epigrams has accompanied
me through life and invaded the margins of my most serious authors.
Mockery is the first puerile form of wit, playing with surfaces without
sympathy: I abounded in it. During the winter of 1880–1881 our class,
then the second class, formed a society to meet once a week in the evening and have a debate. We hired a bare room in Tremont Street, opposite the Common, with a few benches or chairs in it; some one would
propose a resolution or advance an opinion, and the discussion would
follow. When my turn came, I read a little satire on all our teachers, in
verse, saying very much what I have said about them above; only that my
account was more complete, included them all, and treated them less
kindly. It had a great success, and the boys wanted to have it printed.
Printed it was, but not as it originally stood. "Holy Moses," for instance,
which was the nickname current for our headmaster, Moses Merrill, was
changed to the less irreverent and more exact phrase: "lordly Moses,"
and many other things were modified. Then the whole was enveloped in a
tirade, of a sentimental sort, about the Bedford Street Schoolhouse, which
was about to be abandoned for a new building in the South End. A lot
of copies were printed, perhaps two or three hundred; and on the day of
our Farewell Public Declamation in the Hall, the Headmaster somehow
got wind of its existence, and said, "We hear that one of the boys has
written a poem about leaving this old Schoolhouse: will he get up and
read it." I had a copy in my pocket: I got up, and read the longish senti-

mental part and then sat down again, leaving out the personalities. For the moment all was well; but other boys and some outsiders got copies; and the disrespectful gibes at the teachers became public under their noses.

It was a day or two before Christmas, and the School was not to meet again for ten days or more: however, after consulting with the family at home, I went to see the Headmaster at his own house, and explained how everything had happened. He wasn't severe; I had been really very complimentary to him, and had come spontaneously to apologize. But he said I had better write to the various teachers, explaining that I had only intended the thing as a private joke, without any thought that it would become public; and that I must particularly apologize to Mr. Chadwick, whom I had spoken of unkindly, and who felt the blow. When School met again, Mr. Merrill made us a long speech; but nothing more happened, and official sentiment towards me was not unfavorably affected. This appeared at the opening of the next term. My class had to elect the Lieutenant Colonel of the Boston School Regiment, the Colonel that year coming from the English High School; and by a majority of one vote they elected Dick Smith, and then me unanimously for Major of our Battalion. But the Headmaster reversed the order, and appointed me Lieutenant Colonel and Dick Smith Major, without giving reasons, at which legal but arbitrary exhibition of favoritism on the Headmaster's part Dick Smith's father took him out of the School; and I became both Lieutenant Colonel and Major, both offices being almost sinecures.

TALKS ON ART

WILLIAM MORRIS HUNT

———◆◆◆———

Boston painters at one time constituted an important school in this country. One of the most brilliant, both as painter and critic, was William Morris Hunt, born in Vermont (1824–1879). His iconoclastic Talks on Art, *full of gibes at Boston, stirred the art world of New England, and still offers excellent counsel to those who seek art as above the arty. An excerpt follows.*

WITH BRUSH IN HAND

WHY draw more than you see? We must sacrifice in drawing as in everything else.

You thought it needed more work. It needs less. You don't get mystery because you are too conscientious! When a bird flies through the air you see no feathers! Your eye would require more than one focus: one for the bird, another for the feathers. You are to draw not reality, but the appearance of reality!

In your sketches keep the first vivid impression! Add no details that shall weaken it! Look first for the big things!
1st. Proportions!
2d. Values—or masses of light and shade.
3d. Details that will not spoil the beginnings!

You can always draw as well as you know how to. I flatter myself that I know and feel more than I express on canvas; but I know that it is not so.

This doing things to suit people! They'll hate you, and you won't suit them. Most of us live for the critic, and he lives on us. He don't sacrifice himself. He gets so much a line for writing a criticism. If the birds should read the newspapers they would all take to changing their notes. The parrots would exchange with the nightingales, and what a farce it would be!

Work as long as you know what to do. Not an instant longer!

Be carefully careless!
Avoid certain petty, trivial details which people call "finish." They are of the nature of things with which one would confuse a child, deceive a fly, or amuse an idiot!

The struggle of one color with another produces color.

I tell you it's no joke to paint a portrait! I wonder that I am not more timid when I begin! I feel almost certain that I can do it. It seems very simple. I don't think of the time that is sure to come, when I almost despair; when the whole thing seems hopeless. Into the painting of every picture that is worth anything, there comes, sometime, this period of despair!

I have disliked pictures so much that I afterwards found were good, that I want to hint to you that you may, some day, want an outlet from the opinions you now hold.

The fact is, we must take, in the works of these men, what you call
faults, and ask ourselves if they were not perhaps *qualities.*

What a time has been made over Michael Angelo's "Moses," with his
horns! Michael Angelo felt that *Moses must have horns!* To represent him
he must have something more than a man with a full beard, and you must
accept these horns just as you would a word which some poet had felt
the need of, and had coined. As Michael Angelo was the greatest creator
that ever worked in art, hadn't we better decide that we'll wait fifteen
minutes before passing judgment upon him, or upon what he did?

The painter knows what is necessary in literature better than the *lit-
térateur* knows what is needful in painting. Shakespeare could not paint
with brushes as well as I can write a poem. A painter is necessarily a poet;
but a poet is not a painter. Emerson can describe a forest in words better
than I can; but I can make one in paint better than he. If he is a full man
he will understand both; and if I am a full man I can understand his
description as well as my own.

That's where Cambridge is short! Such knowledge counts for nothing.
They forget the song that painting has sung, and listen only to Homer.
A Greek professor who doesn't know what Greek Art is, isn't a Greek
scholar. I don't know just what Greek was a ruler during a certain period,
but I have some literary science and *ensemble.* Ignorant as I am, I know
more about Homer than a Greek professor can know about Pheidias. He
might tell me when he was born. Well, a rat was born about that time.

Emerson says, "It is better to write a poor poem than a good criticism."
True. And I had rather paint a poor picture than write a good criticism.
It is the critics that make us so timid. You don't quite dare to paint as you
see and feel. You can't get rid of the thought of what people will say of
your work. That's why you struggle so hard for form. But you must not
work for that alone. That is what the academies, the world over, are
striving for; and when they get it, what is it worth?

Don't mind what your friends say of your work. In the first place, they
all think you're an idiot; in the next place, they expect great things of
you; in the third place, they wouldn't know if you did a good thing. Until
we come to study Art, we are not aware of the ignorance there is about
it. Artists have to create their audiences. They have to do their own work
and educate the public at the same time. Nobody cared for Corot's pictures at first. He had to teach people how to like them. The same with
Raphael. His pictures were not understood; but he went on painting,
and in time he was appreciated.

I like painting on panel for a change from canvas, and on rough canvas
for a change from smooth. Anything to keep you from a "way" of doing

things. After you have been painting for fun for a while, it's good to do some hard digging. And the reverse is true as well.

Why are you doing that?
"You told me to, the other day."
Well, I didn't tell you to do so forever.

If you are determined to paint, you won't mind what kind of things you use to paint with. I remember when I sketched that ploughing-scene I had only a butter-box for a palette, a brush or two, and a palette-knife. For rubbing in a velvet coat, sometimes nothing works better than the palm of your hand.

Get your mind off of your work for a minute, and then go at it like a cataract.

Perfect simplicity of expression! In this country only martyrs attain to it. Abraham Lincoln had it. John Brown had it. I saw the latter refuse oysters once at a party, because "he was not hungry." I said to a friend,— and Brown was not celebrated then, not having been hanged!—"There's something remarkable about that man! Did you ever know a man to refuse oysters at a party because he was not hungry?" He did not take champagne, because he was "not thirsty." Held the glass as you would hold a doll for a baby. Was not going to gorge himself,—a man with such a destiny and such a work before him!

Here is a photograph of my "Bather," which you may call Youth, or Summer, going forth, seeming to walk miraculously on the surface of the water, but supported by a power which has reached firm footing; balancing himself gracefully, it may be a long, long time, but never getting anywhere until he has made his dive into the Unknown.
I was thinking of this subject of Eternity the other night, when I looked at the moon, and saw, before it, a church-spire, a finger pointing upward into space. Next the spire, the moon. Beyond the moon, a fixed star. Next—what? Eternity.

A ripple closes over us.

AN INTERNATIONAL EPISODE

HENRY JAMES

———◆◆◆———

In the latter half of the nineteenth century, Newport was not only a fashionable watering place but rivaled Boston and Concord as a center for writers and painters. Hazards (with whom Rhode Island waters so abound), La Farges, Howes, Holmeses, Jameses, were among the literary and artistic people identified with the resort not only in the summer but, some of them, all year round.

Henry James, the novelist (1843–1919), lived in Newport for some years as a young man, and in The American Scene, *a travel book, has an essay "On Newport." I have chosen for inclusion here, however, an excerpt from his novelette* An International Episode, *partly because of the picture it gives of one of the steamers which used to ply the waters of the various resorts—Bar Harbor, Dark Harbor, the islands in Casco Bay. They were by no means all so gorgeous as the Newport boat James describes, but they had infinite charm and gaiety as—painted white, flags flying, little orchestra playing on deck, passengers strolling about—their whistles blew and they came up to some sunny dock where the hostesses in their shady hats had come down to meet guests at the boat.*

It was indeed, as Mr. Westgate had said, a big boat, and his leadership in the innumerable and interminable corridors and cabins, with which he seemed perfectly acquainted, and of which any one and every one appeared to have the entrée, was very grateful to the slightly bewildered voyagers. He showed them their state-room—a spacious apartment, embellished with gas-lamps, mirrors *en pied,* and sculptured furniture— and then, long after they had been intimately convinced that the steamer was in motion and launched upon the unknown stream that they were about to navigate, he bade them a sociable farewell.

"Well, good-bye, Lord Lambeth," he said; "good-bye, Mr. Percy Beaumont. I hope you'll have a good time. Just let them do what they want with you. I'll come down by-and-by and look after you."

The young Englishmen emerged from their cabin and amused themselves with wandering about the immense labyrinthine steamer, which struck them as an extraordinary mixture of a ship and a hotel. It was

densely crowded with passengers, the larger number of whom appeared
to be ladies and very young children; and in the big saloons, ornamented
in white and gold, which followed each other in surprising succession, beneath the swinging gaslight, and among the small side passages where
the negro domestics of both sexes assembled with an air of philosophic
leisure, every one was moving to and fro and exchanging loud and familiar observations. Eventually, at the instance of a discriminating black,
our young men went and had some "supper" in a wonderful place arranged like a theatre, where, in a gilded gallery, upon which little boxes
appeared to open, a large orchestra was playing operatic selections, and,
below, people were handing about bills of fare, as if they had been pro-
grammes. All this was sufficiently curious; but the agreeable thing, later,
was to sit out on one of the great white decks of the steamer, in the warm,
breezy darkness, and, in the vague starlight, to make out the line of low,
mysterious coast. The young Englishmen tried American cigars—those of
Mr. Westgate—and talked together as they usually talked, with many odd
silences, lapses of logic, and incongruities of transition, like people who
have grown old together, and learned to supply each other's missing
phrases; or, more specially, like people thoroughly conscious of a common point of view, so that a style of conversation superficially lacking in
finish might suffice for reference to a fund of associations in the light of
which everything was all right.

"We really seem to be going out to sea," Percy Beaumont observed.
"Upon my word, we are going back to England. He has shipped us off
again. I call that 'real mean.'"

"I suppose it's all right," said Lord Lambeth. "I want to see those pretty
girls at Newport. You know he told us the place was an island; and aren't
all islands in the sea?"

"Well," resumed the elder traveller after a while, "if his house is as
good as his cigars, we shall do very well indeed."

"He seems a very good fellow," said Lord Lambeth, as if this idea just
occurred to him.

"I say, we had better remain at the inn," rejoined his companion,
presently. "I don't think I like the way he spoke of his house. I don't
like stopping in the house with such a tremendous lot of women."

"Oh, I don't mind," said Lord Lambeth. And then they smoked a while
in silence. "Fancy his thinking we do no work in England!" the young
man resumed.

"I dare say he didn't really think so," said Percy Beaumont.

"Well I guess they don't know much about England over here!" declared Lord Lambeth, humorously. And then there was another long
pause. "He was devilish civil," observed the young nobleman.

"Nothing, certainly, could have been more civil," rejoined his companion.

"Littledale said his wife was great fun," said Lord Lambeth.

"Whose wife—Littledale's?"

"This American's—Mrs. Westgate. What's his name? J. L."

Beaumont was silent a moment. "What was fun to Littledale," he said at last, rather sententiously, "may be death to us."

"What do you mean by that?" asked his kinsman. "I am as good a man as Littledale."

"My dear boy, I hope you won't begin to flirt," said Percy Beaumont.

"I don't care. I dare say I sha'n't begin."

"With a married woman, if she's bent upon it, it's all very well," Beaumont expounded. "But our friend mentioned a young lady—a sister, a sister-in-law. For God's sake, don't get entangled with her!"

"How do you mean entangled?"

"Depend upon it she will try to hook you."

"Oh, bother!" said Lord Lambeth.

"American girls are very clever," urged his companion.

"So much the better," the young man declared.

"I fancy they are always up to some game of that sort," Beaumont continued.

"They can't be worse than they are in England," said Lord Lambeth, judicially.

"Ah, but in England," replied Beaumont, "you have got your natural protectors. You have got your mother and sisters."

"My mother and sisters——" began the young nobleman, with a certain energy. But he stopped in time, puffing at his cigar.

"Your mother spoke to me about it, with tears in her eyes," said Percy Beaumont. "She said she felt very nervous. I promised to keep you out of mischief."

"You had better take care of yourself," said the object of maternal and ducal solicitude.

"Ah," rejoined the young barrister, "I haven't the expectation of a hundred thousand a year, not to mention other attractions."

"Well," said Lord Lambeth, "don't cry out before you're hurt!"

It was certainly very much cooler at Newport, where our travellers found themselves assigned to a couple of diminutive bedrooms in a far-away angle of an immense hotel. They had gone ashore in the early summer twilight, and had very promptly put themselves to bed; thanks to which circumstance, and to their having, during the previous hours in their commodious cabin slept the sleep of youth and health, they began to feel, towards eleven o'clock, very alert and inquisitive. They looked out of their windows across a row of small green fields, bordered with low stone walls of rude construction, and saw a deep blue ocean lying beneath a deep blue sky, and flecked now and then with scintillating patches of foam. A strong, fresh breeze came in through the curtainless casements, and prompted our young men to observe generally that it didn't seem half a bad climate. They made other observations after they had emerged from their rooms in pursuit of breakfast—a meal of which they partook in a huge bare hall, where a hundred negroes in white jackets were shuffling about upon an uncarpeted floor; where the flies were superabundant, and the tables and dishes covered over with a strange, voluminous integument of coarse blue gauze; and where several little boys and girls, who had risen late, were seated in fastidious solitude at the morning repast. These young persons had not the morning paper before them, but they were engaged in languid perusal of the bill of fare.

The latter document was a great puzzle to our friends, who, on reflecting that its bewildering categories had relation to breakfast alone, had an uneasy prevision of an encyclopædic dinner list. They found a great deal of entertainment at the hotel, an enormous wooden structure, for the erection of which it seemed to them that the virgin forests of the West must have been terribly deflowered. It was perforated from end to end with immense bare corridors, through which a strong draught was blowing—bearing along wonderful figures of ladies in white morning-dresses and clouds of valenciennes lace, who seemed to float down the long vistas with expanded furbelows like angels spreading their wings. In front was a gigantic veranda, upon which an army might have encamped—a vast wooden terrace, with a roof as lofty as the nave of a cathedral. Here our young Englishmen enjoyed, as they supposed, a glimpse of American society, which was distributed over the measureless expanse in a variety of sedentary attitudes, and appeared to consist largely of pretty young girls, dressed as if for a *fête champêtre*, swaying to and fro in rocking chairs, fanning themselves with large straw fans, and enjoying an enviable exemption from social cares. Lord Lambeth had a theory, which it might be interesting to trace to its origin, that it would be not only agreeable, but easily possible, to enter into relations with one of these young ladies; and his companion (as he had done a couple of days before) found occasion to check the young nobleman's colloquial impulses.

"You had better take care," said Percy Beaumont, "or you will have an offended father or brother pulling out a bowie-knife."

"I assure you it is all right," Lord Lambeth replied. "You know the Americans come to these big hotels to make acquaintances."

"I know nothing about it, and neither do you," said his kinsman, who, like a clever man, had begun to perceive that the observation of American society demanded a readjustment of one's standard.

"Hang it, then, let's find out!" cried Lord Lambeth, with some impatience. "You know I don't want to miss anything."

"We will find out," said Percy Beaumont, very reasonably. "We will go and see Mrs. Westgate, and make all the proper inquiries."

And so the two inquiring Englishmen, who had this lady's address inscribed in her husband's hand upon a card, descended from the veranda of the big hotel and took their way, according to direction, along a large, straight road, past a series of fresh-looking villas embosomed in shrubs and flowers, and enclosed in an ingenious variety of wooden palings. The morning was brilliant and cool, the villas were smart and snug, and the walk of the young travellers was very entertaining. Everything looked as if it had received a coat of fresh paint the day before—the red roofs, the green shutters, the clean, bright browns and buffs of the house fronts. The flower beds on the little lawns seemed to sparkle in the radiant air, and the gravel in the short carriage sweeps to flash and twinkle. Along the road came a hundred little basket-phaetons, in which, almost always, a couple of ladies were sitting—ladies in white dresses and long white gloves, holding the reins and looking at the two Englishmen—whose nationality was not elusive—through thick blue veils tied tightly about their faces, as if to guard their complexions. At last the young men came within sight of the sea again, and then, having interrogated a gardener over the paling of a villa, they turned into an open gate. Here they found themselves face to face with the ocean and with a very picturesque structure, resembling a magnified chalet, which was perched upon a green embankment just above it. The house had a veranda of extraordinary width all around it, and a great many doors and windows standing open to the veranda. These various apertures had, in common, such an accessible, hospitable air, such a breezy flutter within of light curtains, such expansive thresholds and reassuring interiors, that our friends hardly knew which was the regular entrance, and, after hesitating a moment, presented themselves at one of the windows. The room within was dark, but in a moment a graceful figure vaguely shaped itself in the rich-looking gloom, and a lady came to meet them. Then they saw that she had been seated at a table writing, and that she had heard them and had got up. She stepped out into the light; she wore a frank, charming smile, with which she held out her hand to Percy Beaumont.

"Oh, you must be Lord Lambeth and Mr. Beaumont," she said. "I have heard from my husband that you would come. I am extremely glad to see you." And she shook hands with each of her visitors. Her visitors were a little shy, but they had very good manners; they responded with smiles and exclamations, and they apologized for not knowing the front door. The lady rejoined, with vivacity, that when she wanted to see people very much she did not insist upon these distinctions, and that Mr. Westgate had written to her of his English friends in terms that made her really anxious. "He said you were so terribly prostrated," said Mrs. Westgate.

"Oh, you mean by the heat?" replied Percy Beaumont. "We were rather knocked up, but we feel wonderfully better. We had such a jolly—a—voyage down here. It's so very good of you to mind."

"Yes, it's so very kind of you," murmured Lord Lambeth.

Mrs. Westgate stood smiling; she was extremely pretty. "Well, I did mind," she said; "and I thought of sending for you this morning to the Ocean House. I am very glad you are better, and I am charmed you have arrived. You must come round to the other side of the piazza." And she led the way, with a light, smooth step, looking back at the young men and smiling.

The other side of the piazza was, as Lord Lambeth presently remarked, a very jolly place. It was of the most liberal proportions, and with its awnings, its fanciful chairs, its cushions and rugs, its view of the ocean, close at hand, tumbling along the base of the low cliffs whose level tops intervened in lawn-like smoothness, it formed a charming complement to the drawing-room. As such it was in course of use at the present moment; it was occupied by a social circle. There were several ladies and two or three gentlemen, to whom Mrs. Westgate proceeded to introduce the distinguished strangers. She mentioned a great many names very freely and distinctly; the young Englishmen, shuffling about and bowing, were rather bewildered. But at last they were provided with chairs—low, wicker chairs, gilded, and tied with a great many ribbons—and one of the ladies (a very young person, with a little snub-nose and several dimples) offered Percy Beaumont a fan. The fan was also adorned with pink love-knots; but Percy Beaumont declined it, although he was very hot. Presently, however, it became cooler; the breeze from the sea was delicious, the view was charming, and the people sitting there looked exceedingly fresh and comfortable. Several of the ladies seemed to be young girls, and the gentlemen were slim, fair youths, such as our friends had seen the day before in New York. The ladies were working upon bands of tapestry, and one of the young men had an open book in his lap. Beaumont afterwards learned from one of the ladies that this young man had been reading aloud; that he was from Boston, and was very fond of reading aloud. Beaumont said it was a great pity that they had interrupted him; he should like so much (from all he had heard) to hear a Bostonian read. Couldn't the young man be induced to go on?

"Oh no," said his informant, very freely; "he wouldn't be able to get the young ladies to attend to him now."

There was something very friendly, Beaumont perceived, in the attitude of the company; they looked at the young Englishmen with an air of animated sympathy and interest; they smiled, brightly and unanimously, at everything either of the visitors said. Lord Lambeth and his companion felt that they were being made very welcome. Mrs. Westgate seated herself between them, and, talking a great deal to each, they had occasion to observe that she was as pretty as their friend Littledale had promised. She was thirty years old, with the eyes and the smile of a girl of seventeen, and she was extremely light and graceful—elegant, exquisite. Mrs. Westgate was extremely spontaneous. She was very frank and demonstrative, and appeared always—while she looked at you delightedly with her beautiful young eyes—to be making sudden confessions and concessions after momentary hesitations.

"We shall expect to see a great deal of you," she said to Lord Lambeth, with a kind of joyous earnestness. "We are very fond of Englishmen here —that is, there are a great many we have been fond of. After a day or two you must come and stay with us; we hope you will stay a long time. Newport's a very nice place when you come really to know it—when you know plenty of people. Of course you and Mr. Beaumont will have no difficulty about that. Englishmen are very well received here; there are almost always two or three of them about. I think they always like it, and I must say I should think they would. They receive ever so much attention. I must say I think they sometimes get spoiled; but I am sure you and Mr. Beaumont are proof against that."

THE RISE OF SILAS LAPHAM

WILLIAM DEAN HOWELLS

One myth about Boston prevalent in the rest of the country is that Boston is snobbish. I don't believe this to be true, if snobbishness is to be equated with a sense of social superiority. Boston society was always in the literal sense exclusive, more because its members were so contented with one another that they were not interested in meeting anybody new than because outsiders were looked down upon. There is also the matter of Boston diffidence. My father used to say, "Bostonians are too shy to ask anyone to marry them but their cousins."

The following excerpt from W. D. Howells' The Rise of Silas Lapham —perhaps the best of all his novels—gives an encounter between Bostonians of the entrenched sort, and a parvenu family.

A DINNER PARTY

THE Coreys were one of the few old families who lingered in Bellingham Place, the handsome, quiet old street which the sympathetic observer must grieve to see abandoned to boarding-houses. The dwellings are stately and tall, and the whole place wears an air of aristocratic seclusion, which Mrs. Corey's father might well have thought assured when

he left her his house there at his death. It is one of two evidently designed by the same architect who built some houses in a characteristic
taste on Beacon Street opposite the Common. It has a wooden portico,
with slender fluted columns, which have always been painted white, and
which, with the delicate mouldings of the cornice, form the sole and sufficient decoration of the street front; nothing could be simpler, and
nothing could be better. Within, the architect has again indulged his
preference for the classic; the roof of the vestibule, wide and low, rests on
marble columns, slim and fluted like the wooden columns without, and
an ample staircase climbs in a graceful, easy curve from the tesselated
pavement. Some carved Venetian *scrigni* stretched along the wall; a rug
lay at the foot of the stairs; but otherwise the simple adequacy of the
architectural intention had been respected, and the place looked bare to
the eyes of the Laphams when they entered. The Coreys had once kept a
man, but when young Corey began his retrenchments the man had
yielded to the neat maid who showed the Colonel into the reception-
room and asked the ladies to walk up two flights.

He had his charges from Irene not to enter the drawing-room without
her mother, and he spent five minutes in getting on his gloves, for he had
desperately resolved to wear them at last. When he had them on, and
let his large fists hang down on either side, they looked, in the saffron tint
which the shop-girl said his gloves should be of, like canvased hams. He
perspired with doubt as he climbed the stairs, and while he waited on the
landing for Mrs. Lapham and Irene to come down from above before
going into the drawing-room, he stood staring at his hands, now open
and now shut, and breathing hard. He heard quiet talking beyond the
portière within, and presently Tom Corey came out.

"Ah, Colonel Lapham! Very glad to see you."

Lapham shook hands with him and gasped, "Waiting for Mis' Lapham," to account for his presence. He had not been able to button his
right glove, and he now began, with as much indifference as he could
assume, to pull them both off, for he saw that Corey wore none. By
the time he had stuffed them into the pocket of his coat-skirt his wife
and daughter descended.

Corey welcomed them very cordially too, but looked a little mystified.
Mrs. Lapham knew that he was silently inquiring for Penelope, and she
did not know whether she ought to excuse her to him first or not. She said
nothing, and after a glance toward the regions where Penelope might
conjecturably be lingering, he held aside the *portière* for the Laphams to
pass, and entered the room with them.

Mrs. Lapham had decided against low-necks on her own responsibility,
and had entrenched herself in the safety of a black silk, in which she
looked very handsome. Irene wore a dress of one of those shades which
only a woman or an artist can decide to be green or blue, and which to

other eyes looks both or neither, according to their degree of ignorance. If it was more like a ball dress than a dinner dress, that might be excused to the exquisite effect. She trailed, a delicate splendour, across the carpet in her mother's sombre wake, and the consciousness of success brought a vivid smile to her face. Lapham, pallid with anxiety lest he should some-how disgrace himself, giving thanks to God that he should have been spared the shame of wearing gloves where no one else did, but at the same time despairing that Corey should have seen him in them, had an unwonted aspect of almost pathetic refinement.

Mrs. Corey exchanged a quick glance of surprise and relief with her husband as she started across the room to meet her guests, and in her gratitude to them for being so irreproachable, she threw into her manner a warmth that people did not always find there. "General Lapham?" she said, shaking hands in quick succession with Mrs. Lapham and Irene, and now addressing herself to him.

"No, ma'am, only Colonel," said the honest man, but the lady did not hear him. She was introducing her husband to Lapham's wife and daughter, and Bromfield Corey was already shaking his hand and saying he was very glad to see him again, while he kept his artistic eye on Irene, and apparently could not take it off. Lily Corey gave the Lapham ladies a greeting which was physically rather than socially cold, and Nanny stood holding Irene's hand in both of hers a moment, and taking in her beauty and her style with a generous admiration which she could afford, for she was herself faultlessly dressed in the quiet taste of her city, and looking very pretty. The interval was long enough to let every man present confide his sense of Irene's beauty to every other; and then, as the party was small, Mrs. Corey made everybody acquainted. When Lapham had not quite understood, he held the person's hand, and, leaning urbanely forward, inquired, "What name?" He did that because a great man to whom he had been presented on the platform at a public meeting had done so to him, and he knew it must be right.

A little lull ensued upon the introductions, and Mrs. Corey said quietly to Mrs. Lapham, "Can I send any one to be of use to Miss Lapham?" as if Penelope must be in the dressing-room.

Mrs. Lapham turned fire-red, and the graceful forms in which she had been intending to excuse her daughter's absence went out of her head. "She isn't upstairs," she said, at her bluntest, as country people are when embarrassed. "She didn't feel just like coming to-night. I don't know as she's feeling very well."

Mrs. Corey emitted a very small "O!"—very small, very cold,—which began to grow larger and hotter and to burn into Mrs. Lapham's soul before Mrs. Corey could add, "I'm very sorry. It's nothing serious, I hope?"

Robert Chase, the painter, had not come, and Mrs. James Bellingham was not there, so that the table really balanced better without Penelope;

but Mrs. Lapham could not know this, and did not deserve to know it. Mrs. Corey glanced round the room, as if to take account of her guests, and said to her husband, "I think we are all here, then," and he came forward and gave his arm to Mrs. Lapham. She perceived then that in their determination not to be the first to come they had been the last, and must have kept the others waiting for them.

Lapham had never seen people go down to dinner arm-in-arm before, but he knew that his wife was distinguished in being taken out by the host, and he waited in jealous impatience to see if Tom Corey would offer his arm to Irene. He gave it to that big girl they called Miss Kingsbury, and the handsome old fellow whom Mrs. Corey had introduced as her cousin took Irene out. Lapham was startled from the misgiving in which this left him by Mrs. Corey's passing her hand through his arm, and he made a sudden movement forward, but felt himself gently restrained. They went out the last of all; he did not know why, but he submitted, and when they sat down he saw that Irene, although she had come in with that Mr. Bellingham, was seated beside young Corey, after all.

He fetched a long sigh of relief when he sank into his chair and felt himself safe from error if he kept a sharp lookout and did only what the others did. Bellingham had certain habits which he permitted himself, and one of these was tucking the corner of his napkin into his collar; he confessed himself an uncertain shot with a spoon, and defended his practice on the ground of neatness and common-sense. Lapham put his napkin into his collar too, and then, seeing that no one but Bellingham did it, became alarmed and took it out again slyly. He never had wine on his table at home, and on principle he was a prohibitionist; but now he did not know just what to do about the glasses at the right of his plate. He had a notion to turn them all down, as he had read of a well-known politician's doing at a public dinner, to show that he did not take wine; but, after twiddling with one of them a moment, he let them be, for it seemed to him that would be a little too conspicuous, and he felt that every one was looking. He let the servant fill them all, and he drank out of each, not to appear odd. Later, he observed that the young ladies were not taking wine, and he was glad to see that Irene had refused it, and that Mrs. Lapham was letting it stand untasted. He did not know but he ought to decline some of the dishes, or at least leave most of some on his plate, but he was not able to decide; he took everything and ate everything.

He noticed that Mrs. Corey seemed to take no more trouble about the dinner than anybody, and Mr. Corey rather less; he was talking busily to Mrs. Lapham, and Lapham caught a word here and there that convinced him she was holding her own. He was getting on famously himself with Mrs. Corey, who had begun with him about his new house; he was telling her all about it, and giving her his ideas. Their conversation naturally included his architect across the table; Lapham had been delighted and secretly surprised to find the fellow there; and at something Seymour said the talk spread suddenly, and the pretty house he was building for Colonel Lapham became the general theme. Young Corey testified to its loveliness, and the architect said laughingly that if he had been able to make a nice thing of it, he owed it to the practical sympathy of his client.

"Practical sympathy is good," said Bromfield Corey; and, slanting his head confidentially to Mrs. Lapham, he added, "Does he bleed your husband, Mrs. Lapham? He's a terrible fellow for appropriations!"

Mrs. Lapham laughed, reddening consciously, and said she guessed the Colonel knew how to take care of himself. This struck Lapham, then draining his glass of sauterne, as wonderfully discreet in his wife.

Bromfield Corey leaned back in his chair a moment. "Well, after all, you can't say, with all your modern fuss about it, that you do much better now than the old fellows who built such houses as this." . . .

Lapham leaned a little toward Mrs. Corey, and said of a picture which he saw on the wall opposite, "Picture of your daughter, I presume?"

"No; my daughter's grandmother. It's a Stewart Newton; he painted a great many Salem beauties. She was a Miss Polly Burroughs. My daughter *is* like her, don't you think?" They both looked at Nanny Corey and then at the portrait. "Those pretty old-fashioned dresses are coming in again. I'm not surprised you took it for her. The others"—she referred to the other portraits more or less darkling on the walls—"are my people; mostly Copleys."

These names, unknown to Lapham, went to his head like the wine he was drinking; they seemed to carry light for the moment, but a film of deeper darkness followed. He heard Charles Bellingham telling funny stories to Irene and trying to amuse the girl; she was laughing, and seemed very happy. From time to time Bellingham took part in the general talk between the host and James Bellingham and Miss Kingsbury and that minister, Mr. Sewell. They talked of people mostly; it astonished Lapham to hear with what freedom they talked. They discussed these persons unsparingly; James Bellingham spoke of a man known to Lapham for his business success and great wealth as not a gentleman; his cousin Charles said he was surprised that the fellow had kept from being governor so long. . . .

It was not an elaborate dinner; but Lapham was used to having everything on the table at once, and this succession of dishes bewildered him; he was afraid perhaps he was eating too much. He now no longer made any pretence of not drinking his wine, for he was thirsty, and there was no more water, and he hated to ask for any. The ice-cream came, and then the fruit. Suddenly Mrs. Corey rose, and said across the table to her husband, "I suppose you will want your coffee here." And he replied, "Yes; we'll join you at tea."

The ladies all rose, and the gentlemen got up with them. Lapham started to follow Mrs. Corey, but the other men merely stood in their places, except young Corey, who ran and opened the door for his mother. Lapham thought with shame that it was he who ought to have done that; but no one seemed to notice, and he sat down again gladly, after kicking out one of his legs which had gone to sleep.

They brought in cigars with coffee, and Bromfield Corey advised Lapham to take one that he chose for him. Lapham confessed that he liked a good cigar about as well as anybody, and Corey said: "These are new. I had an Englishman here the other day who was smoking old cigars in the superstition that tobacco improved with age, like wine."

"Ah," said Lapham, "anybody who had ever lived off a tobacco country could tell him better than that." With the fuming cigar between his lips he felt more at home than he had before. He turned sidewise in his chair and, resting one arm on the back, intertwined the fingers of both hands, and smoked at large ease.

James Bellingham came and sat down by him. "Colonel Lapham, weren't you with the 96th Vermont when they charged across the river in front of Pickensburg, and the rebel battery opened fire on them in the water?"

Lapham slowly shut his eyes and slowly dropped his head for assent, letting out a white volume of smoke from the corner of his mouth.

"I thought so," said Bellingham. "I was with the 85th Massachusetts, and I sha'n't forget that slaughter. We were all new to it still. Perhaps that's why it made such an impression."

"I don't know," suggested Charles Bellingham. "Was there anything much more impressive afterward? I read of it out in Missouri, where I was stationed at the time, and I recollect the talk of some old army men about it. They said that death-rate couldn't be beaten. I don't know that it ever was."

"About one in five of us got out safe," said Lapham, breaking his cigar-ash off on the edge of a plate. James Bellingham reached him a bottle of Apollinaris. He drank a glass, and then went on smoking.

They all waited, as if expecting him to speak, and then Corey said: "How incredible those things seem already! You gentlemen *know* that they happened; but are you still able to believe it?" . . .

"I suppose it isn't well for us to see human nature at white heat habitually," continued Bromfield Corey, after a while. "It would make us vain of our species. Many a poor fellow in that war and in many another has gone into battle simply and purely for his country's sake, not knowing whether, if he laid down his life, he should ever find it again, or whether, if he took it up hereafter, he should take it up in heaven or hell. Come, parson!" he said, turning to the minister, "what has ever been conceived of omnipotence, of omniscience, so sublime, so divine as that?"

"Nothing," answered the minister quietly. "God has never been imagined at all. But if you suppose such a man as that was Authorised, I think it will help you to imagine what God must be."

"There's sense in that," said Lapham. He took his cigar out of his mouth, and pulled his chair a little toward the table, on which he placed his ponderous fore-arms. "I want to tell you about a fellow I had in my own company when we first went out. We were all privates to begin with; after a while they elected me captain—I'd had the tavern stand, and most of 'em knew me. But Jim Millon never got to be anything more than corporal; corporal when he was killed." The others arrested themselves in various attitudes of attention, and remained listening to Lapham with an interest that profoundly flattered him. Now, at last, he felt that he was holding up his end of the rope. "I can't say he went into the thing from the highest motives, altogether; our motives are always pretty badly mixed, and when there's such a hurrah-boys as there was then, you can't tell which is which. I suppose Jim Millon's wife was enough to account for his going, herself. She was a pretty bad assortment," said Lapham, lowering his voice and glancing round at the door to make sure that it was shut, "and she used to lead Jim *one* kind of life. Well, sir," continued Lapham, synthetising his auditors in that form of address, "that fellow used to save every cent of his pay and send it to that woman. Used to get me to do it for him. I tried to stop him. 'Why, Jim,' said I, 'you know what she'll do with it.' 'That's so, Cap,' says he, 'but I don't know what she'll do without it.' And it did keep her straight—straight as a string—as long as Jim lasted. Seemed as if there was something mysterious about it. They had a little girl,—about as old as my oldest girl,—and Jim used to talk to me about her. Guess he done it as much for her as for the mother; and he said to me before the last action we went into, 'I should like to turn tail and run, Cap. I ain't comin' out o' this one. But I don't suppose it would do.' 'Well, not for you, Jim,' said I. 'I want to live,' he says; and he bust out crying right there in my tent. 'I want to live for poor Molly and Zerrilla' —that's what they called the little one; I dunno where they got the name. 'I ain't ever had half a chance; and now she's doing better, and I believe we should get along after this.' He set there cryin' like a baby. But he wan't no baby when he went into action. I hated to look at him after it was over, not so much because he'd got a ball that was meant for me by a sharpshooter—he saw the devil takin' aim, and he jumped to warn me— as because he didn't look like Jim; he looked like—fun; all desperate and savage. I guess he died hard."

The story made its impression, and Lapham saw it. "Now I say," he resumed, as if he felt that he was going to do himself justice, and say something to heighten the effect his story had produced. At the same time he was aware of a certain want of clearness. He had the idea, but it floated vague, elusive, in his brain. He looked about as if for something to precipitate it in tangible shape.

"Apollinaris?" asked Charles Bellingham, handing the bottle from the other side. He had drawn his chair closer than the rest to Lapham's, and was listening with great interest. When Mrs. Corey asked him to meet Lapham, he accepted gladly. "You know I go in for that sort of thing, Anna. Since Leslie's affair we're rather bound to do it. And I think we meet these practical fellows too little. There's always something original about them." He might naturally have believed that the reward of his faith was coming.

"Thanks, I will take some of this wine," said Lapham, pouring himself a glass of Madeira from a black and dusty bottle caressed by a label bearing the date of the vintage. He tossed off the wine, unconscious of its preciousness, and waited for the result. That cloudiness in his brain disappeared before it, but a mere blank remained. He not only could not remember what he was going to say, but he could not recall what they had been talking about. They waited, looking at him, and he stared at them in return. After a while he heard the host saying, "Shall we join the ladies?"

Lapham went, trying to think what had happened. It seemed to him a long time since he had drunk that wine.

Miss Corey gave him a cup of tea, where he stood aloof from his wife, who was talking with Miss Kingsbury and Mrs. Sewell; Irene was with Miss Nanny Corey. He could not hear what they were talking about; but if Penelope had come, he knew that she would have done them all credit. He meant to let her know how he felt about her behaviour when he got home. It was a shame for her to miss such a chance. Irene was looking beautiful, as pretty as all the rest of them put together, but she was not talking, and Lapham perceived that at a dinner-party you ought to talk. He was himself conscious of having talked very well. He now wore an air of great dignity, and, in conversing with the other gentlemen, he used a grave and weighty deliberation. Some of them wanted him to go into the library. There he gave his ideas of books. He said he had not much time for anything but the papers; but he was going to have a complete library in his new place. He made an elaborate acknowledgment to Bromfield Corey of his son's kindness in suggesting books for his library; he said that he had ordered them all, and that he meant to have pictures. He asked Mr. Corey who was about the best American painter going now. "I don't set up to be a judge of pictures, but I know what I like," he said. He lost the reserve which he had maintained earlier, and began to boast. He himself introduced the subject of his paint, in a natural transition from pictures; he said Mr. Corey must take a run up to Lapham with him some day, and see the Works; they would interest him, and he would drive him round the country; he kept most of his horses up there, and he could show Mr. Corey some of the finest Jersey grades in the country. He told about his brother William, the judge at Dubuque; and a farm he had out there that paid for itself every year in wheat. As he cast off all fear, his voice rose, and he hammered his arm-chair with the thick of his hand for emphasis. Mr. Corey seemed impressed; he sat perfectly

quiet, listening, and Lapham saw the other gentlemen stop in their talk
every now and then to listen. After this proof of his ability to interest
them, he would have liked to have Mrs. Lapham suggest again that he
was unequal to their society, or to the society of anybody else. He surprised himself by his ease among men whose names had hitherto overawed him. He got to calling Bromfield Corey by his surname alone. He
did not understand why young Corey seemed so preoccupied, and he
took occasion to tell the company how he had said to his wife the first
time he saw that fellow that he could make a man of him if he had him
in the business; and he guessed he was not mistaken. He began to tell
stories of the different young men he had had in his employ. At last he
had the talk altogether to himself; no one else talked, and he talked unceasingly. It was a great time; it was a triumph.

He was in this successful mood when word came to him that Mrs.
Lapham was going; Tom Corey seemed to have brought it, but he was not
sure. Anyway, he was not going to hurry. He made cordial invitations to
each of the gentlemen to drop in and see him at his office, and would not
be satisfied till he had exacted a promise from each. He told Charles
Bellingham that he liked him, and assured James Bellingham that it had
always been his ambition to know him, and that if any one had said when
he first came to Boston that in less than ten years he should be hobnob-
bing with Jim Bellingham, he should have told that person he lied. He
would have told anybody he lied that had told him ten years ago that a
son of Bromfield Corey would have come and asked him to take him into
the business. Ten years ago he, Silas Lapham, had come to Boston a little
worse off than nothing at all, for he was in debt for half the money that he
had bought out his partner with, and here he was now worth a million,
and meeting you gentlemen like one of you. And every cent of that was
honest money,—no speculation,—every copper of it for value received.
And here, only the other day, his old partner, who had been going to the
dogs ever since he went out of the business, came and borrowed twenty
thousand dollars of him! Lapham lent it because his wife wanted him to:
she had always felt bad about the fellow's having to go out of the
business.

He took leave of Mr. Sewell with patronising affection, and bade him
come to him if he ever got into a tight place with his parish work; he
would let him have all the money he wanted; he had more money than
he knew what to do with. "Why, when your wife sent to mine last
fall," he said, turning to Mr. Corey, "I drew my cheque for five hundred
dollars, but my wife wouldn't take more than one hundred; said she
wasn't going to show off before Mrs. Corey. I call that a pretty good joke
on Mrs. Corey. I must tell her how Mrs. Lapham done her out of a cool
four hundred dollars."

He started toward the door of the drawing-room to take leave of the
ladies; but Tom Corey was at his elbow, saying, "I think Mrs. Lapham is

waiting for you below, sir," and in obeying the direction Corey gave him toward another door he forgot all about his purpose, and came away without saying good-night to his hostess.

Mrs. Lapham had not known how soon she ought to go, and had no idea that in her quality of chief guest she was keeping the others. She stayed till eleven o'clock, and was a little frightened when she found what time it was; but Mrs. Corey, without pressing her to stay longer, had said it was not at all late. She and Irene had had a perfect time. Everybody had been very polite; on the way home they celebrated the amiability of both the Miss Coreys and of Miss Kingsbury. Mrs. Lapham thought that Mrs. Bellingham was about the pleasantest person she ever saw; she had told her all about her married daughter who had married an inventor and gone to live in Omaha—a Mrs. Blake.

"If it's that car-wheel Blake," said Lapham proudly, "I know all about him. I've sold him tons of the paint."

"Pooh, papa! How you do smell of smoking!" cried Irene.

"Pretty strong, eh?" laughed Lapham, letting down a window of the carriage. His heart was throbbing wildly in the close air, and he was glad of the rush of cold that came in, though it stopped his tongue, and he listened more and more drowsily to the rejoicings that his wife and daughter exchanged. He meant to have them wake Penelope up and tell her what she had lost; but when he reached home he was too sleepy to suggest it. He fell asleep as soon as his head touched the pillow, full of supreme triumph.

But in the morning his skull was sore with the unconscious, night-long ache; and he rose cross and taciturn. They had a silent breakfast. In the cold grey light of the morning the glories of the night before showed poorer. Here and there a painful doubt obtruded itself and marred them with its awkward shadow. Penelope sent down word that she was not well, and was not coming to breakfast, and Lapham was glad to go to his office without seeing her.

He was severe and silent all day with his clerks, and peremptory with customers. Of Corey he was slyly observant, and as the day wore away he grew more restively conscious. He sent out word by his office-boy that he would like to see Mr. Corey for a few minutes after closing. The typewriter girl had lingered too, as if she wished to speak with him, and Corey stood in abeyance as she went toward Lapham's door.

"Can't see you to-night, Zerrilla," he said bluffly, but not unkindly. "Perhaps I'll call at the house, if it's important."

"It is," said the girl, with a spoiled air of insistence.

"Well," said Lapham, and, nodding to Corey to enter, he closed the door upon her. Then he turned to the young man and demanded: "Was I drunk last night?"

1885-1914

THE TOWN POOR

SARAH ORNE JEWETT

———◆•◆———

*The short stories of Sarah Orne Jewett (1849–1909), one of which follows,
are concerned with the old, rural New England life already dying. She
was born in South Berwick, Maine, the port town where John Paul Jones
had recruited his sailors; and, while driving about the countryside with
her doctor father, had absorbed the atmosphere and feeling of old-time
New England, which she was to express ever more poignantly in the
course of her development as a natural storyteller. She forms an interesting
link in the history of writing, since she was, when young, greatly influenced by H. B. Stowe's Oldtown stories, and when old was an influence
on Willa Cather, who met her at the house of Miss Jewett's great friend
Mrs. James T. Fields, wife of the publisher, in Boston.*

Mrs. William Trimble and Miss Rebecca Wright were driving along
Hampden east road, one afternoon in early spring. Their progress was
slow. Mrs. Trimble's sorrel horse was old and stiff, and the wheels were
clogged by clay mud. The frost was not yet out of the ground, although
the snow was nearly gone, except in a few places on the north side of the
woods, or where it had drifted all winter against a length of fence.

"There must be a good deal o' snow to the nor'ard of us yet," said
weather-wise Mrs. Trimble. "I feel it in the air; 't is more than the
ground-damp. We ain't goin' to have real nice weather till the up-
country snow's all gone."

"I heard say yesterday that there was good sleddin' yet, all up through
Parsley," responded Miss Wright. "I shouldn't like to live in them northern
places. My cousin Ellen's husband was a Parsley man, an' he was obliged,
as you may have heard, to go up north to his father's second wife's
funeral; got back day before yesterday. 'T was about twenty-one miles, an'

they started on wheels; but when they'd gone nine or ten miles, they found 't was no sort o' use, an' left their wagon an' took a sleigh. The man that owned it charged 'em four an' six, too. I should n't have thought he would; they told him they was goin' to a funeral; an' they had their own buffaloes an' everything."

"Well, I expect it's a good deal harder scratchin', up that way; they have to git money where they can; the farms is very poor as you go north," suggested Mrs. Trimble kindly. "'T ain't none too rich a country where we be, but I've always been grateful I wa'n't born up to Parsley."

The old horse plodded along, and the sun, coming out from the heavy spring clouds, sent a sudden shine of light along the muddy road. Sister Wright drew her large veil forward over the high brim of her bonnet. She was not used to driving, or to being much in the open air; but Mrs. Trimble was an active business woman, and looked after her own affairs herself, in all weathers. The late Mr. Trimble had left her a good farm, but not much ready money, and it was often said that she was better off in the end than if he had lived. She regretted his loss deeply, however; it was impossible for her to speak of him, even to intimate friends, without emotion, and nobody had ever hinted that this emotion was insincere. She was most warm-hearted and generous, and in her limited way played the part of Lady Bountiful in the town of Hampden.

"Why, there's where the Bray girls lives, ain't it?" she exclaimed, as beyond a thicket of witch-hazel and scrub-oak, they came in sight of a weather-beaten, solitary farmhouse. The barn was too far away for thrift or comfort, and they could see long lines of light between the shrunken boards as they came nearer. The fields looked both stony and sodden. Somehow, even Parsley itself could be hardly more forlorn.

"Yes'm," said Miss Wright, "that's where they live now, poor things. I know the place, though I ain't been up here for years. You don't suppose, Mis' Trimble—I ain't seen the girls out to meetin' all winter. I've re'lly been covetin' "—

"Why, yes, Rebecca, of course we could stop," answered Mrs. Trimble heartily. "The exercises was over earlier 'n I expected, an' you 're goin' to remain over night long o' me, you know. There won't be no tea till we git there, so we can't be late. I'm in the habit o' sendin' a basket to the Bray girls when any o' our folks is comin' this way, but I ain't been to see 'em since they moved up here. Why, it must be a good deal over a year ago. I know 't was in the late winter they had to make the move. 'T was cruel hard, I must say, an' if I had n't been down with my pleurisy fever I'd have stirred round an' done somethin' about it. There was a good deal o' sickness at the time, an'—well, 't was kind o' rushed through, breakin' of 'em up, an' lots o' folks blamed the selec'men; but when 't was done, 't was done, an' nobody took holt to undo it. Ann an' Mandy looked same 's ever when they come to meetin', 'long in the summer,—kind o' wishful, perhaps. They've always sent me word they was gittin' on pretty comfortable."

"That would be their way," said Rebecca Wright. "They never was any hand to complain, though Mandy's less cheerful than Ann. If Mandy 'd been spared such poor eyesight, an' Ann had n't got her lame wrist that wa'n't set right, they'd kep' off the town fast enough. They both shed tears when they talked to me about havin' to break up, when I went to see 'em before I went over to brother Asa's. You see we was brought up neighbors, an' we went to school together, the Brays an' me. 'T was a special Providence brought us home this road, I've been so covetin' a chance to git to see 'em. My lameness hampers me."

"I'm glad we come this way, myself," said Mrs. Trimble.

"I'd like to see just how they fare," Miss Rebecca Wright continued. "They give their consent to goin' on the town because they knew they'd got to be dependent, an' so they felt 't would come easier for all than for a few to help 'em. They acted real dignified an' right-minded, contrary to what most do in such cases, but they was dreadful anxious to see who would bid 'em off, town-meeting day; they did so hope 't would be somebody right in the village. I just sat down an' cried good when I found Abel Janes's folks had got hold of 'em. They always had the name of bein' slack and poor-spirited, an' they did it just for what they got out o' the town. The selectmen this last year ain't what we have had. I hope they've been considerate about the Bray girls."

"I should have be'n more considerate about fetchin' of you over," apologized Mrs. Trimble. "I've got my horse, an' you 're lame-footed; 't is too far for you to come. But time does slip away with busy folks, an' I forgit a good deal I ought to remember."

"There's nobody more considerate than you be," protested Miss Rebecca Wright.

Mrs. Trimble made no answer, but took out her whip and gently touched the sorrel horse, who walked considerably faster, but did not think it worth while to trot. It was a long, round-about way to the house, farther down the road and up a lane.

"I never had any opinion of the Bray girls' father, leavin' 'em as he did," said Mrs. Trimble.

"He was much praised in his time, though there was always some said his early life hadn't been up to the mark," explained her companion. "He was a great favorite of our then preacher, the Reverend Daniel Longbrother. They did a good deal for the parish, but they did it their own way. Deacon Bray was one that did his part in the repairs without urging. You know 't was in his time the first repairs was made, when they got out the old soundin'-board an' them handsome square pews. It cost an awful sight o' money, too. They had n't done payin' up that debt when they set to alter it again an' git the walls frescoed. My grandmother was one that always spoke her mind right out, an' she was dreadful opposed to breakin' up the square pews where she 'd always set. They was countin' up what 't would cost in parish meetin', an' she riz right up an' said 't would n't cost nothin' to let 'em stay, an' there wa'n't a house carpenter left in the parish that could do such nice work, an' time would come when the great-grandchildren would give their eye-teeth to have the old meetin'-house look just as it did then. But haul the inside to pieces they would and did."

"There come to be a real fight over it, did n't there?" agreed Mrs. Trimble soothingly. "Well, 't wa'n't good taste. I remember the old house well. I come here as a child to visit a cousin o' mother's, an' Mr. Trimble's folks was neighbors, an' we was drawed to each other then, young 's we was. Mr. Trimble spoke of it many's the time,—that first time he ever see me, in a leghorn hat with a feather; 't was one that mother had, an' pressed over."

"When I think of them old sermons that used to be preached in that old meetin'-house of all, I'm glad it 's altered over, so 's not to remind folks," said Miss Rebecca Wright, after a suitable pause. "Them old brimstone discourses, you know, Mis' Trimble. Preachers is far more reasonable, nowadays. Why, I set an' thought, last Sabbath, as I listened, that if old Mr. Longbrother an' Deacon Bray could hear the difference they'd crack the ground over 'em like pole beans, an' come right up 'long side their headstones."

Mrs. Trimble laughed heartily, and shook the reins three or four times by way of emphasis. "There's no gitting round you," she said, much pleased. "I should think Deacon Bray would want to rise, any way, if 't was so he could, an' knew how his poor girls was farin'. A man ought to provide for his folks he 's got to leave behind him, specially if they 're women. To be sure, they had their little home; but we 've seen how, with all their industrious ways, they had n't means to keep it. I s'pose he thought he 'd got time enough to lay by, when he give so generous in collections; but he did n't lay by, an' there they be. He might have took lessons from the squirrels: even them little wild creatur's makes them their winter hoards, an' menfolks ought to know enough if squirrels does. 'Be just before you are generous:' that's what was always set for the B's in the copy-books, when I was to school, and it often runs through my mind."

"'As for man, his days are as grass,'—that was for A; the two go well together," added Miss Rebecca Wright soberly. "My good gracious, ain't this a starved-lookin' place? It makes me ache to think them nice Bray girls has to brook it here."

The sorrel horse, though somewhat puzzled by an unexpected deviation from his homeward way, willingly came to a stand by the gnawed corner of the door-yard fence, which evidently served as hitching-place.

Two or three ragged old hens were picking about the yard, and at last a face appeared at the kitchen window, tied up in a handkerchief, as if it were a case of toothache. By the time our friends reached the side door next this window, Mrs. Janes came disconsolately to open it for them, shutting it again as soon as possible, though the air felt more chilly inside the house.

"Take seats," said Mrs. Janes briefly. "You'll have to see me just as I be. I have been suffering these four days with the ague, and everything to do. Mr. Janes is to court, on the jury. 'T was inconvenient to spare him. I should be pleased to have you lay off your things."

Comfortable Mrs. Trimble looked about the cheerless kitchen, and could not think of anything to say; so she smiled blandly and shook her head in answer to the invitation. "We'll just set a few minutes with you, to pass the time o' day, an' then we must go in an' have a word with the Miss Brays, bein' old acquaintance. It ain't been so we could git to call on 'em before. I don't know 's you 're acquainted with Miss R'becca Wright. She 's been out of town a good deal."

"I heard she was stopping over to Plainfields with her brother's folks," replied Mrs. Janes, rocking herself with irregular motion, as she sat close to the stove. "Got back some time in the fall, I believe?"

"Yes 'm," said Miss Rebecca, with an undue sense of guilt and conviction. "We've been to the installation over to the East Parish, an' thought we'd stop in; we took this road home to see if 't was any better. How is the Miss Brays gettin' on?"

"They're well 's common," answered Mrs. Janes grudgingly. "I was put out with Mr. Janes for fetchin' of 'em here, with all I 've got to do, an' I own I was kind o' surly to 'em 'long to the first of it. He gits the money from the town, an' it helps him out; but he bid 'em off for five dollars a month, an' we can't do much for 'em at no such price as that. I went an' dealt with the selec'men, an' made 'em promise to find their firewood an' some other things extra. They was glad to get rid o' the matter the fourth time I went, an' would ha' promised 'most anything. But Mr. Janes don't keep me half the time in oven-wood, he's off so much, an' we was cramped o' room, any way. I have to store things up garrit a good deal, an' that keeps me trampin' right through their room. I do the best for 'em I can, Mis' Trimble, but 't ain't so easy for me as 't is for you, with all your means to do with."

The poor woman looked pinched and miserable herself, though it was evident that she had no gift at house or home keeping. Mrs. Trimble's heart was wrung with pain, as she thought of the unwelcome inmates of such a place; but she held her peace bravely, while Miss Rebecca again gave some brief information in regard to the installation.

"You go right up them back stairs," the hostess directed at last. "I'm glad some o' you church folks has seen fit to come an' visit 'em. There ain't been nobody here this long spell, an' they've aged a sight since they come. They always send down a taste out of your baskets, Mis' Trimble, an' I relish it, I tell you. I'll shut the door after you, if you don't object. I feel every draught o' cold air."

"I've always heard she was a great hand to make a poor mouth. Wa'n't she from somewheres up Parsley way?" whispered Miss Rebecca, as they stumbled in the half-light.

"Poor meechin' body, wherever she come from," replied Mrs. Trimble, as she knocked at the door.

There was silence for a moment after this unusual sound; then one of the Bray sisters opened the door. The eager guests stared into a small, low room, brown with age, and gray, too, as if former dust and cobwebs could not be made wholly to disappear. The two elderly women who stood there looked like captives. Their withered faces wore a look of apprehension, and the room itself was more bare and plain than was fitting to their evident refinement of character and self-respect. There was an uncovered small table in the middle of the floor, with some crackers on a plate; and, for some reason or other, this added a great deal to the general desolation.

But Miss Ann Bray, the elder sister, who carried her right arm in a sling, with piteously drooping fingers, gazed at the visitors with radiant joy. She had not seen them arrive.

The one window gave only the view at the back of the house, across the fields, and their coming was indeed a surprise. The next minute she was laughing and crying together. "Oh, sister!" she said, "if here ain't our dear Mis' Trimble!—an' my heart o' goodness, 't is 'Becca Wright, too! What dear good creatur's you be! I've felt all day as if something good was goin' to happen, an' was just sayin' to myself 't was most sundown now, but I would n't let on to Mandany I'd give up hope quite yet. You see, the scissors stuck in the floor this very mornin' an' it's always a reliable sign. There, I've got to kiss ye both again!"

"I don't know where we can all set," lamented sister Mandana. "There ain't but the one chair an' the bed; t' other chair's too rickety; an' we've been promised another these ten days; but first they 've forgot it, an' next Mis' Janes can't spare it,—one excuse an' another. I am goin' to git a stump o' wood an' nail a board on to it, when I can git outdoor again," said Mandana, in a plaintive voice. "There, I ain't goin' to complain o' nothin', now you've come," she added; and the guests sat down, Mrs. Trimble, as was proper, in the one chair.

"We've sat on the bed many's the time with you, 'Becca, an' talked over our girl nonsense, ain't we? You know where 't was—in the little back bedroom we had when we was girls, an' used to peek out at our beaux through the strings o' mornin'-glories," laughed Ann Bray delightedly, her thin face shining more and more with joy. "I brought some o' them mornin'-glory seeds along when we come away, we'd raised 'em so many years; an' we got 'em started all right, but the hens found 'em out. I declare I chased them poor hens, foolish as 't was; but the mornin'-glories I'd counted on a sight to remind me o' home. You see, our debts was so large, after my long sickness an' all, that we did n't feel 't was right to keep back anything we could help from the auction."

It was impossible for any one to speak for a moment or two; the sisters felt their own uprooted condition afresh, and their guests for the first time really comprehended the piteous contrast between that neat little village house, which now seemed a palace of comfort, and this cold, unpainted upper room in the remote Janes farmhouse. It was an unwelcome thought to Mrs. Trimble that the well-to-do town of Hampden could provide no better for its poor than this, and her round face flushed with resentment and the shame of personal responsibility. "The girls shall be well settled in the village before another winter, if I pay their board myself," she made an inward resolution, and took another almost tearful look at the broken stove, the miserable bed and the sisters' one hair-covered trunk, on which Mandana was sitting. But the poor place was filled with a golden spirit of hospitality.

Rebecca was again discoursing eloquently of the installation; it was so much easier to speak of general subjects, and the sisters had evidently been longing to hear some news. Since the late summer they had not been to church, and presently Mrs. Trimble asked the reason.

"Now, don't you go to pouring out our woes, Mandy!" begged little old Ann, looking shy and almost girlish, as if she insisted upon playing that life was still all before them and all pleasure. "Don't you go to spoilin' their visit with our complaints! They know well's we do that changes must come, an' we 'd been so wonted to our home things that this come hard at first; but then they felt for us, I know just as well's can be. 'T will soon be summer again, an' 't is real pleasant right out in the fields here, when there ain't too hot a spell. I 've got to know a sight o' singin' birds since we come."

"Give me the folks I've always known," sighed the younger sister, who looked older than Miss Ann, and less even-tempered. "You may have your birds, if you want 'em. I do re'lly long to go to meetin' an' see folks go by up the aisle. Now, I will speak of it, Ann, whatever you say. We need, each of us, a pair o' good stout shoes an' rubbers,—ours are all wore out; an' we 've asked an' asked, an' they never think to bring 'em, an' "—

Poor old Mandana, on the trunk, covered her face with her arms and sobbed aloud. The elder sister stood over her, and patted her on the thin shoulder like a child, and tried to comfort her. It crossed Mrs. Trimble's mind that it was not the first time one had wept and the other had comforted. The sad scene must have been repeated many times in that long, drear winter. She would see them forever after in her mind as fixed as a picture, and her own tears fell fast.

"You did n't see Mis' Janes's cunning little boy, the next one to the baby, did you?" asked Ann Bray, turning round quickly at last, and going cheerfully on with the conversation. "Now, hush, Mandy, dear; they'll think you're childish! He's a dear, friendly little creatur', an' likes to stay with us a good deal, though we feel 's if it 't was too cold for him, now we are waitin' to get us more wood."

"When I think of the acres o' woodland in this town!" groaned Rebecca Wright. "I believe I'm goin' to preach next Sunday, 'stead o' the minister, an' I'll make the sparks fly. I've always heard the saying, 'What's everybody's business is nobody's business,' an' I've come to believe it."

"Now, don't you, 'Becca. You've happened on a kind of a poor time with us, but we've got more belongings than you see here, an' a good large cluset, where we can store those things there ain't room to have about. You an' Miss Trimble have happened on a kind of poor day, you know. Soon's I git me some stout shoes an' rubbers, as Mandy says, I can fetch home plenty o' little dry boughs o' pine; you remember I was always a great hand to roam in the woods? If we could only have a front room, so 't we could look out on the road an' see passin', an' was shod for meetin', I don' know 's we should complain. Now we're just goin' to give you what we've got, an' make out with a good welcome. We make more tea 'n we want in the mornin', an' then let the fire go down, since 't has been so mild. We've got a *good* cluset" (disappearing as she spoke), "an' I know this to be good tea, 'cause it's some o' yourn, Mis' Trimble. An' here's our sprigged chiny cups that R'becca knows by sight, if Mis' Trimble don't. We kep' out four of 'em, an' put the even half dozen with the rest of the auction stuff. I've often wondered who'd got 'em, but I never asked, for fear 't would be somebody that would distress us. They was mother's, you know."

The four cups were poured, and the little table pushed to the bed, where Rebecca Wright still sat, and Mandana, wiping her eyes, came and joined her. Mrs. Trimble sat in her chair at the end, and Ann trotted about the room in pleased content for a while, and in and out of the closet, as if she still had much to do; then she came and stood opposite Mrs. Trimble. She was very short and small, and there was no painful sense of her being obliged to stand. The four cups were not quite full of cold tea, but there was a clean old tablecloth folded double, and a plate with three pairs of crackers neatly piled, and a small—it must be owned, a very small—piece of hard white cheese. Then, for a treat, in a glass dish, there was a little preserved peach, the last—Miss Rebecca knew it instinctively—of the household stores brought from their old home. It was very sugary, this bit of peach; and as she helped her guests and sister Mandy, Miss Ann Bray said, half unconsciously, as she often had said with less reason in the old days, "Our preserves ain't so good as usual this year; this is beginning to candy." Both the guests protested, while Rebecca added that the taste of it carried her back, and made her feel young again. The Brays had always managed to keep one or two peach-trees alive in their corner of a garden. "I've been keeping this preserve for a treat," said her friend. "I'm glad to have you eat some, 'Becca. Last summer I often wished you was home an' could come an' see us, 'stead o' being away off to Plainfields."

The crackers did not taste too dry. Miss Ann took the last of the peach on her own cracker; there could not have been quite a small spoonful, after the others were helped, but she asked them first if they would not have some more. Then there was a silence, and in the silence a wave of tender feeling rose high in the hearts of the four elderly women. At this moment the setting sun flooded the poor plain room with light; the un-painted wood was all of a golden-brown, and Ann Bray, with her gray hair and aged face, stood at the head of the table in a kind of aureole. Mrs. Trimble's face was all aquiver as she looked at her; she thought of the text about two or three being gathered together, and was half afraid.

"I believe we ought to 've asked Mis' Janes if she would n't come up," said Ann. "She's real good feelin', but she's had it very hard, an gits discouraged. I can't find that she's ever had anything real pleasant to look back to, as we have. There, next time we'll make a good heartenin' time for her too."

The sorrel horse had taken a long nap by the gnawed fence-rail, and the cool air after sundown made him impatient to be gone. The two friends jolted homeward in the gathering darkness, through the stiffening mud, and neither Mrs. Trimble nor Rebecca Wright said a word until they were out of sight as well as out of sound of the Janes house. Time must elapse before they could reach a more familiar part of the road and resume conversation on its natural level.

"I consider myself to blame," insisted Mrs. Trimble at last. "I have n't no words of accusation for nobody else, an' I ain't one to take comfort in calling names to the board o' selec'men. I make no reproaches, an' I take it all on my own shoulders; but I'm goin' to stir about me, I tell you! I shall begin early to-morrow. They're goin' back to their own house,—it's been standin' empty all winter,—an' the town's goin' to give 'em the rent an' what firewood they need; it won't come to more than the board's pay-in' out now. An' you an' me'll take this same horse an' wagon, an' ride an go afoot by turns, an' git means enough together to buy back their furniture an' whatever was sold at that plaguey auction; an' then we'll put it all back, an' tell 'em they've got to move to a new place, an' just carry 'em right back again where they come from. An' don't you never tell, R'becca, but here I be a widow woman, layin' up what I make from

my farm for nobody knows who, an' I'm goin' to do for them Bray girls
all I'm a mind to. I should be sca't to wake up in heaven, an' hear anybody there ask how the Bray girls was. Don't talk to me about the town o'
Hampden, an' don't ever let me hear the name o' town poor! I'm ashamed
to go home an' see what's set out for supper. I wish I'd brought 'em right
along."

"I was goin' to ask if we could n't git the new doctor to go up an' do
somethin' for poor Ann's arm," said Miss Rebecca. "They say he 's very
smart. If she could get so 's to braid straw or hook rugs again, she'd soon
be earnin' a little somethin'. An' may be he could do somethin' for
Mandy's eyes. They did use to live so neat an' ladylike. Somehow I could
n't speak to tell 'em there that 't was I bought them six best cups an'
saucers, time of the auction; they went very low, as everything else did,
an' I thought I could save it some other way. They shall have 'em back
an' welcome. You're real whole-hearted, Mis' Trimble. I expect Ann'll be
sayin' that her father's child'n wa'n't goin' to be left desolate, an' that all
the bread he cast on the water's comin' back through you."

"I don't care what she says, dear creatur'!" exclaimed Mrs. Trimble. "I'm
full o' regrets I took time for that installation, an' set there seepin' in a
lot o' talk this whole day long, except for its kind of bringin' us to the
Bray girls. I wish to my heart 't was to-morrow mornin' a'ready, an' I
a-startin' for the selec'men."

MRS. JACK GARDNER?

F. MARION CRAWFORD

*One of the most famous figures of post-Civil War, cosmopolitan Boston
was Mrs. Jack Gardner. Patron of the fine arts, for whom Bernard Beren-
son, a pupil of Charles Eliot Norton's, bought pictures; painted by Sargent (with whom her name was sometimes linked in gossip), she built the
beautiful, Italianate house always called, in Boston, "Mrs. Gardner's
Palace" (not Fenway Court), which is now a museum. When I was a child
she still lived there, and one could occasionally catch a glimpse of the
legendary old lady as one was led about the galleries to absorb art.*

*She was a controversial figure at all times. By some idolized, always
imitated, she had also her detractors. Many Boston ladies felt envious.
Some of the painters she sought out did not care to be patronized. There
is a story of the late Frank Benson, at one of her soirées, becoming quite*

drunk and following his hostess from room to room until she turned and said, "Mr. Benson, why are you following me around?" He replied with dignity, "Because you're sho damned rich."

Old-line Bostonians, moreover—remembering that Mrs. Gardner, for all her social grandeur, was heiress to the Stewart chocolates fortune— would sing, to a music-hall tune of the day:

> *"She's full of piety,*
> *And fond of s'ciety,*
> *And her father keeps a little candy store!"*

The following fictional portrait, possibly of "Mrs. Jack," is by F. Marion Crawford (1854–1909) and is excerpted from his novel An American Politician, *which concerns political corruption. Crawford, a nephew of Julia Ward Howe, himself gifted in many ways, was a clever storyteller who also, in adopting a luxurious way of life, marked the change from the simplicity of earlier New England writers to a more grandiose conception of a literary career.*

Mrs. Sam Wyndham was generally at home after five o'clock. The established custom whereby the ladies who live in Beacon Street all receive their friends on Monday afternoon did not seem to her satisfactory. She was willing to conform to the practice, but she reserved the right of seeing people on other days as well.

Mrs. Sam Wyndham was never very popular. That is to say, she was not one of those women who are seemingly never spoken ill of, and are invited as a matter of course, or rather as an element of success, to every dinner, musical party, and dance in the season. Women did not all regard her with envy, all young men did not think she was capital fun, nor did all old men come and confide to her the weaknesses of their approaching second childhood. She was not invariably quoted as the standard authority on dress, classical music, and Boston literature, and it was not an unpardonable heresy to say that some other women might be, had been, or could be, more amusing in ordinary conversation. Nevertheless, Mrs. Sam Wyndham held a position in Boston which Boston acknowledged, and which Boston insisted that foreigners such as New Yorkers, Philadelphians and the like, should acknowledge also in that spirit of reverence which is justly due to a descent on both sides from several signers of the Declaration of Independence, and to the wife of one of the ruling financial spirits of the aristocratic part of Boston business.

As a matter of fact, Mrs. Wyndham was about forty years of age, as all her friends of course knew; for it is as easy for a Bostonian to conceal a

question of age as for a crowned head. In a place where one half of society calls the other half cousin, and went to school with it, every one
knows and accurately remembers just how old everybody else is. But Mrs.
Wyndham might have passed for younger than she was among the world
at large, for she was fresh to look at, and of good figure and complexion.
Her black hair showed no signs of turning gray, and her dark eyes were
bright and penetrating still. There were lines in her face, those micro-
scopic lines that come so abundantly to American women in middle age,
speaking of a certain restless nervousness that belongs to them especially;
but on the whole Mrs. Sam Wyndham was fair to see, having a dignity of
carriage and a grace of ease about her that at once gave the impression
of a woman thoroughly equal to the part she had to play in the world,
and not by any means incapable of enjoying it.

For the rest, Mrs. Sam led a life very much like the lives of many rich
Americans. She went abroad frequently, wandered about the continent
with her husband, went to Egypt and Algiers, stayed in England, where
she had a good many friends, avoided her countrymen and countrywomen
when away from home, and did her duty in the social state to which she
was called in Boston. She read the books of the period, and generally
pronounced them ridiculous; she believed in her husband's politics, and
aristocratically approved the way in which he abstained from putting
theory into practice, from voting, and in a general way from dirtying his
fingers with anything so corrupt as government, or so despicable as elections; she understood Boston business to some extent, and called it
finance, but she despised the New York Stock Market and denounced its
doings as gambling. She made fine distinctions, but she was a woman of
sense, and was generally more likely to be right than wrong when she
had a definite opinion, or expressed a definite dislike. Her religious
views were simple and unobtrusive, and never changed.

Her custom of being at home after five o'clock was perhaps the only
deviation she allowed herself from the established manners of her native
city, and since two or three other ladies had followed her example, it had
come to be regarded as a perfectly harmless idiosyncrasy for which she
could not be properly blamed. The people who came to see her were
chiefly men, except, of course, on the inevitable Monday.

A day or two before Christmas, then, Mrs. Sam Wyndham was at home
in the afternoon. The snow lay thick and hard outside, and the sleigh
bells tinkled unceasingly as the sleighs slipped by the window, gleaming
and glittering in the deep red glow of the sunset. The track was well
beaten for miles away, down Beacon Street and across the Milldam to the
country, and the pavements were strewn with ashes to give a foothold
for pedestrians. For the frost was sharp and lasting. But within, Mrs.
Wyndham sat by the fire with a small table before her, and one companion by her side, for whom she was pouring tea.

"Tell me all about your summer, Mr. Vancouver," said she, teasing the flame of the spirit-lamp into better shape with a small silver instrument.

Mr. Pocock Vancouver leaned back in his corner of the sofa and looked at the fire, then at the window, and finally at his hostess, before he answered. He was a pale man and slight of figure, with dark eyes, and his carefully brushed hair, turning gray at the temples and over his forehead, threw his delicate, intelligent face into relief.

"I have not done much," he answered, rather absently, as though trying to find something interesting in his reminiscences; and he watched Mrs. Wyndham as she filled a cup. He was not the least anxious to talk, it seemed, and he had an air of being thoroughly at home.

"You were in England most of the time, were you not?"

"Yes—I believe I was. Oh, by the bye, I met Harrington in Paris; I thought he meant to stay at home."

"He often goes abroad," said Mrs. Wyndham indifferently. "One lump of sugar?"

"Two, if you please—no cream—thanks. Does he go to Paris to convert the French, or to glean materials for converting other people?" inquired Mr. Vancouver languidly.

"I am sure I cannot tell you," answered the lady, still indifferently. "What do you go to Paris for?"

"Principally to renew my acquaintance with civilized institutions and humanizing influences. What does anybody go abroad for?"

"You always talk like that when you come home, Mr. Vancouver," said Mrs. Wyndham. "But nevertheless you come back and seem to find Boston bearable. It is not such a bad place after all, is it?"

"If it were not for half a dozen people here, I would never come back at all," said Mr. Vancouver. "But then, I am not originally one of you, and I suppose that makes a difference."

"And pray, who are the half dozen people who procure us the honor of your presence?"

"You are one of them, Mrs. Wyndham," he answered, looking at her.

"I am much obliged," she replied, demurely. "Any one else?"

"Oh—John Harrington," said Vancouver with a little laugh.

"Really?" said Mrs. Wyndham, innocently; "I did not know you were such good friends."

Mr. Vancouver sipped his tea in silence for a moment and stared at the fire.

"I have a great respect for Harrington," he said at last. "He interests me very much, and I like to meet him." He spoke seriously, as though thoroughly in earnest. The faintest look of amusement came to Mrs. Wyndham's face for a moment.

"I am glad of that," she said; "Mr. Harrington is a very good friend of mine. Do you mind lighting those candles? The days are dreadfully short."

Pocock Vancouver rose with alacrity and performed the service required.

"By the way," said Mrs. Wyndham, watching him, "I have a surprise for you."

"Indeed?"

"Yes, an immense surprise. Do you remember Sybil Brandon?"

"Charlie Brandon's daughter? Very well—saw her at Newport some time ago. Lily-white style—all eyes and hair."

"You ought to remember her. You used to rave about her, and you nearly ruined yourself in roses. You will have another chance; she is going to spend the winter with me."

"Not really?" ejaculated Mr. Vancouver, in some surprise, as he again sat down upon the sofa.

"Yes; you know she is all alone in the world now."

"What? Is her mother dead too?"

"She died last spring, in Paris. I thought you knew."

"No," said Vancouver, thoughtfully. "How awfully sad!"

"Poor girl," said Mrs. Wyndham; "I thought it would do her good to be among live people, even if she does not go out."

"When is she coming?" There was a show of interest about the question.

"She is here now," answered Mrs. Sam.

"Dear me!" said Vancouver. "May I have another cup?" His hostess began the usual series of operations necessary to produce a second cup of tea.

"Mrs. Wyndham," began Vancouver again after a pause, "I have an idea —do not laugh, it is a very good one, I am sure."

"I am not laughing."

"Why not marry Sybil Brandon to John Harrington?"

Mrs. Wyndham stared for a moment.

"How perfectly ridiculous!" she cried at last.

"Why?"

"They would starve, to begin with."

"I doubt it," said Vancouver.

"Why, I am sure Mr. Harrington never had more than five thousand a year in his life. You could not marry on that, you know—possibly."

"No; but Miss Brandon is very well off—rich, in fact."

"I thought she had nothing."

"She must have thirty or forty thousand a year from her mother, at the least. You know Charlie never did anything in his life; he lived on his wife's money, and Miss Brandon must have it all."

Mrs. Wyndham did not appear surprised at the information; she hardly seemed to think it of any importance.

"I knew she had something," she repeated; "but I am glad if you are right. But that does not make it any more feasible to marry her to Mr. Harrington."

"I thought that starvation was your objection," said Vancouver.

"Oh, no; not that only. Besides, he would not marry her."

"He would be very foolish not to, if he had the chance," remarked Vancouver.

"Perhaps he might not even have the chance—perhaps she would not marry him," said Mrs. Wyndham, thoughtfully. "Besides, I do not think John Harrington ought to marry yet; he has other things to do."

Mr. Vancouver seemed about to say something in answer, but he checked himself; possibly he did not speak because he saw some one enter the room at that moment, and was willing to leave the discussion of John Harrington to a future time. In fact, the person who entered the room should have been the very last to hear the conversation that was taking place, for it was Miss Brandon herself, though Mr. Vancouver had not recognized her at once.

There were greetings and hand-shakings, and then Miss Brandon sat down by the fire and spread out her hands as though to warm them. She looked white and cold.

There are women in the world, both young and old, who seem to move among us like visions from another world, a world that is purer and fairer, and more heavenly than this one in which the rest of us move. It is hard to say what such women have that marks them so distinctly; sometimes it is beauty, sometimes only a manner, often it is both. It is very certain that we know and feel their influence, and that many men fear it as something strange and contrary to the common order of things, a living reproach and protest against all that is base and earthly and badly human.

Most people would have said first of Sybil Brandon that she was cold, and many would have added that she was beautiful. Ill-natured people sometimes said she was deathly. No one ever said she was pretty. Vancouver's description—lily-white, all eyes and hair—certainly struck the principal facts of her appearance, for her skin was whiter than is commonly natural, her eyes were very deep and large and blue, and her soft brown hair seemed to be almost a burden to her from its great quantity. She was dressed entirely in black, and being rather tall and very slight of figure, the dress somewhat exaggerated the ethereal look that was natural to her. She seemed cold, and spread out her delicate hands to the bright flame of the blazing wood-fire. Mrs. Wyndham and Pocock Vancouver looked at her in silence for a moment. Then Mrs. Wyndham rose with a cup of tea in her hand, and crossed to the other side of the fireplace where Sybil was sitting and offered it to her.

"Poor Sybil, you are so cold. Drink some tea." The elder woman sat down by the young girl, and lightly kissed her cheek. "You must not be sad, darling," she whispered sympathetically.

"I am not sad at all, really," answered Miss Brandon aloud, quite naturally, but pressing Mrs. Wyndham's hand a little, as though in acknowledgment of her sympathy.

"No one can be sad in Boston," said Vancouver, putting in a word. "Our city is altogether too wildly gay." He laughed a little.

"You must not make fun of us to visitors, Mr. Vancouver," answered Mrs. Wyndham, still holding Sybil's hand.

"It is Mr. Vancouver's ruling passion, though he never acknowledges it," said Miss Brandon, calmly. "I remember it of old."

"I am flattered at being remembered," said Mr. Vancouver, whose delicate features betrayed neither pleasure nor interest, however. "But," he continued, "I am not particularly flattered at being called a scoffer at my own people—"

"I did not say that," interrupted Miss Brandon.

"Well, you said my ruling passion was making fun of Boston to visitors; at least, you and Mrs. Wyndham said it between you. I really never do that, unless I give the other side of the question as well."

"What other side?" asked Mrs. Sam, who wanted to make conversation.

"Boston," said Vancouver with some solemnity. "It is not more often ridiculous than other great institutions."

"You simply take one's breath away, Mr. Vancouver," said Mrs. Wyndham, with a good deal of emphasis. "The idea of calling Boston 'an institution'!"

"Why, certainly. The United States are only an institution after all. You could not soberly call us a nation. Even you could not reasonably be moved to fine patriotic phrases about your native country, if your ancestors had signed twenty Declarations of Independence. We live in a great institution, and we have every right to flatter ourselves on the success of its management; but in the long run this thing will not do for a nation."

Miss Brandon looked at Vancouver with a sort of calm incredulity. Mrs. Wyndham always quarreled with him on points like the one now raised, and accordingly took up the cudgels.

"I do not see how you can congratulate yourself on the management of your institution, as you call it, when you know very well you would rather die than have anything to do with it."

"Very true. But then, you always say that gentlemen should not touch anything so dirty as politics, Mrs. Wyndham," retorted Vancouver.

"Well, that just shows that it is not an institution at all, and that you are quite wrong, and that we are a great nation supported and carried on by real patriotism."

"And the Irish and German votes," added Vancouver, with that scorn which only the true son of freedom can exhibit in speaking of his fellow-citizens.

"Oh, the Irish vote! That is always the last word in the argument," answered Mrs. Sam.

"I do not see exactly what the Irish have to do with it," remarked Miss Brandon, innocently. She did not understand politics.

Vancouver glanced at the clock and took his hat.

"It is very simple," he said, rising to go. "It is the bull in the china shop —the Irish bull amongst the American china—dangerous, you know. Good evening, Mrs. Wyndham; good evening, Miss Brandon." And he took his leave. Miss Brandon watched his slim figure disappear through the heavy curtains of the door.

"He has not changed much since I knew him," she said, turning again to the fire. "I used to think he was clever."

"And have you changed your mind?" asked Mrs. Wyndham, laughing.

"Not quite, but I begin to doubt. He has very good manners, and looks altogether like a gentleman."

"Of course," said Mrs. Wyndham. "His mother was a Shaw, although his father came from South Carolina. But he is really very bright; Sam always says he is one of the ablest men in Boston."

"In what way?" inquired Sybil.

"Oh, he is a lawyer, don't you know?—great railroad man."

"Oh," ejaculated Miss Brandon, and relapsed into silence.

Mrs. Wyndham rose and stood before the fire, and pushed a log back with her small foot. Miss Brandon watched her, half wondering whether the flames would not catch her dress.

"I have been to see that Miss Thorn," said Sybil presently.

"Oh," exclaimed Mrs. Sam, with sudden interest, "tell me all about her this minute, dear. Is not she the most extraordinary creature?"

"I rather like her," answered Miss Brandon. "She is very pretty."

"What style? Dark?"

"No; not exactly. Brown hair, and lots of eyebrows. She is a little thing, but very much alive, you know."

"Awfully English, of course," suggested Mrs. Sam.

"Well—yes, I suppose so. She is wild about horses, and says she shoots. But I like her—I am sure I shall like her very much. She does not seem very pleased with her aunt."

"I do not wonder," said Mrs. Sam. "Poor little thing—she has nobody else belonging to her, has she?"

"Oh, yes," answered Sybil, with a little tremor in her voice; "she has a mother in England."

"I want to see her ever so much," said Mrs. Sam. "Bring her to luncheon."

"You will see her to-night, I think; she said she was going to that party."

"I hate to leave you alone," said Mrs. Wyndham. "I really think I had better not go."

"Dear Mrs. Wyndham," said Sybil, rising, and laying her hands on her hostess's shoulders, half affectionately, half in protest, "this idea must be stopped from the first, and I mean to stop it. You are not to give up any party, or any society, or anything at all for me. If you do I will go away again. Promise me, will you not?"

"Very well, dear. But you know you are the dearest girl in the world." And so they kissed, and agreed that Mrs. Wyndham should go out, and that Sybil should stay at home.

Mrs. Wyndham was really a very kind-hearted woman and a loving friend. That might be the reason why she was never popular. Popularity is a curious combination of friendliness and indifference, but very popular people rarely have devoted friends, and still more rarely suffer great passions. Everybody's friend is far too apt to be nobody's, for it is impossible to rely on the support of a person whose devotion is liable to be called upon a hundred times a day, from a hundred different quarters. The friendships that mean anything mean sacrifice for friendship's sake; and a man or a woman really ready to make sacrifices for a considerable number of people is likely to be asked to do it very often, and to be soon spent in the effort to be true to every one.

But popularity makes no great demands. The popular man is known to be so busy in being popular that his offenses of omission are readily pardoned. His engagements are legion, his obligations are innumerable, and far more than he can fulfil. But, meet him when you will, his smile is as bright, his greeting as cordial, and his sayings as universally good-natured and satisfactory as ever. He has acquired the habit of pleasing, and it is almost impossible for him to displease. He enjoys it all, is agreeable to every one, and is never expected to catch cold in attending a friend's funeral, or otherwise to sacrifice his comfort, because he is quite certain to have important engagements elsewhere, in which the world always believes. There is probably no individual more absolutely free and untrammeled than the thoroughly popular man.

WITH THE FIRST ARBUTUS

EMILY DICKINSON

The pure strain of New England poet, in the late nineteenth century, came out as if miraculously in the work of Emily Dickinson (1830–1886) of Amherst, Massachusetts. Was this purity the result of so hiding herself from the world that she never went out of the house, was seen, even by neighbors, only in glimpses, and all because of having in early life conceived an inconceivable attraction for a married clergyman in Philadelphia? Critics will never be sure. The only thing sure is that other poets of her time were well-fed and prosperous-seeming, not only in their persons but in their verse, while Emily's poetry, like her person, is strange, delicate, remote; above all is simple, as theirs had ceased to be.

Her poems might never even have come to the world's eyes at all had it not been for the encouragement of Thomas Wentworth Higginson, Unitarian minister and writer, who issued an appeal for new poets in the Atlantic Monthly *to which the Amherst elf replied, obliquely, by sending some poems in one envelope and her name in another. In 1890 Higginson actually managed to edit one volume, then next year another, of her poems.*

Any one of them would serve to illustrate a facet of the New England quality. I have chosen the short poem below (they are all short) because in it she comes especially close to the facts of what is dear to the New England heart.

Pink, small, and punctual,
Aromatic, low,
Covert in April,
Candid in May,

Dear to the moss,
Known by the knoll,
Next to the robin
In every human soul.

Bold little beauty,
Bedecked with thee,
Nature forswears
Antiquity.

WRECK OF THE S.S. PORTLAND

The loss of the steamer Portland *with all on board was one of the nightmare wrecks that still haunt New England memory. Bound for Portland, Maine, from Boston, November 29, 1898,* Portland *was beaten back by a wind so violent that the actual disaster occurred off the south coast of Cape Cod. The following fragments of newspaper accounts are from the Boston* Daily Advertiser.

A lantern that used to light the porch of the house where I summered as a child was part of wreckage washed ashore and still bore, faintly, the painted legend S.S. Portland. The gale that destroyed her, one of the most monstrous of modern times, was always referred to by Gloucester fishermen with typical understatement as "the Portland Breeze."

THE PORTLAND LOST?

150 People Must Have Perished at Sea in the Gale.

Freighter Fairfax a Total Wreck—29 Vessels Wrecked at Vineyard Haven.

FATAL WORK OF THE STORM.

ESTIMATED LOSS OF LIFE AT SEA DURING THE STORM, 150.

STEAMER PORTLAND, BOSTON AND PORTLAND BOAT, PROBABLY LOST WITH 60 LIVES.

CONSOLIDATED COAL CO. BARGES 1 AND 4 ASHORE AT PT. ALLERTON. THREE LIVES LOST.

UNKNOWN SCHOONER SUNK AT NANTASKET BEACH WITH ALL HANDS.

SCHR. ISLAND CITY, ROCKLAND, ME., CAPT. NELSON, LOST OFF COTTAGE CITY. CAPTAIN AND CREW OF THREE DROWNED.

CAPT. ROBERTS OF SCHR. LEORA THURLOW OF BATH, ME., PERISHED FROM EXPOSURE IN VINEYARD HAVEN HARBOR.

TUG MARS. CAPT. MILES, OF PHILADELPHIA, WITH BARGES DANIEL I. TENNEY AND DELAWARE, PROBABLY LOST OFF MINOT'S LIGHT WITH 16 SOULS.

MRS. WILBUR OF RAYNHAM SWEPT AWAY BY THE SEA AT SCITUATE.

SCHR. VIRGINIA WRECKED ON THOMPSON'S ISLAND. CAPT. STANLEY AND PALMER FREEMAN DROWNED.

SCHR. BESSIE H. GROSS LOST ON FRESH ISLAND. CAPT. WALLACE THURSTON, HIS FATHER AND HIS SON PERISH.

TWO UNKNOWN BARGES ASHORE ON BLACK ROCK. FIVE MEN LOST.

SCHR. KITTIE OF GREENPORT, N. Y., SUNK AT SAYBROOK, CONN., WITH ALL HANDS.

SCHR. CALVIN BAKER ASHORE ON SHAG ROCKS, NEAR BOS-
TON LIGHT. FOUR MEN DROWNED.

THE PORTLAND'S AWFUL FATE.

The steamer Portland, with 100 souls on board, was pounded to pieces
in Massachusetts bay Sunday. Most and almost certainly all of her passengers and crew have perished.

This much is made certain by the news developments of yesterday and
last night. Only details remain in doubt.

There remains the bare possibility that by some miracle some of the
Portland's 100 lives may have been saved. The chance is of the slenderest.

There is also doubt as to the precise chain of events that led up to the
Portland's terrible drift across Massachusetts bay, battered by terrific seas
and at the mercy of the blinding gale, until what was left of her found its
final resting place in the merciless breakers on Peaked Hill bars. This can
be definitely determined only in the improbable event of some survivors
being found somewhere in the sand hills of Cape Cod.

Briefly, the Portland, Capt. Blanchard, sailed from her Boston dock for
Portland Saturday at 7 P.M. The Maine fisherman, Maud S., Capt.
Thomas, reports sighting her at 9 P.M. off Eastern Pt., making good
weather of it. At that time she had not yet met the full force of the storm,
being protected in a measure from the growing gale by the bluff promontory of Cape Ann.

It is argued by mariners who were out in the bay Saturday night that
the gale did not break in its full fury till shortly after 9 P.M. Then the
wind increased quickly to a hurricane, and the sea made fast.

It was just after this that Capt. Stearns of the Gloucester fisherman,
Florence Stearns, reports passing a side-wheel steamer eastward of
Thatcher's Island, headed west. If this was the Portland, and no other
paddle-wheel steamer is known to have been in the Portland's track on
Saturday night, Capt. Blanchard had given up his attempt to reach Portland, had changed his course, either willingly or unwillingly, and was
seeking safety.

From this time no living soul is known to have seen the ill-fated steamer.
Nothing more was heard from her until her wreckage began to come
ashore on the back side of Cape Cod on Sunday. Even this was not known
in Boston until yesterday afternoon, all communication with the cape
being cut off by the ruin wrought by the storm.

Now, the whole of the back side of Cape Cod, from Race Pt. to Nanset,
and even Orleans, is strewn with wreckage from the Portland; bodies
have been washing ashore with life belts on marked with the steamer's
name; and the revenue cutter Dallas reports having sighted what is left of
the wreck on Peaked Hill bars.

The wreckage is of every description. It comprises packages from the cargo, furniture from the saloons, bodies of passengers and crew, the ship's wheel and all the awful debris that Cape Cod knows too well. It is reported that the steamer Longfellow, which came up from Province-town yesterday, sighted a portion of the Portland's deck house floating in the bay this side of Provincetown.

Last night, as means of communication with the Cape gradually be-came better, the same story of wreckage marked Portland, and of bodies washed ashore, came from all along the back side of the Cape, but never a place reported a survivor of the catastrophe. Hope that some have been saved fades with every station heard from.

About this skeleton of fact, experience of seafaring men and knowledge of the conditions that prevailed outside, combine to build a structure that is more than conjecture though less than fact.

It is believed by seafaring men that the Portland, when the full force of the hurricane struck her, had reached a position north of Thatcher's Island, off Ipswich bay, the most exposed position on the Cape Ann Shore.

Here they figure that the Portland either became disabled or was whirled by the force of the gale into the trough of the sea. Disabled or not, if broadside to the sea, the Portland, being a side-wheel steamer, would be equally helpless.

Men of long experience on paddle-wheel steamers say that when such a steamer falls into the trough of the sea it is almost impossible to bring her up into the wind again. Of shallow draft and with high guards as a target for the gale, she would roll down on her beam ends in such a sea-way; and with one wheel out of water the other would spin about like a top.

Helpless from one cause or the other, sailors believed the Portland drifted before the awful gale, edging out to windward all she could to get off the lee shore.

The horror of that night no one can tell, no one can even imagine. A helpless steamer driving with 100 terror-stricken souls before a snow-laden hurricane in weather so thick that no one could see 10 ft. into the gray terror whence they were drifting; wallowing helplessly in merciless seas that pummelled her remorselessly, beat her down, swept away one pitiful wretch after another from her shivering decks and tore great pieces from her superstructure; drifting on and on and on, not knowing whither; her people standing face to face with death for hours and know-ing that he must be met at the last, whether in the tempestuous waters of the bay or, when death came to most, in the roaring malestrom where the sea's white horses charged the rampart that Peaked Hill sets up against the inroads of the ocean; and then, at the end, the crash into the breakers, the parting of the few last timbers and the short bitter struggle in the billowing seas that claimed every victim as due sacrifice—no, the story of that night can never be told, for they that saw life slipping away from them during those awful hours now lie in Ocean's greatest graveyard, the old Cape Cod.

The ocean has given up some of the Portland's dead. How many it is impossible to say. Early reports yesterday said 34 bodies had been washed ashore at Highland Light. Later advices do not bear this out.

The dead lies (*sic*) strewn along 60 miles of coast from Race Point to Orleans. The full count may not be made for some days yet, and many bodies will doubtless never be recovered.

PAINFUL SUSPENSE

Almost Certain That the Portland Was Wrecked.

There is every reason to fear that the steamer Portland of the Portland line, which sailed from Boston last Saturday for Portland, is lost with the 60 people on board.

No news had been received up to a late hour this morning as to the whereabouts of the overdue steamer. She had a passenger list of 25, a crew of 33 men, and two attendants.

When her sister ship, the Bay State, came into the dock yesterday from Portland, and Capt. Dennison reported that he had seen no trace of the lost steamer, Agent Williams took immediate steps to ascertain if the steamer lay disabled in some remote harbor on the northern New England coast.

Every port accessible by telegraph or telephone was questioned, but the answers were in the negative.

Then arrangements were perfected with the United States cutter service to despatch two vessels, and last night the cutter Woodbury was sent out from Portland to cruise down towards Cape Ann, and the cutter Dallas, Capt. Clark, sailed from Salem to explore the shoals and harbors of the south shore and the bight of Massachusetts Bay.

There is no doubt that disaster of some sort has befallen the steamer, as yesterday was a favorable opportunity for venturing out of any harbor in which she may have previously sought shelter.

The names of the 25 passengers on the steamer are known only to the purser on the vessel, as no list is kept in the local office. One name is known, G. B. Kenniston, Jr., of Boothbay.

The officers of the vessel are: Capt. H. H. Blanchard of East Deering, Me.; pilots, Lewis Strout, East Boston; Lewis Nelson, Portland; purser, T. A. Ingraham; clerk, Horace Moore; mate, Edward Deering; second mate, John McKay; all of Portland; watchmen, R. Blake, T. Sewell; 1st eng., Thomas Morrell; 2d eng., John Walter; 3d eng., C. Verrill; all of

Portland; steward, A. B. Matthews; 2d steward, Eben Horton; two colored stewardesses.

The steamer carries a crew of 15 men. Arthur Stran is the only name known here belonging to the crew.

The Portland has a cargo of about 100 tons of miscellaneous merchandise, and total value of vessel and cargo is about $250,000, fully insured. She was built in 1890 by the New England Shipbuilding Co. at Bath, Me., and is 280 ft. 9 in. in length, 42 ft. 1 in. beam, and 15 ft. 5 in. depth of hold. The steamer's net tonnage is 1517 tons.

Capt. Dennison of the Bay State, which sailed last night for Portland, was instructed to keep a sharp lookout on his northern trip for the missing vessel.

LOST WITH ALL ON BOARD.

Nantasket Beach, Nov. 28.—Some time this morning a greater part of the schooner Bessie H. Gross, which was wrecked at Manchester, was thrown up on the beach, having drifted clear across the bay. No one was seen on board, but it was subsequently learned that two were lost when she went ashore and two others taken off by lifesavers at Manchester.

An unknown schooner struck the rocks below the Atlantic House yesterday afternoon and before she went to pieces one man was seen in the rigging making frantic signals towards shore.

Those on the beach, however, were powerless to aid him, and the vessel broke up before their very eyes in a very few minutes. So completely was the schooner ground to pieces on the rocks that not the slightest trace of her name could be found on any of the small fragments.

DIRE DEVASTATION.

THE STORM WAS THE MOST DESTRUCTIVE EVER KNOWN HERE.

The most appalling disaster that has ever overtaken the coastwise shipping of the United States was the fearful record of Sunday's storm in Boston Bay and along the New England coast.

Tales of death and destruction continue to come in from all along the coast and the many points at present unheard from are expected to send direful news when communication can be again restored.

It is known definitely tonight that over 70 lives have been lost in the wrecks of tugs, schooners and coal barges, and if the steamer Portland has also gone down, as now seems probable, the work of the storm will carry the casualties up to 150, with over 100 vessels of all descriptions ashore, two score of them total wrecks, and an unknown number probably beneath the waves of Massachusetts Bay.

There is scarcely a bay, harbor or inlet from the Penobscot to New London that has not on its shores the bones of some staunch craft, while along Massachusetts Bay, and especially Boston harbor, the beaches are piled high with the wreckage of schooners and coal barges. And yet the record is incomplete, for that ocean graveyard of Cape Cod is still to be heard from, and as it has never yet failed to give up some grim tale at such a time, it probably will not be found lacking on such an occasion.

The islands of Boston harbor are without exception strewn with wrecks and wreckages, no less than 29 vessels are ashore at Gloucester, over 20 in a supposed safe harbor of Vineyard Haven parted their anchor chains yesterday, and are high and dry on the beach. Nantasket Beach saw two schooners and a coal barge dashed to pieces on its sands; the rocks of Cohasset claimed a staunch fisherman; Scituate, a well known pilot boat; Manchester, a down-east lumberman, while one tug and three barges known to have been between Cape Cod and Boston, are unaccounted for and probably lost.

FOR THOSE IN PERIL ON THE SEA

RUDYARD KIPLING

Rudyard Kipling (1865–1936) lived for a short period in a house over-looking Gloucester harbor, in Massachusetts; the interest he took in the Gloucester fishing industry led to his writing Captains Courageous, *one of the two or three great classics of the sea for children. The conclusion of the book depicts a ceremony enacted every August, when (nowadays) wreaths are cast on the outgoing tide in memory of Gloucester fishermen dead at sea.*

When I first attended this moving service, as a child, dozens of fishermen were lost each year. In the last century, the count was often over a hundred. In the year in which I am writing this, only three Gloucester fishermen were lost at sea and none by drowning.

I have appended here the program of this year's service. The ceremony would not have been so good if it had been more expert: the oratory was awkward, the singing not always on key, the brass band tiny, the mariners ancient. But the heart was in it.

Disko had no use for public functions where appeals were made for charity, but Harvey pleaded that the glory of the day would be lost, so far as he was concerned, if the *We 're Heres* absented themselves. Then Disko made conditions. He had heard—it was astonishing how all the world knew all the world's business along the water-front—he had heard that a "Philadelphia actress-woman" was going to take part in the exercises; and he mistrusted that she would deliver "Skipper Ireson's Ride." Personally, he had as little use for actresses as for summer boarders; but justice was justice, and though he himself (here Dan giggled) had once slipped up on a matter of judgment, this thing must not be. So Harvey came back to East Gloucester, and spent half a day explaining to an amused actress with a royal reputation on two seaboards the inwardness of the mistake she contemplated; and she admitted that it was justice, even as Disko had said.

Cheyne knew by old experience what would happen; but anything of the nature of a public palaver was meat and drink to the man's soul. He saw the trolleys hurrying west, in the hot, hazy morning, full of women in light summer dresses, and white-faced straw-hatted men fresh from Boston desks; the stack of bicycles outside the post-office; the come-and-go of busy officials, greeting one another; the slow flick and swash of bunting in the heavy air; and the important man with a hose sluicing the brick sidewalk.

"Mother," he said suddenly, "don't you remember—after Seattle was burned out—and they got her going again?"

Mrs. Cheyne nodded, and looked critically down the crooked street. Like her husband, she understood these gatherings, all the West over, and compared them one against another. The fishermen began to mingle with the crowd about the town-hall doors—blue-jowled Portuguese, their women bare-headed or shawled for the most part; clear-eyed Nova Scotians, and men of the Maritime Provinces; French, Italians, Swedes, and Danes, with outside crews of coasting schooners; and everywhere women in black, who saluted one another with a gloomy pride, for this was their day of great days. And there were ministers of many creeds,— pastors of great, gilt-edged congregations, at the seaside for a rest, with shepherds of the regular work,—from the priests of the Church on the Hill to bush-bearded ex-sailor Lutherans, hail-fellow with the men of a score of boats. There were owners of lines of schooners, large contributors to the societies, and small men, their few craft pawned to the mast-heads, with bankers and marine-insurance agents, captains of tugs and water-boats, riggers, fitters, lumpers, salters, boat-builders, and coopers, and all the mixed population of the water-front.

They drifted along the line of seats made gay with the dresses of the summer boarders, and one of the town officials patrolled and perspired

till he shone all over with pure civic pride. Cheyne had met him for five
minutes a few days before, and between the two there was entire
understanding.

"Well, Mr. Cheyne, and what d' you think of our city?—Yes, madam,
you can sit anywhere you please.—You have this kind of thing out West,
I presume?"

"Yes, but we are n't as old as you."

"That's so, of course. You ought to have been at the exercises when we
celebrated our two hundred and fiftieth birthday. I tell you, Mr. Cheyne,
the old city did herself credit."

"So I heard. It pays, too. What's the matter with the town that it don't
have a first-class hotel, though?"

"—Right over there to the left, Pedro. Heaps o' room for you and your
crowd.—Why, that's what *I* tell 'em all the time, Mr. Cheyne. There's big
money in it, but I presume that don't affect you any. What we want is—"

A heavy hand fell on his broadcloth shoulder, and the flushed skipper
of a Portland coal-and-ice coaster spun him half round. "What in thunder
do you fellows mean by clappin' the law on the town when all decent
men are at sea this way? Heh? Town's dry's a bone, an' smells a sight
worse sence I quit. 'Might ha' left us one saloon for soft drinks, anyway."

"'Don't seem to have hindered your nourishment this morning, Carsen.
I'll go into the politics of it later. Sit down by the door and think over
your arguments till I come back."

"What good's arguments to me? In Miquelon champagne's eighteen
dollars a case, and—" The skipper lurched into his seat as an organ-prelude
silenced him.

"Our new organ," said the official proudly to Cheyne. "'Cost us four
thousand dollars, too. We'll have to get back to high-license next year
to pay for it. I was n't going to let the ministers have all the religion at
their convention. Those are some of our orphans standing up to sing. My
wife taught 'em. See you again later, Mr. Cheyne. I'm wanted on the
platform."

High, clear, and true, children's voices bore down the last noise of
those settling into their places.

"*O all ye Works of the Lord, bless ye the Lord: praise him, and
magnify him for ever!*"

The women throughout the hall leaned forward to look as the reiterated
cadences filled the air. Mrs. Cheyne, with some others, began to breathe
short; she had hardly imagined there were so many widows in the world;
and instinctively searched for Harvey. He had found the *We're Heres*
at the back of the audience, and was standing, as by right, between
Dan and Disko. Uncle Salters, returned the night before with Penn, from
Pamlico Sound, received him suspiciously.

"Hain't your folk gone yet?" he grunted. "What are you doin' here, young feller?"

"*O ye Seas and Floods, bless ye the Lord: praise him, and magnify him for ever!*"

"Hain't he good right?" said Dan. "He's bin there, same as the rest of us."

"Not in them clothes," Salters snarled.

"Shut your head, Salters," said Disko. "Your bile 's gone back on you. Stay right where ye are, Harve."

Then up and spoke the orator of the occasion, another pillar of the municipality, bidding the world welcome to Gloucester, and incidentally pointing out wherein Gloucester excelled the rest of the world. Then he turned to the sea-wealth of the city, and spoke of the price that must be paid for the yearly harvest. They would hear later the names of their lost dead—one hundred and seventeen of them. (The widows stared a little, and looked at one another here.) Gloucester could not boast any overwhelming mills or factories. Her sons worked for such wage as the sea gave; and they all knew that neither Georges nor the Banks were cow-pastures. The utmost that folk ashore could accomplish was to help the widows and the orphans; and after a few general remarks he took this opportunity of thanking, in the name of the city, those who had so public-spiritedly consented to participate in the exercises of the occasion.

"I jest despise the beggin' pieces in it," growled Disko. "It don't give folk a fair notion of us."

"Ef folk won't be fore-handed an' put by when they 've the chance," returned Salters, "it stands in the nature o' things they *hev* to be 'shamed. You take warnin' by that, young feller. Riches endureth but for a season, ef you scatter them araound on lugsuries—"

"But to lose everything—everything," said Penn. "What can you do *then?* Once I"—the watery blue eyes stared up and down, as looking for something to steady them—"once I read—in a book, I think—of a boat where every one was run down—except some one—and he said to me—"

"Shucks!" said Salters, cutting in. "You read a little less an' take more int'rust in your vittles, and you 'll come nearer earnin' your keep, Penn."

Harvey, jammed among the fishermen, felt a creepy, crawly, tingling thrill that began in the back of his neck and ended at his boots. He was cold, too, though it was a stifling day.

"'That the actress from Philadelphia?" said Disko Troop, scowling at the platform. "You 've fixed it about old man Ireson, hain't ye, Harve? Ye know why naow."

It was not "Ireson's Ride" that the woman delivered, but some sort of poem about a fishing-port called Brixham and a fleet of trawlers beating in against storm by night, while the women made a guiding fire at the head of the quay with everything they could lay hands on.

> "They took the grandam's blanket,
> Who shivered and bade them go;
> They took the baby's cradle,
> Who could not say them no."

"Whew!" said Dan, peering over Long Jack's shoulder. "That's great! Must ha' bin expensive, though."

"Ground-hog case," said the Galway man. "Badly lighted port, Danny."

.   .   .   .   .   .

> "And knew not all the while
> If they were lighting a bonfire
> Or only a funeral pile."

The wonderful voice took hold of people by their heartstrings; and when she told how the drenched crews were flung ashore, living and dead, and they carried the bodies to the glare of the fires, asking: "Child, is this your father?" or "Wife, is this your man?" you could hear hard breathing all over the benches.

> "And when the boats of Brixham
> Go out to face the gales,
> Think of the love that travels
> Like light upon their sails!"

There was very little applause when she finished. The women were looking for their handkerchiefs, and many of the men stared at the ceiling with shiny eyes.

"H'm," said Salters; "that 'u'd cost ye a dollar to hear at any theater— maybe two. Some folk, I presoom, can afford it. 'Seems downright waste to me. . . . Naow, how in Jerusalem did Cap Bart Edwardes strike adrift here?"

"No keepin' him under," said an Eastport man behind. "He 's a poet, an' he 's baound to say his piece. 'Comes from daown aour way, too."

He did not say that Captain B. Edwardes had striven for five consecutive years to be allowed to recite a piece of his own composition on Gloucester Memorial Day. An amused and exhausted committee had at last given him his desire. The simplicity and utter happiness of the old man, as he stood up in his very best Sunday clothes, won the audience ere he opened his mouth. They sat unmurmuring through seven-and-thirty hatchet-made verses describing at fullest length the loss of the schooner *Joan Hasken* off the Georges in the gale of 1867, and when he came to an end they shouted with one kindly throat.

A far-sighted Boston reporter slid away for a full copy of the epic and an interview with the author; so that earth had nothing more to offer Captain Bart Edwardes, ex-whaler, shipwright, master-fisherman, and poet, in the seventy-third year of his age.

"Naow, I call that sensible," said the Eastport man. "I've bin over that graound with his writin', jest as he read it, in my two hands, and I can testify that he 's got it all in."

"If Dan here could n't do better 'n that with one hand before breakfast, he ought to be switched," said Salters, upholding the honor of Massachusetts on general principles. "Not but what I'm free to own he 's considerable litt'ery—fer Maine. Still—"

"Guess Uncle Salters goin' to die this trip. Fust compliment he 's ever paid me," Dan sniggered. "What's wrong with you, Harve? You act all quiet and you look greenish. Feelin' sick?"

"Don't know what 's the matter with me," Harvey replied. " 'Seems if my insides were too big for my outsides. I 'm all crowded up and shivery."

"Dispepsy? Pshaw—too bad. We 'll wait for the readin', an' then we 'll quit, an' catch the tide."

The widows—they were nearly all of that season's making—braced themselves rigidly like people going to be shot in cold blood, for they knew what was coming. The summer-boarder girls in pink and blue shirtwaists stopped tittering over Captain Edwardes's wonderful poem, and looked back to see why all was silent. The fishermen pressed forward as that town official who had talked with Cheyne bobbed up on the platform and began to read the year's list of losses, dividing them into months. Last September's casualties were mostly single men and strangers, but his voice rang very loud in the stillness of the hall.

"September 9th.—Schooner *Florrie Anderson* lost, with all aboard, off the Georges.

"Reuben Pitman, master, 50, single, Main Street, City.

"Emil Olsen, 19, single, 329 Hammond Street, City; Denmark.

"Oscar Stanberg, single, 25, Sweden.

"Carl Stanberg, single, 28, Main Street, City.

"Pedro, supposed Madeira, single, Keene's boardinghouse, City.

"Joseph Welsh, alias Joseph Wright, 30, St. John's, Newfoundland."

"No—Augusty, Maine," a voice cried from the body of the hall.

"He shipped from St. John's," said the reader, looking to see.

"I know it. He belongs in Augusty. My nevvy."

The reader made a penciled correction on the margin of the list, and resumed:

"Same schooner, Charlie Ritchie, Liverpool, Nova Scotia, 33, single.

"Albert May, 267 Rogers Street, City, 27, single.

"September 27th.—Orvin Dollard, 30, married, drowned in dory off Eastern Point."

That shot went home, for one of the widows flinched where she sat, clasping and unclasping her hands. Mrs. Cheyne, who had been listening with wide-opened eyes, threw up her head and choked. Dan's mother, a few seats to the right, saw and heard and quickly moved to her side. The reading went on. By the time they reached the January and February wrecks the shots were falling thick and fast, and the widows drew breath between their teeth.

> "February 14th.—Schooner *Harry Randolph* dismasted on the way home from Newfoundland; Asa Musie, married, 32, Main Street, City, lost overboard.
> "February 23d.—Schooner *Gilbert Hope;* went astray in dory, Robert Beavon, 29, married, native of Pubnico, Nova Scotia."

But his wife was in the hall. They heard a low cry, as though a little animal had been hit. It was stifled at once, and a girl staggered out of the hall. She had been hoping against hope for months, because some who have gone adrift in dories have been miraculously picked up by deep-sea sailing-ships. Now she had her certainty, and Harvey could see the policeman on the sidewalk hailing a hack for her. "It 's fifty cents to the depot"—the driver began, but the policeman held up his hand—"but I 'm goin' there anyway. Jump right in. Look at here, Alf; you don't pull me next time my lamps ain't lit. See?"

The side-door closed on the patch of bright sunshine, and Harvey's eyes turned again to the reader and his endless list.

> "April 19th.—Schooner *Mamie Douglas* lost on the Banks with all hands.
> "Edward Canton, 43, master, married, City.
> "D. Hawkins, alias Williams, 34, married, Shelbourne, Nova Scotia.
> "G. W. Clay, colored, 28, married, City."

And so on, and so on. Great lumps were rising in Harvey's throat, and his stomach reminded him of the day when he fell from the liner.

> "May 10th.—Schooner *We 're Here* [the blood tingled all over him]. Otto Svendson, 20, single, City, lost overboard."

Once more a low, tearing cry from somewhere at the back of the hall.

"She should n't ha' come. She should n't ha' come," said Long Jack, with a cluck of pity.

"Don't scrowge, Harve," grunted Dan. Harvey heard that much, but the rest was all darkness spotted with fiery wheels. Disko leaned forward and spoke to his wife, where she sat with one arm round Mrs. Cheyne, and the other holding down the snatching, catching, ringed hands.

"Lean your head daown—right daown!" she whispered. "It 'll go off in a minute."

"I ca-an't! I do-don't! Oh, let me—" Mrs. Cheyne did not at all know what she said.

"You must," Mrs. Troop repeated. "Your boy 's jest fainted dead away. They do that some when they 're gettin' their growth. 'Wish to tend to him? We can git aout this side. Quite quiet. You come right along with me. Psha', my dear, we 're both women, I guess. We must tend to aour men-folk. Come!"

The *We 're Heres* promptly went through the crowd as a body-guard, and it was a very white and shaken Harvey that they propped up on a bench in an anteroom.

"Favors his ma," was Mrs. Troop's only comment, as the mother bent over her boy.

"How d' you suppose he could ever stand it?" she cried indignantly to Cheyne, who had said nothing at all. "It was horrible—horrible! We should n't have come. It 's wrong and wicked! It—it isn't right! Why—why could n't they put these things in the papers, where they belong? Are you better, darling?"

That made Harvey very properly ashamed. "Oh, I 'm all right, I guess," he said, struggling to his feet, with a broken giggle. "Must ha' been something I ate for breakfast."

"Coffee, perhaps," said Cheyne, whose face was all in hard lines, as though it had been cut out of bronze. "We won't go back again."

"Guess 't would be 'baout 's well to git daown to the wharf," said Disko. "It 's close in along with them Dagoes, an' the fresh air will fresh Mrs. Cheyne up."

Harvey announced that he never felt better in his life; but it was not till he saw the *We 're Here*, fresh from the lumper's hands, at Wouverman's wharf, that he lost his all-overish feelings in a queer mixture of pride and sorrowfulness. Other people—summer boarders and such-like— played about in catboats or looked at the sea from pier-heads; but he understood things from the inside—more things than he could begin to think about. None the less, he could have sat down and howled because the little schooner was going off. Mrs. Cheyne simply cried and cried every step of the way, and said most extraordinary things to Mrs. Troop, who "babied" her till Dan, who had not been "babied" since he was six, whistled aloud.

And so the old crowd—Harvey felt like the most ancient of mariners— dropped into the old schooner among the battered dories, while Harvey slipped the stern-fast from the pier-head, and they slid her along the wharf-side with their hands. Every one wanted to say so much that no one said anything in particular. Harvey bade Dan take care of Uncle

Salters's sea-boots and Penn's dory-anchor, and Long Jack entreated Harvey to remember his lessons in seamanship; but the jokes fell flat in the presence of the two women, and it is hard to be funny with green harbor-water widening between good friends.

"Up jib and fores'l!" shouted Disko, getting to the wheel, as the wind took her. " 'See you later, Harve. Dunno but I come near thinkin' a heap o' you an' your folks."

Then she glided beyond ear-shot, and they sat down to watch her up the harbor. And still Mrs. Cheyne wept.

"Psha', my dear," said Mrs. Troop; "we 're both women, I guess. Like 's not it 'll ease your heart to hev your cry aout. God He knows it never done me a mite o' good; but then He knows I 've had something to cry fer!"

Fishermen's Memorial Service

SUNDAY, AUGUST 5, 1962, at 3:00 P. M.

WESTON U. FRIEND, Officer of the Day

The Band will leave the Fishermen's Institute at 2:30 p.m. and march to the statue of Gloucester Fisherman.

BAND—"Before the Mast"   Larendeau

AT STATUE

BAND—"Jesus Saviour Pilot Me"   Goldman

LAYING OF WREATHS

Capt. Colin Powers
Representing Master Mariners' Association

Capt. Lemuel R. Firth
Representing Gloucester Fishing Masters and Producers Association

Alphonsus F. Hayes
Representing Atlantic Fishermens Union

BAND—"Son of My Soul"   Monk

MARCH TO BLYNMAN BRIDGE
EXERCISES AT THE BRIDGE

BAND—"Eternal Father Strong to Save"

INVOCATION   Father Daniel G. Sullivan
St. Ann's Church

SOLO—"My Soul Is Athirst For God"　　　　　　　　Gaul
　　　　　　　Robert F. Churchill

BAND—"I know that my Redeemer Liveth"

ADDRESS　　　　　Rev. Charles M. Charlton, Captain, U.S.N. Retd.
　　　　　　　　　　　　　　Chaplain in Chief, U.S.W.V.

DUET—"The Wings of Morning"　　　　　　　　　Scott
　　　　　Mrs. Ronald Maciel and Robert F. Churchill

MEMORIAL PRAYER　　　　　　　Rev. Frank S. Murray
　　　　　　　　　　　　　Ravenswood Community Chapel

SINGING BY THE AUDIENCE　　　Leader—Robert F. Churchill

"SCATTER FLOWERS ON THE WAVES" (Mary Brooks)

1. Scat-ter flow-ers on the waves; There our fa-thers found their graves,
2. Ebb-ing tide of sum-mer day, Bear these blos-soms on their way,

Broth-ers, sons and hus-bands sleep; Strew your gar-lands o'er the deep.
North and east to bank and coast Where they lie whom we love most.

FLOWER CEREMONY

READING OF THE ROLL OF THE DEAD　　　Mrs. Isabel Gray

In memory of all the seamen who through all the years, have found a last resting place in the waters that wash every shore, we lovingly strew these flowers.

Participants standing along the waterway will cast their bouquets of flowers upon the water.

WREATH FROM MASTER MARINERS' ASSOCIATION
Capt. Colin Powers, V.P.

WREATH FROM GLOUCESTER FISHING MASTERS AND
PRODUCERS ASSOCIATION   Capt. Lemuel R. Firth

WREATH FROM ATLANTIC FISHERMEN'S UNION
Alphonsus F. Hayes

WREATH FROM GLOUCESTER FISHERMEN'S INSTITUTE
Leslie F. Yelland

WREATH FROM THE CITY OF GLOUCESTER
AND REMARKS   Councilman John Stanley Boudreau

BENEDICTION   Dr. Glenn Barker
Community Church, East Gloucester

TAPS—Arthur Lufkin and Jack Ramos

BAND—"Anchors Aweigh"

PRESIDENT ELIOT OF HARVARD

MARK A. DEWOLFE HOWE

———◆•◆———

*Mark Antony DeWolfe Howe (1864–1959) was a full-scale professional
literary figure of our own as well as the past century. He knew everybody,
and everybody loved him. Author of dozens of volumes, he was the
raconteur, poet, editor, and biographer of New England; from his* Classic
Shades *I have taken the following excerpt from an essay on President
Charles William Eliot of Harvard (1834–1926).*

*I remember President-Emeritus Eliot, when he used to come, once a
year, to speak at assembly to the girls at Miss Winsor's School. By that
time he was frail and white-skinned. He seemed, indeed he was, a figure
out of a bygone age with his side whiskers and gray, hairy hard hat with
its squared-off top.*

THE education of President Eliot for his work in the world began, in
accordance with the familiar prescription of Dr. Holmes, long before his
birth. His Harvard lineage was impeccable. Back of his father, Samuel
Atkins Eliot, Treasurer of Harvard College for the eleven years ended

with the graduation of his distinguished son, and thus a member of the Harvard Corporation,—that compact body of final authority in which a recent English observer has shrewdly recognized a "government by seven cousins,"—extended a line of Eliots and Lymans reaching far back into New England history, with a goodly number of Eliots in the earlier Harvard classes. It is, by the way, an amusing circumstance that in the latest edition of the *Harvard Quinquennial Catalogue* (1925) an ingenious misprint gives the middle name of President Eliot's uncle, William *Havard* Eliot, of the Class of 1815, when it appears in the Index of Graduates at the end of the volume, as *Harvard*—as if to say that his family must not escape complete identification with the University. . . .

Not until young Eliot had arrived at man's estate did financial misfortune overtake his father and abridge the pleasant indoor and outdoor activities of Boston winters and Nahant summers. But the roots of the son's being had already struck down so deep into what he described many years later as "the durable satisfactions of life" that outward circumstances had little power to disturb him. The personal handicaps of imperfect vision and the disfigurement of a facial birthmark were accepted with equal unconcern.

Even with eyes that cut him off from reading during a large portion of his junior year in Harvard College, the studious, self-contained youth graduated second in his Class of 1853. To mathematics and chemistry he gave as much of his time as the rigid curriculum of the day would permit, the more to chemistry through gaining access—while laboratories were still the sacred precincts of professors only—to the private laboratory of Professor Josiah P. Cooke. He applied himself besides to the mastery of written and spoken English, and trained his classmates in the singing of a graduation ode. For a year after the completion of his college course he was a tutor in mathematics, and then for five years Assistant Professor of Mathematics and Chemistry in the Lawrence Scientific School at Harvard. . . .

The modestly paid professorship of chemistry on which he entered . . . at the newly established Massachusetts Institute of Technology held his thoughts to the field of education—and the fruits of his thinking, shown forth in two articles in the *Atlantic Monthly* for February and March, 1869, are counted the *causa causans* of his election to the presidency of Harvard a few months later. . . .

The anonymity of *Atlantic* contributions was not so dark a secret but that the young professor in the Institute of Technology could easily be identified with the "New Education" articles. It was a new voice which spoke of "the recognized text-books, mostly of exquisite perverseness, but backed by the reputation of their authors and the capital of their publishers," and of "crude communities where hasty culture is as natural as fast eating." It was a voice both new and prophetic which declared that the American university has not yet "grown out of the soil," and proceeded:—

> It cannot be transplanted from England or Germany in full leaf and bearing. It cannot be run up, like a cotton mill, in six months to meet a quick demand. Neither can it be created by the energetic use of the inspired editorial, the advertising circular, and the frequent telegram. Numbers do not constitute it, and no money can make it before its time. There is more of the University about the eight or ten Yale graduates who are studying in the Yale Department of Philosophy and the Arts, than in as many hundred raw youths who do not know more than a fair grammar school may teach. When the American university appears, it will not be a copy of foreign institutions, or a hot-bed plant, but the slow and natural outgrowth of American social and political habits, and an expression of the average aims and ambitions of the better educated classes. The American college is an institution without a parallel; the American university will be equally original.

Though these articles on "The New Education" had to do primarily with the scientific, "practical" training of schools like the new Massachusetts Institute, it was not strange that, through passages such as the one just quoted, they gave the Harvard Corporation good reason to consider the writer, already well known for his character and scholarship, as a possible successor to President Thomas Hill, who resigned in September of 1868.

Accordingly the Corporation elected him in the following March to the vacant post. Under the regulations of the University the election had to be confirmed by the Board of Overseers, of which Eliot himself was then a member. This larger governing body, elected by the graduates of the College, might have been expected to welcome what has since come to be called a "progressive" in education. On the contrary, the Overseers at two meetings following soon upon Eliot's election by the Corporation refused to ratify that action. But the Corporation persisted in its choice of a president, and on May 19 the Board, on the third time of asking, gave its consent to the election. It was highly characteristic of the magnanimity of the new president that in his Inaugural Address in the following October he expressed himself on this wise with respect to the functions of the Board of Overseers: "The Overseers should always hold toward the Corporation an attitude of suspicious vigilance. They ought always to be pushing and prying."

The new "boy president," as the many doubters liked to call him, was only thirty-five years old. Even after the lapse of nearly sixty years, his Inaugural Address conveys to the reader of it that sharp sense of youth which accompanies the forthright expressions of ideas perennially modern. It is an amazing document, its youthfulness of spirit tempered with the maturity of one who had thought much and clearly on the fundamentals of the problem he was about to face; and it is even more amazing in the retrospect than it could have been at the moment of delivery, for it may now be read as one reads a programme not before but after a performance, when all the promises have been fulfilled. . . .

At the time of Eliot's retirement from the Harvard presidency, forty years later, a Phi Beta Kappa poet, Barrett Wendell,—who could be counted upon to disagree with him at many points,—bore testimony to the lifelong inveterate quality of optimism in him:—

> Truly assured, when others doubted still,
> That human good surpasses human ill.

And with the optimism went a confidence—when it came to his favorite subject of elective studies—which Wendell did not fail to note:—

> Election
> He held, almost with Calvin, was the one
> Way to salvation, and he dared to expect
> Boys to be god-like, and like him to elect.

It is impossible in the compass of a brief study to trace the unhurried, unresting steps by which President Eliot, still obeying at eve the voice he obeyed at prime, pressed on to his goal. The elements contributing to his great achievements were easy to recognize. First of all, there was the gift of an extraordinary personality. . . . It is true that personality is a hard thing to keep alive. But in this regard the chances of President Eliot are surely among the best. The picture of his noble presence, dignified by his height of more than six feet and by the carriage of one who made a lifelong practice of exercise in the open air, rowing, sailing, riding, both horse and bicycle; the sound of his distinctive voice, of a husky, quiet depth and richness that made it the perfect medium for the carefully chosen and measured words he was wont to utter—these are certain to remain vivid memories so long as any such things can last.

The manners of "a gentleman who is also a democrat"—and manners are surely to be counted among the expressions of personality—were the subject of a talk he once made to new students at Harvard. He knew these manners well, for they were his own. "Considerate attention," he said, "is always an important part of good manners." He was himself an inveterate asker of questions, but, unlike many such inquirers, he did not in the least resemble Pilate, who "would not stay for an answer." His listening was as notable as his asking, and that was so notorious as to become the subject of a significant anecdote, often told by word of mouth before it was printed in a posthumous book by the late Paul Revere

Frothingham. This story has it that when the Reverend Leighton Parks one evening after a service in Appleton Chapel described to Phillips Brooks the impressive appearance of President Eliot standing in a front pew and singing lustily,

Am I a soldier of the Cross,
A follower of the Lamb?

the chuckling comment of Brooks, quite alive to Eliot's Unitarian sympathies, was, "Asking for information probably." Upon his attentive listening for a reply Brooks would have been among the first to count. It was Eliot's unfailing habit, in faculty meetings and elsewhere, to give careful heed to all expressions of views opposed to his own, but, once his mind was made up, to employ every legitimate means to make his views prevail. . . .

In another talk to new students he once recalled the advice he received from an old friend of his family at the time of his election as president. "Charles," said this friend, "I suppose you think that in your new office the first quality you will need is energy." "Why, yes," came the answer, "I thought that energy was likely to be needed." "No," said his elder friend, "that is not at all the first quality you will need. The first quality is patience, patience, patience." This, as Eliot went on to say, proved clearly to be the case.

His patience was needed particularly in the overcoming of obstacles, often apparently insuperable. So far-reaching a programme of change as that which he proposed, and carried out, could not fail to excite opposition. This was strengthened through many years of his presidency by a positive personal unpopularity in one quarter after another. The established order is dear to the heart not only of university officials but of youth, and to do as many things to the College as Eliot did in the process of liberalizing it, and as many things to the professional schools in lifting them from relative unimportance to the high place they came to occupy under his nourishing and stimulating hand, was sure to provoke antagonism at many a turn. This was conquered only by long and slow degrees. When the Massachusetts Historical Society celebrated in 1923 the fiftieth anniversary of Eliot's becoming a member of it, he referred, in words which I have already quoted elsewhere, to the great change that had come to pass as he was nearing ninety: "In all the early part of my career as a teacher and an educational administrator I was much engaged in controversy, not to say combat, and that at home as well as outside of Harvard. In all my public appearances during those years I had a vivid sense that I was addressing an adverse audience. Now to-day is a very delightful illustration of a change that has come over my experience. For twenty years past, I should think, I have found myself often in the pres-

ence of a favoring audience—of one that wished, at any rate, to agree with
me, or, if they could not, regretted that they could not."

Some measure of the unpopularity that had to be overcome must have
sprung from an undeniable outward coolness of demeanor. The man
whose balanced temperament permits him, as in the case of Eliot, to go
quietly forward to the objects he has in view, unruffled by considerations
personal to himself if only he draws nearer all the time to the final object,
must look upon the common arts of popularity as quite aside from his
main purpose; and this cannot be done without the payment of at least a
temporary penalty. In an unreported speech at a club, devoted primarily
to good-fellowship, which he joined at the age of seventy, I once heard
him lament with a pathetic sincerity the fact that the necessity of working
with unremitting intensity in his earlier years and the handicap of his eyesight had deprived him of human relationships in which he would have
taken a keen enjoyment. The singer that was hushed in the youth who
drilled his classmates in choral song seemed indeed to be speaking. As
one saw him in the later years of his life under conditions favorable to
friendly intercourse, his enjoyment in the give and take of talk and in the
discussion of events, particularly in the light of their human implications,
seemed to relegate the austerity with which he was commonly credited to
the realm of fable. . . .

There were those who complained, and not without reason, that, especially as his years advanced, this specialist in education showed a readiness to appear as a specialist in too many other fields—religion, politics,
labor, health, war, and peace—human relationships of every kind. The
astounding output of his published writings in the decade of his life between eighty and ninety speaks at once for the range of his interests, and,
through the best of these writings, for the distinction of his thought and
expression. The "Harvard Classics" and the memorial inscriptions in the
writing of which he became the acknowledged master throughout the
country; the pervading independence of spirit which made it as natural
for him to adopt the mugwump position in politics as, for a single example, to resist the pressure of a Harvard President of the United States
and Assistant Secretary of State on behalf of Harvard crews weakened
on the eve of their race with Yale by the suspension of two members for
an act of dishonesty at the College Library; his certainty to be found, for
all his personal "superiority," on the essentially democratic side of every
question—it was precisely through such manifestations of his favorite
quality of "serviceableness" that he came to occupy, long before his death,
the place of "the first citizen" of the country, a place to which no single
successor has yet appeared. Of course he was often misjudged—as by the
Yale man who exclaimed after Harvard had won the Varsity boat race
immediately following the episode just mentioned, "How in hell did old
Eliot know that he was putting a better No. 2 into the boat!" The com-

plete independence that brings buffets brings also its rewards, both outward and inward; and at the funeral service in Appleton Chapel, a few days after President Eliot's death at his beloved Northeast Harbor on August 22, 1926, the great company that joined in the singing of

> How happy is he born and taught,
> That serveth not another's will,

must have been at one in feeling that Sir Henry Wotton's noble words had never been more fully illustrated than in the life just ended. . . .

President Eliot retired from office in 1909, after forty years in the presidency, with seventeen years of extraordinary activity still before him. More than any other single person of his time he had stood before the world as the embodiment of Harvard, and, looking back over his whole career, Harvard men are proud to have it so.

HOW TO MAKE JONNY-CAKE

THOMAS ROBINSON HAZARD

Thomas Robinson Hazard (1797–1886), member of the literary circle at Newport, was one of at least forty contemporaneous Thomas Hazards in Rhode Island, and was called Shepherd Tom to distinguish him from Nailer Tom, College Tom, Little Neck Tom, and others. (The vast Hazard family attracts nicknames; when I was a child visiting in Rhode Island I used to hear about a lady called Mrs. Bellerin' Hazard, to distinguish her, I assume, from cousins with lesser vocal resources.)

A reformer and spiritualist, this Hazard is best remembered for his Jonny-Cake Papers *(which he wrote at the age of eighty-three), an excerpt from which follows. I consider it an item of great sociological importance, since there is something about the subject of jonny-cake which arouses Rhode Islanders of old family to accesses of emotion. Walking down the street in Charlottesville, Virginia, one day, I fell into conversation with a gentleman named Greene, from Providence; we had not been talking three minutes before he was off on jonny-cake and the proper way to make it—a way which, of course, differed from Hazard's way. No two Rhode Islanders ever agree about any detail of jonny-cake and its making.*

FIRST BAKING

White Indian meal is very nice, as all Rhode Islanders know, but we should like to ask Thomas R. Hazard how much his cost him in his farming days? Providence Journal, January 16, 1879.

AND where, let me ask in turn, did the Journal learn that white Indian meal is very nice? Not certainly outside of Washington and Newport counties, for nowhere else on the globe was the real article ever to be found. The Southern epicures crack a good deal about hoe-cakes and hominy made from their white flint corn, the Pennsylvanians of their mush, the Boston folks of their Boston brown bread, whilst one Joel Barlow, of New Haven, or somewhere else in Connecticut, used to sing a long song in glorification of New England hasty pudding; but none of these reputed luxuries are worthy of holding a candle to an old-fashioned Narragansett jonny-cake made by an old-time Narragansett colored cook, from Indian corn meal raised on the southern coast of Rhode Island, the fabled Atlantis, where alone the soft, balmy breezes from the Gulf Stream ever fan the celestial plant in its growth, and impart to the grain that genial softness, that tempting fragrance and delicious flavor, that caused the Greeks of old to bestow upon Narragansett corn meal the name of Ambrosia, imagining it to be a food originally designed and set apart by the gods exclusively for their own delectation.

But alas, since the introduction of coal fires, cooking stoves, common schools, and French and Irish bedeviling cooks, the making and baking of a jonny-cake has become one of the lost arts. And yet I can remember when its preparation and completion deservedly stood at the very acme of the fine arts of Rhode Island. My grandfather used to have in his kitchen an old cook by the name of Phillis, originally from Senegambia, or Guinea, who probably made as good a jonny-cake in her day as any other artist known, whether white or black, or in short, as was ever made outside of heaven. Her process, so far as I could gather from observation, was as follows:—premising that she always insisted on having white Narragansett corn, ground at what is now called Hammond's Mill, which is situated on the site of the elder Gilbert Stuart's snuff mill, just above the head of Pettaquamscutt pond or lake.

Nor could Phillis be induced by any persuasion to touch meal ground at any other mill, for the reason, as she averred, that the mills in the more immediate vicinity made harsh feeling round meal, whereas that particular mill made soft feeling flat meal. I may perhaps just as well here digress to say that there are no other mill-stones on earth that will grind corn meal fit for a genuine jonny-cake, except those made from the Narragansett granite rock, most of which is of a peculiarly fine grain, varying, however, in quality, from which arose the distinction of round and flat meal. For instance, the mill-stones at Coon's old mill, now Wake-field, being coarse grained, made round meal, and for that reason ama-teurs in jonny-cakes, who lived within a few rods only of that mill, used to tote their grists on their shoulders, or on horseback, way off to Ham-mond's or Mumford's mills, some eight to twelve miles distant, where the grain of the mill-stones, being of a finer grade, made the flat meal. The idea that a burr stone can grind meal even out of the best of Rhode Is-land white corn, that an old-fashioned Narragansett pig would not have turned up his nose at in disgust, is perfectly preposterous. Rushed through the stones in a stream from the hopper as big as your arm, and rolled over and over in its passage, the coarse, uneven, half-ground stuff falls into the meal box below, hot as ashes and as tasteless as sawdust. I am sure it would have done the Journal's heart good to have stood by and watched the proceedings of an old-fashioned Narragansett miller, after he had turned the grist he, the Journal, had just brought on his back to be ground. The object of the miller then was not to see how much corn he could run through his mill in a given time, but how well he could grind it, let the time required to do it be what it might! See the white-coated old man now first rub the meal, as it falls, carefully and thoughtfully between his fingers and thumb, then graduate the feed and raise or lower the upper stone, with that nice sense of adjustment, observance, and discretion that a Raphael might be supposed to exercise in the mix-ing and grinding of his colors for a Madonna, or a Canova in putting the last touch of his chisel to the statue of a god, until, by repeated han-dling, he had found the ambrosia to have acquired exactly the desired coolness and flatness—the result of its being cut into fine slivers by the nicely-balanced revolving stones—rather than rolled, re-rolled, tumbled, and mumbled over and over again, until all its life and sweetness had been vitiated or dispelled.

I used to be told when I was a boy, how old Benny Rodman, whose buttonwood horsewhip may now be seen growing in the mill-dam at Peace Dale, just a few steps from the north-west corner of where his grist mill then stood, used to turn his bushel of grist in the hopper of an after-noon, and after graduating the mill-stones so as to make flat-fine-nice-cool meal, walk leisurely to Tower Hill, two miles away, where he would take tea with the widow Brown and do an hour's courting, and then return in time to turn up another grist before the other was all out of the hopper. And this was the kind of meal that since my remembrance used to be carried by the farmers of Narragansett and sold in the Newport market, in preference to selling their corn at the same price, for the reason that a cent or two per bushel was gained by the difference of weight, allowed by law between the two, over and above the two quarts taken for toll per bushel. . . .

It is said by some that the Narragansett smelt, cooked in the only proper way, was in pagan times one of the two relishes or condiments that the gods alone indulged in whilst reveling in jonny-cake made of Narragansett white corn meal, the other being Pettaquamscutt eels caught in the months of January and February with spears thrust into the mud beneath the ice, where they lie. The glorious excellence of these eels, prepared in the old-time way, I am sure no poet—not even Homer or Byron, with all their glowing powers of description—can portray, much less a simple writer of prose. The method was as follows: A basket of fat, yellow-breasted eels being brought fresh from the frozen river, were first saturated with a handful of live wood ashes. This loosened the coating of slime so that they were readily cleansed. Next the head was taken off, and the eel split down the entire length of the back. They were then washed in clean sea water and hung up the kitchen chimney, with its wide, open fireplace, for one night only. Next morning the eels were cut in short pieces and placed on a gridiron, flesh side next to sweet-smelling, glowing coals, made from green oak, walnut, or maple wood. When sufficiently broiled on that side, they were turned on the gridiron and a small slice of fragrant butter, made from the milk of cows fed on honey-laden white clover and aromatic five-fingers, put on each piece of eel. By this time the family were seated at the breakfast table in the great-room, waiting impatiently for the all-but-divine luxury, the exquisite aroma of which penetrated every nook and cranny of the house. In due time it appears, on a China plate, you may say; by no means! but on the identical gridiron, hot and luscious, with little transparent globules of dew-like nectar sparkling on each piece. Every guest or member of the family helps himself from the hot gridiron, which is then returned to the glowing coals, and again and again replenished until the appetite is surfeited or the supply of eels exhausted; probably the latter, as I never heard of but one instance wherein a fatal surfeit was produced by the dainty dish, which was the case of one of the kings of England, who died from eating too enormously of broiled eels, speared under the ice at the mouth of the river Humber. I am aware that history charges his death to gormandizing on stewed lamprey eels—a transparent mistake—as no man could be tempted to indulge his appetite exorbitantly on eels of any kind—stewed or fried, but only on yellow-breasted eels, speared under the ice and prepared and cooked after the Narragansett mode.

There used to be an old man in Narragansett by the name of Scribbins, who was a great favorite of my grandfather because of his simplicity and honesty. When a small boy, I remember Scribbins's breakfasting at our house, one winter morning, when we had broiled eels. The old man helped himself from the gridiron seventeen times, a steady smile playing over his features every moment that passed between the first and last mouthful. He then looked at my grandfather—Uncle Toby like—blandly and steadily in the face, and significantly nodding his head sideways in the direction of the kitchen door, remarked: "Them 's eels, them is."

As I was saying, after Phillis had sifted a cupful of the flour of the meal for fish coating, she continued with the same sieve to bolt about one-half of what remained for her jonny-cakes, and then transferred the balance to a coarser sieve to be used minus the bran in the making of Rhineinjun bread. This bread, vulgarly called nowadays rye and Indian bread, in the olden time was always made of one quart of unbolted Rhode Island rye meal to two quarts of the coarser grained parts of ambrosia, well kneaded and made into large round loaves of the size of a half-peck measure. There were two ways of baking it. One way was to fill two large iron basins with the kneaded dough, and late in the evening, when the logs in the kitchen were well burned down, to clear a place in the middle of the fire to the hearth and place the two basins of bread, the one on top of the other, so as to inclose their contents, and press them into one loaf. The whole was then carefully covered with hot ashes with coals on top, and left until morning. The difference between brown bread baked in this way with its thick, soft sweet crust, and that baked in the oven of an iron stove, I must leave to abler pens than mine to portray. Another way was to place a number of loaves in iron basins in a long-heated and well-tempered brick oven—stone would not answer as the heat is too brittle—into which a cup of water was also placed to make the soft crust. The oven door was then closed and plastered up. When the door of the oven was opened in the morning it was customary to raise one or two windows in the kitchen, the fragrance from the bread being so enrapturing as sometimes to affect persons whose nerves were not very strong.

Even before the Boston brown bread had become utterly worthless by the introduction of Western corn meal, made often of damaged corn, and tasteless Western rye to match, I remember bringing home with me, after a visit to that city, a loaf of the famous material, that my children might compare its quality with our family bread. They were all delighted at the prospect of tasting the famous luxury they had heard so much of; but after the first mouthful, not one of them seemed disposed to take a second. After breakfast I took the loaf and placed it in the trough for an old Berkshire sow to eat, that I knew was very fond of our Rhineinjun bread, a piece of which I used almost daily to treat her with. The old creature—which had not been fed that morning—dove her nose greedily into it; but at the first taste she dropped the morsel, and regarding me askance, with a suspicious and sinister expression in her eye, she hastened to a stagnant, muddy pool in the corner of the yard, and rinsed her mouth.

As I was saying, after Phillis had sifted the meal for her jonny-cake, she proceeded to carefully knead it in a wooden tray, having first scalded it with boiling water, and added sufficient fluid, sometimes new milk, at other times pure water, to make it of a proper consistence. It was then placed on the jonny-cake board about three-quarters of an inch in thickness, and well dressed on the surface with rich sweet cream to keep it from blistering when placed before the fire. The red oak jonny-cake board was always the middle portion of a flour barrel from five to six inches wide. This was considered an indispensable requisite in the baking of a good jonny-cake. All the old-time colored cooks without exception, hold that the flour barrel was first made for the express purpose of furnishing jonny-cake boards, and that its subsequent application to the holding of flour was merely the result of an afterthought. Be this as it may, no one I feel certain ever saw a regular, first-rate, old-time jonny-cake that was not baked on a red oak board taken from the middle part of the head of a flour barrel. The cake was next placed upright on the hearth before a bright, green hardwood fire. This kind of fire was indispensable also. And so too was the heart-shaped flat-iron that supported it, which was shaped exactly to meet every exigency. First the flat's front smooth surface was placed immediately against the back of the jonny-cake to hold it in a perpendicular position before the fire until the main part of the cake was sufficiently baked. Then a slanting side of the flat-iron was turned so as to support the board in a reclining position until the bottom and top extremities of the cake were in turn baked, and lastly, the board was slewed round and rested partly against the handle of the flat-iron, so as to bring the ends of the cake in a better position to receive the heat from the fire. After a time it was discovered that the flat-iron, first invented as a jonny-cake holder, was a convenient thing to iron clothes with, and has since been used for that purpose very extensively. When the jonny-cake was sufficiently done on the first side, a knife was passed between it and the board, and it was dextrously turned and anointed, as before, with sweet, golden-tinged cream, previous to being placed again before the fire.

Such as I have described was the process of making and baking the best article of farinaceous food that was ever partaken of by mortal man, to wit, an old-fashioned jonny-cake made of white Rhode Island corn meal, carefully and slowly ground with Rhode Island fine-grained granite mill-stones, and baked and conscientiously tended before glowing coals of a quick green hardwood fire, on a red oak barrel-head supported by a flat-iron. With proper materials and care, a decent jonny-cake can be baked on a coal stove, though by no means equal to the old-time genuine article, for the simple reason that wood fires in open fireplaces have become, as a general rule, things of the past, and good, careful, painstaking cooks extinct.

I may at some future time return to the subject of jonny-cakes and old-time cookery, and state come circumstances that would seem to go to establish the fact that Phillis, my grandfather's cook, was the remote cause of the French Revolution, and the death of Louis XVI and Marie Antoinette. But enough for the present.

ON LOUIS AGASSIZ

WILLIAM JAMES

————◆◆◆————

No one understands the character of New England who has not grasped that, in essence, its keynote is simplicity. The magnificent, the elaborate, the luxurious—these may from time to time ornament but are never inherent to the New England scene. Simplicity, moreover, is what New England most treasures in itself. In the passage which follows, taken from a speech on Louis Agassiz given at the reception in Cambridge in 1896 for the American Society of Naturalists by the President and Fellows of Harvard College (simplicity requires that one always say College, not University), note how William James takes pains to stress the simplicity in the great naturalist's personality.

James (1842–1910), himself one of the greatest of all who have ever been identified with New England, was no less simple. There is a famous story about this celebrated Harvard philosopher and writer, that once it fell to him to put up at his Cambridge house a visiting lecturer from Oxford. Each night the Jameses' guest put his boots outside his door to be polished, according to British custom, and each night James would take them downstairs, black them, and put them back again. When the Englishman, having tipped the maid, was saying good-bye to James beside the hack that was to drive him to the South Station, he suddenly said, "Oh! I do wonder if you would mind giving this to your Boots. He performed his duties so silently, and I may say so splendidly, that I've not been able to catch him to give him a tip." James told the story on himself and, when asked what he did with the two dollars the Briton handed him, said, "I kept them myself. I thought I'd earned them."

IT would be unnatural to have such an assemblage as this meet in the Museum and Faculty Room of this University and yet have no public word spoken in honor of a name which must be silently present to the minds of all our visitors.

At some near future day, it is to be hoped some one of you who is well acquainted with Agassiz's scientific career will discourse here concerning it,—I could not now, even if I would, speak to you of that of which you have far more intimate knowledge than I. On this social occasion it has seemed that what Agassiz stood for in the way of character and influence is the more fitting thing to commemorate, and to that agreeable task I have been called. He made an impression that was unrivalled. He left a sort of popular myth—the Agassiz legend, as one might say—behind him in the air about us; and life comes kindlier to all of us, we get more recognition from the world, because we call ourselves naturalists,—and that was the class to which he also belonged.

The secret of such an extraordinarily effective influence lay in the equally extraordinary mixture of the animal and social gifts, the intellectual powers, and the desires and passions of the man. From his boyhood, he looked on the world as if it and he were made for each other, and on the vast diversity of living things as if he were there with authority to take mental possession of them all. His habit of collecting began in childhood, and during his long life knew no bounds save those that separate the things of Nature from those of human art. Already in his student years, in spite of the most stringent poverty, his whole scheme of existence was that of one predestined to greatness, who takes that fact for granted, and stands forth immediately as a scientific leader of men.

His passion for knowing living things was combined with a rapidity of observation, and a capacity to recognize them again and remember everything about them, which all his life it seemed an easy triumph and delight for him to exercise, and which never allowed him to waste a moment in doubts about the commensurability of his powers with his tasks. If ever a person lived by faith, he did. When a boy of twenty, with an allowance of two hundred and fifty dollars a year, he maintained an artist attached to his employ, a custom which never afterwards was departed from,—except when he maintained two or three. He lectured from the very outset to all those who would hear him. "I feel within myself the strength of a whole generation," he wrote to his father at that time, and launched himself upon the publication of his costly "Poissons Fossiles" with no clear vision of the quarter from whence the payment might be expected to come.

At Neuchâtel (where between the ages of twenty-five and thirty he enjoyed a stipend that varied from four hundred to six hundred dollars) he organized a regular academy of natural history, with its museum, managing by one expedient or another to employ artists, secretaries, and assistants, and to keep a lithographic and printing establishment of his own employed with the work that he put forth. Fishes, fossil and living, echinoderms and glaciers, transfigured themselves under his hand, and at thirty he was already at the zenith of his reputation, recognized by all as one of those naturalists in the unlimited sense, one of those folio copies of mankind, like Linnæus and Cuvier, who aim at nothing less than an acquaintance with the whole of animated Nature. His genius for classifying was simply marvellous; and, as his latest biographer says, nowhere had a single person ever given so decisive an impulse to natural history.

Such was the human being who on an October morning fifty years ago disembarked at our port, bringing his hungry heart along with him, his confidence in his destiny, and his imagination full of plans. The only particular resource he was assured of was one course of Lowell Lectures. But of one general resource he always was assured, having always counted on it and never found it to fail,—and that was the good will of every fellow-creature in whose presence he could find an opportunity to describe his aims. His belief in these was so intense and unqualified that he could not conceive of others not feeling the furtherance of them to be a duty binding also upon them. *Velle non discitur,* as Seneca says:— Strength of desire must be born with a man, it can't be taught. And Agassiz came before one with such enthusiasm glowing in his countenance,— such a persuasion radiating from his person that his projects were the sole things really fit to interest man as man,—that he was absolutely irresistible. He came, in Byron's words, with victory beaming from his breast, and every one went down before him, some yielding him money, some time, some specimens, and some labor, but all contributing their applause and their godspeed. And so, living among us from month to month and from year to year, with no relation to prudence except his pertinacious violation of all her usual laws, he on the whole achieved the compass of his desires, studied the geology and fauna of a continent, trained a generation of zoölogists, founded one of the chief museums of the world, gave a new impulse to scientific education in America, and died the idol of the public, as well as of his circle of immediate pupils and friends.

The secret of it all was, that while his scientific ideals were an integral part of his being, something that he never forgot or laid aside, so that wherever he went he came forward as "the Professor," and talked "shop" to every person, young or old, great or little, learned or unlearned, with whom he was thrown, he was at the same time so commanding a presence, so curious and inquiring, so responsive and expansive, and so generous and reckless of himself and of his own, that every one said immediately, "Here is no musty *savant,* but a man, a great man, a man on the heroic scale, not to serve whom is avarice and sin." He elevated the popular notion of what a student of Nature could be. Since Benjamin Franklin, we had never had among us a person of more popularly impressive type. He did not wait for students to come to him; he made inquiry for promising youthful collectors, and when he heard of one, he wrote, inviting and urging him to come. Thus there is hardly one now of the American naturalists of my generation whom Agassiz did not train. Nay, more; he said to every one that a year or two of natural history, studied as he understood it, would give the best training for any kind of mental work. Sometimes he was amusingly *naïf* in this regard, as when he offered to put his whole Museum at the disposition of the Emperor of Brazil if he would but come and labor there. And I well remember how certain officials of the Brazilian empire smiled at the cordiality with which he pressed upon them a similar invitation. But it had a great effect. Natural history must indeed be a godlike pursuit, if such a man as this can so adore it, people said; and the very definition and meaning of the word naturalist underwent a favorable alteration in the common mind.

Certain sayings of Agassiz's, as the famous one that he "had no time for making money," and his habit of naming his occupation simply as that of "teacher," have caught the public fancy, and are permanent benefactions. We all enjoy more consideration for the fact that he manifested himself here thus before us in his day.

1914 —

THE LATE GEORGE APLEY

JOHN P. MARQUAND

———◆•◆———

The Late George Apley, *by John P. Marquand (1893–1961), a great-nephew of Margaret Fuller, is a successful satire on the sort of place Boston, and to some extent New England, had become by the early twentieth century; young intellectuals of spirit were escaping it in droves. The following chapter from the novel reflects some of the attitudes toward liberal ideas in Boston at the time of the First World War.*

It must be pointed out however, that along with Boston stuffiness there has gone always a strain of equally stiff-necked nonconformity. George Apley's diatribes against Germany were characteristic; but so was the defiant posture maintained at the time by a certain very Bostonian lady whose pro-Germanism was a matter of principle. When this lady died, she bequeathed in her will a considerable sum of money the income of which was to be given annually to "any unpopular cause."

WAR DAYS

Dealing with the Difficulties of Living in a

Reluctant and Neutral Nation

The attitude of Boston toward the questions involved in the World War was essentially George Apley's attitude. It would be difficult for this to be otherwise since the conscience of those like Apley was the basis of the Boston reaction. Those who say that New England has become decadent would do well to remember the lessons of the war. The same inherent sense of justice and of differentiation between right and wrong which brought Boston to the forefront in the American Revolution and in the Civil War were to work again with an equal force.

"To any rightly thinking person," George Apley wrote in a letter to the Boston Evening Transcript in the early part of 1915, "there can be no compromise between wrong and right. Germany is wrong and the Allies are right. The devastations of Belgium and the atrocities of the invading horde of barbarians are an outrage to civilized mankind."

This point of view he held in common with all but a few radicals and eccentrics. From the very beginning of hostilities George Apley began to devote the full force of his interest to the Allied cause. As the conflict spread and its vital issues became more pronounced, until it was patent that democracy and all human freedom were in the balance, Apley became more and more bewildered at the indifference of the rest of the country to this truth. He laid it, as many others did, to the vacillating tactics and to the intentional blindness of a Democratic administration. He watched with growing impatience our temporizing with Germany, which must forever be a blot upon this country. He felt it was his duty to express himself freely upon this subject and he was careful to do so on every occasion that offered itself.

Again, as in many other phases of his life, his letters to his friend Walker are of particular value here. He speaks for himself in them, with a spirit of conviction and sacrifice which even his enemies, and he made many in these years, could not but reluctantly admire. For nearly the first time in his life he was confronted with a real cause in which he could act from definite conviction. For the first time in his life he was at his best, a man of militance and fire.

> I cannot understand George [we find Catharine Apley writing]. The war seems to have utterly upset him. He can talk of nothing else, nothing else seems to interest him. At the Caldwells' the other evening we met a Mr. Nixon who had studied at Heidelberg and who had some pro-German leanings. George was so upset by this that I was afraid he would grow violent, particularly when Mr. Nixon said that the German army was better equipped and disciplined than the French. The library at Beacon Street is one great mass of maps stuck with pins to indicate the opposing lines. I do hope for all our sakes that the war will be over in a little while.

Yet Catharine Apley herself was being carried forward on the tide of sentiment. She shared, with many others around her, a deep affection for France and for the cool courage and the debonair spirit of the *Poilu*. Thus we find her writing again in the spring of 1916:

George brought the dearest French officer to dinner, who is over here on a mission to buy munitions. He was so beautiful in his new horizon-blue uniform and hardly older than John. His manners were absolutely perfect and I am so proud of the way Eleanor speaks French with him. Eleanor, of course, wants to be a nurse in France but this is completely absurd.

The present author, who served with Apley on many war committees, noticed a very great change in him, a new assurance, a new decisiveness, and a demand for action which is reflected in his letters to his old school and college friends.

Some of us [he writes] are trying very hard here to prepare public opinion for the inevitable. It is quite clear, from the information we are able to gather through several informal committees of which I am a member, that this country is riddled with German spies and the brains of the system are actually located beneath the very shadow of the Capitol Dome in Washington. There are a number of rumours here, that we are endeavouring to run down, of undercover activity. There are too many Germans in Boston and all of them should be watched, now that they have placed themselves beyond the pale of civilization by their policy of frightfulness. I believe it is absolutely true, as it is rumoured, that concrete emplacements are being built on the hills around here for heavy guns and that there are a number of wirelesses along the coast which signal to submarines. There is nothing to do now, of course, but to wait. In the meanwhile, I for one am very sorry that any tacit approval is given Germany by employing not only a German, but an ardent German sympathizer, as a director of our Symphony Orchestra. It may be true that the man is an artist, if any German can be an artist, which I very much doubt, but any sympathy with him is only a compromise with justice. Besides this, the man is probably a spy besides being a musician. It is shocking to me also that there is a certain amount of tolerance in Harvard University. Thank Heaven, most of the students there take the right position, but John tells me that certain members of the teaching staff actually speak favourably of Germany in lectures. Obviously, a stand for neutrality is absurd in the face of overt hostility. It must be clear to everyone that Germany is endeavouring to embroil us in a war with Mexico, and yet nothing is done about it by the sentimentalists in Washington. Thank Heaven that there are a few voices crying out aloud in the wilderness and I hope that my own is among them.

As one reads these letters in the light of the present, their contents may seem unreal, since much has happened in the way of disillusion. Weary

tolerance has crept over many, which was not present at the time when
George Apley wrote. His sentiments may have been right or wrong, but
this in no way alters the strength of his deep conviction. Like his ancestors, Apley was standing squarely for the right. When the *Lusitania* was
sunk on the seventh of May, 1915, he breathed a sigh of relief, for it was
his opinion that his country would at last stand for the right. The amazingly supine attitude of the nation at large pained him, as did the temporizing tone of President Wilson's notes, which left an actual loophole for
discussion; and his activities in the various protest meetings against the
sinking of the *Lusitania* are very well remembered.

He writes to Walker at about this time:

> There is another ugly phase of the situation here. It has to do with
> our racial situation here in Boston. Since the sinking of the *Lusitania,*
> much of the Irish element, due to the fanatical ideas of certain Irish
> Independence agitators, I suspect, is tacitly in sympathy with Ger-
> many. I heard yesterday that many persons are going about saying
> that Germany did very well to sink the *Lusitania,* that she was an
> armed vessel carrying munitions. This seems incredible, but I have
> reason to believe that it is absolutely true. In the event of war I dread
> that the Germans may stir up something close to strife in Boston. The
> hold of the Catholic Church here is particularly sinister. In the last
> few years a number of religious institutions have been buying tracts
> of land for schools and orphan asylums. It is very noticeable that
> each one of these sites is selected on a piece of rising ground, com-
> manding a view of the country for miles about. It is not reassuring
> to feel that these sites have been chosen with suspicious military
> accuracy. An enormous amount of concrete is being used in these
> constructions and it is even said that gun emplacements are being
> made. It is certainly high time that there should be some sort of pre-
> paredness. I wish there was something active that I might do, but
> instead I have been born at the wrong time. I have already volun-
> teered for the American Ambulance, only to find that there is a need
> for younger men. I had not realized that I was old. I do not feel par-
> ticularly old. All I can do is to contribute as largely as my means will
> allow and I have offered John the opportunity to join this ambulance
> service when he has finished his first year at Law School. I am some-
> what hurt that he does not take the idea as seriously as I do. He has,
> however, agreed to attend the citizens' camp at Plattsburg and this,
> at least, is something. I am anxious to go myself but I am very busy
> with committee work.
>
> A large number of committees are forming here, as I suppose they
> are everywhere else. A great many of us are trying to do what little
> we can in this crisis and in a sense I truly believe it is revitalizing

Boston, that it is imbuing this city with some part of an old spirit, that it is refurbishing ideals. I am aware of a new vitality and a new pride everywhere around me. This is taking a tangible shape in the vast new Technology buildings on the other side of the river. It has a spiritual manifestation in the raising of our enormous new City Club, where every citizen is welcome as a member at a purely nominal cost and where our civic affairs and problems are open to discussion. I have attended several formal luncheons in this fine new building and I must confess that I have found the company there deeply interesting and refreshing. It is made up of individuals of a sort whom I have not an opportunity of meeting every day, but many of them are most congenial. We are in a great brotherhood there for the betterment of Boston. We all realize that we have a stake in this community. There are politicians and newspapermen, some of them very brilliant after one penetrates their rough exterior, lawyers and small businessmen. It helps me very much to form this contact with new minds and I hope that they benefit from me. Yes, it is highly stimulating, this rubbing of elbows intellectually.

And so it is with the war committees, a new burden which we are assuming besides our local charities. Besides several committees which have been formed to stimulate and to encourage positive action on the part of the administration, there are committees collecting funds and supplies of food and clothing for various groups of war sufferers, notably the Belgians, Serbs, and Poles. I regret that there is also a committee raising a fund for milk for German babies, but its efforts have made no great headway. Most of these groups are remarkably democratic; indeed many of their most active workers are persons of whom I have never heard before. This has raised a suspicion that certain persons are using this means to have themselves recognized by a section of society that has been more or less closed to them, but I do not believe this. At any rate, it is no time for social distinctions. I am very glad to see both Catharine and Eleanor, while they are making bandages for the Red Cross, rubbing elbows and laughing with women from the Newtons. It is all a part of this new spirit of camaraderie.

I have spoken to you before of this new spirit [he writes again]. It makes me very proud of the place I live in. Its genuineness is attested by a species of religious revival. We have just received one of the most remarkable men of the day here, of whom I had never heard, but perhaps you may have. The man's name is Billy Sunday, a revivalist with genuine oratorical gifts. He has erected a huge tabernacle on Huntington Avenue—a tent the size of a circus tent. His language is the sort that appeals to everyone. I was induced to go by my son, John, who said I would be interested. I was more than inter-

ested, so much so that after hearing him once I brought Catharine
and Eleanor the next evening. The expressions of this man may be
crude, but their very crudity is convincing enough to sway a multitude to tears and laughter. Although I admit I cannot agree intellectually with his Biblical interpretations, I am in deep sympathy
with what he is trying to do. I met him at the end of one of the revivalist meetings and I shall never forget the interview. Sunday was
seated in a space partitioned off behind the stage from which he had
delivered his strange address. A dressing-gown was thrown over his
shoulders. He was perspiring freely from his exertion. Sitting there
he looked more like an athlete than a preacher. As a matter of fact, I
believe that he is a professional baseball player. For the first few
moments I found it hard to be natural with him. He seized my hand
in a vise-like grip and asked me if I thought he was driving the Devil
out of Boston. After a few moments he seemed quite as interested in
me as I was in him. A middle-aged woman was sitting beside him,
whom he introduced as "Ma." I was glad at the end of the interview
to write him out a check for $5,000, provided he did not mention my
name as a contributor. Yes, I am learning a great deal these days
about all sorts of people. The more I learn, the more I see how much
good there is in everyone. Sunday is coming down next week to give
a ten-minute talk to the men at the Apley Sailors' Home.

It was about this time, as Apley was treading this broader stage, that
he was obliged to make a stand of a very different nature, for he found
himself confronted with a difficulty that concerned his own flesh and
blood, his friend and second cousin John Apley. So much has already been
said about this matter that it may seem like resurrecting useless gossip to
air it in these pages. We include it only in that it illustrates the soundness
of Apley's judgment.

One is safe in saying that Apley's cousin, John Apley, was of a different
type, highly likeable and sought-after in society, but hotblooded and irresponsible. His marriage at the end of his senior year at Harvard, to Georgina Murch of Brookline, had left him comfortably off. The young couple
had moved to the North Shore, where Apley's stables and his hunters are
too well known to require much mention. The family passion, which
amused and somewhat exasperated George Apley, was almost entirely
confined to this peculiar sport.

I have just been to luncheon at my cousin's house [George Apley
writes at about this time], an informal lunch with Catharine and
myself and Mr. and Mrs. Tom Brecking. The luncheon was quite informal and it was more like dining in a stable than a house. Georgina had on a riding habit and John had on riding breeches; so did

the Breckings. Betty Brecking wore breeches without a skirt. The plates had horses' heads upon them and in the centre of the table was a silver horse, presented to John by some hunt club. Nearly every room was decorated with hunting prints and the hall was hung with riding crops and even bridles. After lunch we three men retired for a while to John's study to drink some very good brandy and there I noticed that the inkwell on his desk was made out of a horse's hoof. John talked to me for a while about the stock market and I became quite alarmed at his ideas. Tom Brecking seemed to me to be rather ill at ease. Once the brandy was finished, we joined the ladies and went outside to a field where a number of very fine horses were being led in a line by grooms. Then Betty Brecking and John signified their intention of riding some of these horses over a series of jumps, which they did while the rest of us watched. It seemed to me that neither Georgina nor Brecking appreciated the exhibition.

This quotation may be enough to foreshadow the ensuing situation, although the writer very well knows that it burst upon George Apley like a clap of thunder. Thus, the following letters from his cousin John Apley, which he kept in his files, require no comment.

DEAR GEORGE: I think you ought to know, among the first, that I am leaving Georgina. We have never understood each other. I may add that Betty Brecking is leaving her husband. I suppose this is going to make a complicated situation but I think you may understand it, George, better than most. . . .

DEAR GEORGE: Your answer is incredible. When I consider you and Clara Goodrich, I don't see why you are in any very great position to read me a lecture about family. I know that this is the first time such a thing has happened to the Apleys—and what of it? . . .

DEAR GEORGE: I have thought over our talk of yesterday, as you have suggested that I should, and I am still somewhat shocked by it. Betty and Georgina and Tom and I have all listened to you carefully and I must say I never knew you would have quite the character to lay your cards on the table the way you did. I must say you have us very nearly where you want us. I know that I have been financially obligated to you for a long while and now you have tied my hands. I even admit that you have done so out of your own perverted sense of justice. I admit that you believe in keeping the family together at the risk of ruining lives. Well, you've done it and due to you we are going to go along as though nothing whatsoever had happened. Believe me, my relationship with Betty will be as beautiful as yours but there's one thing that I hope. I hope to heaven some day I may be able to give you a little sound advice and meanwhile I should like

very much to think that I shall never have to speak to you again.
Don't worry. I shall, of course. . . .

Those who were close to Apley at the time know best the pain that
was caused him by this complex affair. In spite of his satisfaction in knowing that the stand he had taken was just, it was hard to pay the cost of
losing the affection of a relative and a lifelong friend. In doing so, however, he gained the respect of many others, among them his uncle, William Apley, who was failing in health.

> In putting the screws to him [the old gentleman says in one of his
> last letters] you did, of course, the only thing possible. I would not
> have known you were capable of it, but now I know you are your
> father's son.

George Apley scarcely alluded to the matter to his own son, as he
naturally considered the less said about such a scandal the better. His
one allusion was indirect. It is contained in a letter written his son during
a vacation in the latter's second year at the Harvard Law School, which
he was spending with friends in New York.

> I have just been confronted with a very difficult family crisis, one
> that has played heavily upon my emotions. Much as I hope it will
> not, it will probably come to your ears some day. If it should I hope
> you will remember that your father acted for the best, according to
> his lights. You are reaching a time when you will find out what my
> own father pointed out to me at a very trying time in my own career:
> that family is more important than the individual, that a family must
> be solid before the world, no matter what the faults may be of a sin-
> gle member, that a family has a heritage to hand down which must
> be protected. I can give you a number of interesting examples of this
> in the lives of people whom you have known always, but you prob-
> ably know of these yourself. Several individuals in my own genera-
> tion have been sent to the South and West, where they are probably
> making new lives for themselves, but here their names are no longer
> mentioned. A girl I knew at dancing school became involved with a
> public-hack driver. I do not believe you would ever know her name,
> because the matter has been kept as silent as the tomb. There is an-
> other man, a friend of mine once, who abstracted family silver from
> the safe-deposit vault and pawned it in order to pay a gambling debt.
> I do not know where he is to-day. These examples may seem harsh to
> you and perhaps somewhat ridiculous. They did to me, when I was
> young, but believe me they will not as you live longer. These matters
> are not actuated by pride because they are beyond pride. There are

some things which one does not speak about and you will learn to follow this same reticence. I am glad to tell you before I leave this subject that there are very few skeletons in our family closet.

I am sorry that you are not here with your mother and sister and me during your vacation. This gadabout habit you have assumed of wandering away from Boston will not pay you in the end. Above all, I cannot imagine what you see in New York. You are not really fitted to cope with the place, and surely you can't like it. You face a foreign philosophy down there, but I suppose one is venturesome when one is young.

Your mother and Eleanor are both well. Eleanor is the centre of a great deal of society but the young men who come to the house do not seem to me particularly worth while and I am sorry that many of them are your friends. Though their manners are interesting enough, very few of them seem to have any definite prospects; and I can find out very little of most of their backgrounds as they nearly all are students from out of town. Eleanor takes the same lofty attitude about this as you do, that such things do not matter. I am not speaking entirely of money, because I hope that you and Eleanor will both be comfortably off. I am speaking of something that money can't buy—congeniality of habits and manners.

This reticence of which George Apley speaks, regarding family matters, did not confine itself to scandals. It was his rule also never to speak of his generosity toward many distant and impoverished branches of the Apley family. Only after his death did it become apparent how many of his relatives had him to thank for saving them through crisis and illness, for educating the younger generation, and, more than anything else, for saving many who became involved in the disastrous crash of 1929. It would be safe to assume that the estate which George Apley left at his death would have been even larger except for his family loyalty, especially as he suffered like so many others from trusting too much to local institutions. It was fortunate for his issue that a large part of his fortune was in trust when the firm of Apley Brothers became involved at that time through the unforeseen machinations of one of its partners; otherwise Apley would have stepped into the breach with all his resources simply because of the family name, for at that time there was no Apley in the firm.

SACCO AND VANZETTI

EDNA ST. VINCENT MILLAY

My personal associations with the Sacco-Vanzetti case, which rocked the country in the twenties and gave Massachusetts a bad name with liberals, are infantile: I walked past the jail in which Sacco and Vanzetti were confined on my way to school every day for years. Sacco and Vanzetti were just there—a fixture—like the high brick wall around the prison grounds.

Their trial for the 1920 murder of a paymaster and his guard was decided against them. In spite of the case review by a committee composed of President Lowell of Harvard, President Stratton of M. I. T., and Judge Robert Grant; in spite of the confession of a condemned criminal that he had committed the murder; in spite of picketing in front of Boston State House by some of the most exalted figures of the day, Sacco and Vanzetti were put to death in 1927. The case and its conclusion inspired much writing: two plays by Maxwell Anderson, a novel by Upton Sinclair, and two sonnets by Edna St. Vincent Millay, one of which follows.

Miss Millay (1892–1950) had been born in Maine but soon escaped New England's confines. Her life in Greenwich Village typified one reaction of young New Englanders, her poetry another—the continuation of a strain of talent innately New England for all its rebellion, in fact partly on account of its rebellion. A paradox was emerging: the most New England thing a young writer could do was to get out of New England.

Sonnet cxxii (Two Sonnets in Memory of Nicola Sacco—
   Bartolomeo Vanzetti, executed August 23, 1927)

As men have loved their lovers in times past
And sung their wit, their virtue and their grace,
So have we loved sweet Justice to the last,
Who now lies here in an unseemly place.
The child will quit the cradle and grow wise
And stare on beauty till his senses drown;
Yet shall be seen no more by mortal eyes
Such beauty as here walked and here went down.

Like birds that hear the winter crying plain
Her courtiers leave to seek the clement south;
Many have praised her, we alone remain
To break a fist against the lying mouth
Of any man who says this was not so:
Though she be dead now, as indeed we know.

THE NEED OF BEING VERSED
IN COUNTRY THINGS

ROBERT FROST

————◆◆◆————

Native New England talent might be leaving New England, but con-
versely, the greatest New England writer of our time came to it from
outside. Robert Frost (1875–1963), born in California, epitomizes in his
poetry all that is best in New England and its tradition: its pithy under-
statement of a mystical fervor and insight, its quality of being at once
idiosyncratic and universal.

The following poem, part of Frost's fourth volume, New Hampshire,
published in 1923, evokes the all-too-familiar scene of ruined or aban-
doned farms where once men struggled so hard, and against such diffi-
culties, to wrest a living from the soil. As in all his poems, Frost says
more here about New England than he appears to.

The house had gone to bring again
To the midnight sky a sunset glow.
Now the chimney was all of the house that stood,
Like a pistil after the petals go.

The barn opposed across the way,
That would have joined the house in flame
Had it been the will of the wind, was left
To bear forsaken the place's name.

No more it opened with all one end
For teams that came by the stony road
To drum on the floor with scurrying hoofs
And brush the mow with the summer load.

The birds that came to it through the air
At broken windows flew out and in,
Their murmur more like the sigh we sigh
From too much dwelling on what has been.

Yet for them the lilac renewed its leaf,
And the aged elm, though touched with fire;
And the dry pump flung up an awkward arm;
And the fence post carried a strand of wire.

For them there was really nothing sad.
But though they rejoiced in the nest they kept,
One had to be versed in country things
Not to believe the phoebes wept.

EDWIN ARLINGTON ROBINSON

AMY LOWELL

———◆◆———

*Amy Lowell (1874–1925) was one Boston poet who stayed in New Eng-
land. More executive than artist, she ran the Imagist movement in poetry
of the early century more or less single-handed. She was a descendant of
James Russell Lowell, a sister of President Lowell of Harvard, and her
personal idiosyncrasies were famous. There is a story that once, her car
having broken down in a back-country hamlet when she had left her
purse at home, she directed a distrustful garage proprietor to telephone to
Cambridge and ask her brother to vouch for her. When he reached the
president's ear, the man said "A woman who says she's your sister is at
my place and wants credit." Lowell asked, "Where is she now?" "Sitting
on the curbstone smoking a cigar," was the answer. "That's my sister," the
president replied.*

The following excerpt from her long work A Critical Fable, *composed
of verse-portraits of her poet contemporaries, analyzes Edwin Arlington
Robinson (1869–1935), a poet who escaped from New England and in the
end came back to her.*

To speak of seclusion is to think of a man
Who is built on a totally otherwise plan.

I mean, and I rather imagine you know it,
Edwin Arlington Robinson, excellent poet,
And excellent person, but vague as a wood
Gazed into at dusk. His preponderant mood
Is withdrawal, and why? For a man of his stamp,
So conscious of people, it seems odd to scamp
Experience and contact, to live in a hollow
Between the four winds and perpetually swallow
The back draughts of air from a swift forward motion.
It takes a huge strength to withstand all emotion,
But Robinson stays with his feet planted square
In the middle of nothing, the vacuum where
The world's swinging starts and whirls out, where is left
The dead root of movement, an emptiness cleft
In the heart of an aim, of all aims, peering out
At the dust and the grass-blades that swirl all about.
He notes who is here, who is coming along,
Who has passed by alone, who is one of a throng.
He peers with intentness bent all into seeing,
A critical eye finely pointed on being.
He is cruel with dispassion, as though he most dreaded
Some shiver of feeling might yet be imbedded
Within him. And if this occurrence should happen,
He would probably see himself with a fool's cap on
And feel himself sinking to shipwreck at once;
Of the two, much preferring disaster to dunce.
For the dunce is contingent on a sort of a curse
He thinks he is doomed with. A curious, perverse
Undercutting of Fate which decrees him observer
And hoods him in ice from all possible fervour.
The slightest conceivable hint of a thaw
Wounds his conscience as though he had broken a law
He had sworn to uphold. Are there demons in hiding
Within his ice-mail? Can he feel them abiding
A time to break loose and disrupt into tatters
The scheme of existence he has taught himself matters,
A barrier raised betwixt him and his satyrs?
For he has them; his quaint, artificial control
Is a bandage drawn tightly to hold down his soul.
Should a nail or a thorn tear the least little mesh, it
Would let all his nature go leaping in freshet
Overflowing his banks and engulfing his dams
In a flurry of life. But the desolate calms
He has cherished so long would be lost in the slams,

The torrential vortices of a swift current
Exploding in motion. Some uncouth, deterrent
Complex in his make-up enforces recoil
Before the fatigue and the wrench of turmoil.
He compounds with inertia by calling it Fate,
Deeply dreading the rush of emotion in spate,
Distrusting his power to outwit disaster
In the realization that with him fast means faster,
And refusing to see that a turbulent strife
Is the valuable paradox given to life
Which only the few may possess. With the prize
In his hand, he turns sadly away, crucifies
His manhood each day with the old dog's-eared lies,
The heritage, left by those Puritan heirs.
His bogies and satyrs are grandsons of theirs.
Could he see them as fruit-trees distorted by mist,
He might unknot himself from the terrible twist
He has suffered through fear of them. Now, with vicarious
Experience in verse, he cheats all the various
Impulses within him which make him a poet;
But, try as he will, his poems all show it.
His tight little verses an inch in diameter,
His quatrains and whole-book-long tales in pentameter,
With never a hint of what he'd call a sham metre,
Though some people style his kind *ad nauseam* metre—
With gimlets for eyes and a sensitive heart,
All battened down tight in the box of his art,
And we have his rare merits and his strange deficiencies
Which mix to a porridge of peculiar efficiencies.
Admired by every one dowered with wit,
He has scarcely the qualifications to hit
The unlettered public, but the fact that his name
Is already spotted with the lichens of fame
Opens up a most fecund and pertinent query
And is one of the pedestals on which my theory
Is based: whether now we have not reached the stage
Of a perfectly genuine coming-of-age.
I am willing to swear that when he has retired
His books will be listed as 'reading required,'
And poor sweltering youths taking examinations
Will crown him with the bays of their wild lamentations.
Our beautiful system is to make every course able
To render delight quite sterile through forcible
Insistence upon it. But these are the laurels

With which no man who's not insane ever quarrels.
Perhaps it's as well not to look at the guerdon
Too closely or no one would shoulder the burden
Of being a poet.

ATAVISM

ELINOR WYLIE

———◆•◆———

The poet Elinor Wylie (1885–1928) spent many summers in Maine at Mt. Desert Island (it is pronounced Mt. Dessert). She was another of the outsiders who, themselves unhampered by weight of New England tradition, could sense the special quality of the place better than its fugitive children. The following poem gives a sense of that presence of the red Indian in the New England forest which is so haunting a phantom.

I always was afraid of Somes's Pond:
Not the little pond, by which the willow stands,
Where laughing boys catch alewives in their hands
In brown, bright shallows; but the one beyond.
There, when the frost makes all the birches burn
Yellow as cow-lilies, and the pale sky shines
Like a polished shell between black spruce and pines,
Some strange thing tracks us, turning where we turn.

You'll say I dream it, being the true daughter
Of those who in old times endured this dread.
Look! Where the lily-stems are showing red
A silent paddle moves below the water.
A sliding shape has stirred them like a breath;
Tall plumes surmount a painted mask of death.

THE BOSTON EVENING TRANSCRIPT

T. S. ELIOT

———◆•◆———

All through my youth in the nineteen thirties and forties, the leading in-fluence in literature was T. S. Eliot (1888–   ). For a long time he could do no wrong, either as poet or critic. Then, in the fifties, I heard my son's friends at Harvard disparaging Eliot, and realized how times, and fashion, march on.

Eliot was born in St. Louis, grandson of a New England Eliot, a clergy-man who had carried Unitarianism to the Middle West. Educated at Harvard, Eliot soon escaped Boston for England where he became in time a British subject and a convert to Anglo-Catholicism. Curiously enough, escaping from Boston and becoming Episcopalian has become characteristically twentieth-century New England behavior. Where once the Puritans fled the Church of England for Boston, their descendants flee Boston for the Church of England.

The following early poem takes for concrete subject the most famous of all New England newspapers. When it expired, in the 1920's, many peo-ple seriously believed that Boston could only go to the dogs. Eliot conveys via the Transcript *his feelings about the Boston from which he escaped.*

The readers of the *Boston Evening Transcript*
Sway in the wind like a field of ripe corn.

When evening quickens faintly in the street,
Wakening the appetites of life in some
And to others bringing the *Boston Evening Transcript*,
I mount the steps and ring the bell, turning
Wearily, as one would turn to nod good-bye to Rochefoucauld,
If the street were time and he at the end of the street,
And I say, "Cousin Harriet, here is the *Boston Evening Transcript*."

CAMBRIDGE LADIES

E. E. CUMMINGS

————◆•◆————

E. E. Cummings (1894–1962) was another one of the poets who fled New England; he dazzled the world and shocked Boston by his brilliant, avant-garde work, compounded by his insistence on eliminating all capitals and punctuation. My mother, however, when his name was mentioned, always used to exclaim, "Oh, that darling little fair-haired boy"— for he was the child of the Rev. Edward Cummings, assistant minister to Edward Everett Hale at the South Congregational Church in Boston (a church which, as it happens, was neither South nor Congregational, but Unitarian and in the Back Bay). The following sonnet goes far to explain why Cummings went to New York to live.

SONNETS—REALITIES I.

the Cambridge ladies who live in furnished souls
are unbeautiful and have comfortable minds
(also, with the church's protestant blessings
daughters, unscented shapeless spirited)
they believe in Christ and Longfellow, both dead,
are invariably interested in so many things—
at the present writing one still finds
delighted fingers knitting for the is it Poles?
perhaps. While permanent faces coyly bandy
scandal of Mrs. N and Professor D
. . . . the Cambridge ladies do not care, above
Cambridge if sometimes in its box of
sky lavender and cornerless, the
moon rattles like a fragment of angry candy

SALT WATER FARM

E. B. WHITE

———◆◆◆———

E. B. White (1899–   ) has been called a sophisticated Thoreau; he often invokes the shade of Thoreau in his writing, in one piece addressing the poet in letter form. But a Thoreau who was sophisticated would not be Thoreau, and actually E. B. White is like no other writer at all—he is a literary artist of his own unparalleled devising.

For years before his retirement from the New Yorker he and his wife, K. S. White (Don't fire until you see the Whites of the New Yorker, used to be safe counsel around Manhattan bars) vacationed at a farm in Maine where they now live and about which the New York-born White has done some of his best writing; it gives the following piece from Harper's Magazine its title. The piece concludes with some remarks about freedom which, while they were written just before the Second World War, make sense any time, and are worthy comment to come out of the country of Sam Adams and Jimmy Otis.

A SEACOAST farm, such as this, extends far beyond the boundaries mentioned in the deed. My domain is arable many miles offshore, in the restless fields of protein. Cultivation begins close to the house with a rhubarb patch, but it ends down the bay beyond the outer islands, handlining for cod and haddock, with gulls like gnats round your ears, and the threat of fog always in the pit of your stomach.

I think it is the expansiveness of coastal farming that makes it so engrossing: the knowledge that your fence, on one side at least, shuts out no neighbor—you may climb it and keep going if you have a boat and the strength to raise a sail. The presence in the offing of the sea's fickle yield, those self-sown crops given up grudgingly to the patient and the brave, is an attraction few men are proof against. Beyond one blue acre is another, each one a little farther from the house than the last. On a summer's day I may start out down the lane with a pail to pick a few berries for my wife's piemaking, but there is always the likelihood that I will turn up hours later with two small flounders and a look of profound accomplishment. A man who has spent much time and money in dreary restaurants moodily chewing fillet of sole on the special luncheon is bound to become unmanageable when he discovers that he can produce the main fish course directly, at the edge of his own pasture, by a bit of trickery on a fine morning.

Below the barn are the asparagus and the potatoes and the potato bugs in season. Beyond is the pasture, where, amid juniper and granite and lambkill, grow the wild strawberries and the tame heifers. Keep walking and you come to the blueberries and the cranberries. Take off your shoes, advance, and you are on the clam beds—the only crop on the place that squirts water at you in time of drought. Beyond the clams are the cunners and the flounders, hanging round the dock piles on the incoming tide. Near the ledges, off the point, are the lobsters. Two miles farther, off the red rocks, are the mackerel, flashing in schools, ready for the Sunday afternoon sociable when the whole village turns out for the harvest of fishes. Mackereling is the accepted Sabbath engagement in summertime; there are two or three spots known to be good and the boats bunch up at these points, a clubby arrangement for man and fish. It is where you meet your friends, and, if the tide serves you, reap the benefit from your friends' toll bait, which drifts down over your hook. Farthest from home are the cod and haddock. You must rise early the day you go to bring them in.

The salt water farms hereabouts give ample evidence that their owners have a great deal on their minds. Rocks and alders are the most conspicuous crops, and if a man can get a job firming the public highway he gives small thought to loosening the soil in his own garden. With the whole sea bottom to rake, he isn't going to spend all his time weeding a bean row. He puts in a vegetable garden in spring, gives it a few vicious pokes with a hoe in June, and devotes the remainder of the year to lustier pursuits—grinding the valves of an old boat-engine, or mending a weir. My neighbor Mr. Dameron, who goes after the lobsters from early spring till late fall, tethers his cow a few paces from his landing, so that he can pick her up handily when he comes in from hauling his traps. The two of them walk up together through the field, he with his empty gas can, she with her full bag of milk.

There is a lively spirit here among us maritime agriculturalists. My neighbors are mostly descendants of sea rovers and are stifled by the confinements of a farm acre. The young men fit easier on an Indian motorcycle than on a disc harrow. And I have noticed that it is the easy-going ones among us who have the best time; in this climate, at the rate a stove eats wood, if a man were to grow too thrifty or forehanded he'd never be able to crawl out from under his own woodpile.

Although winter is still in possession of the land, the days are perceptibly longer. Skating on the frog pond under an early rising moon, I am conscious of the promise of pollywogs under my runners, and my thoughts turn to seeds and the germinal prospect. Snow, which came with a bang at Thanksgiving, is an old story to the little boy now; winter's charms fade slowly out like the picture of Charlie McCarthy on the back of his sweatshirt. Sears Roebuck's midwinter catalogue is shelved in favor of seed catalogues. Before another week is gone I shall have to map out a poultry program and decide whether to reduce my egg farming to reasonable family proportions or step it up to a commercial scale.

Last spring I started eighty-four day-old chicks under a coal brooder stove. I assumed that if I began with eighty-four I might, with good luck, wind up with an even dozen. The others I expected to meet a horrible death, since I had read that this is what always happens when a man starts to keep chickens. As things turned out I lost only three birds. One sickened and died, two were spirited away by a killer in the night. The others—eighty-one of them—grew so tall and handsome, and responded so well to loving-kindness and to rich food, and the young cockerels crowed so loudly at daybreak, that they became the talk of the countryside. We ate or sold forty-five broilers and roasters, and ended up with thirty-six pullets, all laying like a house afire. During the month of November I presented my little family with a frightful total of six hundred and seventy-two eggs, several of them double-yolked. In December production fell off slightly, because of the short days and long cold nights, but on the average we've been getting about twenty eggs a day, of which we consume maybe six or eight. The others have to be disposed of by one means or another. I haven't yet recovered from my surprise.

For a few days, after the barrage of eggs started in the laying pen, my game wife tried to keep pace with the preposterous influx. She scheduled egg dishes daily—all sorts of rather soft, disagreeable desserts, the kind convalescents eat doggedly and without joy. We grimly faced a huge platter of scrambled eggs at breakfast, a floating island or a custard at noon, and at night drank eggnogs instead of Martinis. We even gave raw eggs to the dogs; it would improve their coats, we said. And once I saw my wife slip an egg to the pig when she thought nobody was looking. It was no use. For every egg we ate, my pullets laid two. Secretly I was impressed and delighted, although I got darn sick of floating island.

It was perfectly obvious that we now had a first-rate farm surplus problem on our hands (along with a heating problem, an earning-a-living problem, a Christmas gift problem, and six or eight other problems which bloom in the fall). Unless I proposed to set up a target and throw eggs at it each afternoon for diversion, we should have to act and act quickly. Eggs don't keep. I turned instinctively to Sears Roebuck, and after studying the poultry section sent a hurry call for an egg scale and some cardboard egg cartons, the kind that hold one dozen eggs and have a picture of a hen staring fatuously at a nest. Six days later I timidly presented myself at the local store, bearing three dozen strictly fresh twenty-four-ounce fancy brown eggs, neatly packaged, to be credited to my account. I don't know anything that ever embarrassed me more, unless it was the day in

St. Luke's Hospital when I misunderstood the nurse's instructions and walked into the X-ray room naked except for my socks and garters.

The steady palming off of surplus eggs on a storekeeper who used to be my friend has done more to unnerve me about the country than anything else, although various people have assured me that I exaggerate the gravity of the situation, and some even say that the store turns right round and resells the eggs at a profit. I don't know. I certainly have never *seen* anybody buy an egg in the stores where I trade. I've often hung around watching. It reminded me of the early days of authorhood, when I used to sneak into Brentano's book store and hang around the counter where my book was kept (one copy of it) hoping that I would some day witness a sale. I never did. I have a suspicion the storekeeper takes my eggs home and eats them himself—or throws them at a target. The eggs simply disappear mysteriously behind the counter and show up as a sixty-cent or a ninety-cent credit on my slip. It has reduced my bills appreciably, but it has damn near destroyed my spirit. I am sure it has left its mark on the storekeeper, whose embarrassment equalled mine and to whom for all I know it has meant the difference between operating my account at a profit and at a loss. Anyway, it has shown me clearly that the personal-contact side of agriculture will never be my forte: I can handle production, but someone else will have to take over the marketing if I am to live through the ordeal.

The truth is I am unfit for barter, being of an apologetic rather than an acquisitive nature. And unless I can raise enough eggs so that I can ship them away impersonally in a standard thirty-dozen crate to the Boston market, I shall have to curtail my activities to a mere subsistence basis.

There are of course more ways than one of dealing with a surplus. One of my favorite people around here (although I have never met him) is an old fellow who has a place on the ridge and who is reputed to be a man of original mind. According to report, as I have it, he wears an overcoat winter and summer—just the same in summer as in winter, his theory being that if an overcoat can keep out the cold then by God it can keep out the heat too. A bachelor, he keeps two cows with whom he dwells contentedly, in peace and in filth. He is a master of surplus. There are days when he gets as much as twenty-four quarts of milk. Somebody once asked him what he did with all that milk.

"Drink what I feel like and throw the rest to hell," he replied testily.

Such strength of character is seldom met with on a farm, though a farm is where it is most urgently needed.

I was sorry to hear the other day that a certain writer, appalled by the cruel events of the world, had pledged himself never to write anything that wasn't constructive and significant and liberty-loving. I have an idea that this, in its own way, is bad news.

All word-mongers, at one time or another, have felt the divine necessity of using their talents, if any, on the side of right—but I didn't realize that they were making any resolutions to that effect, and I don't think they should. When liberty's position is challenged, artists and writers are the ones who first take up the sword. They do so without persuasion, for the battle is peculiarly their own. In the nature of things, a person engaged in the flimsy business of expressing himself on paper is dependent on the large general privilege of being heard. Any intimation that this privilege may be revoked throws a writer into a panic. His is a double allegiance to freedom—an intellectual one springing from the conviction that pure thought has a right to function unimpeded, and a selfish one springing from his need, as a breadwinner, to be allowed to speak his piece. America is now liberty-conscious. In a single generation it has progressed from being tooth-brush conscious, to being air-minded, to being liberty-conscious. The transition has been disturbing, but it has been effected, and the last part has been accomplished largely by the good work of writers and artists, to whom liberty is a blessed condition which must be preserved on earth at all costs.

But to return to my man who has foresworn everything but what is good and significant. He worries me. I hope he isn't serious, but I'm afraid he is. Having resolved to be nothing but significant, he is in a fair way to lose his effectiveness. A writer must believe in something, obviously, but he shouldn't join a club. Letters flourish not when writers amalgamate, but when they are contemptuous of one another. (Poets are the most contemptuous of all the writing breeds, and in the long run the most exalted and influential.) Even in evil times, a writer should cultivate only what naturally absorbs his fancy, whether it be freedom or cinch bugs, and should write in the way that comes easy.

The movement is spreading. I know of one gifted crackpot who used to be employed gainfully in the fields of humor and satire, who has taken a solemn pledge not to write anything funny or light-hearted or "insignificant" again till things get straightened around in the world. This seems to me distinctly deleterious and a little silly. A literature composed of nothing but liberty-loving thoughts is little better than the propaganda which it seeks to defeat.

In a free country it is the duty of writers to pay no attention to duty. Only under a dictatorship is literature expected to exhibit an harmonious design or an inspirational tone. A despot doesn't fear eloquent writers preaching freedom—he fears a drunken poet who may crack a joke that will take hold. His gravest concern is lest gaiety, or truth in sheep's clothing, somewhere gain a foothold, lest joy in some unguarded moment be unconfined. I honestly don't believe that a humorist should take the veil to-day; he should wear his bells night and day, and squeeze the uttermost jape, even though he may feel more like writing a strong letter to the *Herald Tribune*.

HURRICANE

JOHN T. WINTERICH

————◆•◆————

Soon after the fearful hurricane of 1938, in the days before hurricanes had names, John T. Winterich (1891–   ), an editor and writer, born in Connecticut, contributed the following piece on the then comparatively unstudied phenomenon of hurricanes, as a Reporter At Large piece for the New Yorker.

Since then New England has been bowled over in different summers by Carol, Edna, Hazel, and many another tempestuous lady. But it is to that first great hurricane of '38 that New Englanders return whenever they get a chance to tell of their hurricane experiences (as they do to me; I was in Virginia at the time). One friend told me he was sick with flu at his house near Point Judith, Rhode Island, on the fatal morning when the storm struck. Rising from his bed, he drove off toward the mooring place of his sailboat, which was laden with government-owned equipment for marine observation. A tree fell on his car as he drove, and he resorted to a small boy's bicycle to reach the harbor, where he found his skiff had cast adrift; so he swam out to his boat and, climbing aboard, managed to keep her afloat during the rest of the day and night by riding the storm out as far off Point Judith as he could keep. When he got home next day, the story concludes, his house was demolished but his flu was gone.

On the morning of September 13th, the navigators of ships then in the region of 19 degrees north and 37 west—mid-Atlantic, on the shipping lane between South America and England—noted in their logs certain evidences of cyclonic circulation. It was the beginning of the hurricane which, eight days later, was to appear so unexpectedly off Long Island, sweeping the coast from there to Boston.

The time was favorable; hurricanes are bred from midsummer to mid-autumn out of the difference in temperature of air and water. There was an area of low atmospheric pressure far out there at sea. The sea-warmed, water-ladened air over this area rose—not straight up, but in a counter-clockwise spiral. Everything north of the equator that is affected by the earth's rotation moves counter-clockwise—smoke rising from a chimney on a still day, a whirlpool, the tiny eddy created over the drain of your bathtub. As the warm air rose, the air that came in from the sides of the low-pressure area took the same circular movement. The moisture in the rising air began to be precipitated as rain, and the dry air then swept up faster than before, adding speed to the rotation of the incoming winds. The hurricane was well started.

A hurricane has two movements: its own rotation and a forward movement of the mass. On the evening of September 16th, this particular hurricane was observed in unhurried progress—12 or 15 miles an hour, perhaps—apparently toward the Leeward Islands. This is information gathered by meteorologists after the event; the first warning received by the United States Weather Bureau came a day later, in the evening, when a ship reported the hurricane about 500 miles northeast of the Leeward Islands. On the eighteenth it was going about 20 miles an hour, in a direction slightly north of west. During the next two days, the nineteenth and twentieth, it veered north and slowed down to 15 miles an hour.

This, so far, was orthodox behavior for a hurricane. Most of the storms headed for the Florida coast (this one was now only a couple of hundred miles off Jacksonville) don't actually reach the coast. In meteorological jargon, they "recur"; i.e., they veer off in a parabolic sweep to the northeast, go up past Newfoundland, and expend themselves harmlessly somewhere in the northern ocean. Their normal rate of speed is 15 or 20 miles an hour, at the start, and they go faster as they proceed. Once they start, their impetus is supplied by the precipitation of moisture, with a consequent uprush of light, dry air. Passing on to land, where the air is dry, they slow down very quickly; it has been observed that hurricanes striking Florida show a marked subsidence in their hundred-mile sweep overland to the Gulf.

Perhaps it might be well to get a clear picture of this hurricane as it was on the evening of September 20th. A billiard ball moving down a table, crowded with right-hand English, might serve to illustrate the forces involved: a very fast circular motion combined with a slow, steady, forward progress. Or, if you could impart the same motion to a doughnut, and imagine it to be about fifty miles from one edge to the other, it would be a better example, because there is a dead spot in the centre of a hurricane where there is no wind or rain—the "eye," meterologists call it. The western half of a northbound hurricane is nowhere near so destructive as the eastern half, because its internal motion is bucking the forward motion of the mass, but it precipitates most of the rain. The other half is comparatively dry and, since the forward motion is added to the force of the whirlwind, very swift and destructive.

Warned by special bulletins from the Weather Bureau, Florida prepared for the big blow, but the hurricane, still behaving with perfect normality, speeded up to 35 miles an hour and, on the evening of September 20th, veered northward enough to miss Florida. On the morning of the twenty-first, it was seventy-five miles off Cape Hatteras, moving at about 50 miles an hour. It was only reasonable to expect that it would continue the curve it had begun to describe and go out to sea. It was walled in, however, by two high-pressure areas that left no outlet but a pathway through Connecticut, Rhode Island, Massachusetts, New Hampshire, Vermont, and Canada. This wasn't predictable, or at least the Weather Bureau didn't predict it. From the time it left Hatteras until it hit West Hampton, it was a lost hurricane. The Weather Bureau had that morning sent out an appeal to coastwise shipping to help it locate the storm centre, but the only tangible result of this had been to send everything afloat in the threatened area scuttling to safer waters.

The path which the hurricane took on September 21st was, though astonishing, not unheard of. Let Nathaniel Morton of the Massachusetts Bay Colony tell about the hurricane of 1635:

> This Year, on Saturday, the fifteenth day of August, was such a mighty storm of Wind and Rain, as none now living in these parts, either English or Indian, had seen the like, being like unto those Hirracanes or Tiffuns that writers mention to be sometimes in the Indies. It began in the morning a little before day, and grew not by degrees, but came with great violence in the beginning, to the great amazement of many; It blew down sundry houses, and uncovered divers others; Divers vessels were lost at Sea in it, and many more in extream danger. It caused the sea to swell in some places to the southward of Plimouth, as that it rose to twenty foot right up and down, and made many of the Indians to climb into Trees for their Safety: It threw down all the Corn to the ground, which never rose more; the which through the mercy of God, it being near harvest time, was not lost, though much the worse: and had the wind continued without shifting, in likelihood it would have drowned some part of the country. It blew down many hundred thousands of Trees, turning up the stronger by the roots, and breaking the high Pine Trees and such like in the midst, and the tall young Oaks and Walnut Trees of good bigness, were wound as a Wyth by it; very strange and fearful to behold: It began in the Southeast and veered sundry wayes, but the greatest force of it at Plimouth, was from the former quarter: it continued not in extremity above five or six hours, ere the violence of it began to abate; the marks of it will remain this many years, in those parts where it was sorest . . .

One hundred and eighty years passed. On September 23, 1815, a southeast wind came howling up Narragansett Bay and hurled many million tons of water into the streets of Providence, together with four ships, nine brigs, seven schooners, and fifteen sloops. Moses Brown, the trader, suffered a million-dollar loss. The hurricane tore onward, snatched the Sunday breeches of Oliver Wendell Holmes (aged six) from a Cambridge clothesline, then blasted a path through the hamlets of southern and central New Hampshire, uprooting trees, flattening crops, killing cattle and men. The people of Providence solemnized the event by setting a bronze tablet in the wall of the Old Market House in Market Square, marking a flood level eleven feet nine and a quarter inches above mean high water.

Last September the high-water level in Market Square stood one foot eleven and three-quarters inches above the record level of 1815.

The hurricane of 1938 followed the pattern set by the two that came before, but outdid them in intensity. It raced from Hatteras to the south shore of Long Island, a gull flight of 425 miles, in slightly less than seven hours; that averages 61 miles an hour, but since the hurricane was gathering momentum all the time, it is probable that it was making 80 when it hit West Hampton. That is merely the speed of the mass, to which you must add the whirlwind's speed in order to get the real velocity. It was well over 150 miles an hour at times.

Fire Island received the full force of the gale first. Though far more damage was done by water than by wind, there was no "tidal wave" there, or anywhere else along the coast. It was simply an elevated mass of water pushed along by the wind—a storm wave, meteorologists call it. The wave washed right over the island, furrowing out several permanent channels and floating off hundreds of the flimsily built summer houses. The storm then leaped northward to the ocean shore of Long Island, the savage eastern half hitting hardest at the Hamptons. The calm centre passed over Brentwood between 2:50 and 3:50 that afternoon. Five minutes later the hurricane reached the Connecticut coast, centering somewhere between Bridgeport and New Haven.

In Manhattan, the wet, gusty weather testified to the presence of the rainy, relatively weak semicircle of the hurricane. At the Battery, the water was about six and a half feet above mean sea level, the backwash of the storm wave. In the Sound, thousands of boats were tossed ashore or broken on the rocks. The clam flats and oyster beds were stirred up and the shellfish either buried or tossed into an aquatic No Man's Land, where anybody could later claim them. The islands in the Sound suffered badly. Gamecock Island, a small, carefully landscaped island off Port Chester, used by its owner, Dr. J. Darwin Nagel, as an experimental garden, suddenly became a heap of rocks. J. P. Morgan's island at Glen Cove was flooded and the private highway leading to it destroyed. The century-old oaks standing on Marshall Field's place in Huntington went down.

The storm centre was moving up toward Rhode Island and Massachusetts. The coast was flooded to depths ranging from twelve to twenty-five feet. The anemometer at the Watch Hill Coast Guard Station recorded a velocity of 121 miles an hour. This region saw the most impressive demonstration of what a hurricane can do. Misquamicut, Quonochontaug, and the Napatree Point section of Watch Hill all have the same kind of shoreline—a twenty-three-mile strip of land backed by salt marshes. On this strip were a concrete highway, grass, shrubbery, trees, and some seven hundred houses. When the wind died down and the water receded, there was nothing left but a bare sandspit. Not even the foundation of a house was to be seen. The Red Cross workers, attempting to locate the bodies of missing residents, found it necessary to use the telephone company's diagram of the region; there was no other way of telling where a house had stood.

September 21st was the day of the "double new-moon tide," when both the sun and the moon exert their greatest pull on the sea. At 5:15 P.M., only an hour and a half before high tide, the storm struck Providence and a man was drowned in front of the City Hall—an incident far more fantastic than if it had happened at the corner of Broadway and Wall Street. The Hen and Chickens lightship rode out the storm, but drifted north to a point where it might as well have been marking Brenton Reef.

Inland, the Connecticut Valley tobacco planters lost almost their entire crop. Three-quarters of the broadleaf had already been picked and was drying in flimsy sheds heated by charcoal braziers. The sheds blew down and many caught fire. The standing plants were all levelled. The oyster beds of Narragansett Bay were stirred up, like the ones off Long Island.

Still moving in its channel between the two walls of high atmospheric pressure, the hurricane headed toward Vermont. The anemometer on Mount Washington recorded 183 miles an hour, with unofficial estimates on some of the gusts running over 200. Dr. Charles F. Brooks, of Harvard's Blue Hill Meteorological Observatory, noted that from four to eight o'clock there occurred seventy-six gusts of 75 miles an hour or better, five of over 100, and several that he estimated at 180—his anemometer couldn't register more than 100. Other anemometers along the coast paid an impressive but scientifically inconclusive tribute to the force of the wind by blowing away, either with or without their supporting roofs.

In the path of the hurricane, all but the strongest trees went down. Ironically enough, the loss of trees was heaviest in parks, village greens, and private estates—places where special attention had been given to the care of growing things. Here the tree roots, instead of having to dig deep for water and nourishment, had remained near the surface, living on the artificial supplies provided for them by man. Where roots had been lopped off to make room for streets or building excavations, the trees were easy victims of the wind. The oaks stood up best, and after them the maples. Vermont lost two-thirds of her sugar maples, New Hampshire half her stand of white pine. Dedham, Massachusetts, lost its famous old Avery Oak, which had been saved by popular vote from being sawed down for use as timber in the frigate Constitution.

The passage overland should have abated the force of the hurricane within a couple of hundred miles, but it was still strong enough to cause serious damage when it reached Montreal. That was the last seen of it; it passed on and died somewhere in northern Ontario. It was followed by a clear, mild night. The weather for the next few days was fine. Nature had struck one quick, clean blow, then rested to allow time for the work of rescue and rebuilding.

Inside of three weeks the superficial cleaning-up had been done. The telephone and telegraph wires were restrung, the roads made passable, and the railroads restored to service. The dead were identified and buried, the missing tabulated. The 63,000 people who had been thrown on the care of the Red Cross and local relief agencies were able, most of them, to go back to their houses, or the places where their houses had been. But we have not even yet heard the last of the hurricane.

THE PROPER BOSTONIANS

CLEVELAND AMORY

Boston-bred Cleveland Amory (1917–   ), in his book The Proper Bostonians, *gets the nuances of Boston society right as no outlander, not even Marquand (who was from Newburyport), could quite do. In the following chapter, Amory (there are two branches of his family, those who pronounce it Aymory, as the rest of the country does, and those who say Emory; the latter branch is subtly the sweller) discusses a very special breed of cat, the Boston woman, who in her pure state must be seen to be believed. For unworldliness, high-mindedness, and thrift, her Puritan ancestors could hardly go her one better.*

One story was told me by a niece of two aged ladies who owned a large slice of Beacon Hill's formidable real estate. My friend, then living in Manhattan, was very anxious for her Aunt Fanny to see the New York production of Shaw's St. Joan (so worthwhile), and got tickets for a matinee on the Saturday after Thanksgiving. Aunt Fanny arrived from Boston Friday evening, spent the night with an old friend, and on Saturday her niece took her to lunch and the theatre. Aunt Fanny enjoyed the play but would not stay for the end of the last act because she had to catch the Five O'clock home. My friend escorted the old lady to Grand Central, saw her onto the train, and found a seat which she considered specially desirable. "It's right next to the dining car," she told her aunt. "You won't have far to walk." "Dining car?" inquired Aunt Fanny. "Why should I go into the dining car?" It turned out that this millionairess had brought a sandwich made out of her Thanksgiving turkey all the way to New York, kept it overnight in her hostess's refrigerator, and proposed to make her Saturday evening meal of it.

THE BOSTON WOMAN

THE one quality with which the female of the Proper Bostonian species has most impressed outsiders—once they are safely beyond the stage of merely staring at her antiquated hat, her stout shoes, and her generally severe exterior—is her incredible vitality. Many years ago a frail young clergyman from some effete hinterland west of Boston was invited to come to the city to deliver a series of lectures. During his stay he was run ragged by the elderly head of the women's committee of the church which had engaged him and became, to his embarrassment, so exhausted he did not know how he could find the strength to complete his work. Feeling that the woman's religion must be the source of her energy and believing he would benefit from hearing her express this source to him, he spoke to her frankly. "Madam," he said, "may I ask what it is that has given you the strength to do all that you do?" The woman regarded his anxious, worn countenance for a moment with some displeasure, then replied stiffly, "Victuals, sir, victuals."

Actually it is more likely that the woman was prescribing for the needs of the young man himself rather than parting with the secret of her own energy. The Boston woman is not by nature an extraordinarily large eater and she is by no means as physically well fortified in appearance as, for example, the typical suburban clubwoman regularly cartooned by Helen Hokinson in the *New Yorker* magazine. But she is energetic and she wears her low-heeled walking shoes for a purpose. It is almost impossible to travel around the Back Bay-Beacon Hill zone without being impressed with the number of Boston's "low-heelers"—a familiar term for First Family ladies—who, many of them being of remarkably advanced years, regularly ply the streets from dawn to dark, and often long after dark, in a resolute manner. Yet when these women stop at their favorite Boston beaneries—such as the Brittany Coffee Shop or the Old English Tea Room—it is usually merely to sip a cup of tea and take a bite or two of an English muffin and then move on again.

Psychologists have long been interested in this problem of the phenomenal activity of the Boston Amazon, and knowing they must look
deeper than the moderate caloric intake of these women, many have come
to the conclusion that energy, pent up by the Puritan inhibitions of Boston life, will, like truth, out in the end. One Boston psychiatrist, whose
mother-in-law was a Cabot, recalls that he used to sit and argue with her
on this subject. He was never able to get far with his research, however,
because, though a woman in her eighties, she would fret like a race horse
as the argument increased in intensity and swing her leg so impatiently
that he was reduced to staring in wonder at her excess energy. First
Family women are known Boston over for their determination to "fill
their life," as the expression is, regardless of their age. A wealthy Welles-
ley widow turned seventy took up painting. She enjoyed it but found it
too sedentary an occupation to use all her time, and recently turned
eighty, took up sculpture as well. Lilla Cabot Perry, another First Family
artist of note, did her best work when approaching her ninetieth birthday
and, painting five hours every day at that age, used to say she felt sure
she was getting better all the time.

Many of Boston's most active women of today seem to feel they must
make up for time lost as a result of an overly restricted Victorian girl-
hood. "We used to be perfectly asinine most of the time," perky First
Family spinster Katharine Homans declares. "We'd spend whole after-
noons sitting in bay windows and watching people walk up and down
Commonwealth Avenue." During World War II Miss Homans, in the
neighborhood of seventy and with a distinctly frail appearance, spent her
Mondays and Fridays running ward errands for four hours a day in the
Massachusetts General Hospital, her Tuesdays travelling all over town for
Boston's Family Welfare Society, and her Thursdays at the Red Cross.
The owner of a country place of thirty acres with only a part-time gardener, she liked to keep her Wednesdays and Saturdays "open," as she
called them, for gardening, but she also sandwiched in regular work at
the heart clinic of another Boston hospital and at the same time managed
to keep up with the pursuits of all true Proper Boston women—lectures,
concerts, indignation meetings, etc.

Up until recently the most remarkable First Family hyperthyroid cases
were those of two of Boston Society's most charming characters, Mrs.
Augustus Hemenway, a sister of the late Bishop Lawrence, and the late
Miss Minna Hall. Friends since debutante days, both were approaching
ninety but continued to lead such active lives that they thought nothing
of a two- or three-mile walk if they had nothing else to occupy their
time. Mrs. Hemenway was a year older than Miss Hall, but the latter
had the distinction of being the only living member of an organization
formed by one of the elder Boston Lowells, known as The Society of
Those Still Living in the House They Were Born In. Miss Hall's home in

Brookline antedated her by a scant ten years. Fifty years ago, together with Mrs. Hemenway, she founded the Massachusetts Audubon Society, which dedicated itself against the then prevalent fashion of women wearing egret feathers in their hats; both women were severe critics of any feathered hats they encountered on Boston streets. The solicitude of these two friends for each other's health was touching, tinged as it was with an entirely unconscious rivalry. "Minna is so busy these days," Mrs. Hemenway would tell a fellow member at an Audubon meeting, "I'm really afraid she's overdoing," while Minna, for her part, cornering a friend at Symphony, would express concern over how tired Harriet Hemenway must be with all her gadding about. "Harriet's a gadder," she used to declare firmly, "she just doesn't know when to stop." Today Mrs. Hemenway is ninety-seven.

With such examples before them it is little wonder that Boston women are known for growing old with zest. Few mind giving their exact ages and many take great pride in their advancing years. Gray hair is not something to be delayed by cheap artifice; it is something to be looked forward to. Life, for the Proper Boston woman, begins at no mere forty; it is more likely to be sixty. Then she can wear her queen-mother hair-do, her inherited hat, and her ankle-length fur coat with the righteous air of knowing she is safely past the draft age of fashion for good. "I love growing old," Susan Hale of Boston's illustrious Hale Family once wrote to a friend. "Each year I come to is the most exciting yet." At the time she wrote she was seventy-four, ill and deaf, but this mattered little to her. "Life," said Julia Ward Howe, who spent a large part of her ninety-one years as a Beacon Streeter, "is like a cup of tea, the sugar is all at the bottom." The author of the *Battle Hymn of the Republic* caught what might be called the true spirit of the Boston woman when, at the age of eighty-seven, she wrote in her diary:

> I pray for many things this year. For myself, I ask continued health of mind and body, work, useful, honorable, remunerative, as it shall please God to send; for my dear family, work of the same description with comfortable wages.

That the First Family ladies of Boston have a tradition of hardihood behind them is undeniable. The very first woman to land in Boston, who came over with Governor Winthrop and his party in 1630, set the pace at the earliest possible moment when she jumped from the bow of the boat onto the beach in order to gain the distinction of being the first ashore. Outliving her husband by fifty years, she supported herself by keeping open house for Harvard students at an inn on Beacon Street and lived to be a hundred and five years old. At the age of a hundred and three she had her portrait painted lest her example of fortitude be lost on future generations of her sex. Fortunately, it was not. It was no easy thing to be a Puritan wife and follow such a schedule as that laid out by one of New England's leading First Family ministers of his day. In his journal for 1719, he notes:

Oct. 30. I marry.
　　　　　We begin to keep house.
　　　　　My proposed order:
1. At 5 get up and go into my study.
2. Pray and read in the Original Bible till 6 and then call up the family.
3. At 6½ Go to Family Prayers and only the Porringer of Chocolate for Breakfast.
4. At 7 go in to my study till 12½ and then do something about the House till 1 to dinner.
5. Dinner at 1.
6. At 2 Dress and go about till Candle Light, except Wednesday after Dinner, do something about the House: Saturday after Dinner visit Dr. Sewall's till 2½ and then Home.
7. At Candle Light and Study to 9½ at 9½ go to Family Prayers and so to Bed: N.B. I eat no supper.*

This sort of thing had undoubtedly something to do with the development of the Boston woman's character, which was to rise to such heights in time of stress. "With your shield, or on it," the Spartan mother used to say to her son knowing that, with the heavy shields Spartan warriors carried, flight was impossible and her son would either return to her victorious or be carried home dead. Echoing this cry, the First Family mother of four good Boston Burnham sons watched them march off to the Revolution with their father and shouted from her doorway: "Never let me hear that one of you was shot in the back." Needless to say, none of them was; coming from such a home, the Army was the Life of Riley to the Burnham boys. Curiously enough, all during the early-day trials and tribulations of Boston, the Boston woman exhibited the same resoluteness of character whichever side she was on. During the Revolution, if a Patriot she scorned to touch a drop of Black Market tea—though no true Boston woman before or since has ever been known to be able to get by five o'clock without it—if a Loyalist she was utterly fearless in facing deportation and confiscation of her property. Few Loyalist women who later were able to return to Boston were ever known to change sides. "My grandmother," James Russell Lowell once observed, "was a Loyalist to her death and whenever Independence Day came around, instead of joining in the general rejoicing, she would dress in deep black, fast all day, and loudly lament our late unhappy differences with his Most Gracious Majesty."

* *Famous Families of Massachusetts,* by Mary Caroline Crawford (Boston: Little Brown) © 1930.

In the golden Family-founding days of the nineteenth century the Boston woman also played a vigorous role, both as merchant mother and sea-captain wife. The mother of Boston's greatest merchant, the elder Colonel Perkins, was early left a widow with eight children to be brought up. Her husband, however, had been engaged in a small export business dealing in furs and imported hats, and the young widow did so well at carrying it on that letters often came to her from Holland addressed to *Mr.* Elizabeth Perkins—the highest possible compliment. The mother of another man who became one of Boston's most successful merchants had fifteen children to look after as well as all the housework to do. In a diary of later years the merchant recalled the picture of his anxious mother stirring the uncovered well on their place with a long stick to see if one of her children she had lost track of had by chance drowned himself. He wrote that his mother was always "greatly relieved" when her stick scraped freely over the bottom of the well. Robert Bennet Forbes, the sea captain, had a particularly sturdy specimen of a mother. Sailing with her young children to join her husband in France, she wrote on the ship, a full five weeks at sea after leaving Boston, a factual account of her difficulties:

> We have just seen five vessels, perhaps privateers to our sorrow. We have been under water most of the time . . . The cabin and my stateroom have been so wet as to compel me to bail out the water constantly. Many days we lived in darkness, or only seeing by the light of a dim lamp. At night I am often obliged to have the boys in my bunk, theirs being wet. I was only seasick three weeks.*

Married early, girls often went to sea side by side with their husband ship captains. At the age of nineteen one wife, sailing from Boston to San Francisco, had her husband suddenly stricken blind with brain fever, and with no other officer on board who understood navigation, was forced to take charge of the ship. Calmly studying in spare moments out of books brought to her from the ship's cabin, not only navigation but also medicine—so that she could care for her husband—she brought the ship around Cape Horn and put into Frisco on time to discharge the cargo. For fifty nights, it is recorded, she never left the deck. One sea captain, whose ship had foundered on a shoal in the China Seas and was being torn to pieces by breakers, ran to his cabin to get his wife. He found her seated on a sea chest dressed in his pants and the mate's coat and vest and ready for any emergency. All she wanted, she told him, was a hat. Amazed, her husband found her one and watched her take a pair of scissors, coolly and quickly cut off her hair close to her head, and put on the hat. "There," she asked cheerfully, "don't I look like a boy?" To-

---

* *Canton Captain*, by James B. Connolly (New York: Doubleday Doran) © 1942.

gether they went on deck, and his wife's calmness, the captain later maintained, was the only thing that restored order among the panic-stricken crew and made the eventual rescue of all of them possible. On still another memorable voyage Mrs. Joseph Coolidge, nineteenth-century matriarch of Boston Coolidges, was sailing as a passenger on a ship commanded by Captain Dumaresq, often called the prince of Boston sea captains. Dumaresq, finding his ship being chased by pirates who appeared to be gaining, graciously deferred to Mrs. Coolidge the decision as to whether, if the pirates caught them, they should allow themselves to be captured or whether he should blow the ship up. "Blow her up," said Mrs. Coolidge abruptly and then went on deck, despite remonstrances from the captain, for a better view of her race for life. This race was only won when the pirates, for no apparent reason, abandoned the chase.

With her physical hardihood established, the Boston woman of the nineteenth century went on to greater things. It seems impossible to realize now, but there was a time in Boston when females were not admitted to lectures. When the Boston Lyceum series of lectures were inaugurated early in the nineteenth century, however, its promoter had an idea. "I will attach a *locomotive* to this Lyceum," he declared, "which shall *make it go.*" His locomotive was the Boston woman, and it is doubtful if anyone has ever given a more accurate description of the female of the Proper Bostonian species. She did, of course, make the Lyceum series go, and regular attendance at lectures has ever since been a ritual in her life. She has always had her favorites—the traveler Burton Holmes is now working on his third generation of Boston women—but through the years she has welcomed to her podium with open ears any author of whatever note and, particularly in these latter days, all manner of international experts. She has made her city a recognized Garden of Eden on the American lecture circuit, and the intense seriousness with which she attends any and all offerings has become proverbial. A brief sample of this was demonstrated during World War II when the Boston author John P. Marquand was on the platform. Marquand, who has been married twice, told his audience he had "one son in the Seventh Army and another in diapers." One lady could not refrain from questioning this. "Mr. Marquand," she asked, "where is Diapers?"

Margaret Fuller, Boston's great feminist of the nineteenth century, was a strong dose in the prescription which has made the Boston woman's character of today. An extremely plain woman who talked in a nasal voice and had a habit of constantly opening and shutting her eyes, she had nonetheless great personal magnetism—the most, Emerson once said, of any woman he ever knew. She began by teaching a class of the twenty-five women she considered most "cultivated" in Boston the art of "mental refinement," and went on from there to refine Boston womanhood on a larger scale. "It is a vulgar error," she once said, "that love, *a* love, is to woman her whole existence. She is also born for Truth and Love in their universal energy."

The Boston woman learned from this sort of thing a zeal for reform which was not long in expressing itself. Women, not men, were the moving spirit in one noted meeting of the day which had no less an object than Universal Reform. If the Proper Boston merchant held sternly aloof from Brook Farm, the country's most distinguished experiment in communal living—what else could he do with an organization which had Nathaniel Hawthorne for head of its finance committee, a man who had never met a payroll in his life?—his sisters, and in some cases, even his wife, did not. First Family women were from the start a real force in the experiment, and if foredoomed to general failure, the Farm succeeded in giving women one ultra-modern landmark in emancipation—the establishment of the first nursery school known in America.

As a general thing, wife-reformers of the nineteenth century did not disturb the tranquillity of the Proper Boston marriage as they have been known to do in later days. This seems to have been at least partly due to the remarkable equanimity of the merchant-husbands involved, who were evidently able to take such things, along with their occasional financial reverses, in stride. One of these merchant-husbands, asked how he felt about the manifold activities of his wife, a well-known reformer of her day, replied briefly that he attended the closer to his own business the more his wife attended to other people's. But the question seems also to have been solved by the fact that many a First Family woman, feeling the urge for reform at an early age, chose for her mate, not a merchant at all but a very different type of man. A young Cabot girl with a reforming bent, for example, married Theodore Parker, a veritable firebrand of reform. Parker, who once devoted an entire sermon to the topic "The Temptations of Milkmen," and who ate no breakfast, but instead started each day by reading five books of the Bible, would have been a match for any wife-reformer. So, too, would have been his friend, George Ripley, founder of Brook Farm. Ripley once stated with some pride that his marriage was "founded not upon any romantic or sudden passion" but instead "upon great respect for her [his wife's] intellectual power, moral worth, deep and true Christian piety and peculiar refinement and dignity of character." Wendell Phillips, the abolitionist, though a son of Boston's first mayor and a First Family man, was still another young bridegroom far removed from the merchant-husband when he admitted that his wife invariably preceded him in the adoption of the various causes he advocated. Leaving his London boardinghouse one day to attend a convention where he was to deliver an address, he went out the door with the parting words of his young wife ringing in his ears: "Wendell, don't shilly shally." Wendell did not. Though the convention was a World Anti-Slavery meeting and had nothing to do with women at all, Phillips ended by delivering the first speech ever made by a man in advocacy of the rights of women.

Along with her reform, the Proper Boston woman has always played a leading part in church activities. The real strength of Boston's First Family churches has apparently always lain in the female head of the women's auxiliary, always the vigorous type of blue-blood feminist, rather than in her male counterpart who, as the impeccable warden or vestryman, may be the nominal leader of the congregation but actually is likely to content himself with passing the collection plate and keeping a weather eye out that the current preacher doesn't get himself out on a limb with any socialistic tommyrot. Denominationally most of the Boston churches started out by being Congregationalist, once the established faith of New England. Then, in the nineteenth century, the Emersons, Channings, Eliots and Lowells brought Unitarianism to a high position of favor among the First Families. Little by little, however, a practical low-church Episcopalianism began to make severe inroads on Boston's home-grown Unitarianism. Many a First Family woman turned with joy to the more definite ritual of this Episcopalianism, which included kneeling for prayer—Unitarians bend and make "slight obeisance" but do not kneel—and belief in the divinity of Christ. Sometimes she brought her husband along with her; sometimes First Families were split on the question. When the handsome young bachelor Phillips Brooks came to Boston in 1869 from Philadelphia, it was the Boston woman who soon made a social as well as an ecclesiastical lion out of him. With ringing rhetoric from his Trinity Church pulpit Brooks soon had even such staunch Unitarian feminists as the daughters of James Russell Lowell and Dr. Oliver Wendell Holmes proudly referring to him as "our bishop"; since Brooks had been born a Unitarian, his success was singularly important in placing Episcopalianism on a par with Unitarianism in the fight for the No. 1 religion of Boston's best.

This struggle has by no means abated, and it is the Boston woman, who relishes such things, who has kept it in focus in the Boston Society picture. Episcopal ladies still regard the God of the Unitarians, as He was once characterized, as "an oblong blur," and delight in such stories as that told of the mother of Harvard's president Eliot who, addressing a friend who had just become an Episcopalian, asked incredulously, "Eliza, do *you* kneel down in church and call yourself a miserable sinner? Neither I nor any member of my family will ever do *that!*" For their part the Unitarian ladies do not find it hard to remember the days when even the great Brooks was characterized as "an Episcopalian—with leanings toward Christianity" and when Emerson made his telling definition of Boston Episcopalianism as the best diagonal line that could be drawn between the life of Jesus Christ and that of the Boston merchant Abbott Lawrence. When Harvard turned from Unitarianism and went non-sectarian—its

Divinity School was once described as consisting of "three mystics, three skeptics and three dyspeptics"—it was, of course, a triumph for the Episcopalians. So was the growth of the First Family fed Episcopal Church Schools which under the leadership of such men as Endicott Peabody of Groton have always been staunchly Episcopalian. But Boston's Unitarian ladies are a strong breed and, if now outnumbered, they still show no signs of submitting to social domination by the upstart Episcopalians. From such sturdy Unitarian redoubts as historic King's Chapel, home of Curtises, Coolidges and in-town Cabots, or Chestnut Hill's First Church, home of Lees, Higginsons, Saltonstalls and out-of-town Cabots, they are still ready to carry the fight to all comers. Chestnut Hill's church is a social match for any church in America of any denomination. So exclusively aristocratic in tone is its congregation that the church's annual meeting is always a "formal" affair, with all women present in evening dresses and all men in tuxedos. Only one member of the church is recognized as underprivileged even by Chestnut Hill standards but there is no question of any embarrassment from this angle. Probably the only church in which no collection plate is ever passed, the First Church handles its finances by a First Family finance committee which decides on a proportionate annual assessment for each family in the parish.

The most recent highlight of this Unitarian-Episcopalian struggle was the case of Dr. Phillips Endecott Osgood. A man in his middle sixties, for many years Boston's outstanding preacher, Dr. Osgood in 1945 rocked all of Proper Boston to its heels with his announced intention to divorce his wife and marry his secretary. An Episcopalian who preached in the wintertime at Boston's in-town Emmanuel Church and in the summer at Emmanuel Church in Manchester-by-the-Sea, he was a First Family Episcopalian stand-by. Shortly after his change in marital plans, however, Dr. Osgood resigned from the Episcopal Church "for theological reasons" and joined the Unitarian Church, in which he was shortly offered a high appointment. Historians were thus afforded an opportunity to compare the reactions of both Churches almost at once under the same storm. Unfortunately the Proper Boston woman of any denomination looks upon divorce with such disfavor that the test was inconclusive. Dr. Osgood soon resigned his Unitarian appointment, and he became to Boston's Unitarian ladies as well as to their Episcopalian sisters simply Dr. "Wasgood."

It is characteristic of the Proper Boston woman that, whether Episcopalian or Unitarian, in a city which has the largest per capita Catholic population in America she barely recognizes Catholicism. She has equally little contact with Christian Scientists; her Boston may be their home, but with the exception of an occasional reading of the *Christian Science Monitor*, generally regarded as the best newspaper in Boston, she is in no way concerned with the faith. As for other Protestant sects, the late Henry

Coit, first headmaster of St. Paul's School, probably spoke her mind as
well as his own when he felt it necessary to rebuke a woman whose son,
for some reason, showed inclinations toward becoming a Presbyterian.
"Never forget, my dear," he said gently, "that in the life to come the
Presbyterians will not be on the same plane as the Episcopalians." The
Oxford Group, with its early emphasis on public confession, has had particularly hard sledding among traditionally inhibited First Family ladies.
Off to a good start with the conversion of the daughter of Episcopal
leader Bishop Lawrence, it had more difficulty in an attempt to duplicate
this feat on another leading First Family Episcopalian. At a banquet the
woman was given the seat of honor next to Frank Buchman, founder of
the movement. After dinner an enthusiastic young Grouper rushed up to
her and demanded to know what she thought of his leader. Receiving a
haughty Episcopalian stare and an abruptly unfavorable verdict he was
crushed—but only for a moment. Then, looking the lady over, he declared
firmly, "Madam, you wouldn't have liked Jesus Christ or St. Paul."

In her own home it did not take the Proper Boston woman long to
emancipate herself from her early nineteenth-century position. Where
once she had played a yes-dear second fiddle to her merchant-husband,
even in the domain of ordering meals and hiring servants, she soon
fought fire with fire and became an executive in her own right. Today in
most First Family homes in Boston it is impossible to say who is the
more dominant character. If the male still assiduously retains his prerogative of keeping his bankbook to himself and holding his wife to a
household budget of his own making, the female brooks no interference in
the actual running of the home. Bishop Lawrence, in the description of
his mother in his *Memoirs,* left a revealing picture of the First Family
Boston housewife. Mrs. Lawrence, her son wrote, was a woman of such
physical stamina that he had once seen her lift a sideboard which two
men refused to touch. She never showed any anxiety in her face or in her
actions. Once in a while, however, she would come down with what she
described as a sick headache, in the treatment of which she took little
stock in the advice of her doctor. Like all good Proper Bostonian Families the Lawrences had, of course, their Family Doctor, but the latter
used to say he was called, in time of sickness of some member of the
family, only to see what medicine Mrs. Lawrence would advise him to
give—and then give it. To the assembled Lawrences at breakfast each
morning Mrs. Lawrence would always ask, in the manner of a general
addressing a group of staff officers, "Now what is the order of perform-
ances today?" Mrs. John T. Sargent, a near contemporary of Mrs. Lawrence, put into a memorable line the Proper Boston woman's pride in her
executive capacities. "I can't do things myself," she used to say, "but I can
manage those who can."

The Proper Boston woman's sphere of managerial capacity is a large one. One curious example of this may be found in her pronunciation of the name of S. S. Pierce, long the city's First Family grocery. Founded many years ago by the Boston Pierce Family, who used the pronunciation "Purse" to distinguish themselves from lesser Pierces, the store soon found the appellation inconvenient for business reasons and announced they wished to be S. S. Pierce—pronounced Pierce. The Boston woman would have none of this, however, and though today Walworth Pierce, present head of the firm, is Pierce to his friends as well as his business acquaintances, no First Family lady ever refers to the store as anything but S. S. Purse. In the matter of the New Haven Railroad, another cherished First Family institution, one Proper Boston woman also showed her mettle. Some years ago, after an unfortunate collision had taken place on the line, she wrote to the president of the railroad and reminded him of the fact that her daughter regularly rode one of his trains; she wished him to speak personally to the engineer about driving carefully. The president wrote back that, much as he would like to do so, it would be impossible for him to make contact with each of his company's thousand or more engineers. Once more he received a letter, the lady taking issue with him on the point. "Furthermore," she added in sharp postscript, she had herself noticed on a recent trip on the railroad that "your man in Providence"—evidently referring to the baggage collector at the station—"is almost constantly in a draft."

Whatever her complaint, and to whomever addressed, the Proper Boston woman expects preferential treatment and immediate action. Remarkably enough, she usually receives it. Many of these women would undoubtedly be inveterate letter-to-the-editor writers were it not for the fact that their names would be published; this, of course, with the exception of the late Boston *Transcript*, would be an unthinkable breach of propriety, and First Family ladies today usually confine themselves to major issues, which they take up on a private basis direct with the top. During World War II Miss Rose Standish Nichols, noted Beacon Hill spinster, did not hesitate to write directly to Admiral King in Washington complaining that his subordinate, Admiral Halsey, who had just referred to the Japanese in his customary colorful manner, was "a disgrace to the Navy." He was, she declared, "not a gentleman." Admiral King not only answered Miss Nichols politely but also told her he had referred her letter to Halsey and said he would appreciate hearing from her what the latter's reply would be. Unfortunately for King's curiosity, this reply was not all it might have been. Even Battling Bill was apparently awed by the Boston spinster. In a letter which contained not so much as a gosh, he told Miss Nichols merely that he had been misquoted.

Basically unembarrassable, the First Family lady is so secure in her position in Boston that she has no fear of looking ridiculous. With rarified aplomb she does not hesitate to carry in public an assortment of bundles which would bring a blush to the cheek of her upstairs maid, and she faces with complete indifference such feminine tragedies as being caught with a run in her stocking or wearing her galoshes on a sunny day. Rules are made for others, not her. She jay-walks freely on Boston streets and in a crowded store, while never pushy in the vulgar sense, she does not hesitate to go direct to the department head for service, rather than wait her turn in line. Carefully brought up never to raise her voice, she rarely lowers it either. In a public place where others are talking in low tones she feels free to carry on a conversation with a friend in the same well-bred but clearly audible pitch she would use in her own drawing room.

The difficulty of controlling such women even for short periods of time was illustrated some years ago when the wife of a prominent Boston surgeon, a woman in her upper sixties, determined to get herself a driver's license. Out on the road, taking her test with a young instructor, she was doing nicely when, climbing a steep hill, she was suddenly ordered by the instructor to stop the car and turn around. It was a routine part of the test but the woman drove on as if she had not heard. Again the instructor repeated his order. At this the woman turned and gave him a sharp glance, then said, "Young man, nobody but a fool would turn around here." The instructor, deciding he had met his match, let her continue up the hill and around to the inspection station. Without another word having passed between them, the woman was handed her license.

Nowhere does the First Family lady show the more forbidding side of her nature more clearly than within the sacrosanct confines of the Chilton Club. Far from being merely one more of Boston's many women's clubs, the Chilton is the real social "must." In the Proper Boston woman's parlance "everybody in Boston" belongs to it, everybody being understood to mean a select five hundred, or about one-tenth of one percent of the city's feminine population. Seemingly patterned on an English men's club rather than the usual American informal type of women's club, the Chilton is in reality Boston's female Somerset—almost equally archaic and in some respects as austere. There are three entrances to the club, one for members only off Commonwealth Avenue, one for members and guests off Dartmouth Street, and one for delivery people and servants off an alley. No member of the press is ever admitted, even from the alley, and Society editors, apparently on pain of not even being permitted to stand outside, are not allowed to mention club activities at all. If a debutante tea takes place in the club they are supposed to write merely that a tea was given and not say where. Submission to such ruling is, of course, merely one more evidence of First Family power in Boston. But Chilton Club power extends even beyond Boston. Legendary in the club is the story of a New Yorker who arrived, by the guest entrance, late one afternoon to give a lecture. Having little time to change her clothes before being due to talk, she asked for a room to dress in and telephoned downstairs for her dinner to be sent up. Just as she had completed her toilet she heard a knock on the door, which she opened to admit, not the expected waiter, but the manager of the club, a formidable woman of the Old School. The latter surveyed the lecturer for some moments in stern silence, then abruptly turned on her heel with the ultimatum, "You are far too well to have dinner served in your room."

Near by the Chilton Club and ranking not far from it as a social haunt of the Proper Boston woman is the ancient and honorable Exeter Street Theatre. The oldest continuously operating movie theatre in Boston, it was built originally as a church and still has regular Sunday morning services. Boston's First Family ladies, who scorn Hollywood and all its works, are nonetheless enticed to this mausoleum-like structure by reason of the fact that its proprietor, a cultivated woman with a degree and an accent from the University of London, features foreign films and runs her business in the homey way she knows all Proper Boston women love. She calls all her regular patrons by name, knows what night they generally want to come and where they wish to sit. She never buys a picture without seeing it first; when her patrons telephone her and ask if they should come—which is general practice—she tells them whether or not she thinks they will have a good time. If they come against her advice, she makes clear that they are on their own. The chances are they will enjoy themselves, for, an astute analyst of the Proper Boston woman's character, she would rather hold over a second-rate import than show a Hollywood Western, a slapstick comedy, or anything "off-color."

Bookstores all over Boston reflect this homey touch First Family ladies love so well. Not for nothing is Boston's most successful book chain called the Personal Bookshop, an outfit with a score of stores two of which, in the Beacon Hill area, face each other on opposite sides of the same street. Many of these Boston bookstores, including the famed Old Corner, Lauriat's and Jordan Marsh, given standing orders by their feminine customers, select a number of books each month, which they know will suit a certain customer's taste, and send them to her. For many years one store has been filling such an order from a Chestnut Hill dowager for "nice novels about nice people." To another bookseller a lady described what she wanted as "books about the kind of people I would have to my own house to dinner." Deploring the moral laxity of modern authors she went further and stated she wanted only the works of authors who knew when to "close the door." Decent people, she felt, closed the door to their own bathrooms and bedrooms, and decent authors should know enough to do the same. A former Proper Boston woman, now living in California, wrote her bookstore she was homesick and wanted everything they had about Boston. Another expatriated dowager asked for "anything you think I should know about." Now living in Maine, she has felt out of

touch with her former home in the center of the world. After some debate
the store recently sent her two books about the atomic bomb. Woe to the
bookseller who trusts blindly to advance publicity and sends such dis-
cerning clients books merely because he knows they are going to be popular. Some years ago, in the heat of a Christmas rush, a salesman sent a
Proper Boston woman a copy of *Kitty Foyle*. He received a prompt
telephone call in which the lady told him curtly she wouldn't allow that
kind of book in her kitchen. "I had my husband take it down to the
furnace," she said, "with my fire tongs." From this sort of book burning,
it might be noted, it was only a step for many of such First Family ladies
to be on the "side of decency" in the recent furore over Boston book
banning.

The herd instinct among Proper Boston women has long been the delight of established Boston institutions and the bane of those wishing to
break into the select circle. Such institutions may even be individuals.
From head to toe—from the hairdresser who for twenty years has been
going from one Proper Boston home to another as "the" hairdresser, to
the chiropodist who for three decades has been "the" chiropodist—First
Family ladies attend to their personal needs in the secure company of
their social equals. For an entire generation, apparently in the belief that
there were no good barbers anywhere else, Proper Boston mothers even
from distant suburbs took their sons to Boston's ancient Hotel Vendome
to have their hair crew cut in the approved pre-Harvard fashion. Today
it is not unusual for such a distant suburbanite to make a special trip in
town to a tiny old-fashioned bakery, where her mother went before her
and where she is sure to see her friends, just to procure such a small order
as a half a dozen cocoanut cakes for tea. A restaurant suddenly becomes
"popular" in Boston—popular, of course, in the restricted sense—not because it serves good food or has an inviting atmosphere, but because some
First Family social leader has "discovered" it, brought her friends, and
made it, as the saying is, a "ladies' and gentlemen's place to eat."

Generally speaking, so restricted is the Proper Boston woman's patron-
age that to her Boston might well be a town of a few thousand people
instead of a city of a million. When shopping in such a city as New York,
where, as she puts it, "no one cares *who* you are," she is particularly unhappy. The more chic and modern the store the more irritated it makes
her. Almost certain to be too ostentatious to suit her Puritan taste, it is
likely to be "cheap," a word she uses for New York in general, though not
of course in the monetary sense. One lady, returning recently from a New
York shopping spree, reported indignantly to her Boston lunch club that
though she had introduced herself to a department head of Bonwit Teller
as Mrs. —— of Boston, she had been met with a blank stare—"as if she'd
never heard the name in her life." Another matron demonstrated how far
out of the swim of modern living the Proper Boston woman often finds

herself, when, on a short trip during the postwar meat shortage, she
stopped at a diner for the first time in her life. Pointing to the meat sandwich being consumed by the man next to her she told the man at the
counter she wished one like it, whatever it was. The man stared at her
for a moment, then called through the slide in a triumphant voice, "Hey,
Joe, come out here and get a load of a dame who's never seen a hamburg!"

The store the Proper Boston woman knows best in her city is R. H.
Stearns. For half a century its first-floor glove counter has been the
meeting place of First Family ladies, and the length of time a woman has
spent waiting here for her friends is a fair barometer of her social
standing. Founded a hundred years ago by the original Stearns, a genial
old-time merchant, the store remained in the hands of his son until the
latter's death in 1939. The present chairman of the board has been with
the company for more than forty years and a personnel survey held some
time before World War II disclosed that, of his eight hundred-odd em-
ployees, more than two hundred had served the store in some capacity
for twenty-five years, and twenty of them for over fifty years. One of these
half-century salesmen was a man who knew without being reminded the
stocking sizes of more than five hundred Boston women. Such a phenomenal memory is not a requisite for a Stearns' salesman, but an increasingly
respectful familiarity with all First Family ladies, and with their mar-
riages and intermarriages, is an almost sure road to advancement in the
store.

Hardly more than a pigmy compared with such large up-to-date Boston
stores as Jordan Marsh and Filene's, Stearns nonetheless does close to a
ten-million-dollar-a-year business in a homey atmosphere which has never
abandoned the nineteenth-century grandmother in catering to the twentieth-century debutante. Its present chairman, now a man in his seventies,
runs his store like a well-bred Boston Family. He lives on Beacon Hill,
walks across the Common each morning—usually without an overcoat
even in the winter—and arrives well before eight o'clock. Each evening
at 5:30 closing time he walks through all eleven floors of his store saying
good night to his clerks and whatever customers may have remained to
that time. He is not quite certain how his store ever cornered Boston's
social market as completely as it has but, knowing his Proper Boston
woman well, he doesn't intend to lose her trade—and unnecessarily increase his overhead—by indulging in such fripperies as lushly décored
windows, French-accented manikins, mirrored-wall dressing rooms, etc.
Stearns has none of these things. But all during World War II, alone of
New England stores, it never forgot that war casualty, the "stylish stout,"
and still today bravely displays, along with sleeker trends, all manner of
old-time merchandise, including pearl chokers, Queen Mary hats, cameo
brooches, high-necked, long-sleeved nightgowns, etc.—and business
thrives.

The penchant for Victorian clothing is an integral part of the Proper Boston woman's character and is apparently as immutable as anything else about that character. Some years ago the father of a girl who with his wife had been present at graduation-day festivities and a dance at St. Mark's School found his daughter in tears after the affair. "I wish Mother would look like a New York mother," the girl sobbed. The father resolved to speak to his wife on the subject. The mother, Boston diarist Edith Forbes Perkins, records the event for posterity. She did indeed buy a "fashionable bonnet" shortly after the affair to please her daughter, but she declares: "Never shall I forget that bonnet—it was a soft gray felt with cherry ribbons, *not a bit like me!*"

This attitude is typical. Whether she is or not, the Proper Boston woman is not loath to think of herself as fundamentally drab and she does not wish her appearance to interfere with her Puritan pleasure. While this modesty has its charm by way of contrast with the *haut monde* peacocks in some other cities it also has its dangers in producing a type of woman who is not only indifferent to, but in extreme instances actually looks down upon, femininity itself. The Proper Boston woman dresses, as a man dresses, for all day and she shops the way a man shops, as quickly and efficiently as possible. She speaks of "doing" stores the way, when travelling, she is likely to speak of "doing" cities. "We have done Rome, Florence, Pisa, and Leghorn," the indefatigable Susan Hale once wrote proudly home to her Boston friends, "all in five days." In the same spirit the Boston woman enters a store, knowing exactly what she wants and out to get just it and nothing else. It is a bold salesgirl who tries to make a sale to such a woman by telling her "everybody is wearing" this or that. To the Proper Boston woman what other people are wearing, particularly the young people, means less than nothing. One Boston sales-girl, significantly not at Stearns but at one of the specialty shops in the Ritz-Carlton district, recently recalled a First Family matron's remark on being shown the latest spring fashions. "Don't you dare sell me anything like that," the woman told her sharply. "I don't like butterfly clothes, and" —she added after a telling pause—"neither does my husband."

The day of days for the Proper Boston woman comes twenty-six times a year—every Friday all winter—at Symphony. Here she blossoms in all her glory, for Symphony—one never speaks of it as "the" Symphony but always just as "Symphony"—is not only Culture with a capital "C" but it is also Society with a capital "S." There is also Symphony every Saturday night, to which some First Family ladies do come, bringing their husbands with them, but the only concerts that really matter for First Family femininity are held on Friday. "Friday afternoons," former Proper Bostonian Lucius Beebe has written, "assume the aspect of holy days dedicated to the classics and a vast craning of necks to be certain that the Hallowells and the Forbeses are in their accustomed stalls." To be a true

Symphony patron one must be a "Friend" of the orchestra—in other words, a contributor to the orchestra's annual deficit as well as a regular attender at the concerts. For many years Major Henry Lee Higginson, who founded Symphony in 1881, made up this deficit himself, but he was finally persuaded to share the privilege with others of Boston's best. Ever since the Major gave in, Boston's First Families have thrown their Yankee caution to the winds, loosened their purse strings and vied for the soul-satisfying distinction of digging deep in the cause of Boston Culture. Once a year Symphony's program announces not only the complete list of Friends but also publishes an Honor Roll of all those who have attended the orchestra under each of its regular conductors, from Sir George Henschel in 1881 to the present Sergei Koussevitsky, who began conducting in 1924. Significantly there are over a hundred women, and only fifteen men, on this Roll.

Outsiders who visit Symphony for the first time rarely remember much about the music, however widely acclaimed Boston's orchestra has been, but they never forget the spectacle of the audience. The Proper Boston woman has a busy day on Friday. She has a Chilton Club lecture and a Chilton Club lunch but she is never late, and seldom early, for Symphony. For more than half a century, attired in her sensible coat, her sensible hat and her sensible shoes, she has entered the hall promptly at 2:25 and swept serenely to her seat in a manner that defies description. If she forgets her ticket it is no tragedy. A large proportion of patrons regularly do this, but they have been so resolutely marching toward the same seats for so many years that no usher, even in a packed hall, would dare attempt to stop them. "You must go," writes guide-book author Eleanor Early, "to see old Boston on parade." But there is no hurry—Symphony will wait for you:

> When I was a small child, a Symphony audience looked exactly as it does today . . . This phenomenon had been going on then for a long time, and it may last forever. I think that when this year's debs are another day's spinsters, they will save all their perfectly good clothes and they will wear them to Symphony on Fridays. They will arrive in the family's old car . . . And they will smile gently at the men who did not marry them. Although they may look bored, they will be quite happy. And their shabbiness will be in the traditional manner. For this is the Boston legend.*

* *And This Is Boston!,* by Eleanor Early (Boston: Houghton Mifflin) © 1938.

TOWN REPORT: 1942

MALCOLM COWLEY

———◆•◆———

Malcolm Cowley (1898–   ) born in Pennsylvania, is a poet, translator, and critic. In 1930 he became an editor of The New Republic *and from that journal the following account of the western Connecticut town where he lives is taken. It is interesting to see what was left when gas rationing and other restrictions of the last war brought life in a New England village back to something like self-reliance.*

THIS isn't a piece about Middletown or Anyburg or Sauk Center. The country towns here in New England all bear a family resemblance to one another, but they also have individual characters that can be learned only by living in them. They are more or less united as communities, more or less friendly to newcomers, more or less dominated by cliques that are more or less conservative and sometimes corrupt. But all of them are different from small towns in other parts of the country, and I suspect that all of them have been rapidly changing since the war, in fashions that are not always apparent to their own inhabitants.

I suspect, but I can't be certain. One effect of this war has been to broaden our political interests while narrowing our ˊsocial horizons. Friends who live within thirty miles of us used to be regarded as neighbors; now we can see them only by saving gasoline for weeks to have a little surplus. Our cousins in Pennsylvania might as well be living in Omaha, or the moon. And so, in setting down the wartime record of one little town, I wonder whether it is at all unusual or whether it is typical of the country as a whole.

Sheridan is a town only in the New England sense; in New York it would be an unincorporated village, in Pennsylvania a township and farther west nothing more than a school district. It consists of about twenty-five square miles of land shaped like a narrow slice of pie—a valley ten miles long with a lake in the south, farmland in the north and a range of wooded hills on either side. The back roads are full of abandoned farms like those described in Slater Brown's novel, "The Burning Wheel." North of the village, locally called the Center, there are twenty fairly prosperous dairy farms. Summer cottages are clustered along the shores of the lake and scattered through the hills. The winter population is about 450.

Small as it is, the town has its own probate judge and its own representative in the Connecticut General Assembly. As for local officials, it has so many of them that I have never been able to make an accurate count, although thirty-five are listed by name in the annual report, which doesn't bother to mention three or four constables. Most of these officials are elected for terms of one or two years, but a few are appointed, including the dog warden, who happens to be a Democrat. The first selectman, who acts as a mayor or burgess, more than earns his salary of $500 a year. With a few exceptions, the other officials either serve without pay or else receive fees for the work they actually perform. One of them makes a living by holding three town offices and driving the school bus.

Except for Republican politics, Sheridan has no native industries, and there are only three products of any importance: milk, scenery and good roads. About one-third of the inhabitants are supported by dairy farming and most of the others either work on the roads, which are maintained or subsidized by the state, or else they supply various goods and services to the summer people who come to enjoy the scenery. At least that is what they used to do before the war.

Sheridan today has twenty-nine men and two women in the armed forces—about seven percent of its people and substantially more than the average for the nation. About one-third of them enlisted voluntarily, including an aviation cadet and two army nurses, besides half a dozen men in the navy. I heard that one boy thought seriously of becoming a conscientious objector, but he changed his mind at the last moment, and it now seems that he has become an uncommonly good soldier. Most of the men neither try very hard to get into the army nor take any steps to keep out of it. There is a somewhat passive attitude, as if they said—and in fact I have heard more than one man saying—"When Uncle Sam wants me, he'll come and get me and I'll be ready to go."

Uncle Sam doesn't want the farmers, most of whom are now in their fifties, but they complain of not being able to find help, and this at a time when they are being asked to keep bigger herds. The summer people had to mow their own lawns or let them grow into hay. To keep a maid is a dream that most of the housewives have forgotten. Building has stopped completely, and many of the carpenters and plumbers are finding jobs in airplane factories; at any rate they are moving to Bridgeport and Hartford. Sheridan has only two war workers now living here, a grandfather more than seventy years old and one of his younger sons. They work twelve hours on the night shift at Bridgeport, besides driving fifty miles each way.

It is surprising how little talk one hears about the war. Maybe it's because I don't get around as much as I should, or don't catch everything that is said. I note, however, that the radio at the grocery store was turned on for the World's Series but not for news reports of the fighting in the Solomons. Ten years ago when farmers on the backroads talked about "the war," they meant the American Revolution, during which this countryside was infested with marauding Tories. The Civil War and the First World War left no such lasting impressions, for the fighting was far away —and New Guinea is even farther. What is near at hand is food and fuel rationing, high prices and the shortage of unrationed articles like prunes and alarm clocks and bacon. About all these matters there is grumbling, but rather less than I expected to hear. Sometimes a man will say, "Those people in Washington . . ." as if he blamed them for everything that was going wrong; but the same man will volunteer as an airplane spotter or a fire warden. Nobody thinks that we will lose the war, but there are signs of deep uncertainty about the future. People say, "It's no use making plans any more," and that is a bitter remark for New Englanders, who like to know what they will be doing in twenty years.

So far the most obvious change in Sheridan life has been produced by the rationing of gasoline and tires. Eight miles from a railroad station, the town had learned to live on rubber. There is a state highway two hundred yards from my house, and I used to hear the hum of tires as cars shot past at seventy miles an hour. Now the highway is empty half the morning, and then a car passes as slowly and silently as if it were driving behind a hearse. Nobody can take long trips. Hardly anybody thinks of driving to New Milford or Danbury—the nearest large towns—without inviting his neighbors to come too.

At first the church suffered from gasoline rationing, but I understand that with people learning to share rides, attendance is almost back to normal. Sunday school has been resumed, after being abandoned during the summer; the children are now taken there in the school bus. There is absolutely no sign, however, of the religious revival that is supposed to be felt in wartime. Activities that used to be connected with the church are now centered in the town hall.

Indeed, that little white Gothic chickencoop has become more important than any other building in Sheridan. It used to stand empty from week to week, being opened only for town meetings and an occasional square dance or chicken supper. The town clerk kept his books and papers at home. Now the hall is open every day, with the clerk at his desk, the selectmen or the assessors meeting and the rationing board receiving applications (which, incidentally, it handles with great fairness). In the evenings the hall is lighted for meetings connected with war or politics—for lectures on gas masks, fire protection or first aid; for Republican caucuses and rallies of the fire company. One feels that the community has been drawn together by the new tasks it is called upon to perform.

Some of its former activities have been discontinued; for example, there are not many purely social gatherings. Sheridan used to be known as the eatingest town in Connecticut. Two years ago its women compiled and published a Sheridan Cookbook, with local recipes that are widely followed—and they are good ones, too. It used to be that every event was celebrated and every organization was financed by a covered-dish luncheon, a clambake, a turkey dinner or a cake and jelly sale. But public meals are difficult to arrange in wartime, and many of the organizations that depended on them for support have become inactive.

Meanwhile the war has created new organizations—too many of them by far, and with functions that in some cases are vague or conflicting. The rationing board, however, has a definite job and is doing it well; it will end by exercising a tremendous power over civilian lives. The observation post has been in continuous operation since the day after Pearl Harbor. It has the services of 150 airplane spotters in summer and 90 in winter, each of them standing guard for three hours a week. A service committee has been forwarding letters and packages to the Sheridan boys in the armed forces.

The local defense council is charged with supervising a host of activities, those listed in its report as Air Raid Wardens, Agriculture, Auxiliary Police, Emergency Housing and Evacuation, Finance, Fire Wardens, Courses, Medical, Women's Division and Salvage—in other words, the whole complicated pattern created in Washington by the Office of Civilian Defense, on the model of what had been done in England. The trouble is that events here aren't following the English model. Serious air raids are becoming more unlikely and it is the countryside instead of the cities that is being evacuated. I should guess that the muddle in civilian defense cost the administration more votes than the loss of the Philippines.

And yet new organizations continue to proliferate. An hour ago I was interrupted by a visitor who urged my wife to become the coördinator of something or other; I didn't catch all of the high-sounding title. The actual work involved was organizing a course in forest-fire prevention to compete with courses already being given in first aid, home nursing and nutrition, not to mention others. In spite of having a coördinator, the new course would apparently not be coördinated with earlier activities, even those of the local fire wardens. The visitor, who was very nice and rather apologetic, had to carry out his instructions from Washington, where the course had been carefully and no doubt soundly planned, but without any notion of what is actually being done in towns like this.

A great deal is being done, and done willingly, in spite of all the confusion. Although some of the defense activities are being performed in a perfunctory fashion, as perhaps they deserve to be, others are taking root in local life. To mention one example, the naming of fire wardens led naturally to the organization of a local fire company, a step that had been hopefully discussed for several years. Until the war we had been forced to depend on the fire company from New Milford, which does excellent work in its own town, but which is so far from Sheridan that often a house burned down before it arrived—and even then it charged $50 for making the trip. After the chief fire warden suggested that we could do the work ourselves, the selectmen appropriated $1,500 to buy a secondhand fire truck, and the firemen collected money to buy hose. A firehouse is being built by volunteer labor, with materials furnished by the town. It is an achievement like those we used to admire in travelers' stories from Russia.

When the time came for the national scrap collection, it was the fire company that undertook to do the job. We gathered at nine o'clock one Sunday morning—twenty-five or thirty men and seven or eight trucks, each with a route assigned to it. The driver of the truck on which I rode was the Republican candidate for the General Assembly. I was running against him and we joked about it sometimes during the morning, when we weren't too busy carrying old iron, but nobody was much concerned about our political rivalry, considering that no Democrat has carried the town since Cleveland's second term. At almost every house a pile of scrap was waiting. People said, "I had three old cars, too, but I guess they were shipped to Japan." Or else, "The Japs got in ahead of you, Howard. You'll have to go out to the Solomon Islands if you want to find my tractor." For people here, the scrap iron sold to Japan has come to stand for all the errors in our foreign policy.

From one house we hauled away a weatherbeaten Ford that was rooted in weeds and looked like an enormous vegetable; from another we drove off in a caravan, with a hayrake hitched to the back of the truck and a buggy hitched to the hayrake. The big pile in a corner of the schoolyard had been growing all morning and afternoon; it was now about as large as a brownstone house lying on its side. Digging into it, one could reconstruct almost everything the town had ever been. There were saws and axes, ox chains, farming implements (some used for crops no longer grown in western Connecticut), dozens of heavy milk cans, old trucks and tires, kiddie cars, a box of tennis balls—in all, the record of a town that had passed from lumbering to herding to general farming, and then to a mixed economy of dairying and providing vacations for city people; that had traveled in a century and a quarter from pioneering to week-ending—and now was moving in what direction? If it had not been for the war, Sheridan might have become an outer suburb, with gentlemen's estates in the midst of desolate fields. So far, the war has preserved its farms and has carried Sheridan backward in time through the automobile age toward the period when it was an isolated community furnishing most of its own food and its own amusements. It is in most ways a better and friendlier town in wartime than it was in peace.

That Sunday we collected twenty-five tons of its relics, or about 110 pounds for each inhabitant. It was more than the state or the national average, but less than we might have collected if we had planned our work more carefully or continued it longer. And that might stand as a general comment on our effort in wartime: it is better than the average, and in spite of some confusion it is probably better organized, like the community itself, but it is not half the effort we are capable of making or will have to make before the end of the war. As for what is being done in towns bigger and smaller than Sheridan, I haven't heard and I would like to know.

WAKING IN THE BLUE

ROBERT LOWELL

———◆◆◆———

There used to be a macabre definition of what constituted a real Boston family: to possess two seats for the Friday Symphony, to subscribe to the Boston Transcript, *and to have at least one member in the McLean Asylum. It is of the latter institution that Robert Lowell (1917–   ) writes in the poem that follows. Lowell, a great-grandson of James Russell Lowell and possibly the most important American poet of today, demonstrates the curious vitality of a New England strain, despite all sneering and all jokes to the contrary. Lowell, Saltonstall, Cabot, Howe, Warren, Storey, Homans, Adams, Forbes—these and many other names, through their present-day representatives, are not only still going but going strong.*

The night attendant, a B.U. sophomore,
rouses from the mare's-nest of his drowsy head
propped on *The Meaning of Meaning.*
He catwalks down our corridor.
Azure day
makes my agonized blue window bleaker.
Crows maunder on the petrified fairway.
Absence! My heart grows tense
as though a harpoon were sparring for the kill.
(This is the house for the "mentally ill.")

What use is my sense of humor?
I grin at Stanley, now sunk in his sixties,

once a Harvard all-American fullback,
(if such were possible!)
still hoarding the build of a boy in his twenties,
as he soaks, a ramrod
with the muscle of a seal
in his long tub,
vaguely urinous from the Victorian plumbing.
A kingly granite profile in a crimson golf-cap,
worn all day, all night,
he thinks only of his figure,
of slimming on sherbet and ginger ale—
more cut off from words than a seal.

This is the way day breaks in Bowditch Hall at McLean's;
the hooded night lights bring out "Bobbie,"
Porcellian '29,
a replica of Louis XVI
without the wig—
redolent and roly-poly as a sperm whale,
as he swashbuckles about in his birthday suit
and horses at chairs.

These victorious figures of bravado ossified young.

In between the limits of day,
hours and hours go by under the crew haircuts
and slightly too little nonsensical bachelor twinkle
of the Roman Catholic attendants.
(There are no Mayflower
screwballs in the Catholic Church.)

After a hearty New England breakfast,
I weigh two hundred pounds
this morning. Cock of the walk,
I strut in my turtle-necked French sailor's jersey
before the metal shaving mirrors,
and see the shaky future grow familiar
in the pinched, indigenous faces
of these thoroughbred mental cases,
twice my age and half my weight.
We are all old-timers,
each of us holds a locked razor.

NEW ENGLAND INDUSTRY

JOHN F. KENNEDY

———◆•◆———

After emotional and intellectual assessments of New England's twentieth-century position, it is refreshing to read the following matter-of-fact assessment of New England's industrial plight in 1953, written by that master of the refreshing view and phrase John F. Kennedy, then Senator from Massachusetts, later President of the United States. It appeared as an article in the New York Times Magazine *in the fall of that year.*

"NEW ENGLAND," wrote Bernard DeVoto nearly twenty years ago, "is a finished place . . . it is the first American section to be finished, to achieve stability in the conditions of its life. It is the first old civilization and the first permanent civilization in America."

Obviously this comment suffers somewhat from exaggeration, but it does point up the fact that there are areas in the nations that have become comparatively old economically—and as such, despite their prestige, raise special problems. These areas are not limited to the six northeastern states, nor even to the Middle Atlantic area. Cincinnati and St. Louis—once the booming river towns of the Middle West—the coal fields of Pennsylvania and West Virginia, industrial cities in the Mohawk Valley, heads of navigation on rivers such as Cumberland on the Potomac in Maryland, are samples of this same economic phenomenon.

But the impact of economic maturity and economic stability in industrial development without a corresponding stability in employment is to be found primarily in an area such as New England, where industrialization has been more pronounced and more continuous. The results are that machinery is old, methods are perforce old, and too frequently management is old. Community after community has relied for years upon one or two industries, and a decline in the world market for the products of these industries may take place. Some fast-growing industries have settled elsewhere, leaving areas of serious unemployment and of economic stagnation in our generally prosperous country.

This is not to say that New England as a whole is economically depressed. In terms of per capita income and standard of living, and the absolute growth of our industries and manufacturing employment, the region is neither depressed nor undeveloped. New England remains highly industrialized and productive, vital to the rest of the nation and the world as a market for raw materials and as a source of manufactured products. The average New England worker, particularly since the rise in defense-inspired prosperity, enjoys an hourly income and standard of living not equaled in many parts of the country.

However, region-wide statistics on high employment do not reveal the acute unemployment of individual communities. Defense prosperity conceals long-range declines in particular industries. Contracts in the aircraft and electrical machinery industries and inflated Government payrolls cover up the static position of the private civilian economy of the region. In 1953 the immediate outlook has been much improved; but soft spots remain in the economy, defense plants are completing orders and laying off workers, and large-scale unemployment, although at least temporarily lessened, continues to be a reality in several communities.

These problems are not new. They have plagued New England since the close of World War II and, to a lesser extent, since World War I. From 1919 to 1950 the nation gained 46 per cent in manufacturing jobs while New England lost 6 per cent; much of this was prior to 1939. The region's economic growth, industrialization, population, per capita income, manufacturng employment and share in particular industries have not kept pace with the rest of the country.

The problems of the textile industry, employing some 250,000 workers in New England, are not primarily regional problems, but their effect is felt heavily in New England because of the concentration of that industry in the region. Between 1929 and 1950 New England textiles lost 149,000 jobs, many of them to other areas of the country in a pattern of industrial migration and dislocation which has become particularly acute in the past few years. Since 1946, in Massachusetts alone, seventy textile mills have been liquidated, generally for migration or disposition of their assets to plants in other sections of the country.

A second New England industry facing a rapid decline in recent years is America's oldest—the New England fishing industry. Increased imports, increased difficulty in securing favored species of fish and a lag in market development and research have all hit the famous fishing villages of New England. The Boston fleet is now but half as great in number as in 1939.

New England's once predominant leather and shoe industry lost 44,000 jobs between 1929 and 1950. Industrial migrations have taken place among electrical goods and apparel concerns. Business men and workers in various lines all over New England have expressed to me their concern over what the future holds for them.

How acute these problems can become community-wide can be seen only by looking at the individual cities and towns. Take, for instance, Lawrence, Mass., not because it is typical (for the distress there is far greater than anywhere else in the country) but because it dramatically illustrates the impact of these forces on one community. Lawrence is a world-famous textile center. The long-range decline of the textile industry and the migration of mills out of Lawrence to other areas have brought in their wake mass unemployment, wasted productive capacity and drains upon public funds.

Post-war liquidations and migrations caused approximately one-fifth of all Lawrence workers to be without jobs continually from 1947 to early 1953—this during the greatest prosperity in American history. Indeed, the heavy mobilization year of 1951 actually brought an increase of unemployment. Nearly 5,000,000 square feet of industrial plant stood idle. Over $11 million annually had been paid out in unemployment insurance benefits; and over 50 per cent of the unemployed workers exhausted their benefits and faced debt and public relief. This year has seen some improvement, but Lawrence remains the nation's number one labor surplus area.

What is true of Lawrence is only to a lesser degree true of New Bedford and Fall River, Nashua and Pawtucket, Saco in Maine and Danielson in Connecticut.

Basically, the problems of the New England economy stem from its status as America's "first old civilization." Without more new industries to replace the old—new job skills, new investments and techniques—this situation will not revise itself but continue to be a drag on our entire economy. The obvious remedy for these conditions is either the attraction of new industries or the reshaping of those economic factors that will make for the retention of the old. But the shaping of that remedy must have regard to competition that New England faces from other sections of this country.

Cheaper power costs, cheaper labor, tax advantages and incentives, more efficient transportation arrangements and other inducements offered by these areas are factors which no manufacturer considering a move into or out of New England can overlook.

Clearly New England cannot oppose the industrial development of any other section of the country, nor can it shrink from competition with other areas. But we believe that competition should be fair. We cannot approve the abandonment of plants and thousands of workers for what we consider to be the exploitation of unfair methods of competition.

Fair competition cannot be obtained when our Federal social legislation permits exploitation of labor through inadequate labor standards. Whether such workers are nonunion, in sweatshops, children, learners, Negroes or Puerto Ricans, or whether they are denied adequate wages, pensions, or unemployment benefits, the effect is to damage the well-being of not only those workers but employers, employes, and the public in other areas.

Nor can fair competition be obtained when transportation rates discriminate against New England. For example, a quantity less than a truck load of cotton and rayon may be shipped from Greensboro, N. C., to Detroit, at a rate one-third cheaper than from Lowell, Mass., to Detroit, approximately the same distance. With the recent exception of grain, inland cities sending materials to the ports of Philadelphia, New York and Baltimore by rail have rates more favorable than those shipping to Boston. At the same time, Boston, nearly 2,000 miles closer to Bordeaux than New Orleans and 500 miles closer to Buenos Aires than New Orleans, is forbidden the competitive advantage of ocean shipping rates that such a geographical position should afford.

Nor is it fair competition for the Federal Government to award a disproportionate amount of defense contracts and tax amortization benefits to plants migrating to other parts of the country, despite the existence of over-capacity in the industries themselves. Not one of the eight Southeastern states had as small a share of Federal construction contracts, facilities and projects as Massachusetts (1 per cent), which led all New England states. Despite New England's substantial contribution to the defense effort, its percentage of tax amortization certificates is about one-fourth of its share in terms of defense contracts, value added by manufacturer and manufacturing potential.

When municipal bonds, free from Federal taxes, are used to build tax-free or low-rent plants to induce industries to move to a new community; when the Federal program of unemployment compensation is administered by the several states with standards so greatly at variance with each other as to distribute areawise unequally the cost of such programs; and when Federal laws freeze the unionization of employes by making more difficult the organization of workers in more recently industrialized areas, then it is clear that the competition between areas and between sections of this country has ceased to be fair and unduly favors one against the other.

A letter from a Southern community recently offered a leading Massachusetts textile manufacturer a tax-free modern factory financed by tax-exempt municipal bonds, inexpensive Tennessee Valley Authority power and cheap nonunion labor. The firm could utilize a Federal tax amortization certificate for its machinery and subminimum learner rates for its initial work crew, while taking advantage of lower unemployment compensation taxes and cheaper transportation rates.

In advocating that the Federal Government turn its attention to the elimination of these methods of unfair competition, I am not asking for the intervention of that Government in new fields. Nor am I asking for any system of regional preference or sectional discrimination. Indeed, these "islands of surplus labor" are not confined to New England nor are the effects of unfair competition limited to that area.

Although these problems may be of more concern now to the older communities in the Middle Atlantic and East North Central states, they involve problems national in scope and character. They demonstrate that the Federal Government still has an important role in developing and conserving the resources of a region and that fair competition in the long run is important to the Southwest and Southeast as well as New England.

This view is not shared by all segments of New England public opinion. There are those who refuse to recognize or discuss its problems and deplore my frankness in calling the nation's attention to them, believing somehow that a spiritual regeneration of New England is all that is necessary to revivify its essential might. There are other confirmed pessimists who believe that the period of decline has set in and believe it is hopeless to attempt to stem it.

And finally there are those who would reject outside assistance on the ground that they fear its "paternalistic" import. Their solution is to deprive other areas of the benefits obtained from the various forms of Federal assistance and so bring them down to a level where they can look only to local initiative for the development of their human and natural resources.

These views seem to be totally unrealistic in modern society. I believe that we must speak frankly about the problems that confront us and I believe that the Federal Government has a role to play in the alleviation of those problems in its position as catalyst and conservator of the resources of the entire nation.

In May of this year, I presented to the Senate an analysis of these problems and a 40-point program for Congressional action. The steps which I suggested fell into the following categories.

First, I stressed the Government's role in making possible the diversification and expansion of commercial and industrial activity. Tax amortization incentives to replace outmoded industrial plant, Government loans and technical assistance to small business and aids to state and local industrial development corporations would be important steps toward the rebuilding of the distressed one-industry towns.

An adequate job-retraining program could provide the skills necessary to fill the thousands of job opportunities in new industries now unavailable to the unemployed in their own communities. Through the fullest utilization of our natural resources, New England—which has not a single one of the 156 Federal hydroelectric projects in the country—could develop an adequate supply of low-cost power, an important element in industrial development.

Second, the Government's role as an arbiter of fair competition must be strengthened to prevent further industrial dislocation. The present outmoded minimum wage of 75 cents an hour must be increased, the Walsh-Healey and other fair labor standards must be strengthened; certain sections of the Taft-Hartley Law which have tended to freeze unionization in older industrial areas must be revised; and more adequate nation-wide non-discriminatory standards for our unemployment compensation and other social security programs must be adopted. Competitive abuses of tax loopholes used as inducements for migration or liquidation of industry, such as plants financed by tax-free municipal bonds or sold to tax-free foundations, must be corrected.

Federal business incentives, including defense contracts and tax amortization certificates, must be equitably distributed in recognition of these problems. Discrimination in transportation rates, excessive speculation in raw materals, and inadequate use of available Federal research funds for the fishing industry, for example, must be prevented.

Third, as we strengthen the economy with these measures, we must not forget those who may still become victims of economic misfortune. Our unemployment compensation program must be strengthened. Our social security and other measures for our elder and less fortunate citizens must be improved to provide real security.

Here is a program born out of the necessities, as I have learned to know them, of the state and the region that I represent. It is in no way a substitute for incentive and hard work. It offers nothing in the way of subsidy. It calls for no undue regional advantage. It provides instead a basic framework within which our regional economies can take full advantage of their own resources, their own initiative and their own enterprise and can free themselves from the burdens that unfair competition these days presses down upon them.

HOMAGE TO NEW ENGLAND

DAVID MCCORD

I would like to round out this volume with a tribute to New England paid her by the poet David McCord (1897–   ), which follows. It was delivered as a speech at the 1960 opening of Old Sturbridge Village in Massachusetts, a colonial restoration. Although he was born in Pennsylvania, McCord has spent most of his adult life in New England, working for his alma mater, Harvard.

And for the things I see
I trust the things to be.
Whittier

NOTHING in my life since childhood has ever outweighed the land unless it be the sky. "The sky is the daily bread of the eyes," said Emerson, and I may suppose that I have been close to my mother's Emersonian father all my days simply by looking at the sky which, in its endless dissolving and affirmation of cloudlike form, gives meaning to another Concord line: "People forget that it is the eye which makes the horizon." . . .

I have long been persuaded that anyone insensitive to the values of land and sky is unprepared to experience the total harmony of a village, a town, or a city. Henry James quite beautifully could describe the interior of the Boston Public Library, for I think he was happier inside a building than out of it. George Santayana is to me another such. Santayana could speak of Hollis and Stoughton Halls at Harvard, in their Euclidean simplicity, as "the architecture of sturdy poverty, looking through thrift in the direction of wealth. It [the architecture] well matched the learning of early New England," he said, "traditionally staunch and narrow, yet also thrifty and tending to positivism; a learning destined as it widened to be undermined and to become, like the architecture, flimsy and rich." Somehow it was Oxford in the *Soliloquies,* was it not, that suited Santayana? I cannot imagine him exalted among the potatoes in Aroostook County down in Maine. But clearly do I see him here in Cambridge reading by his fire which, he says with universal truth, "made poetry of indoor life."

I cite these two internationalists because, though they valued New England, they stand at such variance with the native New Englander as I know him. Of course the New Englander himself does not show you his country; if he did, he would not be a New Englander. He never boasts about its size, quality, resources, achievement, history, scenery, architecture; about its learning or its weather. The native remains a native, whether he springs from New Haven or Hartford, from Boston or Providence, Salem or Portland, or from Chatham, Williamstown, Unity, Orford, or Windsor. Although it takes all of New England plus New York, Pennsylvania, New Jersey, and possibly a slice of Ohio to equal the area of our now diminished Texas, New England is another country first, and six states only when the newcomer cares to press for details. New England is the authorized version of America: her land and people chapter and verse for more than 300 years.

In acknowledging a nearly lifelong debt to this morainic, comely, indivisible region and its people, I cannot assert, as M. Sainte-Beuve wrote to Matthew Arnold in the last years of his life: "Vous avez traversé notre vie et notre littérature par une ligne intérieure, profonde, qui fait les initiés, et que vous ne perdrez jamais." "You have passed through our life and literature by a deep inner line, which confers initiation, and which you will never lose." That I have passed through New England life, and to some extent New England literature, art, and architecture, I persuade myself is true. I only wish that I had done it by "a deep inner line." But

I have done it by making an infinite series of pilgrimages, by the "daily straight and yearly oblique path" as North Andover's Anne Bradstreet said in speaking of an astronomical matter.

My first excursions beyond Cambridge were endless walks in Boston or out into Lexington and the sand plain of Concord. After that it progressed to train journeys north and west and boat excursions down the coast. George Blake, the Glasgow novelist, once told me that he hoped to traverse every road in Scotland before he died. I have had no such ambition, but the web which I have spun across the face of my adopted country by now seems adequately complicated. I have reached the point where, from year to year, I feel the sudden urge to retrace and revisit as well as to explore; but just as Havelock Ellis declared that he never wished to finish reading Herodotus and so come to the end of that delightful journey, I have kept certain sections of New England willfully unexplored. I am weakest in Connecticut and Rhode Island, strongest in Massachusetts, New Hampshire, and Vermont, and reasonably familiar with the State of Maine.

Outside of New England I have always felt that I was walking or traveling over endless mountains, across an endless plain, and that the states themselves were in no sense boundaries or walls. "Others will see the islands large and small," as Whitman says; but before I came to live in New England, nothing in America geographically seemed enisled. Not so today: I see and feel an outer wall enclosing my six New England states; I look across the water of Lake Champlain at Burlington, across and into the Adirondacks, into the deeps and varied levels of the tumid sunset clouds, and the flashing swords of evening light that play among them and seem not at all to realize that I am looking into the state where I was born. I am the landsman gazing across one boundary of my country as I once stood at Kyle of Loch Alsh for the first time and perceived the ancestral misty Isle of Skye but with only a wild and atavistic sense of looking home. But the lines of demarcation for me between Maine and New Hampshire, New Hampshire and Vermont, Massachusetts and Rhode Island, Massachusetts and Connecticut, and so on, are as real at point after point as if there were a witness tree to sustain my intuition. Were I a true New Englander, I should also feel a boundary sense of counties. I do feel in the instance of Essex County in Massachusetts, in Aroostook County in Maine, in Coös County in New Hampshire, in Windsor County in Vermont, but that is all.

I see New England for the most part in relief as on a map. I see her from the tops of certain mountains which I shall never climb again. I see her in all the lights and weathers I have known in the vicinity of Katahdin, the Presidentials, the Sandwich Range, up the Green Mountains from Pico to the Camel's Hump and Mount Mansfield, down the Berkshires from Mount Greylock south; but most especially I see her in the contours of Chocorua, Monadnock, Wachusett, and the Warner slope of Kearsarge.

After the mountains, the rivers: the Connecticut first because it is the Mississippi, the St. Lawrence, and the Columbia of New England, all in one. To a fly fisherman, Melville's salty notion that "meditation and water are wedded for ever" explains the fascination of a river road. The oxbows of such streams as the Charles, the Pemigewasett, and the upper Connecticut are apt to keep the traveler and his waterway at a respectful distance. But along such rivers as the Merrimac, the Connecticut, the Housatonic, the Deerfield, the Ottauquechee, the Kennebec, Penobscot, Androscoggin, Saco, Winooski, and the Amonoosuc, run my endless ribbons of delight. The wilder rivers, such as the Allegash, Kennebago Stream, the west branch of the Penobscot and the upper Kennebec, the Denys and Machias and all such riblike drainage of the State of Maine, are dear and distant with my fly rod all at once. So are the bass and bittern tidal inlets from Rhode Island to Kennebunkport; and such as the St. Croix at Calais where the late Professor Copeland found a certain strangeness mixed with beauty. And after the rivers, of course, the valleys leading one to another through notches in New Hampshire, gulfs and gaps in Vermont, or cradled safely in a nest of mountains under the name of Intervale.

New England, I sometimes think, is my walled-in house and garden. I am not sure of all the rooms in the house save that Massachusetts is most certainly my library, Maine my bedroom opening on the sea, Boston my Bulfinch dining room, Connecticut and Rhode Island my guest rooms, New Hampshire my front porch, and Vermont my ample garden. My bouldered walls are the Atlantic, the Empire State, Quebec, New Brunswick. From almost any vantage point, at almost any window, I can look at once upon the summer dunes and beaches southward from the Cape, hear the foundry hammers in the surf below the northern rocks, stare level as the sun's ray into the green wilderness of New Brunswick across the noble St. John, or north and down upon the peneplain of the St. Lawrence, or west and over beyond the Catskills and the Adirondacks to the vast reach of Parkman's America whence the wagons, the canal barge, glistening irons, and the vapor trails each in their turn and after him have borne away what New England of herself could spare.

Sometimes when I am weary with the congestion and fever of Boston, I return for a day or so to Manhattan where I was born; but after that brief moment, viewing in the words of Phyllis McGinley,

> Viewing with idolatry more then lenience
> The City of Infinite Inconvenience,

I return to the Back Bay wondering why I ever left that sleepy village where the hoods of cars are the shells of snails and where the pace is

regular, unimpeded, and reflective. If Boston and New England towns
and cities are not precisely in the image of my exaggeration, at least they
know how to preserve their commons, greens, and inner sanctuaries. Take
New Haven and take Yale:

> The gnathic index as a useful measure
> Of cranial bones suggests the word we need:
> The Gothic index to New Haven treasure
> Reveals the flower of mediaeval seed.

Trinity in Hartford, Brown in Providence, a yard of colleges, universities,
and institutions in Boston and Cambridge, the University of Vermont in
Burlington, Bates in Lewiston: they are each and all as snug as Oxford in
her now shrill, clamorous valley. And there is the converse in New England; the peaceful towns and little cities which are the rational suburbs of
learning: Hanover, Amherst, Brunswick, Williamstown, Middletown, Or-
ono, Andover, Exeter, Deerfield, Wallingford, Lakeville, and others. It
seems to me I owe them all some special debt for their existence, their
Thoreauvian independence, their legal federation in the mind's democracy. I think especially of those landmarks set apart on hills or otherwise
withdrawn: the stony strength of Middlebury above the quiet town, the
pinnacle of Tufts above the Medford sprawl, the new brick symmetry of
Colby looking far across the idle Kennebec into the farms and lodgepole
wilderness of Maine. I think of Groton, St. George's, and the Kent School
shapely within a landscape to themselves. For these are all clear syllables
in the essential text of this passage out of John Jay Chapman:

> New York is not a civilization; it is a railway station. . . . The present
> in New York is so powerful that the past is lost. There is no past. Not
> a bookshelf, nor a cornice, nor a sign, nor a face, nor a type of mind
> endures for a generation, and a New York boy who goes away to
> boarding school returns to a new world at each vacation. . . .

> Now in Massachusets there has been a consecutive development of
> thought since colonial times. Her links with the past have never been
> broken. The influx of new blood and new idea has not overwhelmed
> the old blood and old idea. There is in New England a traceable con-
> nection between the whole historic volume and stream of human
> culture—that moving treasury of human thought and experience
> which flows down out of antiquity and involves us, surrounds and
> supports us and makes us the thing we are, no matter how we may
> struggle or how little we may understand. In Massachusetts you may
> still stop the first man you meet in the street and find in his first re-
> mark the influence of Wyclif or Samuel Adams. The spiritual life in
> New England has never been luxuriant. It is one-sided, sad, and in-
> expressive in many ways. But it has coherence, and this is what makes

it valuable for the young American. . . . You cannot go to Harvard or indeed to any New England College without getting into some sort of contact with a logical civilization.

If I speak in such terms of one aspect of New England education, I do so in no Utopian sense. "The more we live by our intellect, the less we understand the meaning of life," warns William James. It is the concentration of so many institutions in so small an area that is to me significant. Chapman does not speak—but I do—of the old line academies, high schools, parochial schools, schools with historic names such as the Boston, Cambridge, and Roxbury Latin, the multiplicity of trade schools, and the whole dominion of the small New England schoolhouse. But the important words to remember in the Chapman passage are the pandemic words about "contact with a logical civilization."

Among my other New England debts is the museum debt—not only the network of fine art centers from Hartford to Rockland, from Providence to Williamstown, but the incredible number and variety of museums for the specialist: whaling in New Bedford, the South Seas in Salem, ships in Mystic, artifacts in Deerfield, carriages and coaches at Newport, Americana in Peterborough; Fruitlands, immaculate above the Nashua valley, for the visible evidence of Bronson Alcott's transcendental survival; and above all the great and detailed reconstructions of the past here in Sturbridge Village, down in Plymouth, and up in Shelburne, Vermont. Just as Boston is unique in the marriage of a historic Common and a Public Garden, so is much of New England prodigal in public reservations, parks, bird and wildlife sanctuaries, and in private forests like Harvard's in Petersham, and the Dartmouth Grant. It made the month of this September for me to see on Plum Island three American egrets, snow-white against the dunes behind which they were wading. As to that, most islands on the New England coast are sanctuaries to some, and often to considerable, extent. If Martha's Vineyard failed to prevent the meeting between the heath hen and extinction, it has admirably preserved simplicity and self-esteem. My personal acknowledgment to islands includes the private privacy of Naushon, the public privacy of Nantucket, the theological privacy of the Isles of Shoals, and the social privacy of Mount Desert.

Lakes, of course, are the counterparts of islands, and to me the difference between the four great lakes of New England—Champlain, Moosehead, Winnipesaukee, and Sebago—is almost as marked as the difference between the Frog Pond in Boston Common, where Francis Parkman in his youth caught horned pout, and Thoreau's Walden, in which he lost his axe. Nor would I for one moment overlook the man-made wonder of the vast Quabbin Reservoir—New England's southern lake, and in its concept and protective planting one of the truly decent, dignified, and sensible projects that any state has ever engineered.

I am naturally shocked, as all of us must be, by the hideous ribbon-development—in the English phrase—which exists along such highways as Route 1, to name no other; but some of the proud industrial cities of New England—Lawrence, Lowell, Manchester, Holyoke, Fall River, for example—exert upon me a curious antique charm, not for what their sweatshops stood for, but for the bastion quality of architecture above their rivers and canals, and the ingenuity in many instances with which the mills have been revived, unspoiled in silhouette, to modern use.

Disgusted as we are by the long history of pollution of our rivers, I am cheered by the fact that the salmon are returning to some of the familiar streams in Maine, and by the mild assurance that one day (as I heard in a night broadcast last week while driving from Augusta to Portland) the pulp mills may appear in their stunning jackstraw outline as but harmless evidence of a time when the birling logger, his peavy, and the black bateau were part of the wild spring life in northern waters.

Into my mind from time to time flash images as clear as leaf venation in the fall: the purple base and cool grey cloudy top of Mt. Katahdin when the sun peered under his carnival tent; quake grass at its only-known New Hampshire station—by the doorsill of the house of Arthur Stanley Pease near Randolph; the strangely different cry of druid loons in moonlight on the Third Connecticut Lake; the rapturous play of fireflies one May evening up near Wolfeboro; the voice of Palfrey Perkins in or out of the pulpit; the always suddenness of Lake Willoughby from the south; white steeples, weathered barns, and salt box houses for the poetry and metaphysics of proportion; red newts on brown leaves after rain; elm seed blowing down a city street; ventriloquy of all white-throated sparrows above timber line; the four-chutney menu in the lost Cheshire House in Keene; the Dirigo window in the railway station at Augusta; the first week in October in New England anywhere; catching a frog with nothing but a long-stemmed black-eyed Susan from which the petals have been removed; one solitary monumental oak somewhere near North Hero; the Harvard Yard in spring mist when the lights come on; one cecropia moth at midnight in the rain on Mount Greylock; dawn and the sea gulls over Boston; dusk and the smoke bush out by country doorways; the hand of Samuel McIntire in Salem; cedar waxwings along the Kennebago's boneyard; maple redness of the spring; the western Promenade in Portland; New England's signature—an old white pine against her hardwood hills.

Spring on the Cape and the running of the alewives. They come in the lap of the tide, over a spit of sand perhaps, up into a curving creek; they come in the stem and froth of waters, under the shadowing wings of hundreds of gulls. They come by the whispering thousands, over the lip of falls and the water step of ladder, the vast quaking wake of them filling

a small stream (as I have seen it) from bank to bank: tails, dorsals showing above the eddies, a living current of silver, blue, and gun-metal gray.

> Boston: I like the way the old red face of her peers through the
> blue mist in the morning and dissolves into the dark when the sun
> drains out of the solvent streets. I like the slant of light at midday
> on the thousand chimney pots on the one hand and the smoky gran-
> ite on the other. I like the white plumes of steam that issue swirling
> from her downtown roof tops on a cold and blowing November
> afternoon. I like the gentle look of rain on her doorstep. I like the
> deep laryngal sound of harbor whistles floating in on the cold damp
> easterly, just ahead of enveloping fog. I like the fellowship of church
> bells on a Sunday morning and the spell of chimes and carillon hymn
> tunes drifting north across the Back Bay. I like the inexhaustible
> freshness of an October day and the strongest March winds that ever
> blew in any city east of Michigan. I like the flight of lavender win-
> dowpanes on Beacon Street and the two or three on Commonwealth,
> and the sudden glimpse of red and blue and yellow in the inner gar-
> dens back of unexpected windows. I like the occasional iron handrails
> to help the old and young down slippery streets on slippery days. I
> like the narrowness of streets that should be wide and the wideness
> of streets that might be narrow. I like the old-fashioned faded let-
> tering on the signs of shops and warehouses leaning toward the
> harbor. I like the market set off by Greek New England buildings,
> and general bedlam, and open carts so openly arrived at, blending
> the exuberance of fish with the indestructibility of garlic. I like the
> many steps on Blackstone Street leading down by night to lighted
> markets underground. I like the multiple names of stores that read
> like the multiple names of distinguished law firms. I like the patch-
> work of old and honest iron and brass surviving into a century that
> greatly prefers a chromium front and the cheap streamline of fake
> obsidian.

But, I sometimes ask myself: Have I seen these things? Have I experienced them? "Is it a true thing?" as Touchstone says; or is it all a borrow-
ing, an enlargement, an aberration, a distillation of what I have read and
forgotten, of what I have read and re-remembered, of what I have read
and discarded of my New England authors? I have always been fearful
of the books, as any writer has to be—fearful that they would obtrude
and leave me an outsider to myself. "Earth's the right place for love; I
don't know where it's likely to go better," says Robert Frost in *Birches*.
Of course he was saying it in New England. I'd say for once he was saying
it *for* New England. Well, this is the right brief place for books—and what
should I do without them? I need not name them if I name their authors:
Melville, Emerson, Thoreau, Whittier, Sarah Orne Jewett, Frost and Rob-

inson, Emily Dickinson, Henry Beston, E. B. White, Edmund Ware Smith, Annie Trumbull Slosson, Samuel Eliot Morison, Elizabeth Coatsworth, Van Wyck Brooks, and Arthur Stanley Pease.

"Do no dishonor to the earth lest you dishonor the spirit of man," says Henry Beston. "Hold your hands out over the earth as over a flame." I know not where the flame of earth burns brighter than here in New England. I wish I could be aphoristic about it. What would I say? And would I need to name the states?

Acknowledgments

Any anthology represents the concerted efforts of a number of specially informed and equipped people who have helped its editor in producing his end result. It seems to me that I am more than ordinarily in debt to those who have so generously assisted me in the present anthology. Most of all I am grateful to my brilliant research assistant, Ruthe Smith, who worked in close collaboration with me on the selection of texts, and to Anne Freudenberg of the Manuscripts Division of the Alderman Library of the University of Virginia, who found the very pictures I wanted.

The entire English Department of the University of Virginia has my gratitude for its kind interest in and suggestions for this volume. In particular I want to thank the distinguished scholars of American literature, Professor Floyd Stovall and Professor James B. Colvert. Also Professor Martin Battestin and Mr. Donald Mull, Professor Robert Ganz, Professor Lester Beaurline, Dean Irby Cauthen, and Professor Fredson Bowers, my husband.

Equally, the Alderman Library has given generous help, and I thank the Library collectively, and in particular Mr. John Cook Wyllie, its Librarian, and Mr. William Runge, Curator of Rare Books, and his staff in the McGregor and Barrett Collections. I would like also to express my gratitude to Mr. Clifton Waller Barrett, donor of the Barrett Collection of American literature to the Alderman Library.

My thanks are also due to many who have made valuable suggestions and given bibliographical assistance, particularly Mr. Nolan E. Smith. Also Professor Bernard Mayo and Professor Thomas Cary Johnson, of the History Department of the University of Virginia, and Mr. Stephen T. Riley, Director of the Massachusetts Historical Society, who also helped in the collection of pictures.

I must also acknowledge special assistance given me by Marjorie Wynne, Librarian at the Rare Book Room of the Yale University Library; William Maxwell of *The New Yorker*; Professor Kenneth Murdock of Harvard; Mr. Bertram K. Little, Director of the Society for the Preservation of New England Antiquities; Mr. Abbott L. Cummings, Assistant Director of that institution; and Mr. Walter Muir Whitehill, Director of the Boston Athenaeum. I want also to thank Mr. William Raney, and Miss

Clementine Paddleford of the New York *Herald-Tribune*. Great help was given me by the General Reference Department of the Boston Public Library.

When it came to finding and selecting the pictures for this volume, special assistance was rendered me by Mr. and Mrs. Paul B. Victorius and Mr. Richard M. Bigelow of Charlottesville, Virginia, and by Mr. Zachary Taylor of the Camera Center in Charlottesville; Mrs. W. A. Hartman of the Metropolitan Museum of Art's Photographic Sales Department; Mrs. Marcia E. Moss, Reference Librarian, Concord Free Public Library; The Essex Institute; Mr. George M. Cushing; Mr. Harold S. Sniffen, Assistant Director, The Mariners Museum, Newport News, Virginia; Miss Helen Chillman, Assistant to the Art Librarian, Yale University Art Library; Mr. Allan Ludwig; and the distinguished American painters Leon Kroll and Gardner Cox.

Also Mr. Bartlett H. Hayes, Director, Addison Gallery of American Art; Miss Virginia Gunter, Museum of Fine Arts, Boston; Miss Helen H. Sevagian, Chief of Information Office, Boston Public Library; Mr. Philip C. Beam, Director, Bowdoin College Museum of Art; Mrs. Mary W. Ranby, Brown University Library; Miss Charlotte Johnson, Assistant Librarian, Concord Free Public Library; Mr. Bruce McKain, Director, Provincetown Art Association; Mrs. Otis C. Nash, Executive Secretary, Star Island; the Reverend Lyman Rutledge; Mr. Harold Hugo, Manager, Meriden Gravure Co.; Mr. Robert C. Sale, State Librarian, Connecticut State Library; Mr. George O'Connell, Director, Dartmouth College News Service; Mrs. Jean Jackson, Secretary, Fogg Art Museum; Mrs. Henry W. Howell, Jr., Librarian, Frick Art Reference Library; Miss Charlotte D. Conover, Librarian, Sawyer Free Library, Gloucester, Massachusetts; Miss Elizabeth Droppers, Reference Librarian, Harvard College Library; Miss Elizabeth B. McIntire, Director, House of Seven Gables Settlement Association; Miss Sally Carroll, Permissions Department, Little, Brown & Co.; Mr. Odell Shepard; Miss Marian Rowe, Librarian, Maine Historical Society; Mrs. James Shokoff, Photograph Sales Department, Metropolitan Museum of Art; Miss Marian de Grasse, Secretary to the Director, Montclair Art Museum; Mr. J. T. Rankin, First Assistant, Art and Architecture Division, The New York Public Library; Mr. M. V. Brewington, Assistant Director, The Peabody Museum; Mrs. Leonoard J. Panaggio, Public Relations Director, The Preservation Society of Newport County; Mr. Harold I. Lessem, Superintendent, Salem Maritime National Historic Site; Senator Leverett Saltonstall; Mr. Thomas E. Andres, Archivist, The Society for the Preservation of New England Antiquities; Mr. Thomas G. Brown, Jr., Vice President, State Street Bank and Trust Co., Boston; Miss Elva B. McCormick, The Wadsworth Atheneum; Mr. Ralph R. Renzi, News Director, Williams College; Mr. Julain B. Doggett, Wiscasset Public Library; Mr. Curtis P. Fields, President, The Woodstock, Vermont, Historical Society, Inc.; Mr. Frank H. Teagle, Jr., The Elm Tree Press; and Miss Louisa Dresser, Curator, Worcester Art Museum.

I want, too, to thank members of my family—my mother, Lilian Westcott Hale, my son, William Wertenbaker, and my aunt, Mrs. E. G. Littell—for reminding me of stories and bits of lore about New England that I might otherwise have forgotten.

In addition, I want, in lieu of furnishing a bibliography, to acknowledge the help given me by those books I used most in compiling this anthology, both to find what I wanted and to inform myself of critical opinion:

Perry Miller, *The New England Mind: The 17th Century*
 The New England Mind: From Colony to Province
 Errand Into the Wilderness
 Jonathan Edwards
Perry Miller and Thomas H. Johnson, editors, *The Puritans*
Perry Miller, editor, *The American Transcendentalists*
Samuel Eliot Morison, *The Puritan Pronaos; studies in the intellectual life of New England in the 17th century;* reissued in paperback under the title *The Intellectual Life of Colonial New England*
Samuel Eliot Morison, editor, *Of Plymouth Plantation,* by William Bradford
Morison and Henry Steele Commager, *The Growth of the American Republic*
Richard Morris and Commager, editors, *The Spirit of 'Seventy-Six*
Van Wyck Brooks, *The Flowering of New England, 1815–1865*
 New England, Indian Summer, 1865–1915
Commager, editor, *The Blue and The Gray*
Edmund C. Stedman and Ellen M. Hutchinson, editors, *Library of American Literature,* in 10 vols.